Scott Foresman - Addison Wesley

MATH

AUTHORS

RANDALL I. CHARLES

Carne S. Barnett **Diane J. Briars** **Warren D. Crown**
Martin L. Johnson **Steven J. Leinwand** **John Van de Walle**

Charles R. Allan • Dwight A. Cooley • Portia C. Elliott
Pearl Ling • Alma B. Ramírez
Freddie Lee Renfro • Mary Thompson

Scott Foresman
Addison Wesley

Editorial Offices: Menlo Park, California • Glenview, Illinois
Sales Offices: Reading, Massachusetts • Atlanta, Georgia • Glenview, Illinois
Carrollton, Texas • Menlo Park, California

http://www.sf.aw.com

The friendly characters who help you in this book with math tips, remembering, and problem solving are Zoombinis™. They are used with the permission of Brøderbund Software and can be found in the interactive problem-solving software, *Logical Journey of the Zoombinis®*, © 1996 Brøderbund Software and TERC, available from Brøderbund Software, Novato, California. For more information, write Brøderbund at P.O. Box 6125, Novato, CA 94948-6125, or call (415) 382-4740.

Cover artist Robert Silvers was taking photographs and playing with computers by the time he was ten. Eventually he melded his interests in computer programming and photography to produce a program that divides images into a grid and matches them with images from a database. The results are mosaics such as the one on this cover.

Printed in the United States of America

ISBN 0-201-69013-6

1 2 3 4 5 6 7 8 9 10-VH-01 00 99 98 97

CHAPTER 1

Data, Graphs, and Facts Review 6

Theme **Getting to Know You**

Data File 6

Team Project A Hand Print Vote 8

Technology Resources

SECTION A Reading Graphs and Facts Review 9

1-1	**Reading Pictographs** Mixed Review: Basic Facts	10
1-2	**Reading Bar Graphs** Mixed Review: Basic Facts	12
1-3	**Reading Line Graphs** Mixed Review: Basic Facts	14
1-4	**Problem Solving** Analyze Word Problems: Introduction to Problem Solving	16
1-5	**Problem Solving** Analyze Word Problems: Choose an Operation	18
1-6	**Exploring Algebra: What's the Rule?**	20
STOP	**Stop and Practice: Basic Facts**	22
A	**Review and Practice**	24

Problem Solving
Look for a Pattern,
Make a Table

Connections
Data, Science, Journal

SECTION B Making Graphs and Facts Review 25

1-7	**Exploring Organizing Data** Mixed Review: Basic Facts	26
1-8	**Exploring Making Pictographs** Mixed Review: Basic Facts	28
1-9	**Exploring Making Bar Graphs** Mixed Review: Basic Facts	30
1-10	**Problem Solving** Decision Making: Collect and Analyze Data	32
	Technology Making Graphs	34
STOP	**Stop and Practice: Basic Facts**	36
1-11	**Problem Solving** Analyze Strategies: Look for a Pattern Mixed Review: Basic Facts	38
B	**Review and Practice**	42

Problem Solving
Draw a Picture,
Make a Table

Connections
Data, Geometry, Music, Patterns, Social Studies, Journal

Chapter Resources

Your Choice	43
Ch 1 Review/Test	44
Performance Assessment	45
Math Magazine	46
Ch 1 Cumulative Review	47

Review and Maintenance appears in green type; **Problem Solving** in red type

CHAPTER 2

Place Value and Time 48

Theme

Data File 48
Team Project Bug Mural 50
Technology Resources

SECTION A Understanding Place Value 51

- 2-1 **Place Value Through Hundreds** 52
  Mixed Review and Test Prep
- 2-2 **Exploring Place Value Relationships** 54
- 2-3 **Place Value Through Thousands** 56
  Mixed Review and Test Prep
- 2-4 **Place Value Through Hundred Thousands** 58
  Mixed Review and Test Prep
- 2-5 **Problem Solving** Analyze Strategies: Make an Organized List 60
- A **Review and Practice** 62

Problem Solving
Look for a Pattern,
Use Objects/Act It Out

Connections
Algebra, Data, Geometry,
Logic, Measurement, Patterns,
Literature, Science,
Journal

SECTION B Building Number Sense 63

- 2-6 **Comparing Numbers** Mixed Review and Test Prep 64
- 2-7 **Ordering Numbers** Mixed Review and Test Prep 66
- 2-8 **Rounding to Tens** Mixed Review and Test Prep 68
- 2-9 **Rounding to Hundreds** 70
  Mixed Review and Test Prep
- B **Review and Practice** 72

Connections
Algebra, Data, Logic, Time,
Geography, History,
Science, Journal

SECTION C Understanding Time 73

- 2-10 **Time to the Nearest Five Minutes** 74
  Mixed Review and Test Prep
- 2-11 **Exploring Time to the Nearest Minute** 76
- 2-12 **Time to the Half Hour and Quarter Hour** 78
  Mixed Review and Test Prep
- 2-13 **Elapsed Time** Mixed Review and Test Prep 80
- 2-14 **Ordinal Numbers and the Calendar** 82
  Mixed Review and Test Prep
- 2-15 **Problem Solving** Decision Making: Make a Schedule 84
- C **Review and Practice** 86

Problem Solving
Guess and Check,
Use Objects/Act It Out

Connections
Algebra, Data, Estimation,
Patterns, Time, Careers,
Literature, Journal

Chapter Resources

Your Choice	87
Ch 2 Review/Test	88
Performance Assessment	89
Math Magazine	90
Ch 1–2 Cumulative Review	91

CHAPTER 3 Adding Whole Numbers and Money 92

Theme **DIGS AND FINDS**

Data File 92
Team Project Time Capsule 94
Technology Resources

SECTION A Developing Addition Number Sense 95

3-1 **Exploring Addition Patterns** 96
3-2 **Exploring Adding on a Hundred Chart** 98
3-3 **Exploring Algebra: Missing Numbers** 100
3-4 **Estimating Sums** Mixed Review and Test Prep 102
A Review and Practice 104

Problem Solving
Guess and Check, Look for a Pattern, Use Objects/Act It Out

Connections
Algebra, Calculator, Data, Estimation, Geometry, Logic, Measurement, Mental Math, Money, Patterns, Music, Journal

SECTION B Adding Greater Numbers and Money 105

3-5 **Exploring Adding with Regrouping** 106
3-6 **Adding 2-Digit Numbers** Mixed Review and Test Prep 108
3-7 **Adding 3-Digit Numbers** Mixed Review and Test Prep 110
STOP Stop and Practice 114
3-8 **Adding 4-Digit Numbers: Choose a Calculation Method** Mixed Review and Test Prep 116
3-9 **Column Addition** Mixed Review and Test Prep 118
3-10 **Problem Solving** Analyze Strategies: Guess and Check 120
B Review and Practice 122

Problem Solving
Look for a Pattern, Use Objects/Act It Out

Connections
Algebra, Data, Estimation, Geometry, Mental Math, Patterns, Time, Geography, Literature, Journal

SECTION C Extending Addition 123

3-11 **Mental Math** Mixed Review and Test Prep 124
3-12 **Counting Coins** Mixed Review and Test Prep 126
3-13 **Using Dollars and Cents** Mixed Review and Test Prep 128
3-14 **Exploring Making Change** 130
Practice Game **The Greatest Sum Game** 132
3-15 **Adding Money** Mixed Review and Test Prep 134
3-16 **Front-End Estimation** Mixed Review and Test Prep 136
3-17 **Problem Solving** Analyze Word Problems: Exact Answer or Estimate? 138
C Review and Practice 140

Problem Solving
Guess and Check, Use Objects/Act It Out

Connections
Algebra, Data, Mental Math, Money, Patterns, Science, Time, Journal

Chapter Resources
Your Choice 141
Ch 3 Review/Test 142
Performance Assessment 143
Math Magazine 144
Ch 1–3 Cumulative Review 145

CHAPTER 4

Subtracting Whole Numbers and Money 146

Theme **Fun PLACES TO VISIT**

Data File 146
Team Project How Many? 148
Technology Resources

SECTION A Developing Subtraction Number Sense 149

4-1 Reviewing the Meaning of Subtraction 150
Mixed Review and Test Prep
4-2 Exploring Subtraction Patterns 152
4-3 Exploring Subtracting on a Hundred Chart 154
4-4 Estimating Differences 156
Mixed Review and Test Prep
4-5 Exploring Regrouping 158
A Review and Practice 160

Problem Solving
Look for a Pattern,
Use Objects/Act It Out

Connections
Algebra, Data, Estimation, Measurement, Mental Math, Money, Patterns, Time, Music, Sports, Journal

SECTION B Subtracting Greater Numbers and Money 161

4-6 Exploring Subtracting 2-Digit Numbers 162
4-7 Subtracting 2-Digit Numbers 164
Mixed Review and Test Prep
4-8 Exploring Subtracting 3-Digit Numbers 166
4-9 Subtracting 3-Digit Numbers 168
Mixed Review and Test Prep
4-10 Subtracting with 2 Regroupings 170
Mixed Review and Test Prep
4-11 Subtracting Across 0 174
Mixed Review and Test Prep
STOP Stop and Practice 176
B Review and Practice 178

Problem Solving
Look for a Pattern,
Use Objects/Act It Out

Connections
Algebra, Calculator, Data, Estimation, Money, Patterns, Time, Geography, History, Science, Journal

SECTION C Extending Subtraction 179

4-12 Subtracting 4-Digit Numbers: Choose a Calculation Method 180
Mixed Review and Test Prep
Practice Game What's the Difference? 182
4-13 Problem Solving Analyze Word Problems: Multiple-Step Problems 184
4-14 Mental Math Mixed Review and Test Prep 186
4-15 Subtracting Money Mixed Review and Test Prep 188
4-16 Problem Solving Analyze Strategies: Use Objects 190
Mixed Review and Test Prep
C Review and Practice 194

Connections
Algebra, Data, Estimation, Logic, Mental Math, Money, Patterns, Time, History, Literature, Science, Journal

Chapter Resources
Your Choice 195
Ch 4 Review/Test 196
Performance Assessment 197
Math Magazine 198
Ch 1–4 Cumulative Review 199

CHAPTER 5

Multiplication Concepts and Facts 200

Theme

Data File 200

Team Project Tale of a Pig 202

Technology Resources

Section A Understanding Multiplication 203

5-1 **Exploring Equal Groups** 204

5-2 **Writing Multiplication Sentences** 206
Mixed Review and Test Prep

5-3 **Exploring Multiplication Stories** 208

A **Review and Practice** 210

Problem Solving
Draw a Picture,
Use Objects/Act It Out

Connections
Data, Geometry, Money, Science,
Social Studies, Journal

Section B Multiplying with 0, 1, 2, 5, and 9 as Factors 211

5-4 **2 as a Factor** 212
Mixed Review and Test Prep

5-5 **5 as a Factor** 214
Mixed Review and Test Prep

5-6 **Exploring Patterns on a Hundred Chart: 2s and 5s** 216

5-7 **Exploring 0 and 1 as Factors** 218

5-8 **9 as a Factor** 220
Mixed Review and Test Prep

STOP **Stop and Practice** 222

5-9 **Problem Solving** Analyze Word Problems: Too Much or Too Little Information 224

5-10 **Problem Solving** Analyze Strategies: Draw a Picture 226
Mixed Review and Test Prep

B **Review and Practice** 230

Problem Solving
Look for a Pattern,
Use Objects/Act It Out

Connections
Data, Geometry, Money, Patterns,
Time, Health, History, Language Arts,
Music, Science, Journal

Chapter Resources

Your Choice 231

Ch 5 Review/Test 232

Performance Assessment 233

Math Magazine 234

Ch 1–5 Cumulative Review 235

CHAPTER 6

More Multiplication Facts 236

Theme WHAT'S TO EAT?

Data File 236
Team Project Sweet & Spicy Ginger-ade 238
Technology Resources

SECTION A Multiplying with 3, 4, 6, 7, and 8 as Factors 239

6-1 **3 as a Factor: Using Known Facts** 240
Mixed Review and Test Prep

6-2 **4 as a Factor: Doubling** 242
Mixed Review and Test Prep

6-3 **6 as a Factor: Using Known Facts** 244
Mixed Review and Test Prep

6-4 **7 and 8 as Factors** 246
Mixed Review and Test Prep

Stop and Practice 248

6-5 **Problem Solving** Decision Making: Planning Meals 250

A Review and Practice 252

Connections
Algebra, Data, Money, Patterns, Health, Music, Science, Social Studies, Journal

SECTION B Extending Multiplication 253

6-6 **Exploring Patterns on a Hundred Chart: 3s and 6s** 254

6-7 **Exploring Patterns on a Fact Table** 256

6-8 **Multiplying with 3 Factors** 258
Mixed Review and Test Prep

Practice Game Product Cross Off 260

6-9 **Problem Solving** Compare Strategies: Look for a Pattern and Draw a Picture 262

Technology Doubling with a Calculator 264

B Review and Practice 266

Problem Solving
Look for a Pattern, Make a Table

Connections
Algebra, Data, Geometry, Measurement, Patterns, Science, Social Studies, Journal

Chapter Resources

Your Choice 267
Ch 6 Review/Test 268
Performance Assessment 269
Math Magazine 270
Ch 1–6 Cumulative Review 271

CHAPTER 7 Division Concepts and Facts 272

Theme **COOL COLLECTIONS**

Data File 272
Team Project Send & Deliver 274
Technology Resources

SECTION A Understanding Division 275

7-1 **Exploring Division as Sharing** 276
7-2 **Exploring Division as Repeated Subtraction** 278
7-3 **Exploring Division Stories** 280
A **Review and Practice** 282

Problem Solving
Draw a Picture, Use Objects/Act It Out

Connections
Algebra, Data, Money, Fine Arts, Science, Journal

SECTION B Using Multiplication Facts to Find Division Facts 283

7-4 **Connecting Multiplication and Division** 284
Mixed Review and Test Prep
7-5 **Dividing by 2** 286
Mixed Review and Test Prep
7-6 **Dividing by 5** 288
Mixed Review and Test Prep
7-7 **Dividing by 3 and 4** 290
Mixed Review and Test Prep
7-8 **Exploring Dividing with 0 and 1** 292
Practice Game **The Secret Divisor Game** 294
7-9 **Problem Solving** Analyze Word Problems: Choose an Operation 296
B **Review and Practice** 298

Problem Solving
Look for a Pattern

Connections
Algebra, Data, Money, Patterns, Time, Science, Social Studies, Journal

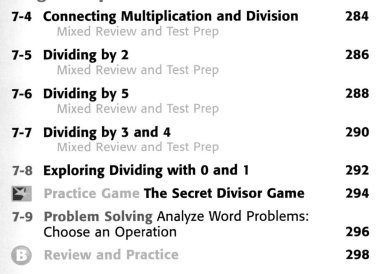

SECTION C Finding More Division Facts 299

7-10 **Dividing by 6 and 7** 300
Mixed Review and Test Prep
7-11 **Dividing by 8 and 9** 302
Mixed Review and Test Prep
STOP **Stop and Practice** 304
7-12 **Exploring Even and Odd Numbers** 306
7-13 **Problem Solving** Compare Strategies: Use Objects and Make an Organized List 308
7-14 **Exploring Algebra: Balancing Scales** 310
C **Review and Practice** 312

Problem Solving
Look for a Pattern, Make a Table, Use Objects/Act It Out

Connections
Algebra, Data, Money, Time, Journal

Chapter Resources
Your Choice 313
Ch 7 Review/Test 314
Performance Assessment 315
Math Magazine 316
Ch 1–7 Cumulative Review 317

CHAPTER 8

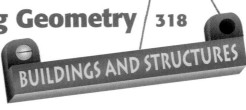

Using Geometry 318

Theme BUILDINGS AND STRUCTURES

Data File 318
Team Project Still Life Collage 320
Technology Resources

SECTION A Shapes and Solids 321

8-1 Exploring Solids 322
8-2 Exploring Solids and Shapes 324
8-3 Lines and Line Segments 326
Mixed Review and Test Prep
8-4 Exploring Angles 328
8-5 Exploring Slides, Flips, and Turns 330
8-6 Exploring Symmetry 332
Technology Congruence and Symmetry 334
8-7 Problem Solving Analyze Strategies: Solve a Simpler Problem 336
A Review and Practice 338

Problem Solving
Draw a Picture,
Use Objects/Act It Out

Connections
Data, Logic, Patterns, Time,
Fine Arts, Geography, Journal

SECTION B Perimeter, Area, and Volume 339

8-8 Exploring Perimeter 340
8-9 Exploring Area 342
8-10 Problem Solving Decision Making: Estimating Area 344
8-11 Exploring Volume 346
8-12 Coordinate Grids 348
Mixed Review and Test Prep
B Review and Practice 350

Problem Solving
Draw a Picture,
Use Objects/Act It Out

Connections
Algebra, Data, Geometry,
Mental Math, Patterns, Geography,
Social Studies, Journal

Chapter Resources
Your Choice 351
Ch 8 Review/Test 352
Performance Assessment 353
Math Magazine 354
Ch 1–8 Cumulative Review 355

Review and Maintenance appears in green type; **Problem Solving** in red type

CHAPTER 9 Multiplying and Dividing 356

Theme

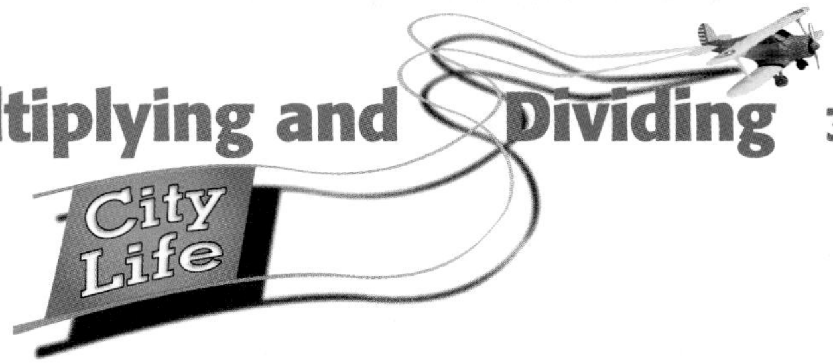

Data File 356

Team Project City Planning 358

Technology Resources

SECTION A Developing Multiplication Number Sense 359

9-1 Exploring Multiplying Tens 360

9-2 Exploring Multiplication Patterns 362

9-3 Estimating Products 364

Mixed Review and Test Prep

9-4 Exploring Multiplication with Arrays 366

A Review and Practice 368

Problem Solving
Draw a Picture, Look for a Pattern, Use Objects/Act It Out

Connections
Algebra, Data, Estimation, Geometry, Mental Math, Careers, Geography, Social Studies, Journal

SECTION B Multiplying by 1-Digit Factors 369

9-5 Multiplying: Partial Products 370

Mixed Review and Test Prep

9-6 Multiplying 2-Digit Numbers 372

Mixed Review and Test Prep

STOP Stop and Practice 376

9-7 Multiplying 3-Digit Numbers 378

Mixed Review and Test Prep

9-8 Multiplying Money 380

Mixed Review and Test Prep

9-9 Mental Math 382

Mixed Review and Test Prep

Practice Game Target Products! 384

9-10 Problem Solving Analyze Strategies: Make a Table 386

B Review and Practice 388

Connections
Algebra, Data, Mental Math, Measurement, Money, Time, Health, Science, Social Studies, Journal

SECTION C Dividing with 1-Digit Divisors 389

9-11 Exploring Division Patterns 390

9-12 Estimating Quotients 392

Mixed Review and Test Prep

9-13 Exploring Division with Remainders 394

9-14 Dividing 396

Mixed Review and Test Prep

9-15 Problem Solving Decision Making: Plan a Marathon 398

Technology Dividing with a Calculator 400

C Review and Practice 402

Problem Solving
Look for a Pattern, Use Objects/Act It Out

Connections
Data, Estimation, Geometry, Measurement, Mental Math, Money, Time, History, Science, Social Studies, Journal

Chapter Resources

Your Choice 403

Ch 9 Review/Test 404

Performance Assessment 405

Math Magazine 406

Ch 1–9 Cumulative Review 407

CHAPTER 10

Fractions and Customary Linear Measurement 408

Theme

SPORTS AND GAMES

Data File 408

Team Project Coin Olympics 410

Technology Resources

SECTION A Understanding Fractions 411

10-1 **Exploring Equal Parts** 412

10-2 **Naming and Writing Fractions** 414
Mixed Review and Test Prep

10-3 **Exploring Equivalent Fractions** 416

10-4 **Exploring Comparing and Ordering Fractions** 418

10-5 **Estimating Fractional Amounts** 420
Mixed Review and Test Prep

A **Review and Practice** 422

Problem Solving
Draw a Picture, Look for a Pattern, Use Objects/Act It Out

Connections
Algebra, Data, Patterns, Time, History, Music, Journal

SECTION B Extending Fraction Concepts 423

10-6 **Fractions and Sets** 424
Mixed Review and Test Prep

10-7 **Exploring Finding a Fraction of a Number** 426

10-8 **Mixed Numbers** 428
Mixed Review and Test Prep

10-9 **Exploring Adding and Subtracting Fractions** 430

10-10 **Problem Solving** Decision Making: Plan a Team Party 432

B **Review and Practice** 434

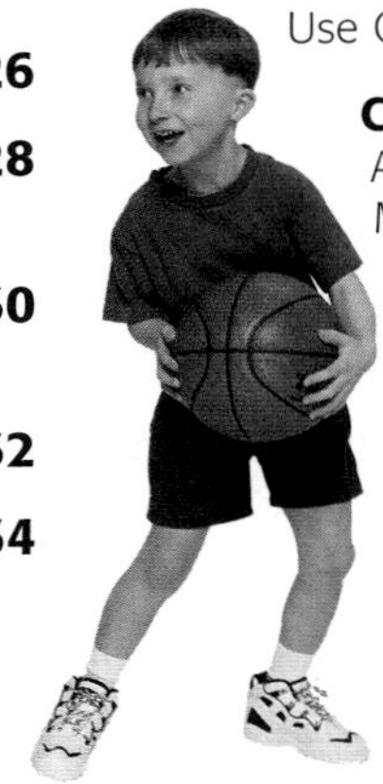

Problem Solving
Look for a Pattern, Use Objects/Act It Out

Connections
Algebra, Data, Money, Time, Science, Journal

SECTION C Customary Linear Measurement 435

10-11 **Exploring Length** 436

10-12 **Measuring to the Nearest $\frac{1}{2}$ Inch and $\frac{1}{4}$ Inch** 438
Mixed Review and Test Prep

10-13 **Exploring Length in Feet and Inches** 440

10-14 **Feet, Yards, and Miles** 442
Mixed Review and Test Prep

10-15 **Problem Solving** Analyze Strategies: Use Logical Reasoning 444

C **Review and Practice** 446

Problem Solving
Look for a Pattern, Use Objects/Act It Out

Connections
Data, Estimation, Geometry, Logic, Measurement, Money, Patterns, Health, Science, Journal

Chapter Resources

Your Choice 447

Ch 10 Review/Test 448

Performance Assessment 449

Math Magazine 450

Ch 1–10 Cumulative Review 451

CHAPTER 11 Decimals and Metric Linear Measurement 452

Theme *On the Fast Track*

Data File 452
Team Project Treasure Hunt 454
Technology Resources

SECTION A Understanding Decimals 455

11-1 **Exploring Tenths** 456
11-2 **Hundredths** 458
Mixed Review and Test Prep
11-3 **Exploring Adding and Subtracting Decimals** 460
11-4 **Connecting Decimals and Money** 462
Mixed Review and Test Prep
Technology Fractions and Decimals on a Calculator 464
11-5 **Problem Solving** Decision Making: Plan a Day 466
A **Review and Practice** 468

Problem Solving
Draw a Picture,
Use Objects/Act It Out

Connections
Algebra, Data, Money, Patterns, Health, History, Science, Journal

SECTION B Metric Linear Measurement 469

11-6 **Exploring Centimeters and Decimeters** 470
11-7 **Meters and Kilometers** 472
Mixed Review and Test Prep
11-8 **Problem Solving** Compare Strategies: Use Objects and Draw a Picture 474
B **Review and Practice** 476

Problem Solving
Use Objects/Act It Out

Connections
Algebra, Data, Geometry, Journal

Chapter Resources

Your Choice 477
Ch 11 Review/Test 478
Performance Assessment 479
Math Magazine 480
Ch 1–11 Cumulative Review 481

CHAPTER 12 Measurement and Probability 482

Theme **Around the HOUSE**

Data File 482
Team Project Penny Weight 484
Technology Resources

SECTION A Capacity, Weight, and Temperature 485

12-1 **Exploring Capacity: Customary Units** 486
12-2 **Measuring Capacity: Metric Units** 488
Mixed Review and Test Prep
12-3 **Exploring Weight: Customary Units** 490
12-4 **Grams and Kilograms** 492
Mixed Review and Test Prep
12-5 **Temperature** Mixed Review and Test Prep 494
12-6 **Problem Solving** Decision Making: Packing for Backpacking 496
A **Review and Practice** 498

Problem Solving
Make a Table, Use Objects/Act It Out

Connections
Data, Geometry, Patterns, Geography, Health, Journal

SECTION B Probability 499

12-7 **Exploring Likely and Unlikely** 500
12-8 **Exploring Predictions** 502
12-9 **Exploring Probability** 504
12-10 **Exploring Fair and Unfair** 506
Technology Testing Predictions 508
12-11 **Problem Solving** Analyze Strategies: Work Backward 510
B **Review and Practice** 512

Problem Solving
Guess and Check, Make a Table, Use Logical Reasoning, Use Objects/Act It Out

Connections
Data, Geometry, Time, Journal

Chapter Resources

Your Choice 513
Ch 12 Review/Test 514
Performance Assessment 515
Math Magazine 516
Ch 1–12 Cumulative Review 517

Student Resources

Welcome to Math Class 1
Reviewing Skills 2
Problem Solving
Introduction to Strategies 4
Skills Practice Bank Chapter 1 518
Skills Practice Bank Chapter 2 519
Skills Practice Bank Chapter 3 520
Skills Practice Bank Chapter 4 521
Skills Practice Bank Chapter 5 522
Skills Practice Bank Chapter 6 523
Skills Practice Bank Chapter 7 524
Skills Practice Bank Chapter 8 525
Skills Practice Bank Chapter 9 526
Skills Practice Bank Chapter 10 527
Skills Practice Bank Chapter 11 528
Skills Practice Bank Chapter 12 529
Table of Measures 530
Glossary 531
Credits 537
Index 539

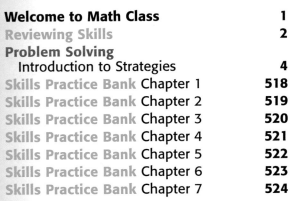

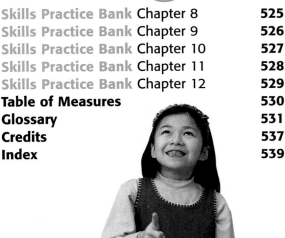

GET READY!

Welcome to Math Class

Welcome back to math class! I'm the Get Ready Zoombini. My friends and I are here to help you this year.
I'll help you remember. You won't forget with me around!
STAY SHARP!
I like to give helpful math tips!
I'll help with problem solving!
Did you know? I know lots of fun facts!

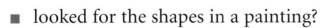

Just think, math helps us understand the world around us. Have you ever:

- wondered how far monarch butterflies travel every winter?
- figured out how much smaller a volcano is after an eruption?
- looked for the shapes in a painting?
- discovered about how many miles of road the ancient Anasazi built?
- changed a favorite recipe to make enough for the whole class?

NORTH
SOUTH
Chaco Canyon

We will do all that, and more, as we explore the math that real students use every day!

Reviewing Skills

You Will Meet
real students, like these, who use math skills in their everyday lives

Meet Becky and her artwork on page 123.

Frank works with computers. See him on page 283.

Here's a little warm-up before we begin.

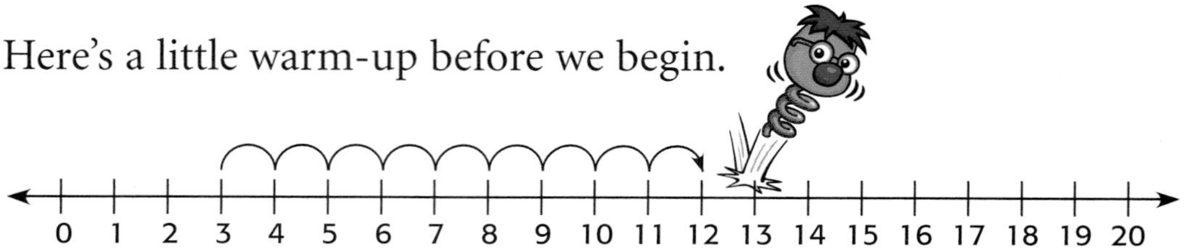

Review addition facts. Find each sum. You may use the number line to help.

1. $3 + 9$	**2.** $2 + 6$	**3.** $1 + 4$	**4.** $3 + 5$	**5.** $4 + 7$
6. $8 + 7$	**7.** $8 + 8$	**8.** $5 + 6$	**9.** $9 + 8$	**10.** $6 + 4$
11. $2 + 8$	**12.** $3 + 6$	**13.** $7 + 6$	**14.** $5 + 8$	**15.** $9 + 2$
16. $6 + 9$	**17.** $9 + 7$	**18.** $8 + 4$	**19.** $7 + 1$	**20.** $2 + 5$
21. $5 + 5$	**22.** $2 + 7$	**23.** $5 + 9$	**24.** $3 + 2$	**25.** $9 + 1$

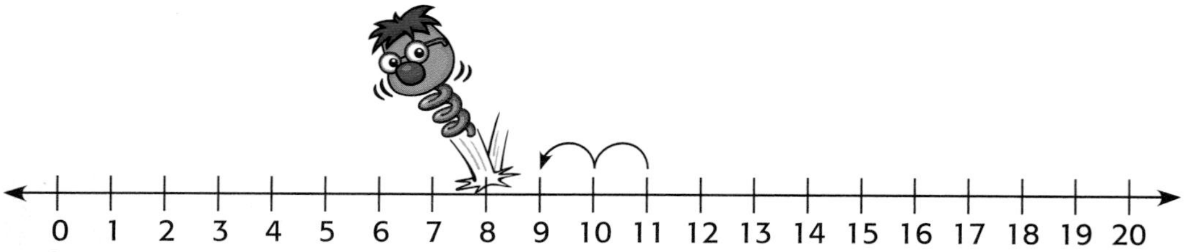

Review subtraction facts. Find each difference. You may use the number line to help.

26. $11 - 2$	**27.** $6 - 4$	**28.** $10 - 5$	**29.** $9 - 1$	**30.** $18 - 9$
31. $17 - 9$	**32.** $13 - 5$	**33.** $8 - 5$	**34.** $13 - 4$	**35.** $9 - 4$
36. $10 - 2$	**37.** $14 - 7$	**38.** $15 - 7$	**39.** $11 - 5$	**40.** $5 - 4$
41. $7 - 4$	**42.** $8 - 4$	**43.** $16 - 7$	**44.** $9 - 3$	**45.** $10 - 8$
46. $11 - 4$	**47.** $12 - 8$	**48.** $17 - 8$	**49.** $10 - 3$	**50.** $6 - 3$

Review skip counting. Copy and complete each pattern.

51. 2, 4, 6, ■, ■

52. 3, 6, 9, ■, ■

53. 10, 20, 30, ■, ■

54. 10, 8, 6, ■, ■

55. 5, 10, 15, ■, ■

56. 100, 200, 300, ■, ■

Complete the pattern.

57.  ____ ____ ____

58. 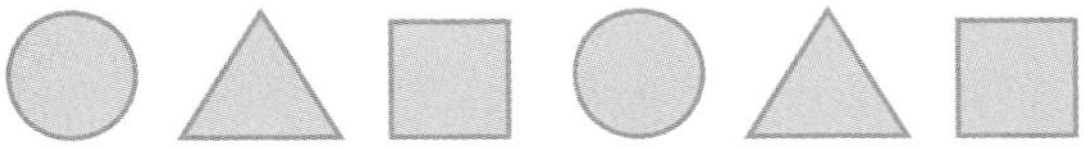 ____ ____ ____

Add and subtract to solve the riddle. Match each letter to its answer in the blank below. Some of the letters are not used.

59. 6 + 8 [L]

60. 12 − 8 [A]

61. 9 + 4 [N]

62. 7 − 6 [R]

63. 3 + 7 [E]

64. 13 − 6 [S]

65. 4 + 3 [I]

66. 14 − 8 [D]

67. 7 + 2 [T]

____ ____ ____ ____ ____ ____ ____
4 13 4 6 6 10 1

PRACTICE AND APPLY

Problem Solving

Introduction to Strategies

Problem Solving Strategies

- Use Objects/Act It Out
- Draw a Picture
- Look for a Pattern
- Guess and Check
- Use Logical Reasoning
- Make an Organized List
- Make a Table
- Solve a Simpler Problem
- Work Backward

Choose a Tool

There are many ways to solve most problems. A **strategy** is a plan to help you solve a problem. You will learn about strategies that can help solve problems you've never seen before!

Theresa has 5 balloons. How many balloons does she have after Ethan gives her 12 balloons?

See how Ethan and Theresa solved the problem.

Use Objects/Act It Out

I used objects to solve.

First I showed a group of 5 counters. Then I showed 12 more. I counted both groups. There are 17 counters all together.

The answer is 17 balloons!

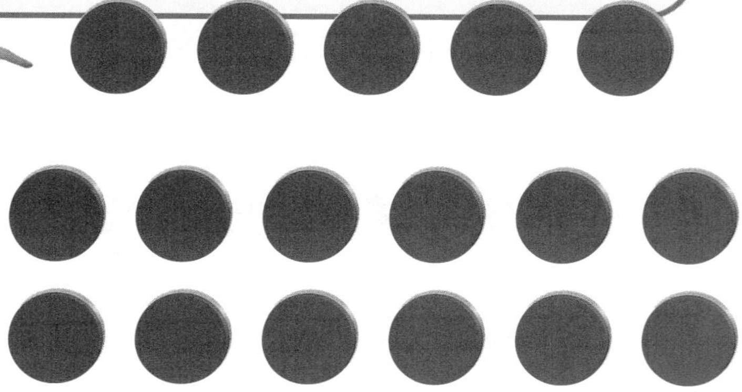

Draw a Picture

I drew a picture to solve.

First I drew 5 **O**s to show 5 balloons. Then I drew 12 more **O**s. I counted the **O**s.

There are 17 **O**s, so there are 17 balloons!

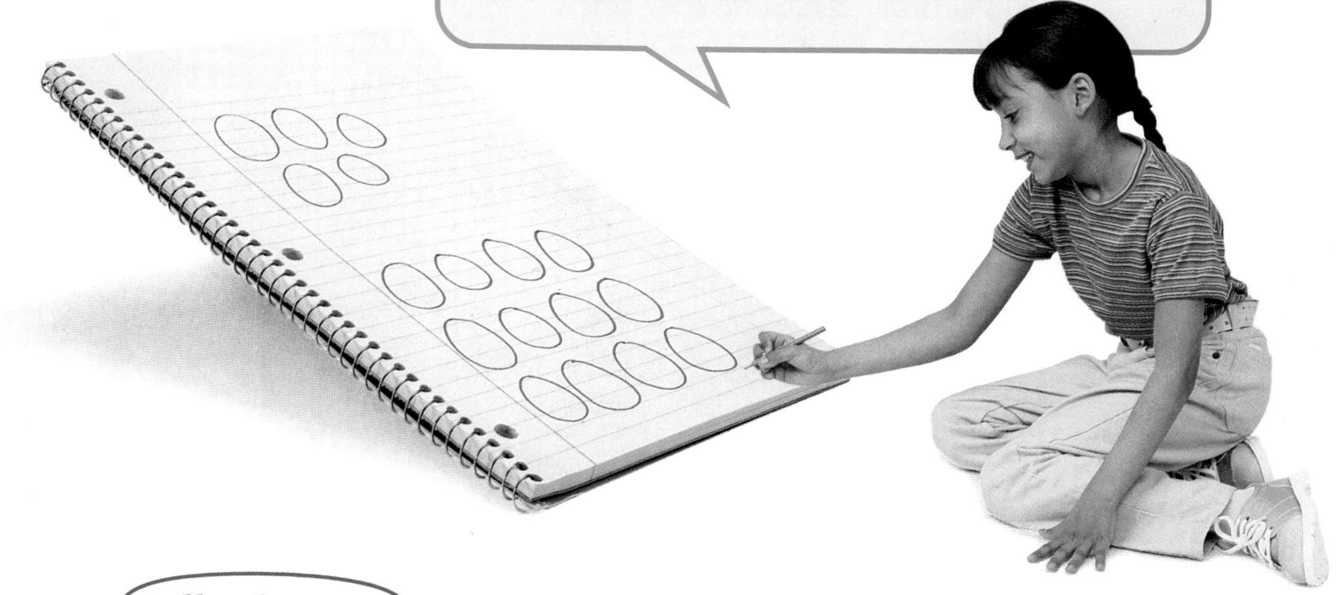

Talk About It

1. Can you use either strategy to solve the problem? Explain.
2. Which strategy would you have chosen? Why?

Try These

Use any strategy to solve.

1. Jed has 4 marbles. How many marbles does Jed have after Alice gives him 14 more?
2. Janice has 22 toy trucks. How many toy trucks does Janice have after she gives 7 to Francis?
3. Kurt had 12 crayons. He gives 2 to Laura and gets 5 from Frank. How many crayons does he have now?
4. **Journal** Throughout the year you'll keep a math journal. You can start by writing a few sentences telling what you already know about math. What do you want to learn this year? Remember to check your journal during the year to see your progress!

DATA FILE

Chapter 1

Data, Graphs, and Facts Review

Getting to Know You

SECTION A

Students at Shoreline Elementary School
Page 9

9

Reading Graphs and Facts Review

How much sleep do you get every night? This pictograph shows the amount of sleep people usually need at different ages. At what age do people need the least amount of sleep?

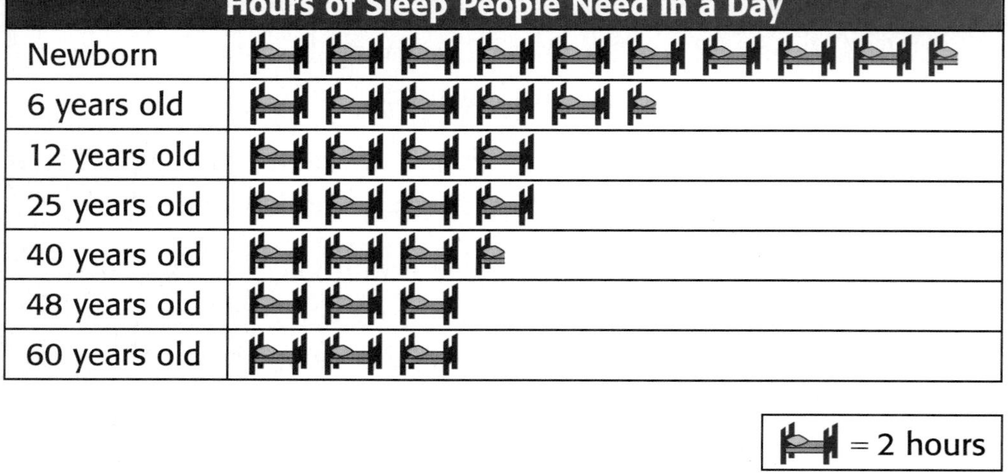
Hours of Sleep People Need in a Day
Newborn
6 years old
12 years old
25 years old
40 years old
48 years old
60 years old
= 2 hours

SECTION B

Making Graphs and Facts Review

Some third, fourth, and fifth grade students spoke out about what they like to do in their spare time. Which activity is the most popular?

Things Students Like to Do	
Activity	**Number of Votes**
Play basketball	9
Play video games	10
Play with friends	11
Play with pets	3
Swim	10
Watch TV	9

Surfing the World Wide Web!

What's your favorite activity? Find out how your choice compares with other students' choices around the country. Use the data you find at **www.mathsurf.com/3/ch1** to report the top three activities.

Students at Kennerly School

Page 25

Prese

8

TEAM PROJECT

A Hand Print Vote

Materials

large sheet of butcher paper, tape, markers or crayons, scissors

You can make a graph to record a vote.

Make a Plan

- Choose a topic for the whole class to vote on. It could be a favorite color, a favorite food, or a favorite book.
- List the choices everyone will vote for.

Carry It Out

1. Everyone in the class should trace his or her hand and cut out the tracing.
2. Make a graph like the one shown here. Use your own choices and title.

Favorite Colors	
Blue	
Green	
Red	

3. Take the vote. Tape your hand tracing to the graph to show your vote.

Talk About It

- Can you tell which choice is the favorite without counting the actual number of votes? Explain.

nt the Project

- Display the graph in your classroom. What does the graph tell about your classmates?

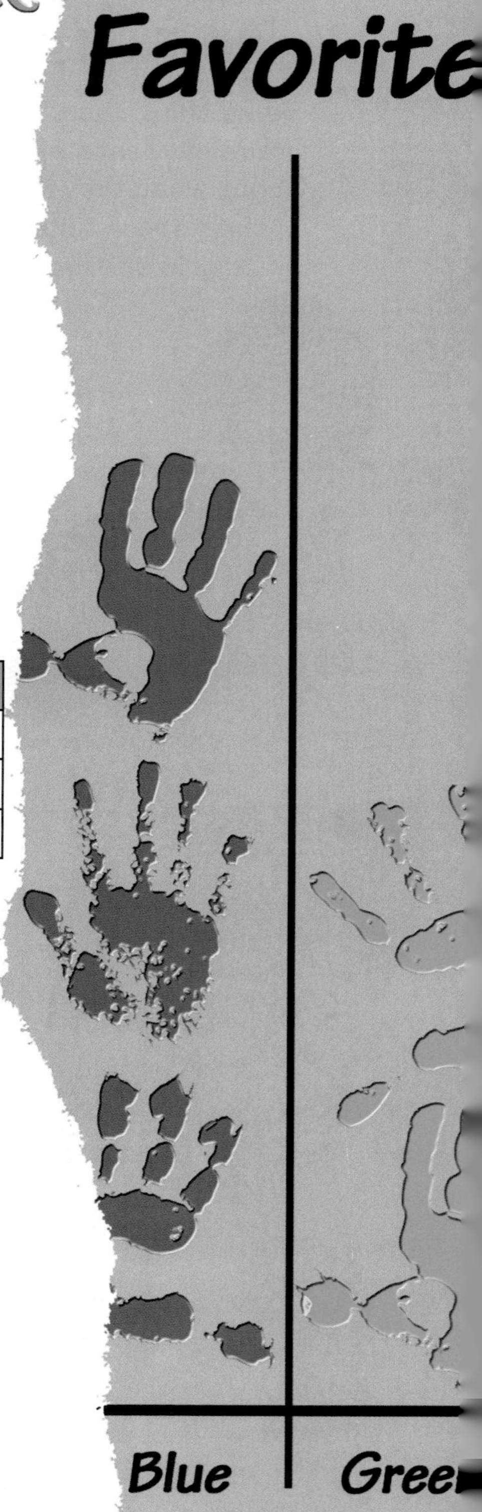

CHAPTER 1

SECTION

A Reading Graphs and Facts Review

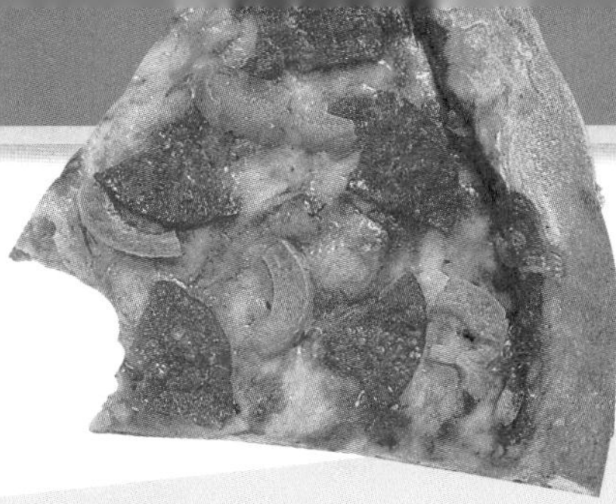

Students at Shoreline Elementary School in Whitehall, Michigan, voted for their favorite pizza topping. What are some ways you could show the results of their survey?

Reading Graphs

Review counting. Continue each pattern.

1. 0, 2, 4, 6, ■, ■, ■

2. 10, 20, 30, ■, ■, ■

3. 5, 10, 15, 20, ■, ■, ■

4. 70, 80, 90, ■, ■, ■

Skills Checklist

In this section, you will:

- ❒ Review Basic Addition and Subtraction Facts
- ❒ Read Pictographs, Bar Graphs, and Line Graphs
- ❒ Solve Problems by Using a Guide
- ❒ Solve Problems by Choosing an Operation
- ❒ Explore Algebra

Reading Pictographs

You Will Learn
how to read a pictograph

Vocabulary

pictograph
a graph that uses pictures, or symbols, to show data

key
part of a pictograph that tells what each symbol shows

symbol
a picture in a pictograph that shows a given number of objects

Learn

What's the best thing to put on a pizza? Third graders at Shoreline Elementary School in Whitehall, Michigan, had lots of ideas. How many students chose pepperoni?

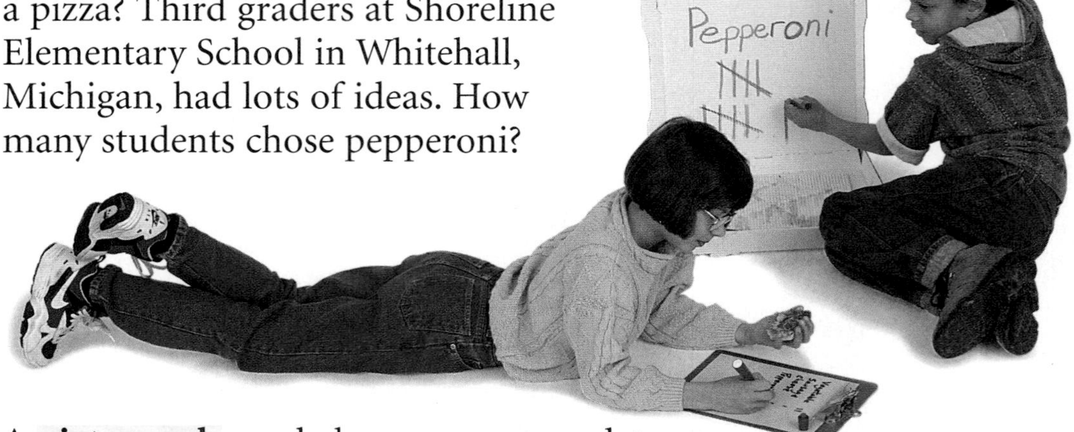

A **pictograph** can help you compare data.

Favorite Pizza Toppings	
Sausage	⊛ ◖
Vegetables	◖
Extra cheese	⊛ ⊛ ⊛ ◖
Pepperoni	⊛ ⊛ ⊛ ⊛ ⊛ ◖

Title
Symbol
Key

⊛ = 2 votes

The **key** tells you that each **symbol** shows 2 votes. Since ⊛ shows 2 votes, ◖ shows 1 vote. So, 11 students chose pepperoni.

Talk About It

How can you tell what each symbol shows in a pictograph?

Check

Use the pictograph to answer each question.

1. Which pizza topping had the fewest votes?
2. Which pizza topping had 7 votes?
3. **Reasoning** If 10 students voted for onions, how many symbols would there be for onions? Explain.

Practice

Skills and Reasoning

Use the pictograph to answer **4–10.**

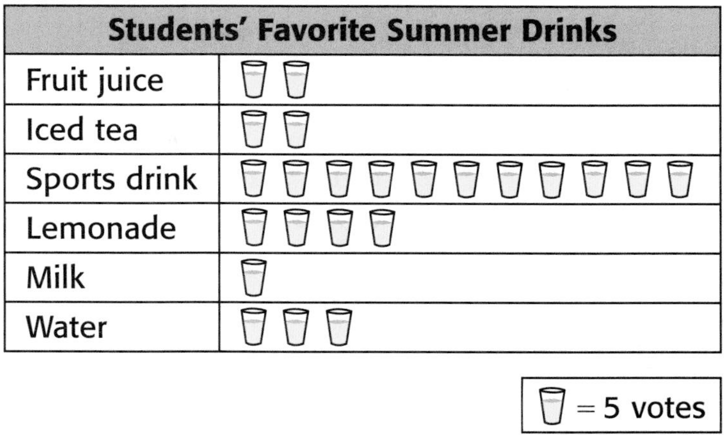

4. Which drink had the most votes?

5. Which two drinks had the same number of votes?

6. Which drink had 20 votes?

7. Which drink had the fewest votes?

8. How many more students voted for fruit juice than milk?

9. Suppose 25 students voted for water. How many symbols would water have?

Problem Solving and Applications

10. Critical Thinking Suppose the key was missing in the pictograph above. What kinds of information would you still know?

11. Write Your Own Problem Write a problem that uses one of the pictographs from this lesson. Trade your problem with a classmate and then solve.

Using Data Use the Data File on page 6 to answer **12** and **13.**

12. How many hours of sleep does a 40-year-old person need?

13. How many more hours of sleep does a 6-year-old need than a 60-year-old?

Mixed Review: Basic Facts

Find each sum or difference. Count on or count back to help.

14. 6 + 2	**15.** 8 + 1	**16.** 5 − 3	**17.** 4 + 3	**18.** 4 − 1
19. 3 + 1	**20.** 5 − 2	**21.** 8 − 2	**22.** 7 + 2	**23.** 5 + 2
24. 11 − 2	**25.** 9 − 1	**26.** 8 + 3	**27.** 7 − 2	**28.** 6 − 2
29. 9 + 2	**30.** 10 − 2	**31.** 6 + 2	**32.** 2 + 7	**33.** 9 − 2

Reading Bar Graphs

You Will Learn
how to read a bar graph

Vocabulary

bar graph
a graph that uses bars to show data

scale
the numbers that show the units used on a bar graph

Math Tip
Think of each bar as a ruler that measures the number of votes

Learn

What kind of music gets your feet tapping? Some students voted for their favorite type of music. The results are shown on this **bar graph**. Which type of music has 10 votes?

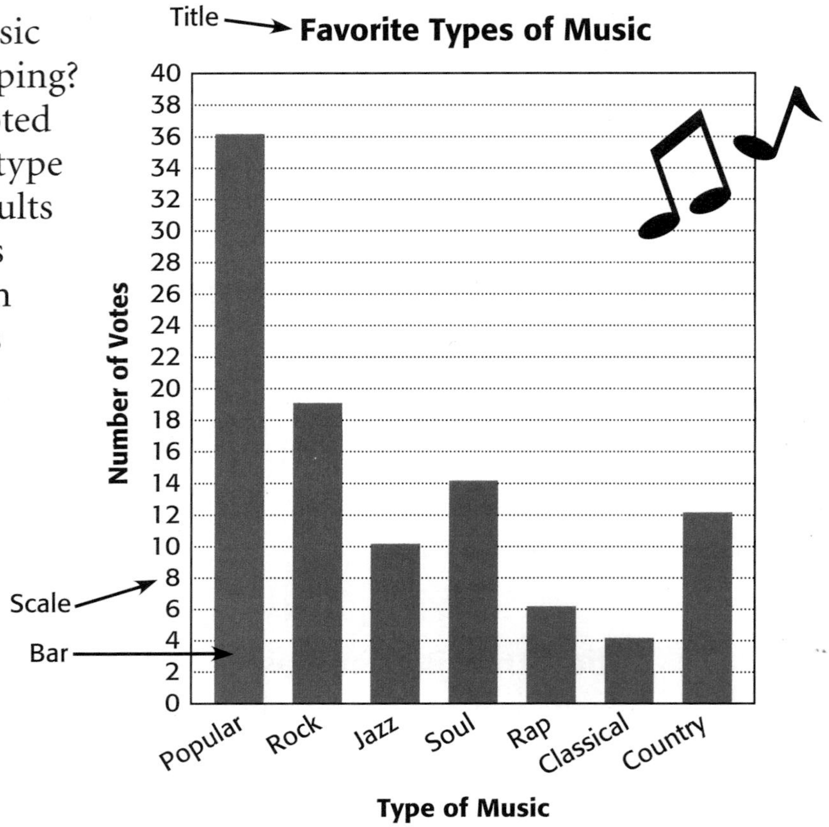

A bar graph is another way to help you compare data. Bar graphs use bars to show data. In this graph, each type of music has its own bar.

You can find the type of music that has 10 votes by looking at the **scale**.

Find the number 10 on the scale. Find the bar that ends at that number. The type of music that has 10 votes is jazz.

Talk About It

1. How can you use the scale to find the type of music that has the most votes?
2. How does a bar graph help you to compare data?

Check

Use the bar graph on page 12 to answer each question.

1. Which type of music has the fewest votes?

2. Which type of music has 19 votes?

3. **Reasoning** Suppose five students voted for folk music. Would there be more votes for folk music or for rap?

Practice

Skills and Reasoning

Use the bar graph to answer each question.

4. What does each bar on the graph show?

5. What do the numbers on the scale stand for?

6. Do any two animals jump the same distance? How can you tell?

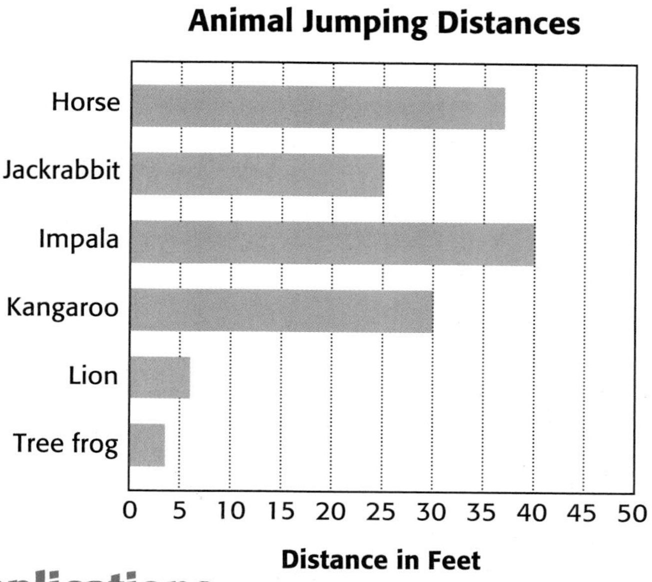

Problem Solving and Applications

Science Use the bar graph above to answer **7–9.**

7. Which animals jump less than 10 feet?

8. How many feet does the jackrabbit jump?

9. About how far does a tree frog jump?

10. **Journal** Describe how bar graphs and pictographs are alike and how they are different.

Mixed Review: Basic Facts

Find each sum or difference. Think about doubles to help.

11. 6 + 6	**12.** 5 + 4	**13.** 16 − 8	**14.** 18 − 9	**15.** 15 − 7
16. 9 + 8	**17.** 4 + 3	**18.** 5 − 2	**19.** 5 + 6	**20.** 7 + 7
21. 12 − 6	**22.** 9 + 9	**23.** 5 + 5	**24.** 14 − 6	**25.** 6 + 7

Reading Line Graphs

You Will Learn
how to read a line graph

Vocabulary
line graph
a graph that connects points to show how data changes over time

Math Tip
Use a ruler to help match each point on the graph with a number on the scale.

Learn

Kevin's family keeps a record of his height. Kevin made a **line graph** to show how his height has changed. How many inches long was Kevin when he was born?

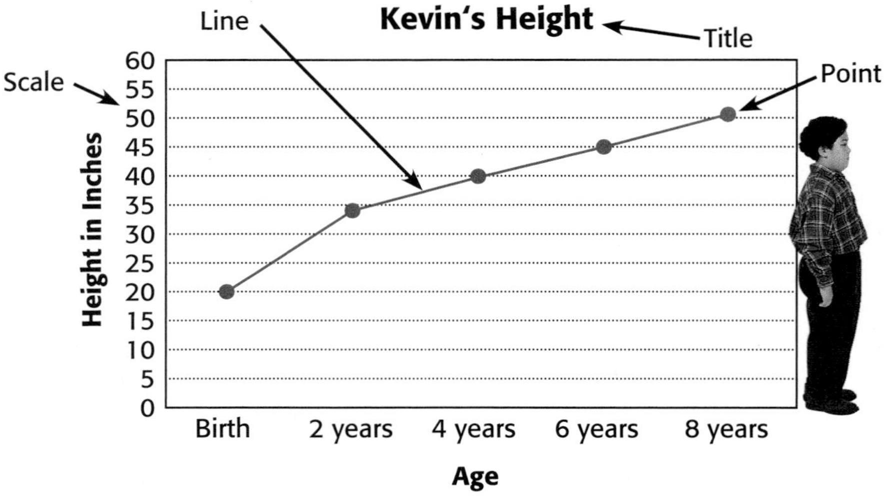

A line graph shows how data changes over time. The points are connected to help show how the data changes.

Find the point that marks Kevin's height at birth. Match the point with the scale to read his height.

Kevin was 20 inches when he was born.

Talk About It

Suppose you couldn't see the numbers of inches on the graph. What information could you still get from the graph?

Check

Use the line graph above to answer each question.

1. How old was Kevin when he was 34 inches tall?
2. How tall was Kevin when he was 4 years old?
3. **Reasoning** What do you think Kevin's height will be when he is 10 years old?

Practice

Skills and Reasoning

Use the line graph to answer each question.

Andrea keeps track of the number of apples on her apple tree. The line graph shows how many apples she counted from August through November.

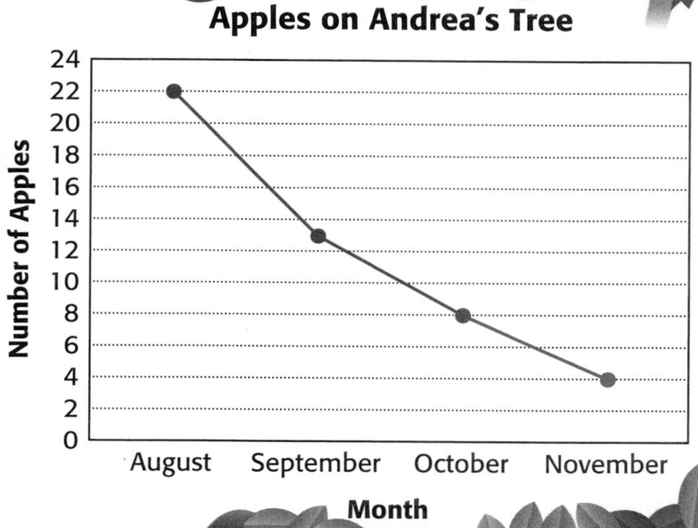

4. How many apples were on the tree in August?

5. When did Andrea count only four apples on the tree?

6. Do you think there will be more or less than four apples in December? Explain.

7. Why do you think the line in the graph goes down? What could be happening to the apples?

Problem Solving and Applications

Use the line graph above to answer **8** and **9**.

8. How many more apples were on Andrea's tree in September than in October?

9. How many apples fell off the tree or were picked between October and November?

10. **Write Your Own Problem** Write a problem that uses data from one of the line graphs in this lesson. Trade problems with a classmate and then solve.

Mixed Review: Basic Facts

Find each sum.

11. 9 + 3	**12.** 7 + 9	**13.** 6 + 9	**14.** 9 + 1	**15.** 2 + 8
16. 5 + 9	**17.** 9 + 4	**18.** 9 + 8	**19.** 8 + 3	**20.** 7 + 8
21. 2 + 9	**22.** 9 + 9	**23.** 8 + 8	**24.** 6 + 8	**25.** 8 + 4

Problem Solving

Analyze Word Problems: Introduction to Problem Solving

You Will Learn
how to solve problems

Did You Know?
The bottlenose whale can hold its breath for 120 minutes!

Learn

Using a guide can help you solve problems.

How much longer can a muskrat hold its breath than a sea otter?

How Long Animals Can Hold Their Breath

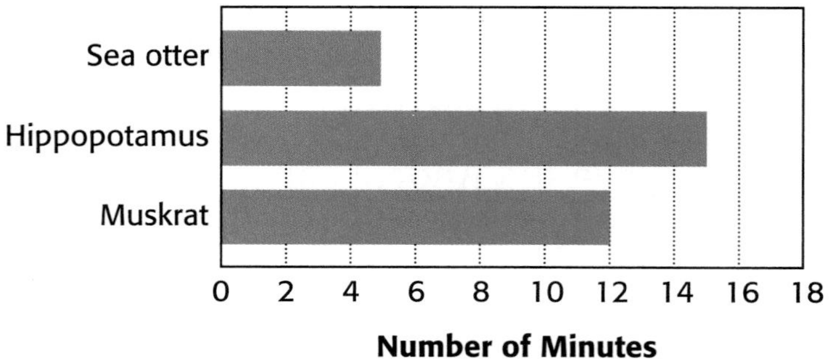

Work Together

▶ Understand

What do you know?

Muskrats hold their breath for 12 minutes. Sea otters hold their breath for 5 minutes.

What do you need to find out?

How much longer a muskrat can hold its breath.

▶ Plan

Decide how you will find out.

Compare how long muskrats and sea otters hold their breath. Subtract.

▶ Solve

Find the answer.

$12 - 5 = 7$

Write your answer.

A muskrat can hold its breath 7 minutes longer than a sea otter.

▶ Look Back

Check to see if your answer makes sense.

Add to check. $7 + 5 = 12$
So, the answer is correct.

Talk About It

How did the guide help you to solve the problem?

Check

Plan how you will solve each problem. Then solve.

1. How many students all together like CDs or cassettes?

2. How many more students like to listen to music on CDs than on the radio?

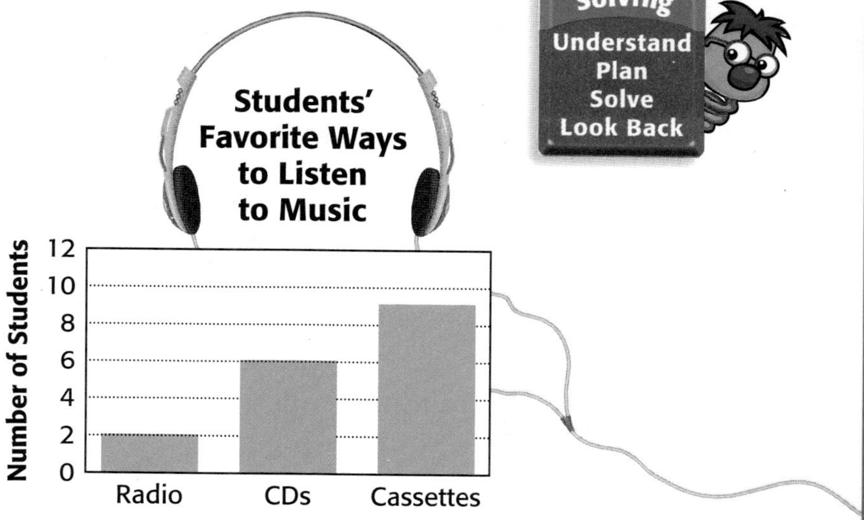

Problem Solving
Understand
Plan
Solve
Look Back

Problem Solving Practice

Plan how you will solve each problem. Then solve.

Using Data Use the pictograph to answer **3–6.**

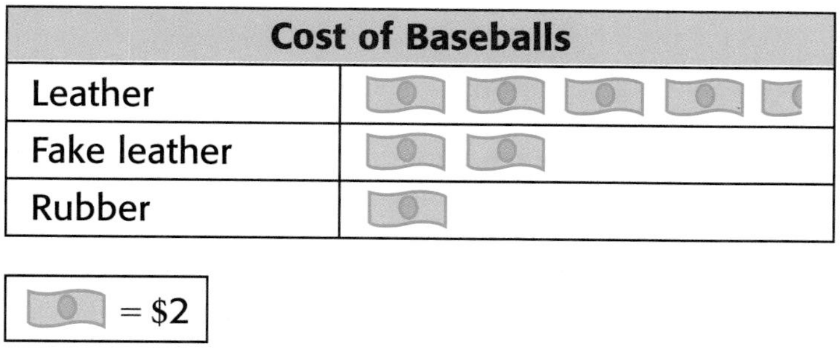

Problem Solving Strategies

- Use Objects/Act It Out
- Draw a Picture
- Look for a Pattern
- Guess and Check
- Use Logical Reasoning
- Make an Organized List
- Make a Table
- Solve a Simpler Problem
- Work Backward

Choose a Tool

3. How much more does a leather baseball cost than a fake leather baseball?

4. How much would it cost to buy a fake leather baseball and a rubber baseball?

5. Sam's team needs 3 rubber baseballs for practice. How much will they cost?

6. **Write Your Own Problem** Write a problem about buying baseballs. Trade problems with a classmate and solve.

7. **Journal** Write a real-world problem that could be solved using the Problem Solving guide. Explain how the guide can help you solve it.

Chapter 1 Lesson 5

Problem Solving

Analyze Word Problems: Choose an Operation

You Will Learn

how to choose the operation needed to solve a problem

Problem Solving Hint

Operation Sense

Addition
- put together

Subtraction
- take away
- compare
- find a missing part

Learn

If you could spend time with anyone you wanted to, who would you choose? This bar graph shows the choices of some students. How many students want to spend time with a friend or a pet?

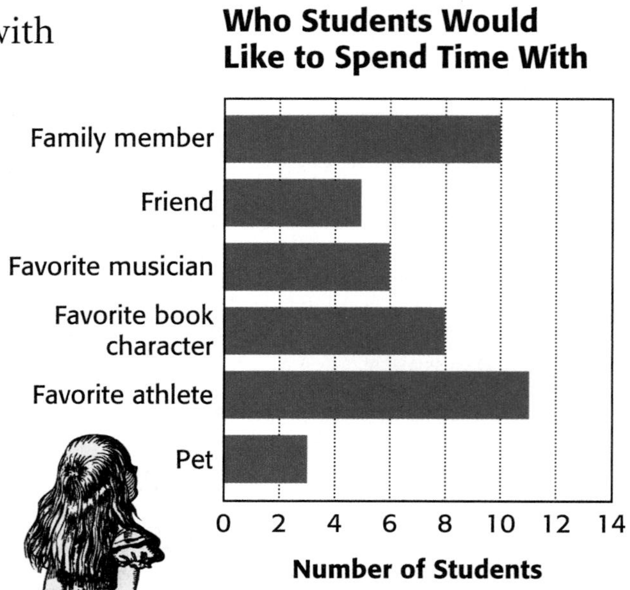

Work Together

Alice is the main character in *Alice's Adventures in Wonderland,* written in 1865 by Lewis Carroll.

▶ Understand What do you know?

What do you need to find out?

▶ Plan How will you find out?

Since you are putting together groups to find the total, you can add.

▶ Solve What's the answer?

$5 + 3 = 8$

8 students would choose to spend time with a friend or a pet.

▶ Look Back Does your answer make sense?

Talk About It

How can you tell whether you need to add or subtract?

Check

Problem Solving
Understand
Plan
Solve
Look Back

Choose the number sentence you would use to solve. Explain.

1. Tara watched 5 hours of TV last weekend. She watched 2 hours of TV this weekend. How many more hours did she watch TV last weekend?

   Ⓐ $5 + 2 = 7$ Ⓑ $5 - 2 = 3$

Write which operation you would use. Then solve.

2. Diego walked his dog for 7 minutes on Saturday and 9 minutes on Sunday. How many minutes did he walk his dog on both days?

Problem Solving Practice

Problem Solving Strategies
- Use Objects/Act It Out
- Draw a Picture
- Look for a Pattern
- Guess and Check
- Use Logical Reasoning
- Make an Organized List
- Make a Table
- Solve a Simpler Problem
- Work Backward

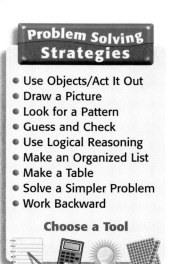

Choose a Tool

Choose the number sentence you would use to solve. Explain.

3. Steffi practiced piano for 2 hours on Monday and 1 hour on Tuesday. How many hours did she practice on both days?

   Ⓐ $2 + 1 = 3$ Ⓑ $2 - 1 = 1$

4. Andre is riding in a bike-a-thon. The trail is 10 miles long. Andre has ridden his bike 7 miles. How many more miles does he need to ride?

   Ⓐ $10 + 7 = 17$ Ⓑ $10 - 7 = 3$

Write which operation you would use. Then solve.

5. The chorus sang 4 songs in the first half of the show. Then they sang 6 songs in the second half. How many songs did they sing during the show?

6. **Using Data** How many more students would choose to spend time with their favorite book character than their friends? Use the graph on page 18.

7. **Journal** Write an addition problem using the numbers 5, 8, and 13. Then write a subtraction problem using the same numbers. Solve each one.

Exploring Algebra: What's the Rule?

Problem Solving Connection
- Look for a Pattern
- Make a Table

Materials
counters

Problem Solving Hint
Look for patterns in the table to help you.

Explore

Here is a special machine that works with numbers. Put a number **In** the machine and look at what comes **Out.** Look at the tables to see if you can figure out what each machine does.

Work Together

Copy and complete each table. Use counters to help.

1.

In	4	5	6	7	10	20
Out	7	8	9			

2.

In	2	3	4	5	9	10
Out	6	7	8			

3.

In	5	6	7	8	10	12
Out	3	4	5			

Talk About It

In the first table, what do you have to do to each **In** number to find the **Out** number? In the second table? In the third table?

Connect

A rule describes what to do to the **In** number to get the **Out** number.

In	5	6	7	11	12	13
Out	1	2	3	7	8	9

$5 - \mathbf{4} = 1$
$6 - \mathbf{4} = 2$
$7 - \mathbf{4} = 3$

The rule for this table is to subtract 4.

Practice

Copy and complete each table. Write the rule for each.

1.

In	2	3	4	5	7	10
Out	4	5	6			

2.

In	1	3	7	8	12	13
Out	5	7	11			

3.

In	12	11	10	9	6	5
Out	7	6	5			

4.

In	10	15	17	22	27	30
Out	9	14	16			

5.

In	5	6	7	8	10	12
Out	11	12	13			

6.

In	0	1	2	3	4	5
Out		8		10		12

7. **Write Your Own Problem** Make your own table. Have a classmate find the rule.

8. **Journal** Explain how looking for a pattern can help you find the rule.

STOP and Practice: Basic Facts

Find each sum or difference.

1. $7 + 2$	**2.** $6 - 5$	**3.** $9 - 7$	**4.** $4 + 5$	**5.** $7 - 1$
6. $6 + 7$	**7.** $4 + 4$	**8.** $5 + 9$	**9.** $6 + 6$	**10.** $7 - 2$
11. $9 - 3$	**12.** $9 + 6$	**13.** $3 + 4$	**14.** $5 - 1$	**15.** $7 + 9$
16. $9 + 5$	**17.** $8 - 2$	**18.** $9 - 4$	**19.** $8 + 7$	**20.** $7 + 7$
21. $6 - 3$	**22.** $7 + 6$	**23.** $5 + 6$	**24.** $4 - 2$	**25.** $6 + 9$
26. $\begin{array}{r} 8 \\ +2 \\ \hline \end{array}$	**27.** $\begin{array}{r} 8 \\ +8 \\ \hline \end{array}$	**28.** $\begin{array}{r} 4 \\ +1 \\ \hline \end{array}$	**29.** $\begin{array}{r} 9 \\ -8 \\ \hline \end{array}$	**30.** $\begin{array}{r} 7 \\ -1 \\ \hline \end{array}$
31. $\begin{array}{r} 7 \\ +8 \\ \hline \end{array}$	**32.** $\begin{array}{r} 6 \\ -2 \\ \hline \end{array}$	**33.** $\begin{array}{r} 5 \\ -3 \\ \hline \end{array}$	**34.** $\begin{array}{r} 9 \\ +9 \\ \hline \end{array}$	**35.** $\begin{array}{r} 9 \\ +4 \\ \hline \end{array}$
36. $\begin{array}{r} 1 \\ +9 \\ \hline \end{array}$	**37.** $\begin{array}{r} 5 \\ -4 \\ \hline \end{array}$	**38.** $\begin{array}{r} 5 \\ +5 \\ \hline \end{array}$	**39.** $\begin{array}{r} 4 \\ +9 \\ \hline \end{array}$	**40.** $\begin{array}{r} 8 \\ +9 \\ \hline \end{array}$
41. $\begin{array}{r} 8 \\ -1 \\ \hline \end{array}$	**42.** $\begin{array}{r} 2 \\ +3 \\ \hline \end{array}$	**43.** $\begin{array}{r} 9 \\ +2 \\ \hline \end{array}$	**44.** $\begin{array}{r} 6 \\ -1 \\ \hline \end{array}$	**45.** $\begin{array}{r} 4 \\ -1 \\ \hline \end{array}$
46. $\begin{array}{r} 9 \\ -2 \\ \hline \end{array}$	**47.** $\begin{array}{r} 3 \\ +1 \\ \hline \end{array}$	**48.** $\begin{array}{r} 3 \\ +3 \\ \hline \end{array}$	**49.** $\begin{array}{r} 9 \\ -1 \\ \hline \end{array}$	**50.** $\begin{array}{r} 5 \\ -2 \\ \hline \end{array}$

Error Search

51. Find each sum or difference that is not correct. Write it correctly and explain the error.

a. $6 - 3 = 9$ **b.** $8 + 1 = 7$ **c.** $7 - 2 = 5$

d. $5 + 6 = 11$ **e.** $5 + 3 = 2$ **f.** $4 + 3 = 1$

"May I Take Your Order?"

Add or subtract to solve the puzzle. Match each letter to its answer to find out what this customer is really ordering. Some letters are not used.

I'd like a bowl of red and a glass of city juice.

52. 6 + 9 [F]	**53.** 9 + 8 [E]	**54.** 5 + 5 [I]	**55.** 8 − 2 [T]
56. 5 − 2 [B]	**57.** 5 + 9 [L]	**58.** 6 + 6 [C]	**59.** 4 + 1 [N]
60. 9 + 9 [H]	**61.** 9 − 5 [W]	**62.** 9 − 1 [G]	**63.** 9 + 2 [J]
64. 10 − 3 [K]	**65.** 9 + 4 [D]	**66.** 8 + 8 [R]	**67.** 10 − 1 [A]

___ ___ ___ ___ ___   ___ ___ ___   ___ ___ ___ ___ ___

12 18 10 14 10   9 5 13   4 9 6 17 16

Remember the Facts!

Use these activities anytime to help you remember your addition and subtraction facts.

1. **Catch the Ball** Practice basic facts when you're outside! Sit in a circle with three or more students. Think of a basic fact like 6 + 4. Call out the fact and throw a ball to one of your classmates. Your classmate should try to catch the ball and say the answer at the same time. Continue playing.

2. **Fact "Address" Book** Make an "address" book of facts. Instead of ordering the book by letters, order the book by numbers. Page 1 should have all the 1s facts listed. Page 2 should have all the 2s facts, and so on. Then look up your facts anytime you need to in your fact "address" book!

SECTION A
Review and Practice

(Lesson 1) Use the pictograph to answer each question.

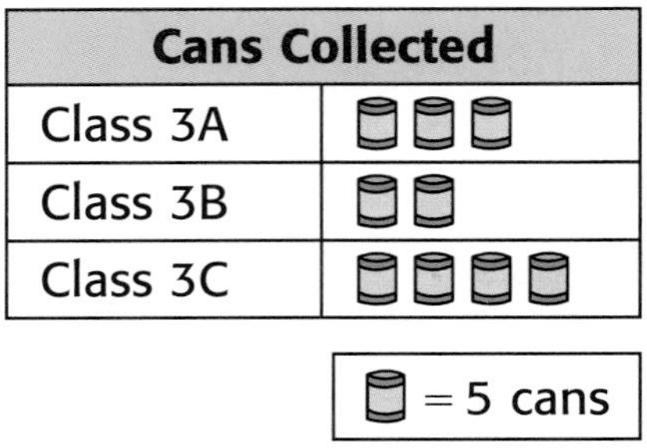

1. Which class collected the most cans?
2. How many cans did Class 3B collect?
3. **Reasoning** Suppose [can symbol] = 10 cans. How many symbols would there be for Class 3C?

(Lesson 2) Use the bar graph to answer each question.

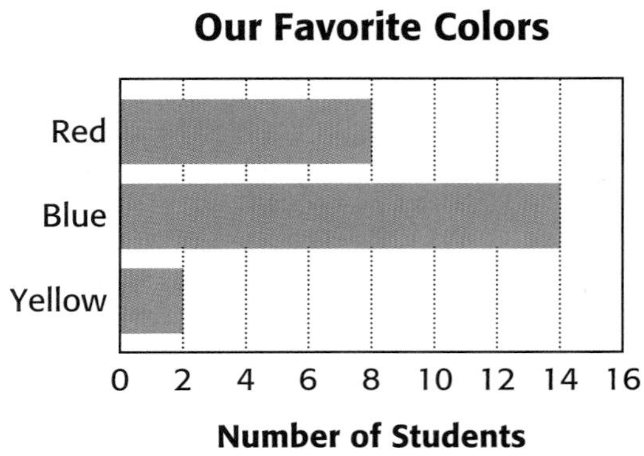

4. How many more students voted for red than yellow?
5. Which color had the fewest votes?
6. Which color did 14 students vote for?

(Lesson 3) Use the line graph to answer each question.

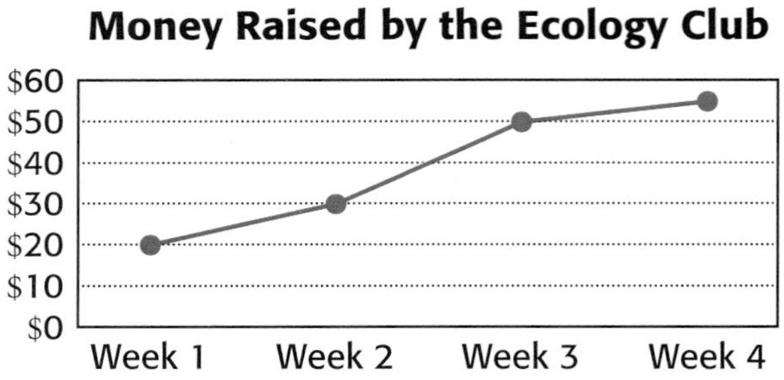

7. How much money was raised by Week 2?
8. By what week did the Ecology Club raise $50?

(Lesson 5) Choose the number sentence you would use to solve the problem. Explain.

9. The Wu family recycled 15 cans last week and 9 cans this week. How many more cans did they recycle last week?

   Ⓐ $15 - 9 = 6$ Ⓑ $15 + 9 = 24$

10. **Journal** How does a graph help you compare data?

Skills Checklist

In this section, you have:

- ☑ Reviewed Basic Addition and Subtraction Facts
- ☑ Read Pictographs, Bar Graphs, and Line Graphs
- ☑ Solved Problems by Using a Guide
- ☑ Solved Problems by Choosing an Operation
- ☑ Explored Algebra

CHAPTER 1

SECTION B

Making Graphs and Facts Review

Students at Kennerly School in St. Louis, Missouri, took a survey of their hobbies. How would you show the results of their survey?

Making Graphs

Review reading graphs. Use the Data File on page 6 to answer each question.

1. How old is a person who needs 7 hours of sleep?
2. Who needs more sleep, a 25-year-old or a 60-year-old?

Skills Checklist

In this section, you will:

- ❒ Review Basic Addition and Subtraction Facts
- ❒ Explore Organizing Data
- ❒ Explore Making Pictographs and Bar Graphs
- ❒ Make Decisions by Collecting and Analyzing Data
- ❒ Solve Problems by Looking for a Pattern

Exploring Organizing Data

Problem Solving Connection
Make a Table

Vocabulary
tally mark
a mark used to record votes or other items

Explore

Do you have a favorite animal? You can take a survey of your classmates to find out which animal is the most popular.

Math Tip
You can write the total number of votes for each animal at the bottom of each column.

Work Together

1. Think of different animals your classmates can vote for. Make a table to show the choices.

Favorite Animals		
Rabbit	Dog	Elephant

2. Take the survey. Write your classmates' names in the table to show their choices.
3. Use the table to answer these questions.
   a. How many students voted for each animal?
   b. Which animal had the most votes? Which had the fewest votes?
   c. Did any two animals have the same number of votes?
   d. Did everyone in the class vote? How do you know?

Talk About It

Suppose you want to take a survey of all of the students in your school. How would you keep track of all of the votes?

Connect

You can use **tally marks** to help count and organize data.

| means 1 vote.

卌 means 5 votes.

This tally table shows students' votes for their favorite family members.

Favorite Family Members		
Family Member	**Tally**	**Number**
Grandmother	卌 卌 ||	12
Grandfather	卌 卌 |	11
Aunt	||||	4
Uncle	卌	5

Practice

1. Copy and complete the tally table. Use the data to help. The votes for "Morning" have already been counted.

Our Favorite Times of Day		
Time of Day	**Tally**	**Number**
Morning	|||	3
Lunchtime		
Afternoon		
Evening		
Nighttime		

evening
afternoon
afternoon
evening
afternoon
lunchtime
evening
afternoon

morning
afternoon
morning
lunchtime
morning
afternoon
nighttime
afternoon

2. Reasoning How does grouping tally marks in groups of 5 help you count the number of votes?

3. Journal Do you think it is better to record votes by using tally marks or by writing out names? Explain.

Mixed Review: Basic Facts

Copy and complete each fact family.

4. $3 + 5 = ■$
$5 + 3 = ■$
$8 - 5 = ■$
$8 - 3 = ■$

5. $4 + 7 = ■$
$■ + 4 = 11$
$11 - 7 = ■$
$■ - 4 = 7$

6. $8 + 6 = ■$
$6 + ■ = 14$
$14 - ■ = 8$
$14 - 8 = ■$

7. $2 + ■ = 11$
$9 + 2 = ■$
$■ - 9 = 2$
$11 - 2 = ■$

Exploring Making Pictographs

Problem Solving Connection
- Draw a Picture
- Make a Table

Materials
grid paper

Remember
The key tells you what each symbol shows.

Explore

This tally table shows students' votes for their favorite breakfast foods. Make a pictograph to make the data easier to read.

Our Favorite Foods for Breakfast		
Food	**Tally**	**Number**
Fruit	||	2
Rice	||||	4
Bagels	卌 卌 ||||	14
Cereal	卌 卌 卌 卌 卌 卌 卌 卌 ||	42
Eggs	卌 |	6
Pancakes	||||	4

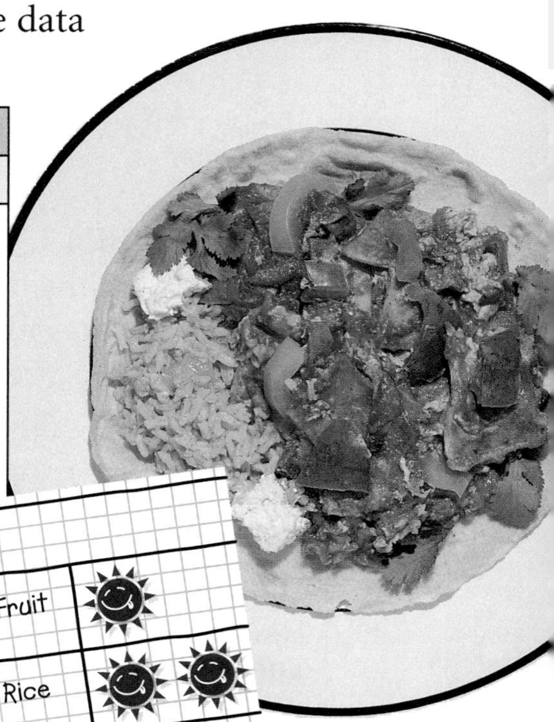

Mexican chiliquillas

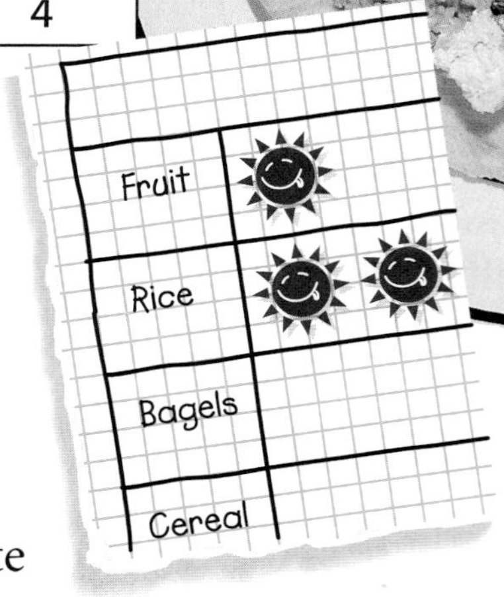

Work Together

1. Use grid paper to make a pictograph.
2. Decide what symbol to use on your pictograph. Have each symbol = 2 votes. Write a key for your pictograph.
3. Make sure your pictograph has a title.
4. How many symbols will you draw to show votes for cereal? How many symbols will you draw to show votes for bagels?
5. Complete your pictograph.

Vietnamese noodle soup, phō

Talk About It

How did you know how many symbols to draw for each breakfast food?

South Indian dosa

Connect

Symbols on a pictograph can show any number. The key shows what each symbol means. Kara and Ryan each used a different key to show the same data.

Kara's Way

Sports We Like to Watch	
Basketball	●●●●●●●●
Football	●●●●
Ice hockey	●●

● = 5 votes

Ryan's Way

Sports We Like to Watch	
Basketball	●●●●
Football	●●
Ice hockey	●

● = 10 votes

Practice

1. **Music** An orchestra has many different kinds of instruments. Copy and complete the pictograph. Use the data in the table.

Some Instruments in an Orchestra	
Bassoons	♪♪
Cellos	

♪ = 2 instruments

2. **Reasoning** Suppose you used this key for your pictograph. How many symbols would there be for cellos?

♪ = 5 instruments

Some Instruments in an Orchestra		
Instrument	**Tally**	**Number**
Bassoons	IIII	
Cellos	~~IIII~~ ~~IIII~~	
Basses	~~IIII~~ III	
Violins	~~IIII~~ ~~IIII~~ ~~IIII~~ I	

3. **Journal** Suppose your class serves breakfast at school for a week. Use the pictograph you made on page 28 to plan a menu. Explain how you decided what to serve.

Mixed Review: Basic Facts

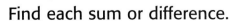

Find each sum or difference.

4. $2 + 6$ **5.** $8 - 6$ **6.** $3 - 2$ **7.** $3 + 9$ **8.** $6 + 3$

9. $1 - 1$ **10.** $5 + 7$ **11.** $4 - 4$ **12.** $9 - 5$ **13.** $8 + 7$

Exploring Making Bar Graphs

Problem Solving Connection
- Draw a Picture
- Make a Table

Materials
grid paper

Explore

Students in one class at Kennerly Elementary School took a survey about the kinds of things they like to collect.

Suppose these students wanted to share their data with another class. To present the data clearly, they could make a bar graph.

Great Things to Collect		
Collection	**Tally**	**Number**
Stamps	𝍷	1
Rocks	𝍷𝍷𝍷𝍷	4
Sports cards	𝍸 𝍷𝍷𝍷	8
Dolls	𝍷𝍷	2
Pins	𝍷	1
Stickers	𝍷	1
Other	𝍸	5

Students at Kennerly School in St. Louis, Missouri

Math Tip
The end of each bar should match each number of votes.

Work Together

Use grid paper and data in the table to make a bar graph.

1. Number the scale for your graph. Start at 0. Count by 2s.
2. Make sure you label your graph and give it a title.
3. Choose an item. Draw the bar. Where should the bar end?
4. Complete your bar graph.

Talk About It

5. How did you know where each bar should end?
6. Where did your scale end? How did you know where to stop?

Connect

You can use any scale for a bar graph. Here are two bar graphs that show the same data with different scales.

Kim uses a scale of 2.

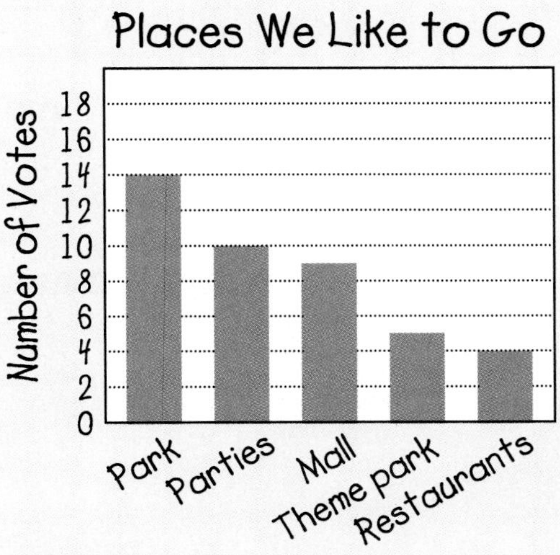

Darryl uses a scale of 5.

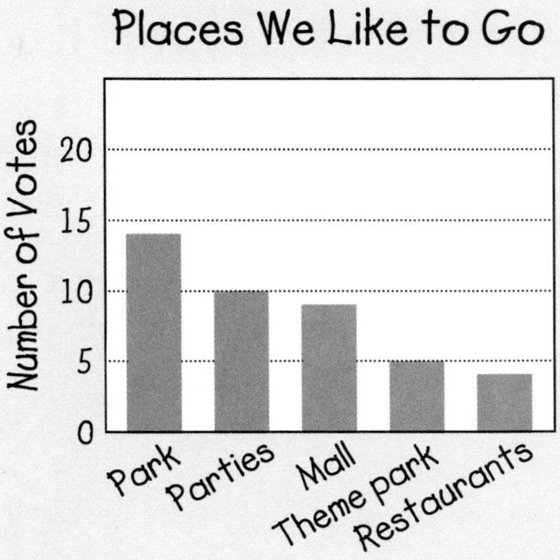

Practice

Using Data Use the Data File on page 7 for **1** and **2**.

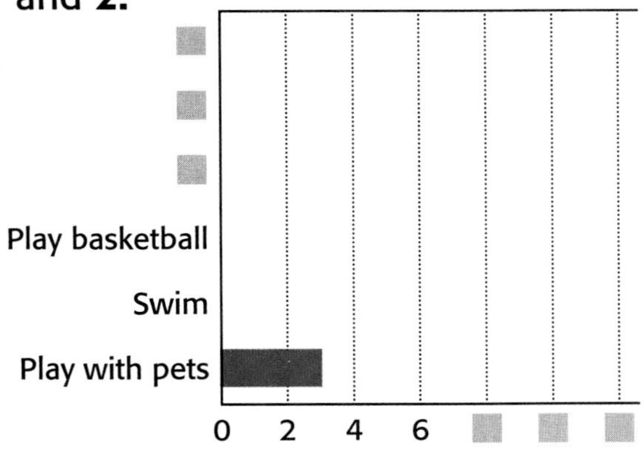

1. Copy and complete the bar graph. Make sure you label it and give it a title.
2. How many more students voted for swimming than playing basketball?
3. **Journal** Compare making a bar graph with making a pictograph. How is it the same? How is it different?

Mixed Review: Basic Facts

Add or subtract.

4. 8 + 9	**5.** 12 − 3	**6.** 6 + 6	**7.** 18 − 9	**8.** 14 − 7
9. 5 + 8	**10.** 3 + 7	**11.** 4 − 2	**12.** 8 − 3	**13.** 15 − 6
14. 9 − 4	**15.** 6 + 2	**16.** 12 − 4	**17.** 17 − 8	**18.** 3 + 3
19. 11 − 2	**20.** 7 + 8	**21.** 14 − 8	**22.** 10 − 8	**23.** 4 + 8

Skills Practice Bank, page 518, Set 2

Chapter 1
Lesson
10

Problem Solving

Decision Making: Collect and Analyze Data

You Will Learn
how to collect and analyze data to help you make decisions

Explore

Do you have ideas about how to improve your school? Suppose the principal wants to know how to make the school better for everyone. You are asked to present three suggestions.

Collect and graph data about your ideas. Then use your graph to decide what your three suggestions will be.

Work Together

Understand

1. What do you need to decide?
2. How can you organize your classmates' ideas?

Plan and Solve

3. Make a tally table to record your classmates' ideas.
4. Look at your data. Will you create a bar graph or a pictograph?
5. What will the title of your graph be?
6. If you make a pictograph, let each symbol show 2 votes. If you make a bar graph, make a scale by counting by 2s.
7. Complete your graph.

Make a Decision

8. Use your graph to choose three suggestions to make to your principal about improvements to your school.

Present Your Decision

9. Record your suggestions in a list. Explain why you are making each suggestion and how the graph helped you decide.
10. Suppose you meet with the principal to present your ideas. How could your graph help you explain your choices?

Students in Seattle, Washington, help make their school more beautiful.

Technology

Making Graphs

Darren's class is having a party to welcome new students. Darren is in charge of ordering Big Bite Sandwiches for the party. He took a survey to find out what kinds of sandwiches his classmates like. Help Darren decide what kinds of sandwiches he should order.

Materials
DataWonder! or other graphing software

Big Bite Sandwich Shop
Four Cheese
Peanut Butter & Jelly
Meatball
Ham & Cheese
Turkey & Cheese

Work Together

Making a graph with a computer can help you make decisions.

1. Create a Simple Data Table in a graphing program. Copy this data into your table.

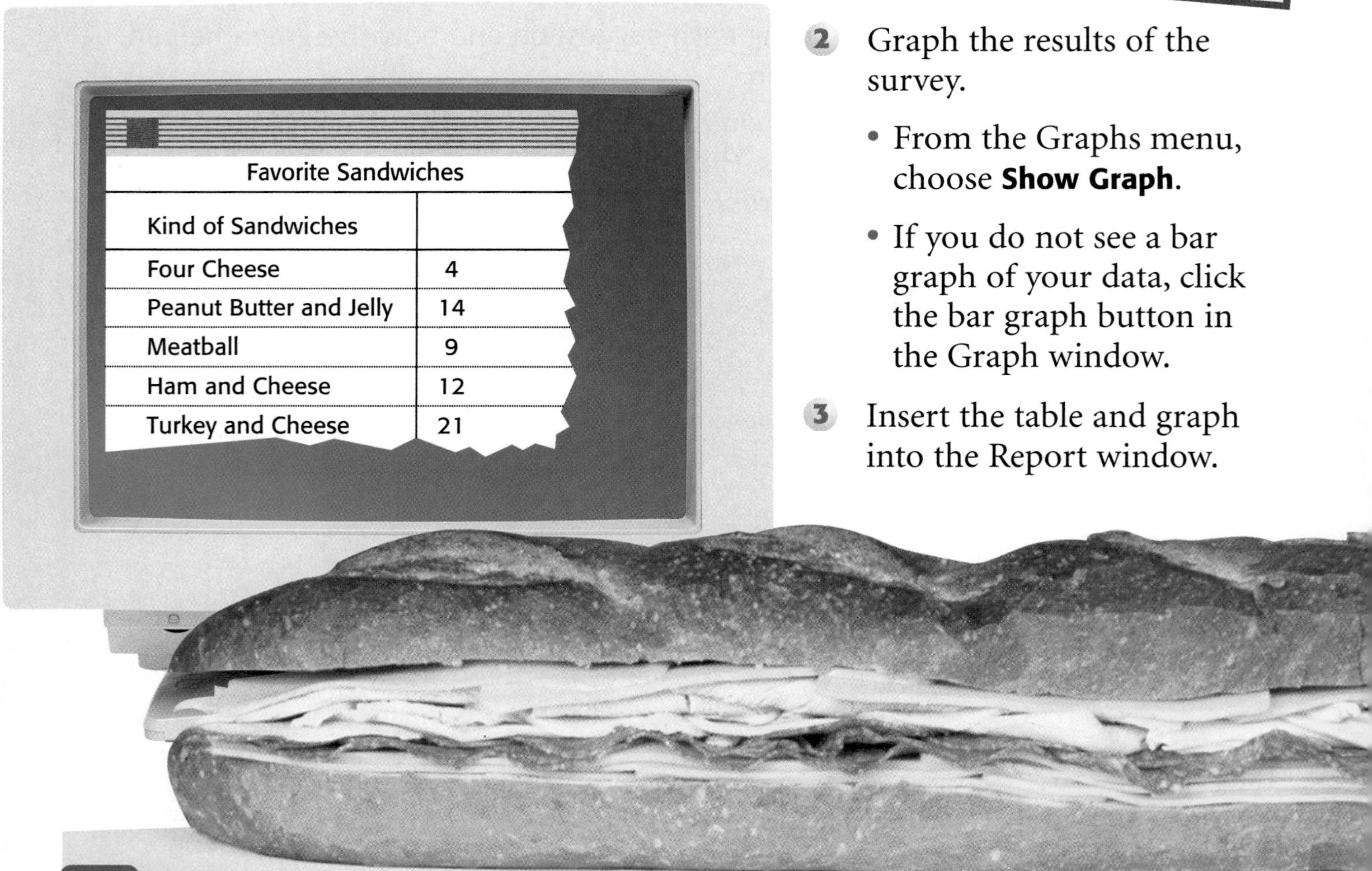

Favorite Sandwiches	
Kind of Sandwiches	
Four Cheese	4
Peanut Butter and Jelly	14
Meatball	9
Ham and Cheese	12
Turkey and Cheese	21

2. Graph the results of the survey.
   - From the Graphs menu, choose **Show Graph**.
   - If you do not see a bar graph of your data, click the bar graph button in the Graph window.
3. Insert the table and graph into the Report window.

Exercises

Answer 1–3 in the Report window below your graph. When you are finished, choose Print Report from the File menu.

1. Which sandwich had the most votes?
2. Which sandwich had the fewest votes?
3. If Darren needs to order 12 sandwiches, how many of each type should he order? Explain.

Extensions

4. The cast of the school play wants to order Big Bite Sandwiches. Use your graphing software to make a data table and a bar graph of the cast's survey results. Use the tally table to help.

Favorite Sandwiches	
Kind of Sandwich	**Tally**
Four cheese	|||
Peanut butter and jelly	𝍸 |
Meatball	𝍸 𝍸 |
Ham and cheese	𝍸 𝍸 |||
Turkey and cheese	𝍸 ||

Insert the data table and graph for 4 in the Report window. Answer 5 and 6 in the Report window. Print Report when you are finished.

5. The cast needs to order eight sandwiches. How many of each kind of sandwich do you think the cast should order?
6. **Reasoning** When the cast members order their sandwiches, they find out that the Big Bite Shop ran out of peanut butter. Will they need to change their order? If so, how will they change it?

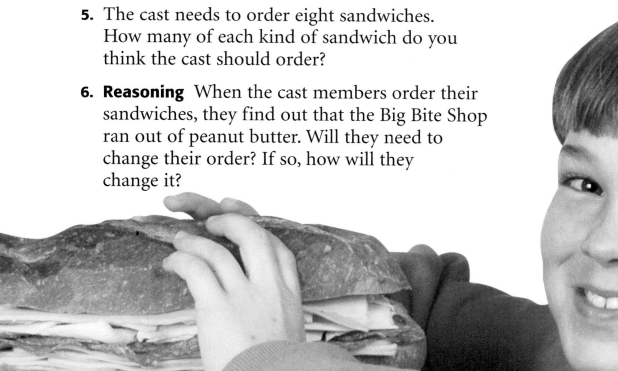

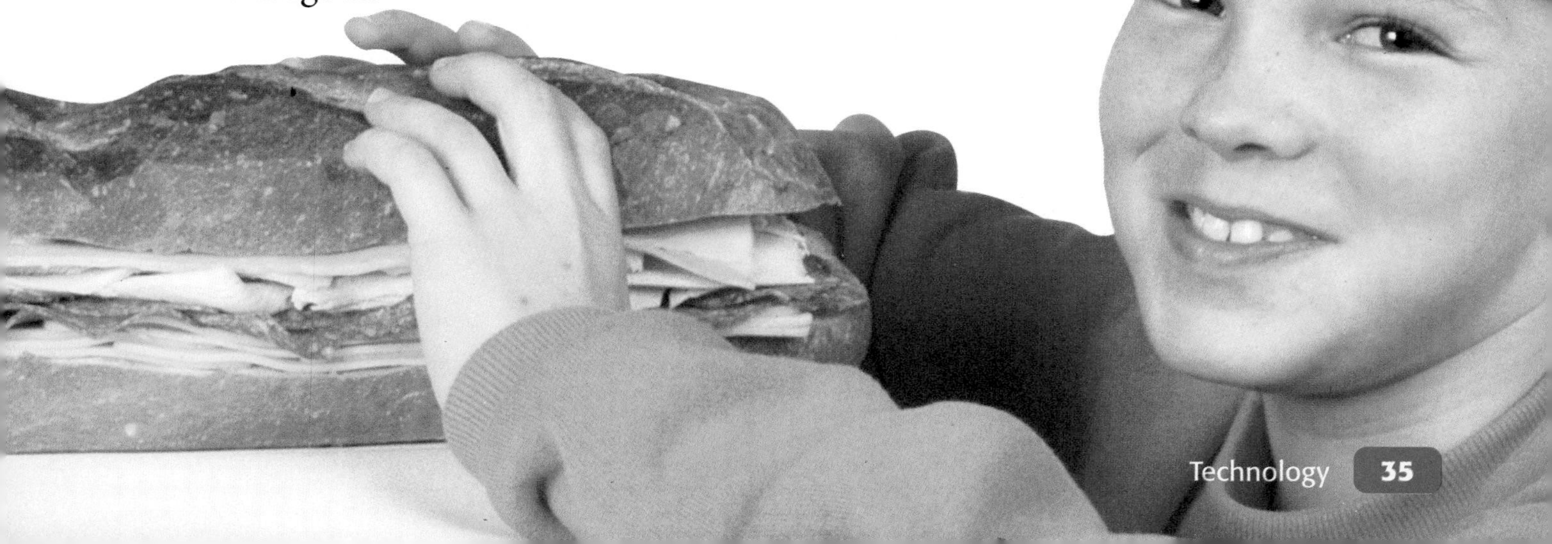

STOP and Practice: Basic Facts

Find each sum or difference.

1. $10 - 8$	**2.** $9 + 7$	**3.** $13 - 7$	**4.** $7 + 7$	**5.** $14 - 9$
6. $12 - 4$	**7.** $16 - 8$	**8.** $5 + 9$	**9.** $6 + 5$	**10.** $13 - 5$
11. $11 - 7$	**12.** $10 - 6$	**13.** $12 - 7$	**14.** $10 - 2$	**15.** $15 - 7$
16. $13 - 4$	**17.** $8 + 8$	**18.** $13 - 8$	**19.** $9 + 2$	**20.** $17 - 9$
21. $8 + 2$	**22.** $9 + 5$	**23.** $14 - 6$	**24.** $18 - 9$	**25.** $8 + 5$

26. $16 - 9$	**27.** $6 + 7$	**28.** $2 + 9$	**29.** $8 + 7$	**30.** $15 - 9$
31. $14 - 7$	**32.** $8 - 5$	**33.** $15 - 6$	**34.** $12 - 3$	**35.** $5 + 4$
36. $14 - 5$	**37.** $6 + 1$	**38.** $8 + 3$	**39.** $17 - 8$	**40.** $16 - 7$
41. $12 - 5$	**42.** $11 - 4$	**43.** $9 + 4$	**44.** $13 - 9$	**45.** $10 - 4$
46. $7 - 3$	**47.** $7 + 3$	**48.** $13 - 6$	**49.** $9 + 8$	**50.** $12 - 8$

Error Search

51. Find each sum or difference that is not correct. Write it correctly and explain the error.

a. $9 - 2 = 6$	**b.** $10 - 3 = 13$	**c.** $15 - 7 = 8$	**d.** $6 + 1 = 6$
e. $9 + 2 = 7$	**f.** $8 + 4 = 12$	**g.** $9 - 4 = 13$	**h.** $3 + 5 = 35$

Remember the Facts!

Use these activities anytime to help you remember your addition and subtraction facts.

1. **Fact Trains** Make a fact card for each difficult fact. Make a fact train with your cards. Say each fact. When you know it, add it to the train. If you miss, start over. See who can make the longest train.

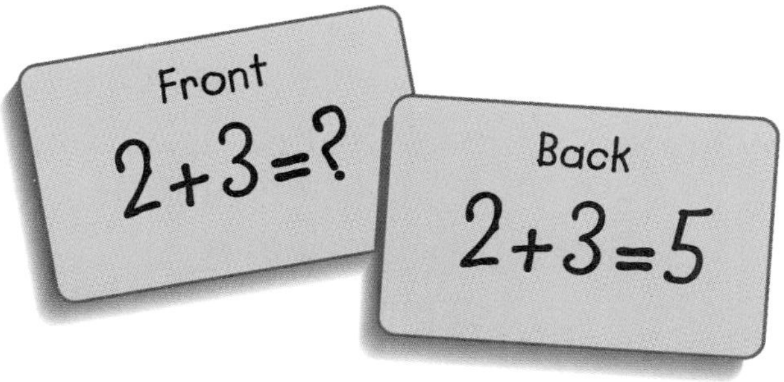

2. **Pocket Math** On a card, write a fact that is difficult to remember. Put the card in your pocket. Every hour, think about your fact. Do you remember it? If not, take the card out and check. When you've learned it, try it with another fact!

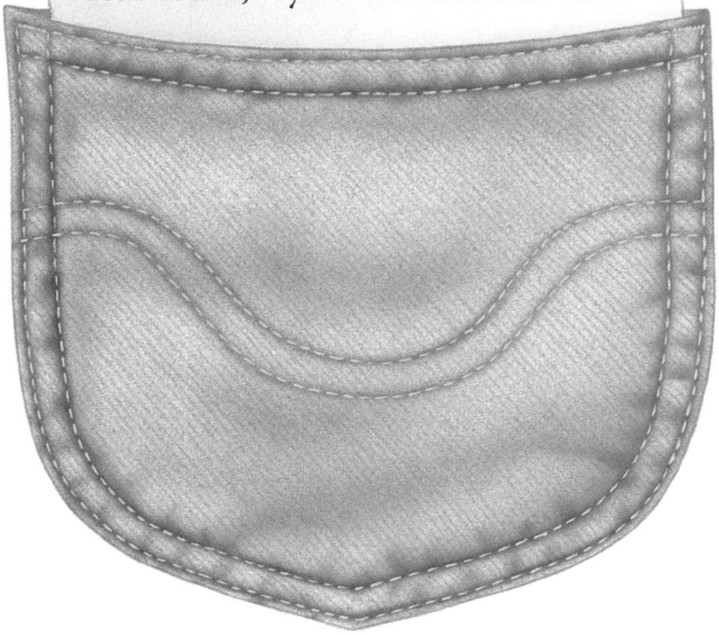

3. **Fact Relay** Have a fact relay with two or more teams. One student from each team starts by writing down a fact. The next student on each team must write the correct answer. If the answer is correct, the student who wrote the correct answer writes down another. Continue playing until everyone has had a few turns.

Chapter 1 Lesson 11

Problem Solving

Analyze Strategies: Look for a Pattern

You Will Learn
how finding a pattern can help you solve problems

Learn

The *shekere* (SHA-ker-ay) is a West African instrument. It is made from a dried, hollowed-out gourd and covered with a net of beads. On this shekere net, what beads would you use next?

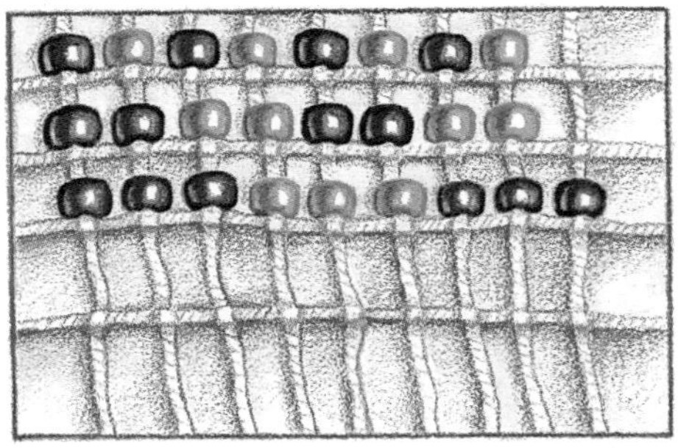

When shaken to the beat of the music, the beads make a rattling sound.

Work Together

▶ Understand
What do you know?
What do you need to find out?

▶ Plan
How will you find out?
Look for a pattern that will help you solve the problem.

▶ Solve
Find a pattern.
Each row of beads has one more of each color in each group than the row before. The beads go from groups of black to groups of blue to groups of black and so on.

The next row of beads should be 4 black, 4 blue.

Write the answer.
You should use 4 black beads next.

▶ Look Back
Check to see if your answer makes sense.

Another Example

What are the next two numbers?

2, 5, 8, 11, ▒, ▒

Look for a number pattern.

Try skip counting.

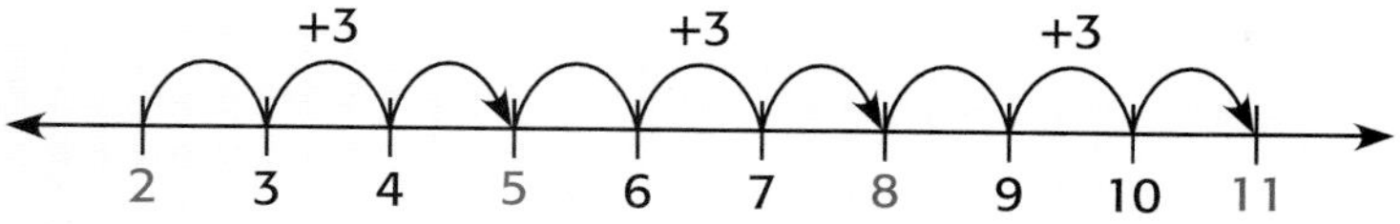

Each number is 3 more than the one before.

Use the pattern to find the next two numbers.

$11 + 3 = 14$

$14 + 3 = 17$

So, the next two numbers are 14 and 17.

Talk About It

How can looking for a pattern help you to solve problems?

Check

1. If the pattern continues, which bead should come next?

Ⓐ    Ⓑ 

2. How many yellow beads should come next?

3. What are the next three numbers?
   12, 10, 8, ▒, ▒, ▒

4. What are the next three numbers?
   1, 3, 5, 7, ▒, ▒, ▒

5. **Reasoning** Jamal says, "The next picture in this pattern should be an apple." Do you agree or disagree? Explain.

Problem Solving Practice

Apply the Strategy

Look for a pattern to help you solve each problem.

6. Lisa is making the border for her quilt. What are the next three shapes in her pattern?

Ⓐ 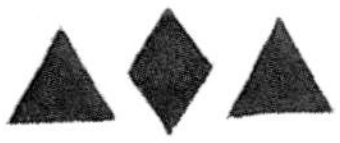

Ⓑ 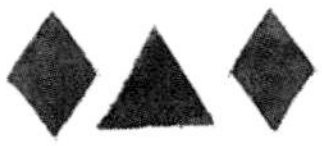

> **Problem Solving Strategies**
> - Use Objects/Act It Out
> - Draw a Picture
> - Look for a Pattern
> - Guess and Check
> - Use Logical Reasoning
> - Make an Organized List
> - Make a Table
> - Solve a Simpler Problem
> - Work Backward
>
> **Choose a Tool**
>
> 

7. Josie and her friends played a game. Josie clapped her hands like this: 4 claps, 8 claps, 12 claps. Jon continued the pattern. What will he clap next? Explain.

8. What are the next three numbers?

12, 14, 16, 18, ■, ■, ■

9. What are the next three numbers?

20, 25, 30, 35, ■, ■, ■

Choose a Strategy

Look for a pattern or use any strategy to help you solve each problem.

10. The Snail-Mail Service uses a pattern to number their mailboxes. What number should be on the next two mailboxes?

11. The art teacher buys paint by the jar. She bought 8 jars of blue paint and 9 jars of red paint. How many jars of paint did she buy?

12. Dan made a bracelet for his mother. He used 5 yellow beads and 13 white beads. How many more white beads did he use?

13. Geometry Readiness How many ■ will be in the next figure?

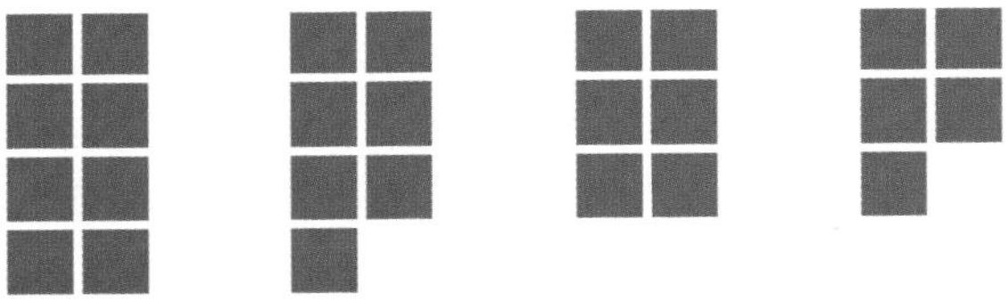

____

Problem Solving and SOCIAL STUDIES

Patterns can be found in many places. Baskets made with grass, feathers, bits of shell, and beads can have patterns with colors and shapes.

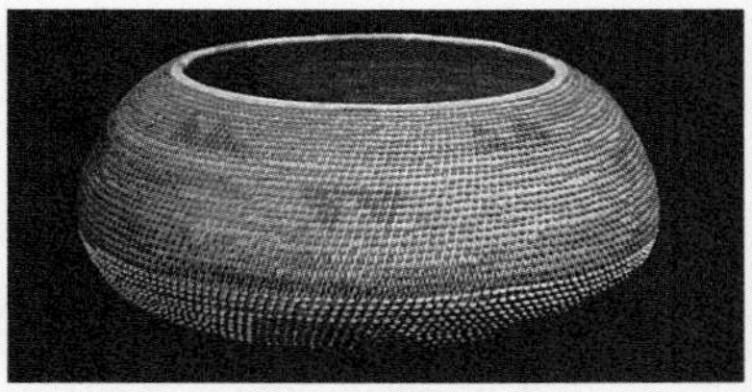
Pomo basket

14. Which pattern was used on the Pomo basket?

Ⓐ 

Ⓑ 

Ⓒ 

15. Suppose the Hopi basket in the picture were flattened. Which shows the complete basket pattern?

Ⓐ 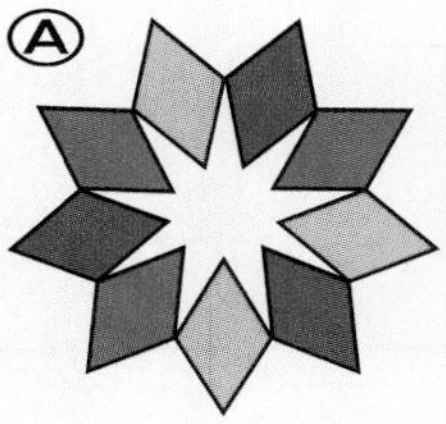

Ⓑ 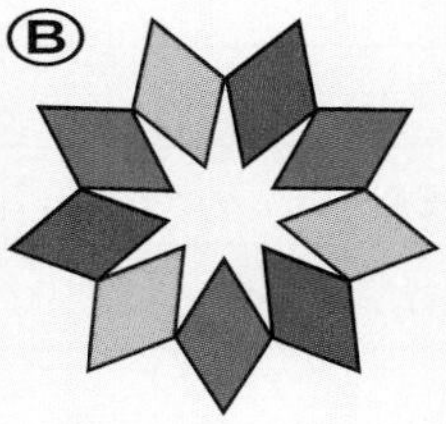

Ⓒ 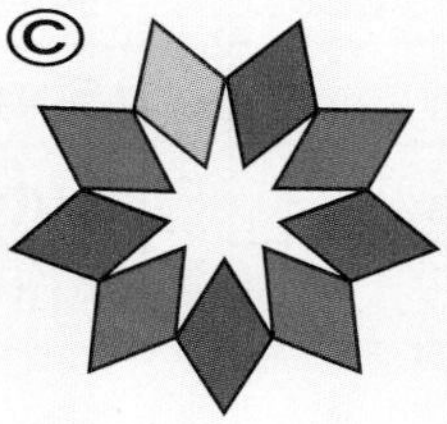

Hopi basket

16. Write Your Own Problem Make up your own pattern. You can use colors or numbers. Trade patterns with a classmate. Continue your classmate's pattern.

17. Journal When might you look for a pattern to solve a problem?

Mixed Review: Basic Facts

Find each sum or difference.

18. 13 − 9	**19.** 9 + 8	**20.** 8 + 7	**21.** 4 + 4	**22.** 11 − 7
23. 18 − 9	**24.** 7 − 4	**25.** 6 + 5	**26.** 9 − 3	**27.** 10 − 6
28. 4 + 7	**29.** 14 − 6	**30.** 3 + 9	**31.** 15 − 7	**32.** 5 + 7
33. 2 + 9	**34.** 6 + 8	**35.** 14 − 7	**36.** 3 + 6	**37.** 16 − 8
38. 13 − 6	**39.** 5 + 5	**40.** 7 + 9	**41.** 17 − 9	**42.** 9 + 3

Skills Practice Bank, page 518, Set 4

SECTION B
Review and Practice

(Lesson 7) Make a tally table.

1. Copy and complete the tally table with the ages shown below.

7, 8, 8, 7, 9, 7, 7, 8, 7, 9, 7, 7, 8, 8, 9, 7, 8, 7, 9

Ages of Scouts		
Age	**Tally**	**Number**
7		
8		
9		

(Lesson 8) Make a pictograph.

2. Use the data in the table. Copy and complete the pictograph.

Our Favorite Season	
Season	**Number of Votes**
Winter	4
Spring	8
Summer	10
Autumn	6

Our Favorite Season	
Winter	
Spring	
Summer	
Autumn	

 = 2 votes

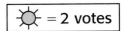

(Lesson 9) Make a bar graph.

3. Use the data in the table. Copy and complete the bar graph.

Lamar's Trumpet Practice	
Day of Week	**Number of Minutes**
Monday	15
Wednesday	10
Friday	15

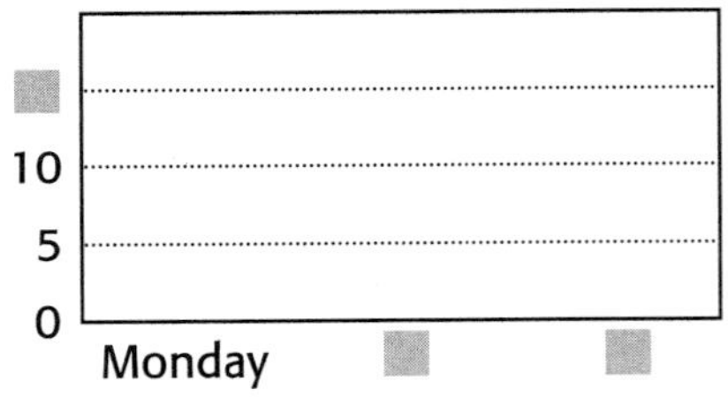

(Lesson 11) Solve. Use any strategy.

4. **Patterns** Hugo is taking piano lessons. The first day, he played for 5 minutes. Every day, he plays for 5 minutes more than the day before. When will he play for 30 minutes?

5. **Journal** What kind of graph would you use to show how many times you and four friends can jump rope without missing? Explain.

Skills Checklist

In this section, you have:

- ☑ Reviewed Basic Addition and Subtraction Facts
- ☑ Explored Organizing Data
- ☑ Explored Making Pictographs and Bar Graphs
- ☑ Collected and Analyzed Data
- ☑ Solved Problems by Looking for a Pattern

YOUR CHOICE

Choose at least one. Use what you have learned in this chapter.

1 Snail Survey

Help a scientist read this pictograph. What three things could the scientist report about the snail population?

Snail Population	
Mirror Lake	🐌🐌
West Lake	🐌🐌🐌🐌🐌🐌🐌🐌
Miller's Pond	🐌🐌🐌🐌🐌🐌🐌🐌🐌

🐌 = 5 snails

2 Data Hunt

Use the World Wide Web to find data about three of your favorite animals. Then make a bar graph to show something about the animals. Your graph might show how much they weigh, how long they live, how tall or long they are, or something else.

3 Collect It

At Home Take a survey about your family's favorite dinner. Make a pictograph to show the results. Then treat your family and help prepare their favorite meal!

4 Pet Power

The bar graph shows the pets that Tad has at home. Use this information to write a question for each answer.

a. 5

b. 11

c. 13

d. 10

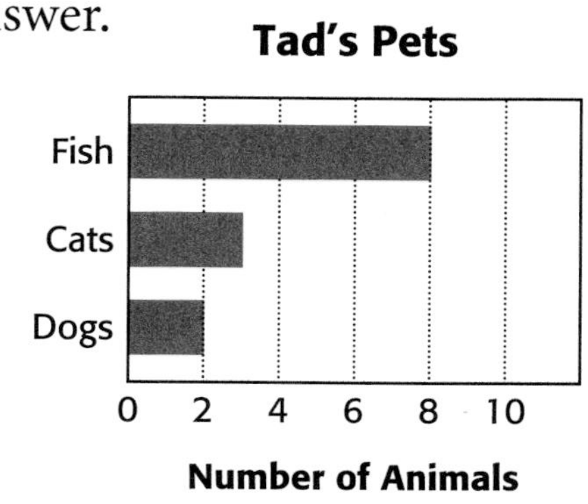

5 Picture That!

Cut out pictures from old magazines or newspapers and paste them on paper to show some basic facts. Write the basic fact below each picture.

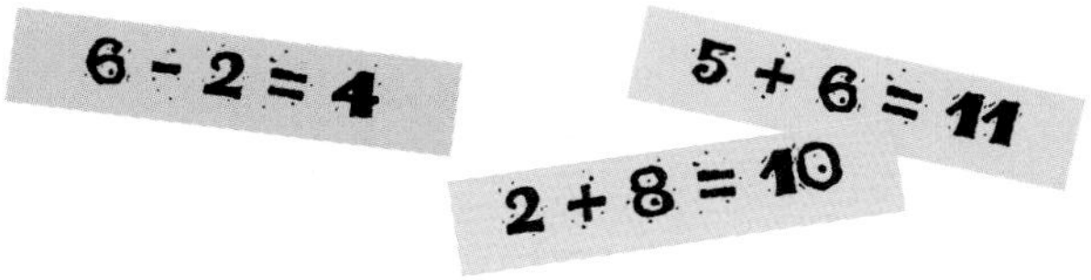

CHAPTER 1
Review/Test

Vocabulary Match each with its meaning.

1. bar graph — **a.** a graph that uses pictures, or symbols, to show data

2. pictograph — **b.** part of a pictograph that tells what each symbol shows

3. key — **c.** a graph that uses bars to show data

(Lessons 1–3) Use the graphs to answer **4–7.**

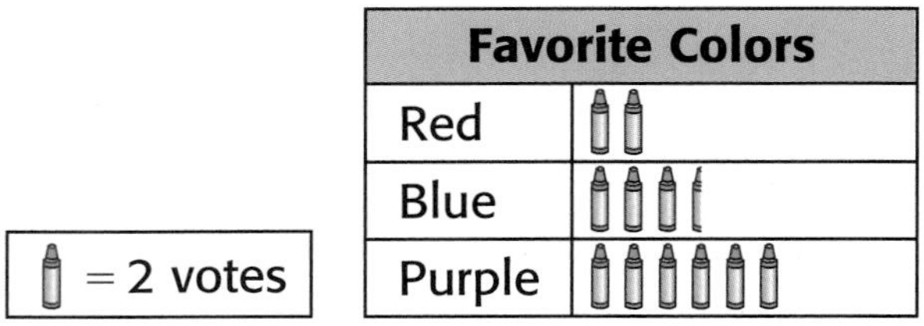

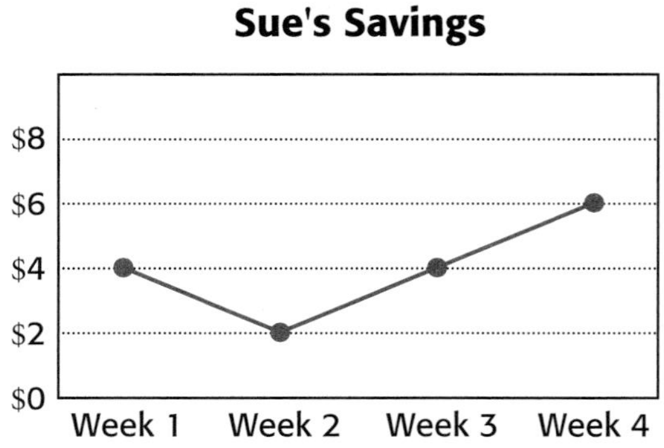

4. How many students chose red as their favorite color?

5. How many students chose blue as their favorite color?

6. How much had Sue saved by Week 3?

7. When did Sue have $6?

(Lesson 5) Tell which operation you would use. Then solve.

8. Diana wants a soccer ball that costs $10. She has $7. How much more money does she need?

(Lesson 9) Make a bar graph.

9. Copy and complete the bar graph. Include a title and labels.

Favorite Types of Books	
Type of Book	**Number of Votes**
Nonfiction	𝍸
Science fiction	𝍸
Mystery	𝍸 𝍸 𝍸 𝍸
Humor	𝍸 𝍸 𝍸

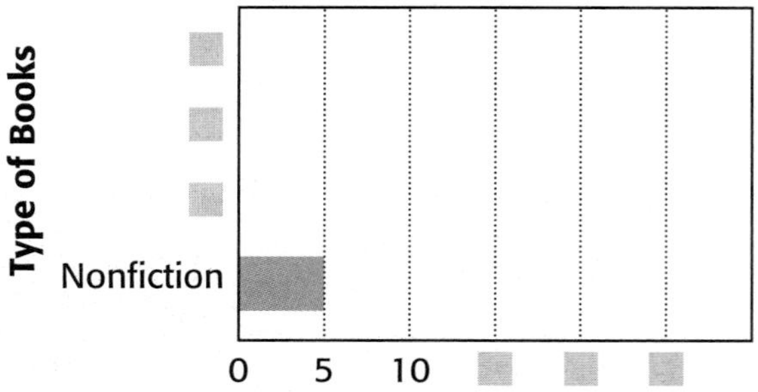

(Lesson 11) Solve. Use any strategy.

10. Otis did 3 sit-ups on Monday, 6 on Tuesday, and 9 on Wednesday. Find a pattern. How many will he do on Friday?

CHAPTER 1
Performance Assessment

Suppose a group of parents wants to donate books to your school library. They need to know what kinds of books students like to read. Ask your classmates what their favorite type of book is. Then make a graph to help the parents decide what to donate.

1. **Decision Making** List different types of books students can vote for. Make a table to record the votes.

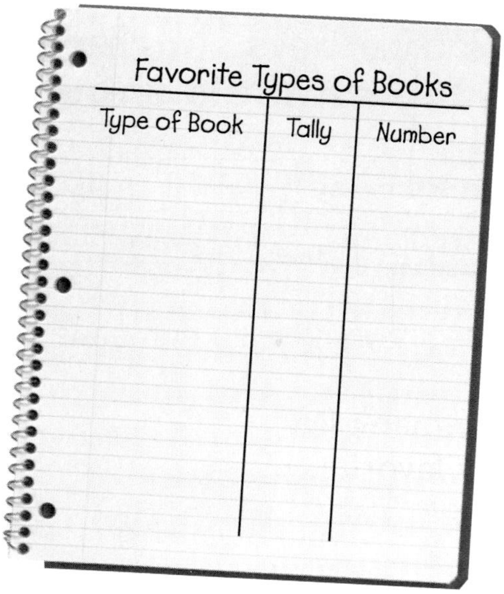

2. **Recording Data** Record students' votes on your table using tally marks. Make a pictograph of the data you collected using this key.
   ★ = 1 vote

3. **Explain Your Thinking** What do you think the parents will learn from your graph? What are the top three choices of books? What types of books do you think the parents should donate to the library?

4. **Critical Thinking** How are your table and graph different? Could the parents have read the same information from the table and the graph? Explain.

Math Magazine

Clock Talk **Today we use digits like 1, 2, and 3 to name numbers. Many years ago, pictures of objects or other symbols were used to name numbers. Ancient Romans used the symbols shown below.**

Roman Numeral	I	II	III	IV	V	VI	VII	VIII	IX	X	XI	XII
Standard Form	1	2	3	4	5	6	7	8	9	10	11	12

The table shows Roman numerals for 1–12.

Here's the key: I = 1

V = 5

X = 10

Here's what happens when I comes after V or X.

VI Think of this as V + I 5 + 1 = 6

XI Think of this as X + I 10 + 1 = 11

Here's what happens when I comes before V or X.

IV Think of this as V − I 5 − 1 = 4

IX Think of this as X − I 10 − 1 = 9

You might see Roman numerals on a watch.

Try These!

Write each Roman numeral in standard form.

1. XV **2.** XIII **3.** XVI **4.** XX

CHAPTER 1
Cumulative Review

I can test each of the answer choices to see which one works.

12 − 6 is 6.
6 + 4 is 10—not correct.

14 − 6 is 8.
8 + 4 is 12—not correct.

11 − 6 is 5.
5 + 4 is 9—correct!
So the answer is Ⓒ, 11.

Test Prep Strategy: Work Backward from an Answer

Replace the missing number with each choice.
I am a 2-digit number. If you subtract 6 from me and add 4 to me, you will get 9. What number am I?

Ⓐ 12 Ⓑ 14 Ⓒ 11 Ⓓ 10

Test Prep Strategies
- Read Carefully
- Follow Directions
- Make Smart Choices
- Eliminate Choices
- Work Backward from an Answer

Write the letter of the correct answer. Work backward from an answer or use any strategy to help.

1. Luis had nine pencils. After he gave some away, he had five pencils left. How many did he give away?

Ⓐ 5 Ⓑ 4 Ⓒ 14 Ⓓ 9

2. Complete the pattern.

6, 8, ■, 12, 14.

Ⓐ 15 Ⓑ 6 Ⓒ 10 Ⓓ 18

Use the bar graph to answer **3** and **4.**

3. How many more students have brown eyes than hazel eyes?

Ⓐ 3 students Ⓑ 9 students
Ⓒ 12 students Ⓓ 14 students

4. How many students do NOT have brown eyes?

Ⓐ 5 students Ⓑ 14 students
Ⓒ 12 students Ⓓ 9 students

Color of Students' Eyes

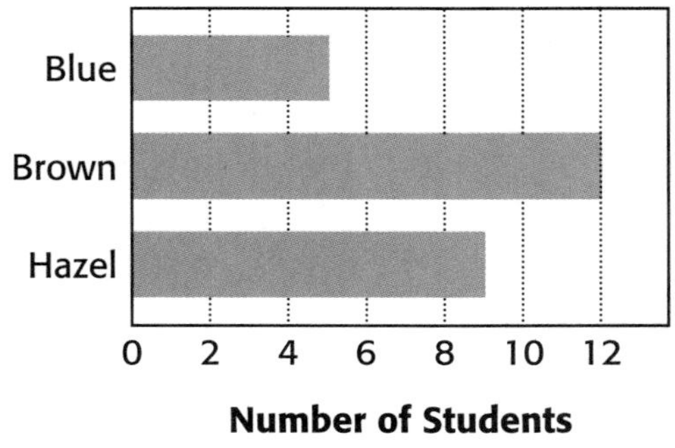

5. Which has the same sum as $6 + 9$?

Ⓐ $5 + 8$ Ⓑ $9 - 6$ Ⓒ $8 + 7$ Ⓓ $4 + 10$

6. What is the missing number in ■ $+ 5 = 11$?

Ⓐ 3 Ⓑ 11 Ⓒ 5 Ⓓ 6

REVIEW AND PRACTICE

DATA FILE

Chapter 2

Place Value and Time

BUGS AND BUG EATERS

SECTION A

The Royal Ontario Museum

Page 51

Understanding Place Value 51

If you want to see lots of bugs, go to the Royal Ontario Museum in Canada. Why? They have thousands of creepy crawlers! How many beetles does the museum have?

Insects and Spiders at The Royal Ontario Museum	Number
Spiders	27,185
Common flies	96,725
Beetles	110,475
Caddis flies	245,755
Grasshoppers and crickets	21,478
Stone flies	17,093
Butterflies and moths	125,541

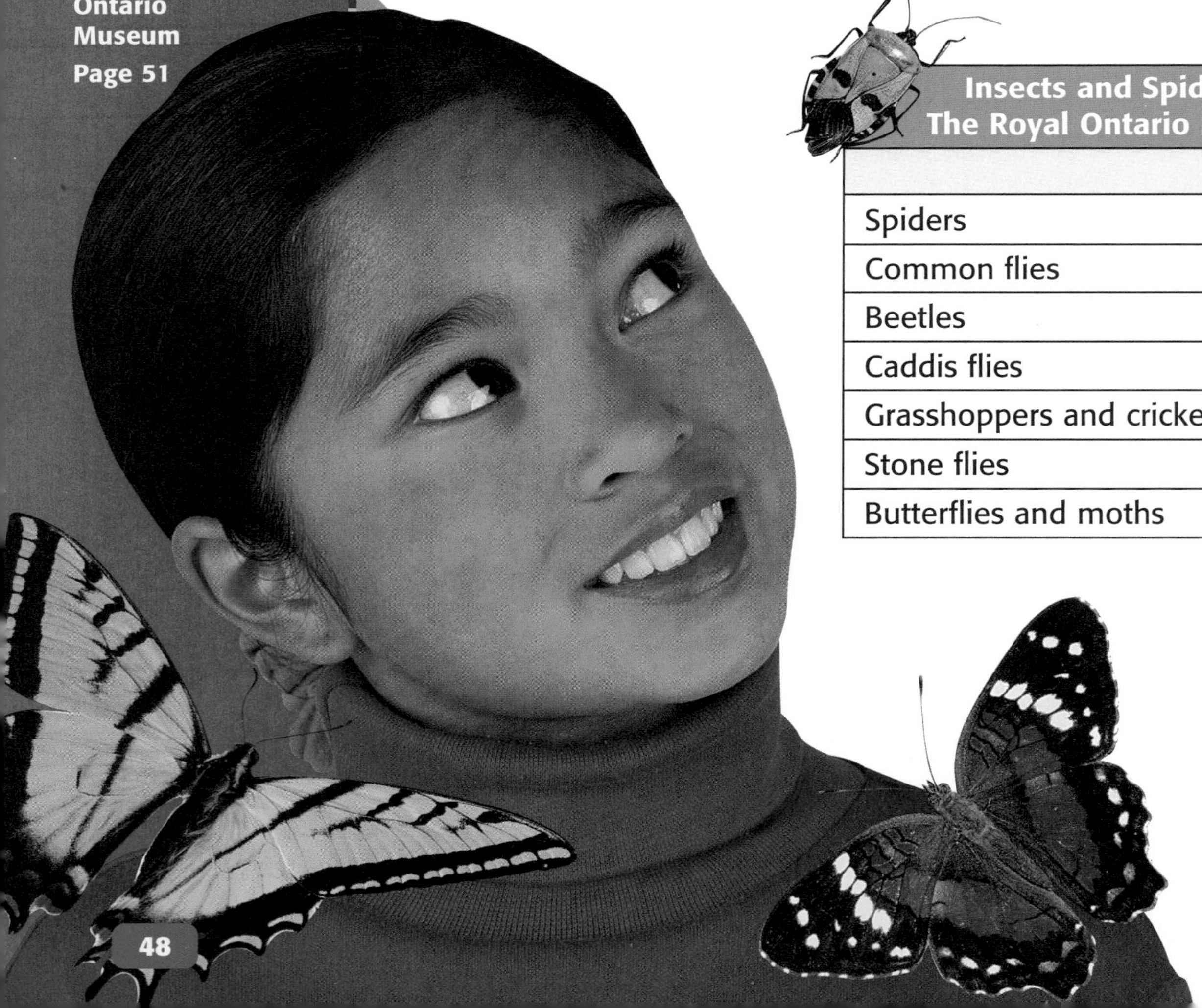

Building Number Sense

63

How long does it take a centipede to travel 100 meters?

Time to Travel 100 Meters	
Snail	124 minutes
Giant tortoise	22 minutes
Three-toed sloth	22 minutes
Centipede	3 minutes
Spider	9 minutes

Giant tortoise
Page 63

Surfing the World Wide Web!

Pick a bug to research using the World Wide Web and record some data you find. Start your research at **www.mathsurf.com/3/ch2**.

Understanding Time

73

For a book called *Egg*, writers watched while animals hatched from their shells. Which animal took the longest time to hatch?

Time Taken to Hatch

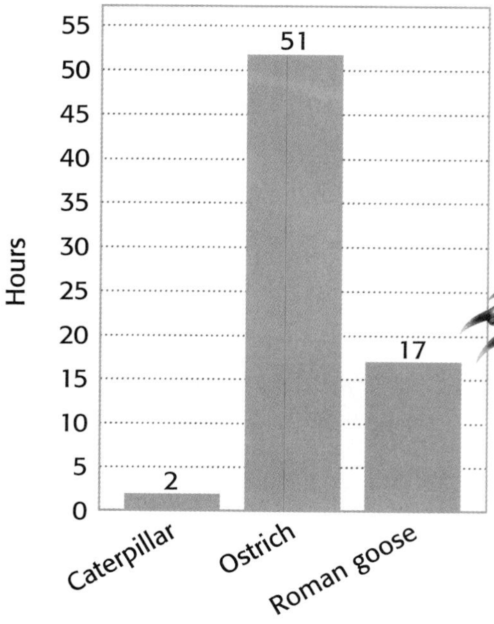

Baby ostrich
Page 73

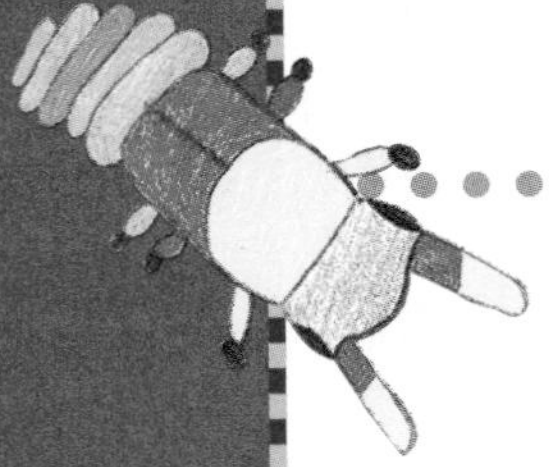

TEAM PROJECT

BUGS

Materials
large sheet of paper; crayons, colored pencils, or markers

If you've ever visited a tropical rain forest, you know that you can find some amazing insects. Now you can bring some incredible bugs into your classroom! Make a mural with 500 bugs.

Make a Plan

- How can the class decide how many bugs each group should draw?
- How can your group decide how many bugs each person should draw?
- How can you decide how much paper you will need?

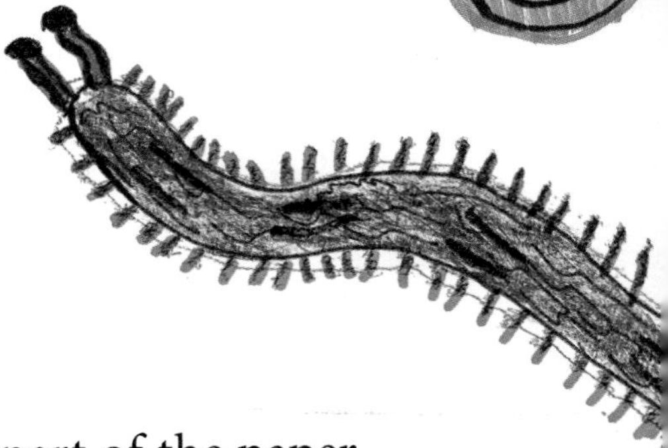

Carry It Out

- With your group, draw bugs on your part of the paper. Make them look real or imaginary. Have fun!

Talk About It

- How long did it take your class to draw the bugs?
- How long do you think it would take the class to draw 1,000 bugs?
- How much paper do you think you would need to draw 1,000 bugs?

Present the Project

- Display your mural in the classroom. Be proud of it!
- How can you describe how big 500 is?

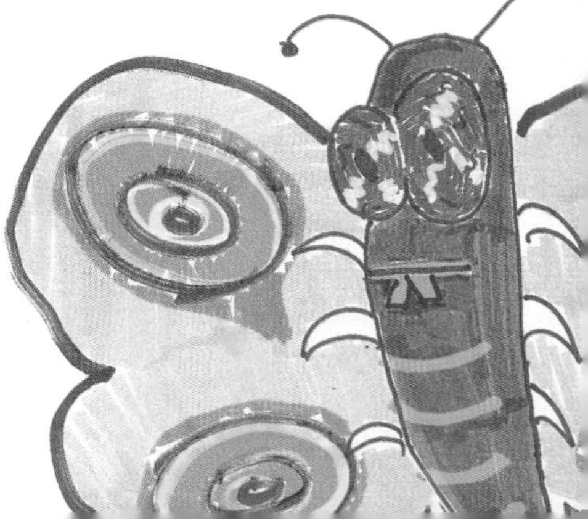

CHAPTER 2 SECTION A

Understanding Place Value

You can find butterflies, moths, and more at the Royal Ontario Museum in Canada.

How many butterflies do you think are on this page?

Skills Checklist

In this section, you will:

- ❐ Learn About Place Value Through Hundreds
- ❐ Explore Place Value Relationships
- ❐ Learn About Place Value Through Thousands
- ❐ Learn About Place Value Through Hundred Thousands
- ❐ Solve Problems by Making an Organized List

Naming and Writing Greater Numbers

Review counting on and skip counting by tens and hundreds. Continue each pattern.

1. 1, 2, 3, ■, ■, ■

2. 10, 20, 30, ■, ■, ■

3. 100, 200, 300, ■, ■, ■

Chapter 2
Lesson
1

Place Value Through Hundreds

You Will Learn
how to read and write numbers in the hundreds

Vocabulary
place value
the value given to the place a digit has in a number

digit
0, 1, 2, 3, 4, 5, 6, 7, 8, and 9

Ways to Show a Number
expanded form
standard form

Remember

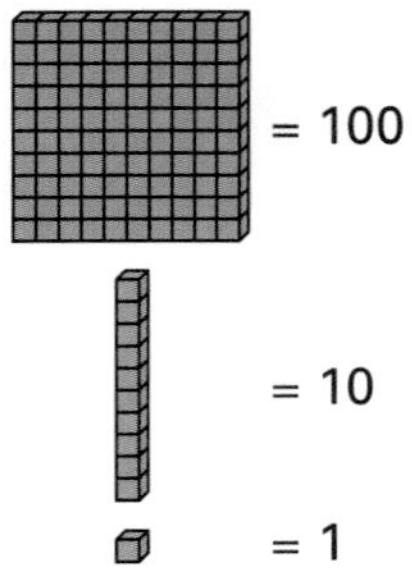

Learn

The word *centipede* means "a hundred feet." But centipedes don't really have exactly 100 feet. In fact some centipedes can have as many as 354 feet.

Place value can help you understand this number. To tell the value of each **digit**, look at its place in the number.

hundreds	tens	ones
3	5	4
The value of the 3 is 3 hundreds, or 300.	The value of the 5 is 5 tens, or 50.	The value of the 4 is 4 ones, or 4.

Here are some ways you can show this number.

place-value blocks:

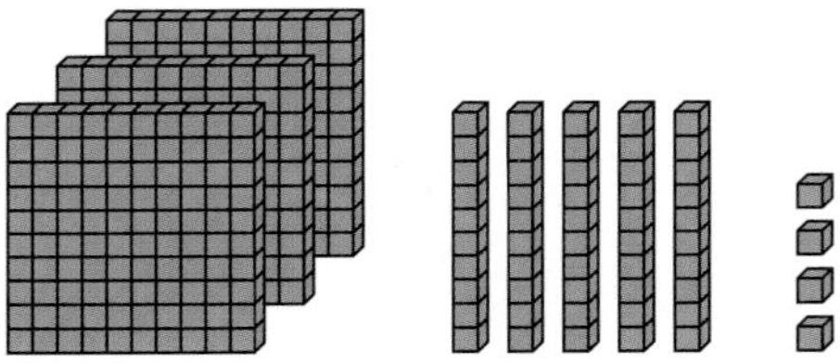

expanded form: 300 + 50 + 4

standard form: 354

word name: three hundred fifty-four

Talk About It

Are 345 and 354 the same number? Explain.

Check

Write each number in standard form.

1. two hundred nineteen

2. 400 + 50 + 8

3. Reasoning What is the value of the 3 in 235? Explain.

Practice

Skills and Reasoning

Write each number in standard form.

4. 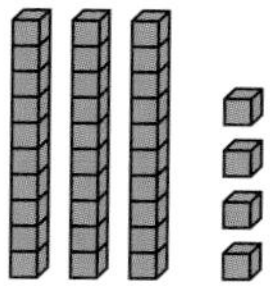

5. 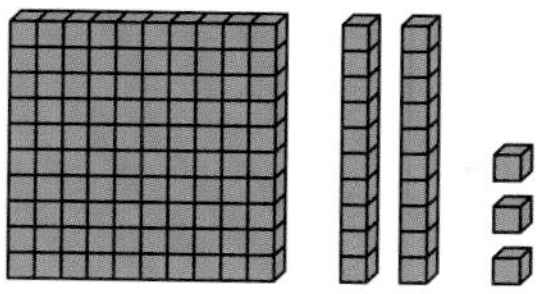

6. fifty-three **7.** nineteen **8.** 300 + 40

9. two hundred four **10.** 100 + 50 + 2 **11.** 200 + 20 + 6

Write the word name for each number.

12. 89 **13.** 300 + 70 + 6 **14.** 402 **15.** 100 + 10 + 2

16. To write the number two hundred five, do you need a 0? Explain.

17. Which digit has the greatest value in 359? Explain.

Problem Solving and Applications

18. Science Centipedes grow new legs in pairs. If a centipede grows two pairs of new legs, how many new legs does it have?

19. Measurement How much longer can a centipede grow than a millipede?

20. Literature *Around the World in 80 Days* is a popular adventure by Jules Verne. Write the word name for 80.

Longest Centipedes and Millipedes

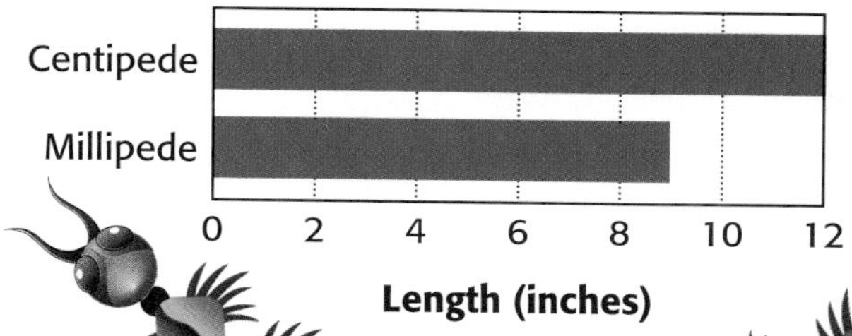

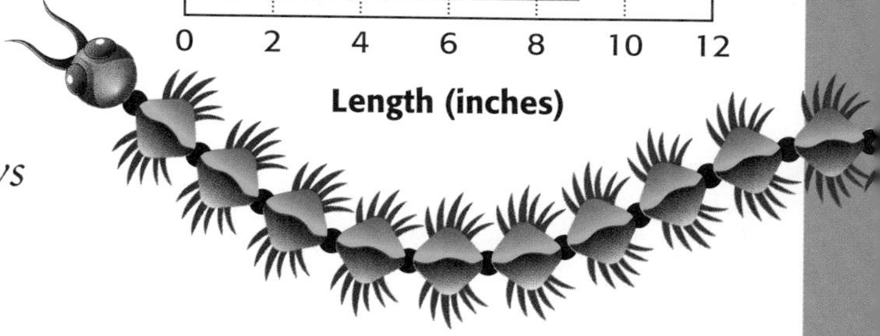

21. Journal How can you tell how many hundreds, tens, and ones a number has?

22. Patterns Complete the pattern.
10, 20, 30, ■, ■, 60, ■, 80, ■, ■

Mixed Review and Test Prep

Add or subtract.

23. 2 + 9 **24.** 14 − 5 **25.** 5 + 5 **26.** 6 + 9 **27.** 18 − 9

28. Judy had 9 strawberries and gave 2 away. How many strawberries did she have left?

Ⓐ 11 Ⓑ 2 Ⓒ 7 Ⓓ not here

Chapter 2
Lesson
2

Exploring Place Value Relationships

Problem Solving Connection
- Look for a Pattern
- Use Objects/Act It Out

Materials
- place-value blocks
- number cubes labeled 1–6

Math Tip
You can skip count by tens and add on ones to find the total.

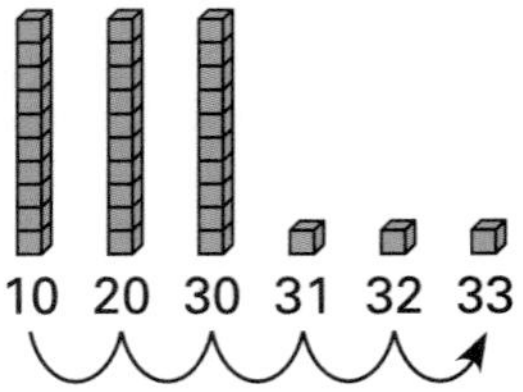

Explore

You can use place-value blocks to learn about number patterns.

Play "Race to 200."

Work Together

1. Use two different colored number cubes. Decide which cube shows the tens and which cube shows the ones.
2. Roll the cubes. Record the number rolled. Use tens and ones blocks to show the number. Write the total value of the blocks you have.
3. Now it's your partner's turn to roll the cubes and take blocks. Your partner records on his or her own table.

Roll	Number Rolled	Total
1	14	14
2	52	66
3		

Exchange blocks to find the total.

4. Keep taking turns. When you have 10 ones blocks, exchange them for 1 tens block. When you have 10 tens blocks, exchange them for 1 hundreds block.
5. The first player to reach a total of 200 wins.
6. Play the game three more times.

Talk About It

How did exchanging ones for tens and tens for hundreds help you find the total?

Connect

Our place-value system is based on groups of ten.

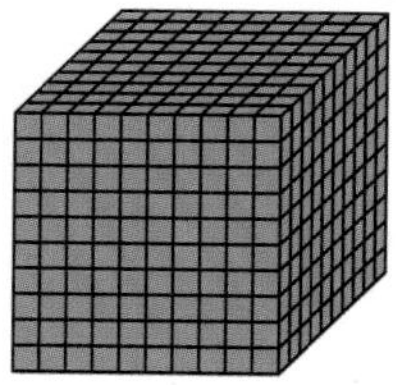	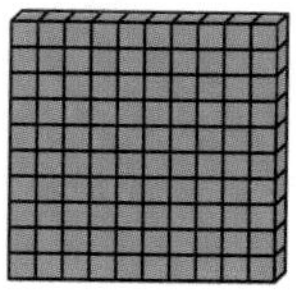	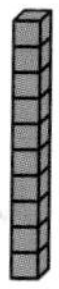	
1,000 one thousand 1 thousand = 10 hundreds	100 one hundred 1 hundred = 10 tens	10 one ten 1 ten = 10 ones	1 one

Practice

Write each number in standard form.

1. 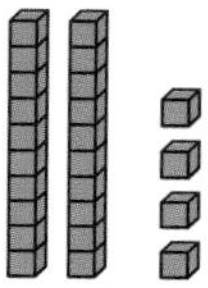

2. 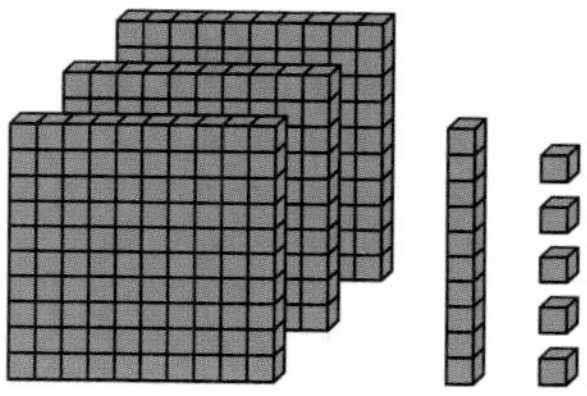

3. 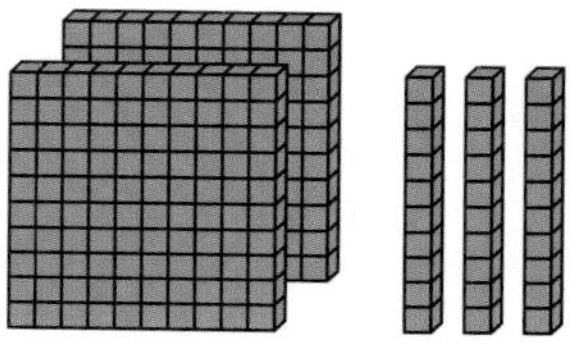

Copy and complete the table.

	Number	Number of Ones	Number of Tens	Number of Hundreds
4.	300	300		
5.	800		80	
6.	200			2
7.	400			
8.	900			

9. 2 tens = ▒ ones 10. 5 hundreds = ▒ tens 11. 7 hundreds = ▒ ones

12. **Geometry Readiness** Continue the pattern.

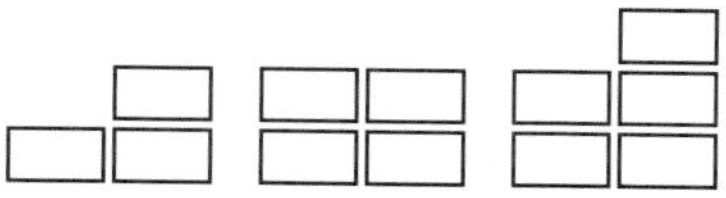 ______ ______ ______

13. **Journal** Suppose you had to stack 100 T-shirts in groups of ten for a school fund-raiser. Write a story and draw a picture that tells how many shirts were in each stack, and how many stacks you made.

Chapter 2
Lesson
3

Place Value Through Thousands

You Will Learn
how to read and write numbers through thousands

Learn

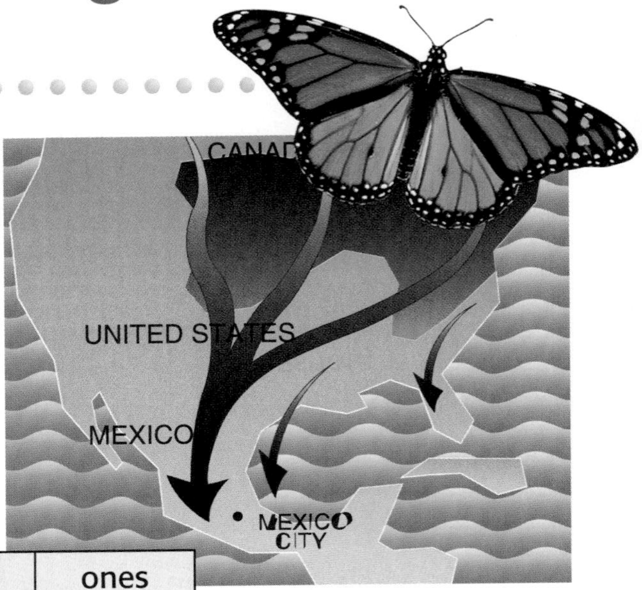

Monarch butterflies think cold weather is for the birds! Each winter monarchs fly south to warmer places. They have been known to fly as far as 1,870 miles.

Place value can help you understand this number.

thousands	hundreds	tens	ones
1 ,	8	7	0

Some monarchs travel long distances to find warmer weather.

Remember

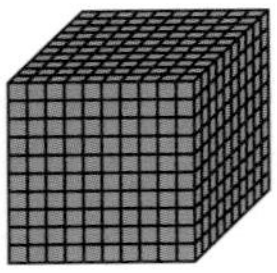 = 1,000

Here are some ways to show this number.

place-value blocks:

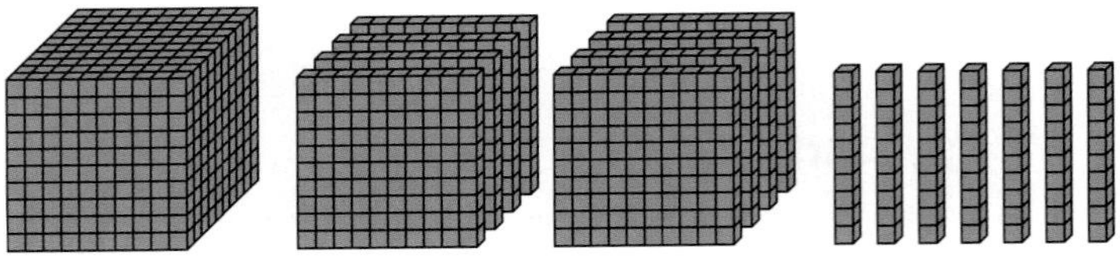

expanded form: 1,000 + 800 + 70

standard form: 1,870

word name: one thousand, eight hundred seventy

Talk About It

If you showed the number two thousand, four hundred two with place-value blocks, would you need a tens block? Explain.

Check

Write each number in standard form.

1. 7,000 + 400 + 50 + 6
2. three thousand, two hundred fifty
3. **Reasoning** How could you show 1,000 using hundreds blocks?

Practice

Skills and Reasoning

Write each number in standard form.

4. 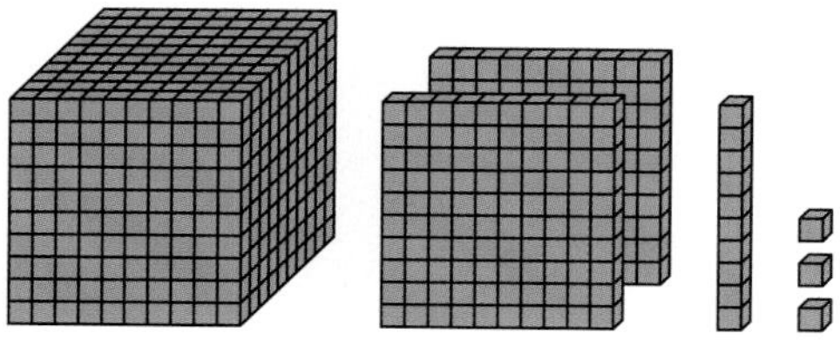

5. 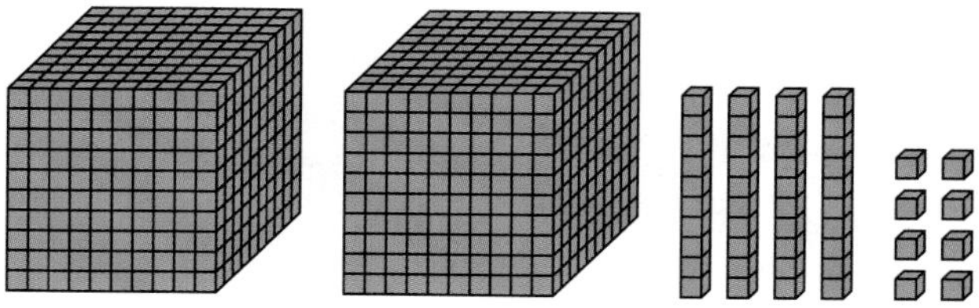

6. 1,000 + 600 + 70 + 2

7. four thousand, two hundred fourteen

Write the word name for each number.

8. 8,201 9. 222 10. 9,049 11. 949 12. 8,970

Copy and complete the table.

	Number	100 More	100 Less
13.	5,242		
14.	3,102		
15.	1,722		

16. Is fourteen hundred the same amount as one thousand, four hundred? Explain.

17. Is 1,000 the same amount as 10 tens or 10 hundreds?

Problem Solving and Applications

18. **Science** A brown bat can eat about 600 bugs in one hour. Can a brown bat eat thousands of bugs in one hour? Explain.

19. **Journal** Why do you need to use a zero when you write four hundred five in standard form?

Mixed Review and Test Prep

Add or subtract.

20. 8 + 3 21. 2 + 6 22. 16 − 7 23. 10 − 7 24. 6 − 5

25. 14 − 6 26. 6 + 5 27. 5 + 6 28. 7 − 5 29. 4 + 9

30. What is the value of the red digit in 578?

Ⓐ 7 Ⓑ 70 Ⓒ 700 Ⓓ not here

Chapter 2
Lesson
4

Place Value Through Hundred Thousands

You Will Learn
how to read and write numbers through hundred thousands

Vocabulary
period
group of three digits in a number, separated by a comma

Learn

If you want to see *lots* of bugs, go to the Royal Ontario Museum in Toronto, Canada. It has 125,541 butterflies and moths!

Place value can help you understand this number.

Thousands Period			Ones Period		
hundred thousands	ten thousands	thousands	hundreds	tens	ones
1	2	5 ,	5	4	1

Did You Know?
Butterflies can travel as far as 80 miles in a day.

The value of the 2 is 2 ten thousands, or 20,000.

expanded form: 100,000 + 20,000 + 5,000 + 500 + 40 + 1

standard form: 125,541

word name: one hundred twenty-five thousand, five hundred forty-one

Talk About It

What is the value of each 5 in 125,541?

Check

Write each number in standard form.

1. one hundred fifty-seven thousand, nine hundred eighty
2. 800,000 + 30,000 + 8,000 + 400 + 2
3. **Reasoning** Write a number with 3 in the ten thousands place.

Practice

Skills and Reasoning

Write each number in standard form.

4. thirty-eight thousand, four hundred twelve

5. three hundred forty-four thousand, nine hundred eleven

6. $10{,}000 + 8{,}000 + 700 + 90 + 1$ **7.** $500{,}000 + 6{,}000 + 800 + 5$

Write the value of each red digit.

8. 39,041 **9.** 29,467 **10.** 820,193 **11.** 709,436

12. In the number 63,458, which digit has the greatest value?

13. Using only the digits 1, 5, and 7, write a number with a 7 in the hundred thousands place and a 5 in the tens place.

Problem Solving and Applications

14. Logic What are the greatest and least numbers you can write using these digits?

2	9	1	4	8

15. Using Data Use the Data File on page 48. Which bugs does the Royal Ontario Museum have more than one hundred thousand of?

16. Algebra Readiness Continue the pattern. Then write the rule.

In	1,100	1,200	1,300	1,400	1,500	1,600
Out	1,110	1,210	1,310			

17. Journal How does the comma in the number 624,031 help you find the place value of each digit?

Mixed Review and Test Prep

Algebra Readiness Find each missing number.

18. $7 + \square = 10$ **19.** $4 + \square = 8$ **20.** $\square + 9 = 11$

Write the value of each red digit.

21. 8,765 **22.** 3,675 **23.** 998 **24.** 2,112 **25.** 9,191

26. Choose the number that has a 4 in the thousands place.

Ⓐ 45,987 Ⓑ 421,801 Ⓒ 94,212 Ⓓ not here

Chapter 2
Lesson
5

Problem Solving

Analyze Strategies: Make an Organized List

You Will Learn
how to make an organized list to help solve problems

Learn

Bzzzz ...Urp! There's no need for a flyswatter at Marilee and Peter's place! They raise bug-eating plants such as Venus flytraps and sundews and send them all over the country.

Suppose Marilee packed 54 Venus flytraps in boxes that hold 10 plants or 1 plant. How many ways could she pack the boxes?

Work Together

▶ Understand

What do you know?

What do you need to find out?

▶ Plan

Write one way to box the plants. 4 tens boxes and 14 ones boxes.

Write other ways. 5 tens boxes and 4 ones boxes, or 3 tens boxes and 24 ones boxes

▶ Solve

Use a pattern to organize your list.

List all possible ways.

Tens Boxes	5	4	3	2	1	0
Ones Boxes	4	14	24	34	44	54

What is your answer? There are 6 ways to pack the flytraps.

▶ Look Back

How can you check your answer?

Talk About It

Why was it helpful to organize the list?

Check

Problem Solving
Understand
Plan
Solve
Look Back

Make a list to help solve.

1. Suppose Marilee used tens and ones boxes to pack 32 sundews. How many ways could she pack the boxes?

2. Suppose you are allowed to pick 2 plants. You can pick 2 of the same plant. How many different combinations could you choose?

ON SALE!
Venus Flytrap
Sundew
Bladderwort

Problem Solving Practice

Make a list or use any strategy to help solve each.

3. Suppose Peter wants to order 45 pounds of soil. He can order the soil in 10-pound bags or 1-pound bags. How many ways could he order the soil?

4. You spent hours finding pill bugs, ants, and slugs to feed your sundew plant. You want to feed it 2 bugs a day. You cannot feed it two of the same bugs on one day. How many different combinations of bugs can you feed it?

5. Suppose Marilee needed 31 gallons of water. If water comes in 10-gallon and 1-gallon containers, what is the least number of containers she could buy? What is the greatest number of containers?

6. Peter arranged a sundew, a purple pitcher plant, and a cobra plant on a shelf. The sundew was farthest left. The cobra plant was to the right of the purple pitcher plant. Which plant was in the middle?

7. Marilee counted her plants and found she had 5 more cobra plants than sundews. If she had 9 sundews, how many cobra plants did she have?

Problem Solving Strategies

- Use Objects/Act It Out
- Draw a Picture
- Look for a Pattern
- Guess and Check
- Use Logical Reasoning
- Make an Organized List
- Make a Table
- Solve a Simpler Problem
- Work Backward

Choose a Tool

Marilee Maertz and Peter D'Amato own a carnivorous plant greenhouse in Forestville, California.

Skills Practice Bank, page 519, Set 6

SECTION A

Review and Practice

Vocabulary Match each word with its meaning.

1. place value **a.** 0, 1, 2, 3, 4, 5, 6, 7, 8, and 9
2. digit **b.** the value given to the place a digit has in a number
3. period **c.** group of three digits, separated by a comma

(Lesson 1) Write the word name for each number.

4.

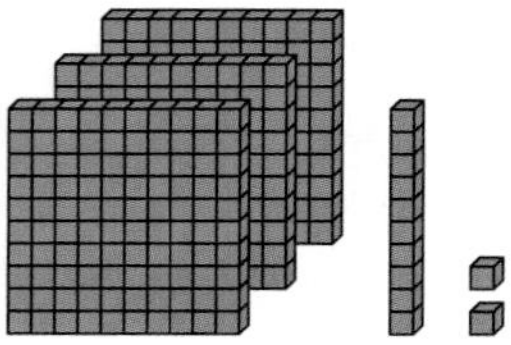

5.

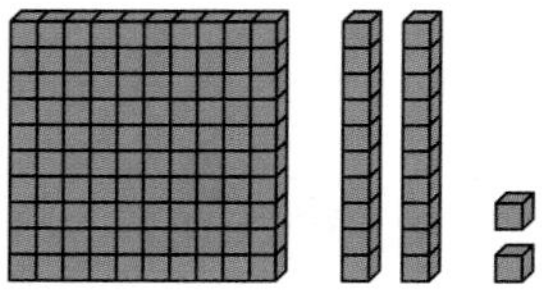

6. 324 **7.** 700 + 40 + 5 **8.** 51 **9.** 200 + 5

(Lesson 2) Write each missing value.

10. 30 ones = ▢ tens **11.** ▢ ones = 2 hundreds **12.** ▢ ones = 5 tens

13. 40 tens = ▢ hundreds **14.** ▢ tens = 200 ones **15.** ▢ tens = 3 hundreds

(Lesson 3) Write each number in standard form.

16. Eight thousand, nine hundred ten **17.** 2,000 + 300 + 40 + 8

18. 7,000 + 20 + 1 **19.** six thousand, seven hundred eighty-one

20. 900 + 80 + 7 **21.** one hundred eleven

(Lesson 4) Write the value of each red digit.

22. 147,583 **23.** 219,460 **24.** 37,052

(Lesson 5) Make a list to help solve.

25. Joan needs to pack 47 plants into boxes that hold 10 plants or 1 plant. How many ways can she pack the boxes?

26. Gema needs to order 17 pounds of soil. She can buy the soil in 10-pound or 1-pound bags. How many ways can she order the soil?

27. Journal How can place-value patterns help you read the number 235,684?

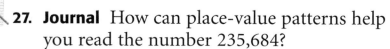

Skills Checklist

In this section, you have:

- ☑ Learned About Place Value Through Hundreds
- ☑ Explored Place Value Relationships
- ☑ Learned About Place Value Through Thousands
- ☑ Learned About Place Value Through Hundred Thousands
- ☑ Solved Problems by Making an Organized List

CHAPTER 2
SECTION

B Building Number Sense

A giant tortoise might move more slowly than a rabbit, but do you think it moves faster than a snail?

The giant tortoise comes from the Galapagos Islands off the coast of South America and can weigh up to 500 pounds.

Comparing, Ordering, and Rounding Numbers

Review place value. Write each number in standard form.

1. 50 + 6 **2.** 2,000 + 500 + 40 + 2

3. 300 + 10 + 4 **4.** 6,000 + 800 + 1

Skills Checklist

In this section, you will:

- ❒ Compare Numbers
- ❒ Order Numbers
- ❒ Round to Tens
- ❒ Round to Hundreds

Chapter 2
Lesson
6

Comparing Numbers

You Will Learn
how to compare numbers

Vocabulary

compare
to decide which of two numbers is greater

Learn

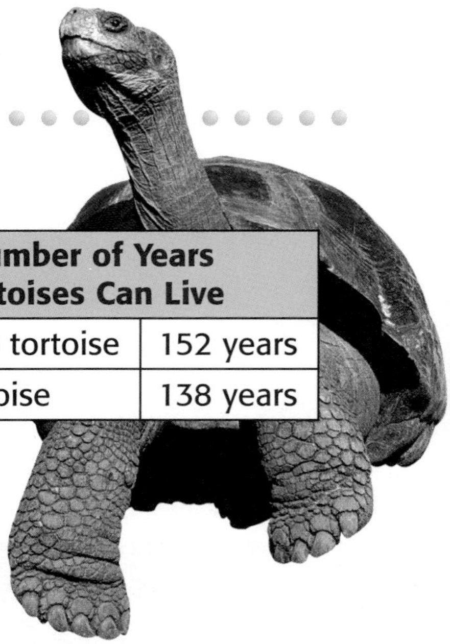

Slurrrp! Some tortoises love to eat snails and slugs. They can eat a lot of them in a lifetime because they live to be so old!

Number of Years Tortoises Can Live	
Marion's tortoise	152 years
Box tortoise	138 years

Which can live longer, a box tortoise or a Marion's tortoise? You can **compare** numbers to find out.

Example 1

Compare 152 and 138.

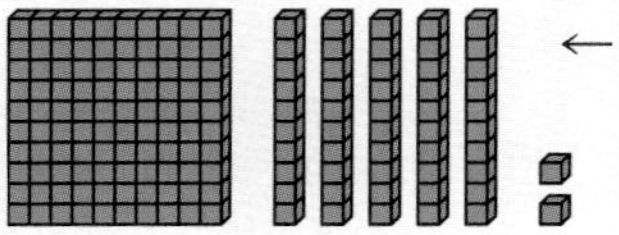

← Same number of hundreds. →

← More tens.

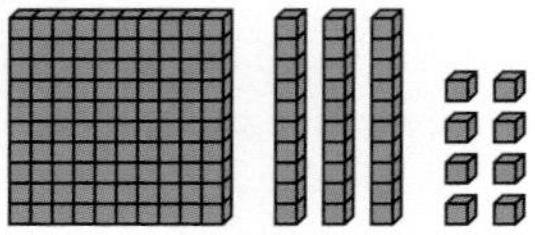

152 **138**

152 **is greater than** 138.

152 > 138

138 **is less than** 152.

138 < 152

So, a Marion's tortoise can live longer than a box tortoise.

You can also compare numbers using place value.

Example 2

Compare 1,550 and 1,830.

Step 1

Begin at the left.
Compare.

1,550
1,830

Both numbers have 1 thousand.

Step 2

Find the first place where the digits are different. Compare.

1,**5**50
1,**8**30

5 hundreds is less than 8 hundreds.

So, 1,550 < 1,830 or 1,830 > 1,550.

Math Tip
You can use these steps to compare numbers with any number of digits.

Talk About It

Since 5 is greater than 2, is 5,360 greater than 26,314? Explain.

Check

Compare. Use <, >, or =.

1. 245 ● 254 **2.** 1,485 ● 1,583 **3.** 3,021 ● 2,301 **4.** 1,001 ● 101

5. Reasoning For 195 and 1,002, can you tell which number is greater by comparing the first digit in each number? Explain.

PRACTICE AND APPLY

Practice

Skills and Reasoning

Compare. Use <, >, or =.

6. 34 ● 54 **7.** 198 ● 109 **8.** 1,190 ● 1,709 **9.** 9,235 ● 8,399

10. 100 ● 99 **11.** 1,305 ● 135 **12.** 3,512 ● 3,512 **13.** 492 ● 4,032

Write "is less than," "is greater than," or "equals."

14. 78 ● 87 **15.** 299 ● 301 **16.** 331 ● 331 **17.** 91 ● 89

18. 312 and 231 have the same digits, but in a different order. Do they have the same value? Explain.

19. Could you compare the 9 in 391 with the 8 in 280 to find which number is greater? Explain.

Problem Solving and Applications

Using Data Use the Data File on page 49 for **20–22.**

20. Which travels 100 meters faster, a giant tortoise or a snail?

21. Which two animals take the same amount of time to travel 100 meters?

22. How much longer does it take a spider to travel 100 meters than a centipede?

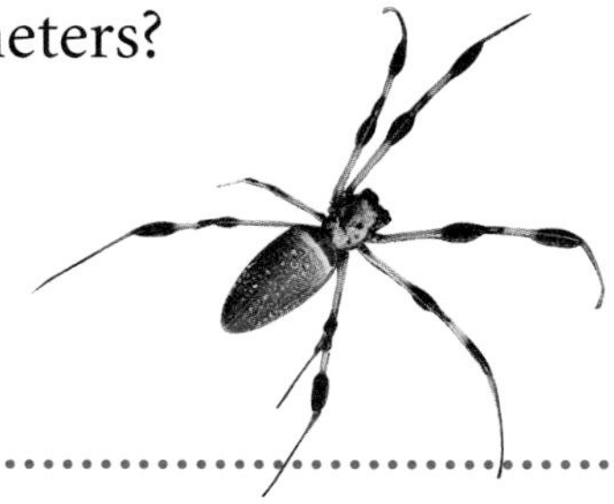

Mixed Review and Test Prep

Write the word name for each number.

23. 7,392 **24.** 9,430 **25.** 101 **26.** 8,011 **27.** 555

28. 400 + 20 + 1 **29.** 5,000 + 40 **30.** 2,000 + 500 + 10 + 1

31. Algebra Readiness Find the missing number. 8 + ■ = 12

Ⓐ 2 Ⓑ 4 Ⓒ 6 Ⓓ 8

Chapter 2
Lesson
7

Ordering Numbers

You Will Learn
how to order numbers

Vocabulary
order
to place numbers from least to greatest or greatest to least

Learn

A shadow passes across the ground and a small animal dives for cover. Why? An eagle is on the hunt! Eagles are birds that soar through the air and catch prey.

Which bird is fastest? Which bird is slowest? You can **order** the numbers to find out.

Speeds of Birds	
Eagle	120 miles per hour
Swift	106 miles per hour
Falcon	168 miles per hour

Example 1

Order the numbers on a number line.

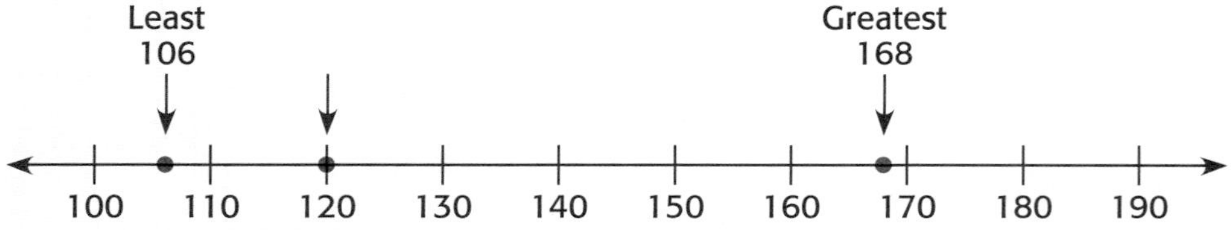

The fastest bird is the falcon. The slowest bird is the swift.

You can also order numbers by comparing them two at a time.

Example 2

Order 5,231, 4,132, and 5,219 from greatest to least.

Compare to find the greatest number.

5,231 > 4,132
5,231 > 5,219

Compare the other numbers.

5,219 > 4,132

5,231 is the greatest.

The order from greatest to least is 5,231, 5,219, 4,132.

Remember
Always start with the greatest place value when comparing numbers.

Talk About It

Could you order 235, 321, and 511 by just comparing tens? Explain.

Check

Order from least to greatest.

1. 430, 380, 410 **2.** 360, 440, 390 **3.** 111, 121, 112

Order from greatest to least.

4. 981, 1,001, 1,045 **5.** 4,073, 3,740, 4,037 **6.** 2,021, 2,201, 2,102

7. **Reasoning** Can a number with 5 in the tens place be greater than a number with 9 in the tens place? Explain.

Practice

Skills and Reasoning

Order from least to greatest.

8. 274, 742, 247 **9.** 87, 107, 71 **10.** 621, 216, 612

Order from greatest to least.

11. 1,450, 1,350, 1,430 **12.** 1,380, 1,480, 1,420 **13.** 96, 690, 609

14. Write a number that is between 1,960 and 3,906.

15. Were you born between the years 1985 and 2002? Explain.

Problem Solving and Applications

16. **Time** Selma has a collection of nature magazines from these years: 1967, 1966, and 1951. Find the order from oldest to newest.

17. **Logic** I am a 1-digit number. When you add 2 to me, and then subtract 4, the answer is 5. What number am I?

Mixed Review and Test Prep

Algebra Readiness Write <, >, or =.

18. 6 + 4 ○ 6 + 5 **19.** 9 − 3 ○ 8 − 2 **20.** 7 + 8 ○ 14 − 6

Write each number in standard form.

21. four hundred thirty-four **22.** ninety-eight **23.** 600 + 30 + 3

24. Lois had 13 cookies and ate 7. How many were left?

Ⓐ 11 Ⓑ 6 Ⓒ 7 Ⓓ 3

Chapter 2
Lesson
8

Rounding to Tens

You Will Learn

how to round 2-digit and 3-digit numbers to the nearest ten

Vocabulary

estimate
to find a number that is close to the exact number

rounding
replacing a number with a number that tells about how many or how much

Learn

You can **estimate** when you need to know about how many or about how much. **Rounding** is one way to estimate.

Place	Distance
Insect Institute	53 miles
Spider House	58 miles
Natural History Museum	55 miles

You must decide about how far away each place is, so you can plan the time needed for science club field trips.

About how far away is each place?

Round to the nearest ten to find out.

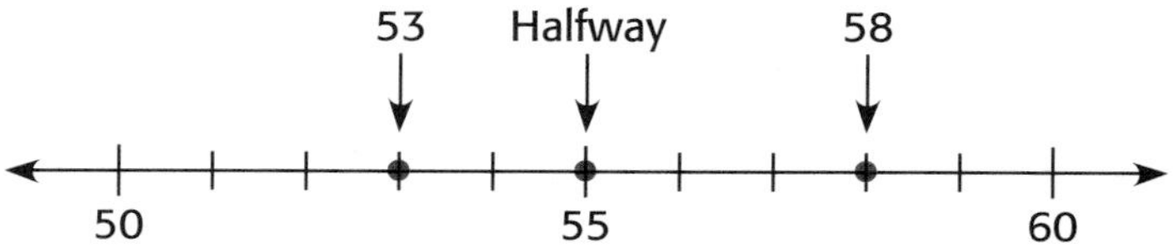

- **53** is between 50 and 60, but closer to 50. So the Insect Institute is about 50 miles away.
- **58** is between 50 and 60, but closer to 60. So the Spider House is about 60 miles away.
- When a number is halfway between two tens, round to the greater ten. So the Natural History Museum is about 60 miles away.

Katydid

Math Tip

Round to the greater ten if the ones digit is 5 or more.

Other Examples

You can also round three-digit numbers to the nearest ten.

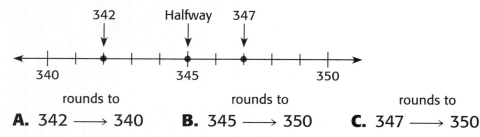

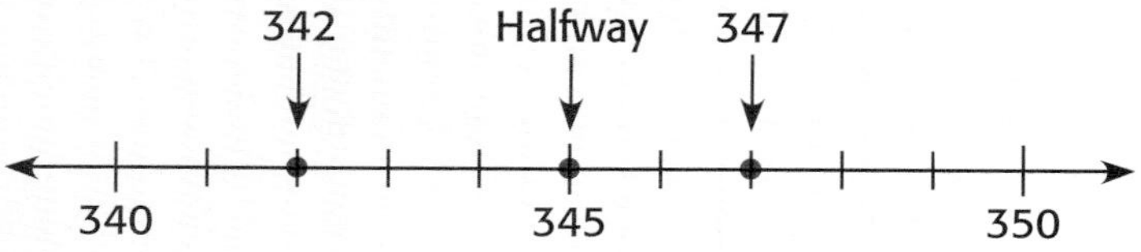

A. 342 $\xrightarrow{\text{rounds to}}$ 340 **B.** 345 $\xrightarrow{\text{rounds to}}$ 350 **C.** 347 $\xrightarrow{\text{rounds to}}$ 350

Talk About It

What number is halfway between 70 and 80?

Check

Round to the nearest ten.

1. 67 **2.** 84 **3.** 65 **4.** 70 **5.** 19

6. 23 **7.** 55 **8.** 189 **9.** 464 **10.** 597

11. **Reasoning** Write four numbers that would round to 100.

Practice

Skills and Reasoning

Round to the nearest ten.

12. 93 **13.** 59 **14.** 25 **15.** 95 **16.** 505

17. 107 **18.** 287 **19.** 854 **20.** 31 **21.** 119

22. Ashaki waited 12 minutes to meet Jerry after school. Ashaki said that she was waiting about 20 minutes. Is this correct? Explain.

23. What digits must be in the ones place in order to round to the greater ten?

Problem Solving and Applications

24. **Geography** While on a car trip in Salisbury, Maryland, you may see this sign.

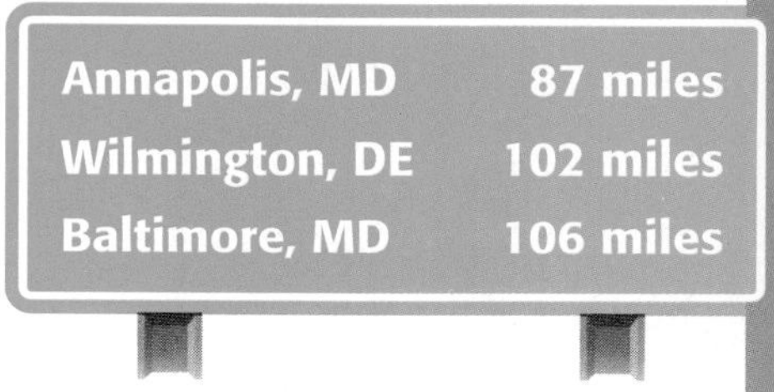

a. Which city is about 110 miles away?

b. About how many miles away is Wilmington?

c. Which is farther away, Baltimore or Annapolis?

Mixed Review and Test Prep

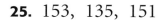

Order the numbers from least to greatest.

25. 153, 135, 151 **26.** 301, 331, 313 **27.** 689, 698, 599

Compare. Write <, >, or =.

28. 435 ● 415 **29.** 732 ● 1,723 **30.** 1,212 ● 1,121

31. Which of these numbers is the greatest?

Ⓐ 1,033 Ⓑ 1,303 Ⓒ 1,330 Ⓓ 330

Rounding to Hundreds

You Will Learn
how to round numbers to the nearest hundred

Learn

In the book *Charlotte's Web*, Charlotte is a spider who helps Wilbur the pig. Near the end of the story, Charlotte counts 514 eggs in her egg sac.

Example 1

About how many eggs did Charlotte count? Round 514 to the nearest hundred to find out.

To round to the nearest hundred, find the closer hundred.

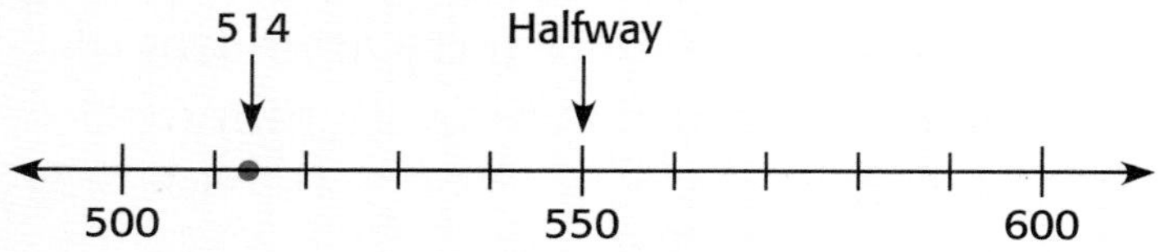

514 is between 500 and 600. It is closer to 500.

514 rounds to 500. So, Charlotte has about 500 eggs.

If a number is halfway between two hundreds, round to the greater hundred.

Math Tip
Round to the greater hundred if the tens digit is 5 or more.

Other Examples

A. 450 $\xrightarrow{\text{rounds to}}$ 500 **B.** 479 $\xrightarrow{\text{rounds to}}$ 500 **C.** \$422 $\xrightarrow{\text{rounds to}}$ \$400

Talk About It

What is the closest hundred to 967?

Check

Round to the nearest hundred.

1. 487 **2.** 307 **3.** \$401 **4.** 956 **5.** 617

6. Reasoning Write the number halfway between 300 and 400.

Practice

Skills and Reasoning

Round to the nearest hundred.

7. 149 **8.** 849 **9.** 750 **10.** 680 **11.** 393

12. 138 **13.** $940 **14.** 262 **15.** $50 **16.** 556

17. 150 **18.** $505 **19.** 945 **20.** 353 **21.** 61

22. Round 82 to the nearest hundred.

23. Round 250 to the nearest hundred.

24. Write the greatest number that rounds to 500 when you round to the nearest hundred.

25. Write five numbers that round to 1,000 when you round to the nearest hundred.

Problem Solving and Applications

26. Science A spider of typical size lays about 100 eggs. Could the exact number be 103?

27. Critical Thinking Can a two-digit number round to 100? Explain.

28. History The zipper was invented in 1913. Is that closer to the year 1900 or 2000?

Using Data Use the table to answer **29** and **30.**

Trekker Bike	
Klein's Sports	$298
State Sports	$275
Mudville Bike Shop	$329
Bikes & Stuff	$309

29. Round the cost of each bike to the nearest hundred dollars. About how much does a Trekker bike cost?

30. In which store does the Trekker cost most? In which store does it cost least?

Mixed Review and Test Prep

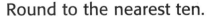

Round to the nearest ten.

31. 75 **32.** 14 **33.** 38 **34.** 66 **35.** 94

Order the numbers from greatest to least.

36. 1,089, 980, 1,980 **37.** 123, 213, 277 **38.** 998, 790, 689

39. What is the value of the red digit in 11,025?

Ⓐ 100 Ⓑ 10,000 Ⓒ 10 Ⓓ 1,000

SECTION B
Review and Practice

Vocabulary Choose the best word for each sentence.

1. One way to estimate is to ____.
2. When you ____ numbers, you place them from least to greatest or greatest to least.
3. You ____ to tell which of two numbers is greater.

Word List
order
round
compare

(Lesson 6) Compare. Use <, >, or =.

4. 512 ● 521   **5.** 3,100 ● 320   **6.** 2,056 ● 2,056

7. 488 ● 484   **8.** 962 ● 1,026   **9.** 3,447 ● 3,744

(Lesson 7) Order from least to greatest.

10. 271, 712, 286   **11.** 1,043, 1,137, 919   **12.** 5,280, 5,185, 5,275

Order from greatest to least.

13. 507, 512, 498   **14.** 838, 8,130, 831   **15.** 4,112, 4,212, 4,121

16. History Order the countries where television was first used from the earliest date to the latest date.

When Television Was First Used in Different Countries	
England	1936
Cuba	1950
United States	1939

(Lesson 8) Round to the nearest ten.

17. 65   **18.** 72   **19.** $61   **20.** 179

(Lesson 9) Round to the nearest hundred.

21. 830   **22.** $725   **23.** 870   **24.** $752

25. Journal Write a story about how you and two friends guess how many pennies are in the jar. In the story, order the guesses from least to greatest.

Skills Checklist

In this section, you have:

- ☑ Compared Numbers
- ☑ Ordered Numbers
- ☑ Rounded to Tens
- ☑ Rounded to Hundreds

CHAPTER 2

SECTION

C Understanding Time

Wow, this is tough work! This baby ostrich has to peck its way out of a shell that could hold two people standing on it!

An ostrich takes more than 50 hours to hatch. Do you think it hatches during daylight and nighttime?

Ostriches can be found in central and southern Africa.

Telling Time

Review skip counting by 5s and 10s. Continue each pattern.

1. 5, 10, 15, ■, ■, ■, ■, ■, ■, ■, ■, ■

2. 10, 20, 30, ■, ■, ■

Skills Checklist

In this section, you will:

- ❒ Learn About Telling Time to the Nearest Five Minutes
- ❒ Explore Time to the Nearest Minute
- ❒ Learn About Telling Time to the Half Hour and Quarter Hour
- ❒ Learn About Elapsed Time
- ❒ Learn About Ordinal Numbers and the Calendar
- ❒ Solve Problems by Making Decisions

Time to the Nearest Five Minutes

You Will Learn
how to tell time to the nearest 5 minutes

Learn

"The bus comes in five minutes!" called Jon's mother. Jon finished tying his shoe and looked at his messy bed. "That's just enough time to make the bed," he thought.

seven o'clock
7:00

5 minutes past 7
7:05

40 minutes past 10
20 minutes before 11

10:40
ten-forty

It takes the minute hand 5 minutes to move from one number on the clock to the next. There are 60 minutes in 1 hour.

Talk About It

Why is it incorrect to write "4:60" or to say "60 minutes past four"? Explain.

Check

Write each time two ways.

1. 

2. 

3. 

4. **Reasoning** Suppose it's 2:55. What time would it be 5 minutes later?

Practice

Skills and Reasoning

Write each time two ways.

5. 

6. 

7. 

8. 

9. 

10. 

11. 

12. 

13. How many minutes are between 11:15 and 11:20?

14. What's another way you could write 5 minutes before 4?

Problem Solving and Applications

15. Critical Thinking Suppose you want to get to the 11:35 movie as close to the start as possible. Which bus should you take?

Bus Schedule

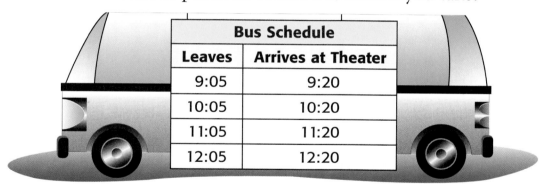

Leaves	Arrives at Theater
9:05	9:20
10:05	10:20
11:05	11:20
12:05	12:20

16. Patterns Continue each pattern.

a. 30, 35, 40, ▒, ▒, ▒, ▒ **b.** 10, 20, 30, ▒, ▒, ▒ **c.** 55, 50, 45, ▒, ▒, ▒

Mixed Review and Test Prep

Algebra Readiness Find each missing number.

17. 18 − ▒ = 9 **18.** 4 + ▒ = 10 **19.** 12 − ▒ = 4 **20.** 9 + ▒ = 17

21. What is 63 rounded to the nearest ten?

Ⓐ 65 Ⓑ 100 Ⓒ 60 Ⓓ 63

Chapter 2
Lesson
11

Exploring Time to the Nearest Minute

Explore

Problem Solving Connection
- Use Objects/ Act It Out
- Guess and Check

Tiffanee knows how to hop to it! She won an American Heart Association jump-a-thon award. She can jump rope 50 times in one minute.

How long is 1 minute?

Tiffanee is from Detroit, Michigan. She likes reading, traveling, ballet, and playing basketball and piano.

Work Together

Here are some activities to help you think about 1 minute.

Did You Know?
It takes about a minute to count to 60.

1. How many times do you think you can write your name in 1 minute? First estimate how many times. Then try it.

2. How many times do you think you can blink your eyes in 1 minute? First estimate how many times. Then try it.

3. How many times do you think you can tap your foot in 1 minute? First estimate how many times. Then try it.

Talk About It

What activities can you think of that take about a minute?

Connect

It takes 1 minute for the minute hand to move 1 mark on the clock.

It is 10:05. In 1 minute, it will be 10:06.

six-seventeen

17 minutes past 6

6:17

two thirty-eight

38 minutes past 2

2:38

Practice

Write each time two ways.

1. 
2. 
3. 
4. 
5. 
6. 
7. 
8. 

9. **Estimation** Suppose you waited 21 minutes in line. About how many minutes did you wait if you round to the nearest ten minutes?

10. **Reasoning** Soccer practice starts at 3:45. Kerry arrived at 3:32. Was she early or late?

11. **Reasoning** If it is 3:55, in how many minutes will it be 4:00?

12. How many minutes does it take the minute hand to move 3 marks on the clock?

13. **Journal** How could you describe to someone about how long 1 minute is?

14. **Critical Thinking** In 1 minute, it will be 2:00. What time is it now?

Chapter 2
Lesson
12

Time to the Half Hour and Quarter Hour

You Will Learn

how to tell time to the nearest 15 minutes

Vocabulary

A.M.
times from midnight to noon

P.M.
times from noon to midnight

Learn

"Now be sure to watch the clock," said Mrs. Quimby, "and leave for school at exactly quarter past eight." What time should Ramona leave?

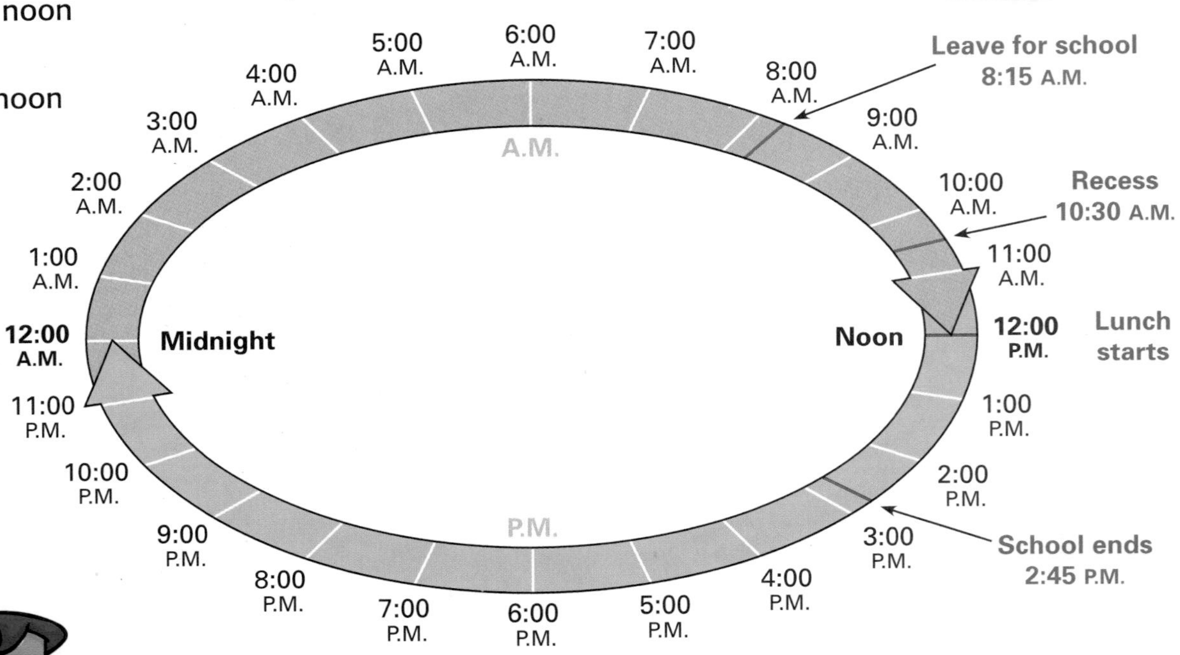

Math Tip

Quarter past eight means the same thing as 15 minutes past 8.

quarter past eight
8:15 **A.M.**

half past ten
10:30 A.M.

noon
12:00 **P.M.**

quarter to three
2:45 P.M.

Ramona should leave at 8:15 A.M.

Talk About It

What are two ways you can name this time?

Check

Write each time two ways. Write A.M. or P.M.

1. 
play soccer

2. 
dinner time

3. 
sun rises

4. 
stars shine

5. Reasoning When it is quarter to two, what number is the minute hand pointing to?

Practice

Skills and Reasoning

Write each time two ways. Write A.M. or P.M.

6. 
sun sets

7. 
breakfast time

8. 
go shopping

9. 
lunch ends

10. Write a time that comes between 7:15 A.M. and quarter to eight A.M.

11. How many times in one day will the clock show 3:15? Explain.

Problem Solving and Applications

12. Journal List four things you do during the A.M. hours. List four things you do during the P.M. hours. Write a time for each thing you list.

13. Literature In *Ramona the Pest,* Ramona leaves for school at 8:25 A.M. Her mother said to leave at quarter past eight. Did she leave at the correct time? Explain.

Mixed Review and Test Prep

Add or subtract.

14. 8 − 5 **15.** 13 − 4 **16.** 6 + 6 **17.** 7 + 2 **18.** 17 − 9

19. What is $450 rounded to the nearest hundred dollars?

Ⓐ $550 Ⓑ $400 Ⓒ $500 Ⓓ not here

Chapter 2
Lesson
13

Elapsed Time

You Will Learn
how to find ending time and the time between events

Remember
You can skip count by 5s to add or count on minutes.

Learn

Some animals have to work hard to hatch from their eggs. Scientists measured the hatching times of several animals.

Example 1

After a baby pigeon cracks the egg, it takes about 6 hours and 25 minutes to hatch. If a pigeon begins hatching at 5:00 A.M., what time will it finish?

Step 1

Start at 5:00 A.M.

Add the hours.

Step 2

Add the minutes.

The baby pigeon will hatch at 11:25 A.M.

Here's an example where you find the time that has passed.

Example 2

Suppose a baby Japanese quail starts hatching at 9:00 P.M. and finishes at 10:35 P.M. How long does it take the baby quail to hatch?

Step 1

Start at 9:00.

Count the hours.

Step 2

Count the minutes.

It takes 1 hour and 35 minutes for the Japanese quail to hatch.

Talk About It

How can skip counting help you count the minutes?

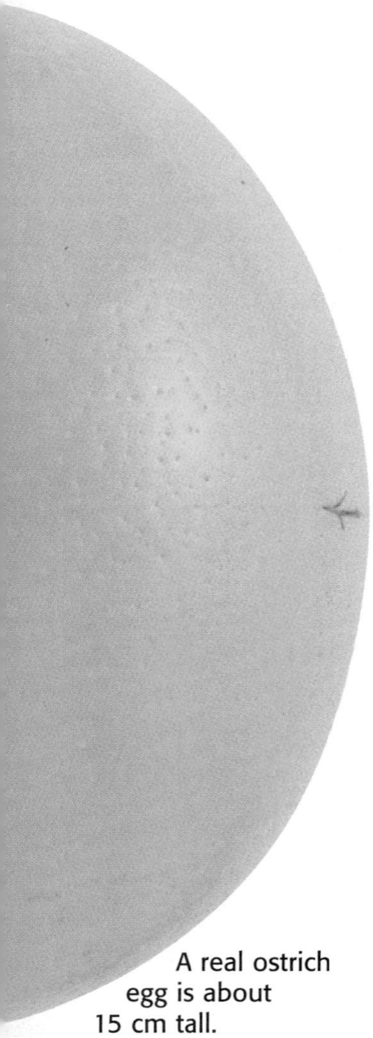

A real ostrich egg is about 15 cm tall.

Check

1. Jeff's family left at 9:00 A.M. for the beach. They drove for 1 hour and 10 minutes. What time did they arrive?

2. Hannah did homework from 5:00 P.M. to 5:44 P.M. How long did she do homework?

3. **Reasoning** Suppose it is 4:00 P.M. What will the time be in 60 minutes?

Practice

Skills and Reasoning

4. Ryoko puts cookies in the oven at 2:00 P.M. They should cook for 13 minutes. What time should she take them out?

5. Ben rents a video that is 1 hour and 21 minutes long. If he starts watching at 7:00 P.M., what time will the movie be over?

6. Suppose it is 4:25 P.M. What time was it 60 minutes ago?

Problem Solving and Applications

7. **Career** "Pet sitters" will visit your home and take care of your pets. If a pet sitter must walk a dog at 7:00 A.M. and leave for her next stop at 8:20 A.M., for how long can she walk the dog?

8. **Using Data** Use the Data File on page 49 to help solve.
   a. Which animal takes longest to hatch? Which animal takes the least amount of time?
   b. Suppose a caterpillar started hatching at 12:15 P.M. What time would it finish?

9. **Algebra Readiness** Write each missing time.
   a. 3:25 P.M. is ▢ minutes after 3:00 P.M.
   b. 6:17 A.M. is ▢ hours and ▢ minutes after 4:00 A.M.

Mixed Review and Test Prep

Add or subtract.

10. 9 + 2 **11.** 17 − 8 **12.** 6 + 3 **13.** 13 − 8 **14.** 5 + 6

15. What is standard form for 30,000 + 700 + 90 + 8?

Ⓐ 3,798 Ⓑ 30,798 Ⓒ 300,798 Ⓓ 7,398

Chapter 2
Lesson
14

Ordinal Numbers and the Calendar

You Will Learn
how to read a calendar

Vocabulary
ordinal numbers
numbers used for ordering

Learn

This calendar shows some unusual holidays. Scream Day is on October 12th. 12th is an **ordinal** number. You can use ordinal numbers to name days on a calendar.

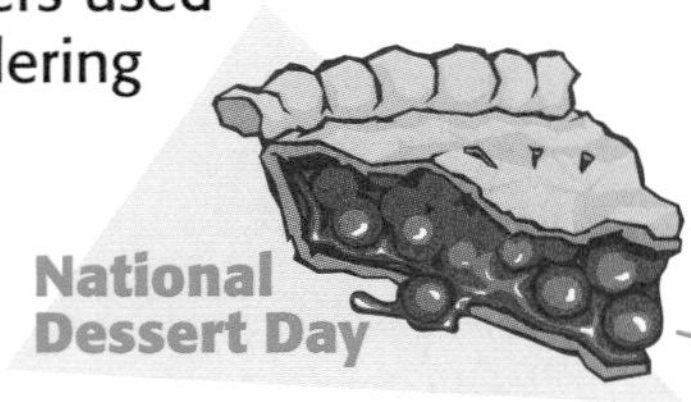

OCTOBER

Sunday	Monday	Tuesday	Wednesday	Thursday	Friday	Saturday
		1	2	3	4	5
6	7	8	9	10	11	12
13	14	15	16	17	18	19
20	21	22	23	24	25	26
27	28	29	30	31		

Each group of 7 days is 1 week.

There are about 4 weeks in one month.

Some Ordinal Numbers							
first 1st	second 2nd	third 3rd	fourth 4th	fifth 5th	sixth 6th	seventh 7th	eighth 8th
	twelfth 12th		twentieth 20th	twenty-first 21st		thirty-first 31st	

Did You Know?
Month comes from *moon.* There are about 29 days between full moons. That's about one month.

Here are the months of the year in order:

There are 12 months in one year.

There are 52 weeks in one year.

January
February
March
April
May
June
July
August
September
October
November
December

Talk About It

Is October more or less than 4 weeks long?

Check

1. What is the month after February?

2. How many days are there in 3 weeks?

3. Write an ordinal number for the last day of October.

4. **Reasoning** Use the calendar on page 82. What day of the week will November 1st be?

Practice

Skills and Reasoning

Use the calendar on page 82 to answer **5–8.**

5. How many Mondays are there in this October?

6. Write the date that is 5 days after October 4th.

7. What day of the week is the 23rd of October?

8. On what day of the week is National Dessert day?

9. Name the ninth month.

10. Which month comes before June?

11. A "weekend" is Saturday and Sunday. How many weekends are there in a year?

12. Suppose that the first day of October is Monday. What day will the last day of October be?

Problem Solving and Applications

13. **Collecting Data** Cinco de Mayo is a Mexican holiday. It is celebrated on May 5th. Use a calendar to find what day of the week that will be this year.

14. Rigo is playing tag with friends. He needs to start his homework at 6:30 P.M. If it is 6:00 P.M. now, how long can he play tag?

Mixed Review and Test Prep

Round to the nearest hundred.

15. 98 **16.** 125 **17.** 588 **18.** 248 **19.** 150

20. 665 **21.** 646 **22.** 718 **23.** 901 **24.** 491

25. **Time** If it is now 2:35 P.M., what will the time be in an hour?

Ⓐ 3:35 A.M. Ⓑ 2:35 A.M. Ⓒ 3:00 P.M. Ⓓ 3:35 P.M.

Chapter 2
Lesson
15

Problem Solving
Decision Making: Make a Schedule

You Will Learn
how to make a schedule

Vocabulary
schedule
a list to help organize tasks

Explore

Suppose you want to make some extra money by helping take care of your neighbor's house and pets.

You will arrive at your neighbor's house right after school at 3:00 P.M. and you must leave for soccer practice at 4:45 P.M. Before you take the job, you need to decide if you have time to do all the tasks. Make a **schedule** to help you decide.

To Do
1. Bring in mail and newspaper
2. Feed Fred the lizard
3. Walk Rowdy the dog for half an hour
4. Give Sam the cat fresh food and water
5. Give Rowdy fresh food and water
6. Water five plants in the house
7. Water the grass for ten minutes

Work Together

▶ Understand

1. What do you know?
2. What do you need to decide?
3. How will the list help you decide?

Plan and Solve

4. How much time do you have to do all the tasks?
5. How can you tell how long the tasks will take all together?
6. Do you know for sure how long any of the tasks will take?
7. Should you include time to go home and change for soccer practice?
8. What if Rowdy knocks over his water bowl! Do you need to build in extra time in case of problems? What other problems might happen?

Make a Decision

9. Make a schedule showing how long each task will take and the times to start each task. Write your schedule like this:

3:00 P.M. Arrive at neighbor's house

___:___ P.M. ______________________

___:___ P.M. ______________________

Present Your Decision

10. Show the class your schedule. According to your schedule, do you have time to take the job?
11. Explain how you decided about how long each task would take. Explain how you planned for possible problems.

SECTION C
Review and Practice

Vocabulary Match each term with its example.

1. A.M.	**a.** first, second, third, ...
2. P.M.	**b.** time for breakfast
3. ordinal numbers	**c.** bedtime

(Lessons 10 and 11) Write each time two ways.

4. 

5. 

6. 

(Lesson 12) Write each time two ways. Write A.M. or P.M.

7. 
lunch time

8. 
dinner time

9. 
breakfast time

(Lesson 13) Write each time.

10. Ralph woke up at 6 A.M. and left 1 hour and 45 minutes later. What time did he leave?

11. A movie started at 7 P.M. and ended at 9:50 P.M. How long was the movie?

(Lesson 14) Use the calendar to answer **12** and **13.**

12. How many Tuesdays are in the month shown?

13. What day of the week is the 14th?

SEPTEMBER

Sun	Mon	Tues	Wed	Thu	Fri	Sat
					1	2
3	4	5	6	7	8	9
10	11	12	13	14	15	16
17	18	19	20	21	22	23
24	25	26	27	28	29	30

14. Journal Name four activities you do during the day. Write the time you start and finish. Tell how long each takes.

Skills Checklist

In this section, you have:

- **Learned About Telling Time to the Nearest Five Minutes**
- **Explored Time to the Nearest Minute**
- **Learned About Telling Time to the Half Hour and Quarter Hour**
- **Learned About Elapsed Time**
- **Learned About Ordinal Numbers and the Calendar**
- **Solved Problems by Making Decisions**

YOUR CHOICE

Choose at least one. Use what you learned in this chapter.

1 Number Juggler

Use the digits shown below to make the three greatest 4-digit numbers you can. Use each digit only once in a number.

5 6 8 2

2 Calculator Challenge

Work with a partner. Enter a 4-digit number on a calculator. Challenge your partner to press keys to make the tens digit a 0. Now trade and keep playing!

3 Can Do!

Fill in the blanks. Then write your own story that compares numbers.

I collected ____ cans over a month for the school fund-raiser. Sarah was absent for a week so she had many fewer cans. She only collected ____ of them. But Ronald collected a lot more than I did. He had ____ cans!

4 Draw the Number

At Home Some numbers name things instead of telling how much or how many. This number tells **how many** ants.

This number **names** the location of a house. It does not tell how many houses.

Find a number in a newspaper that names something. Then draw a picture to show the number and what it names.

CHAPTER 2

Review/Test

Vocabulary Write true or false.

1. **Place value** means replacing a number with a number that tells about how many or how much.
2. When you **round** you place numbers from least to greatest.
3. **Ordinal numbers** are numbers used for ordering.

(Lessons 1–4) Write each number in standard form.

4. six hundred four **5.** 8,000 + 700 + 60 + 3 **6.** one thousand, two

(Lesson 5) Make a list to help solve.

7. Lois has 63 flowers to pack in boxes of 10 or 1. Show all the ways she can pack the boxes.

(Lesson 6) Compare. Use $<$, $>$, or $=$.

8. 345 ● 347 **9.** 2,709 ● 2,981 **10.** 103 ● 89 **11.** 1,201 ● 1,120

(Lesson 7) Order from least to greatest.

12. 4,138, 4,326, 4,126 **13.** 659, 569, 965 **14.** 321, 3,021, 41

15. 772, 719, 712 **16.** 101, 99, 59 **17.** 2,720, 2,101, 1,293

(Lesson 8) Round to the nearest ten.

18. 319 **19.** 25 **20.** 12 **21.** 178 **22.** 197

(Lesson 9) Round to the nearest hundred.

23. 319 **24.** 258 **25.** 152 **26.** 78 **27.** 121

(Lessons 10–12) Write each time two ways.

28.

29.

30.

31.

(Lesson 13) Solve.

32. School starts at 8:00 A.M. and recess is at 10:15 A.M. How long do you have to wait for recess?

(Lesson 14)

33. What month comes after May?

CHAPTER 2
Performance Assessment

Suppose you want to do a science project for the science fair. Your mother says she will drive you to one of these places to do research.

Think about where you would like to go. What time would you leave your house to get there? What time would you arrive?

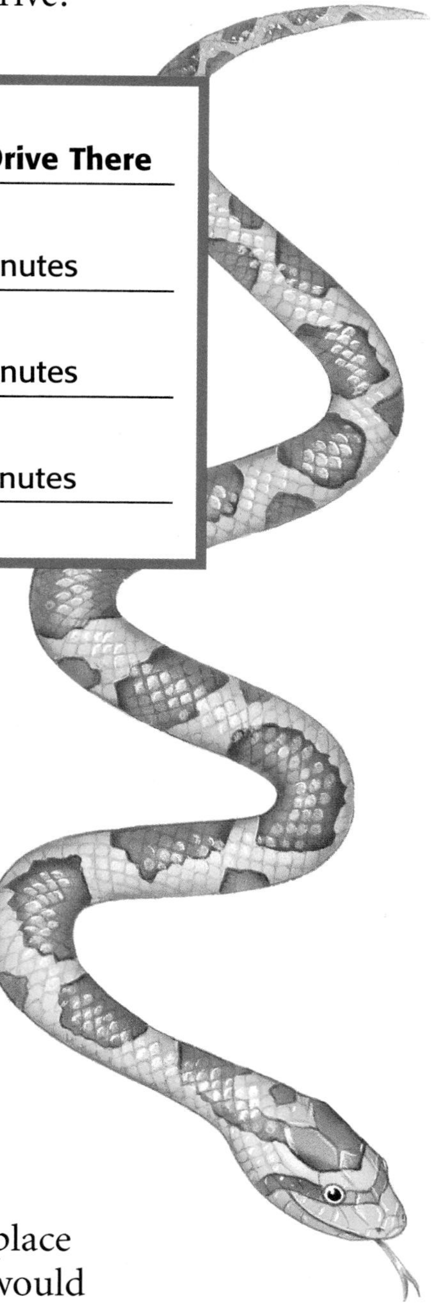

Place	Miles Away	Time It Takes to Drive There
Insect Museum	140	2 hours and 50 minutes
Reptile Park	122	2 hours and 40 minutes
Dinosaur Institute	125	2 hours and 35 minutes

1. **Decision Making** Decide where you want to go. Think about how far away each place is and how long it will take to get there.

2. **Recording Data** Write which place you chose and why. Then copy and complete the schedule.

   __:__ A.M. Leave for _____.

   __:__ _.M. Arrive at _____.

3. **Explain Your Thinking** How did you decide where to go? How did you decide what time to leave and when you would arrive?

4. **Critical Thinking** Suppose you decided to go to the place that took the least amount of driving time. Where would you go? If you left at 8:00 A.M., what time would you get there?

Math Magazine

Ancient Abacus Some kinds of calculators don't need batteries or the sun to work! The Chinese abacus has been used for thousands of years to help people calculate quickly.

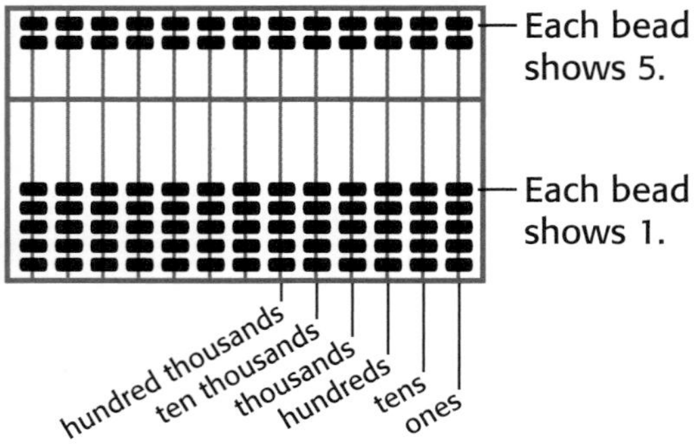

Move the beads to show numbers on the abacus.

This is how to show 46 on an abacus.

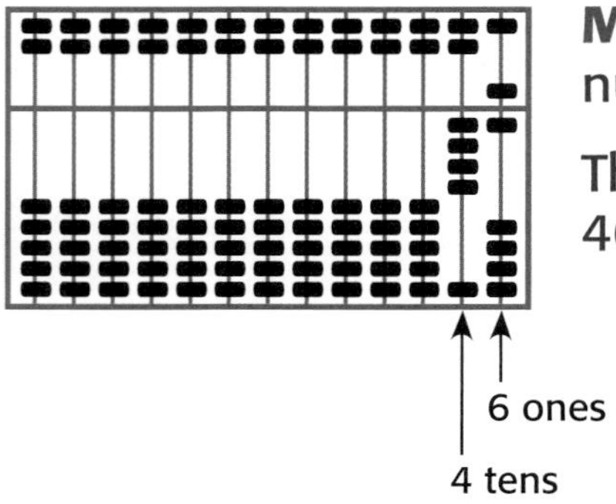

This is how to show 1,246.

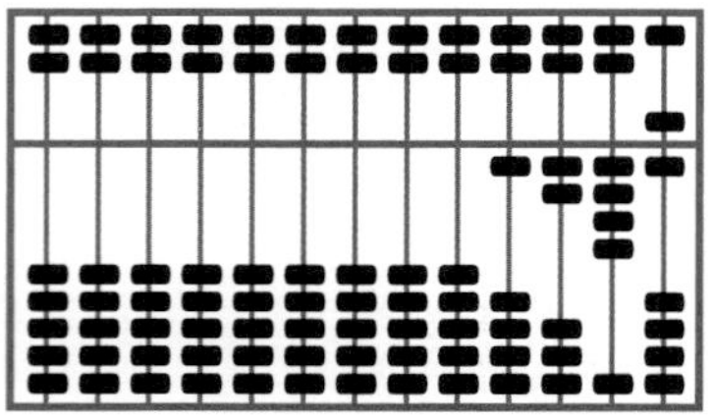

Try These!

What number does each abacus show?

1. 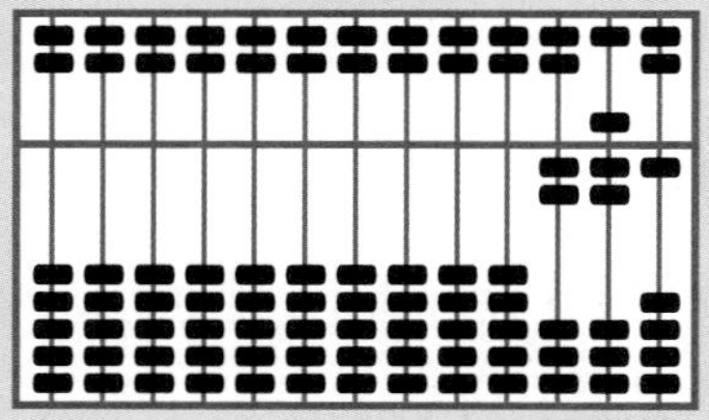

2. 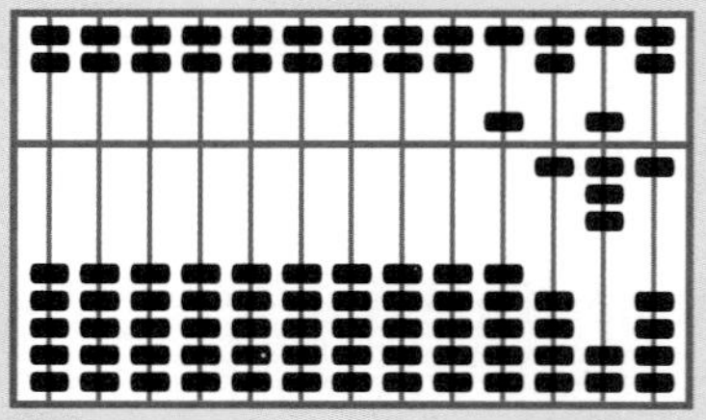

3. Work with a partner. Name a number and have your partner draw a picture of an abacus to show it. Take turns.

Cumulative Review

Test Prep Strategy: Follow Directions

Watch for words like *not*.

Which group of numbers is NOT ordered from least to greatest?

Ⓐ 367, 377, 385 Ⓑ 429, 529, 629

Ⓒ 124, 120, 115 Ⓓ 494, 495, 496

If I read carefully I can see that I must look for numbers that are NOT ordered from least to greatest. I'll pick Ⓒ.

Write the letter of the correct answer. You may use any strategy to help.

Test Prep Strategies

- Read Carefully
- Follow Directions
- Make Smart Choices
- Eliminate Choices
- Work Backward from an Answer

1. What is the value of the second 3 in 23,583?

Ⓐ 3 Ⓑ 30 Ⓒ 300 Ⓓ 3,000

2. Jack has 8 baseball cards and gives 2 to Elise. Now Elise has 10 baseball cards. How many cards does Jack have?

Ⓐ 3 Ⓑ 8 Ⓒ 6 Ⓓ not here

3. How many stickers are NOT red?

Ⓐ 6 Ⓑ 4

Ⓒ 8 Ⓓ not here

Number of Stickers	
Red	★ ★ ★ ★
Blue	★
Green	★ ★

★ = 2 stickers

4. Which of the following numbers is between 3,750 and 3,920?

Ⓐ 3,570 Ⓑ 3,280 Ⓒ 2,426 Ⓓ 3,840

5. What is 788 rounded to the nearest ten?

Ⓐ 700 Ⓑ 800 Ⓒ 780 Ⓓ not here

6. It takes 1 hour and 10 minutes to take the bus from Ernest's house to his grandmother's house. If he wants to be at his grandmother's by 6:10 P.M., which of these times could he leave?

Ⓐ 5:00 P.M. Ⓑ 7:20 P.M. Ⓒ 6:00 P.M. Ⓓ 6:30 P.M.

Chapter 3

Adding Whole Numbers and Money

DIGS AND FINDS

SECTION A

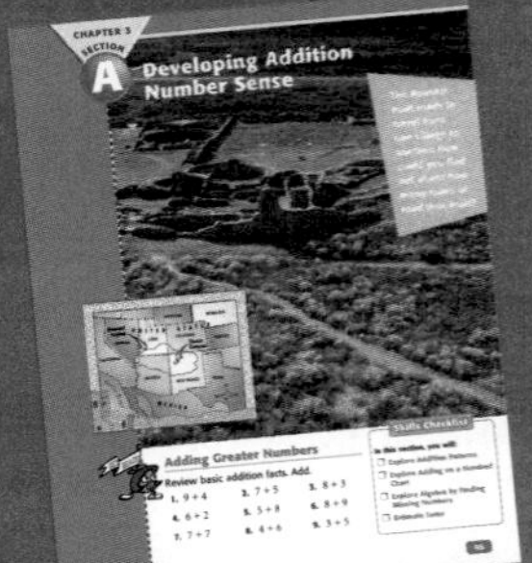

Anasazi roads
Page 95

Developing Addition Number Sense

95

The Anasazi built homes with sandstone and mud called *pueblos*. Most Anasazi pueblos have large underground rooms called *kivas*. Which pueblo has the most kivas?

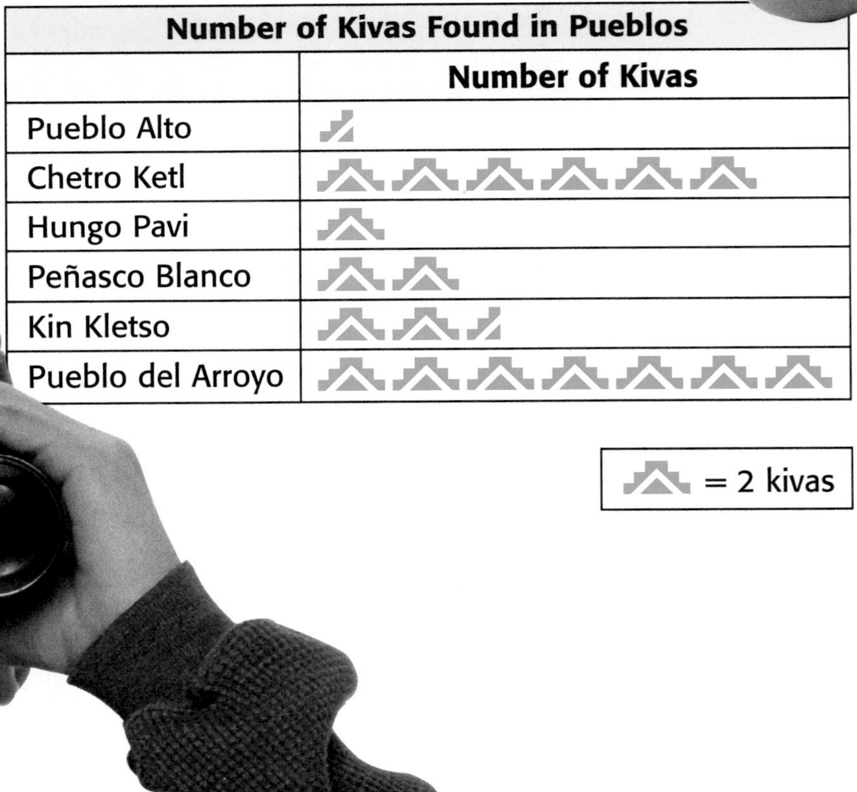
Number of Kivas Found in Pueblos
Number of Kivas
Pueblo Alto
Chetro Ketl
Hungo Pavi
Peñasco Blanco
Kin Kletso
Pueblo del Arroyo
= 2 kivas

SECTION B

Adding Greater Numbers and Money

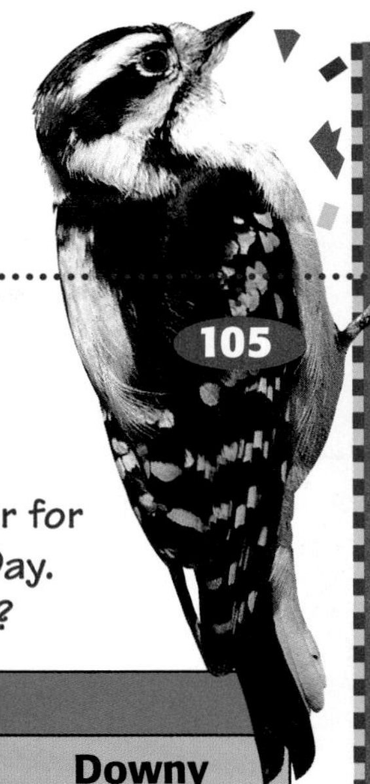

105

People all over North America count birds once a year for the National Audubon Society's Annual Bird Count Day. What two areas spotted the most American Robins?

Annual Bird Count Day Results

	Mallard Duck	American Robin	Downy Woodpecker
Long Point, Ontario, Canada	532	28	74
Austin, Texas	37	915	47
Denver, Colorado	1,482	513	80
St. Marks, Florida	124	1,337	34
Folsom, California	952	1,813	35
Cape Cod, Massachusetts	987	364	79

Elizabeth and Vivian have found thousands of birds' nests.

Page 105

Surfing the World Wide Web!

What kinds of birds are in your neighborhood? Do some bird-watching for a week. Write down the names of the birds and record them at **www.mathsurf.com/3/ch3**.

Compare your results with those of other students around the country to see which of the same birds live in different places.

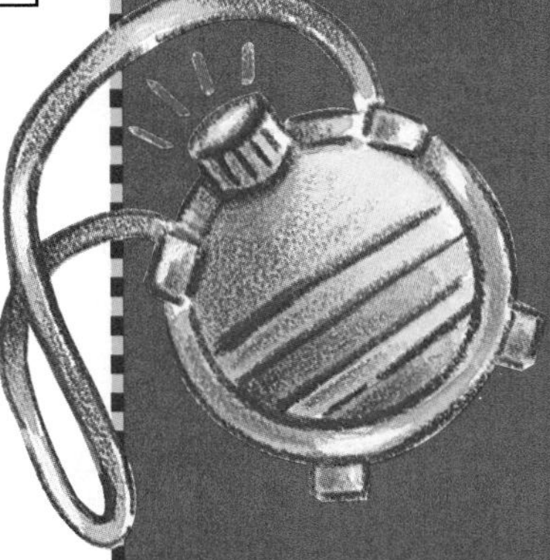

SECTION C

Extending Addition

123

If you're hot on the trail for an adventure, then you might need some of these supplies. Which item costs the most? Which item costs the least?

Supply List	
Pop-up binoculars	$5.25
Flashlight	$7.16
Shovel	$3.89
Bucket	$5.14
Notebook	$1.03
Canteen	$5.14
Pencil	$0.25

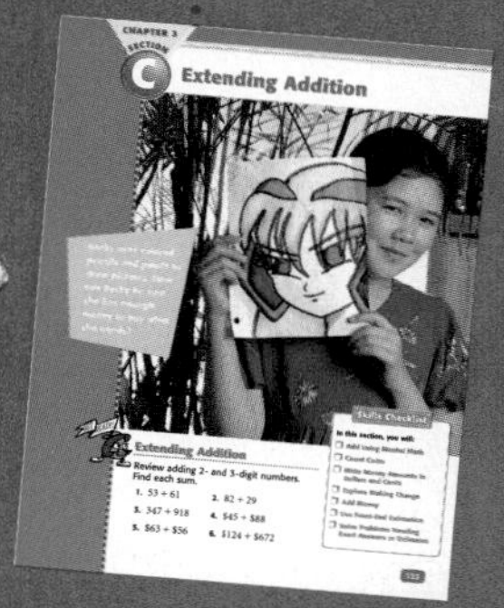

Becky buys supplies to use for her paintings.

Page 123

TEAM PROJECT
Time Capsule

Materials
container

Have you ever wondered what life was like 10, 20, or 30 years ago? Make a time capsule to help people in the future understand what life is like now. It can hold letters, photos, or even cassette tapes.

Make a Plan

- What will you use for your time capsule? How big should it be?
- What will you put in your time capsule? Think about what you would like to find in a time capsule.

Carry It Out

1. Get a box or other container for your time capsule.
2. Write a letter that tells about you and how you live.
3. Collect items to put in the time capsule.

Talk About It

- What did you put in the time capsule?
- How old will you be if you open your time capsule in 10 years? 20 years? 30 years?

Present the Project

- Explain how the items in your time capsule will help people in the future learn about you and your life.
- Seal your time capsule and put it in a safe place.

CHAPTER 3

SECTION

A Developing Addition Number Sense

The Anasazi built roads to travel from one village to another. How could you find out about how many miles of road they built?

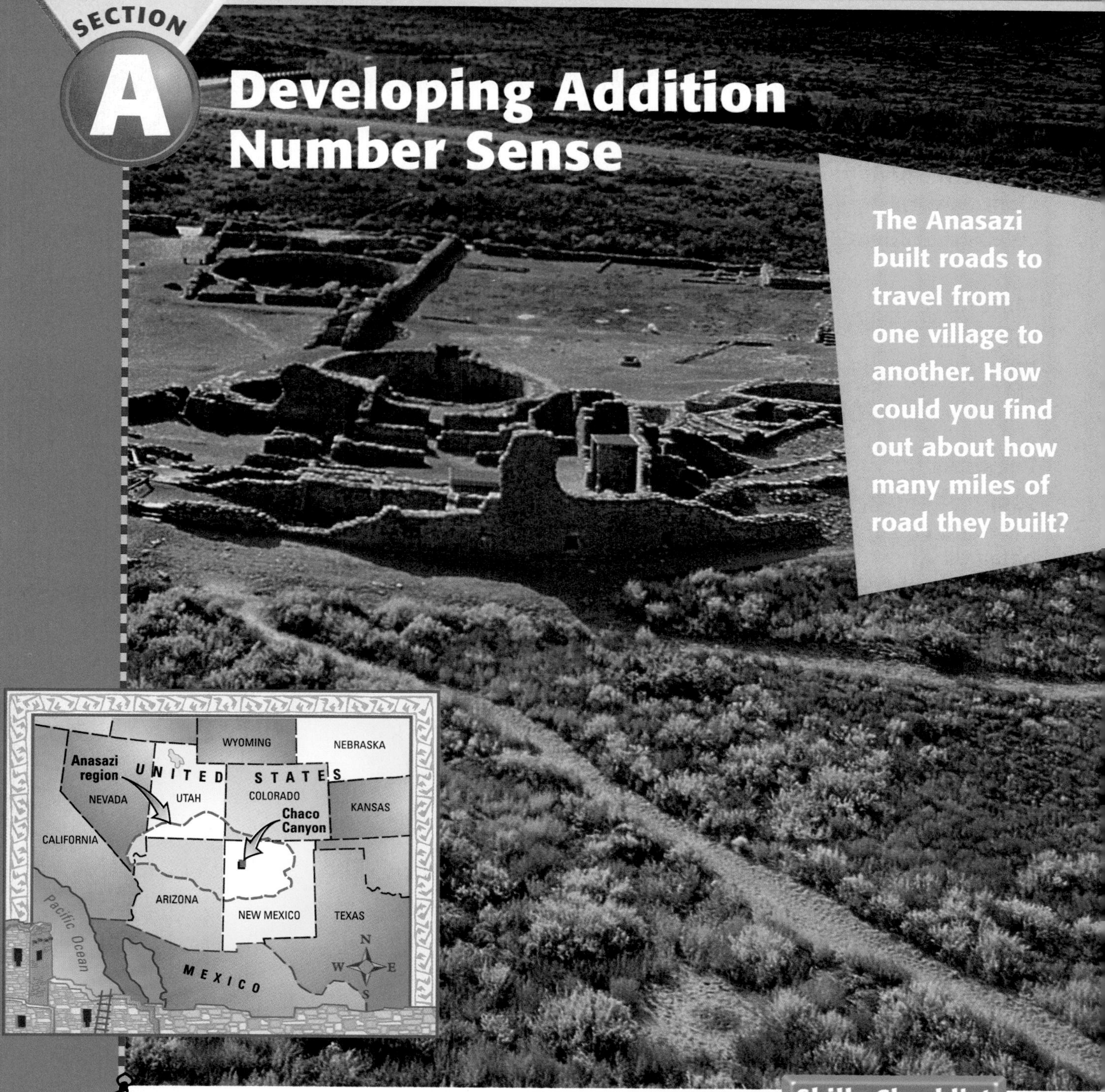

Adding Greater Numbers

Review basic addition facts. Add.

1. $9 + 4$	**2.** $7 + 5$	**3.** $8 + 3$
4. $6 + 2$	**5.** $5 + 8$	**6.** $8 + 9$
7. $7 + 7$	**8.** $4 + 6$	**9.** $3 + 5$

Skills Checklist

In this section, you will:

- ❐ Explore Addition Patterns
- ❐ Explore Adding on a Hundred Chart
- ❐ Explore Algebra by Finding Missing Numbers
- ❐ Estimate Sums

Chapter 3
Lesson
1

Exploring Addition Patterns

Problem Solving Connection
Look for a Pattern

Materials
calculator

Vocabulary
sum
the number obtained when adding numbers

Explore

You can use basic facts and place-value patterns to add greater numbers.

Work Together

1. Use a calculator to find each **sum.** Look for patterns.

   a. 5 + 4 = ■ 50 + 40 = ■ 500 + 400 = ■
   b. 7 + 8 = ■ 70 + 80 = ■ 700 + 800 = ■
   c. 9 + 5 = ■ 90 + 50 = ■ 900 + 500 = ■

2. Use patterns to find each sum. Check with a calculator.

   a. 2 + 6 = ■ 20 + 60 = ■ 200 + 600 = ■
   b. 5 + 5 = ■ 50 + 50 = ■ 500 + 500 = ■
   c. 3 + 8 = ■ 30 + 80 = ■ 300 + 800 = ■
   d. 8 + 9 = ■ 80 + 90 = ■ 800 + 900 = ■
   e. 9 + 7 = ■ 90 + 70 = ■ 900 + 700 = ■
   f. 6 + 7 = ■ 60 + 70 = ■ 600 + 700 = ■

Remember
To tell the value of a digit, look at its place in the number.

Talk About It

3. What patterns did you find?
4. What basic fact can you use to find 300 + 500? Explain.
5. What basic fact can you use to find \$60 + \$20? Explain.

Connect

Basic facts and place value can help you add.

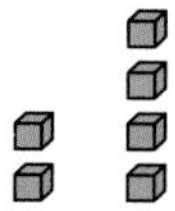

2 + 4 = 6

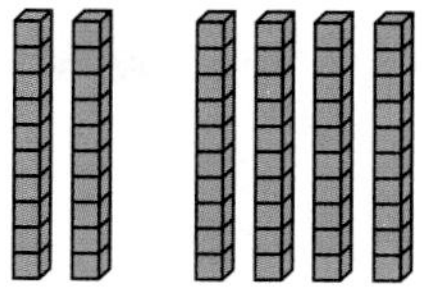

20 + 40 = 60

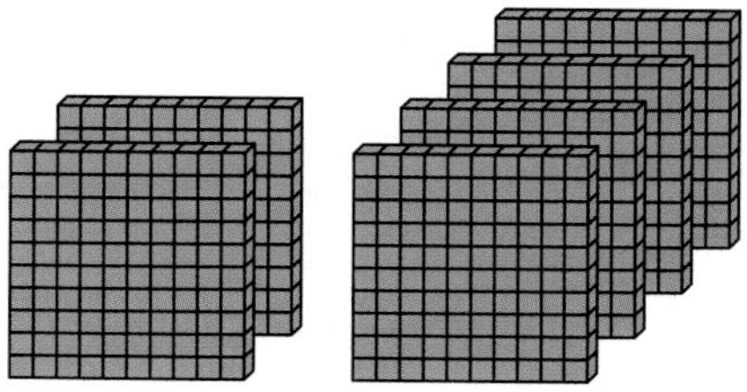

200 + 400 = 600

You can also use mental math to add.

30 + 80

Think: 3 + 8 = 11.

So, 3 tens + 8 tens = 11 tens, or 30 + 80 = 110.

300 + 800

Think: 3 + 8 = 11.

So, 3 hundreds + 8 hundreds = 11 hundreds, or 300 + 800 = 1,100.

Practice

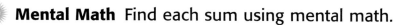

Copy and complete.

1. 2 + 7 = ■
20 + ■ = 90
■ + 700 = 900

2. 4 + 8 = ■
■ + 80 = 120
400 + ■ = 1,200

3. \$5 + \$■ = \$8
\$50 + \$30 = \$■
\$■ + \$300 = \$800

Mental Math Find each sum using mental math.

4. \$40 + \$50 **5.** 800 + 100 **6.** 60 + 30 **7.** \$300 + \$300

8. 50 + 90 **9.** \$400 + \$700 **10.** \$90 + \$20 **11.** 700 + 900

12. Reasoning Can you use the basic fact 7 + 2 to find 70 + 200? Explain.

13. A new bike costs \$80. A new helmet costs \$20. How much would it cost to buy the bike and helmet?

14. Geometry Readiness Continue the pattern.

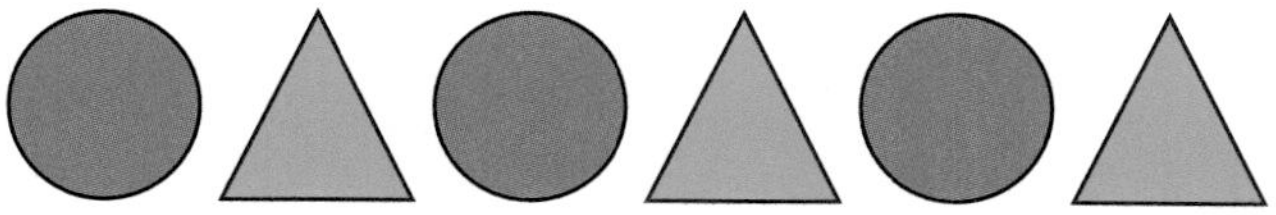

____ ____ ____ ____

15. Critical Thinking Jen said, "If you add hundreds, like 600 and 300, the sum will always have only 2 zeros." Is she correct? Explain.

16. Journal Explain how you can use basic facts to find 700 + 200.

Chapter 3
Lesson
2

Exploring Adding on a Hundred Chart

Problem Solving Connection
- Look for a Pattern
- Use Objects/ Act It Out

Materials
hundred chart

Explore

You can use a hundred chart to find sums.

27 + 20 = ▒

Start at 27.

Move forward 2 tens.

27 + 20 = 47

Work Together

Math Tip
Think about counting by tens.

1. Use a hundred chart to find each sum.

a. 34 + 5 = ▒	**b.** 60 + 8 = ▒	**c.** 44 + 23 = ▒
d. 53 + 19 = ▒	**e.** 72 + 20 = ▒	**f.** 25 + 33 = ▒
g. 16 + 80 = ▒	**h.** 80 + 16 = ▒	**i.** 17 + 29 = ▒

Talk About It

2. What do you notice about the sums of 16 + 80 and 80 + 16?

3. Explain two ways to find 53 + 19 on a hundred chart.

4. How could you use a hundred chart to find $18 + $37?

Connect

You can think about adding numbers in different ways.

Matt thinks:

40 + 28

40 and 20 more is 60.
60 and 8 more is 68.

Krista thinks:

40 + 28

Start at 28 and move down four rows, or 40. Count down the column **38, 48, 58, 68.**

1	2	3	4	5	6	7	8	9	10
11	12	13	14	15	16	17	18	19	20
21	22	23	24	25	26	27	28	29	30
31	32	33	34	35	36	37	38	39	40
41	42	43	44	45	46	47	48	49	50
51	52	53	54	55	56	57	58	59	60
61	62	63	64	65	66	67	68	69	70
71	72	73	74	75	76	77	78	79	80
81	82	83	84	85	86	87	88	89	90
91	92	93	94	95	96	97	98	99	100

You can add numbers in any order and get the same sum.

40 + 28 = 68 and 28 + 40 = 68

Practice

Find each sum. You may use a hundred chart to help.

1. 32 + 10 **2.** 39 + 5 **3.** 5 + 39 **4.** 78 + 21

5. 54 + 29 **6.** $62 + $24 **7.** $87 + $11 **8.** 35 + 30

9. $30 + $35 **10.** 15 + 76 **11.** 76 + 15 **12.** 28 + 49

13. 28 + 55 **14.** 61 + 39 **15.** $18 + $43 **16.** 25 + 35

17. Find the sum of 81 and 16. **18.** Add 24 and 46.

19. Reasoning If you know the sum of 53 + 26, how can you find the sum of 26 + 53? Explain.

20. Music A piano has 52 white keys and 36 black keys. How many keys are there all together?

21. Mental Math Explain how you would find 31 + 30 using mental math.

22. Algebra Readiness Suppose you start at 30. What number would you add to get a sum of 68?

23. Journal Describe two different ways you can find the sum of 36 + 28.

Chapter 3
Lesson
3

Exploring Algebra: Missing Numbers

Problem Solving Connection
- Use Objects/ Act It Out
- Guess and Check

Materials
color cubes

Explore

For ■ + 4 = 20 to be true, each side of the number sentence must be equal.

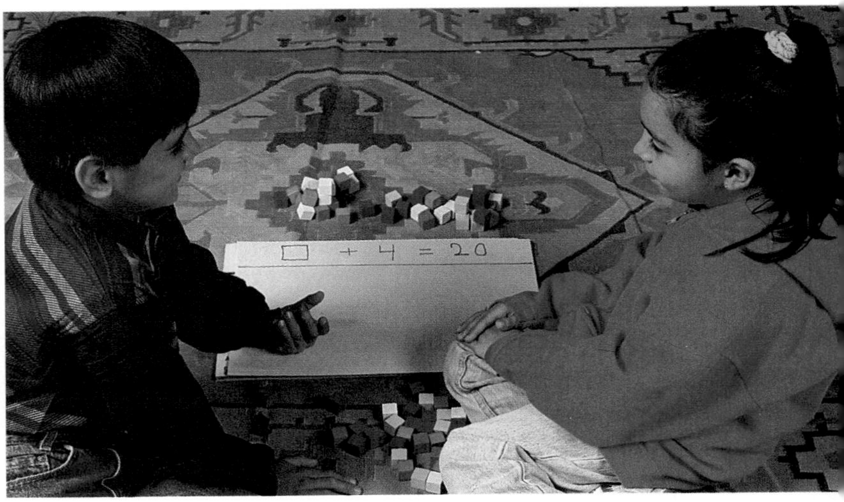

Work Together

1. Find the missing number.
■ + 4 = 20

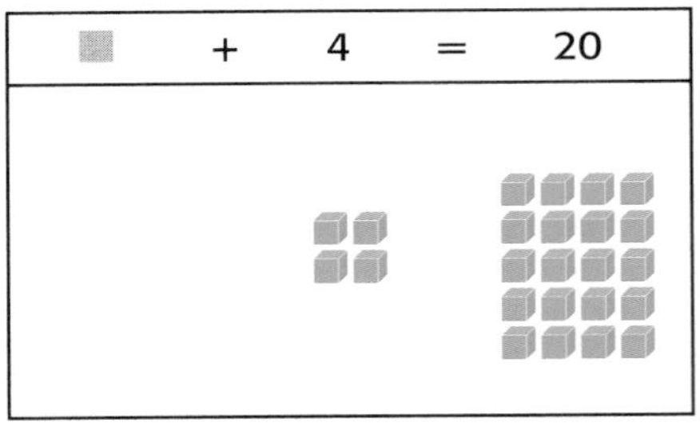

a. Make a workmat to help you.
b. Use color cubes to find the missing number.
c. How many cubes did you put on the workmat to make both sides equal?

Problem Solving Hint
You can use objects to help you find a missing number in a number sentence.

2. Use color cubes to find each missing number.

a. ■ + 9 = 24 **b.** ■ + 5 = 18 **c.** 7 + ■ = 23
d. 11 + ■ = 19 **e.** ■ + 2 = 16 **f.** 14 + ■ = 17

Talk About It

3. Explain how you found the missing numbers.

4. Is 16 + 5 = 22 true? Explain how you know.

Connect

Here are two ways to find the missing number in 6 + ■ = 22.

Tanya's way

I matched 6 cubes on one side with 6 on the other.

I need 16 cubes to make both sides equal. So, 6 + 16 = 22.

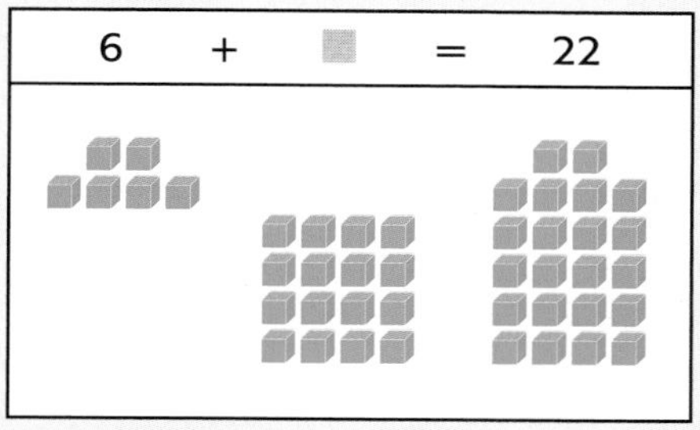

Kelsey's way

I already have 6 on one side, so I can count on from 6 until I have 22.

I counted on 16 more cubes. So, 6 + 16 = 22.

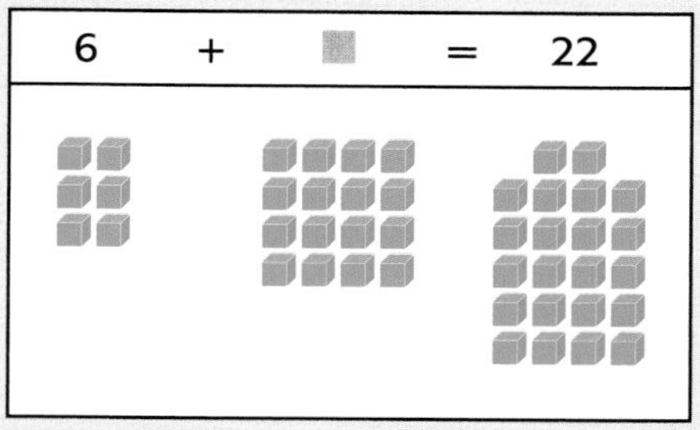

Practice

Find each missing number. You may use color cubes to help.

1. ■ + 5 = 21 **2.** ■ + 9 = 25 **3.** 2 + ■ = 14 **4.** 3 + ■ = 16

5. 15 + ■ = 22 **6.** 4 + ■ = 18 **7.** ■ + 7 = 20 **8.** ■ + 4 = 25

9. ■ + 6 = 19 **10.** ■ + 22 = 25 **11.** 17 + ■ = 23 **12.** 8 + ■ = 24

13. Reasoning Is the missing number in ■ + 3 = 15 the same as the missing number in 3 + ■ = 15? Explain.

14. Patterns Find each missing number.

a. ■ + 4 = 19 **b.** ■ + 5 = 19 **c.** ■ + 6 = 19 **d.** ■ + 7 = 19

15. Measurement Find the missing length. Explain how you know.

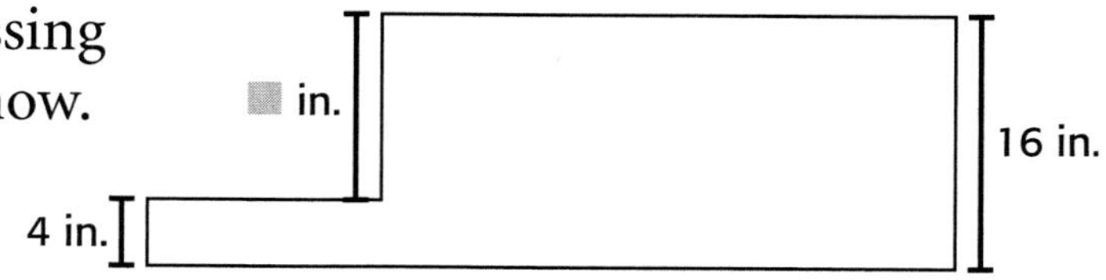

16. Calculator Use a calculator to find the missing number in 14 + ■ = 35.

17. Journal Explain how you would find the missing number in ■ + 5 = 23.

Problem Solving Hint

Take a guess to get you started.

Estimating Sums

You Will Learn
how to use rounding to estimate sums

Vocabulary

estimate
to find a number that is close to an exact number

addend
a number that is added to find a sum

Learn

Over 700 years ago, the Anasazi built long, straight roads through Chaco Canyon. Use the map to find about how many miles of road the Anasazi built.

Since you don't need to find the exact number of miles, you can **estimate**.

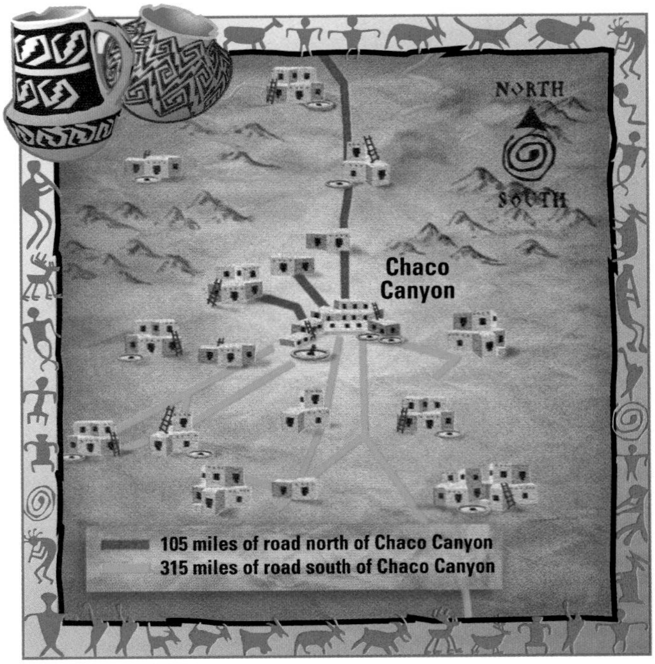

Remember
You can think of a number line to help you round numbers.

Estimate the sum of 315 and 105 by rounding each **addend** to the nearest hundred.

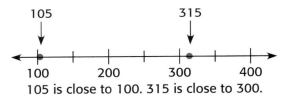

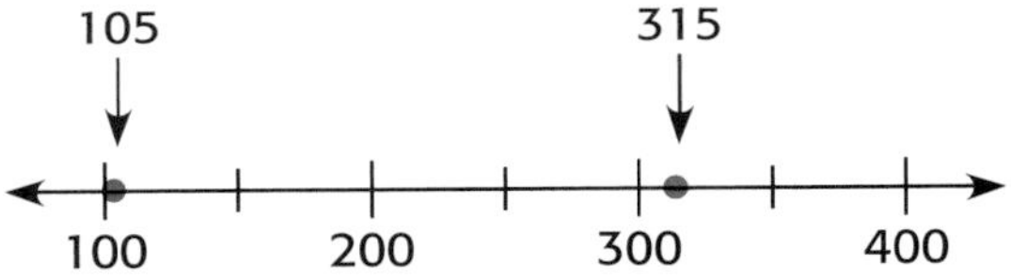

105 is close to 100. 315 is close to 300.

$$\begin{array}{r} 315 \\ +\ 105 \\ \hline \end{array} \longrightarrow \begin{array}{r} 300 \\ +\ 100 \\ \hline 400 \end{array}$$

So, the Anasazi built about 400 miles of road.

Other Examples

A. Estimate by rounding to the nearest hundred dollars.

$$\begin{array}{r} \$578 \\ +\ 150 \\ \hline \end{array} \longrightarrow \begin{array}{r} \$600 \\ +\ 200 \\ \hline \$800 \end{array}$$

B. Estimate by rounding to the nearest ten.

$$\begin{array}{r} 47 \\ +\ 32 \\ \hline \end{array} \longrightarrow \begin{array}{r} 50 \\ +\ 30 \\ \hline 80 \end{array}$$

Talk About It

Why didn't you need to find the exact number of miles of road the Anasazi built?

Check

Estimate each sum.

1. 93 + 58 **2.** 734 + 178 **3.** 387 + 377 **4.** 501 + 461

5. \$41 + \$85 **6.** \$621 + \$247 **7.** 82 + 64 **8.** 26 + 99

9. Reasoning Write two addends that have a sum of about 60.

Practice

Skills and Reasoning

Estimate each sum.

10. 36 + 57 **11.** 823 + 146 **12.** \$253 + \$341 **13.** \$67 + \$81

14. 12 + 43 **15.** 512 + 694 **16.** 71 + 95 **17.** 419 + 726

18. Estimate the sum of 906 and 259.

19. Estimate the sum of 65 and 23.

20. Two addends have a sum of about 900. What are two possible addends?

21. Round to find which two numbers have a sum of about 800.

352	298	409	178	737

Problem Solving and Applications

Using Data Use the Data File on page 92 to answer **22–24.**

22. Which pueblo has the fewest kivas?

23. How many kivas are there in Chetro Ketl and Pueblo del Arroyo?

24. How many kivas can be found in Hungo Pavi?

Kiva ruins at Chaco Canyon

Mixed Review and Test Prep

Add or subtract.

25. 9 + 3 **26.** 12 − 5 **27.** 15 − 6 **28.** 8 + 7 **29.** 11 − 2

30. 17 − 8 **31.** 2 + 9 **32.** 5 + 6 **33.** 12 − 8 **34.** 7 + 6

35. How many more students wore T-shirts than sweatshirts?

Ⓐ 4 students Ⓑ 5 students

Ⓒ 6 students Ⓓ 7 students

Shirts Worn in Class 3A	
Sweatshirts	𝍸 |||
T-shirts	𝍸 𝍸 |||

SECTION A

Review and Practice

Word List
sum addend estimate

Vocabulary Choose the best word for each sentence.

1. A number that is added is called the ____.
2. When you only need to know about how many, you can find an ____.
3. In the number sentence $14 + 23 = 37$, the number 37 is called the ____.

(Lesson 1) Copy and complete.

4. $2 + 5 = \blacksquare$
   $20 + \blacksquare = 70$
   $\blacksquare + 500 = 700$
5. $8 + 6 = \blacksquare$
   $\blacksquare + 60 = 140$
   $800 + \blacksquare = 1{,}400$
6. $\$6 + \$\blacksquare = \$9$
   $\$60 + \$30 = \$\blacksquare$
   $\$\blacksquare + \$300 = \$900$

7. **Reasoning** What basic fact can you use to find $400 + 900$? Explain.

(Lesson 2) Find each sum. You may use a hundred chart to help.

8. $54 + 20$
9. $46 + 9$
10. $35 + 21$
11. $16 + 19$
12. $\$47 + \$39$
13. $\$60 + \$27$
14. $27 + 60$
15. $73 + 18$

(Lesson 3) Find each missing number. You may use color cubes to help.

16. $\blacksquare + 6 = 25$
17. $3 + \blacksquare = 21$
18. $14 + \blacksquare = 25$
19. $\blacksquare + 8 = 27$

20. **Logic** I am a 2-digit number. If you add me to 4 you will get a sum of 25. What number am I?

(Lesson 4) Estimate each sum.

21. $23 + 44$
22. $\$431 + \$509$
23. $55 + 29$
24. $621 + 132$
25. $53 + 82$
26. $357 + 924$

27. **Journal** Explain how basic facts and place-value patterns can help you estimate sums of greater numbers.

Skills Checklist

In this section, you have:

- ☑ Explored Addition Patterns
- ☑ Explored Adding on a Hundred Chart
- ☑ Explored Algebra by Finding Missing Numbers
- ☑ Estimated Sums

CHAPTER 3

SECTION

B Adding Greater Numbers and Money

Elizabeth and Vivian compete each year to see who finds the most birds' nests. What are some ways to keep track of the number of nests they find?

Adding Greater Numbers

Review adding tens and hundreds. Find each sum.

1. 50 + 30 **2.** 60 + 70

3. 80 + 40 **4.** 600 + 900

5. 200 + 500 **6.** 700 + 800

Skills Checklist

In this section, you will:

- ❒ Explore Adding with Regrouping
- ❒ Add 2-, 3-, and 4-Digit Numbers
- ❒ Learn About Column Addition
- ❒ Solve Problems by Guessing and Checking

Chapter 3
Lesson
5

Exploring Adding with Regrouping

Problem Solving Connection
- Use Objects/ Act It Out
- Look for a Pattern

Materials
place-value blocks

Vocabulary
regroup
to name a number in a different way

Remember
10 ones = 1 ten
10 tens = 1 hundred

Explore

You can use place-value blocks to add 2-digit numbers.

Work Together

1. Find 37 + 28. Use place-value blocks.

a. Show 37 and 28 with place-value blocks. Put the two groups together.

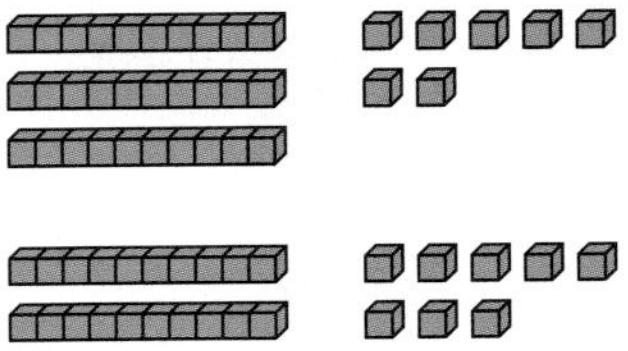

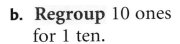

b. **Regroup** 10 ones for 1 ten.

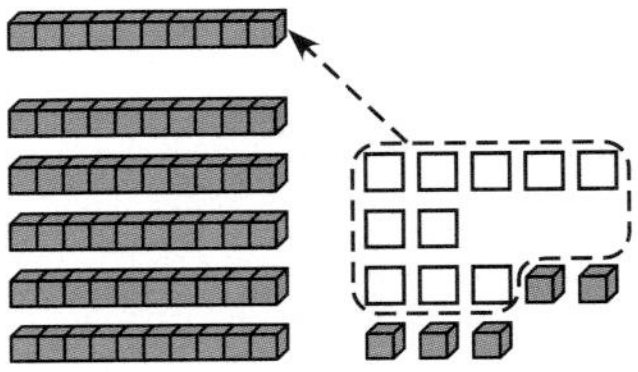

c. What is the sum of 37 + 28?

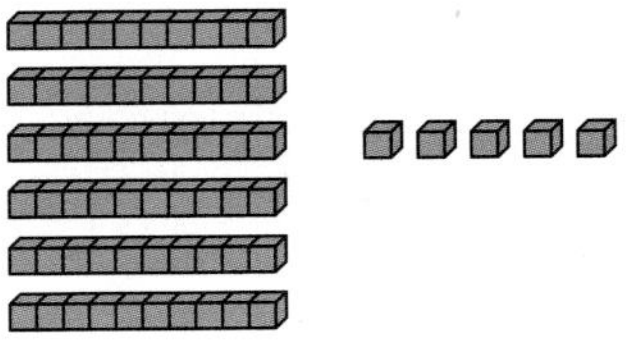

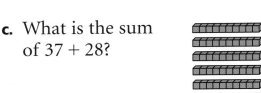

2. Use place-value blocks to find each sum.

a. 21 + 32 = ☐ **b.** 42 + 29 = ☐
c. 14 + 65 = ☐ **d.** 62 + 83 = ☐
e. 74 + 16 = ☐ **f.** 37 + 35 = ☐

Talk About It

3. If you add 24 and 57, do you have to regroup ones for tens? Explain.

4. Name two 2-digit numbers that you can add together without regrouping. Explain.

Connect

You can use what you know about place value and regrouping to add numbers.

Find 25 + 37.

You Show | **You Write**

Add the ones. Regroup as needed.

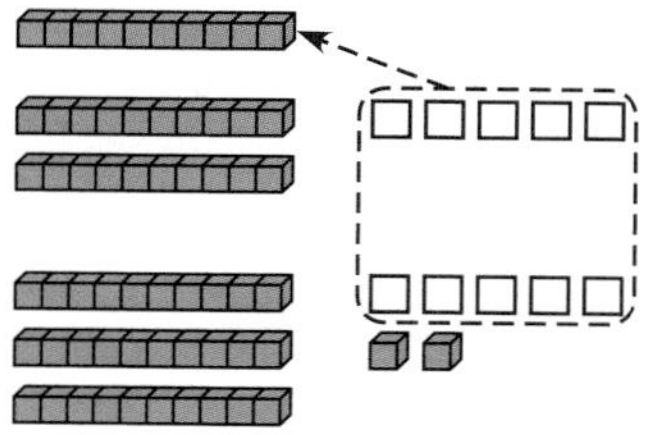

$5 + 7 = 12$ ones, or 1 ten, 2 ones

$$\begin{array}{r} \scriptstyle 1 \\ 25 \\ +\,37 \\ \hline 2 \end{array}$$

Add the tens.

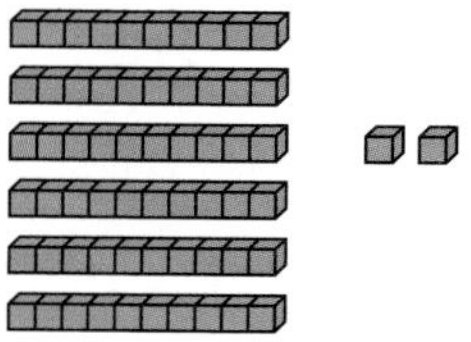

1 ten + 2 tens + 3 tens = 6 tens

$$\begin{array}{r} \scriptstyle 1 \\ 25 \\ +\,37 \\ \hline 62 \end{array}$$

25 + 37 = 62

Practice

Find each sum. You may use place-value blocks to help.

1. 23 + 48

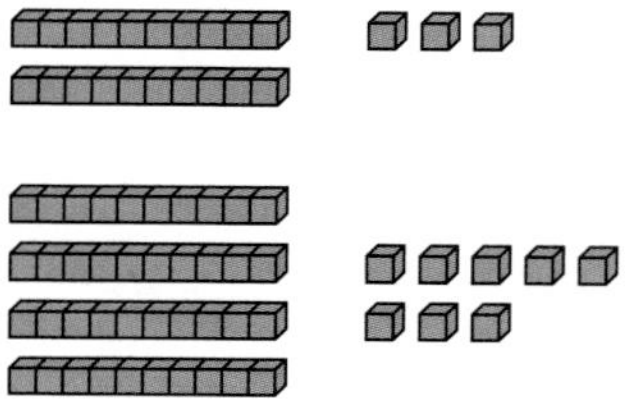

2. 37 + 15

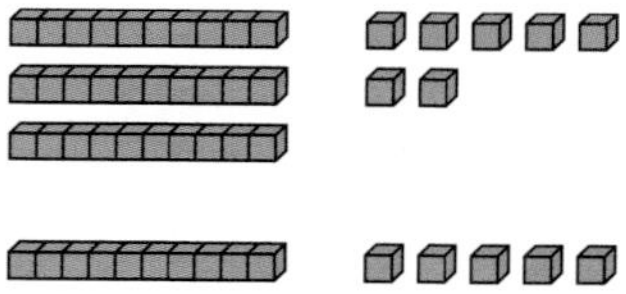

3. 17 + 55

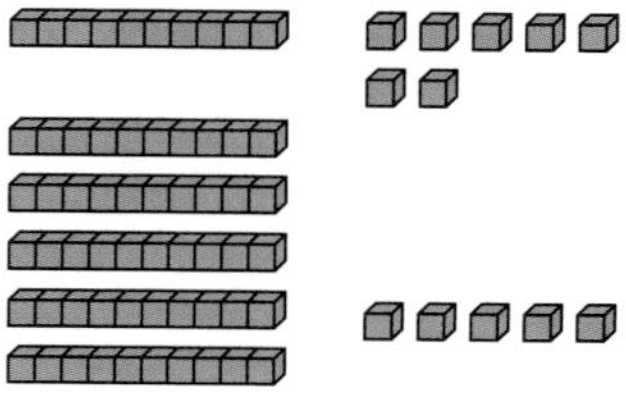

4. 28 + 32

5. 19 + 64

6. 46 + 79

7. 75 + 27

8. 91 + 33

9. 82 + 46

10. **Reasoning** Do you need to regroup 10 ones for 1 ten when you find 64 + 38? Explain.

11. **Geometry Readiness** Continue the pattern.

______

12. **Journal** How would you find 86 + 15? Explain if you need to regroup 10 ones for 1 ten. You may draw a picture to help.

Adding 2-Digit Numbers

You Will Learn
how to add 2-digit numbers

Learn

King Tut lived over 3,000 years ago. But buried in his tomb were lots of the same kinds of clothes worn today, including gloves, socks, and hats!

Clothes Found in King Tut's Tomb	
Gloves	28
Hats	25
Shawls	24
Socks	4
Sashes	15

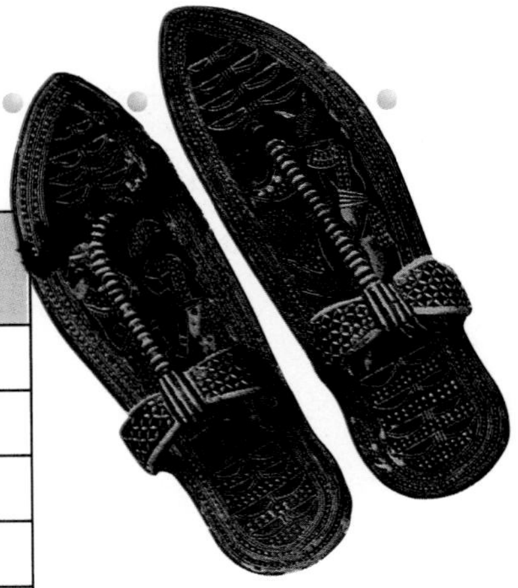

Example

How many gloves and hats were found in King Tut's tomb?

Since you are putting together groups of items, you add.

Find 28 + 25.

Step 1

Add the ones. Regroup as needed.

$$\begin{array}{r} \scriptstyle 1 \\ 28 \\ +\,25 \\ \hline 3 \end{array}$$

8 + 5 = 13 ones, or 1 ten, 3 ones

Step 2

Add the tens.

$$\begin{array}{r} \scriptstyle 1 \\ 28 \\ +\,25 \\ \hline 53 \end{array}$$

1 ten + 2 tens + 2 tens = 5 tens

28 + 25 = 53

Estimate to check. 30 + 30 = 60
Since 53 is close to 60, the answer is reasonable.

So, 53 gloves and hats were found.

Talk About It

What does the small 1 above the 2 in the tens place mean?

Check

Add. Estimate to check.

1. 33 + 16 **2.** $65 + $28 **3.** 86 + 5 **4.** 72 + 93

5. **Reasoning** Do you need to regroup 10 ones for 1 ten to find 44 + 79? Explain.

Practice

Skills and Reasoning

Add. Estimate to check.

6.	7.	8.	9.	10.
52 + 24	37 + 41	\$41 + \$59	34 + 8	78 + 65

11.	12.	13.	14.	15.
63 + 7	\$28 + 43	96 + 36	\$57 + 4	25 + 15

16. 19 + 72 **17.** \$43 + \$89 **18.** \$82 + \$42 **19.** 67 + 26

20. Find the sum of 45 and 33.

21. Add 36 and 28.

22. Write two numbers that add to 60 without regrouping.

23. When you find 32 + 9 do you start by finding 3 + 9? Explain.

Problem Solving and Applications

Use the table on page 108 for **24** and **25**.

24. How many shawls and sashes were found in King Tut's tomb?

25. Were more shawls than hats found in the tomb? Explain.

26. Write Your Own Problem Write and solve an addition word problem that uses regrouping. Use two 2-digit numbers.

In 1922, King Tut's tomb was found in Egypt.

Mixed Review and Test Prep

Mental Math Find each sum.

27. 300 + 500 **28.** \$800 + \$400 **29.** \$900 + \$800 **30.** 200 + 800

Estimation Round to the nearest ten.

31. 79 **32.** 15 **33.** 61 **34.** 183 **35.** 266

36. Estimate the sum of 48 + 23.

Ⓐ 80 Ⓑ 611 Ⓒ 60 Ⓓ 70

Adding 3-Digit Numbers

You Will Learn
how to add 3-digit numbers

Learn

Students at Somerset School think about the future. They wrote letters and put them in a time capsule. Students in kindergarten through second grade wrote 197 letters. Third through sixth grade students wrote 278 letters.

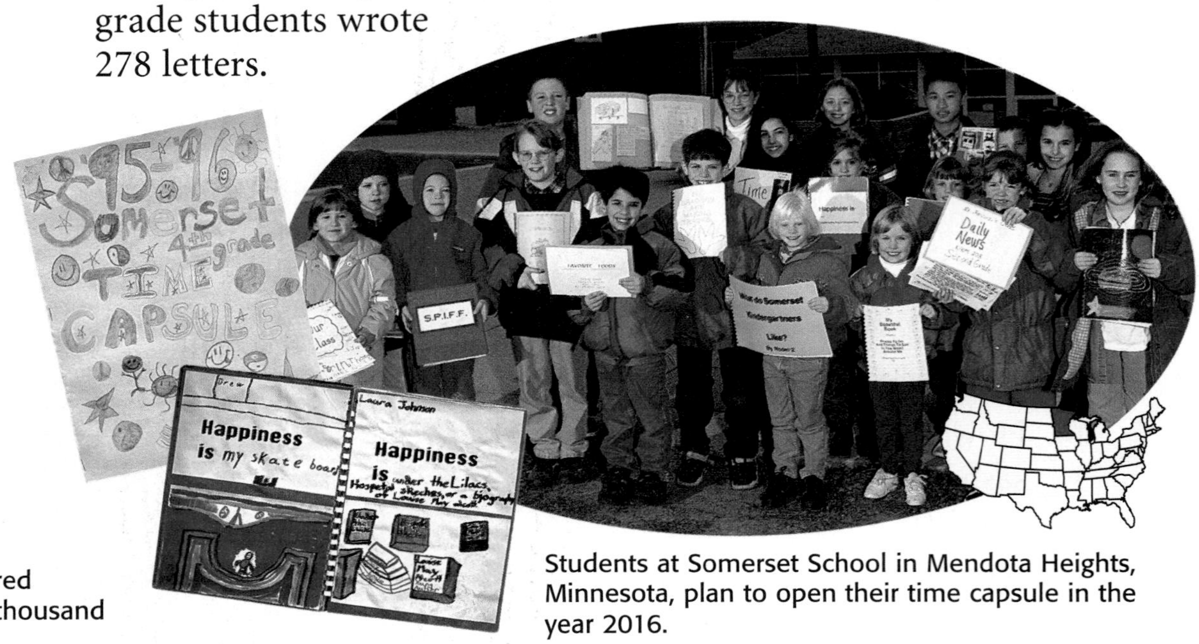

Students at Somerset School in Mendota Heights, Minnesota, plan to open their time capsule in the year 2016.

Remember
10 ones = 1 ten
10 tens = 1 hundred
10 hundreds = 1 thousand

Example 1

How many letters were put in the time capsule?

Since you want to find the total number of letters, you add.

Find 197 + 278.

Step 1	Step 2	Step 3
Add the ones. Regroup as needed.	Add the tens. Regroup as needed.	Add the hundreds.
$\begin{array}{r} \scriptstyle 1 \\ 197 \\ +\,278 \\ \hline 5 \end{array}$	$\begin{array}{r} \scriptstyle 1\,1 \\ 197 \\ +\,278 \\ \hline 75 \end{array}$	$\begin{array}{r} \scriptstyle 1\,1 \\ 197 \\ +\,278 \\ \hline 475 \end{array}$

197 + 278 = 475

Estimate to check. 200 + 300 = 500
Since 475 is close to 500, the answer is reasonable.

So, 475 letters were put in the time capsule.

Example 2

Find 718 + 675.

Step 1	Step 2	Step 3
Add the ones. Regroup as needed.	Add the tens. Regroup as needed.	Add the hundreds.
$\begin{array}{r} \scriptstyle 1 \\ 718 \\ +675 \\ \hline 3 \end{array}$	$\begin{array}{r} \scriptstyle 1 \\ 718 \\ +675 \\ \hline 93 \end{array}$	$\begin{array}{r} \scriptstyle 1 \\ 718 \\ +675 \\ \hline 1{,}393 \end{array}$

718 + 675 = 1,393

The students included letters, graphs, and pictures in their time capsule.

Talk About It

If you are adding 385 and 432, would you need to regroup ones for tens? Would you need to regroup tens for hundreds? Explain.

Check

Copy and complete.

1. $\begin{array}{r} \scriptstyle 1 \\ 415 \\ +\ \ 78 \\ \hline \square\square 3 \end{array}$
2. $\begin{array}{r} \scriptstyle 1 \\ \$227 \\ +\ \ \ 65 \\ \hline \$\square 9\square \end{array}$
3. $\begin{array}{r} \scriptstyle 1 \\ 346 \\ +861 \\ \hline \square,\square 0\square \end{array}$
4. $\begin{array}{r} \scriptstyle 1 \\ 525 \\ +591 \\ \hline 1{,}1\square\square \end{array}$
5. $\begin{array}{r} \scriptstyle 1 \\ 876 \\ +\ \ 31 \\ \hline \square 07 \end{array}$

Add. Estimate to check.

6. $\begin{array}{r} 434 \\ +129 \\ \hline \end{array}$
7. $\begin{array}{r} 971 \\ +453 \\ \hline \end{array}$
8. $\begin{array}{r} 208 \\ +\ \ 91 \\ \hline \end{array}$
9. $\begin{array}{r} 676 \\ +518 \\ \hline \end{array}$
10. $\begin{array}{r} \$565 \\ +\ \ 23 \\ \hline \end{array}$

11. $\begin{array}{r} 547 \\ +328 \\ \hline \end{array}$
12. $\begin{array}{r} 166 \\ +253 \\ \hline \end{array}$
13. $\begin{array}{r} 634 \\ +217 \\ \hline \end{array}$
14. $\begin{array}{r} 816 \\ +\ \ 44 \\ \hline \end{array}$
15. $\begin{array}{r} 368 \\ +416 \\ \hline \end{array}$

16. Find the sum of 149 and 370.

17. Find the sum of $634 and $182.

18. Reasoning Do you think the sum of 825 and 221 has 3 or 4 digits? Use estimation to help you decide. Explain.

19. Reasoning Do you need to regroup 10 tens for 1 hundred to find 348 + 271? Explain.

Practice

Skills and Reasoning

Copy and complete.

20. $\begin{array}{r} \scriptsize{1\ 1} \\ 1\ 7\ 4 \\ +\ 3\ 4\ 6 \\ \hline \square\ 2\ 0 \end{array}$ **21.** $\begin{array}{r} \scriptsize{1} \\ 5\ 2\ 1 \\ +\ \ \ 6\ 9 \\ \hline 5\ \square\ \square \end{array}$ **22.** $\begin{array}{r} \scriptsize{1} \\ \$2\ 7\ 3 \\ +\ \ \ 4\ 2 \\ \hline \$\ \square\ 1\ \square \end{array}$ **23.** $\begin{array}{r} \scriptsize{1} \\ 1\ 5\ 8 \\ +\ 4\ 9\ 1 \\ \hline \square\ \square\ \square \end{array}$ **24.** $\begin{array}{r} \scriptsize{1} \\ \$3\ 4\ 6 \\ +\ \ 8\ 1\ 5 \\ \hline \$\ \square,\square\ \square\ 1 \end{array}$

Add. Estimate to check.

25. $\begin{array}{r} 782 \\ +\ 276 \\ \hline \end{array}$ **26.** $\begin{array}{r} \$96 \\ +\ 79 \\ \hline \end{array}$ **27.** $\begin{array}{r} 345 \\ +\ \ 91 \\ \hline \end{array}$ **28.** $\begin{array}{r} \$851 \\ +\ 149 \\ \hline \end{array}$ **29.** $\begin{array}{r} 634 \\ +\ \ 58 \\ \hline \end{array}$

30. $\begin{array}{r} 248 \\ +\ 728 \\ \hline \end{array}$ **31.** $\begin{array}{r} 371 \\ +\ \ 87 \\ \hline \end{array}$ **32.** $\begin{array}{r} \$455 \\ +\ 693 \\ \hline \end{array}$ **33.** $\begin{array}{r} 89 \\ +\ 57 \\ \hline \end{array}$ **34.** $\begin{array}{r} \$168 \\ +\ 479 \\ \hline \end{array}$

35. 46 + 34 **36.** 273 + 167 **37.** 812 + 773 **38.** \$47 + \$53

39. Find the sum of 547 and 234. **40.** Find the sum of 625 and 97.

41. Write two addends with a sum of 352.

42. Estimate to decide which sum is greater than 1,000:
647 + 315 or 555 + 735.

Problem Solving and Applications

43. 156 elementary students wrote letters for a time capsule. Then 106 middle school students added their letters. How many letters were put in the capsule?

44. Literature In *The 500 Hats of Bartholomew Cubbins,* Bartholomew takes off 135 hats on his way to the castle. He takes off 364 more inside. How many hats has he taken off?

45. Time Look for a pattern in the table to decide if you think a president will be elected in the year 2006. Explain.

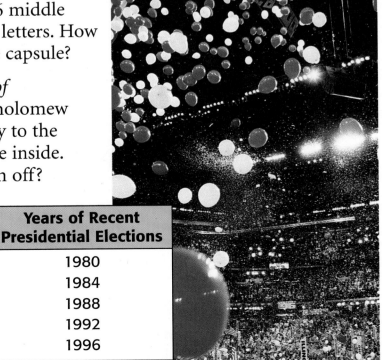

Years of Recent Presidential Elections
1980
1984
1988
1992
1996

Problem Solving and GEOGRAPHY

The fastest way to get iron from Duluth to Cleveland is by water. Many ships carry cargo over the Great Lakes. The Great Lakes make up one of the largest freshwater systems in the world.

46. A ship with a cargo of iron ore travels from Duluth to Cleveland. It then returns to Duluth. How far does it travel?

47. A ship loaded with grain travels from Chicago to Milwaukee and then to Buffalo. How far does it travel?

48. **Write Your Own Problem** Use the data in the table. Write a question that can be answered by using addition.

Distances by Water Between Cities	
Duluth to Cleveland	833 miles
Chicago to Milwaukee	85 miles
Milwaukee to Buffalo	828 miles
Detroit to Cleveland	106 miles

49. **Journal** Explain how adding 3-digit numbers is like adding 2-digit numbers. How is it different?

Mixed Review and Test Prep

Use the bar graph to answer **50–52.**

50. How long does a sloth sleep in one day?

51. How long does a cat sleep in one day?

52. Which two animals sleep the same number of hours in a day?

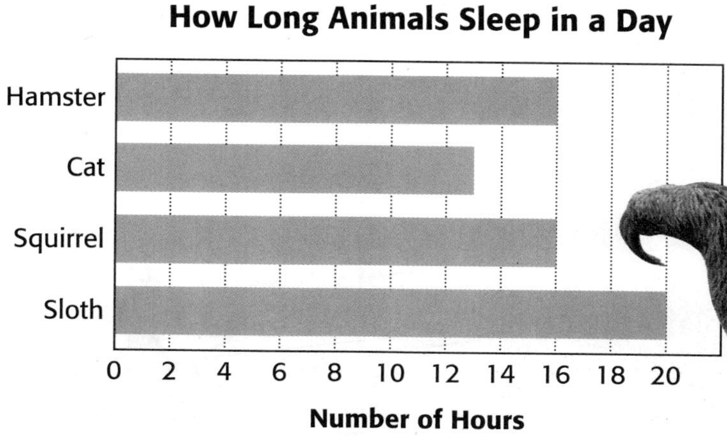

53. **Mental Math** What is the sum of 600 + 300?

Ⓐ 900 Ⓑ 3,000 Ⓒ 9,000 Ⓓ 90,000

STOP and Practice

Find each sum.

1. 126 + 270	**2.** 36 + 24	**3.** \$736 + 196	**4.** \$613 + 875	**5.** 169 + 43
6. 81 + 13	**7.** \$562 + 345	**8.** 45 + 40	**9.** 231 + 316	**10.** 75 + 55
11. 428 + 224	**12.** 63 + 79	**13.** \$614 + 98	**14.** 547 + 539	**15.** 602 + 138
16. 94 + 87	**17.** 382 + 244	**18.** 78 + 35	**19.** \$954 + 417	**20.** 89 + 35
21. 178 + 683	**22.** \$59 + 62	**23.** 22 + 51	**24.** 823 + 367	**25.** 751 + 64
26. 449 + 58	**27.** 833 + 179	**28.** 22 + 8	**29.** \$315 + 872	**30.** 470 + 188
31. \$96 + 6	**32.** 75 + 82	**33.** \$691 + 557	**34.** 257 + 431	**35.** 56 + 44

Error Search

36. Find each sum that is not correct. Write it correctly and explain the error.

a. 300 + 20 = 500	**b.** 566 + 188 = 754	**c.** 737 + 419 = 1,146	**d.** 489 + 241 = 630

Bird Watching!

Add. Match each letter to its answer in the blank below to solve the riddle. Some letters are not used.

What bird has two toes on each foot?

37. 95 + 36 [R]
38. 271 + 326 [V]
39. 269 + 583 [I]
40. 26 + 28 [T]
41. 388 + 694 [B]
42. 18 + 79 [C]
43. 73 + 50 [O]
44. 761 + 402 [A]
45. 318 + 497 [S]
46. 40 + 41 [N]
47. 405 + 157 [H]
48. 943 + 860 [K]
49. 519 + 720 [W]
50. 534 + 958 [E]
51. 458 + 326 [F]

___ ___   ___ ___ ___ ___ ___ ___ ___

1,163 81   123 815 54 131 852 97 562

Number Sense Estimation and Reasoning

Copy and complete. Write <, >, or =.

52. 345 + 298 ● 298 + 345
53. 276 + 402 ● 286 + 402
54. 521 + 236 ● 482 + 116
55. 478 + 343 ● 468 + 393
56. 940 + 825 ● 825 + 940
57. 377 + 641 ● 402 + 377
58. 525 + 443 ● 578 + 651
59. 934 + 728 ● 944 + 718

Adding 4-Digit Numbers: Choose a Calculation Method

You Will Learn
how to add 4-digit numbers

Learn

Elizabeth and Vivian are always on the lookout for birds' nests. Elizabeth has found 4,380 nests, and Vivian has found 6,743 nests. How many nests have they found all together?

Since you want to put groups together, you add.

Elizabeth's way

First I estimated.

4,000 + 7,000 = 11,000

Then I used a calculator.

4380 [+] 6743 [=] 11123

11,123 is close to 11,000.

So, they have found 11,123 birds' nests.

Elizabeth Brooks and Vivian Mills Pitzrick volunteer to help scientists keep track of birds' nests in New York state.

Math Tip
You can round to the nearest thousand the same way you round to the nearest hundred.

Talk About It

Why did Elizabeth estimate before she used the calculator?

Check

Add.

1. 8,134 + 1,726 **2.** \$6,623 + \$3,511 **3.** \$3,000 + \$4,600

4. **Reasoning** Estimate to decide if the sum of 2,801 + 2,099 is more or less than 6,000. Explain.

Practice

Skills and Reasoning

Choose a tool

Add.

5. 6,592 + 2,135

6. 5,200 + 3,300

7. 2,699 + 1,504

8. $1,863 + 7,100

9. 1,175 + 946

10. 7,301 + 898

11. $3,400 + 4,200

12. 4,402 + 3,174

13. 2,594 + 6,563

14. $9,156 + $567

15. 3,600 + 700

16. Find the sum of 837 and 4,619.

17. Find the sum of 4,400 and 3,000.

18. Estimate to decide if the sum of 8,537 + 1,965 is greater than or less than 10,000.

19. Which two numbers have a sum of 8,000?

3,500	4,500	2,500
5,000	4,000	1,500

Problem Solving and Applications

20. Who found the most birds' nests, Vivian or Elizabeth? Use the information on page 116 to solve. Explain how you know.

21. Time Both women spend between 4 and 8 hours a day searching for nests. If Elizabeth begins searching at 7:15 A.M., what time will it be 8 hours later?

22. Using Data How many American Robins were counted in St. Marks, Florida, and Folsom, California? Use the Data File on page 93 to solve.

23. Journal Choose a method to find 3,801 + 4,100. Explain.

Mixed Review and Test Prep

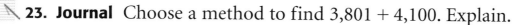

Find each sum.

24. 6 + 8 + 4

25. 3 + 5 + 9

26. 6 + 1 + 7

27. 4 + 8 + 2

Choose the correct sign.

28. 305 + 281 ● 550

Ⓐ >　Ⓑ <　Ⓒ =

29. 416 + 132 ● 648

Ⓐ >　Ⓑ <　Ⓒ =

Column Addition

You Will Learn
how to find the sum of more than 2 addends

Learn

All for one and one for all! The Tree Musketeers planted trees around the border of their town to help keep the air clean.

Trees Planted Each Year	
Year 1	29 trees
Year 2	82 trees
Year 3	44 trees

The Tree Musketeers was started by third graders in El Segundo, California.

Example

How many trees did they plant in these three years?

Since you want to find the total number of trees, you add.

Find 29 + 82 + 44.

Step 1

Line up ones and tens.

$$\begin{array}{r} 29 \\ 82 \\ +\,44 \\ \hline \end{array}$$

Step 2

Add the ones.
Regroup as needed.

$$\begin{array}{r} {}^{1} \\ 29 \\ 82 \\ +\,44 \\ \hline 5 \end{array}$$

Step 3

Add the tens.

$$\begin{array}{r} {}^{1} \\ \text{10 tens} < 29 \\ 82 \\ +\,44 \\ \hline 155 \end{array}$$

29 + 82 + 44 = 155

So, the Tree Musketeers planted 155 trees.

Math Tip
Look for digits that add to 10.

Talk About It

How can looking for digits that make 10 help you add?

Check

Add.

1. 31 + 49 + 65 **2.** 345 + 19 + 202 **3.** 464 + 319 + 66

4. Reasoning Is 10 + 20 + 5 the same as 30 + 5? Explain.

Practice

Skills and Reasoning

Add.

5. $\begin{array}{r}56\\94\\+\ 7\\\hline\end{array}$ **6.** $\begin{array}{r}307\\412\\+\ 231\\\hline\end{array}$ **7.** $\begin{array}{r}63\\176\\+\ 705\\\hline\end{array}$ **8.** $\begin{array}{r}880\\243\\+\ 29\\\hline\end{array}$ **9.** $\begin{array}{r}52\\84\\+\ 3\\\hline\end{array}$

10. $\begin{array}{r}592\\27\\+\ 721\\\hline\end{array}$ **11.** $\begin{array}{r}261\\762\\+\ 863\\\hline\end{array}$ **12.** $\begin{array}{r}677\\352\\+\ 8\\\hline\end{array}$ **13.** $\begin{array}{r}667\\75\\+\ 545\\\hline\end{array}$ **14.** $\begin{array}{r}701\\29\\+\ 880\\\hline\end{array}$

15. $\begin{array}{r}123\\756\\+\ 300\\\hline\end{array}$ **16.** $\begin{array}{r}76\\28\\+\ 51\\\hline\end{array}$ **17.** $\begin{array}{r}94\\845\\+\ 62\\\hline\end{array}$ **18.** $\begin{array}{r}324\\10\\+\ 855\\\hline\end{array}$ **19.** $\begin{array}{r}279\\33\\+\ 61\\\hline\end{array}$

20. 57 + 408 + 197 **21.** 9 + 345 + 41 **22.** 246 + 15 + 89

23. What is the sum of 321, 97, and 584?

24. Add 938, 753, and 864.

25. What is the greatest possible sum using three of these numbers?

83	214	398	809	621

26. To find 54 + 32 + 196, would you start by finding 1 + 5 + 3? Why or why not?

Problem Solving and Applications

27. Did the Tree Musketeers plant the greatest number of trees in the first, second, or third year? Use the table on page 118 to solve.

28. Patterns Use a calculator to skip count by 4s from 43. Record 10 sums. What pattern do you notice in the ones digits? 43 [+] 4 [=] [=] [=]...

Mixed Review and Test Prep

Algebra Readiness Solve.

29. 18 − □ = 9 **30.** □ − 5 = 9 **31.** □ + 8 = 15 **32.** 6 + □ = 14

33. Mental Math What is the sum of 50 + 80?

Ⓐ 1,300 Ⓑ 130 Ⓒ 13 Ⓓ not here

Problem Solving

Analyze Strategies: Guess and Check

You Will Learn
how to guess and check to solve problems

Learn

Rolanda needs to report the score of the last baseball game for her school newspaper, but she can't remember the score. She knows that 35 runs were scored by the Twins and the Tigers and that the scores were 13 runs apart. How many runs did each team score?

Work Together

▶ Understand

What do you know?

What do you need to find out?

▶ Plan

Decide how you will find out.

Since there are many ways to get a sum of 35, guess and check to find 2 numbers that are 13 apart.

▶ Solve

Take a guess and check it.

Keep guessing and checking until you find numbers that work.

Tigers	Twins	Sum	
15	28	43	Too high!
9	22	31	Too low!
10	23	33	Too low!
11	24	35	That's it!

Answer the problem.

The Tigers scored 11 runs, and the Twins scored 24 runs.

▶ Look Back

Check your answer.

Talk About It

Why is guess and check a good strategy to use for this problem?

Check

Problem Solving
Understand
Plan
Solve
Look Back

Guess and check to solve.

1. The Tigers beat the Panthers. The scores were 4 runs apart and there were 20 runs scored in the game. How many runs did each team score?

2. The Tigers lost to the Cubs by 9 runs. There were 19 runs scored in the game. How many runs did the Cubs score?

Problem Solving Practice

Use any strategy to solve.

3. The Tigers beat the Eagles by 5 runs. There were 27 runs scored in the game. How many runs did the Tigers score?

4. The sum of two numbers is 80. The numbers are 2 apart. What are they?

5. The sum of two numbers is 55. The numbers are 7 apart. What are they?

6. Jamie brought in 48 doughnuts for treats during the class play. Jose brought 24 more doughnuts. How many doughnuts did the two students bring?

Problem Solving Strategies

- Use Objects/Act It Out
- Draw a Picture
- Look for a Pattern
- Guess and Check
- Use Logical Reasoning
- Make an Organized List
- Make a Table
- Solve a Simpler Problem
- Work Backward

Choose a Tool

Using Data Use the prices in the table to solve **7–10.**

Item	Cost
Pennant	$5
Baseball	$9
Cap	$13
Sunglasses	$15

7. Rolanda bought two souvenirs at the baseball game. She spent $24. What did Rolanda buy?

8. How much would it cost to buy a cap and sunglasses?

9. Does a baseball cost more or less than a cap?

10. How much more does a cap cost than a baseball?

11. The Sports Club is trying to sell 950 tickets to the game. So far, they have sold 620 tickets. How many more tickets do they need to sell?

SECTION B

Review and Practice

(Lesson 5) Find each sum. You may use place-value blocks to help.

1. $67 + 25$ **2.** $58 + 18$ **3.** $34 + 93$ **4.** $28 + 44$

(Lessons 6 and 7) Add. Estimate to check.

5. $24 + 51$ **6.** $291 + 54$ **7.** $455 + 276$ **8.** $67 + 39$ **9.** $584 + 77$

10. $605 + 105$ **11.** $87 + 3$ **12.** $499 + 264$ **13.** $30 + 32$ **14.** $159 + 79$

15. $324 + 139$ **16.** $72 + 18$ **17.** $65 + 47$ **18.** $614 + 33$

19. $627 + 177$ **20.** $525 + 398$ **21.** $46 + 58$ **22.** $38 + 6$

23. Reasoning Do you need to regroup 10 tens for 1 hundred when you find 164 + 282?

(Lesson 8) Add.

24. $2{,}834 + 615$ **25.** $1{,}821 + 2{,}145$ **26.** $5{,}300 + 3{,}100$ **27.** $4{,}029 + 956$

28. Geography The highest point in Atlanta, Georgia, is 1,050 feet above sea level. The highest point in Denver, Colorado, is 4,444 feet higher. How high is the highest point in Denver?

(Lesson 9) Add. **Choose a tool**

29. $23 + 14 + 36$ **30.** $442 + 25 + 67$ **31.** $537 + 121 + 244$

(Lesson 10) Guess and check to solve.

32. The sum of 2 numbers is 57. The numbers are 5 apart. What are they?

33. Journal Explain how you would find 319 + 188.

Skills Checklist

In this section, you have:

- ☑ Explored Adding with Regrouping
- ☑ Added 2-, 3-, and 4-Digit Numbers
- ☑ Learned About Column Addition
- ☑ Solved Problems by Guessing and Checking

REVIEW AND PRACTICE

CHAPTER 3

SECTION

C Extending Addition

Becky uses colored pencils and paints to draw pictures. How can Becky be sure she has enough money to buy what she needs?

Skills Checklist

In this section, you will:

- ❒ Add Using Mental Math
- ❒ Count Coins
- ❒ Write Money Amounts in Dollars and Cents
- ❒ Explore Making Change
- ❒ Add Money
- ❒ Use Front-End Estimation
- ❒ Solve Problems Needing Exact Answers or Estimates

Extending Addition

Review adding 2- and 3-digit numbers. Find each sum.

1. 53 + 61 **2.** 82 + 29

3. 347 + 918 **4.** \$45 + \$88

5. \$63 + \$56 **6.** \$124 + \$672

Chapter 3
Lesson
11

Mental Math

You Will Learn
different ways to find sums mentally

Learn

Kristian and his brother Erik sell gift wrap for a school fund-raiser. Suppose Kristian knows he's raised $49 so far. Then Erik sells another roll for $7. Here's how they use mental math to find out how much money they raised.

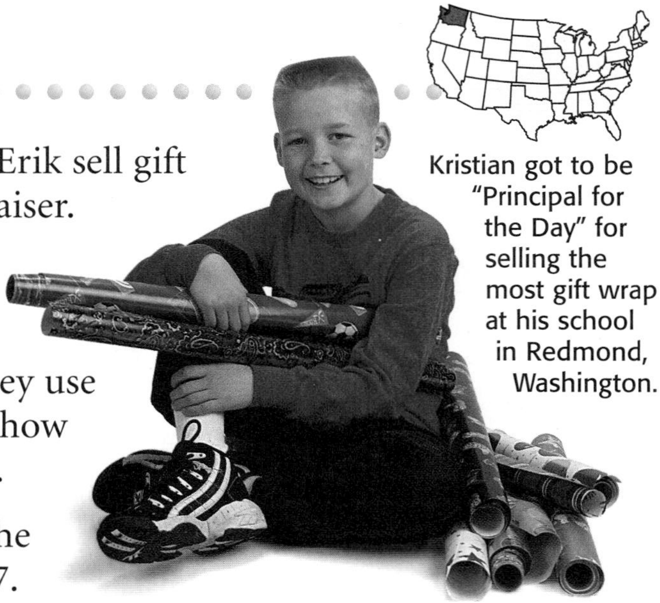

Kristian got to be "Principal for the Day" for selling the most gift wrap at his school in Redmond, Washington.

Since they want to find the total, they add $49 and $7.

Math Tip
Think of numbers that are simpler to add.

Kristian thinks:

I can add $1 to $49 to get $50.

$50 + $7 = $57

Now I must subtract $1.

$57 − $1 = $56

$49 + $7 = $56

So, we raised $56.

Erik thinks:

$7 is the same as $1 + $6.

First I'll add $1.

$49 + $1 = $50

Then I'll add $6.

$50 + $6 = $56

$49 + $7 = $56.

So, we raised $56.

Talk About It

Explain how you would find 28 + 9 mentally. Then tell the sum.

Check

Use mental math to find each sum.

1. 78 + 9 **2.** 99 + 99 **3.** 62 + 8 **4.** 60 + 43

5. **Reasoning** How does knowing 5 + 5 = 10 help you to find 25 + 35 mentally?

Practice

Skills and Reasoning

Use mental math to find each sum.

6. $26 + 8$ **7.** $70 + 65$ **8.** $52 + 9$ **9.** $2 + 37$

10. $25 + 35$ **11.** $49 + 26$ **12.** $31 + 68$ **13.** $56 + 51$

14. $19 + 4$ **15.** $99 + 2$ **16.** $19 + 20$ **17.** $43 + 82$

18. Find the sum of 164 and 9.

19. Add 375 and 15.

20. How does knowing $6 + 4 = 10$ help you to find $86 + 14$ mentally?

21. How can finding digits that add to 10 help you to find $58 + 32$?

Problem Solving and Applications

22. Patterns Use mental math to find each sum. Look for patterns in the addends and sums.

a. $38 + 9$ **b.** $38 + 19$ **c.** $38 + 29$ **d.** $38 + 39$

23. Money A roll of gift wrap costs $7. Suppose Kristian had $14 in orders and sold two more rolls. How much money would he have raised?

24. As principal, Kristian gave an extra recess to students. There were 74 students in his grade and 98 students in the other grades. How many students were given an extra recess?

Mixed Review and Test Prep

Continue each pattern.

25. 20, 25, 30, 35, ■, ■, ■, ■

26. 50, 75, 100, 125, ■, ■, ■, ■

27. 40, 50, 60, 70, ■, ■, ■, ■

28. 85, 90, 95, 100, ■, ■, ■, ■

Find each sum.

29. $25 + 5$ **30.** $49 + 16$ **31.** $35 + 8$ **32.** $57 + 24$ **33.** $86 + 8$

34. Find the sum of 42, 18, and 5.

Ⓐ 63 Ⓑ 110 Ⓒ 55 Ⓓ not here

Counting Coins

You Will Learn
how to find the value of groups of coins

Materials
coins

Vocabulary
Types of coins
half dollar
quarter
dime
nickel
penny

cent
unit of money; 100 cents = one dollar

Learn

Here are five types of coins.

half dollar	quarter	dime	nickel	penny
50¢	25¢	10¢	5¢	1¢
fifty cents	twenty-five cents	ten cents	five cents	one cent

You can count on to find the total value of coins.

50¢, 75¢, 85¢, 90¢, 95¢, 96¢, 97¢, 98¢

The total value written in **cents** is 98¢.

Talk About It

If you count the coins in a different way, will you get the same total? Why or why not?

Did You Know?
People in England used coins called half-pennies until 1984. Two half-pennies were worth the same as a penny.

Check

Write the total value in cents.

1. 

2. 

3. Reasoning How would you make 39¢ with the fewest coins?

Practice

Skills and Reasoning

Write the total value in cents.

4. 

5. 

6. 

7. 

8. Find three ways to make 47 cents.

9. Use the fewest coins to make 31 cents.

Problem Solving and Applications

10. Which coins would you use to buy a small bag of popcorn?

11. Which coins would you use to buy a large bag of popcorn?

12. **Algebra Readiness** Joanne has 67 cents. She has these coins in a pocket. She has 4 other coins. What are they?

13. **Using Data** How many half-pennies would be worth the same as a nickel? Use the fact from *Did You Know?* on page 126.

Mixed Review and Test Prep

Add.

14. 21 + 33
15. 588 + 231
16. \$79 + \$11
17. 363 + 429
18. 88 + 66
19. 125 + 310
20. \$771 + \$435
21. 64 + 15
22. 39 + 52

Choose the correct sign.

23. 122 + 49 ● 50 + 123

Ⓐ > Ⓑ < Ⓒ =

24. 251 + 39 ● 40 + 250

Ⓐ > Ⓑ < Ⓒ =

Chapter 3
Lesson
13

Using Dollars and Cents

You Will Learn
how to write money amounts in dollars and cents

Vocabulary
dollar
a bill or coin worth 100 cents

Learn

Becky spends her free time drawing and painting. She draws cartoons of people's faces. Becky saves money to buy the colored pencils and paints she uses.

Becky lives in Rego Park, New York.

Count	Write	Say
 $1.00, $1.25, $1.35	$1.35 (dollar sign, decimal point)	one dollar and thirty-five cents
 $5.00, $6.00, $6.10, $6.15, $6.16	$6.16	six dollars and sixteen cents

Did You Know?
This coin is worth one dollar. It shows Susan B. Anthony who fought for women's rights in the late 1800s.

You can write amounts less than a **dollar** in dollars and cents. Another way to write 5¢ is $0.05.

Talk About It

1. Name at least two ways to make $5.40 with bills and coins.
2. How would you write 15¢ in dollars and cents?

Check

Write the total value in dollars and cents.

1. 

2. 

3. **Reasoning** Give at least 2 ways to show $5.36.

Practice

Skills and Reasoning

Write the total value in dollars and cents.

4. 

5. 

6. Give at least 2 ways to show $1.45.

7. Keith said, "I lost a coin! I had $2.35. Now I only have 1 one-dollar bill, 5 quarters, and 1 nickel." What coin did Keith lose?

Problem Solving and Applications

8. **Using Data** Suppose someone gives you $2.43 using no bills. What is the least number of coins you could get? Use the fact from *Did You Know?* on page 128 to help.

9. Tom needs change for a dollar. A friend gives him 3 quarters for 1 one-dollar bill. Is this a fair trade? Explain.

Mixed Review and Test Prep

Mental Math Find each sum using mental math.

10. 99 + 10 **11.** 53 + 9 **12.** 28 + 6 **13.** 24 + 37

14. 41 + 23 **15.** 55 + 15 **16.** 36 + 80 **17.** 7 + 49

18. Which two numbers have a sum of about 300?

Ⓐ 113 + 125 Ⓑ 85 + 210 Ⓒ 122 + 78 Ⓓ 282 + 194

Chapter 3
Lesson
14

Exploring Making Change

Problem Solving Connection
- Use Objects/ Act It Out
- Guess and Check

Materials
bills and coins

Explore

A bake sale is a tasty way to raise money for your school. Suppose your class is having a bake sale. You'll need to make change for your customers.

Remember
25¢ and $0.25 name the same amount.

Work Together

1. Use coins to make change for a customer who buys an oatmeal cookie with $1.00.

a. Start at $0.25. Use only nickels. Count on until you reach $1.00. How many nickels did you use? How much change did you give?

b. Make change a different way using any coins. What coins did you use? How much change did you give?

2. Use coins and bills to make change for a customer who buys carrot cake with $5.00.

a. Give two ways to make change. What coins and bills could you use?

b. How much change did you give?

Talk About It

3. How might it help to count on pennies first when making change for $1.38?

Connect

Suppose a customer buys a piece of pumpkin pie with $5.00. How much change should you give?

Count on from the price $1.53 to the amount given. Start with coins that help you count mentally.

$1.54 $1.55 $1.65 $1.75 $2.00 $3.00 $4.00 $5.00

2 pennies, 2 dimes, 1 quarter, and 3 dollar bills is $3.47. So, you should give $3.47 in change.

Practice

Use the prices on page 130 for 1–4. List which coins and bills you would use to make change. Then write the change in dollars and cents.

1. Juan buys an apricot bar with $5.00.
2. Mike buys a brownie with $1.00.
3. At the end of the day, pumpkin pie costs only $1.27. Marisa buys a piece with $2.00.
4. **What If** A customer buys an oatmeal cookie with $5.00. How much change should you give?
5. **Reasoning** Maya buys $3.61 worth of baked goods. She pays with $5.00. List the fewest coins and bills needed to make change.
6. Calvin's purchases total $1.65. He pays with $2.00. Write three ways you could make change. Which way uses the fewest coins?
7. **Journal** Explain how a clerk might make change if you buy a brownie with $5.00.

THE Greatest Sum GAME

Players
2 or more

Materials
digit cards 0–9

0 1 2 3 4
5 6 7 8 9

Object
The object of the game is to make an addition problem with the greatest sum.

How to Play

1. Each player draws an addition grid like the one below. Shuffle the cards and lay them face down.

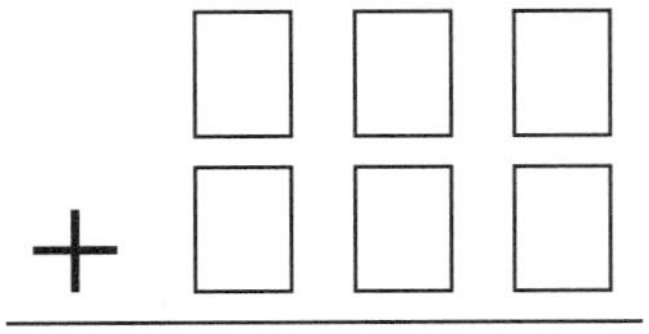

2. One player turns over a card. Each player writes that number in any box on his or her addition grid.

Ken's Grid **Kim's Grid**

3. Continue turning over cards until you have placed numbers in all of the boxes on the grid.

4. Add. The player with the greatest sum wins.

5. Play five or more games. Look for winning strategies.

Talk About It

1. What strategies did you use to get the greatest sum?
2. What card did you most like to turn over? Why?

More Ways to Play

- Play again. Use a grid like this.

$$\begin{array}{rcc} & \square & \square \\ + & \square & \square \\ \hline \end{array}$$

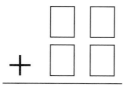

- Play the Least Sum Game. Use either grid. This time the winner is the player with the least sum.
- Play the game using this grid. Try to get a sum that is close to 1,000.

$$\begin{array}{rccc} & \square & \square & \square \\ + & \square & \square & \square \\ \hline \end{array}$$

Reasoning

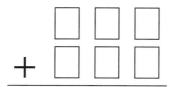

1. Suppose a 9 was turned over, and you could put it in any box on this grid. What strategy would you use if you were playing the Greatest Sum Game?

$$\begin{array}{rccc} & \square & 5 & \square \\ + & \square & \square & \square \\ \hline \end{array}$$

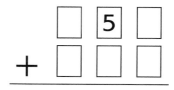

2. Suppose you turn over a 2, and your grid looks like this. What strategy would you use if you were playing the Least Sum Game?

$$\begin{array}{rccc} & \square & 6 & \square \\ + & 3 & \square & 9 \\ \hline \end{array}$$

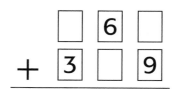

3. Suppose you were playing a game called Closest to 1,000. What number do you hope is picked next? Explain.

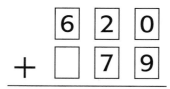

$$\begin{array}{rccc} & 6 & 2 & 0 \\ + & \square & 7 & 9 \\ \hline \end{array}$$

Chapter 3
Lesson
15

Adding Money

You Will Learn
how to add money amounts

Learn

What is your favorite toy? Suppose you want to buy glow-in-the-dark goo and a stunt jet.

Example

How much will both items cost?

Since you want to find the total cost, you add $5.99 and $2.49.

Step 1

Line up the decimal points.

$$\begin{array}{r} \$5.99 \\ +\,2.49 \\ \hline \end{array}$$

Step 2

Add.

$$\begin{array}{r} {\scriptstyle 1\ 1} \\ \$5.99 \\ +\,2.49 \\ \hline 8\ 48 \end{array}$$

Step 3

Write the dollar sign and the decimal point.

$$\begin{array}{r} {\scriptstyle 1\ 1} \\ \$5.99 \\ +\,2.49 \\ \hline \$8.48 \end{array}$$

$5.99 + $2.49 = $8.48

Estimate to the nearest dollar to check.

$$\begin{array}{rcr} \$5.99 & \longrightarrow & \$6.00 \\ +\,2.49 & \longrightarrow & +\,2.00 \\ \hline & & \$8.00 \end{array}$$

Since $8.48 is close to $8.00, the answer is reasonable.

So, both items will cost $8.48.

Math Tip
Make sure to line up the decimal points when adding money amounts.

Talk About It

Explain how adding money is like adding whole numbers.

Check

1. $5.19 + $3.65 **2.** $4.21 + $0.87 **3.** $7.62 + $2.63

4. Reasoning Estimate to decide if $6.00 is enough to buy a giant bottle of bubbles and a stunt jet. Explain.

Practice

Skills and Reasoning

Add. Estimate to check.

5. $6.71 + 2.85 **6.** $5.46 + 3.47 **7.** $9.09 + 3.99 **8.** $4.35 + 0.97 **9.** $6.25 + 5.49

10. $8.95 + 7.49 **11.** $2.57 + 5.84 **12.** $0.14 + 8.32 **13.** $6.86 + 1.78 **14.** $1.99 + 0.67

15. $5.39 + $2.29 **16.** $1.49 + $7.37 **17.** $4.98 + $2.41

18. Find the sum of $3.28 and $4.56.

19. Add $8.46 and $6.51.

20. Will $10.00 be enough to buy a jump rope and a stunt jet? Explain.

21. Which two toys will cost about $9.00?

Problem Solving and Applications

22. Which amount is greater?

a. 3 dollars, 5 dimes, 6 pennies or $3.47

b. 6 dollars, 2 dimes, 8 pennies or $6.82

c. 5 dollars, 6 dimes, 3 pennies or $5.23

23. Amy bought a musical jump rope and glow-in-the-dark goo. How much did both items cost?

24. **Write Your Own Problem** Write an addition problem about two toys you would buy. Then solve.

25. **Using Data** Suppose you are going on a scavenger hunt. You need a bucket and a notebook. How much will both items cost? Use the Data File on page 93 to solve.

26. **Collecting Data** Use a newspaper or a catalog. Find two items that cost less than $10.00 each. How much would they cost all together?

Mixed Review and Test Prep

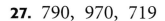

Order from least to greatest.

27. 790, 970, 719 **28.** 515, 151, 551 **29.** 220, 202, 222

30. **Patterns** Choose the next number in the pattern.

50, 45, 40, 35, ▢

Ⓐ 40 Ⓑ 25 Ⓒ 30 Ⓓ 45

Chapter 3
Lesson
16

Front-End Estimation

You Will Learn
how to estimate using front-end estimation

Vocabulary
front-end estimation
using the digits in the greatest place to estimate

Learn

Yuki, her mother, and her grandfather want to visit the Toy Train Museum. Her grandfather is a member of the museum. Will $5.00 be enough to pay for their tickets?

Toy Train Museum Ticket Prices	
Member	$2.75
Nonmember	$3.00
Student	$1.50

Since you don't need to know the exact cost, you can estimate. Use **front-end estimation**.

Example 1

Use front-end estimation to find out if $5.00 is enough.

Add the front digits.

$**1**.50	Yuki's ticket
3.00	Mother's ticket
+ **2**.75	Grandfather's ticket

$**1** + $**3** + $**2** = $6

$6 > $5

So, $5.00 is not enough money.

Example 2

Use front-end estimation to estimate sums of whole numbers.

$$\begin{array}{rcr} 431 & \longrightarrow & 400 \\ 102 & \longrightarrow & 100 \\ +\,356 & \longrightarrow & +\,300 \\ & & \hline 800 \end{array}$$

The sum of 431 + 102 + 356 is about 800.

Math Tip
You can use mental math to add front-end digits.

Talk About It

Do you think the exact sum of money needed for Yuki's museum tickets will be greater than $6? Explain.

Check

Use front-end estimation to estimate each sum.

1. $4.38 + $1.10 **2.** 116 + 204 + 353 **3.** 47 + 13 + 13

4. Reasoning Use front-end estimation to decide if the sum of 265, 128, and 496 is less than 700. Explain.

Practice

Skills and Reasoning

Use front-end estimation to estimate each sum.

5. $\begin{array}{r} \$5.34 \\ +\ 2.40 \\ \hline \end{array}$ **6.** $\begin{array}{r} 242 \\ 467 \\ +\ 309 \\ \hline \end{array}$ **7.** $\begin{array}{r} 617 \\ 155 \\ +\ 828 \\ \hline \end{array}$ **8.** $\begin{array}{r} \$7.10 \\ 3.51 \\ +\ 2.46 \\ \hline \end{array}$ **9.** $\begin{array}{r} 547 \\ 450 \\ +\ 189 \\ \hline \end{array}$

10. $\begin{array}{r} 812 \\ +\ 936 \\ \hline \end{array}$ **11.** $\begin{array}{r} \$9.75 \\ 3.01 \\ +\ 5.22 \\ \hline \end{array}$ **12.** $\begin{array}{r} 493 \\ 621 \\ +\ 330 \\ \hline \end{array}$ **13.** $\begin{array}{r} 249 \\ 154 \\ +\ 712 \\ \hline \end{array}$ **14.** $\begin{array}{r} \$7.58 \\ 1.14 \\ +\ 6.05 \\ \hline \end{array}$

15. 237 + 271 + 586

16. 588 + 576 + 275

17. Use front-end estimation to estimate the sum of 372, 954, and 129.

18. Use front-end estimation to estimate the sum of $6.43, $2.91, and $5.67.

19. Is the sum of $3.56, $8.61, and $4.29 greater than $14.00? Explain.

20. If you buy 2 items that cost $3.55 each, will $5.00 be enough to buy both items? Explain.

Problem Solving and Applications

21. Tickets to the Cincinnati Fire Museum cost $2.50 for adults and $1.50 for students. Is $4.00 enough to buy tickets for 2 adults and 1 student? Explain.

22. **Science** Seventeen-year locusts show up once every 17 years. These locusts came to Connecticut in 1996. In what year will they show up in Connecticut again?

23. **Journal** How would you estimate $3.57 + $2.89 + $5.15 using front-end estimation?

Mixed Review and Test Prep

Add.

24. 23 + 56 **25.** 372 + 318 **26.** 28 + 57 **27.** $42 + $63

28. $128 + $494 **29.** 55 + 41 **30.** 805 + 154 **31.** 278 + 432

32. **Algebra Readiness** Choose the rule for the table.

Ⓐ Add 7 Ⓑ Add 4 Ⓒ Add 3

In	1	2	3	4
Out	4	5	6	7

Problem Solving

Analyze Word Problems: Exact Answer or Estimate?

You Will Learn
how to decide whether you need an estimate or an exact answer to solve a problem

Learn

Blaine is going hunting for minerals. He stops at a shop to get supplies. With $10 in his pocket, can he buy gloves and a guidebook?

Work Together

Supplies	
Hammer	$15.80
Guidebook	$2.95
Gloves	$5.89
Compass	$5.49

▶ Understand

What do you know?

What do you need to find out?

▶ Plan

Decide if you need an exact answer or if an estimate is enough.

You can estimate the sum of $5.89 + $2.95 to find out if $10 is enough.

▶ Solve

Estimate. Think of the closest dollar.

$5.89 is close to $6.00
$2.95 is close to $3.00
$6.00 + $3.00 = $9.00

Compare the estimate to $10.

$9 < $10

Answer the problem.

$10 is enough money to buy both items.

▶ Look Back

Does your answer make sense?

Talk About It

Explain why an estimate is enough to solve this problem.

Check

Problem Solving
Understand
Plan
Solve
Look Back

Write if you need an exact answer or an estimate. Then solve.

1. Blaine has a $20 bill. Does he have enough to buy a hammer and a compass? Explain.

2. How much would it cost to buy one of each item on the supply list?

Problem Solving Practice

Problem Solving Strategies

- Use Objects/Act It Out
- Draw a Picture
- Look for a Pattern
- Guess and Check
- Use Logical Reasoning
- Make an Organized List
- Make a Table
- Solve a Simpler Problem
- Work Backward

Choose a Tool

3. **Critical Thinking** Think of a way to change the problem on page 138 so that it requires an exact answer. Write the new problem and have a classmate solve it.

4. Blaine wants to know if $8.00 is enough to buy a guidebook and a compass. Does he need to find the exact total? Explain.

5. **Collecting Data** Look for money-off coupons in a newspaper. List two coupons that add up to about $1.00 in savings.

6. **Science** Feldspar and mica are minerals. Blaine's collection has 18 pieces of feldspar and mica. How many of each type could there be? Tell what strategy you used to solve.

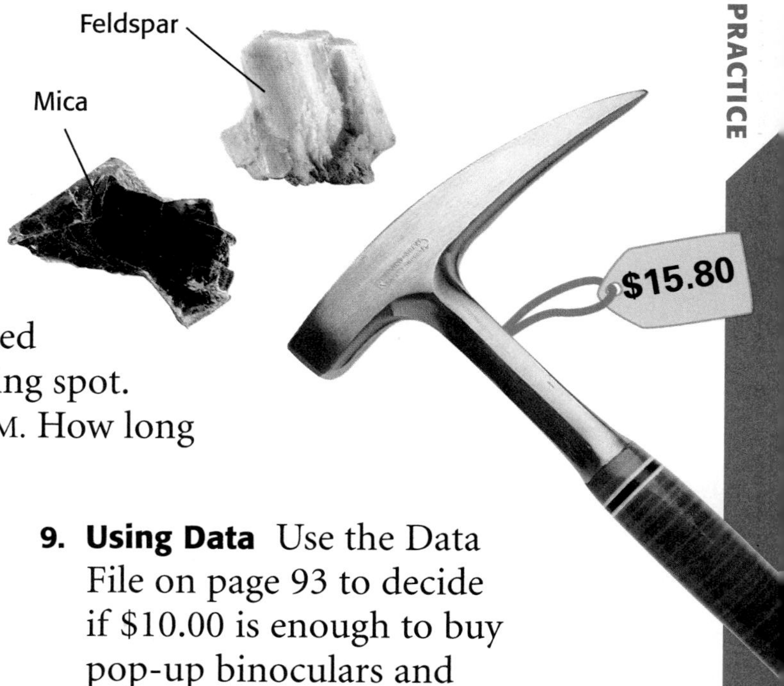

7. **Time** Blaine went to the visitor center at 9:00 A.M. He walked along a trail to his favorite collecting spot. When he got there it was 10:15 A.M. How long did Blaine walk?

8. Three groups signed up for the mineral tour. The groups have 12, 22, and 18 people in them. No more than 55 people can go on the tour. Will Blaine be able to go on the tour? Explain.

9. **Using Data** Use the Data File on page 93 to decide if $10.00 is enough to buy pop-up binoculars and a flashlight. Explain.

SECTION C
Review and Practice

(Lesson 11) Mental Math Use mental math to find each sum.

1. 45 + 9 **2.** 39 + 23 **3.** 67 + 8 **4.** 81 + 26

(Lesson 12) Write the total value in cents.

5.

(Lesson 13) Write the total value in dollars and cents.

6.

(Lesson 14) List which coins and bills you would use to make change. Then write the change in dollars and cents.

7. Odetta buys a granola bar that costs \$0.45. She pays with \$1.00.

8. Ty buys an apple that costs \$0.55. He pays with \$1.00.

(Lesson 15) Add. Estimate to check.

9. \$8.34 + \$1.18 **10.** \$4.29 + \$4.53 **11.** \$3.75 + \$5.35

12. Joe bought a slice of pizza for \$1.25 and a bottle of juice for \$0.85. How much did he pay in all?

(Lesson 16) Use front-end estimation to estimate each sum.

13. 352 + 184 + 917 **14.** 52 + 39 + 76

(Lesson 17) Write if you need an exact answer or an estimate. Then solve.

15. Using Data Will \$6.00 be enough to buy a canteen and a shovel? Use the Data File on page 93 to solve.

16. Journal Explain how mental math can help you find the sum of 65 + 35.

Skills Checklist

In this section, you have:

- ☑ Added Using Mental Math
- ☑ Counted Coins
- ☑ Written Money Amounts in Dollars and Cents
- ☑ Explored Making Change
- ☑ Added Money
- ☑ Used Front-End Estimation
- ☑ Solved Problems Needing Exact Answers or Estimates

YOUR CHOICE

Choose at least one. Use what you have learned in this chapter.

1 Pocket Holes

Have you ever found a hole in your pocket? Linda thinks she's lost a coin. She knows she had 71¢. Here's what she has now.

Has Linda lost a coin? If so, tell what coin she dropped.

2 Invent a Coin!

Did you know that coins in the United States can't be changed for 25 years? Design a new coin. Give your coin a name, tell how many cents it's worth, and draw a picture of it.

3 Digit Detective

Copy and complete. Find each missing digit.

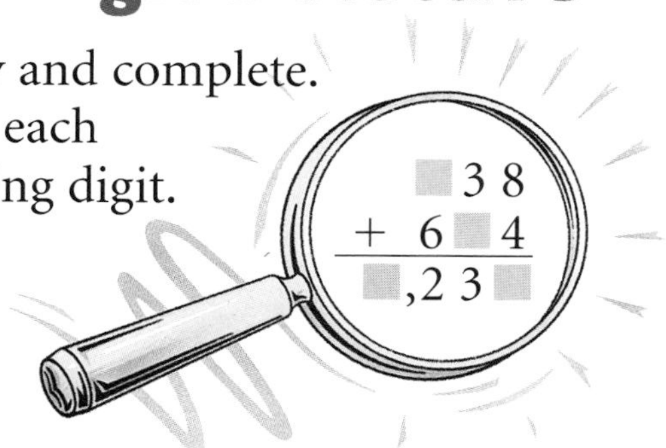

4 A Long Way from Home

At Home Plan a trip with your family. Decide where you will go and how many miles away from home it will be. Use local maps or get information from the library to help.

5 Guess My Number!

I am a 2-digit number. If you add three of me together, the sum is between 115 and 119. What am I?

REVIEW AND PRACTICE

CHAPTER 3
Review/Test

Vocabulary Match each word with its definition.

1. regroup	**a.** a number that is added
2. sum	**b.** the number obtained when adding numbers
3. addend	**c.** to name a number in a different way

(Lesson 1) Mental Math Find each sum using mental math.

4. $10 + 60$ **5.** $\$500 + \$400$ **6.** $200 + 300$ **7.** $700 + 800$

(Lesson 4) Estimate each sum.

8. $68 + 32$ **9.** $577 + 495$ **10.** $419 + 382$ **11.** $40 + 76$

(Lessons 5–9, 11, 15) Add. Estimate to check.

12. $\begin{array}{r} 32 \\ +\ 46 \\ \hline \end{array}$ **13.** $\begin{array}{r} \$4.56 \\ +\ 7.92 \\ \hline \end{array}$ **14.** $\begin{array}{r} 245 \\ +\ 327 \\ \hline \end{array}$ **15.** $\begin{array}{r} 412 \\ +\ 994 \\ \hline \end{array}$ **16.** $\begin{array}{r} 78 \\ +\ 19 \\ \hline \end{array}$

17. $4{,}135 + 2{,}348$ **18.** $49 + 7$ **19.** Add 138, 351, and 76.

(Lesson 10) Guess and check to solve.

20. The Tigers beat the Cubs by 2 runs. There were 18 runs scored in the game. How many runs did the Tigers score?

(Lessons 12, 13) Write the total value in dollars and cents.

21.

(Lesson 14) Write the change in dollars and cents.

22. Judy bought a book for $3.75. She paid with $5.00.

(Lesson 16) Use front-end estimation to estimate each sum.

23. $358 + 227$ **24.** $723 + 431$

(Lesson 17) Write if you need an exact answer or an estimate. Then solve.

25. Three buses took students on a field trip. One bus carried 45 students, another bus carried 38 students, and the third bus carried 37 students. How many students went on the trip?

CHAPTER 3

Performance Assessment

The County Museum's Science Theater seats 250 people. Many school groups want to watch the movie there, but it is only shown 3 times a day. Help the museum staff plan the visits so that everyone can watch. Here are the groups that are coming today.

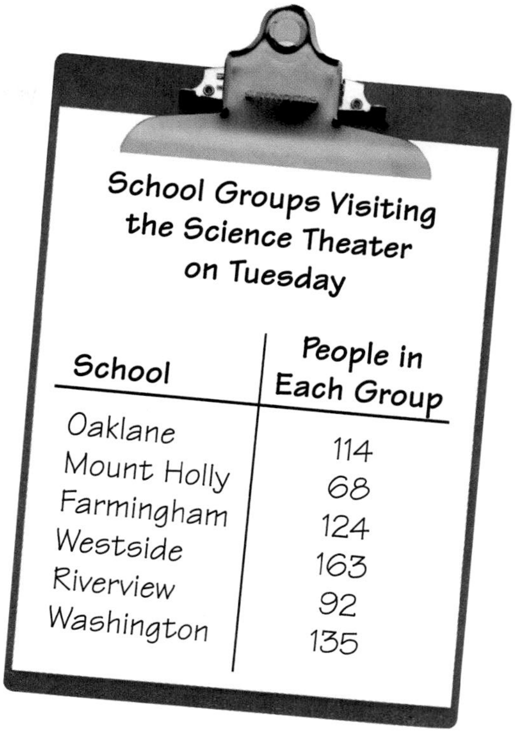

School Groups Visiting the Science Theater on Tuesday

School	People in Each Group
Oaklane	114
Mount Holly	68
Farmingham	124
Westside	163
Riverview	92
Washington	135

1. **Decision Making** Think about which groups can fit in the theater at the same time. Remember, school groups must stay together.

2. **Recording Data** Copy and complete the table to show one way that each group can watch the movie.

Movie Time	Schools	Total Number of People
10:00 A.M.		
12:00 P.M.		
2:00 P.M.		

3. **Explain Your Thinking** How did you decide which groups to place together? How do you know your plan will work?

4. **Critical Thinking** Is it possible for three of these school groups to watch the movie at the same time? Explain.

5. **Decision Making** What would you like to eat for a snack? Would you like more than one item? How much will your snack cost?

Snack Bar	
Pizza	$2.75
Lemonade	$0.60
Frozen yogurt	$1.45

Math Magazine

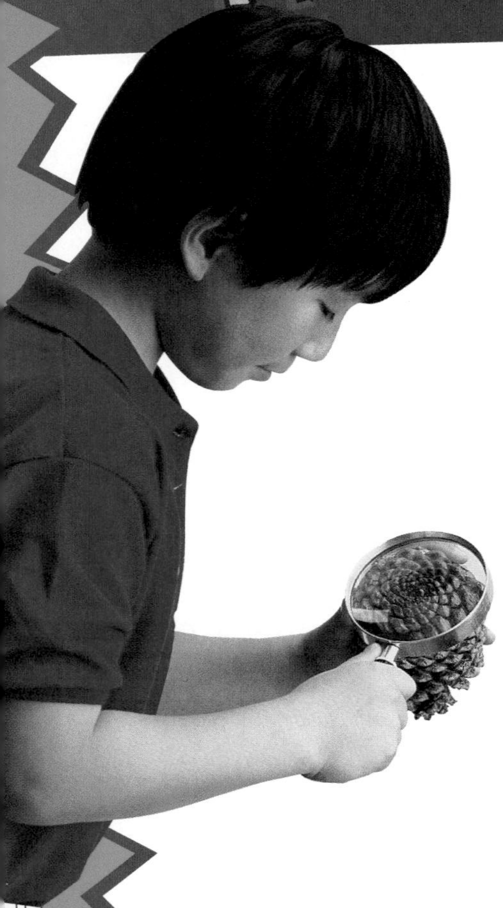

Pine Cone Patterns **Have you ever counted the spiral rows on a pine cone? If so, you've probably found one of the Fibonacci numbers.**

Fibonacci was born in 1175. He was the first person to notice a special number pattern. No one is sure why, but the numbers in the pattern are found in many shapes in nature.

Find the Pattern

Look at these numbers. **0, 1, 1, 2, 3, 5, 8**

0 + 1 = 1
1 + 1 = 2
1 + 2 = 3
2 + 3 = 5
3 + 5 = 8

What pattern do you notice?

Take a closer look.

To get the next Fibonacci number, find the sum of the last two numbers.

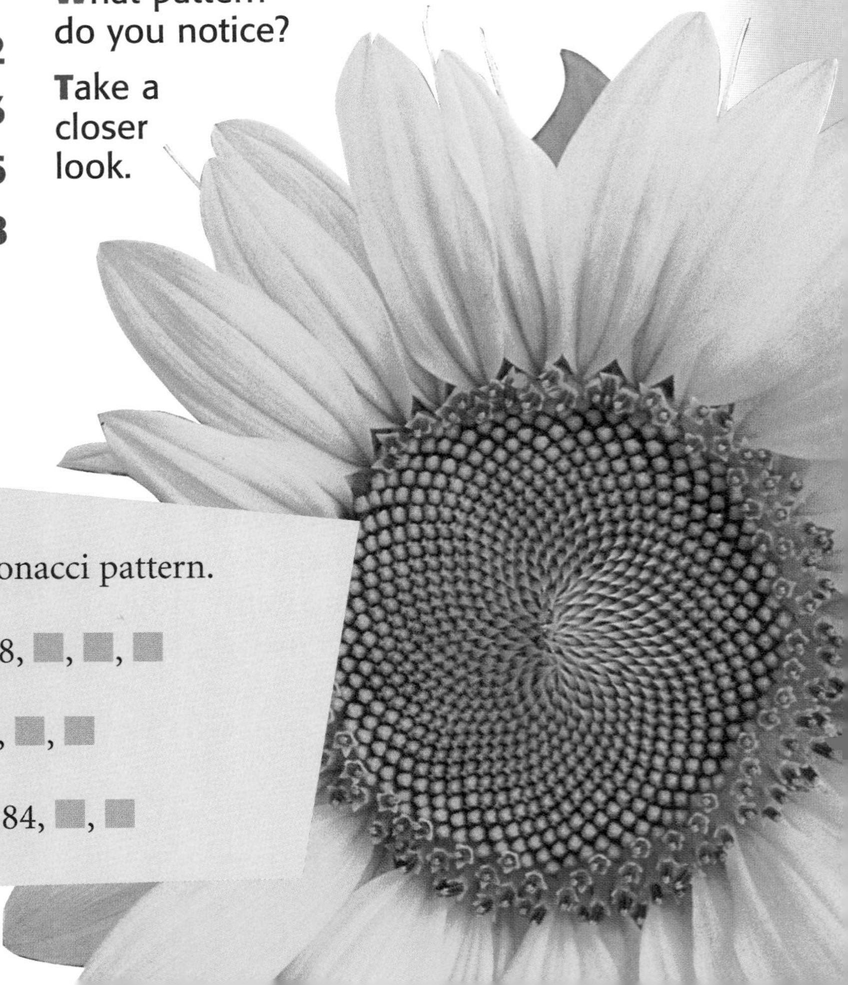

Try These!

Continue each Fibonacci pattern.

1. 0, 1, 1, 2, 3, 5, 8, ■, ■, ■

2. 55, 89, 144, ■, ■, ■

3. 987, 1,597, 2,584, ■, ■

CHAPTERS 1–3

Cumulative Review

Test Prep Strategy: Read Carefully

Watch for tricky problems.

Ted has 2 birds, 3 cats, and 1 dog. How many cats and dogs does he have?

Ⓐ 5 Ⓑ 3 Ⓒ 4 Ⓓ 6

Be sure you answer the right question. The answer is Ⓒ because the question asks only for the number of *cats* and *dogs.*

Write the letter of the correct answer. Read carefully or use any strategy to help.

Test Prep Strategies

- Read Carefully
- Follow Directions
- Make Smart Choices
- Eliminate Choices
- Work Backward from an Answer

1. Gina has 1 one-dollar bill, 2 quarters, 3 dimes, and 1 nickel. How much does she have in quarters and dimes?

   Ⓐ \$1.85 Ⓑ \$0.80 Ⓒ \$0.90 Ⓓ \$0.30

2. The clock shows the time when Luis put some muffins in the oven. They will be done in 25 minutes. What time will it be when the muffins are ready?

   Ⓐ 1:30 Ⓑ 1:25

   Ⓒ 1:55 Ⓓ 1:05

Use the graph to answer **3** and **4.**

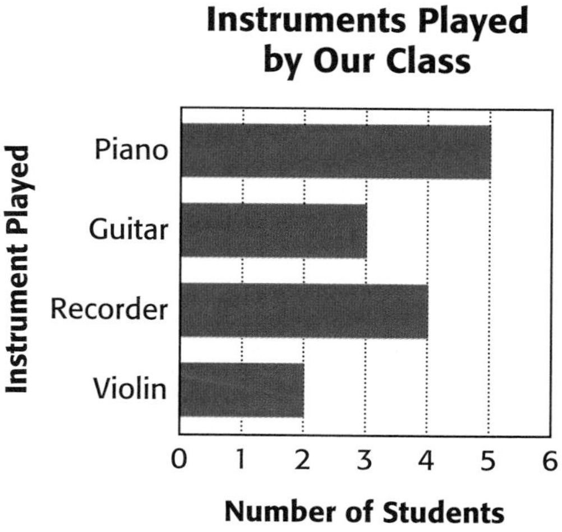

3. How many students in this class play an instrument that is not the piano?

   Ⓐ 5 Ⓑ 9

   Ⓒ 14 Ⓓ not here

4. How many violin and guitar players are there?

   Ⓐ 2 Ⓑ 3

   Ⓒ 5 Ⓓ 7

5. Which of these is not correct?

   Ⓐ $6{,}384 < 6{,}349$ Ⓑ $7{,}700 > 7{,}089$

   Ⓒ $4{,}004 < 4{,}040$ Ⓓ $5{,}812 > 5{,}528$

DATA FILE

Chapter 4

Subtracting Whole Numbers and Money

Fun Places to Visit

SECTION A

Developing Subtraction Number Sense

149

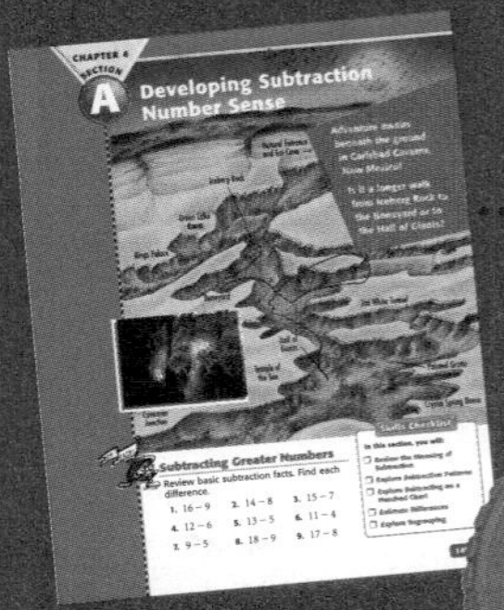

Carlsbad Caverns, New Mexico
Page 149

You can be in over your head when you visit Carlsbad Caverns in New Mexico! Which room has the highest ceiling?

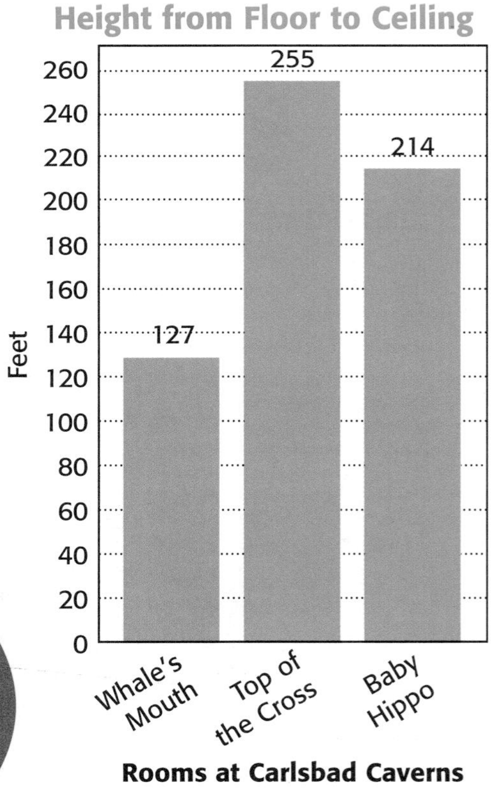

SECTION B

Subtracting Greater Numbers and Money

161

You'll want to roll with surprise after seeing how high these roller coaster rides can reach! Which two rides have the same height?

Roller Coaster Heights

Name of Ride	Location	Height
Texas Giant	Texas	143 feet
Rattler	Texas	179 feet
Gemini	Ohio	125 feet
Mean Streak	Ohio	161 feet
Kumba	Florida	143 feet
Cosmoclock 21	Japan	344 feet

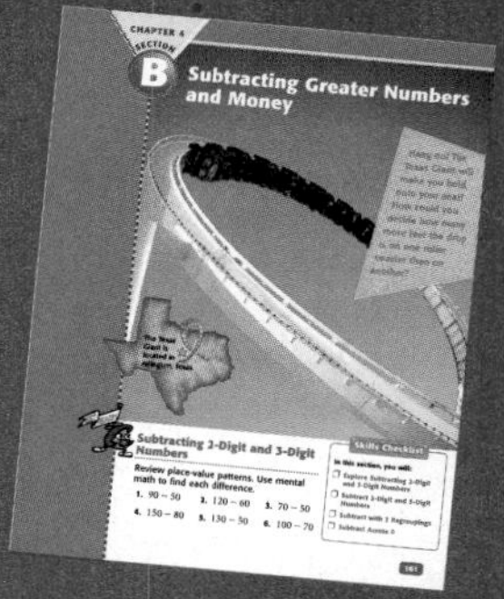

The Texas Giant, Arlington, Texas
Page 161

Surfing the World Wide Web!
Do you know of a great place to visit? Check out **www.mathsurf.com/3/ch4** to let other students know about your favorite spots!

SECTION C

Extending Subtraction

179

Don't blow your top! Instead, take a look at when and where these volcanoes erupted! Name a volcano that has erupted more than once.

Volcano Eruptions

Year	Volcano	Country
79	Mt. Vesuvius	Italy
260	Mt. Ilopango	El Salvador
1631	Mt. Vesuvius	Italy
1792	Mt. Unzen	Japan
1963	Mt. Agung	Indonesia
1980	Mt. St. Helens	United States
1991	Mt. Unzen	Japan
1992	Mt. Pinatubo	Philippines

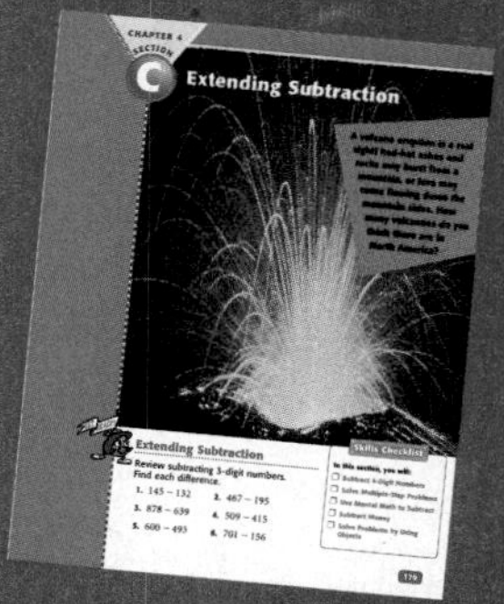

Volcano eruption
Page 179

TEAM PROJECT How Many?

Materials

popcorn, beans, paper clips, or other small objects; jar, plastic bag, or other clear container

Estimate how many objects are in a container. Make a table like this for your game.

Secret Number ______

Group	Guess	How Close?
1		
2		
3		

Actual Number of Objects ______

Make a Plan

- Which kind of object will your class put in the container?

Carry It Out

1. Each group collects some objects. Count the number of objects. This is your group's secret number! Now put all the objects in the container.
2. Once the class has filled the container, each group should estimate the total number of objects. Record each estimate.
3. To find the actual number of objects in the container, add each group's secret number.
4. Now see which group came closest!

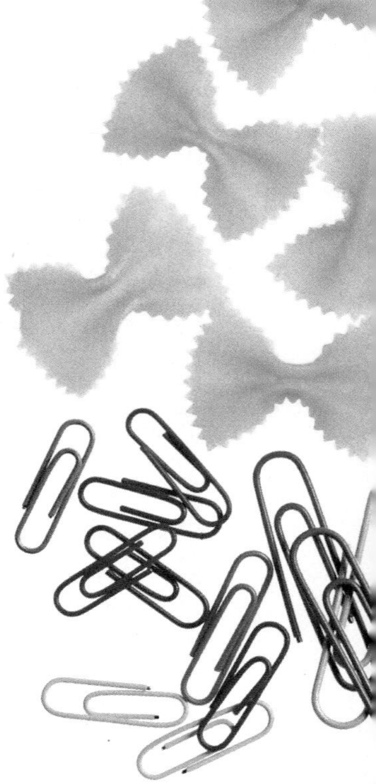

Talk About It

- How did you find the difference between the estimates and the actual number of objects?

Present the Project

- Which group's estimate was closest?

CHAPTER 4

SECTION A

Developing Subtraction Number Sense

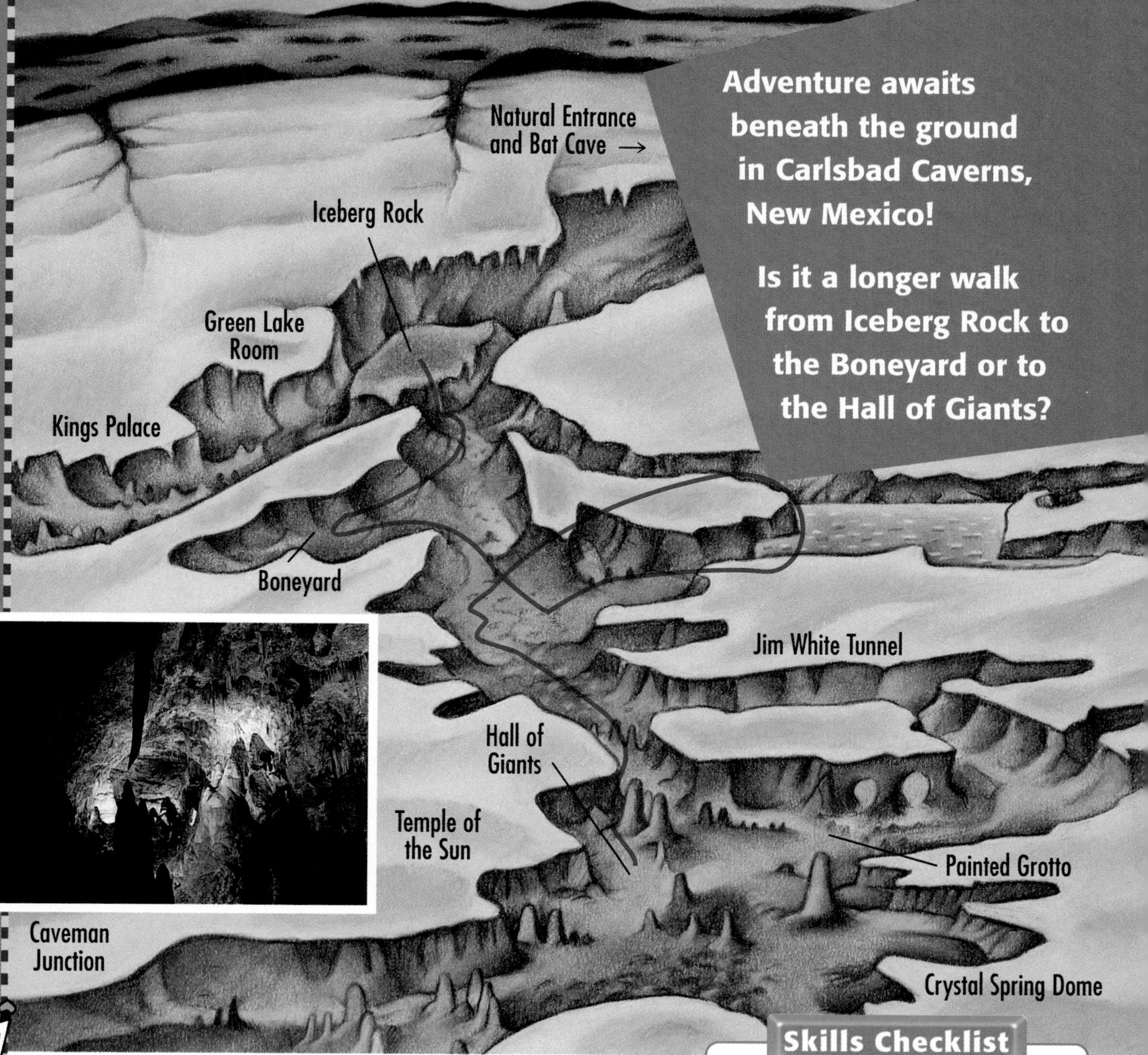

Adventure awaits beneath the ground in Carlsbad Caverns, New Mexico!

Is it a longer walk from Iceberg Rock to the Boneyard or to the Hall of Giants?

Subtracting Greater Numbers

Review basic subtraction facts. Find each difference.

1. $16 - 9$ **2.** $14 - 8$ **3.** $15 - 7$

4. $12 - 6$ **5.** $13 - 5$ **6.** $11 - 4$

7. $9 - 5$ **8.** $18 - 9$ **9.** $17 - 8$

Skills Checklist

In this section, you will:

- ❐ Review the Meaning of Subtraction
- ❐ Explore Subtraction Patterns
- ❐ Explore Subtracting on a Hundred Chart
- ❐ Estimate Differences
- ❐ Explore Regrouping

Chapter 4
Lesson
1

Reviewing the Meaning of Subtraction

You Will Learn
when you need to subtract

Remember
Fact families can help you solve subtraction problems.

$4 + 6 = 10$

$6 + 4 = 10$

$10 - 4 = 6$

$10 - 6 = 4$

Learn

You can use subtraction for three different kinds of actions. Each action can be shown with a number sentence.

Problem	Action	Number Sentence
Five sea otters are sleeping on their backs. Two swim away. How many otters are left?	Take away	$5 - 2 = 3$
There are four adult sea otters and one young otter. How many more adult otters are there?	Compare	$4 - 1 = 3$
There are two otters playing. More otters come to play. Now there are six sea otters. How many otters joined the game?	Find the missing part	$6 - 2 = 4$

Talk About It

Suppose seven otters are hunting, and three otters swim away. What number sentence could you write for this?

Check

Write a number sentence for each. Then solve.

1. Oscar's kickball team has 7 runs. The other team has 5 runs. How many more runs does Oscar's team have?

2. Eva has six crackers. She eats two. How many crackers are there now?

3. Dana collected ten shells and pebbles on the beach. She has six shells. How many pebbles does she have?

4. **Reasoning** Miguel's boat can carry 3 people. Miguel and Ali are in the boat. How many more people can the boat carry?

Practice

Skills and Reasoning

Write a number sentence for each. Then solve.

5. Four campers fit in one canoe. There are two campers in the canoe. How many more can fit?

6. Eight birds are eating from a bird feeder. Three fly away. How many are there now?

Problem Solving and Applications

Choose an Operation Add or subtract.

7. Anita has seven balloons. Three of them pop. How many are left?

8. Chris has 5 balloons. Dennis has 8. How many balloons do they have together?

9. Ray has 12 balloons. He blows up 9 balloons. How many are not blown up?

10. **Write Your Own Problem** Make up two subtraction stories. Use pictures if you want to.

Mixed Review and Test Prep

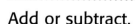

Add or subtract.

11. 50 + 70 **12.** 200 + 600 **13.** 80 + 80 **14.** 30 + 40

15. 17 − 8 **16.** 7 − 6 **17.** 18 − 9 **18.** 16 − 8

19. Which has a sum greater than 5,000?

Ⓐ 2,154 + 2,154 Ⓑ 2,514 + 2,514 Ⓒ 2,000 + 2,000

Exploring Subtraction Patterns

Problem Solving Connection

- Look for a Pattern
- Use Objects/ Act It Out

Materials

calculator

Vocabulary

difference
the number you find when you subtract one number from another

Problem Solving Hint

Find 500 − 100 by using patterns and solving a simpler problem.

Explore

The **difference** is the number you find when you subtract a number from another. You can use basic facts and place-value patterns to find the difference of greater numbers.

Work Together

1. Use a calculator to find each difference. Look for patterns.

a. 8 − 4 = ■	**b.** 13 − 5 = ■	**c.** 17 − 8 = ■
80 − 40 = ■	130 − 50 = ■	170 − 80 = ■
800 − 400 = ■	1,300 − 500 = ■	1,700 − 800 = ■

2. Use patterns to find each difference. Check with a calculator.

a. 5 − 1 = ■	**b.** 11 − 4 = ■	**c.** 16 − 8 = ■
50 − 10 = ■	110 − 40 = ■	160 − 80 = ■
500 − 100 = ■	1,100 − 400 = ■	1,600 − 800 = ■
d. 9 − 8 = ■	**e.** \$10 − \$6 = ■	**f.** 12 − 7 = ■
90 − 80 = ■	\$100 − \$60 = ■	120 − 70 = ■
900 − 800 = ■	\$1,000 − \$600 = ■	1,200 − 700 = ■

Talk About It

3. What patterns did you find?

4. How is 500 − 300 like 5 − 3?

5. What basic fact can you use to find \$80 − \$40? Explain.

Connect

Place-value blocks and patterns can help you subtract.

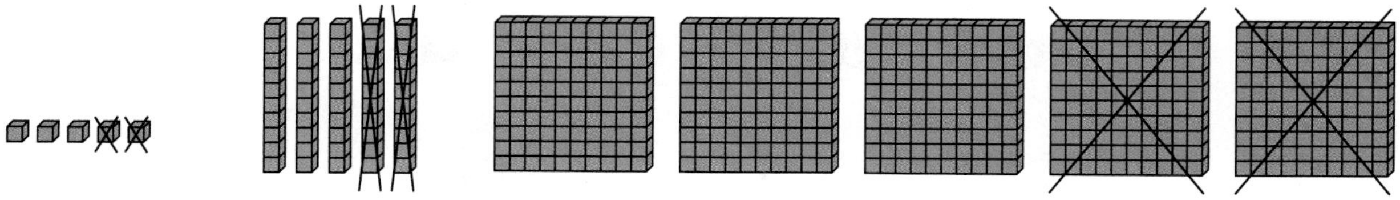

$5 - 2 = 3$ $50 - 20 = 30$ $500 - 200 = 300$

You can also use mental math to subtract.

Find $70 - 40$. **Think:** $7 - 4 = 3$ So, $70 - 40 = 30$

Find $700 - 400$. **Think:** $7 - 4 = 3$ So, $700 - 400 = 300$

Practice

Copy and complete.

1. $7 - 1 =$ ■
   $70 -$ ■ $= 60$
   $700 - 100 =$ ■
2. $15 -$ ■ $= 9$
   $150 - 60 =$ ■
   $1{,}500 - 600 =$ ■
3. \$11 − \$8 = ■
   \$110 − \$80 = ■
   \$1,100 − \$800 = ■

Mental Math Find each difference using mental math.

4. $40 - 30$
5. $600 - 300$
6. \$80 − \$10
7. $1{,}400 - 500$
8. \$700 − \$500
9. $80 - 70$
10. \$1,500 − \$700
11. $90 - 60$
12. $1{,}300 - 900$
13. **Time** Alvaro and Adriana drive to Orlando, Florida. It takes them 90 minutes to get there and 50 minutes to drive back. How long do they spend driving?
14. **Sports** In 1995, Albert Belle hit 50 home runs. Dante Bichette hit 40 home runs. How many more home runs did Albert Belle hit that year?
15. **Reasoning** What basic fact could you use to find $1{,}600 - 900$? Solve.
16. **Money** Simone wants a pair of skates that costs \$90. She has already saved \$70. How much more does she need?
17. **Algebra Readiness** Continue the pattern. Then write the rule.

In	30	40	50	60	70	80
Out	10	20	30			

18. **Journal** Explain how you could find $700 - 500$ mentally.

Exploring Subtracting on a Hundred Chart

Problem Solving Connection
- Look for a Pattern
- Use Objects/ Act It Out

Materials
hundred chart

Explore

You can use a hundred chart to help you subtract.

53 − 20 = ■

Put your finger on 53.

Move back 2 tens, or 20.

The answer is 33.

Work Together

Math Tip
Think about counting by tens.

1. Use a hundred chart to find each difference.

a. 76 − 10 = ■	**b.** 56 − 5 = ■	**c.** 73 − 21 = ■
d. 61 − 30 = ■	**e.** 47 − 10 = ■	**f.** 39 − 7 = ■
g. 38 − 23 = ■	**h.** 71 − 51 = ■	**i.** 52 − 28 = ■
j. 73 − 39 = ■	**k.** 40 − 8 = ■	**l.** 100 − 46 = ■

Talk About It

2. If you move back by rows, what pattern do you see? If you move back by spaces, what pattern do you see?
3. Choose a number greater than 50. What number is 4 less than your number? 14 less than your number? 24 less than your number? Explain.
4. Explain two ways to find 73 − 39 on a hundred chart.

Connect

You can think about subtracting in different ways.

Find 47 − 24.

1 Reggie's Way

I used mental math.

47 minus 20 is 27.

27 minus 4 is 23.

So, 47 − 24 is 23.

2

1	2	3	4	5	6	7	8	9	10
11	12	13	14	15	16	17	18	19	20
21	22	23	24	25	26	27	28	29	30
31	32	33	34	35	36	37	38	39	40
41	42	43	44	45	46	47	48	49	50
51	52	53	54	55	56	57	58	59	60
61	62	63	64	65	66	67	68	69	70
71	72	73	74	75	76	77	78	79	80
81	82	83	84	85	86	87	88	89	90
91	92	93	94	95	96	97	98	99	100

Julia's Way

Start at 47. Move back two rows, or 20, to 27.

Then count back 4 more to 23.

So, 47 − 24 is 23.

Practice

Find each difference. You may use a hundred chart to help.

1. 32 − 20 **2.** 58 − 13 **3.** 96 − 3 **4.** \$39 − \$11

5. 65 − 17 **6.** \$72 − \$11 **7.** 25 − 14 **8.** 100 − 51

Mental Math Use mental math to find each difference.

9. 50 − 30 **10.** \$60 − \$40 **11.** 48 − 20 **12.** 83 − 30

13. 100 − 50 **14.** 70 − 50 **15.** 81 − 51 **16.** \$67 − \$31

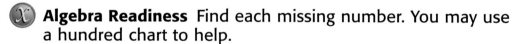

Algebra Readiness Find each missing number. You may use a hundred chart to help.

17. 34 − ▒ = 14 **18.** 58 − ▒ = 38 **19.** 39 − ▒ = 29 **20.** 98 − ▒ = 68

21. Chelsea has 25 points. She needs 45 to win the game. How many more points does she need?

22. **Reasoning** On a hundred chart, Mark starts with his finger on 56. He moves back 4 rows and back 3 spaces. On what number does he land? What number did he subtract?

23. **Music** Susanna is learning to play piano on an electronic keyboard. Her keyboard has 61 keys. A full-size piano has 88 keys. How many fewer keys does Susanna's keyboard have?

24. **Money** Craig wants to buy 2 erasers. Each eraser costs 20¢. How much money will he need to buy the erasers?

25. **Journal** What are two different ways to find the difference of 56 and 25?

Estimating Differences

You Will Learn
how to estimate differences using rounding

Learn

In Carlsbad Caverns, you can walk deep beneath the ground through twisting caves.

The trail from Rock of Ages to Painted Grotto is 425 feet. About how far have you walked when you reach a sign: "143 feet to Painted Grotto"?

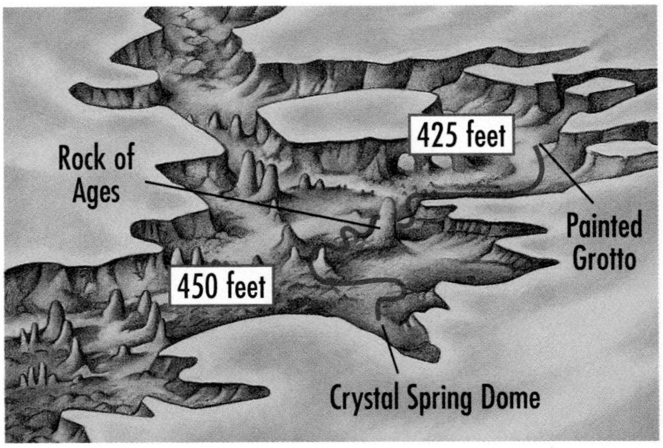

You can estimate.

Round to the nearest hundred.

425 feet	⟶	400 feet
− 143 feet	⟶	− 100 feet
		300 feet

You have walked about 300 feet.

Remember
When you round to the nearest hundred, find the closest hundred.

143 is close to 100.

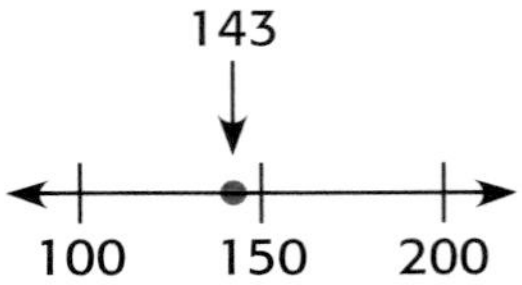

Other Examples

Estimate each difference.

A. Round to the nearest ten.

72	⟶	70
− 28	⟶	− 30
		40

B. Round to the nearest dollar.

$6.15	⟶	$6.00
− 4.95	⟶	− 5.00
		$1.00

Talk About It

How is rounding to the nearest dollar like rounding to the nearest hundred?

Check

Estimate each difference.

1. 578 − 196 **2.** $7.87 − $2.93 **3.** 94 − 15

4. Reasoning The estimated difference of two numbers is 200. One number is 534. What could the other number be?

Practice

Skills and Reasoning

Estimate each difference.

5. 722 − 302 **6.** 271 − 219 **7.** 657 − 439 **8.** 335 − 229

9. 69 − 28 **10.** 85 − 79 **11.** 52 − 37 **12.** 289 − 122

13. 48 − 11 **14.** \$8.75 − \$4.99 **15.** 733 − 318 **16.** \$9.02 − \$5.77

17. Suppose a trip to your aunt's house takes 57 minutes. If you have driven for 19 minutes, do you only have about 10 more minutes to drive? Explain.

18. The estimated difference of two amounts is \$5.00. Give two exact amounts that would make the estimate reasonable.

Problem Solving and Applications

19. Using Data Use the map on page 156 to answer. Suppose you are walking from Crystal Spring Dome to Rock of Ages. About how far have you walked when you reach a sign: "192 feet to Rock of Ages"?

20. Measurement The Bat Cave is 200 feet below ground. The King's Palace is 829 feet below ground. About how many feet lower is the King's Palace than the Bat Cave?

21. Time A tour of the Caverns takes 90 minutes. If you've been on the tour for 43 minutes, about how much longer will it take?

Using Data Use the Data File on page 146 to estimate the difference in the heights of the ceilings of these places.

22. Whale's Mouth and Top of the Cross

23. Whale's Mouth and Baby Hippo

Mixed Review and Test Prep

Find each sum or difference.

24. 89 + 152 + 12 **25.** 17 − 9 **26.** 57 + 39 + 142 **27.** 12 − 5

28. Money Marcus bought a pen for \$0.79 and a notebook for \$1.29. How much did he spend?

Ⓐ \$1.98 Ⓑ \$20.08 Ⓒ \$2.08 Ⓓ \$1.89

Chapter 4
Lesson
5

Exploring Regrouping

Problem Solving Connection
- Use Objects/ Act It Out
- Look for a Pattern

Materials
place-value blocks

Explore

When you subtract, you sometimes need to regroup 1 hundred for 10 tens or 1 ten for 10 ones.

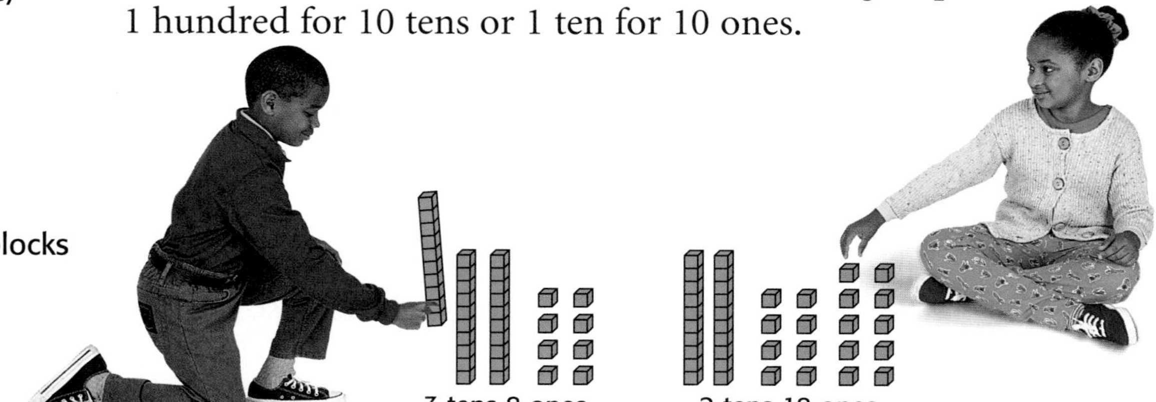

3 tens 8 ones = 2 tens 18 ones

Work Together

1. Use place-value blocks. Regroup 1 ten for 10 ones. Write the number of tens and ones.

a. 4 tens 2 ones = ■ tens ■ ones

b. 7 tens 6 ones = ■ tens ■ ones

c. 5 tens 0 ones = ■ tens ■ ones

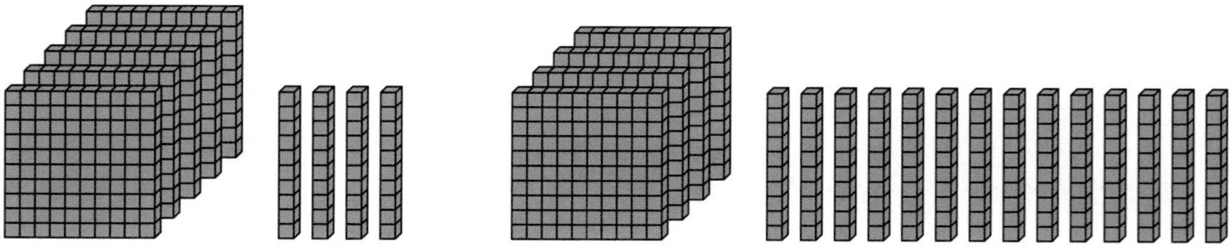

5 hundreds 4 tens = 4 hundreds 14 tens

2. Use place-value blocks. Regroup 1 hundred for 10 tens. Write the number of hundreds and tens.

a. 2 hundreds 3 tens 5 ones = ■ hundred ■ tens 5 ones

b. 4 hundreds 0 tens 2 ones = ■ hundreds ■ tens 2 ones

c. 7 hundreds 1 ten 8 ones = ■ hundreds ■ tens 8 ones

Talk About It

Is fifteen tens the same as one hundred fifty? Explain.

Connect

Here's one way to record how you regroup in subtraction.

Start With	Regroup
52 	is the same as $\overset{4}{\cancel{5}}\ \overset{12}{\cancel{2}}$ One fewer ten, 10 more ones 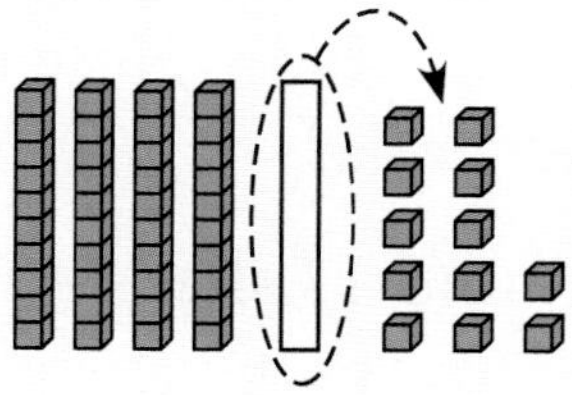
213 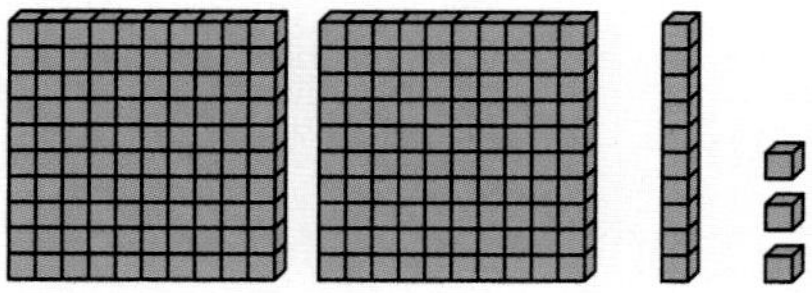	is the same as $\overset{1}{\cancel{2}}\ \overset{11}{\cancel{1}}\ 3$ One fewer hundred, 10 more tens 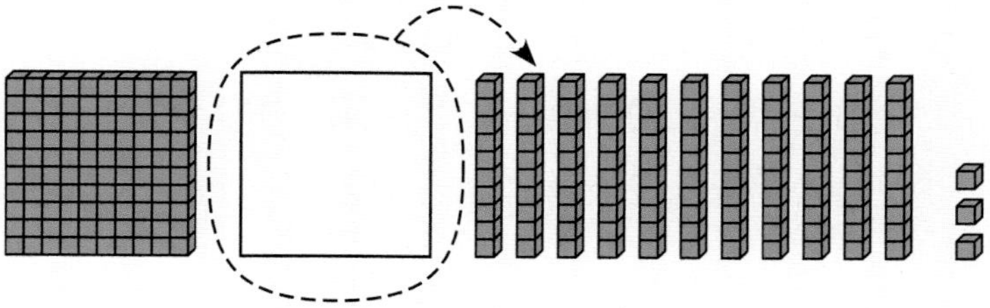

Practice

Regroup 1 ten for 10 ones. You may use place-value blocks or draw a picture to help.

1. $55 = \overset{4}{\cancel{5}}$ tens $\overset{■}{\cancel{5}}$ ones **2.** $37 = \overset{2}{\cancel{3}}$ tens $\overset{■}{\cancel{7}}$ ones **3.** $26 = \overset{1}{\cancel{2}}$ tens $\overset{■}{\cancel{6}}$ ones

4. $\overset{7}{\cancel{8}}\overset{■}{\cancel{8}}$ **5.** $\overset{4}{\cancel{5}}\overset{■}{\cancel{4}}$ **6.** $\overset{2}{\cancel{3}}\overset{■}{\cancel{2}}$ **7.** $\overset{3}{\cancel{4}}\overset{■}{\cancel{2}}$

Regroup 1 hundred for 10 tens. You may use place-value blocks or draw a picture to help.

8. $251 = \overset{1}{\cancel{2}}$ hundreds $\overset{■}{\cancel{5}}$ tens 1 one **9.** $824 = \overset{7}{\cancel{8}}$ hundreds $\overset{■}{\cancel{2}}$ tens 4 ones

10. $\overset{3}{\cancel{4}}\overset{■}{\cancel{4}}3$ **11.** $\overset{2}{\cancel{3}}\overset{■}{\cancel{2}}9$ **12.** $\overset{1}{\cancel{2}}\overset{■}{\cancel{3}}1$ **13.** $\overset{3}{\cancel{4}}\overset{■}{\cancel{6}}2$

14. How could you regroup tens for ones in the number 345?

15. **Journal** Write a 3-digit number. Explain how to regroup 1 hundred into tens or 1 ten into ones.

SECTION A
Review and Practice

(Lesson 1) Write a number sentence for each. Then solve.

1. Billy visited four ghost towns in Arizona and three ghost towns in Colorado. How many more ghost towns did he visit in Arizona?

2. Rachel found 17 shells on the beach. She gave 8 to her mother. How many shells does Rachel have left?

(Lesson 2) Look for a pattern. Copy and complete.

3. $5 - 3 = ■$	**4.** $12 - ■ = 3$	**5.** $15 - 6 = ■$
$50 - ■ = 20$	$120 - 90 = ■$	$150 - 60 = ■$
$500 - ■ = 200$	$1{,}200 - ■ = 300$	$1{,}500 - 600 = ■$

(Lesson 3) Subtract. You may use a hundred chart to help.

6. $28 - 8 = ■$	**7.** $\$53 - \$20 = ■$	**8.** $51 - 20 = ■$	**9.** $49 - 35 = ■$
10. $100 - 25 = ■$	**11.** $82 - 54 = ■$	**12.** $87 - ■ = 20$	**13.** $32 - ■ = 22$
14. $97 - 79 = ■$	**15.** $71 - ■ = 60$	**16.** $64 - ■ = 43$	**17.** $50 - ■ = 25$

(Lesson 4) Estimation Estimate each difference.

18. $514 - 302$ **19.** $\$4.46 - \$1.29$ **20.** $87 - 38$ **21.** $56 - 21$

22. Suppose you are on a 40-minute mule ride. Does it make sense to say you have about 10 minutes left when you've been riding for 28 minutes? Explain.

(Lesson 5) Regroup 1 ten for 10 ones or 1 hundred for 10 tens. You may use place-value blocks or draw a picture to help.

23. $\overset{6}{\not 7}\overset{■}{\not 6}$ **24.** $\overset{2}{\not 3}\overset{■}{\not 5}1$ **25.** $\overset{4}{\not 5}\overset{■}{\not 1}1$

26. Journal Write a way that you can use patterns or mental math to find $120 - 50$.

Skills Checklist

In this section, you have:

- ☑ Reviewed the Meaning of Subtraction
- ☑ Explored Subtraction Patterns
- ☑ Explored Subtracting on a Hundred Chart
- ☑ Estimated Differences
- ☑ Explored Regrouping

CHAPTER 4

SECTION B

Subtracting Greater Numbers and Money

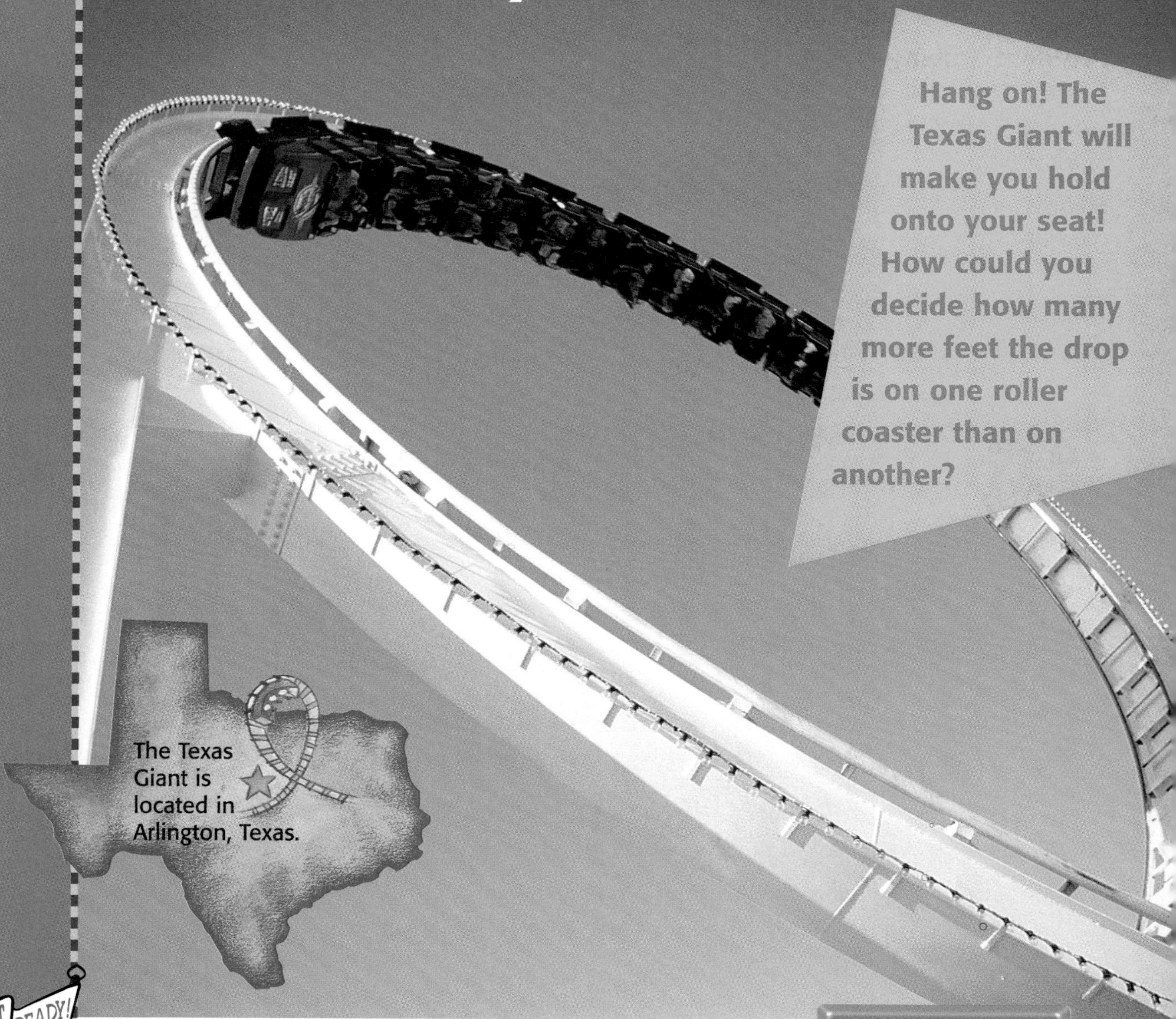

Hang on! The Texas Giant will make you hold onto your seat! How could you decide how many more feet the drop is on one roller coaster than on another?

The Texas Giant is located in Arlington, Texas.

Subtracting 2-Digit and 3-Digit Numbers

Review place-value patterns. Use mental math to find each difference.

1. 90 − 50 **2.** 120 − 60 **3.** 70 − 50

4. 150 − 80 **5.** 130 − 50 **6.** 100 − 70

Skills Checklist

In this section, you will:

- ❒ Explore Subtracting 2-Digit and 3-Digit Numbers
- ❒ Subtract 2-Digit and 3-Digit Numbers
- ❒ Subtract with 2 Regroupings
- ❒ Subtract Across 0

Exploring Subtracting 2-Digit Numbers

Problem Solving Connection
- Use Objects/ Act It Out
- Look for a Pattern

Materials
place-value blocks

Remember
1 ten = 10 ones

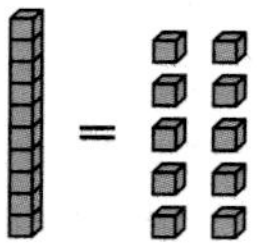

Explore

You can use place-value blocks to subtract 2-digit numbers.

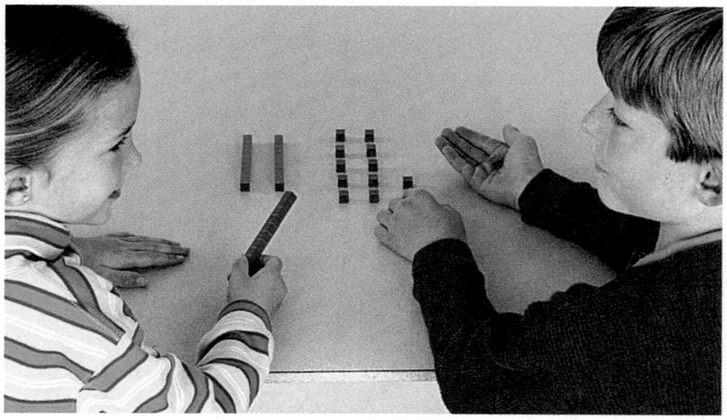

Work Together

1. Find 32 − 18.

a. Use place-value blocks to show 32.

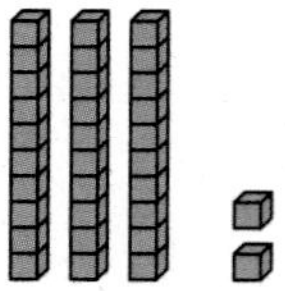

b. Look at the ones. To subtract 8 ones, do you have to regroup? Why?

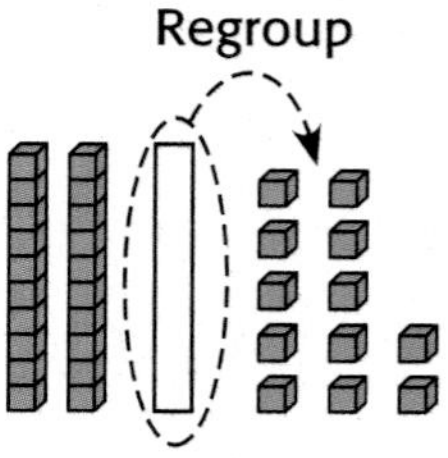

c. Subtract the ones. Subtract the tens.

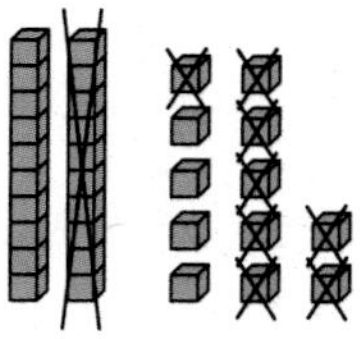

d. What is 32 − 18?

2. Use place-value blocks. Find each difference.

a. 41 − 16 **b.** 23 − 11 **c.** 24 − 9 **d.** 37 − 21
e. 28 − 9 **f.** 40 − 23 **g.** 59 − 37 **h.** 61 − 25

Talk About It

Do you have to regroup to find 41 − 16? Explain.

Connect

You can use what you know about place value and regrouping to subtract numbers.

Find 53 − 26.

You Show | **You Write**

Subtract the ones.
Regroup 1 ten for 10 ones.

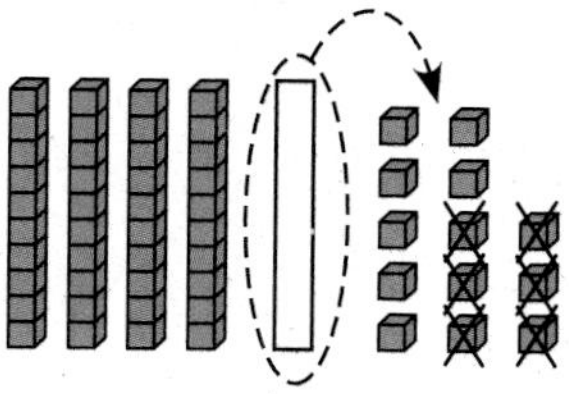

$$\begin{array}{r} \scriptstyle 4\ 13 \\ \not{5}\,\not{3} \\ -\,2\,6 \\ \hline 7 \end{array}$$

Subtract the tens.

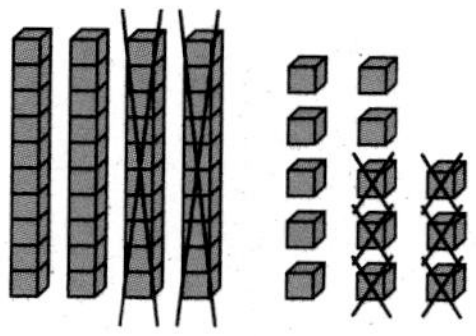

$$\begin{array}{r} \scriptstyle 4\ 13 \\ \not{5}\,\not{3} \\ -\,2\,6 \\ \hline 2\,7 \end{array}$$

Practice

Find each difference. You may use place-value blocks or draw a picture to help.

1. 45 − 29 **2.** 21 − 17 **3.** \$58 − \$35 **4.** 22 − 8

5. \$32 − \$23 **6.** 47 − 6 **7.** 51 − 12 **8.** 43 − 12

9. \$38 − \$19 **10.** 98 − 29 **11.** \$71 − \$8 **12.** 55 − 14

13. Subtract 17 from 34. **14.** Find the difference of 39 and 27.

15. History In 1776, the United States had 13 states. Today there are 50 states. How many more states are there now than in 1776?

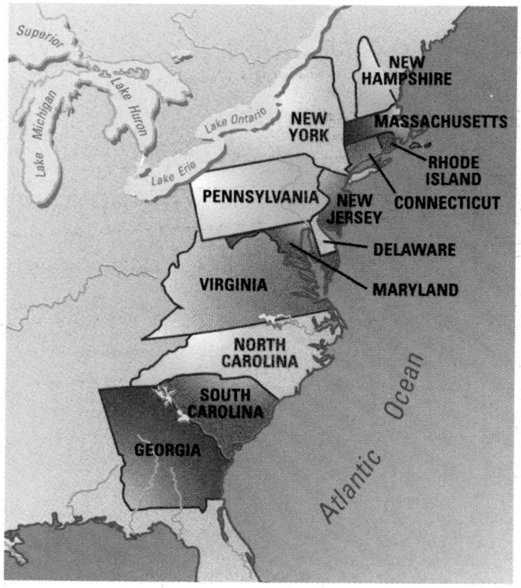

Original thirteen states

16. Estimation Jay wants to spell 200 words correctly to win a prize in a school spell-a-thon. He has learned 114 of the words. About how many more words does he have to learn?

17. Money Suppose you had 2 dimes and 8 pennies. If you found a quarter, how much money would you have?

18. Journal Explain how you would regroup to subtract 29 from 42.

Chapter 4
Lesson
7

Subtracting 2-Digit Numbers

You Will Learn
how to subtract 2-digit numbers

Learn

Yuliana picks up treasures on her travels! She goes as far as Mexico to find blue, pink, yellow, and red rocks!

If Yuliana has found 30 rocks in Texas and 13 rocks in Mexico, how many more rocks has she found in Texas?

Yuliana from Fort Worth, Texas, likes cooking and taking care of her dog.

Example

Find 30 − 13.

Step 1

Subtract the ones.
Regroup as needed.

$$\begin{array}{r} {\scriptstyle 2\ 10} \\ \not{3}\not{0} \\ -\ 1\,3 \\ \hline 7 \end{array}$$

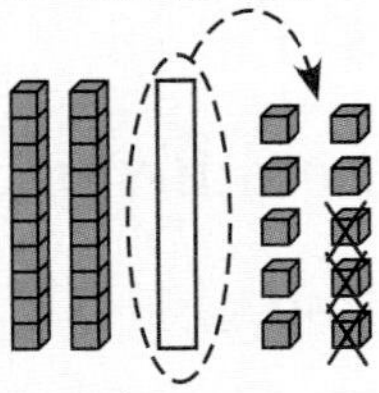

Step 2

Subtract the tens.

$$\begin{array}{r} {\scriptstyle 2\ 10} \\ \not{3}\not{0} \\ -\ 1\,3 \\ \hline 1\,7 \end{array}$$

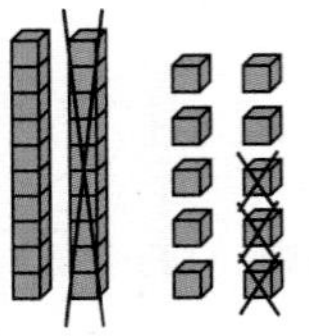

So, she found 17 more rocks in Texas than in Mexico.

You can add to check your answer. 17 + 13 = 30

The answer is correct.

Did You Know?
Rocks are made up of one or more minerals.

Talk About It

How would you check 64 − 28 = 36? Explain.

Check

Subtract. Check each answer.

1. 73 − 32 **2.** 94 − 7 **3.** \$80 − \$73 **4.** 84 − 13 **5.** 56 − 18

6. Reasoning Would you regroup to solve 54 − 23? Explain.

Practice

Skills and Reasoning

Subtract. Check each answer.

7. 89 − 56	**8.** 57 − 38	**9.** 52 − 5	**10.** \$95 − 17	**11.** 45 − 31
12. 33 − 7	**13.** 79 − 25	**14.** \$60 − 14	**15.** 22 − 19	**16.** 31 − 8
17. \$71 − 16	**18.** 59 − 7	**19.** 28 − 17	**20.** 44 − 27	**21.** 80 − 57

22. 38 − 29	**23.** 42 − 15	**24.** 56 − 11	**25.** \$81 − \$39
26. 27 − 8	**27.** \$99 − \$74	**28.** 37 − 18	**29.** 54 − 9
30. 62 − 25	**31.** 83 − 42	**32.** 21 − 12	**33.** \$35 − \$11
34. 20 − 9	**35.** 77 − 8	**36.** 93 − 47	**37.** 40 − 12

38. Find the difference of 40 and 29.

39. Subtract 32 from 51.

40. Write two numbers you could subtract from 26 with regrouping. Then subtract.

Problem Solving and Applications

41. Science The Hubble telescope is a giant telescope in space. It is 44 feet long. A city bus is 35 feet long. How much longer than a city bus is the Hubble telescope?

42. Collecting Data Take a survey. Ask your classmates their favorite place to visit. Make a table showing your findings.

43. Write Your Own Problem Write a subtraction word problem that can be solved by regrouping 1 ten for 10 ones.

Mixed Review and Test Prep

Add.

44. 118 + 127 **45.** 402 + 97 **46.** 391 + 33 **47.** 225 + 134

48. Patterns Continue the pattern. 30, 36, 42, ■, ■, ■

Ⓐ 43, 44, 45 Ⓑ 48, 54, 60 Ⓒ 52, 56, 60 Ⓓ 48, 58, 68

Exploring Subtracting 3-Digit Numbers

Problem Solving Connection
- Use Objects/ Act It Out
- Look for a Pattern

Materials
place-value blocks

Explore

You can use place-value blocks to subtract 3-digit numbers.

Work Together

1. Find 163 − 71.

   a. Use place-value blocks to show 163.

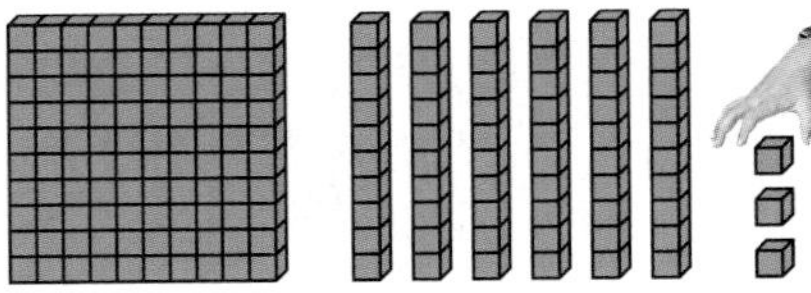

   b. To subtract the ones, do you have to regroup?

   c. To subtract the tens, do you have to regroup?

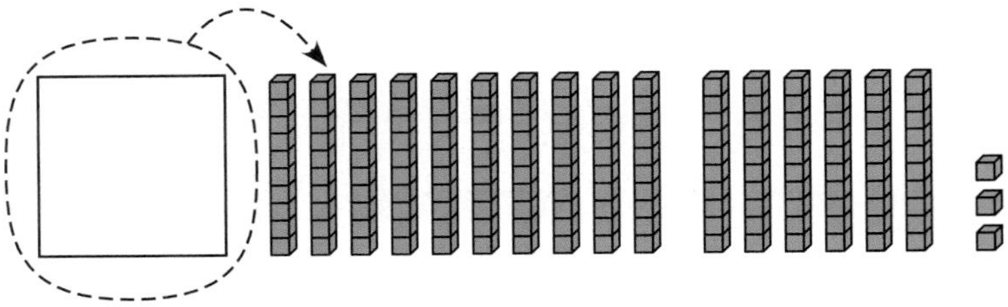

   d. What is 163 − 71?

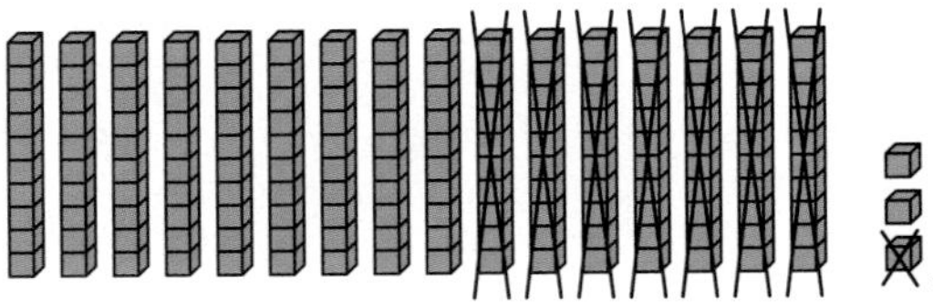

2. Use place-value blocks. Find each difference.

   a. 153 − 16 b. 166 − 139 c. 245 − 62

Remember
You can use addition to check your subtraction.

Talk About It

3. Would you have to regroup to find 151 − 81? Explain.

4. Frank says, "To find 432 − 191, you need to regroup a hundred." Do you agree? Explain.

Connect

Place-value blocks can help you subtract 3-digit numbers.

Find 213 − 42.

	You Show	You Write
Subtract the ones.	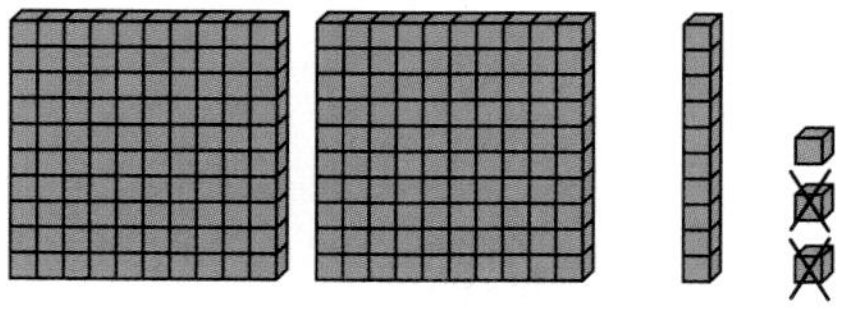	213 − 42 1
Subtract the tens. Regroup 1 hundred for 10 tens.	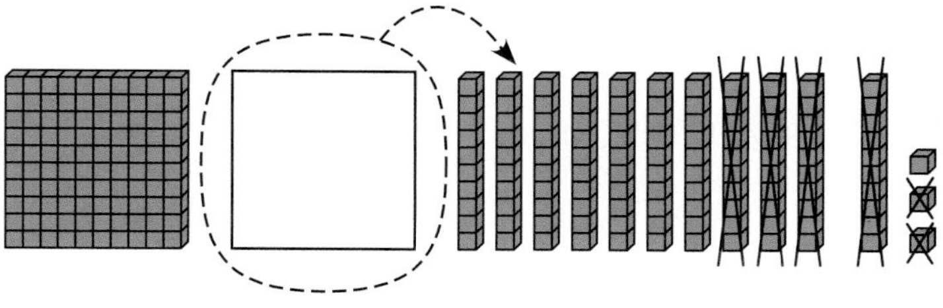	1 11 ~~2~~ ~~1~~ 3 − 4 2 7 1
Subtract the hundreds.	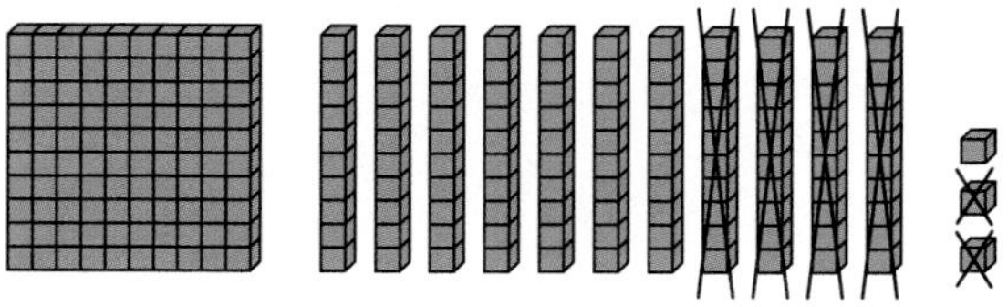	1 11 ~~2~~ ~~1~~ 3 − 4 2 1 7 1

Practice

Find each difference. You may use place-value blocks or draw a picture to help.

1. 137 − 118 **2.** 225 − 23 **3.** 100 − 70 **4.** 148 − 38

5. 321 − 111 **6.** 195 − 77 **7.** 357 − 293 **8.** 218 − 195

9. 383 − 121 **10.** 264 − 115 **11.** 219 − 85 **12.** 196 − 81

13. 439 − 221 **14.** 320 − 40 **15.** 115 − 82 **16.** 200 − 30

17. Subtract 24 from 117. **18.** Subtract 285 from 399.

19. Find the difference of 172 and 111.

20. **History** William H. Harrison was President of the United States for only 32 days in 1841. James Garfield was President for 199 days in 1881. How many more days was Garfield President?

21. **Journal** Suppose you had 3 hundreds blocks, 1 tens block, and 5 ones blocks. Could you subtract 23 without regrouping? Explain.

Chapter 4
Lesson
9

Subtracting 3-Digit Numbers

You Will Learn
how to subtract 3-digit numbers

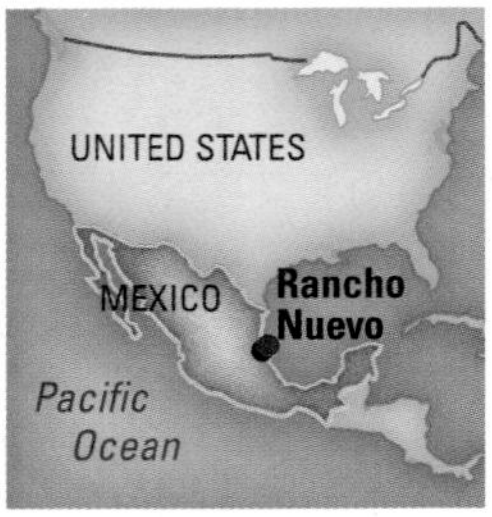

Learn

In Rancho Nuevo, Mexico, experts are helping to keep the beaches a safe place for turtles to nest.

How many more nests were there in 1990 than in 1980?

Since you are comparing how many nests, you subtract.

Rancho Nuevo Turtle Nests

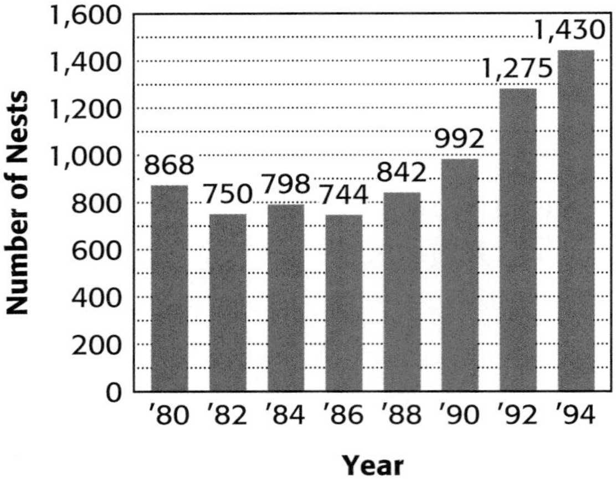

Example 1

Subtract. 992 − 868

Step 1

Subtract the ones. Regroup as needed.

$$\begin{array}{r} \scriptstyle 8\ 12 \\ 9\,\not{9}\,\not{2} \\ -\,8\,6\,8 \\ \hline 4 \end{array}$$

Step 2

Subtract the tens. Regroup as needed.

$$\begin{array}{r} \scriptstyle 8\ 12 \\ 9\,\not{9}\,\not{2} \\ -\,8\,6\,8 \\ \hline 2\,4 \end{array}$$

Step 3

Subtract the hundreds.

$$\begin{array}{r} \scriptstyle 8\ 12 \\ 9\,\not{9}\,\not{2} \\ -\,8\,6\,8 \\ \hline 1\,2\,4 \end{array}$$

There were 124 more nests in 1990 than in 1980.

Example 2

Subtract. 327 − 73

$$\begin{array}{r} \scriptstyle 2\ 12\ \ \\ \not{3}\,\not{2}\,7 \\ -\ \ 7\,3 \\ \hline 2\,5\,4 \end{array}$$

Estimate to check. 300 − 100 = 200
254 is close to 200. So the answer is reasonable.

Talk About It

How would you use addition to check your answers for both examples?

Check

Subtract. Check each answer.

1. 375 − 163
2. 426 − 15
3. 315 − 142
4. \$175 − 90
5. 741 − 81

6. Find the difference of 341 and 127.
7. Subtract 54 from 286.
8. **Reasoning** Suppose you want to find 438 − 146. How would you subtract tens?

Practice

Skills and Reasoning

Subtract. Check each answer.

9. 295 − 186
10. 193 − 172
11. 326 − 142
12. 276 − 91
13. \$681 − 31
14. 266 − 159
15. 74 − 9
16. \$444 − 432
17. 67 − 21
18. 358 − 88
19. 127 − 109
20. \$361 − \$58
21. 958 − 47
22. 392 − 182
23. Find the difference of 319 and 205.
24. Subtract 473 from 591.
25. Explain how to regroup to find 234 − 162.
26. Janet says, "To subtract 105 from 432, I began by subtracting 2 ones from 5 ones." What did she do wrong?

Problem Solving and Applications

27. **Write Your Own Problem** Using the graph on page 168, write a subtraction problem about nests at Rancho Nuevo.
28. **Science** The tallest tree in the United States is 363 feet tall. The second tallest is 329 feet tall. What is the difference?

Mixed Review and Test Prep

Add or subtract.

29. 101 + 203
30. 257 + 634
31. 25 − 18
32. 97 − 9
33. Subtract. \$55 − \$36

Ⓐ \$91 Ⓑ \$29 Ⓒ \$32 Ⓓ \$19

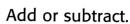

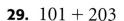

Chapter 4
Lesson
10

Subtracting with 2 Regroupings

You Will Learn
how to regroup more than once when subtracting

Learn

"Aaaaaah!" The passengers on the Mean Streak scream as it whips around a curve. The Mean Streak is a roller coaster that will lift you 161 feet in the air before plunging back to earth. Another coaster, the Blue Streak, lifts you up 78 feet. How much higher does the Mean Streak climb?

Since you want to compare heights, you subtract.

The Mean Streak in Sandusky, Ohio.

Example 1

Subtract. 161 − 78

Step 1

Subtract the ones. Regroup as needed.

$$\begin{array}{r} {\scriptstyle 5\ 11} \\ 1\,\not{6}\,\not{1} \\ -\ \ 7\ 8 \\ \hline 3 \end{array}$$

Step 2

Subtract the tens. Regroup as needed.

$$\begin{array}{r} {\scriptstyle 15} \\ {\scriptstyle \not{5}\ 11} \\ \not{1}\,\not{6}\,\not{1} \\ -\ \ 7\ 8 \\ \hline 8\ 3 \end{array}$$

161 − 78 = 83 **Estimate** to check.

$$\begin{array}{r} 161 \\ -\ 78 \\ \hline \end{array} \longrightarrow \begin{array}{r} 160 \\ -\ 80 \\ \hline 80 \end{array}$$

83 is close to 80. So, the answer is reasonable.

The Mean Streak climbs 83 feet higher than the Blue Streak.

Did You Know?
The Steel Phantom roller coaster in Pittsburgh, Pennsylvania, has a drop of 225 feet. That's as high as a 22-story building!

Example 2

On the Hercules roller coaster, you ride down a drop of 148 feet. The Desperado coaster takes you down 225 feet. How much greater is the drop on the Desperado?

Subtract. 225 − 148

Step 1

Subtract the ones. Regroup as needed.

$$\begin{array}{r} {\scriptstyle 1\ 15} \\ 2\,\not{2}\,\not{5} \\ -\,1\,4\,8 \\ \hline 7 \end{array}$$

Step 2

Subtract the tens. Regroup as needed.

$$\begin{array}{r} {\scriptstyle 11} \\ {\scriptstyle 1\ \not{1}\ 15} \\ \not{2}\,\not{2}\,\not{5} \\ -\,1\,4\,8 \\ \hline 7\,7 \end{array}$$

Step 3

Subtract the hundreds.

$$\begin{array}{r} {\scriptstyle 11} \\ {\scriptstyle 1\ \not{1}\ 15} \\ \not{2}\,\not{2}\,\not{5} \\ -\,1\,4\,8 \\ \hline 7\,7 \end{array}$$

225 − 148 = 77

The drop on the Desperado is 77 feet greater.

Talk About It

How could you use addition to check Example 2?

Check

Subtract.

1. $\begin{array}{r} 282 \\ -194 \\ \hline \square 8 \end{array}$ **2.** $\begin{array}{r} 730 \\ -395 \\ \hline 3\square\square \end{array}$ **3.** $\begin{array}{r} 672 \\ -246 \\ \hline \square\square 6 \end{array}$ **4.** $\begin{array}{r} 851 \\ -\ 95 \\ \hline \square 5 \square \end{array}$ **5.** $\begin{array}{r} 454 \\ -276 \\ \hline 1\square\square \end{array}$

6. 357 − 84 **7.** 521 − 125 **8.** 576 − 297 **9.** 252 − 184

10. Find the difference of 417 and 218.

11. Subtract 391 from 420.

12. Reasoning Do you need to regroup to find 110 − 66? Explain.

Practice

Skills and Reasoning

Subtract. Check each answer.

13. $\begin{array}{r} 453 \\ -284 \\ \hline \square\square 9 \end{array}$ **14.** $\begin{array}{r} 276 \\ -\ 88 \\ \hline \square 8 \square \end{array}$ **15.** $\begin{array}{r} 215 \\ -138 \\ \hline \square 7 \end{array}$ **16.** $\begin{array}{r} 863 \\ -\ 74 \\ \hline 7 \square\square \end{array}$ **17.** $\begin{array}{r} \$935 \\ -821 \\ \hline \$\square 1 \square \end{array}$

18. $\begin{array}{r} 869 \\ -496 \\ \hline \end{array}$ **19.** $\begin{array}{r} 531 \\ -422 \\ \hline \end{array}$ **20.** $\begin{array}{r} 74 \\ -68 \\ \hline \end{array}$ **21.** $\begin{array}{r} \$610 \\ -\ 55 \\ \hline \end{array}$ **22.** $\begin{array}{r} 365 \\ -237 \\ \hline \end{array}$

23. $\begin{array}{r} 543 \\ -345 \\ \hline \end{array}$ **24.** $\begin{array}{r} \$716 \\ -358 \\ \hline \end{array}$ **25.** $\begin{array}{r} 272 \\ -\ 75 \\ \hline \end{array}$ **26.** $\begin{array}{r} 635 \\ -198 \\ \hline \end{array}$ **27.** $\begin{array}{r} 582 \\ -\ 93 \\ \hline \end{array}$

28. $\begin{array}{r} 321 \\ -\ 62 \\ \hline \end{array}$ **29.** $\begin{array}{r} 926 \\ -403 \\ \hline \end{array}$ **30.** $\begin{array}{r} 839 \\ -372 \\ \hline \end{array}$ **31.** $\begin{array}{r} 241 \\ -199 \\ \hline \end{array}$ **32.** $\begin{array}{r} 736 \\ -326 \\ \hline \end{array}$

33. 311 − 267 **34.** 554 − 76 **35.** \$942 − \$335 **36.** 322 − 28

37. 245 − 188 **38.** \$423 − \$382 **39.** 98 − 79 **40.** 873 − 791

41. 332 − 119 **42.** 591 − 283 **43.** 812 − 54 **44.** 297 − 183

45. Find the difference of 562 and 186.

46. Subtract 32 from 154.

47. Find the difference of 651 and 297.

48. Subtract 326 from 672.

49. June subtracted 209 from 848 and found 639. She then added 848 and 209 to check her answer. Did she check her answer correctly? Explain.

50. To find 319 − 129, do you regroup hundreds? Explain.

Problem Solving and Applications

Using Data Use the roller coasters table in the Data File on page 147 to help answer **51–53.**

51. How many feet high is Texas Giant?

52. How many feet higher is Mean Streak than Gemini?

53. How many feet higher is Rattler than Kumba?

54. Texas Star is a Ferris wheel that can carry 244 riders at one time. If 421 people have just bought tickets, how many will have to wait to get a ride?

Problem Solving and HISTORY

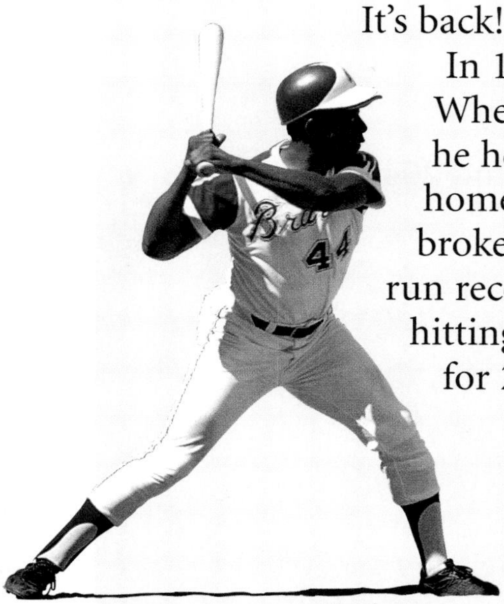

Hank Aaron

It's back! Way back! It's a home run!
In 1927, Babe Ruth hit 60 home runs. When he retired from baseball in 1935 he held the record for hitting the most home runs in a career. Hank Aaron broke Ruth's career home run record and kept hitting balls out of the park for 2 more years.

Player	Career Home Runs
Hank Aaron	755
Babe Ruth	714

Babe Ruth

55. How many more home runs did Hank Aaron hit in his career than Babe Ruth?

56. In 1919 Babe Ruth hit 29 home runs. How many more home runs did he hit in 1927?

57. Critical Thinking It was 39 years after Babe Ruth retired that his career home run record was broken by Hank Aaron. In what year was Ruth's record broken?

58. The most home runs Hank Aaron hit in one season was 44. How many more did he need to equal the number of home runs Babe Ruth hit in 1927?

59. Journal Explain how you would regroup to find 417 − 329.

Mixed Review and Test Prep

Algebra Readiness Find each missing number.

60. 45 + ■ = 56 **61.** 89 + ■ = 119 **62.** 100 + ■ = 300

Compare. Write <, >, or =.

63. 1,562 ● 1,262 **64.** 10,125 ● 11,025 **65.** 138,000 ● 129,999

66. Time A regular year has 365 days. If there are 180 school days in a year, how many days are not school days?

Ⓐ 545 Ⓑ 225 Ⓒ 85 Ⓓ 185

Skills Practice Bank, page 521, Set 3

Subtracting Across 0

You Will Learn
how to subtract 3-digit numbers with zeros

Learn

Ms. Ramirez called on two students to find 204 − 128.

Since there are no tens, I'll regroup hundreds.
Then I can regroup tens.
Now I can subtract ones.

2 hundreds is 20 tens.
1 less ten is 10 more ones.
I'll add to check. 76 + 128 = 204
The answer is correct.

Talk About It

How could you estimate to check 603 − 429?

Remember
2 hundreds is the same as 20 tens.

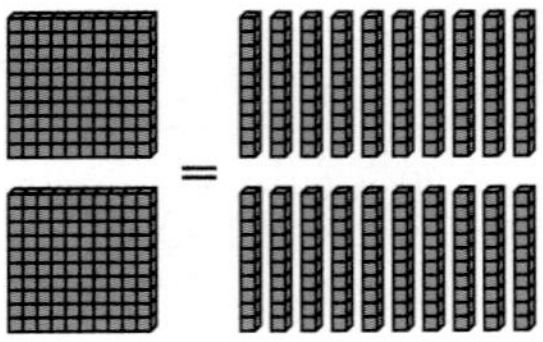

Check

Subtract. Check each answer.

1. 405 − 57 **2.** 904 − 453 **3.** $600 − 342 **4.** 801 − 616 **5.** 700 − 97

6. 702 − 114 **7.** 306 − 147 **8.** 803 − 245

9. What is the difference of 500 and 237?

10. Reasoning In which of these would you not need to regroup?

a. 422 − 112 **b.** 951 − 436 **c.** 470 − 101 **d.** 378 − 276

Practice

Skills and Reasoning

Subtract. Check each answer.

11. $305 - 91$ **12.** $\$603 - 496$ **13.** $700 - 32$ **14.** $\$405 - 267$ **15.** $610 - 278$

16. $203 - 139$ **17.** $802 - 294$ **18.** $507 - 359$ **19.** $723 - 604$ **20.** $103 - 76$

21. $301 - 252$ **22.** $500 - 321$ **23.** $404 - 196$ **24.** $307 - 89$

25. What is 602 minus 317?

26. Subtract 148 from 300.

27. Anthony said, "To find 805 − 396, I can think of 8 hundreds as 80 tens." How might this help him subtract?

28. Write a number you could subtract from 301 without regrouping. Then subtract.

Problem Solving and Applications

29. Money Ms. Chan bought a new lamp for $49. She paid for it with a $100 bill. How much change did she get?

30. Estimation Some students need to wash 100 cars to raise money for a school trip. They have washed 38. About how many more cars do they need to wash?

31. Calculator Enter any 3-digit number. Then press [−] 10 [=]. Record the answer. Press [=] again 2 more times to subtract two more tens. Record each answer. Write about two patterns you see.

32. Career In 1996, astronaut Shannon Lucid spent 188 days in space. Cosmonaut Valeriy Polyakov spent 439 days in space. How many more days did Polyakov spend in space than Lucid?

Mixed Review and Test Prep

Add or subtract.

33. $244 + 646$ **34.** $156 + 765$ **35.** $653 - 154$ **36.** $1{,}876 + 6{,}548$

37. Money Reno buys crackers for $1.69 and milk for $0.45. How much does he spend?

Ⓐ $6.19 Ⓑ $2.14 Ⓒ $1.24 Ⓓ not here

STOP and Practice

Find each difference. Add or estimate to check.

1. $\begin{array}{r} 36 \\ -\ 7 \\ \hline \end{array}$ **2.** $\begin{array}{r} 47 \\ -\ 9 \\ \hline \end{array}$ **3.** $\begin{array}{r} 73 \\ -\ 6 \\ \hline \end{array}$ **4.** $\begin{array}{r} 68 \\ -\ 7 \\ \hline \end{array}$ **5.** $\begin{array}{r} 48 \\ -\ 7 \\ \hline \end{array}$

6. $\begin{array}{r} 48 \\ -\ 36 \\ \hline \end{array}$ **7.** $\begin{array}{r} 21 \\ -\ 15 \\ \hline \end{array}$ **8.** $\begin{array}{r} \$35 \\ -\ 16 \\ \hline \end{array}$ **9.** $\begin{array}{r} 56 \\ -\ 21 \\ \hline \end{array}$ **10.** $\begin{array}{r} 98 \\ -\ 79 \\ \hline \end{array}$

11. $\begin{array}{r} \$129 \\ -\ 72 \\ \hline \end{array}$ **12.** $\begin{array}{r} 433 \\ -\ 92 \\ \hline \end{array}$ **13.** $\begin{array}{r} 379 \\ -\ 54 \\ \hline \end{array}$ **14.** $\begin{array}{r} \$613 \\ -\ 150 \\ \hline \end{array}$ **15.** $\begin{array}{r} 424 \\ -\ 392 \\ \hline \end{array}$

16. $\begin{array}{r} 281 \\ -\ 171 \\ \hline \end{array}$ **17.** $\begin{array}{r} 870 \\ -\ 203 \\ \hline \end{array}$ **18.** $\begin{array}{r} \$205 \\ -\ 178 \\ \hline \end{array}$ **19.** $\begin{array}{r} 503 \\ -\ 257 \\ \hline \end{array}$ **20.** $\begin{array}{r} 600 \\ -\ 74 \\ \hline \end{array}$

21. $\begin{array}{r} \$810 \\ -\ 231 \\ \hline \end{array}$ **22.** $\begin{array}{r} 513 \\ -\ 101 \\ \hline \end{array}$ **23.** $\begin{array}{r} 307 \\ -\ 59 \\ \hline \end{array}$ **24.** $\begin{array}{r} 407 \\ -\ 79 \\ \hline \end{array}$ **25.** $\begin{array}{r} 400 \\ -\ 367 \\ \hline \end{array}$

26. \$41 − \$8 **27.** 133 − 6 **28.** 165 − 61 **29.** 197 − 48

30. 32 − 25 **31.** \$27 − \$14 **32.** 172 − 138 **33.** 88 − 51

34. 432 − 70 **35.** \$516 − \$32 **36.** 327 − 18 **37.** 929 − 62

38. \$693 − \$241 **39.** 748 − 149 **40.** 307 − 194 **41.** 582 − 105

Error Search

Find each difference that is not correct. Write it correctly and explain the error.

42. $\begin{array}{r} 57 \\ -\ 38 \\ \hline 21 \end{array}$ **43.** $\begin{array}{r} 235 \\ -\ 71 \\ \hline 164 \end{array}$ **44.** $\begin{array}{r} 560 \\ -\ 127 \\ \hline 443 \end{array}$ **45.** $\begin{array}{r} 700 \\ -\ 254 \\ \hline 546 \end{array}$

Geography Jumble

Subtract. Match each letter to its answer in the blank below to solve the riddle. Some letters are not used.

What state is round at both ends and tall in the middle?
?

46. 414 − 361 [O]

47. 607 − 113 [W]

48. 522 − 181 [A]

49. 739 − 56 [O]

50. 230 − 108 [D]

51. 77 − 19 [N]

52. 158 − 63 [E]

53. 41 − 36 [M]

54. 167 − 148 [H]

55. 365 − 278 [X]

56. 400 − 65 [C]

57. 528 − 76 [I]

___	___	___	___
53	19	452	683

Number Sense Estimation and Reasoning

Write >, <, or = for each.

58. 500 − 400 ● 500 − 375

59. 650 − 600 ● 625 − 600

60. 715 − 400 ● 730 − 385

61. 475 − 375 ● 575 − 475

62. 400 − 30 ● 400 − 300

63. 560 − 70 ● 560 + 60

64. 295 − 195 ● 285 + 100

65. 902 − 50 ● 900 − 50

SECTION B
Review and Practice

(Lessons 7 and 9) Subtract. Check each answer.

1. 67 − 48 **2.** 82 − 47 **3.** 56 − 38 **4.** 51 − 7 **5.** \$98 − 76

6. 291 − 77 **7.** \$573 − 144 **8.** 325 − 233 **9.** 928 − 37 **10.** 440 − 136

11. 25 − 19 **12.** 127 − 90 **13.** 422 − 331 **14.** \$157 − \$39

15. **Geography** Death Valley, California, is 282 feet below sea level. Salton Sink, California, is 235 feet below sea level. How many feet lower is Death Valley than Salton Sink?

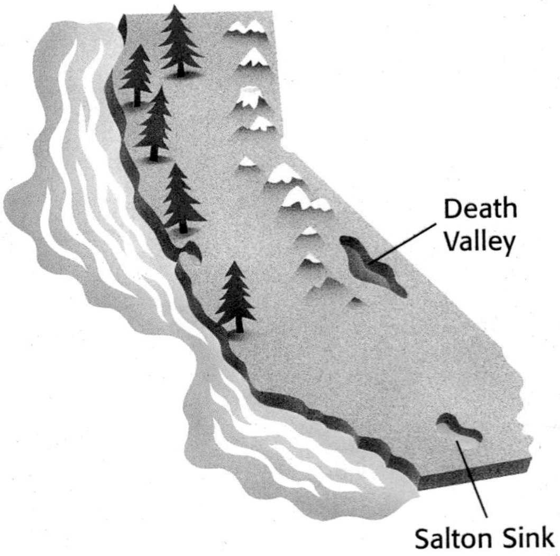

(Lessons 10 and 11) Subtract. Check each answer.

16. 564 − 275 **17.** 705 − 96 **18.** \$700 − 398

19. 301 − 187 **20.** 408 − 219 **21.** 683 − 394

22. \$422 − \$365 **23.** 768 − 87 **24.** 505 − 368

25. Find the difference of 324 and 238. **26.** Subtract 398 from 407.

27. Maria is 48 inches tall. To ride on the roller coaster she must be at least 54 inches tall. How much taller must Maria be to ride the roller coaster?

28. In the Soap Box Derby, a car and driver together must weigh no more than 220 pounds. If Luis weighs 58 pounds, how many pounds can his car weigh?

29. **Journal** How could you explain to a friend a way to find 600 − 23?

Skills Checklist

In this section, you have:

- ☑ Explored Subtracting 2-Digit and 3-Digit Numbers
- ☑ Subtracted 2-Digit and 3-Digit Numbers
- ☑ Subtracted with 2 Regroupings
- ☑ Subtracted Across 0

C Extending Subtraction

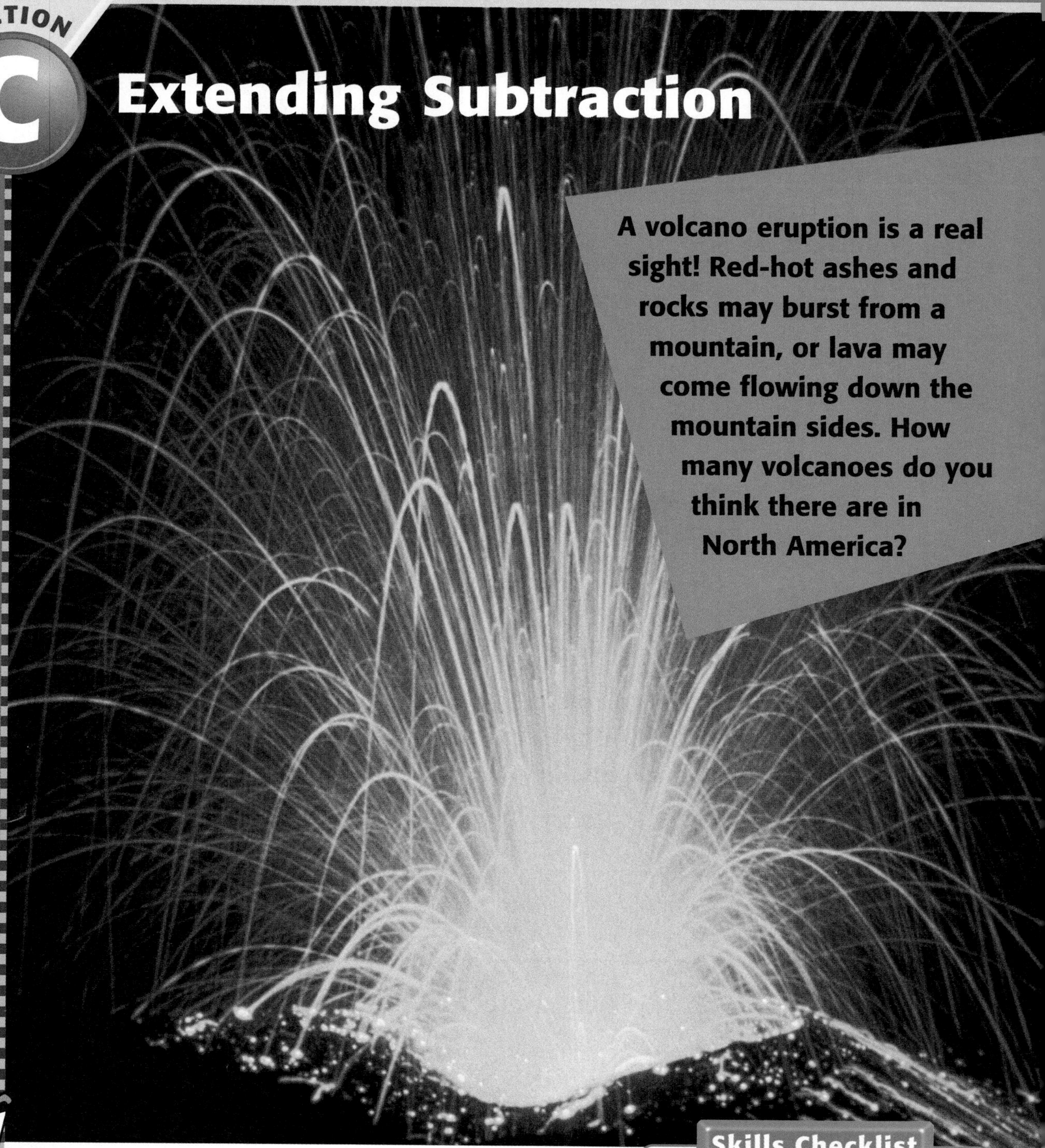

A volcano eruption is a real sight! Red-hot ashes and rocks may burst from a mountain, or lava may come flowing down the mountain sides. How many volcanoes do you think there are in North America?

Extending Subtraction

Review subtracting 3-digit numbers. Find each difference.

1. 145 − 132 **2.** 467 − 195

3. 878 − 639 **4.** 509 − 415

5. 600 − 493 **6.** 701 − 156

Skills Checklist

In this section, you will:

- ❐ Subtract 4-Digit Numbers
- ❐ Solve Multiple-Step Problems
- ❐ Use Mental Math to Subtract
- ❐ Subtract Money
- ❐ Solve Problems by Using Objects

Chapter 4
Lesson
12

Subtracting 4-Digit Numbers: Choose a Calculation Method

You Will Learn
how to subtract 4-digit numbers

Materials
calculator

Learn

Before Mount Saint Helens erupted, it was 9,677 feet high. After it erupted, it was 8,365 feet high. How many feet were blown off the top of the mountain?

Since you want to compare heights you subtract.

Victor's Way

The numbers are too messy for mental math. I used paper and pencil.

$$\begin{array}{r} 9{,}677 \\ -\ 8{,}365 \\ \hline 1{,}312 \end{array}$$

Tara's Way

First I estimated.

$$\begin{array}{r} 9{,}677 \\ -\ 8{,}365 \\ \hline \end{array} \longrightarrow \begin{array}{r} 9{,}700 \\ -\ 8{,}400 \\ \hline 1{,}300 \end{array}$$

Then I used a calculator.

9687 [−] 8365 [=] [1312].

My answer seems reasonable.

So 1,312 feet were blown off the top of the mountain.

Did You Know?
Mount Saint Helens is in Washington State. There are 53 major active volcanoes in North America. 42 of them are in Alaska.

Talk About It

What method would you use to find 2,500 − 1,732? Why?

Check

Choose a calculation method to solve. Check each answer.

1. $\begin{array}{r} 3{,}124 \\ -\ 2{,}870 \\ \hline \end{array}$ **2.** $\begin{array}{r} \$4{,}115 \\ -\ 2{,}110 \\ \hline \end{array}$ **3.** $\begin{array}{r} 5{,}700 \\ -\ 600 \\ \hline \end{array}$ **4.** $\begin{array}{r} 7{,}270 \\ -\ 2{,}300 \\ \hline \end{array}$

5. Reasoning How can you estimate if the difference of 2,801 and 2,099 is greater than or less than 500?

Practice

Skills and Reasoning

Choose a tool

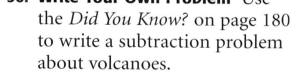

Solve. Check each answer.

6. $5{,}394 - 2{,}617$ **7.** $4{,}100 - 3{,}000$ **8.** $7{,}264 - 4{,}213$ **9.** $8{,}750 - 7{,}285$ **10.** $3{,}569 - 2{,}740$

11. $\$2{,}175 - 1{,}150$ **12.** $5{,}598 - 1{,}650$ **13.** $7{,}200 - 4{,}500$ **14.** $\$1{,}558 - 300$ **15.** $8{,}500 - 900$

16. $4,537 − $2,100 **17.** 9,340 − 1,228 **18.** $2,350 − $550

19. 5,300 − 3,210 **20.** 1,925 − 1,023 **21.** 3,201 − 405

22. 8,602 − 7,002 **23.** 4,537 − 2,913 **24.** 3,900 − 1,000

25. How could you use mental math to find 1,600 − 700?

26. Lisa subtracted 112 from 1,234 on her calculator and found 114. Estimate to check. Is her answer reasonable?

Problem Solving and Applications

Using Data Use the Data File on page 147 to answer **27** and **28.**

27. How many years apart were the two eruptions shown for Mt. Vesuvius?

28. Which two volcanoes erupted 200 years apart?

29. Journal Write a story about using mental math to find the difference of two 4-digit numbers.

30. Write Your Own Problem Use the *Did You Know?* on page 180 to write a subtraction problem about volcanoes.

Mixed Review and Test Prep

Add or subtract.

31. $1.56 + $0.73 **32.** 549 − 299 **33.** $3.32 + $4.95

34. 571 − 340 **35.** 7,612 − 876 **36.** 1,081 − 979

Order from greatest to least.

37. 1,243, 124, 1,351 **38.** 702, 1,005, 897 **39.** 89, 45, 450

40. Estimation Estimate 241 + 769 to the nearest hundred.

Ⓐ 1,100 Ⓑ 1,000 Ⓒ 950 Ⓓ 1,200

WHAT'S the Difference?

Players
2 or more

Materials
3 number cubes with digits
0–5, 2–7, and 4–9

Object
The object of the game is to score 1,000 points by totaling the differences from subtraction problems.

How to Play

1. The first player rolls three number cubes. Both players use the numbers showing to write a 3-digit number. Players don't show each other the number they make.

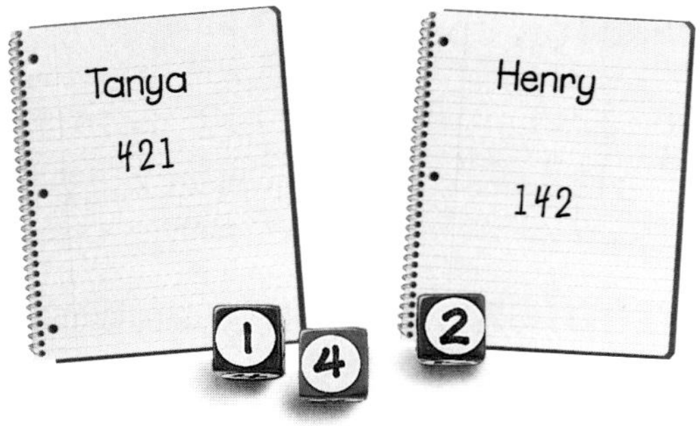

2. The second player rolls the cubes. Both players make another 3-digit number. Each player then subtracts the lesser number from the greater number.

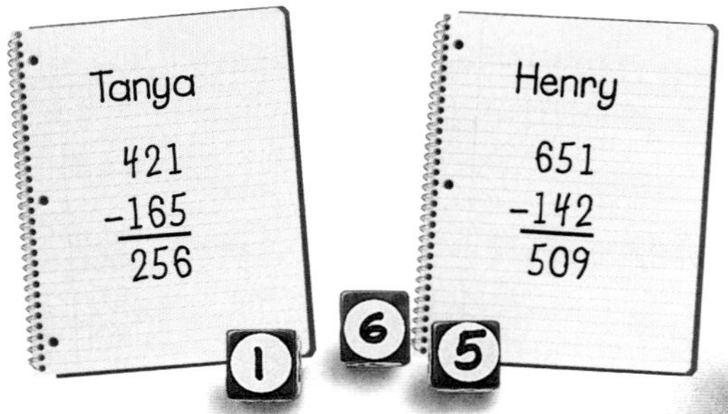

3. Each player's difference is his or her score for that round. Record each score on a score sheet.

4. Keep taking turns. Add the differences on the score sheet as you play. The first player to reach 1,000 or greater wins.

Talk About It

1. Did you always write the greatest 3-digit number possible?

2. What strategies did you use when writing the second number?

More Ways to Play

- Play again. Use only two number cubes. The winner is the first player to reach 100.

- Play another game. Use three number cubes. Play only to 500. But this time, the winner is the *last* player to reach 500.

- Play the game with two number cubes. The winner is the player who reaches 100 exactly. If a player goes over 100, his or her score goes back down to 50.

Reasoning

1. Suppose that this is the first roll of the First to 1,000 game.

What number would you write? Explain.

2. Suppose for your first number you have written 426. This is the second roll.

What number would you write for your second number? Explain.

3. Suppose your paper looks like this in a game called First to Reach 500. What do you hope is rolled next?

Chapter 4
Lesson
13

Problem Solving

Analyze Word Problems: Multiple-Step Problems

You Will Learn
how to solve problems with more than one step

Learn

Suppose you are helping to plan a family trip to Bryce Canyon National Park in Utah. There are four members of your family.

How much more is the total entrance fee if you all ride bikes rather than take a car when you go into the park?

Bryce Canyon Entrance Fees

$5 per car
$2 per person on bicycle
$30 per bus

Work Together

▶ Understand

What do you know?

What do you need to find out?

▶ Plan

How can you begin? Add to find out how much 4 people on bikes would cost.

What's the next step? Subtract to compare this number with the price for taking a car.

▶ Solve

Cost if we bring bikes:

Step 1: Add. $\$2 + \$2 + \$2 + \$2 = \$8$

Step 2: Subtract. $\$8 - \$5 = \$3$

What's the answer? It costs $3 less to drive in.

▶ Look Back

Does your answer make sense?

Talk About It

Why did this problem have to be solved in two steps?

Check

Problem Solving
Understand
Plan
Solve
Look Back

Solve each problem.

1. A third-grade class may take either a bus or 5 cars to Bryce Canyon. Use the data on page 184.
   a. How much is the entrance fee for 5 cars?
   b. How much more will it cost to take the bus than to drive the cars?

2. The park ranger is leading a tour. 15 people signed up to take the tour, but 4 people didn't show up. Then 6 more people asked to come. How many are going on the tour now?

Problem Solving Practice

Problem Solving Strategies

- Use Objects/Act It Out
- Draw a Picture
- Look for a Pattern
- Guess and Check
- Use Logical Reasoning
- Make an Organized List
- Make a Table
- Solve a Simpler Problem
- Work Backward

Choose a Tool

Solve. Use the data on page 184 to help solve **3** and **4.**

3. Suppose a family with 3 people is going to Bryce Canyon. Will the entrance fee be more if they go in by car or by bike?

4. **Money** A group of people went to Bryce Canyon. Thirteen people rode in 3 cars and 29 rode on a bus. How much did they pay to get in?

5. **Time** Joy hiked in Bryce Canyon for an hour. She took one 10-minute rest and one 13-minute rest. How many minutes did she walk?

6. **Estimation** It takes 37 minutes to walk the first mile of a 3-mile trail. About how long will it take to walk the entire trail?

7. **History** Bryce Canyon National Park was founded in 1924. How many years ago was that?

8. **Science** This giant crater is about 600 feet deep. If a ten-story building is 100 feet tall, how many ten-story buildings would fit stacked on top of each other in Meteor Crater?

Meteor Crater in Arizona is a 4,000-foot-wide pit caused by a meteor hitting the earth thousands of years ago.

PROBLEM SOLVING PRACTICE

Chapter 4
Lesson
14

Mental Math

You Will Learn
how to use equal additions to subtract mentally

Learn

If you add the same number to both numbers you are subtracting, the difference is the same! Choose a number to add so you don't have to regroup.

I can use mental math to find 48 − 19. I just add 1 to **both** numbers. 49 − 20 is a much simpler problem. I can do it in my head!

49 − 20 = 29

I see! I can use that way to find 22 − 7. I should choose a number to add that makes the subtraction a simpler problem. If I add 3 to **both** numbers, then I have 25 − 10. I don't have to regroup!

25 − 10 = 15

Talk About It

Look at the number sentences. How did adding let you subtract mentally?

Check

Write what number you would add to each in order to subtract mentally. Subtract.

1. 43 − 19 **2.** 67 − 18 **3.** 72 − 28 **4.** 81 − 39

5. Reasoning Would you add on to help you find 84 − 27? Explain.

Practice

Skills and Reasoning

Write what number you would add to each in order to subtract mentally. Subtract.

6. 27 − 18 **7.** 145 − 27 **8.** 93 − 38 **9.** 52 − 26

10. 197 − 88 **11.** 42 − 17 **12.** 67 − 39 **13.** 176 − 58

14. 91 − 47 **15.** 238 − 9 **16.** 43 − 17 **17.** 94 − 48

18. What could you add on to help you find 940 − 480? Explain.

19. Nathan says, "I can find 160 − 59 by adding 1 to 59 and then subtracting to get 100." What did Nathan do wrong?

Problem Solving and Applications

20. **Science** The Popigai crater in Russia measures 62 miles across. Another crater at Kara, also in Russia, measures 37 miles across. How much bigger is the crater at Popigai?

21. **Logic** The United States has 50 states. Rhode Island is the smallest state. How many states are larger than Rhode Island?

22. **Patterns** Find each difference by adding on. Then write two problems that follow the pattern.

a. $\begin{array}{r} 25 \\ -\ 8 \\ \hline \end{array}$ **b.** $\begin{array}{r} 35 \\ -\ 18 \\ \hline \end{array}$ **c.** $\begin{array}{r} 45 \\ -\ 28 \\ \hline \end{array}$

23. **Journal** Explain how you could find the difference of 195 and 49 mentally.

Mixed Review and Test Prep

Mental Math Use mental math to add.

24. 40 + 75 **25.** 50 + 100 **26.** 20 + 40 **27.** 40 + 90

Compare. Write $<$, $>$, or $=$.

28. 363 ● 336 **29.** 250 ● 255 **30.** 159 ● 195 **31.** 121 ● 121

32. **Estimation** Which is a reasonable estimate of 438 + 620?

Ⓐ 800 Ⓑ 2,000 Ⓒ 1,500 Ⓓ 1,000

Chapter 4
Lesson
15

Subtracting Money

You Will Learn
to subtract money

Learn

Suppose you have $5.00 to spend at Fanny's Fabulous Toys.

Example

You want to buy a jumping spider. How much change will you get back? Subtract. $5.00 – $2.75

Step 1	Step 2	Step 3
Line up the decimal points.	Subtract.	Write the dollar sign and the decimal point.
$\begin{array}{r} \$5.00 \\ -\ 2.75 \\ \hline \end{array}$	$\begin{array}{r} \$5.00 \\ -\ 2.75 \\ \hline 2\ 25 \end{array}$	$\begin{array}{r} \$5.00 \\ -\ 2.75 \\ \hline \$2.25 \end{array}$

Estimate to the nearest dollar to check.

$$\begin{array}{rcr} \$5.00 & \longrightarrow & \$5.00 \\ -\ 2.75 & \longrightarrow & -\ 3.00 \\ \hline & & \$2.00 \end{array}$$

$2.25 is close to $2.00, so the answer is reasonable.

Remember
$5.00 is the same as $5.

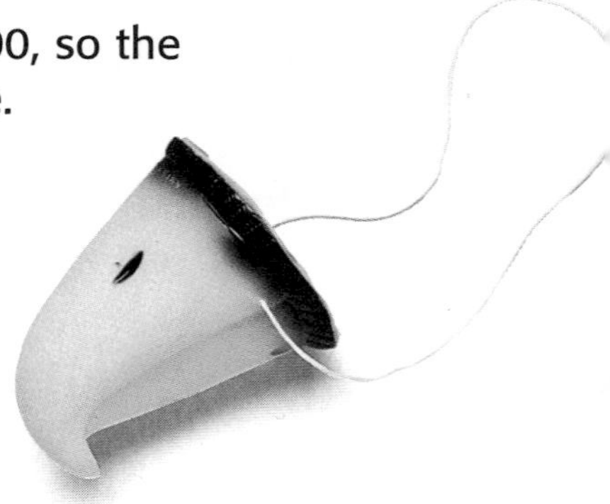

Talk About It

Explain how subtracting money is like subtracting whole numbers.

Check

Subtract.

1. $8.00 – $7.49 **2.** $10.00 – $3.65 **3.** $4.25 – $1.18

4. **Reasoning** Ted bought an item from the list and paid with 2 one-dollar bills. He got $0.40 change. What did he buy?

Practice

Skills and Reasoning

Subtract.

5. $6.75 − 2.54
6. $10.00 − 6.14
7. $9.00 − 8.23
8. $20.00 − 7.89
9. $4.99 − 3.58
10. $8.25 − 4.28
11. $5.75 − 3.45
12. $7.25 − 6.97
13. $12.00 − 4.69
14. $24.95 − 12.99
15. $4.50 − $2.39
16. $14.55 − $8.32
17. $9.50 − $4.26

Using Data Use the price list on page 188 to answer **18** and **19.**

18. Norma paid $5.00 for one item and got $1.50 in change. What did Norma buy?

19. If you buy a finger puppet instead of a jumping spider, how much will you save?

Problem Solving and Applications

Using Data Use the price list on page 188 to answer **20–22.**

20. **Critical Thinking** Merritt bought two fake bugs and paid with a five-dollar bill. How much change did she get?

21. **Write Your Own Problem** Which toy would you buy? Write a subtraction problem about buying an item.

22. **Estimation** Estimate to decide if $4.00 is enough to buy a jumping spider and a wind-up duck.

23. **Literature** In the story *A Jar of Dreams,* each person in Rinko's family saves coins in a jar. Suppose Rinko's brother has $1.80 in his jar. Rinko has 5 quarters, 2 dimes, and 6 nickels in her jar. Who has more? How much more?

Mixed Review and Test Prep

24. 25 + 65 + 40
25. 256 + 365 + 487
26. 562 + 847 + 747

Round to the nearest hundred.

27. 569
28. 331
29. 97
30. 812
31. 550

32. **Estimation** Which is a reasonable estimate of 336 + 156 + 857?

Ⓐ 400 Ⓑ 1,400 Ⓒ 1,000 Ⓓ 2,000

Chapter 4
Lesson
16

Problem Solving

Analyze Strategies: Use Objects

You Will Learn
how using objects can help you solve problems

Learn

Amy and her big brother Santiago are visiting New York City. They want to peek out of the crown of the Statue of Liberty. They walk up many steps to get there.

Santiago goes up 3 steps at a time. Amy goes up 2 steps at a time. When Amy has gone up 12 steps, how many steps has Santiago gone up?

You must climb 354 steps to get to the top of the crown in the Statue of Liberty.

Work Together

▶ Understand

What do you know?

What do you need to find out?

Problem Solving Hint
Using objects can help you understand the information given.

▶ Plan

Decide what each counter will show.

Each counter can show 1 step.

▶ Solve

Use the counters to show the problem.

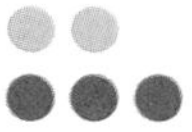

Amy
Santiago

Continue the pattern with the counters.

What's the answer?

When Amy has gone up 12 steps, Santiago has gone up 18 steps.

▶ Look Back

What other ways could you solve this problem?

Another Example

On Saturday, Amy and Santiago had 6 subway tokens and bought 2 more. They used 5 tokens. On Sunday, they bought more tokens so that they had 10 tokens. How many tokens did they buy on Sunday?

What You Read	What You Do
a. On Saturday, they had 6 tokens and bought 2 more.	
b. They used 5 tokens.	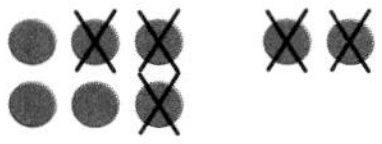
c. On Sunday they bought more tokens so they had 10.	
d. How many tokens did they buy on Sunday?	

They bought 7 tokens on Sunday.

Talk About It

How can using objects help you solve a problem?

Check

Use objects to help solve each problem.

1. Amy and her mother walk next to each other in the park. Amy takes 2 long steps for every 5 steps her mother takes.
   - **a.** When Amy has taken 4 steps, how many steps has her mother taken?
   - **b.** When Amy has taken 8 steps, how many steps has her mother taken?
2. Amy waits to buy tickets to the Statue of Liberty. She counts 14 people ahead of her. 5 people buy tickets and leave. 3 people leave without buying anything. How many people are ahead of her now?

Problem Solving Practice

Apply the Strategy

Use objects to help you solve each problem.

3. The trip from Alexandria, Virginia, to Jacksonville, Florida, takes 13 hours in the car. Suppose you read a book, and then sleep for 2 hours. Then you do puzzles for the last 3 hours.
   a. How long did you spend sleeping and doing puzzles?
   b. How long did you read the book?

4. Amy is 6 steps ahead of Santiago. If she goes up one step at a time and Santiago goes up 2 steps at a time, in how many steps will Santiago reach her?

Problem Solving Strategies

- Use Objects/Act It Out
- Draw a Picture
- Look for a Pattern
- Guess and Check
- Use Logical Reasoning
- Make an Organized List
- Make a Table
- Solve a Simpler Problem
- Work Backward

Choose a Tool

Choose a Strategy

Use any strategy to help you solve each problem.

5. Amy, Santiago, and their mother and father are in line for the ferry to the Statue of Liberty. Amy is the only person between her mother and father. Santiago is directly behind his mother. Who is first in line?

6. Amy goes up 3 steps, then back down 2 steps to pick up a pamphlet she dropped. She goes up 5 steps, then down 3 to take a mint from her mother. How many steps has she gone up?

7. Amy and her mom are waiting to take a tour of the Statue of Liberty. There are 9 other people waiting with them. Three more people join the group, then 1 person leaves. How many people are taking the tour now?

8. Santiago is ordering a sandwich. He can have whole wheat bread or sourdough bread. He can have ham, chicken, or turkey in the sandwich. How many different kinds of sandwiches could he order?

Problem Solving and SCIENCE

A roadrunner is great on the ground, but not so great in the air. Its wings are too short for much flying, but it can run a mile in about 5 minutes. A roadrunner's body is about 24 inches long. It also has 2-inch feathers on its head that stand up when it's curious. Roadrunners eat lots of other animals, including tarantulas, scorpions, and lizards.

9. Roadrunners can run long distances at a speed of 1 mile in 5 minutes. In how many minutes could they run 2 miles?

10. About how much longer is a roadrunner's body than its head feathers?

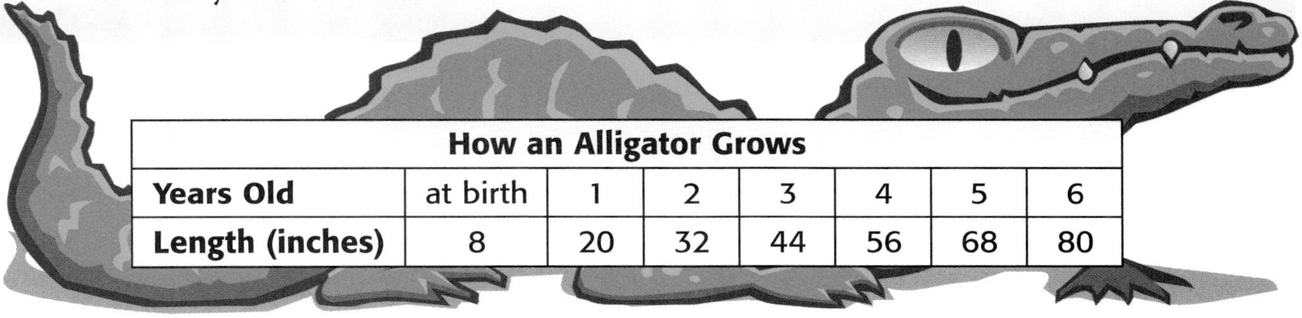

How an Alligator Grows							
Years Old	at birth	1	2	3	4	5	6
Length (inches)	8	20	32	44	56	68	80

Using Data Use the table for **11–13.**

11. How much does an alligator grow from birth to 6 years old?

12. Suppose an alligator measures 42 inches. About how old is the alligator?

13. Algebra Readiness Write a rule that tells about how many inches alligators grow each year in their first 6 years.

14. Journal When might you use objects to solve a problem?

Mixed Review and Test Prep

Mental Math Compare. Write >, <, or =.

15. 435 − 300 ● 430 − 200 **16.** 550 − 200 ● 550 − 199

17. Patterns Which numbers continue the pattern?

30, 25, 20, ■, ■, ■

Ⓐ 5, 10, 15 Ⓑ 15, 10, 0 Ⓒ 10, 5, 0 Ⓓ not here

SECTION C

Review and Practice

(Lesson 12) Solve. Check each answer.

1. 6,123 − 3,577 **2.** 7,200 − 5,000 **3.** 6,000 − 589

4. 3,856 − 1,211 **5.** 5,940 − 4,389 **6.** 1,275 − 1,108

Using Data Use the table to solve.

7. How many feet higher is Colorado Springs than El Paso?

8. How many feet higher is Denver than Amarillo?

9. Is Colorado Springs more than 1,000 feet higher than Salt Lake City?

City	Feet Above Sea Level
Colorado Springs, CO	5,980 feet
Denver, CO	5,280 feet
El Paso, TX	3,695 feet
Amarillo, TX	3,685 feet
Salt Lake City, UT	4,390 feet
Atlanta, GA	1,050 feet

(Lesson 13) Solve.

10. Money It costs $4 for a child's ticket and $7 for an adult ticket at the movies. Joel's dad buys tickets for 2 children and 2 adults. How much does he pay?

(Lesson 14) Write what number you would add to each in order to subtract mentally. Subtract.

11. 34 − 18 **12.** 283 − 69 **13.** 96 − 27 **14.** 68 − 39 **15.** 351 − 28

(Lesson 15) Subtract.

16. $3.59 − 1.22 **17.** $7.11 − 3.29 **18.** $8.00 − 7.65 **19.** $9.68 − 4.91

(Lesson 16) Use objects or any strategy to solve.

20. Jessica is on a 6-hour car ride. She played cards for 2 hours, did a puzzle for 1 hour, then slept. When she woke there was 1 hour to go. How long did she sleep?

21. Journal Explain how you would subtract the year you were born from 2010.

Skills Checklist

In this section, you have:

- ☑ Subtracted 4-Digit Numbers
- ☑ Solved Multiple-Step Problems
- ☑ Used Mental Math to Subtract
- ☑ Subtracted Money
- ☑ Solved Problems by Using Objects

YOUR CHOICE

Choose at least one. Use what you have learned in this chapter.

1 Let's Go!

Pick a state you'd like to visit. Then go to **www.mathsurf.com/3/ch4** to find information about the state. Plan a trip to the state. Where would you stay? What sites would you see? How long would you stay? About how much money would you need for your trip?

2 Math Reporter

At Home Interview a family member to find out when he or she has used subtraction and why. Write an example to present to the class.

3 Picture This

Draw pictures to show each problem. Write each difference.

a. 59 − 42

b. 150 − 30

c. 246 − 106

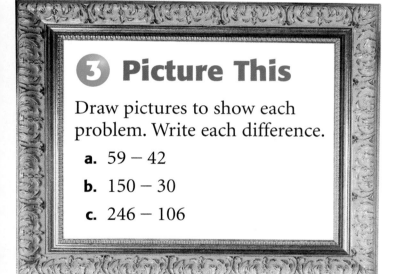

4 Sum Difference!

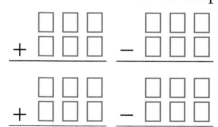

Arrange the digits 3, 4, 5, 6, 7, and 8 to form two 3-digit numbers that have the (a) greatest sum, (b) least sum, (c) greatest difference, and (d) least difference. Use each digit only once. Use a calculator to help you.

5 Acting Up

Write and act out a play about going on rides at a fun park. In the play, actors should start with 6 ride tickets, then spend 3, then buy more tickets so that they have a total of 10. Be sure the actors tell how many tickets they need to buy!

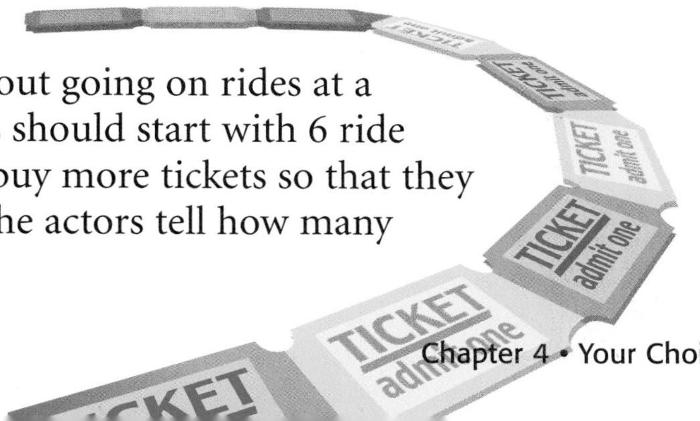

CHAPTER 4

Review/Test

(Lesson 1) Solve.

1. On a trip, Glen counted 8 license plates from Florida and 6 license plates from Georgia. How many more Florida plates did Glen count?

(Lesson 2) Mental Math Find each difference using mental math.

2. 70 – 10 3. 900 – 400 4. \$30 – \$20 5. 150 – 90

(Lesson 4) Estimation Estimate each difference.

6. 436 – 295 7. \$8.19 – \$4.29 8. 76 – 11 9. 617 – 499

(Lessons 7, 9–12) Subtract. Check each answer.

10. 93 – 78 11. 25 – 19 12. 90 – 69 13. 387 – 323

14. 667 – 248 15. 825 – 631 16. 342 – 167 17. 135 – 76

18. 803 – 27 19. 700 – 144 20. 6,000 – 4,500 21. 4,567 – 1,238

(Lesson 13) Solve.

22. Linda has 2 sets of markers with 8 markers in each set. She also has a box of 12 crayons. How many more markers than crayons does she have?

(Lesson 14) Write what number you would add to each in order to subtract mentally. Subtract.

23. 57 – 29 24. 496 – 39 25. 75 – 38

(Lesson 15) Subtract.

26. \$12.95 – \$2.75 27. \$5.75 – \$3.97 28. \$4.09 – \$1.99

29. \$2.61 – \$0.44 30. \$8.00 – \$4.36 31. \$19.86 – \$7.97

(Lesson 16) Use objects or any strategy to solve.

32. Jerry took 2 steps for every 4 steps his little brother took. After Jerry has walked 12 steps, how many steps has his little brother walked?

33. There are 258 steps to the top of the fire lookout station. Tori has walked up 89 steps. Is it correct to say that Tori still has over 160 steps before she reaches the top? Explain.

CHAPTER 4

Performance Assessment

You need to decide some places to visit with your History Club. The tour bus can only travel 350 miles before it needs more gas. The bus must only be filled with gas from a pump at the school. How many places can you visit before going back to school to fill the tank with gas?

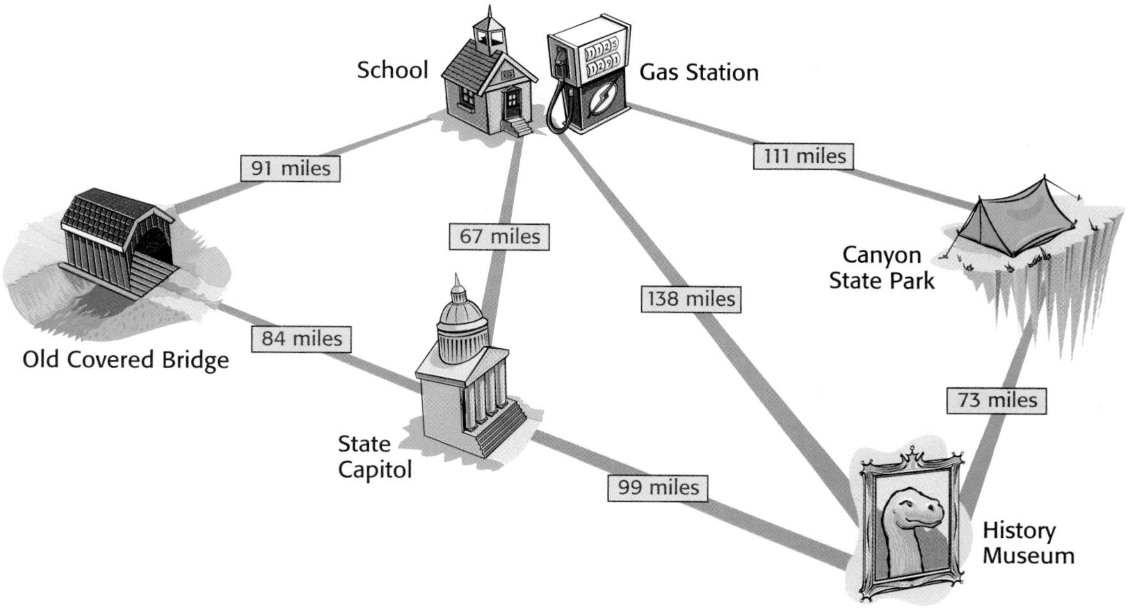

1. **Decision Making** Choose the places you'd like your class to visit.

2. **Recording Data** Make your own travel log like this one to show where you'll go.

Travel Log		
Travel	Distance	Miles Remaining for Travel
School to Bridge	91 miles	350 − 91 = 259
Bridge to State Capitol	84 miles	259 − 84 = 175
State Capitol to School	67 miles	175 − 67 = 108

3. **Explain Your Thinking** How did you know how many more miles you could travel after each stop?

4. **Critical Thinking** Is there another route you could have taken that would have allowed you to travel to more places? Explain.

REVIEW/TEST

Math Magazine

The Puzzle of Magic Squares **The idea of magic squares is thousands of years old. According to legend, the first magic square was found on a turtle's shell in ancient China. Since then, people all over the world have played with and thought about magic squares.**

The mystery about magic squares is that the numbers in any row, column or diagonal add up to the same sum. The sum is called the magic constant.

In this square, the magic constant is 15.

1. All the rows add up to 15.

4	9	2	$4 + 9 + 2 = 15$
3	5	7	$3 + 5 + 7 = 15$
8	1	6	$8 + 1 + 6 = 15$

2. All the columns add up to 15.

4	9	2
3	5	7
8	1	6

$2 + 7 + 6 = 15$

$9 + 5 + 1 = 15$

$4 + 3 + 8 = 15$

3. All the diagonals add up to 15.

$8 + 5 + 2 = 15$

4	9	2
3	5	7
8	1	6

$4 + 5 + 6 = 15$

You can use subtraction to discover other magic constants!

Try These!

Find the missing numbers in each magic square. Write the magic constant.

1.

8	?	4
1	5	?
?	7	2

Magic Constant = ■

2.

9	?	11
?	8	6
5	12	?

Magic Constant = ■

3.

?	70	?
90	50	10
40	?	80

Magic Constant = ■

CHAPTERS 1–4

Cumulative Review

Test Prep Strategy: Eliminate Choices

Check the ones digit first.

What is the difference of 632 and 120?

Ⓐ 521 Ⓑ 512 Ⓒ 510 Ⓓ 752

If I subtract 0 from 2 ones, I will get 2 ones. So, eliminate Ⓐ and Ⓒ. The difference of 632 and 120 is less than 632. Eliminate Ⓓ. The answer is Ⓑ.

Test Prep Strategies

- Read Carefully
- Follow Directions
- Make Smart Choices
- Eliminate Choices
- Work Backward from an Answer

Write the letter of the correct answer. Eliminate choices or use any strategy to help.

1. Armando has 118 newspapers to deliver on his route. If he delivers 65 papers, how many does he have left?

   Ⓐ 183 Ⓑ 163 Ⓒ 53 Ⓓ 153

2. What is the difference of 546 and 123?

   Ⓐ 429 Ⓑ 569 Ⓒ 679 Ⓓ 423

3. Mei bought a map of Carlsbad Caverns for $3.95 and a pin for $1.79. How much money did she spend?

   Ⓐ $2.24 Ⓑ $4.66 Ⓒ $5.74 Ⓓ $6.00

4. What is the sum of 790 and 318?

   Ⓐ 472 Ⓑ 1,108 Ⓒ 3,708 Ⓓ 5,970

Use the graph to solve **5** and **6**.

Length of Water Animals

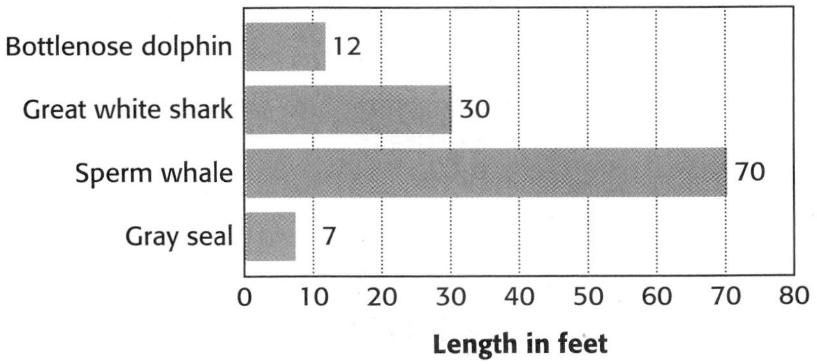

5. Which animal is 18 feet longer than a bottlenose dolphin?

   Ⓐ great white shark
   Ⓑ gray seal
   Ⓒ sperm whale
   Ⓓ not here

6. How much longer is a sperm whale than a great white shark?

   Ⓐ 63 feet Ⓑ 58 feet Ⓒ 100 feet Ⓓ 40 feet

DATA FILE

Chapter 5

Multiplication Concepts and Facts

SECTION A

Understanding Multiplication 203

Be crafty when you buy art supplies! Here are some arts and crafts items. Which two items cost the same amount?

Craft Supplies	
Item	**Price**
Glue (1 bottle)	$2
Pearl-colored beads (1 bag)	$4
Wired ribbon (1 roll)	$7
Pipe cleaners (1 box)	$3
Yarn (1 roll)	$6
Paints (1 box)	$5
Google eyes (1 bag)	$2

Christine's craft creations include beaded bracelets and rings.
Page 203

SECTION B

Multiplying with 0, 1, 2, 5, and 9 as Factors

211

Everyone wants a part in a puppet play. Which story needs the most puppets?

Finger Puppet Characters	
Charlotte's Web	● ● ● ● ●
Jumanji	● ● ● ● ● ● ● ● ●
More Stories Julian Tells	● ●
Mufaro's Beautiful Daughters	● ● ● ●
Ramona Forever	● ● ●
Winnie-the-Pooh	● ● ● ● ◖

● = 2 puppets

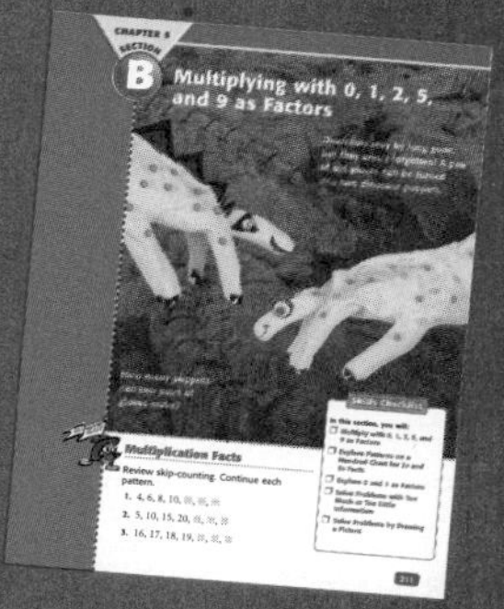

Gloves become dinosaur puppets.
Page 211

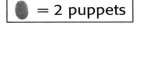

Surfing the World Wide Web!

Want to have fun with arts and crafts? Check out the World Wide Web for art projects. Start at **www.mathsurf.com/3/ch5**. Use the data you find to make a materials list for a group project.

TEAM PROJECT
Tale of a Pig

Materials

yogurt container, beans, construction paper, pipe cleaners, glue

In this arts and crafts project each member of your team will make a pig. Help your group by collecting the materials needed for the pig's body, eyes, ears, nose, legs, or tail.

Make a Plan

- Which material will you help collect for your group?
- How many pigs will your group make?

Carry It Out

1. Make a table to decide how many of each kind of material your group will need.

	Number Needed for One Pig	Number Needed for Group
Containers for body	1	
Beans for eyes	2	
Paper for ears	2	
Pipe cleaners for legs and tail	5	
Paper for nose	1	

2. Make your pig.

Talk About It

- How did you find the total number of each kind of material your group needed?

Present the Project

- Show your pig to the class. Explain how you used multiplication or addition to make your pig.

CHAPTER 5
SECTION

A Understanding Multiplication

Christine makes beaded jewelry like bracelets, anklets, and rings.

If she uses the same number of beads on each bracelet, how could you find the number of beads she needs for 5 bracelets?

Multiplication

Review addition. Find each sum.

1. $7 + 7 + 7$ **2.** $6 + 6 + 6$

3. $4 + 4 + 4 + 4$ **4.** $5 + 5 + 5 + 5$

5. $2 + 2 + 2 + 2 + 2$ **6.** $3 + 3 + 3$

Skills Checklist

In this section, you will:

- ❒ Explore Multiplication
- ❒ Write Multiplication Sentences
- ❒ Explore Multiplication Stories

Exploring Equal Groups

Problem Solving Connection
- Use Objects/ Act It Out
- Draw a Picture

Materials
counters

Explore

Christine makes beaded jewelry for her friends. She uses beads and string to make bracelets and anklets.

Christine makes rings, bracelets, and anklets in Kailua, Hawaii.

Problem Solving Hint
Use objects to show groups of beads.

Work Together

Use counters or draw pictures to solve.

1. Christine wants to make 6 bracelets like these.
   a. How many red beads should be on each bracelet?
   b. How many red beads does Christine need in all?
2. Christine wants to make 3 anklets like this one.
   a. How many blue beads should be on each anklet?
   b. How many blue beads does Christine need in all?

3. Write your own problem about Christine.

Talk About It

4. Tell how you found how many red beads were needed for 6 bracelets.
5. Tell how you found how many blue beads were needed for 3 anklets.

Connect

When you put together equal groups, you can use repeated addition.

$5 + 5 + 5 + 5 = 20$

4 rows of 5 equals 20.

$5 + 5 + 5 + 5 = 20$

4 groups of 5 equals 20.

Practice

Copy and complete.

1. 

a. ■ + ■ + ■ = ■

b. ■ groups of ■ equals ■.

2. 

a. ■ + ■ + ■ + ■ = ■

b. ■ rows of ■ equals ■.

3. 

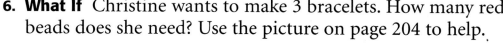

a. ■ + ■ + ■ = ■

b. ■ groups of ■ equals ■.

4. 

a. ■ + ■ + ■ = ■

b. ■ rows of ■ equals ■.

5. Reasoning Do these counters show equal groups? Explain.

6. What If Christine wants to make 3 bracelets. How many red beads does she need? Use the picture on page 204 to help.

7. Geometry Readiness Continue the pattern. Describe what the next two beads will look like.

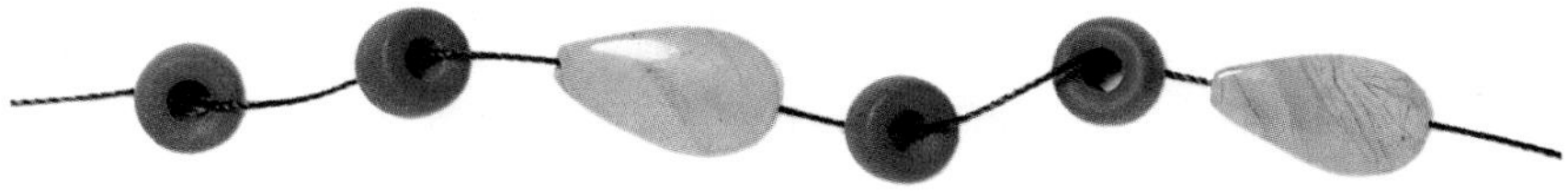

8. Journal Draw a picture and write an addition sentence to show 3 groups of 4 beads. Then tell how many beads there are all together.

Chapter 5
Lesson
2

Writing Multiplication Sentences

You Will Learn
how to write multiplication sentences

Vocabulary

array
objects arranged in rows and columns

factor
one of the numbers multiplied

product
the number obtained when multiplying

Learn

These students are growing grass in eggshells.

When you put together equal groups, you can multiply.

You can show multiplication using equal groups or an **array**.

Example 1

Equal Groups

$2 + 2 + 2 + 2 + 2 + 2 = 12$

6 groups of 2

Say: 6 times 2 equals 12

Write: $6 \times 2 = 12$ (multiplication sentence)

6 ↑ factor, 2 ↑ factor, 12 ↑ product

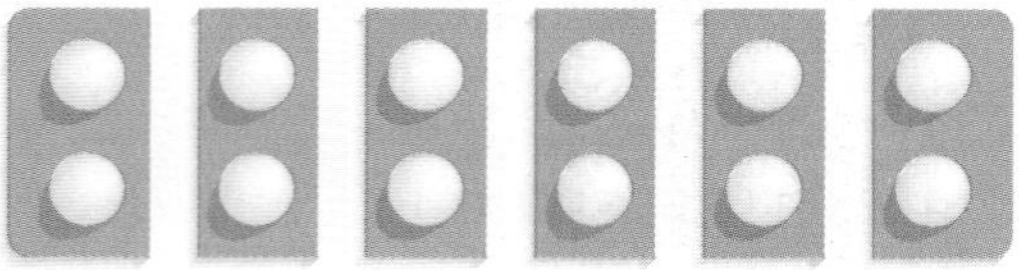

Example 2

Array

$6 + 6 = 12$

2 rows of 6

Say: 2 times 6 equals 12

Write: $2 \times 6 = 12$

2 ↑ factor, 6 ↑ factor, 12 ↑ product

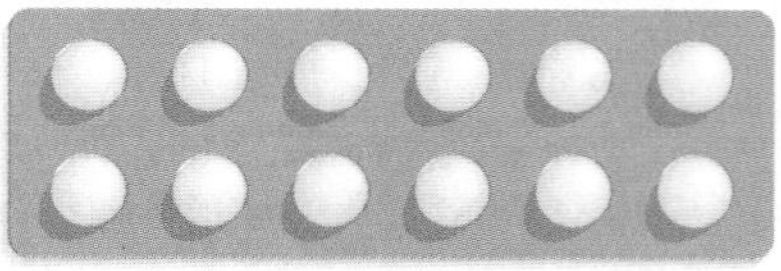

Math Tip
Since you are putting together equal groups, you can add *or* multiply.

You can multiply two **factors** in any order and get the same **product**.

Talk About It

Is the product of 2×3 the same as the product of 3×2? Explain.

Check

Copy and complete.

1. 

   a. ■ + ■ = ■

   b. ■ × ■ = ■

2. 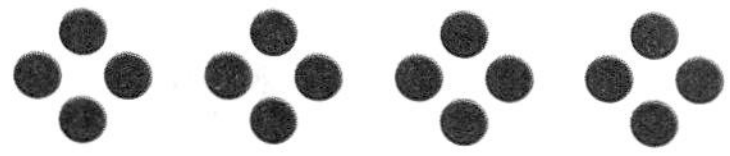

   a. ■ + ■ + ■ + ■ = ■

   b. ■ × ■ = ■

3. **Reasoning** Can you multiply to find the sum of 2 + 2 + 3? Explain.

Practice

Skills and Reasoning

Copy and complete.

4. 

   a. ■ + ■ + ■ = ■

   b. ■ × ■ = ■

5. 

   a. ■ + ■ + ■ = ■

   b. ■ × ■ = ■

6. 

   a. ■ + ■ + ■ + ■ = ■

   b. ■ × ■ = ■

7. Draw a picture that shows 2 × 7. Find the product.
8. Can you multiply to find the total of 7 + 7 + 7 + 7? Explain.

Problem Solving and Applications

9. **Science** Armadillos always have 4 babies at a time. Suppose 5 armadillos have babies. How many babies are there?
10. Joey has a garden with 4 green plants, 6 flowering plants, and 1 sunflower plant. How many plants does Joey have?

Mixed Review and Test Prep

Add or subtract.

11. 4 + 4 + 4 **12.** 8 + 8 + 8 **13.** 12 − 5 **14.** 5 + 5 + 5

15. 17 − 8 **16.** 13 − 7 **17.** 6 + 6 + 6 + 6 **18.** 15 − 6

19. What is the sum of \$1.05 and \$3.63?

Ⓐ \$4.67 Ⓑ \$4.68 Ⓒ \$4.78 Ⓓ 468

Exploring Multiplication Stories

Problem Solving Connection
- Draw a Picture
- Use Objects/ Act It Out

Materials
counters

Explore

Julie wrote a multiplication story to show $2 \times 9 = 18$.

I borrowed 2 boxes of crayons from my friend. She told me there were 9 crayons in each box. When I dropped them by mistake, I thought "how many crayons will I have to pick up?"

Try writing your own multiplication stories. You may use counters to help you solve them.

Math Tip
Make sure your story has a question to answer.

Work Together

1. Write your own story for $2 \times 9 = 18$.
2. Write a multiplication story for each and solve.
   a. 7×2 **b.** 5×3 **c.** 8×4

Talk About It

3. Tell how your story for $2 \times 9 = 18$ is like Julie's story. Tell how it is different.
4. Explain how you know your stories are multiplication stories.

Connect

Here are two multiplication stories. Each has equal groups.

Mai had a bag of peanuts to share with her friends. She gave 3 friends 4 peanuts each. How many peanuts did Mai give away?

$3 \times 4 = 12$

Mai gave away 12 peanuts.

Tyler planted 6 rows of cabbage plants. Each row had 5 cabbage plants. How many cabbage plants did he plant?

$6 \times 5 = 30$

Tyler planted 30 cabbage plants.

Practice

Write a multiplication story for each. You may use counters to solve.

1. 5×5 **2.** 3×4 **3.** 2×6 **4.** 3×7

5. Money Tyler has 7 five-dollar bills. A set of gardening tools costs 25 dollars. Does Tyler have enough money to buy the tools? Explain.

6. Science Each year in the fall, house martins fly south. In one day they can fly for 8 hours. How many hours can a house martin fly in 3 days?

House Martin

7. Social Studies Early American carriages were pulled by a team of 6 horses. Each horse wore 4 horseshoes. How many horseshoes were needed for 1 team?

8. Using Data Mai wants to buy a package of pearl-colored beads and a box of pipe cleaners. How much will she spend? Use the Data File on page 200 to solve.

9. Each person in Mai's group brought 3 buttons to class. There are 5 people in Mai's group. How many buttons were brought to class?

10. Science A termite weighs about 3 milligrams. About how many milligrams would 5 termites weigh?

11. What If Yolanda has 3 roses. Marissa has 4 times as many roses as Yolanda. How many roses does Marissa have?

12. Journal Draw a picture to show what 3×4 means. Write about your picture using these words: factor, product, and multiply.

SECTION A
Review and Practice

Vocabulary Use $3 \times 5 = 15$ to answer **1–3.**

1. Write the product.
2. Write the factors.
3. Show the multiplication sentence with an array.

(Lessons 1 and 2) Copy and complete.

4. 

   a. ■ + ■ + ■ = ■
   b. ■ groups of ■ equals ■.
   c. ■ × ■ = ■

5. 

   a. ■ + ■ = ■
   b. ■ rows of ■ equals ■.
   c. ■ × ■ = ■

6. 

   a. ■ + ■ = ■
   b. ■ groups of ■ equals ■.
   c. ■ × ■ = ■

7. 

   a. ■ + ■ + ■ = ■
   b. ■ groups of ■ equals ■.
   c. ■ × ■ = ■

8. **Science** A spider lives for about 3 years. A snake can live 4 times as long as a spider. About how long can a snake live?
9. Dennis has a garden with 3 rows of plants. If there are 5 plants in each row, how many plants are in the garden?
10. **Reasoning** Is the product of 4×5 the same as the product of 5×4? Explain.

(Lesson 3) Write a multiplication story for each. You may use counters to solve.

11. 6×5 **12.** 2×7 **13.** 3×6 **14.** 2×8

15. **Journal** When can you use multiplication instead of addition to find a total? Give an example.

Skills Checklist

In this section, you have:

- ☑ **Explored Multiplication**
- ☑ **Written Multiplication Sentences**
- ☑ **Explored Multiplication Stories**

CHAPTER 5

SECTION

B Multiplying with 0, 1, 2, 5, and 9 as Factors

Dinosaurs may be long gone, but they aren't forgotten! A pair of old gloves can be turned into two dinosaur puppets.

How many puppets can two pairs of gloves make?

Skills Checklist

In this section, you will:

- ❐ Multiply with 0, 1, 2, 5, and 9 as Factors
- ❐ Explore Patterns on a Hundred Chart for 2s and 5s Facts
- ❐ Explore 0 and 1 as Factors
- ❐ Solve Problems with Too Much or Too Little Information
- ❐ Solve Problems by Drawing a Picture

Multiplication Facts

Review skip-counting. Continue each pattern.

1. 4, 6, 8, 10, ■, ■, ■
2. 5, 10, 15, 20, ■, ■, ■
3. 16, 17, 18, 19, ■, ■, ■

Chapter 5
Lesson
4

2 as a Factor

You Will Learn
how to multiply with 2 as a factor

Learn

You can turn old gloves into new toys! Rhonda brought four pairs of dishwashing gloves to the Craft Club. How many dinosaur puppets can the club members make?

Since you are putting together 4 groups of 2, you can multiply.

$4 \times 2 = \square$

You can skip count by 2s on a number line to help you find the product.

$2 + 2 + 2 + 2 = 8$

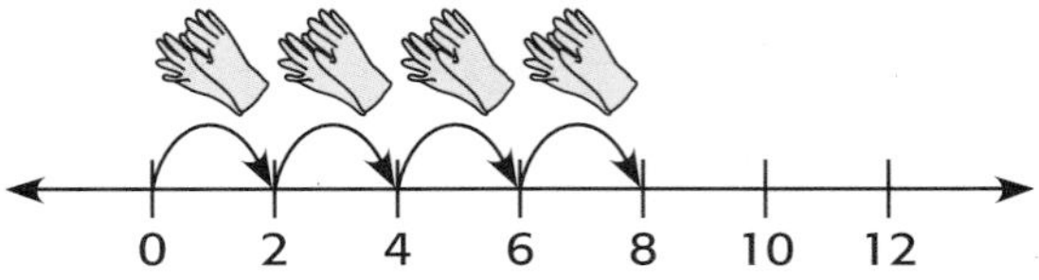

$4 \times 2 = 8$

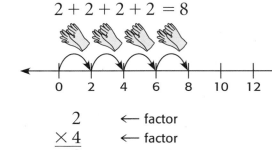

You can also write:

$$\begin{array}{r} 2 \\ \times 4 \\ \hline 8 \end{array}$$
← factor
← factor
← product

Math Tip
You can write 4 times 2 as 4×2 or $\begin{array}{r} 2 \\ \times 4 \\ \hline \end{array}$

So, the club can make 8 dinosaur puppets.

Talk About It

How is skip counting like adding equal groups?

Check

Find each product.

1. 6×2 **2.** 2×8 **3.** 9×2 **4.** 2×7 **5.** 2×4

6. Find the product of 2 and 2. **7.** Multiply 3 and 2.

8. **Reasoning** How can $5 \times 2 = 10$ help you find 6×2?

Practice

Skills and Reasoning

Find each product.

9. 2×4 **10.** 7×2 **11.** 2×6 **12.** 1×2 **13.** 2×9

14. 2×5 **15.** 2×1 **16.** 2×8 **17.** 5×2 **18.** 2×3

19. $\begin{array}{r} 3 \\ \times 2 \\ \hline \end{array}$ **20.** $\begin{array}{r} 8 \\ \times 2 \\ \hline \end{array}$ **21.** $\begin{array}{r} 2 \\ \times 2 \\ \hline \end{array}$ **22.** $\begin{array}{r} 6 \\ \times 2 \\ \hline \end{array}$ **23.** $\begin{array}{r} 2 \\ \times 7 \\ \hline \end{array}$

24. Find the product of 9 and 2. **25.** Find the product of 4 and 2.

26. Is the product of 2×4 the same as the sum of $4 + 4$? Explain.

27. Draw a picture to show that the product of 2×8 is the same as the product of 8×2.

Problem Solving and Applications

Using Data Use the Data File on page 200 to answer **28–30.**

28. The Craft Club needs google eyes for their dinosaurs. How much would it cost for 8 bags of google eyes?

29. Rhonda has \$3 to spend. What items can she buy?

30. How much would it cost to buy 2 rolls of wired ribbon?

31. **Language Arts** A *tandem* bike can carry 2 riders. How many riders can ride on 5 tandem bikes?

Mixed Review and Test Prep

Patterns Complete each pattern.

32. 5, 10, ■, ■, 25 **33.** 0, 5, ■, ■, 20 **34.** ■, ■, 20, 25, 30

35. 40, 45, ■, ■, 60 **36.** 0, 9, 18, ■, ■ **37.** 27, 36, 45, ■, ■

Add or subtract.

38. $196 - 115$ **39.** $551 - 259$ **40.** $625 - 439$ **41.** $232 - 116$

42. $296 + 238$ **43.** $121 + 752$ **44.** $476 + 382$ **45.** $508 + 207$

46. What is the sum of $890 + 257$?

Ⓐ 1,417 Ⓑ 1,174 Ⓒ 1,147 Ⓓ 1,047

5 as a Factor

You Will Learn
how to multiply with 5 as a factor

Learn

Paintings aren't always found in picture frames. Arie paints his designs on sweatshirts, pants, hats, and socks. Suppose it takes Arie 5 hours to paint 1 sweatshirt. How long will it take him to finish 6 sweatshirts?

Arie from Chicago, Illinois, likes to paint scenes of city life.

Since you want to find 6 groups of 5, you can multiply.

$$\begin{array}{r} 5 \\ \times\, 6 \\ \hline \square \end{array}$$

Skip count by 5s.

$5 + 5 + 5 + 5 + 5 + 5 = 30$

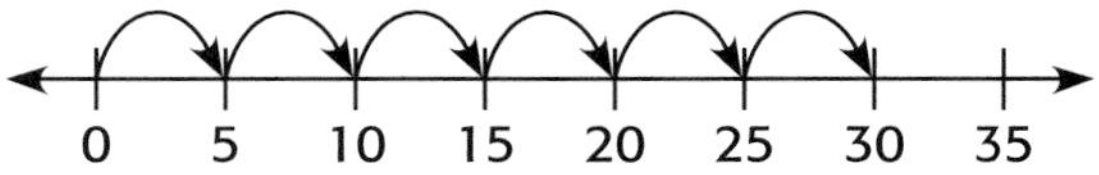

Remember
To skip count by 5s, count: 5, 10, 15 ...

$6 \times 5 = 30$

It will take Arie 30 hours to finish.

Talk About It

Tell at least two ways to find 5×2.

Check

Find each product.

1. 5×5 **2.** 2×5 **3.** 5×6 **4.** 5×7 **5.** 9×5

6. Find the product of 5 and 8. **7.** Multiply 5 by 1.

8. Reasoning How could you use $3 \times 5 = 15$ to find 4×5?

Practice

Skills and Reasoning

Find each product.

9. 5×4 **10.** 5×2 **11.** 6×5 **12.** 5×8 **13.** 5×9

14. 2×9 **15.** 2×2 **16.** 5×3 **17.** 7×5 **18.** 2×7

19. $\begin{array}{r} 3 \\ \times 5 \\ \hline \end{array}$ **20.** $\begin{array}{r} 2 \\ \times 4 \\ \hline \end{array}$ **21.** $\begin{array}{r} 2 \\ \times 5 \\ \hline \end{array}$ **22.** $\begin{array}{r} 6 \\ \times 2 \\ \hline \end{array}$ **23.** $\begin{array}{r} 2 \\ \times 3 \\ \hline \end{array}$

24. $\begin{array}{r} 5 \\ \times 9 \\ \hline \end{array}$ **25.** $\begin{array}{r} 6 \\ \times 5 \\ \hline \end{array}$ **26.** $\begin{array}{r} 7 \\ \times 5 \\ \hline \end{array}$ **27.** $\begin{array}{r} 2 \\ \times 8 \\ \hline \end{array}$ **28.** $\begin{array}{r} 5 \\ \times 5 \\ \hline \end{array}$

29. Find the product of 5 and 4.

30. Multiply 5 by 6.

31. If you know the product of 7×5, how can you use it to find 8×5?

32. Is the product of 5×5 greater than or less than the product of 4×5? Explain.

Remember
A week has 7 days.

Problem Solving and Applications

33. What If Arie paints sweatshirts for 2 friends. How many hours will it take Arie to make both sweatshirts? Use information on page 214 to help.

34. Time Eva eats 5 carrots each day. How many carrots does she eat in a week?

35. Money Suppose you have 6 nickels in your pocket. How much money do you have?

36. Music Nara makes banjos in her shop. Each banjo has 5 strings. How many strings does she need for 4 banjos?

Mixed Review and Test Prep

Subtract.

37. $58 - 56$ **38.** $98 - 12$ **39.** $42 - 26$ **40.** $39 - 16$

41. $27 - 11$ **42.** $70 - 39$ **43.** $487 - 251$ **44.** $699 - 347$

45. Money Corey bought stickers that cost \$0.76. He paid with \$1.00. How much change should he get?

Ⓐ \$0.24 Ⓑ \$0.14 Ⓒ \$0.23 Ⓓ \$0.26

Exploring Patterns on a Hundred Chart: 2s and 5s

Problem Solving Connection
- Look for a Pattern
- Use Objects/ Act It Out

Materials
- hundred chart
- red and blue pencils

Vocabulary
multiple
the product of a given whole number and any other whole number

Explore

You can use patterns on a hundred chart to help you learn multiplication facts.

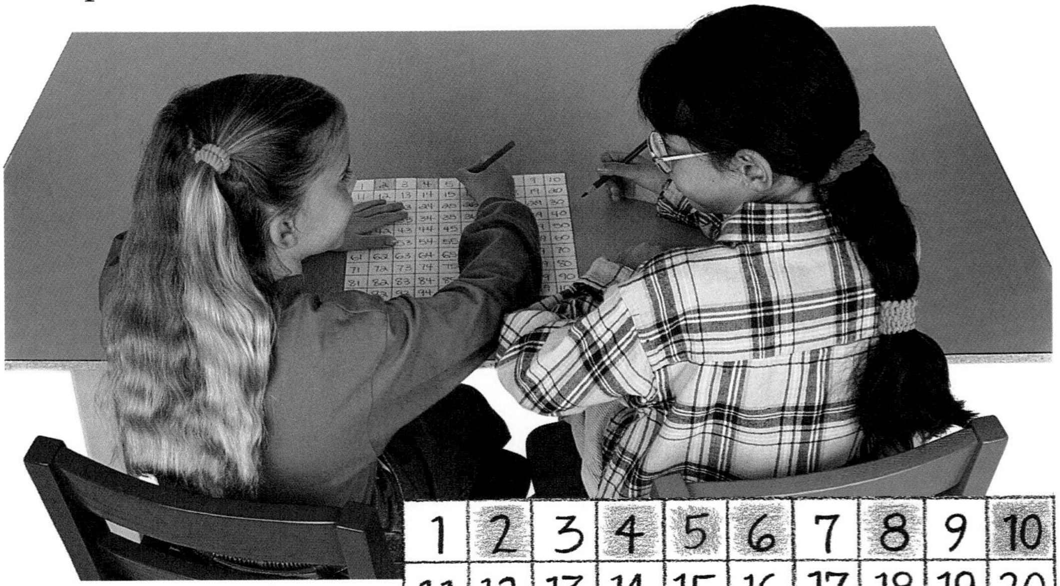

1	2	3	4	5	6	7	8	9	10
11	12	13	14	15	16	17	18	19	20
21	22	23	24	25	26	27	28	29	30
31	32	33	34	35	36	37	38	39	40
41	42	43	44	45	46	47	48	49	50
51	52	53	54	55	56	57	58	59	60

Work Together

Use a hundred chart. Look for patterns as you shade in numbers.

1. Skip count by 2s to find **multiples** of 2. Shade each multiple of 2 red. What patterns do you notice?
2. Skip count by 5s to find multiples of 5. Shade each multiple of 5 blue. What patterns do you notice?

Math Tip
Finding patterns can help you remember multiplication facts.

Talk About It

3. Which numbers are shaded twice? What do you notice about these numbers?
4. What other patterns do you see on the hundred chart?

Connect

There are patterns in the multiples of numbers.

2s Facts	
$0 \times 2 = 0$	$5 \times 2 = 10$
$1 \times 2 = 2$	$6 \times 2 = 12$
$2 \times 2 = 4$	$7 \times 2 = 14$
$3 \times 2 = 6$	$8 \times 2 = 16$
$4 \times 2 = 8$	$9 \times 2 = 18$

Multiples of 2 end in 0, 2, 4, 6, or 8.

5s Facts	
$0 \times 5 = 0$	$5 \times 5 = 25$
$1 \times 5 = 5$	$6 \times 5 = 30$
$2 \times 5 = 10$	$7 \times 5 = 35$
$3 \times 5 = 15$	$8 \times 5 = 40$
$4 \times 5 = 20$	$9 \times 5 = 45$

Multiples of 5 end in 0 or 5.

Practice

Find each product.

1. 5×6 **2.** 3×2 **3.** 5×3 **4.** 5×8 **5.** 1×2

6. 2×6 **7.** 5×1 **8.** 5×5 **9.** 2×3 **10.** 2×9

11. 5×9 **12.** 2×2 **13.** 8×2 **14.** 4×5 **15.** 3×5

16. $\begin{array}{r} 4 \\ \times 5 \\ \hline \end{array}$ **17.** $\begin{array}{r} 5 \\ \times 2 \\ \hline \end{array}$ **18.** $\begin{array}{r} 5 \\ \times 7 \\ \hline \end{array}$ **19.** $\begin{array}{r} 2 \\ \times 7 \\ \hline \end{array}$ **20.** $\begin{array}{r} 4 \\ \times 2 \\ \hline \end{array}$

21. $\begin{array}{r} 5 \\ \times 9 \\ \hline \end{array}$ **22.** $\begin{array}{r} 2 \\ \times 8 \\ \hline \end{array}$ **23.** $\begin{array}{r} 5 \\ \times 1 \\ \hline \end{array}$ **24.** $\begin{array}{r} 2 \\ \times 2 \\ \hline \end{array}$ **25.** $\begin{array}{r} 5 \\ \times 8 \\ \hline \end{array}$

26. Find the product of 7 and 5.

27. Multiply 2 and 8.

28. Write three multiples of 2.

29. Write three multiples of 5.

30. **Reasoning** Miranda says that 32 is a multiple of 5 because the digits 3 and 2 add to 5. Do you agree? Explain.

Patterns Continue each pattern.

31. 16, 18, 20, ▒, ▒, ▒

32. 2, 4, 6, ▒, ▒, ▒

33. **Money** Roberto has a handful of nickels. Could he have 45¢? Explain.

34. **Journal** Describe a pattern you found on the hundred chart when looking at multiples of 2. Do you think this pattern will continue?

Chapter 5
Lesson
7

Exploring 0 and 1 as Factors

Problem Solving Connection
Look for a Pattern

Materials
calculator

Problem Solving Hint
Check to see if any patterns you notice also work for other numbers.

Explore

Patterns can help you multiply with the factors 0 and 1.

Work Together

1. Copy and complete each table. Look for patterns. You may use a calculator to help.

   a. Multiply with 1 as a factor.

$1 \times 1 = \square$	$32 \times 1 = \square$
$1 \times 2 = \square$	$1 \times 486 = \square$
$15 \times 1 = \square$	$1{,}536 \times 1 = \square$

   b. Multiply with 0 as a factor.

$0 \times 1 = \square$	$22 \times 0 = \square$
$0 \times 3 = \square$	$0 \times 445 = \square$
$10 \times 0 = \square$	$2{,}693 \times 0 = \square$

2. Make up your own multiplication sentences using 1 and 0 as factors.

Talk About It

3. Tell what you noticed when you multiplied with 1 as a factor.

4. Tell what you noticed when you multiplied with 0 as a factor.

Connect

The product of any number and 1 is that number.

$5 \times 1 = 5$ $\quad$ $1 \times 101 = 101$ $\quad$ $7{,}322 \times 1 = 7{,}322$

The product of any number and 0 is 0.

$4 \times 0 = 0$ $\quad$ $0 \times 2{,}000 = 0$ $\quad$ $328 \times 0 = 0$

Practice

Find each product.

1. 0×6 **2.** 2×1 **3.** 5×2 **4.** 0×8 **5.** 1×5

6. 2×8 **7.** 1×6 **8.** 5×4 **9.** 9×0 **10.** 8×5

11. $\begin{array}{r} 4 \\ \times 1 \\ \hline \end{array}$ **12.** $\begin{array}{r} 3 \\ \times 2 \\ \hline \end{array}$ **13.** $\begin{array}{r} 7 \\ \times 0 \\ \hline \end{array}$ **14.** $\begin{array}{r} 5 \\ \times 3 \\ \hline \end{array}$ **15.** $\begin{array}{r} 1 \\ \times 7 \\ \hline \end{array}$

16. $\begin{array}{r} 2 \\ \times 6 \\ \hline \end{array}$ **17.** $\begin{array}{r} 4 \\ \times 0 \\ \hline \end{array}$ **18.** $\begin{array}{r} 5 \\ \times 7 \\ \hline \end{array}$ **19.** $\begin{array}{r} 2 \\ \times 4 \\ \hline \end{array}$ **20.** $\begin{array}{r} 3 \\ \times 5 \\ \hline \end{array}$

21. Multiply 8 by 1. **22.** Find the product of 0 and 1.

23. **Reasoning** Which is greater, the product of your age times 0 or the product of your age times 1? Explain.

Copy and complete. Write $\times$ or $+$.

24. 6 ● 1 = 6 **25.** 6 ● 0 = 0 **26.** 6 ● 0 = 6 **27.** 6 ● 1 = 7

28. **Health** Foods that are low in fat are healthier for you. A serving of celery has 0 grams of fat. How much fat does 7 servings of celery have?

29. **Geometry Readiness** Continue the pattern.

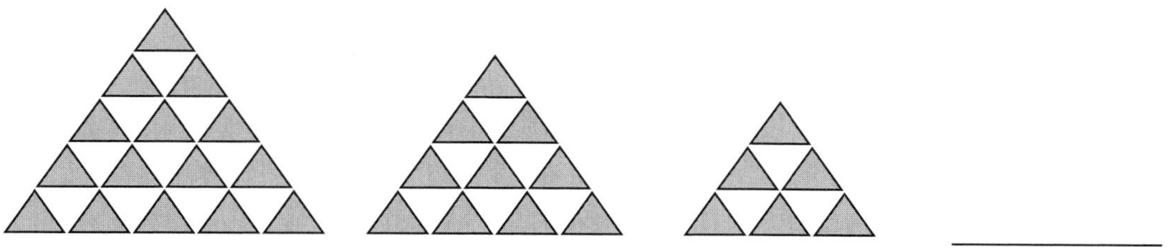

30. **Journal** Suppose you are selling cookies for $7 a box. How much money would you make if you sold 1 box? If you sold 0 boxes? Explain.

Chapter 5
Lesson
8

9 as a Factor

You Will Learn
how to use patterns to multiply with 9 as a factor

Learn

Carlo and Ben used patterns to find the product of 6×9.

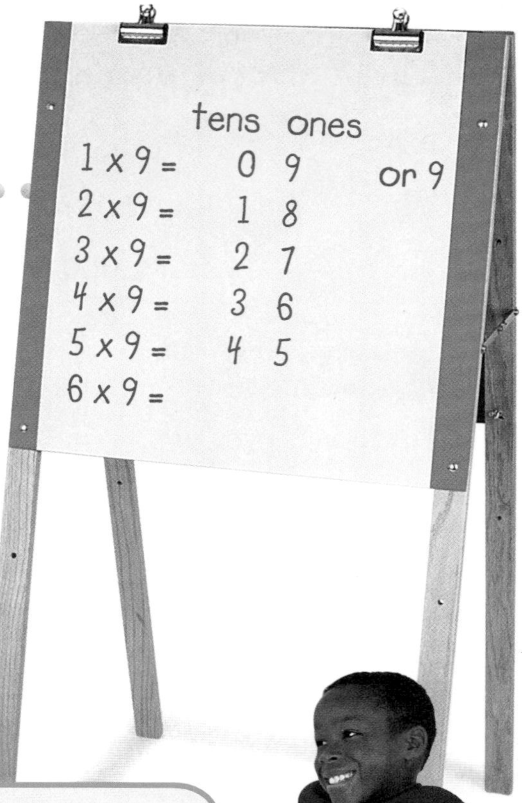

The tens digit in each product counts up by 1. So, the next tens digit is 5.

The ones digits count back by 1. So, the next ones digit is 4.

$6 \times 9 = 54$

The tens digit is 1 less than the first factor. So, the tens digit is 5.

Also, the sum of the tens and ones digits is 9.

So, $6 \times 9 = 54$.

Talk About It

Explain how patterns can help you find 7×9.

Math Tip
Look for patterns in the ones place *and* the tens place.

Check

Find each product.

1. 5×9 **2.** 9×2 **3.** 9×8 **4.** 4×9

5. Find the product of 3 and 9. **6.** Multiply 9 by 6.

7. **Reasoning** Carlo says that the product of 9×9 is 18 because the tens digit and the ones digit add to 9. Is he correct? Explain.

Practice

Skills and Reasoning

Find each product.

8. 9×7 **9.** 6×2 **10.** 9×3 **11.** 5×7 **12.** 4×5

13. 8×9 **14.** 2×7 **15.** 8×5 **16.** 9×9 **17.** 5×3

18. 9×6 **19.** 9×8 **20.** 5×4 **21.** 2×8 **22.** 9×5

23. $\begin{array}{r} 3 \\ \times 9 \\ \hline \end{array}$ **24.** $\begin{array}{r} 5 \\ \times 0 \\ \hline \end{array}$ **25.** $\begin{array}{r} 2 \\ \times 9 \\ \hline \end{array}$ **26.** $\begin{array}{r} 9 \\ \times 1 \\ \hline \end{array}$ **27.** $\begin{array}{r} 9 \\ \times 0 \\ \hline \end{array}$

28. $\begin{array}{r} 9 \\ \times 5 \\ \hline \end{array}$ **29.** $\begin{array}{r} 6 \\ \times 9 \\ \hline \end{array}$ **30.** $\begin{array}{r} 7 \\ \times 9 \\ \hline \end{array}$ **31.** $\begin{array}{r} 9 \\ \times 4 \\ \hline \end{array}$ **32.** $\begin{array}{r} 8 \\ \times 1 \\ \hline \end{array}$

33. Find the product of 9 and 9. **34.** Multiply 9 by 6.

35. How can knowing $7 \times 9 = 63$ help you to find 8×9?

36. Is the product of 7×9 the same as the product of 9×7? Explain.

Problem Solving and Applications

37. Science When a bear sleeps in the winter, its heartbeat slows down to about 9 beats a minute. About how many times will its heart beat in 5 minutes?

38. Using Data Carlo's class wants to put on a finger puppet show of the story *Jumanji*. How many puppets will his class need? Use the Data File on page 201 to help solve.

Mixed Review and Test Prep

Add or subtract.

39. $700 - 156$ **40.** $562 + 381$ **41.** $307 - 225$ **42.** $132 + 689$

43. $642 - 271$ **44.** $436 + 498$ **45.** $205 - 173$ **46.** $53 + 153$

47. $529 - 469$ **48.** $828 + 106$ **49.** $176 - 117$ **50.** $358 + 275$

Patterns Continue the pattern.

51. 150, 125, 100, 75, ■, ■

Ⓐ 50, 35 Ⓑ 25, 50 Ⓒ 60, 50 Ⓓ 50, 25

STOP and Practice

Find each product.

1. 2×7	**2.** 5×3	**3.** 6×0	**4.** 8×9	**5.** 2×3
6. 5×1	**7.** 2×8	**8.** 9×3	**9.** 0×5	**10.** 5×9
11. 8×0	**12.** 1×2	**13.** 2×0	**14.** 9×6	**15.** 7×5
16. 3×1	**17.** 6×2	**18.** 9×2	**19.** 4×5	**20.** 0×4
21. $\begin{array}{r} 8 \\ \times 5 \\ \hline \end{array}$	**22.** $\begin{array}{r} 1 \\ \times 1 \\ \hline \end{array}$	**23.** $\begin{array}{r} 2 \\ \times 5 \\ \hline \end{array}$	**24.** $\begin{array}{r} 9 \\ \times 2 \\ \hline \end{array}$	**25.** $\begin{array}{r} 5 \\ \times 6 \\ \hline \end{array}$
26. $\begin{array}{r} 1 \\ \times 5 \\ \hline \end{array}$	**27.** $\begin{array}{r} 4 \\ \times 9 \\ \hline \end{array}$	**28.** $\begin{array}{r} 0 \\ \times 2 \\ \hline \end{array}$	**29.** $\begin{array}{r} 1 \\ \times 7 \\ \hline \end{array}$	**30.** $\begin{array}{r} 4 \\ \times 1 \\ \hline \end{array}$
31. $\begin{array}{r} 2 \\ \times 4 \\ \hline \end{array}$	**32.** $\begin{array}{r} 9 \\ \times 7 \\ \hline \end{array}$	**33.** $\begin{array}{r} 5 \\ \times 1 \\ \hline \end{array}$	**34.** $\begin{array}{r} 5 \\ \times 9 \\ \hline \end{array}$	**35.** $\begin{array}{r} 7 \\ \times 0 \\ \hline \end{array}$
36. $\begin{array}{r} 6 \\ \times 5 \\ \hline \end{array}$	**37.** $\begin{array}{r} 0 \\ \times 3 \\ \hline \end{array}$	**38.** $\begin{array}{r} 8 \\ \times 1 \\ \hline \end{array}$	**39.** $\begin{array}{r} 5 \\ \times 5 \\ \hline \end{array}$	**40.** $\begin{array}{r} 5 \\ \times 2 \\ \hline \end{array}$
41. $\begin{array}{r} 6 \\ \times 1 \\ \hline \end{array}$	**42.** $\begin{array}{r} 9 \\ \times 9 \\ \hline \end{array}$	**43.** $\begin{array}{r} 2 \\ \times 8 \\ \hline \end{array}$	**44.** $\begin{array}{r} 0 \\ \times 9 \\ \hline \end{array}$	**45.** $\begin{array}{r} 4 \\ \times 2 \\ \hline \end{array}$
46. $\begin{array}{r} 1 \\ \times 0 \\ \hline \end{array}$	**47.** $\begin{array}{r} 9 \\ \times 1 \\ \hline \end{array}$	**48.** $\begin{array}{r} 2 \\ \times 2 \\ \hline \end{array}$	**49.** $\begin{array}{r} 9 \\ \times 8 \\ \hline \end{array}$	**50.** $\begin{array}{r} 0 \\ \times 0 \\ \hline \end{array}$

Error Search

51. Find each product that is not correct. Write it correctly and explain the error.

a. $\begin{array}{r} 5 \\ \times 0 \\ \hline 5 \end{array}$	**b.** $\begin{array}{r} 5 \\ \times 1 \\ \hline 5 \end{array}$	**c.** $\begin{array}{r} 7 \\ \times 5 \\ \hline 12 \end{array}$	**d.** $\begin{array}{r} 1 \\ \times 8 \\ \hline 9 \end{array}$	**e.** $\begin{array}{r} 9 \\ \times 9 \\ \hline 0 \end{array}$	**f.** $\begin{array}{r} 6 \\ \times 2 \\ \hline 12 \end{array}$

"Oink! Oink!"

Multiply. Match each letter to its answer in the blank below to solve the riddle. Some letters are not used.

A healthy dog has a cold, wet nose.
What does a healthy pig have?

52. 2×6 [C] **53.** 9×4 [B] **54.** 5×5 [Y] **55.** 8×2 [L]

56. 1×9 [M] **57.** 5×3 [K] **58.** 7×9 [N] **59.** 0×5 [H]

60. 9×6 [E] **61.** 6×5 [A] **62.** 4×2 [D] **63.** 5×9 [I]

64. 5×4 [R] **65.** 2×5 [T] **66.** 3×9 [U] **67.** 2×7 [F]

68. 2×1 [Q] **69.** 9×8 [G] **70.** 2×9 [P] **71.** 7×5 [J]

___   ___ ___ ___ ___ ___   ___ ___ ___ ___

30   12 27 20 16 25   10 30 45 16

Number Sense Operations and Properties

Write + or ×.

72. 8 ● 0 = 8 **73.** 2 ● 6 = 12 **74.** 6 ● 1 = 6 **75.** 7 ● 0 = 0

76. 8 ● 2 = 10 **77.** 5 ● 1 = 6 **78.** 9 ● 5 = 45 **79.** 3 ● 0 = 3

80. 2 ● 4 = 8 **81.** 0 ● 4 = 4 **82.** 6 ● 5 = 11 **83.** 9 ● 1 = 9

Problem Solving

Analyze Word Problems: Too Much or Too Little Information

You Will Learn
how to decide which information is important when solving a problem

Learn

A male elk, or stag, grows two antlers. A stag is considered fully grown when it has 6 tines on each antler. Elk antlers may measure as much as 5 feet across.

How many tines are on the antlers of a fully grown stag?

Work Together

▶ Understand

What do you know?

What do you need to find out?

▶ Plan

What information do you need? — How many tines are on each antler. How many antlers are on a stag.

Is there any extra information? — You don't need to know how many feet across the antlers are.

▶ Solve

Multiply. — 2 antlers × 6 tines = 12 tines

What's the answer? — A fully grown stag has 12 tines.

▶ Look Back

Does your answer make sense?

Talk About It

How did you know which information you needed to answer the question? Explain.

Check

Decide if the problem has too much or too little information. Then solve.

Problem Solving
Understand
Plan
Solve
Look Back

1. Cougars can travel 20 feet in one leap, and 25 miles in a day. They can also see 6 times as well as humans in the late afternoon light. How many feet could a cougar travel in 2 leaps?

2. Elephants can be as tall as 13 feet. They eat 130 pounds of hay, fruit, and vegetables every day. How many pounds of hay do they eat in 3 days?

Problem Solving Practice

Decide if the problem has too much or too little information. Then solve.

3. Walruses are about 3 feet long when they are born. When they are fully grown they are about 11 feet. They have 4 inches of blubber beneath their skin. About how many feet longer is a full-grown walrus than a walrus when it is first born?

4. An ostrich weighs about 340 pounds and can move up to 15 feet in one stride. How many feet could an ostrich move in 2 strides?

5. Asian elephants have 4 toenails on each hind foot. African elephants have 3 toenails on each hind foot. How many toenails does an Asian elephant have on 2 hind feet?

6. Just like kangaroos, female koalas have a pouch where their babies stay after they are born. A baby koala is 1 inch long when it is born. It lives in its mother's pouch for 7 months. How many inches longer is a mother koala than a newborn koala?

7. A river hippo weighs about 2,500 pounds. It eats about 100 pounds of grass each night. A pygmy hippo weighs about 500 pounds. About how much more does a river hippo weigh than a pygmy hippo?

Problem Solving Strategies

- Use Objects/Act It Out
- Draw a Picture
- Look for a Pattern
- Guess and Check
- Use Logical Reasoning
- Make an Organized List
- Make a Table
- Solve a Simpler Problem
- Work Backward

Choose a Tool

Skills Practice Bank, page 522, Set 6

Chapter 5
Lesson
10

Problem Solving

Analyze Strategies: Draw a Picture

You Will Learn
how to draw a picture to solve problems

Learn

Aaron is making a necklace that will spell his name in letter beads. Between each letter, he will put 5 red beads. He will also put 5 red beads at each end of the name. How many red beads will he need for the necklace?

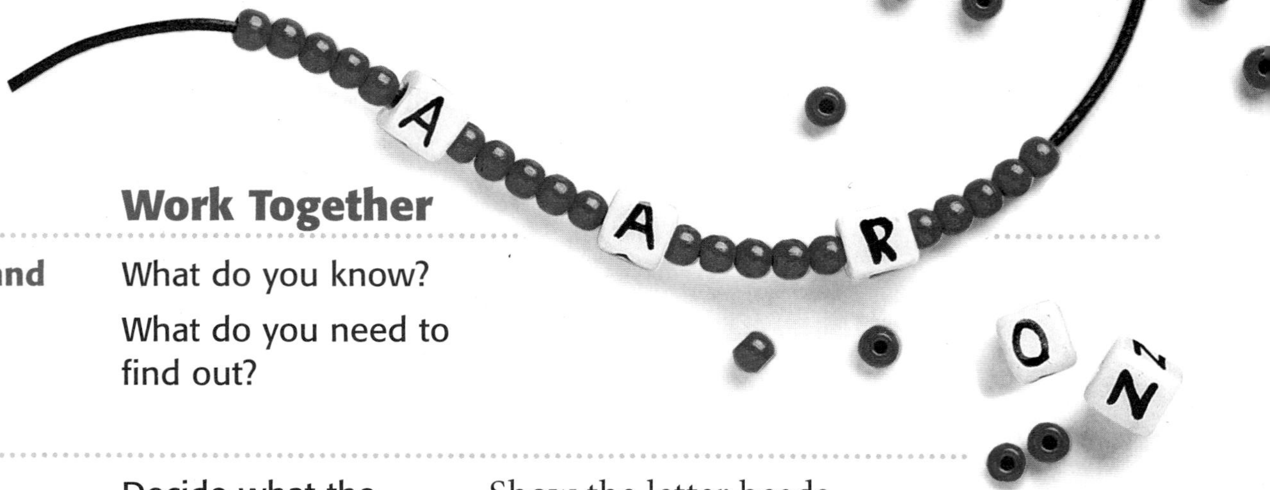

Work Together

▶ Understand

What do you know?

What do you need to find out?

▶ Plan

Decide what the picture needs to show.

Show the letter beads.
Show 5 red beads between each letter and at the beginning and end.

▶ Solve

Draw the picture.

There are 6 groups of 5 red beads.

Use the picture to solve.

$6 \times 5 = 30$

What's your answer?

Aaron needs 30 red beads for the necklace.

▶ Look Back

How can you check your answer?

Another Example

Aaron strings 4 beads on a bracelet. The blue bead is to the left of the gold bead. The red bead is to the left of the blue bead and to the right of the silver bead. Which beads are at the ends of the bracelet?

Draw a picture of the bracelet. Use letters for the beads.

What You Read	What You Do
a. The blue bead is to the left of the gold bead.	—— B —— G ——→
b. The red bead is to the left of the blue bead.	—— R – B —— G ——→
c. The red bead is to the right of the silver bead.	— S – R – B —— G ——→
d. Which beads are at the ends?	—(S)– R – B ——(G)——→

The silver bead and the gold bead are at the ends.

Talk About It

How did drawing pictures help to solve the problems?

Check

Draw a picture to help you solve.

1. Suppose you wanted to make a necklace with 9 strands of beads. The first strand has 2 green beads. The second strand has 7 blue beads. The third strand has 2 green beads, the fourth has 7 blue beads, and so on.
   - **a.** How many strands of blue beads will there be?
   - **b.** How many strands of green beads will there be?
   - **c.** How many blue beads will you use?
   - **d.** How many green beads will you use?
   - **e.** How many beads will you use in all?

2. Suppose you wanted to make a bracelet with the name April. You put 2 red beads between each letter and 4 red beads at each end. How many red beads would you need?

Problem Solving Practice

Apply the Strategy

Draw a picture to help you solve.

3. Annette plans a necklace that will have 8 beads. Beads 1 and 8 will be the same color, beads 2 and 7 will be the same color, and so on. She will not use more than 2 beads of the same color.
   a. How many different colors of beads will Annette use?
   b. Will any two of the same color of bead be next to each other? Explain.

   Necklace plan:

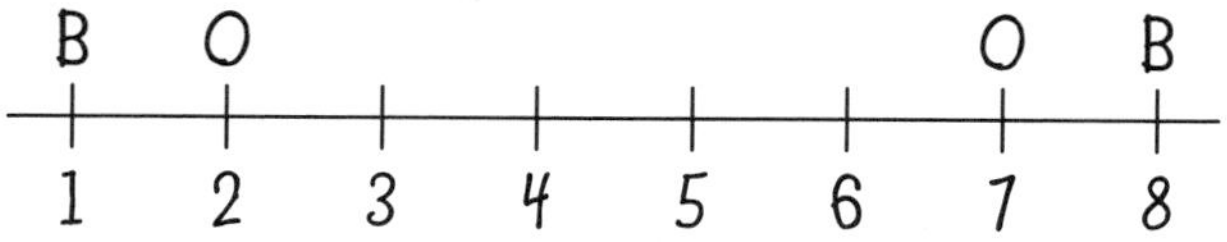

Problem Solving Strategies

- Use Objects/Act It Out
- Draw a Picture
- Look for a Pattern
- Guess and Check
- Use Logical Reasoning
- Make an Organized List
- Make a Table
- Solve a Simpler Problem
- Work Backward

Choose a Tool

Choose a Strategy

Draw a picture or use any strategy to solve.

4. The Craft Club made a banner of paper flowers. There were 9 rows. Here are the first 4 rows.
   a. How many flowers did they make to cover the banner?
   b. Suppose they decide to make the first and last flower of each row yellow. How many red flowers would they need?

5. Annette can use either small or large safety pins to make friendship pins. On each pin she can put one color of beads: blue, green, or silver. How many different kinds of pins can Annette make?

6. In a bracelet, Annette uses 5 more small beads than large beads. She uses 27 beads in all. How many of each kind of bead does she use?

Problem Solving and HISTORY

This timeline shows the dates for some inventions.

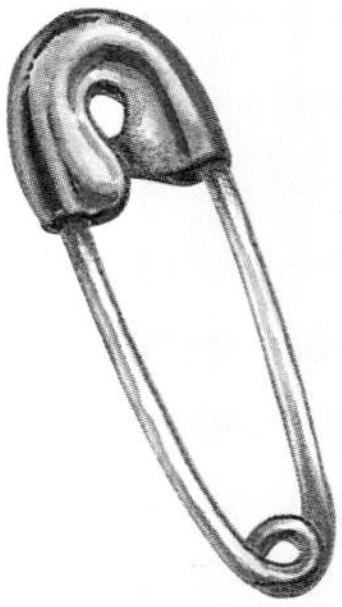

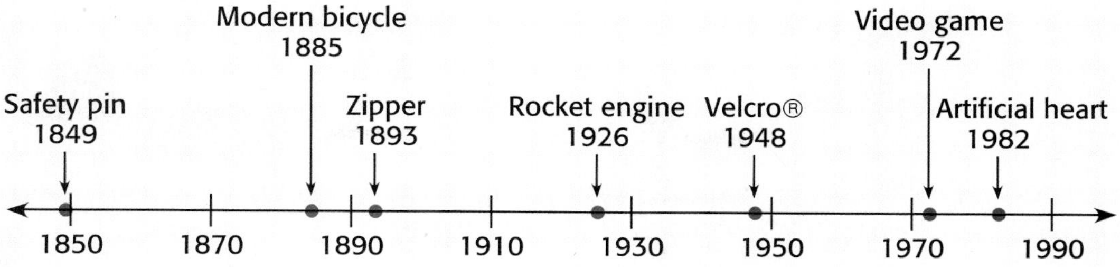

7. Health Twelve years after the invention of the zipper, Madame C. J. Walker invented a hair-care product. When was her product invented?

Madame C. J. Walker

8. Using Data Two years before the modern bicycle was invented, Jan E. Matzeliger invented a machine to increase the production of shoes. What year was this?

Jan E. Matzeliger

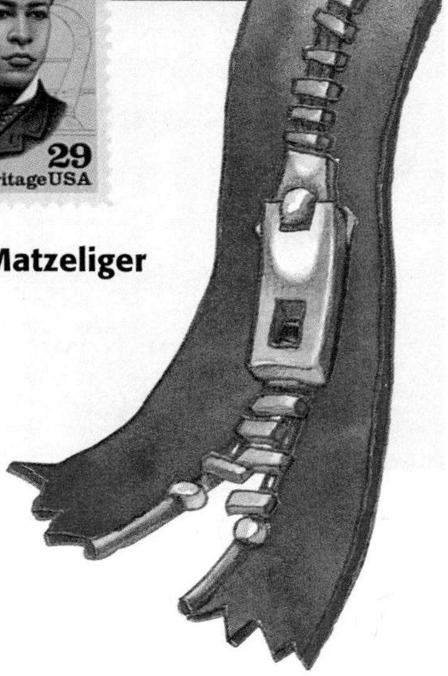

9. Science Robert Goddard invented the first rocket engine 13 years before Igor Sikorsky flew the first helicopter. When did the first helicopter fly?

10. Critical Thinking How many years before you were born was the video game invented?

11. Journal Give an example of how a picture can be used to organize information.

Mixed Review and Test Prep

Find each product.

12. 2×9 **13.** 5×6 **14.** 8×2 **15.** 4×0 **16.** 6×9

Find each difference. Check each answer.

17. 387 − 174 **18.** 549 − 352 **19.** 832 − 477 **20.** 409 − 257

21. What is the sum of $22.98 + $30.05?

Ⓐ $52.93 Ⓑ $5,303 Ⓒ $52.03 Ⓓ $53.03

SECTION B

Review and Practice

(Lessons 4–8) Find each product.

1. 9×2	**2.** 3×9	**3.** 7×5	**4.** 8×1	**5.** 5×6
6. 3×2	**7.** 0×2	**8.** 4×9	**9.** 5×0	**10.** 8×2
11. 5×8	**12.** 6×9	**13.** 7×9	**14.** 0×9	**15.** 5×1
16. 2×6	**17.** 2×2	**18.** 2×7	**19.** 5×3	**20.** 4×1
21. 5×9	**22.** 1×6	**23.** 8×9	**24.** 1×9	**25.** 7×0
26. 9×9	**27.** 2×1	**28.** 2×5	**29.** 5×4	**30.** 5×5

31. Find the product of 0 and 6.

32. Multiply 2 by 4.

33. List 4 multiples of 2.

34. List 4 multiples of 9.

35. List all multiples of 5 between 8 and 24.

36. Reasoning Carol says that if you know the product of 2×5, you also know the product of 5×2. Is she correct? Explain.

(Lessons 9 and 10)

37. Money For lunch, Sal bought a sandwich for $3.95, soup for $1.50, and lemonade for $1.25. How much more did he pay for the soup than the lemonade?

38. Iris sits right behind Quint. Anna is the only person between Quint and Marvin. Who sits in the front?

Patterns Continue each pattern.

39. 0, 5, 10, $\square$, $\square$, $\square$

40. 20, 22, 24, $\square$, $\square$, $\square$

41. Journal Explain how you might use patterns to find 8×9.

Skills Checklist

In this section, you have:

- ☑ Multiplied with 0, 1, 2, 5, and 9 as Factors
- ☑ Explored Patterns on a Hundred Chart for 2s and 5s Facts
- ☑ Explored Patterns When Multiplying with 0 and 1
- ☑ Solved Problems with Too Much or Too Little Information
- ☑ Solved Problems by Drawing a Picture

YOUR CHOICE

Choose at least one of the following. Use what you have learned in the chapter.

1 Pattern Search

a. Find the pattern. Then copy and complete the table.

In	3	4	5	6	7	8
Out	15	20	25			

b. Make up your own multiplication pattern and show it in a table.

2 A Poet and You Know It

Help your classmates remember their multiplication facts. Write a poem or a song about multiplying with 0, 1, 2, 5, or 9 as a factor.

3 Number Mania

See how many multiplication sentences you can write using the digits 0, 1, 2, 5, and 9. Make sure the digits in the product are also 0, 1, 2, 5, or 9.

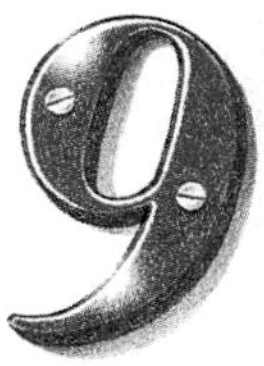

4 Picture It

At Home Make a collage to show one of these number sentences. Use pictures of equal groups from magazines or newspapers, or draw equal groups yourself.

$3 \times 2 = 6$ $4 \times 3 = 12$ $2 \times 8 = 16$

5 Double Trouble

Jeff's sister will let him borrow her roller blades for $1 on the first day, and double the money on every day for 10 more days. Jeff thinks, "That should be less than the $5 a day the store charges!" He'll be soooorrry! Use a calculator to find out why!

CHAPTER 5
Review/Test

Vocabulary Choose the best word for each sentence.

Word List
factor
product
multiple
array

1. A number that is multiplied is called a ____.
2. You know that 30 is a ____ of 5 because it has a 0 in the ones place.
3. In the multiplication sentence $3 \times 5 = 15$, the number 15 is called the ____.

(Lessons 1 and 2) Copy and complete.

4. 

a. ■ + ■ + ■ = ■

b. ■ rows of ■ equals ■.

c. ■ × ■ = ■

5. 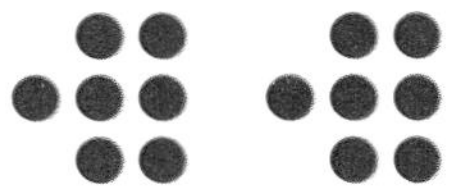

a. ■ + ■ = ■

b. ■ groups of ■ equals ■.

c. ■ × ■ = ■

(Lesson 3) Write a multiplication story for each. Find each product.

6. 5×7 **7.** 4×2 **8.** 9×3 **9.** 2×6

(Lessons 4–8) Find each product.

10. 5×2 **11.** 9×8 **12.** 9×7 **13.** 5×1 **14.** 6×5

15. 4×5 **16.** 2×8 **17.** 6×2 **18.** 5×5 **19.** 7×1

20. 2×4 **21.** 3×2 **22.** 2×0 **23.** 5×7 **24.** 8×2

25. 9×9 **26.** 6×9 **27.** 8×5 **28.** 9×2 **29.** 5×9

(Lessons 9 and 10) Solve. Use any strategy.

30. Cara has two dogs and two cats. Each week her mother buys 7 cans of dog food for each dog. How many cans of dog food does she buy each week?

31. In a family picture, Rose stands beside Bart. Rose is to the left of Bart. Vera is the only person between Bart and Holly. Michael stands to the right of Holly. Who is standing at each end?

CHAPTER 5
Performance Assessment

Suppose your class wants to paint and sell greeting cards to raise money. You have $50 to spend on supplies. How would you spend it?

Supplies	
Box of 10 blank cards with envelopes	$4
Jar of paint	$2
Set of 9 brushes	$5

1. **Decision Making** Decide which items you will buy. Decide how many of each item or set.

2. **Recording Data** Copy and fill out the table below. Remember that your total can be close to $50, but cannot go over.

Item	How Many Items or Sets	Price of One Item or Set	Total Price
		Total Cost:	

3. **Explain Your Thinking** How did you decide how many cards, paints, and brushes to buy?

4. **Critical Thinking** If you sell your cards for $3 each, how much money will you make? Remember to include the cost of cards, paint, and brushes.

Math Magazine

Make a Rakhi **Raksha Bandhan is a festival celebrated in India by Hindu and Sikh families. It's a day when families celebrate their love for each other. On this day, a sister ties a bracelet, or rakhi, around her brother's wrist.**

To make a rakhi you need 3 pieces of ribbon each measuring 9 inches long.

Ashish and Anjali celebrate Raksha Bandhan here in the United States.

Try These!

1. How many total inches of ribbon would you need to make a rakhi?
2. How many pieces of ribbon would you need to make 5 rakhis?
3. How many sequins would you need to make 4 rakhis like the one to the right?

CHAPTERS 1–5
Cumulative Review

Test Prep Strategy: Read Carefully!

Watch for tricky problems.
How many more gift packs did the fourth grade sell than the fifth grade?

Ⓐ 2 Ⓑ 5 Ⓒ 9 Ⓓ 10

When you read a pictograph, be sure to look at the key. Since each symbol stands for 5 packs, the answer is 2 × 5, which is Ⓓ 10.

Test Prep Strategies

- Read Carefully
- Follow Directions
- Make Smart Choices
- Eliminate Choices
- Work Backward from an Answer

Write the letter of the correct answer. You may use any strategy to help.

1. Which is NOT ordered from least to greatest?
   Ⓐ 1,188, 1,088, 1,008 Ⓑ 342, 343, 344
   Ⓒ 900, 1,000, 1,001 Ⓓ 551, 5,510, 55,100

2. At swim practice, Janine swam 38 laps and Mercedes swam 51. How many more laps did Mercedes swim?
   Ⓐ 89 laps Ⓑ 29 laps Ⓒ 13 laps Ⓓ 12 laps

3. How many plastic and paper plates were ordered?
   Ⓐ 3 Ⓑ 9
   Ⓒ 18 Ⓓ 6

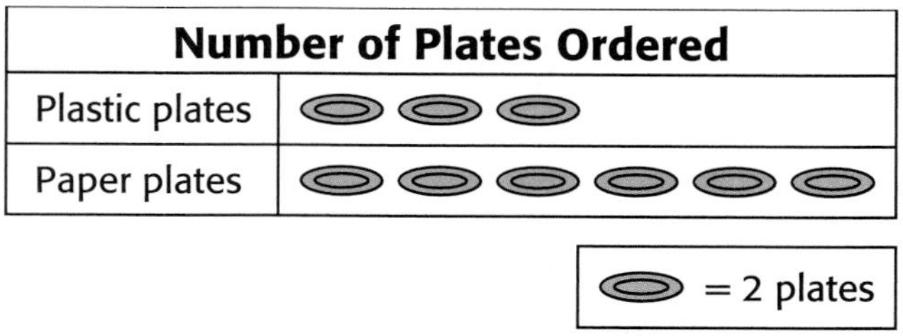

4. How many feet is the track?
   Ⓐ 600 feet Ⓑ 1,320 feet
   Ⓒ 1,440 Ⓓ not here

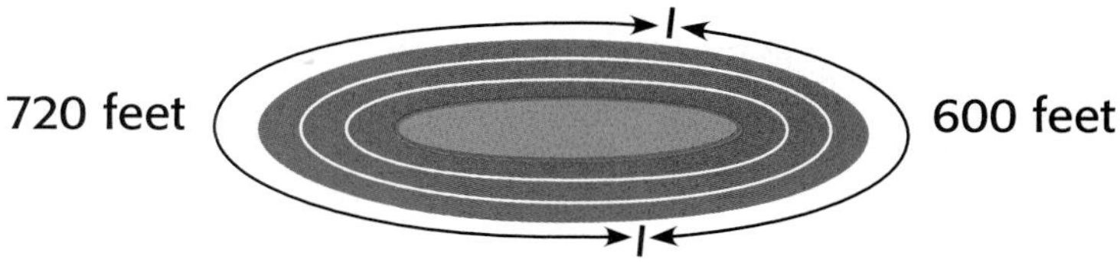

5. Find 302 − 198.
   Ⓐ 296 Ⓑ 116
   Ⓒ 14 Ⓓ not here

REVIEW AND PRACTICE

DATA FILE

Chapter 6

More Multiplication Facts

WHAT'S TO EAT?

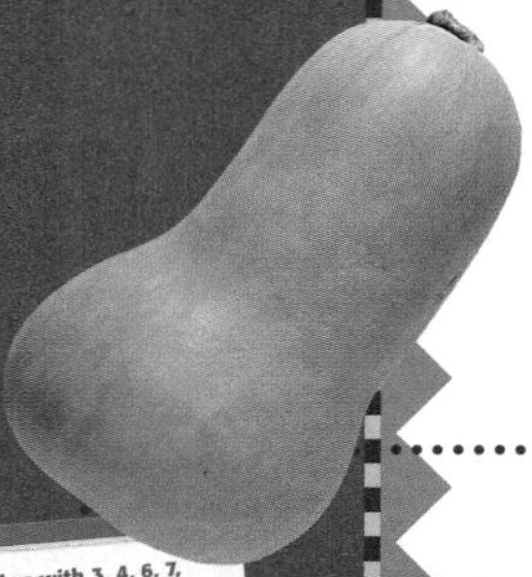

SECTION A

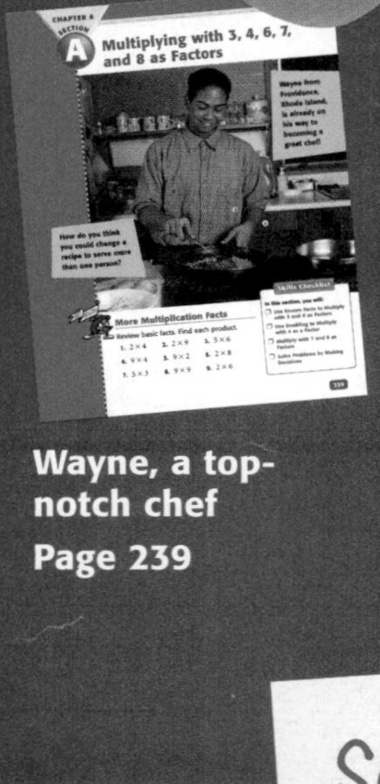

Wayne, a top-notch chef

Page 239

Multiplying with 3, 4, 6, 7, and 8 as Factors

239

People have been living in Pueblo communities in northern New Mexico since long before the Mayflower arrived in America. Summer Squash Soup is one of the delicious recipes that comes from the Pueblo Indians' long history.

How many cloves of garlic would you need for two batches of soup?

Summer Squash Soup

3 medium-sized summer squash
1 clove garlic
$\frac{1}{8}$ teaspoon oregano
$\frac{1}{2}$ teaspoon salt
2 tablespoons butter
1 cup broth

SECTION B

Extending Multiplication

253

Like it or not, you're getting a lot of sugar in packaged foods! How many teaspoons of sugar are in a cup of chocolate milk?

Amount of Sugar Used in Packaged Foods

Food	Teaspoons of Sugar
Bread (one slice)	0
Muffin (one medium)	1
Canned fruit with light syrup	2
Chocolate milk (one cup)	3
Chocolate milk shake	9
Cola (one can)	9

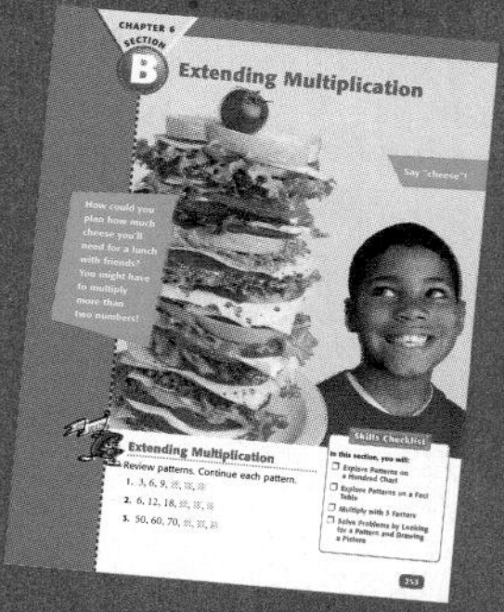

Say cheese!
Page 253

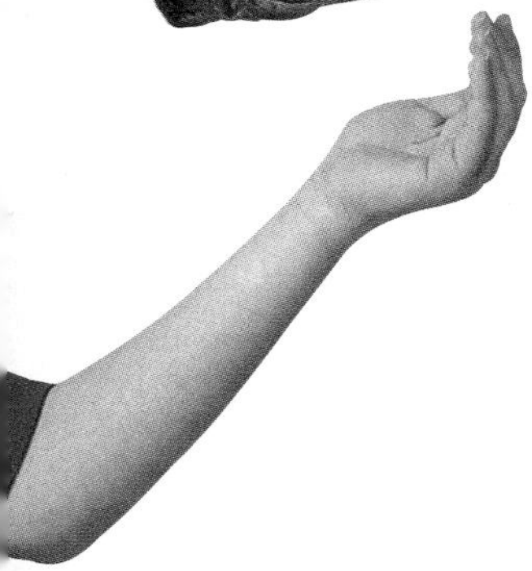

Surfing the World Wide Web!

What kinds of food do you like? Find out what other students like by visiting **www.mathsurf.com/3/ch6**. Use the information there to report on the three most liked foods.

TEAM PROJECT

Sweet & Spicy GINGER-ADE

Materials
large bowl,
measuring cup,
measuring spoons,
water, ginger-water,
lemon juice, honey,
ice cubes

Would you like to try a favorite West African drink? Make a pitcher of ginger-ade with your class. You'll need to decide how much of each of the ingredients you'll need.

Make a Plan

- How many people are in your class? How many servings will you make?
- Will you need to double the recipe? Will you need to multiply the recipe by 3? By 4?

Carry It Out

1. Write your new recipe.
2. Make the drink, following your new recipe.

Talk About It

- Now taste! Does anyone think the drink should be sweeter? Or should it have more lemon or ginger? How could you change the recipe?

Present the Project

- How did you figure out how to change the recipe so everyone got a drink?

Ginger-ade

4 cups ginger-water
8 tablespoons lemon juice
1 cup honey
4 cups water
ice cubes

1. Combine the warm ginger-water, lemon juice, and honey, and let cool.
2. Add the remaining water. Serve over ice.

Makes 9 servings.

CHAPTER 6

SECTION

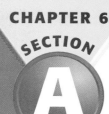

A Multiplying with 3, 4, 6, 7, and 8 as Factors

Wayne from Providence, Rhode Island, is already on his way to becoming a great chef!

How do you think you could change a recipe to serve more than one person?

More Multiplication Facts

Review basic facts. Find each product.

1. 2×4 **2.** 2×9 **3.** 5×6

4. 9×4 **5.** 9×2 **6.** 2×8

7. 5×3 **8.** 9×9 **9.** 2×6

Skills Checklist

In this section, you will:

- ❒ Use Known Facts to Multiply with 3 and 6 as Factors
- ❒ Use Doubling to Multiply with 4 as a Factor
- ❒ Multiply with 7 and 8 as Factors
- ❒ Solve Problems by Making Decisions

3 as a Factor: Using Known Facts

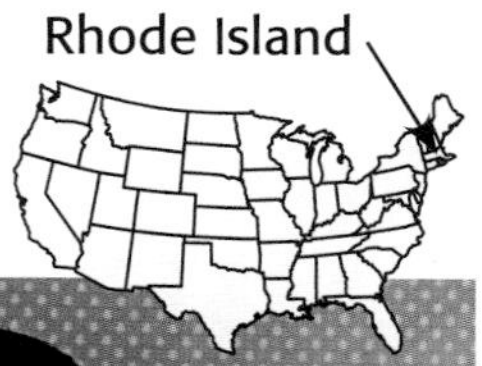

You Will Learn
how to multiply with 3 as a factor

Learn

There's fabulous food at Wayne's house! He likes to cook great meals like *Bim Bim Bap,* a Korean dish.

Wayne from Providence, Rhode Island, spends his free time cooking and playing sports.

Wayne needs 4 small carrots to make one serving of Bim Bim Bap. How many small carrots does he need to make dinner for 3 people?

Since you are putting together 3 groups of 4, multiply.

Use what you know about multiplying by 2 to multiply by 3.

Find 3×4.

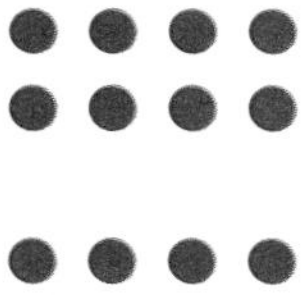

$2 \times 4 = 8$

$1 \times 4 = 4$

$8 + 4 = 12$

$3 \times 4 = 12$ So, Wayne needs 12 small carrots.

Math Tip
3 groups of 4 is the same amount as 2 groups of 4 plus one more group of 4.

Talk About It

How could you find 3×6 if you know 2×6?

Check

Find each product.

1. 3×7 **2.** 3×0 **3.** 3×5 **4.** 1×3 **5.** 3×3

6. Reasoning How could you add to this array to show 3×8?

Practice

Skills and Reasoning

Find each product.

7. 4×3 **8.** 5×3 **9.** 3×8 **10.** 3×4 **11.** 2×4

12. 3×1 **13.** 2×3 **14.** 3×5 **15.** 6×3 **16.** 9×3

17. 3×7 **18.** 3×9 **19.** 2×5 **20.** 3×5 **21.** 2×4

22. 3×6 **23.** 3×8 **24.** 5×9 **25.** 3×4 **26.** 3×1

27. What is the product of 3 and 3?

28. Multiply 4 by 3.

29. If you know the product of 2×7, how can you find the product of 3×7? What is it?

30. Aaron says, "To find 3×9, I can find 2×9 and add one more group of 3." What's wrong?

Problem Solving and Applications

31. Patterns Copy and complete the table. Then name at least one pattern you see in the products.

$3 \times 0 = 0$	$3 \times 5 =$ ■
$3 \times 1 = 3$	$3 \times 6 =$ ■
$3 \times 2 = 6$	$3 \times 7 =$ ■
$3 \times 3 =$ ■	$3 \times 8 =$ ■
$3 \times 4 =$ ■	$3 \times 9 =$ ■

Using Data Use the recipe in the Data File on page 236 to answer **32** and **33.**

32. How many summer squashes do you need to make 6 batches of Summer Squash Soup?

33. How many tablespoons of butter do you need to make 6 batches of the soup?

Mixed Review and Test Prep

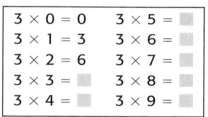

Add or subtract.

34. $919 + 234$ **35.** $492 - 200$ **36.** $108 + 777$ **37.** $935 - 49$

Patterns Continue each pattern.

38. 4, 8, 12, ■, ■, ■ **39.** 36, 32, 28, ■, ■, ■

40. How much money would you have if you had 7 quarters?

Ⓐ \$1.00 Ⓑ \$1.75 Ⓒ \$2.00 Ⓓ \$1.25

4 as a Factor: Doubling

You Will Learn
how to multiply with 4 as a factor

Learn

Bestila is a chicken pie described by Moroccans as "food for a wedding."

If you are ever invited to a wedding in Morocco, go! You can expect to eat a tasty dish called *bestila* (bis-TEE-ya).

It takes 7 eggs to make one bestila. How many eggs would you need for 4 bestilas?

Since you want to find 4 groups of 7, multiply.

To multiply by 4, first multiply by 2. Then double the product.

Math Tip
4×7 is the same as 2×7 and 2×7. It's a "double double"!

Find 4×7.

$2 \times 7 = 14$

$2 \times 7 = 14$

$14 + 14 = 28$

$4 \times 7 = 28$

So, you need 28 eggs to make 4 bestilas.

Talk About It

Why is doubling the product of 2×3 the same as finding 4×3?

Check

Find each product.

1. 4×5 **2.** 4×1 **3.** 4×8 **4.** 2×4 **5.** 9×4

6. Reasoning Rachel said, "I can find 4×6 by doubling 2×6." Is she correct? Explain.

Practice

Skills and Reasoning

Find each product.

7. 3×4 **8.** 2×4 **9.** 7×4 **10.** 4×4 **11.** 4×1

12. 3×3 **13.** 8×4 **14.** 0×4 **15.** 4×5 **16.** 6×4

17. 4×4 **18.** 4×3 **19.** 7×4 **20.** 5×4 **21.** 2×8

22. 6×4 **23.** 8×4 **24.** 4×9 **25.** 7×5 **26.** 4×1

27. 4×7 **28.** 3×8 **29.** 8×5 **30.** 4×0 **31.** 3×4

32. 4×2 **33.** 5×3 **34.** 9×4 **35.** 2×9 **36.** 5×9

37. Multiply 9 by 4.

38. What is the product of 4 and 6?

39. Draw arrays to show that 4×3 is the same amount as 3×4.

40. Could you use doubling to multiply 3×5? Explain.

Problem Solving and Applications

41. Patterns Copy and complete the table. Then name at least one pattern you see in the products.

$4 \times 0 = 0$	$4 \times 5 =$ ▢
$4 \times 1 = 4$	$4 \times 6 =$ ▢
$4 \times 2 = 8$	$4 \times 7 =$ ▢
$4 \times 3 =$ ▢	$4 \times 8 =$ ▢
$4 \times 4 =$ ▢	$4 \times 9 =$ ▢

42. Music A musical group with four people is called a *quartet*. How many people are needed for 3 quartets?

Mixed Review and Test Prep

Patterns Continue each pattern.

43. 25, 30, 35, ▢, ▢, ▢ **44.** 5, 10, 15, ▢, ▢, ▢ **45.** 45, 40, 35, ▢, ▢, ▢

Find each product.

46. 2×6 **47.** 5×6 **48.** 3×6 **49.** 4×6 **50.** 1×6

51. Tyrone is reading a 118-page book. He is on page 79. How many pages does he have left to read?

Ⓐ 49 Ⓑ 39 Ⓒ 29 Ⓓ 197

Chapter 6
Lesson
3

6 as a Factor: Using Known Facts

You Will Learn
how to multiply with 6 as a factor

Learn

Grill it up! You need enough burger buns for 50 people.

Each package has 8 buns. Are 6 packages enough?

Since you want to find 6 groups of 8, you multiply.

Use what you know about multiplying by 5 to multiply by 6.

Math Tip
6 × 8 has the same value as 5 × 8 plus one more group of 8.

Find 6×8.

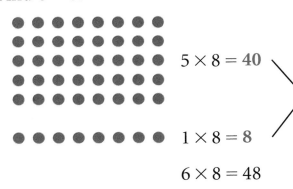

$5 \times 8 = 40$

$1 \times 8 = 8$

$40 + 8 = 48$

$6 \times 8 = 48$

There are 48 buns in 6 packages. So, 6 packages is not enough.

Talk About It

If you know 5×4, how can you find 6×4?

Check

Find each product.

1. 6×4 **2.** 6×5 **3.** 8×6 **4.** 3×6 **5.** 6×6

6. Reasoning Name two facts to help you find 6×7.

Practice

Skills and Reasoning

Find each product.

7. 9×6 **8.** 3×6 **9.** 6×6 **10.** 7×6 **11.** 6×2

12. 6×0 **13.** 9×3 **14.** 8×6 **15.** 5×4 **16.** 5×6

17. 6×2 **18.** 6×9 **19.** 5×6 **20.** 7×6 **21.** 4×8

22. 6×1 **23.** 6×8 **24.** 9×2 **25.** 6×0 **26.** 6×7

27. Find the product of 6 and 1.

28. What is 4 multiplied by 6?

29. Which is greater, 6×8 or 8×5? How can you tell without multiplying?

30. Can you think of a way to use doubling to multiply 6×5? Explain.

Problem Solving and Applications

31. Algebra Readiness Copy and complete the table. Then write the rule.

In	3	5	9	4	2	1	7
Out	18	30	54				

Jerboas live in Africa and Asia.

32. Science Jerboas can travel 9 feet in a single hop. How many feet could they travel in 4 hops?

Mixed Review and Test Prep

Patterns Continue each pattern.

33. 7, 14, 21, ■, ■, ■

34. 8, 16, 24, ■, ■, ■

Add.

35. $76 + 51 + 200$ **36.** $85 + 152 + 49$ **37.** $12 + 81 + 98$

38. $421 + 5 + 50$ **39.** $7 + 3 + 501$ **40.** $82 + 493$

41. What is the difference of 580 and 346?

Ⓐ 925 Ⓑ 246 Ⓒ 234 Ⓓ not here

7 and 8 as Factors

You Will Learn

how to multiply with 7 and 8 as factors

Vocabulary

square number the product when both factors are the same

Learn

Cooking for a grade? Yes! These students made a special meal for a roomful of guests!

You need to make 7 pizzas. Each pizza has 8 onion slices. How many onion slices do you need?

Since you want to find 7 groups of 8, you multiply.

Students in a class at the California Culinary Academy in San Francisco, California.

Example 1

Use 5s facts and 2s facts to find 7×8.

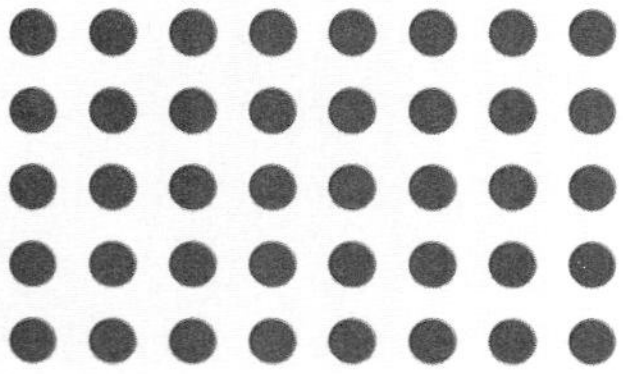

$5 \times 8 = \mathbf{40}$

$2 \times 8 = \mathbf{16}$

$40 + 16 = \mathbf{56}$

$7 \times 8 = 56$

You need 56 onion slices.

Example 2

The product of 8×8 is a **square number.**

Use doubling to find 8×8.

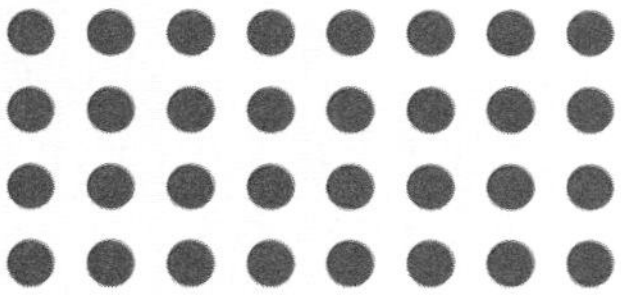

$4 \times 8 = \mathbf{32}$

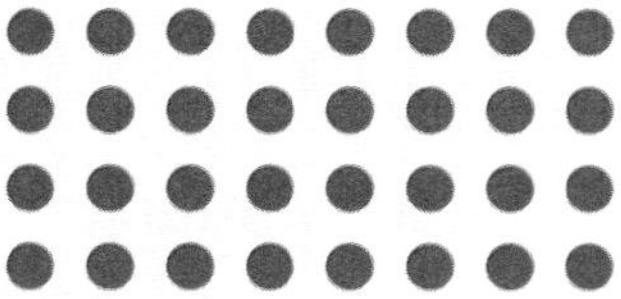

$4 \times 8 = \mathbf{32}$

$32 + 32 = \mathbf{64}$

$8 \times 8 = 64$

Talk About It

Explain one way to use $5 \times 6 = 30$ to find 7×6.

Check

Find each product.

1. 8×4 **2.** 7×3 **3.** 8×7 **4.** 8×5 **5.** 7×7

6. Reasoning Name two facts that can help you find the product of 7×9.

Practice

Skills and Reasoning

Find each product.

7. 9×8 **8.** 6×8 **9.** 7×6 **10.** 7×7 **11.** 2×8

12. 8×5 **13.** 7×1 **14.** 3×8 **15.** 8×7 **16.** 9×7

17. 7×4 **18.** 7×5 **19.** 7×2 **20.** 8×8 **21.** 8×1

22. Find the product of 8 and 6.

23. Find the product of 7 and 4.

24. How could you find the product of 7×7 if you know the product of 5×7?

25. How can you tell that 6×6 is less than 7×9 without multiplying?

Problem Solving and Applications

26. Health You should eat at least 4 servings of fruits and vegetables a day. How many servings is that a week?

Algebra Readiness Write each missing number.

27. $8 \times \square = 24$ **28.** $\square \times 7 = 14$ **29.** $\square \times 9 = 63$

Mixed Review and Test Prep

Add or subtract.

30. $97 - 44$ **31.** $212 + 162$ **32.** $500 - 199$ **33.** $137 + 81$

34. An animal park had 146 animals. During the year 18 animals were born. How many animals were there at the end of the year?

Ⓐ 154 animals Ⓑ 164 animals Ⓒ 226 animals

STOP and Practice

Find each product.

1. $\begin{array}{r} 8 \\ \times 4 \\ \hline \end{array}$	**2.** $\begin{array}{r} 4 \\ \times 3 \\ \hline \end{array}$	**3.** $\begin{array}{r} 6 \\ \times 5 \\ \hline \end{array}$	**4.** $\begin{array}{r} 8 \\ \times 6 \\ \hline \end{array}$	**5.** $\begin{array}{r} 9 \\ \times 8 \\ \hline \end{array}$
6. $\begin{array}{r} 7 \\ \times 5 \\ \hline \end{array}$	**7.** $\begin{array}{r} 8 \\ \times 9 \\ \hline \end{array}$	**8.** $\begin{array}{r} 8 \\ \times 7 \\ \hline \end{array}$	**9.** $\begin{array}{r} 8 \\ \times 3 \\ \hline \end{array}$	**10.** $\begin{array}{r} 9 \\ \times 9 \\ \hline \end{array}$
11. $\begin{array}{r} 7 \\ \times 7 \\ \hline \end{array}$	**12.** $\begin{array}{r} 2 \\ \times 7 \\ \hline \end{array}$	**13.** $\begin{array}{r} 8 \\ \times 5 \\ \hline \end{array}$	**14.** $\begin{array}{r} 7 \\ \times 3 \\ \hline \end{array}$	**15.** $\begin{array}{r} 2 \\ \times 9 \\ \hline \end{array}$
16. $\begin{array}{r} 5 \\ \times 7 \\ \hline \end{array}$	**17.** $\begin{array}{r} 7 \\ \times 1 \\ \hline \end{array}$	**18.** $\begin{array}{r} 9 \\ \times 5 \\ \hline \end{array}$	**19.** $\begin{array}{r} 6 \\ \times 8 \\ \hline \end{array}$	**20.** $\begin{array}{r} 7 \\ \times 8 \\ \hline \end{array}$

21. 3×6	**22.** 3×9	**23.** 3×2	**24.** 3×7	**25.** 3×5
26. 5×4	**27.** 4×9	**28.** 7×4	**29.** 6×4	**30.** 6×9
31. 6×7	**32.** 7×9	**33.** 5×6	**34.** 3×4	**35.** 8×2
36. 0×2	**37.** 5×5	**38.** 9×3	**39.** 2×6	**40.** 6×6
41. 8×1	**42.** 5×4	**43.** 2×7	**44.** 6×2	**45.** 9×4
46. 8×8	**47.** 4×7	**48.** 8×0	**49.** 7×6	**50.** 5×8

Error Search

Find each sentence that is not correct. Write it correctly and explain the error.

51. 19 is a multiple of 7.

52. The product of 4 and 7 is 28.

53. 3×7 is 2×7 and 3 more.

54. 9 multiplied by 3 is 12.

Remember the Facts!

Use these activities anytime to help you remember your multiplication facts.

1. **Around the World** How many multiplication facts can your class complete in a row? Your teacher will ask a student to complete a fact. If correct, the student stands by the next student in the class. Continue around the class until the student misses a fact. If the student sitting down can complete the fact, the students trade places. Can your class make it all the way around without missing a fact?

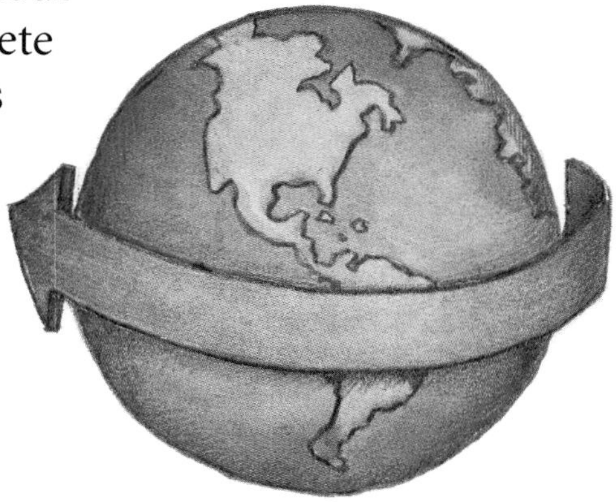

2. **Fact Letters** Make a mailbox to put at your desk. Think of a multiplication fact that you know and write it in a "letter." Drop the letter in a classmate's mailbox. Everyone in the class should receive one letter a day. Try to memorize the fact that is delivered to you by the end of the day. On the next day, deliver the fact letter you received to another student or write a new letter.

3. **Spinner Game** Make a spinner numbered 1–9. With a partner, spin the spinner twice. Take turns telling the product of the two numbers. As you play, write each multiplication sentence on a piece of paper and circle facts you have trouble with. Keep your list to help you study!

Chapter 6
Lesson
5

Problem Solving

Decision Making: Planning Meals

You Will Learn
how to use a table to help make decisions

Explore

Suppose you, a friend, and your grandfather go on an all-day hike. You must make a list for the food you'll bring. The food chart below shows how many servings of each type of food each person must eat. You must choose food from each group.

Work Together

▶ Understand

1. What do you know?
2. What do you need to decide?

▶ Plan and Solve

3. How many people should you buy food for?
4. How can you figure out how many servings of each kind of food you should buy?
5. What kinds of food might be difficult to take along in a backpack?

▶ Make a Decision

6. Copy and complete the table to decide how much and what kind of food you'll buy.

Food Group	Servings per Person	Total Servings for 3 People	Food to Buy
Fats, oils, sweets			
Milk, cheese, yogurt			
Meat, fish, eggs, nuts, beans			
Fruit			
Vegetables			
Breads, cereals, rice, pasta			

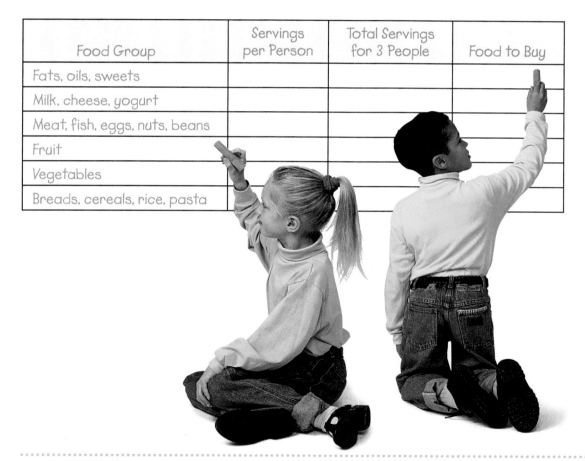

▶ Present Your Decision

7. Share your table with the class. According to your table, what foods will you bring on your hike?

SECTION A
Review and Practice

(Lesson 1) Find each product.

1. 3×7 **2.** 3×4 **3.** 3×5 **4.** 3×3 **5.** 3×8

6. 5×3 **7.** 3×2 **8.** 6×3 **9.** 3×9 **10.** 4×3

11. Naomi, Hong, and Todd are making cookies. If they want to make enough to have five cookies each, how many cookies should they make?

(Lesson 2) Find each product.

12. 4×9 **13.** 4×6 **14.** 4×7 **15.** 4×3 **16.** 4×8

17. 4×2 **18.** 4×5 **19.** 1×4 **20.** 4×4 **21.** 7×4

22. **Social Studies** Alexis wants to be a Senator some day. She knows that Senators serve terms that are 6 years long. If she is elected for 4 terms, how many years will she be in Congress?

(Lesson 3) Find each product.

23. 6×7 **24.** 6×3 **25.** 6×2 **26.** 6×9 **27.** 6×6

28. 6×8 **29.** 5×6 **30.** 6×4 **31.** 3×6 **32.** 9×6

33. **Money** Roberto saves coins in a glass jar. He adds 6 nickels to his jar. How much did Roberto add to his savings?

(Lesson 4) Find each product.

34. 7×5 **35.** 7×9 **36.** 8×6

37. 7×8 **38.** 8×9 **39.** 7×4

40. 8×5 **41.** 6×7 **42.** 8×8

43. You want to make 8 apple pies. You need 6 apples for each pie. How many apples must you buy?

44. **Journal** Write two ways to find the product of 5×8.

Skills Checklist

In this section, you have:

- ☑ Used Known Facts to Multiply with 3 and 6 as Factors
- ☑ Doubled to Multiply with 4 as a Factor
- ☑ Multiplied with 7 and 8 as Factors
- ☑ Solved Problems by Making Decisions

CHAPTER 6
SECTION

B Extending Multiplication

Say "cheese"!

How could you plan how much cheese you'll need for a lunch with friends? You might have to multiply more than two numbers!

Extending Multiplication

Review patterns. Continue each pattern.

1. 3, 6, 9, ▒, ▒, ▒
2. 6, 12, 18, ▒, ▒, ▒
3. 50, 60, 70, ▒, ▒, ▒

Skills Checklist

In this section, you will:

- ☐ Explore Patterns on a Hundred Chart
- ☐ Explore Patterns on a Fact Table
- ☐ Multiply with 3 Factors
- ☐ Solve Problems by Looking for a Pattern and Drawing a Picture

Exploring Patterns on a Hundred Chart: 3s and 6s

Problem Solving Connection
Look for a Pattern

Materials
- hundred chart
- yellow pencil
- blue pencil

Vocabulary
multiple
the product of a given whole number and any other whole number

Remember
To skip count by 3s, start with 3, 6, 9, 12, …

Explore

You can look for patterns to help you multiply with 3 and 6 as factors.

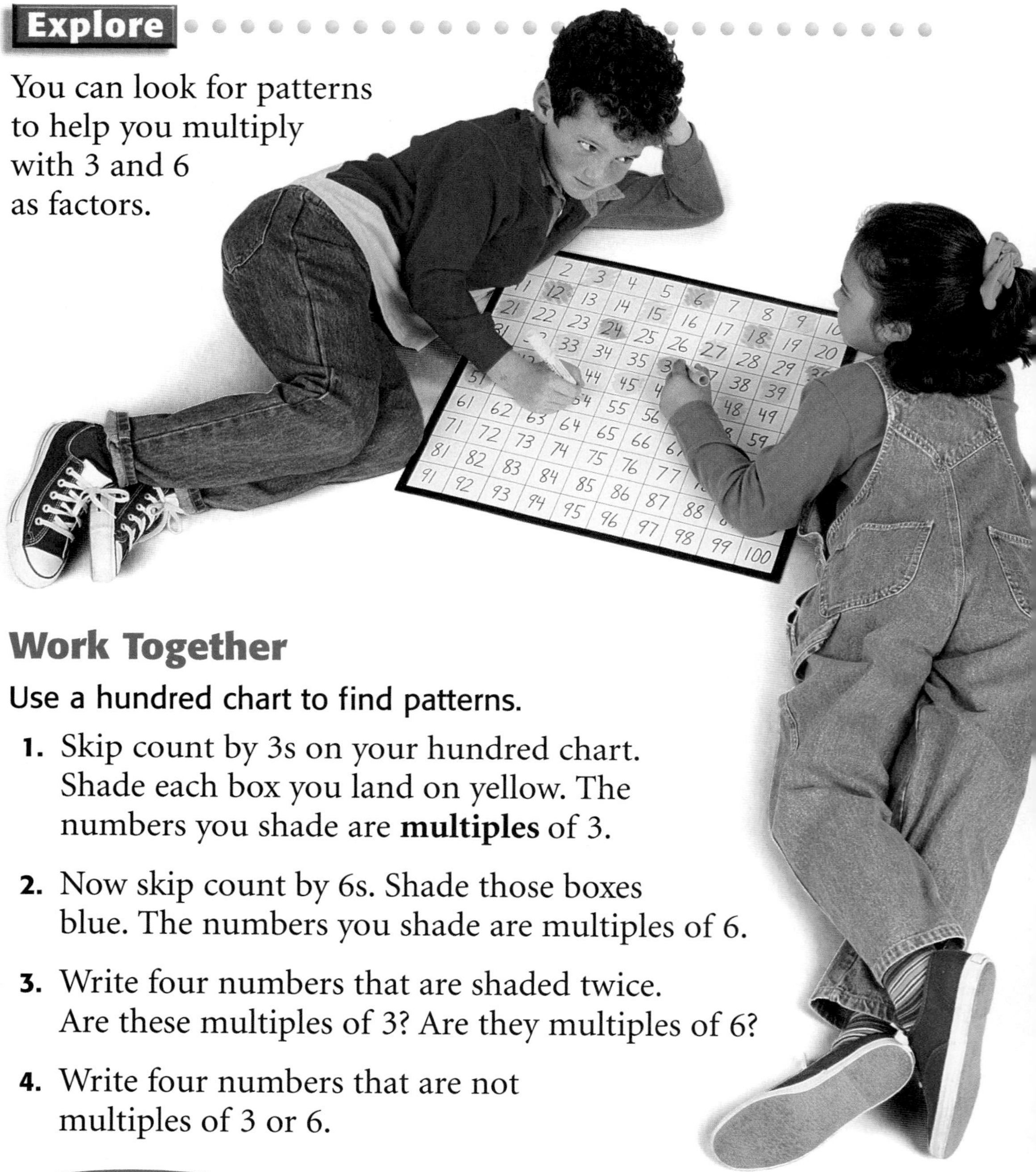

Work Together

Use a hundred chart to find patterns.

1. Skip count by 3s on your hundred chart. Shade each box you land on yellow. The numbers you shade are **multiples** of 3.
2. Now skip count by 6s. Shade those boxes blue. The numbers you shade are multiples of 6.
3. Write four numbers that are shaded twice. Are these multiples of 3? Are they multiples of 6?
4. Write four numbers that are not multiples of 3 or 6.

Talk About It

5. What color patterns do you see in the shaded squares?
6. What patterns do you see in ones digits? In tens digits?

Connect

You can use patterns to help remember multiples of 3 and 6.

All multiples of 6 are also multiples of 3!
The digits in all multiples of 3 and 6 in the hundred chart add to 3, 6, 9, 12, 15, or 18!

Practice

Algebra Readiness Find each missing number. You may use a hundred chart to help.

1. $3 \times \square = 9$ **2.** $\square \times 6 = 36$ **3.** $6 \times \square = 18$ **4.** $\square \times 8 = 48$

Write true or false for **5–8.** If the answer is false, explain why.

5. 44 is a multiple of 3.

6. 12 is a multiple of 3 and a multiple of 6.

7. All multiples of 3 are also multiples of 6.

8. 14 is not a multiple of 3 or 6.

9. Science All spiders have 8 legs and all insects have 6 legs. Could a group of spiders have 24 legs? Could a group of insects have 24 legs? Explain.

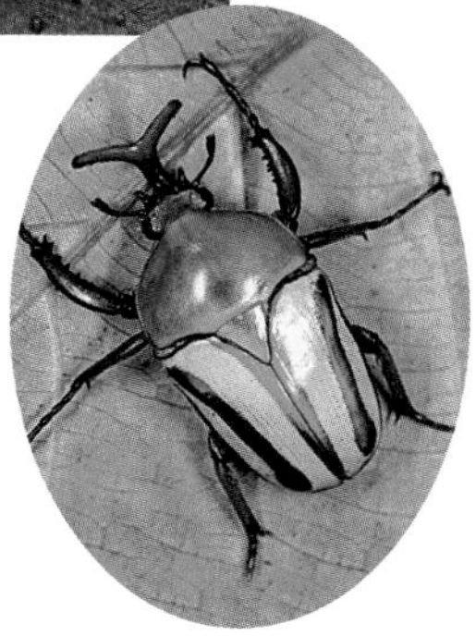

10. Patterns Use a hundred chart or a calculator to help skip count to 96 by 8s. Write at least one pattern you see.

11. Geometry Readiness Continue the pattern.

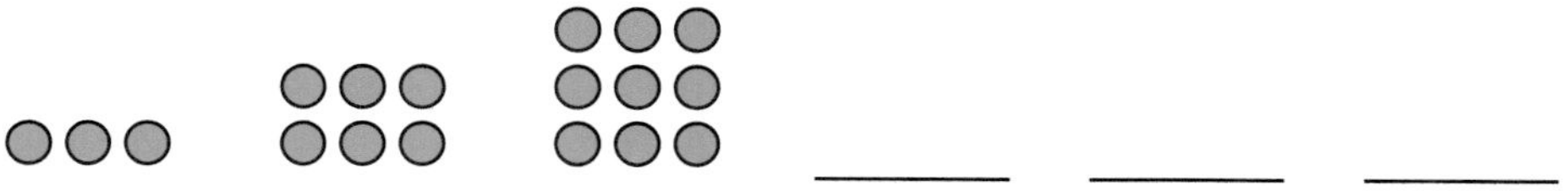

12. Journal Write about a pattern that might help you remember a 3 or 6 fact.

Chapter 6
Lesson
7

Exploring Patterns on a Fact Table

Problem Solving Connection
- Look for a Pattern
- Make a Table

Materials
fact table

Math Tip
You can use addition to find greater multiplication facts.
3×12 is 2×12 plus one more 12.

Explore

Patterns in a multiplication table can help you remember facts.

Work Together

Copy and complete the table.

$2 \times 3 = 6$

×	0	1	2	3	4	5	6	7	8	9	10	11	12
0	0	0	0	0	0	0	0						
1	0	1	2	3	4	5							
2	0	2	4	6									
3	0	3	6										
4													
5													
6													
7													
8													
9													
10													
11													
12													

Talk About It

1. What patterns go across the table?
2. What patterns go down the table?
3. What other patterns can you find?

Connect

Look for patterns in multiples of greater numbers.

10	11	12
10 × 0 = 0	11 × 0 = 0	12 × 0 = 0
10 × 1 = 10	11 × 1 = 11	12 × 1 = 12
10 × 2 = 20	11 × 2 = 22	12 × 2 = 24
10 × 3 = 30	11 × 3 = 33	12 × 3 = 36
10 × 4 = 40	11 × 4 = 44	12 × 4 = 48
10 × 5 = 50	11 × 5 = 55	12 × 5 = 60
10 × 6 = 60	11 × 6 = 66	12 × 6 = 72
10 × 7 = 70	11 × 7 = 77	12 × 7 = 84
10 × 8 = 80	11 × 8 = 88	12 × 8 = 96
10 × 9 = 90	11 × 9 = 99	12 × 9 = 108
10 × 10 = 100	11 × 10 = 110	12 × 10 = 120
10 × 11 = 110	11 × 11 = 121	12 × 11 = 132
10 × 12 = 120	11 × 12 = 132	12 × 12 = 144
↑ Zero is in the ones place.	↑ Ones digit increases by 1 each time.	↑ Ones digit increases by 2 each time.

Practice

Find each product.

1. 10×5 **2.** 11×4 **3.** 10×3 **4.** 12×2 **5.** 10×8

6. 11×7 **7.** 10×9 **8.** 9×8 **9.** 11×4 **10.** 12×5

Patterns Continue each pattern.

11. 40, 50, 60, ■, ■, ■ **12.** 66, 55, 44, ■, ■, ■

13. 12, 24, 36, ■, ■, ■ **14.** 120, 110, 100, ■, ■, ■

15. Journal Charlie made three mistakes in making tables to show 10, 11, and 12 multiplication facts. Write how you know that each is wrong.

a. 33 is in the 10s table.

b. 13 is in the 12s table.

c. 94 is in the 11s table.

16. Measurement Eggs often come 12 to a carton. This is called a *dozen* eggs. How many eggs are in 4 dozen?

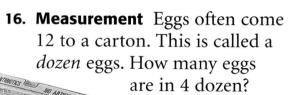

Multiplying with 3 Factors

You Will Learn
how to multiply with 3 factors

Vocabulary
grouping property
When you multiply, you can change the grouping of factors and the product will be the same.

Learn

Suppose you make Super Cheesy Sandwiches for 4 people. Each person gets 2 sandwiches. Each sandwich has 3 slices of cheese. How many slices of cheese will you need?

Here are some ways to find the product of $4 \times 2 \times 3$.

Grouping symbols ( ) tell which factors to multiply first.		**If there are no grouping symbols, you can choose any two factors to multiply first.**
$(4 \times 2) \times 3$	$4 \times (2 \times 3)$	$4 \times 2 \times 3$
8×3	4×6	Try 4×3 first.
$8 \times 3 = 24$	$4 \times 6 = 24$	$12 \times 2 = 24$

Grouping property: You can change the grouping of factors, and the product will be the same.

$4 \times 2 \times 3 = 24$

So, you will need 24 slices of cheese.

Talk About It

Marc says, "The product of $(6 \times 4) \times 1$ is greater than $(1 \times 6) \times 4$." Do you agree or disagree? Explain.

Check

Find each product.

1. $(2 \times 3) \times 6$ **2.** $3 \times (7 \times 1)$ **3.** $5 \times 1 \times 2$ **4.** $1 \times (4 \times 3)$

5. Reasoning Give at least two different ways to find the product of $8 \times 1 \times 7$. Then tell what the product is.

Practice

Skills and Reasoning

6. $(3 \times 2) \times 5$ **7.** $1 \times (4 \times 8)$ **8.** $7 \times 1 \times 7$ **9.** $6 \times (2 \times 0)$

10. $3 \times 1 \times 9$ **11.** $(2 \times 2) \times 6$ **12.** $0 \times 8 \times 8$ **13.** $(2 \times 4) \times 2$

14. $3 \times (4 \times 1)$ **15.** $(3 \times 3) \times 6$ **16.** $9 \times 1 \times 4$ **17.** $(0 \times 3) \times 9$

18. $2 \times (4 \times 2)$ **19.** $(3 \times 3) \times 9$ **20.** $2 \times 2 \times 2$ **21.** $3 \times 5 \times 2$

22. Find the product of 1, 8, and 5. **23.** Find the product of 5, 4, and 0.

24. Does 9×8 have the same product as $3 \times 8 \times 3$? Explain.

25. If you know the product of $4 \times 6 \times 2$, do you also know the product of $2 \times 6 \times 4$? Explain.

Problem Solving and Applications

26. What If You make sandwiches for six people. Each person gets one sandwich. How many slices of cheese will you need? Use the information on page 258 to help.

Using Data Use the Data File on page 237 to answer **27–29.**

27. How many teaspoons of sugar are in 3 slices of packaged bread?

28. How many more teaspoons of sugar are in a can of cola than in a cup of chocolate milk?

29. How many teaspoons of sugar are in 5 chocolate milk shakes?

Algebra Readiness Find each missing factor.

30. $3 \times ■ \times 3 = 18$ **31.** $2 \times 2 \times ■ = 16$ **32.** $■ \times 8 \times 6 = 48$

33. $■ \times 5 \times 4 = 20$ **34.** $2 \times ■ \times 4 = 56$ **35.** $3 \times 1 \times ■ = 27$

Mixed Review and Test Prep

Find each product.

36. 3×9 **37.** 5×6 **38.** 4×7 **39.** 8×2 **40.** 4×0

41. 3×8 **42.** 7×5 **43.** 8×6 **44.** 9×5 **45.** 2×7

46. Find the difference of 521 and 375.

Ⓐ 296 Ⓑ 156 Ⓒ 896 Ⓓ 146

Product Cross Off

Players
2 or more

Materials
- number cube labeled 3–8
- grid paper

Object
The object of this game is to cross out a row of products by thinking of basic multiplication facts.

How to Play

1. Each player makes a product card with 4 rows and 4 columns. Place these products anywhere on your card. Each number should only be used once.

Products			
10	12	14	15
16	18	20	21
24	25	27	28
30	32	35	40

2. One player rolls the number cube to get the first factor. Each player thinks of a multiplication fact using that factor. Record the fact you use. Cross off the product on your product card.

3. Take turns rolling the number cube. Try to be the first player to cross off one row of products.

4 Check each multiplication fact to be sure that the products are correct. Then make new product cards and play again.

Talk About It

How did you decide which multiplication fact to use?

More Ways to Play

- Play the Complete Cross Off Game. This time try to be the first player to cross off all of the products.

- Play the game again using a product card with 5 rows and 5 columns. Place these products anywhere on your card. Each number should only be used once.

Products				
0	3	4	5	6
7	8	9	10	12
14	15	16	18	20
21	24	25	27	28
30	32	35	40	45

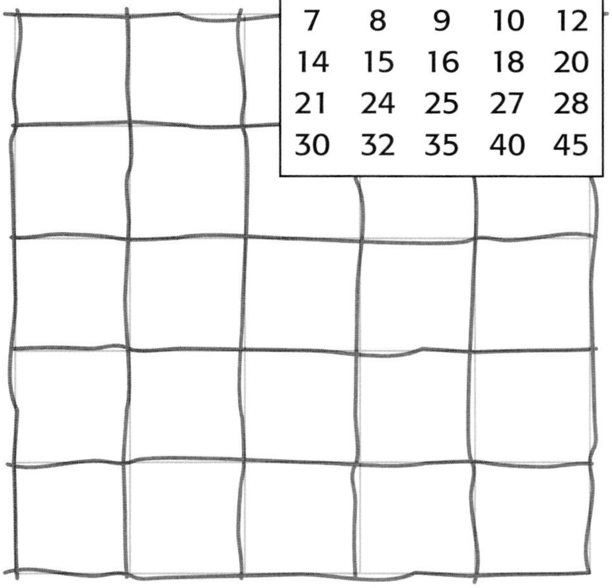

Reasoning

1. Suppose your product card looks like this. What number do you hope is rolled next? What fact would you use? Explain.

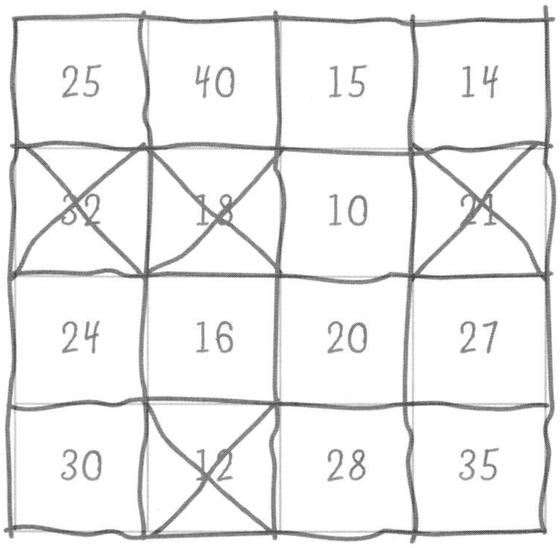

2. Suppose you rolled an 8. What product would you cross off? What fact would you use? Explain.

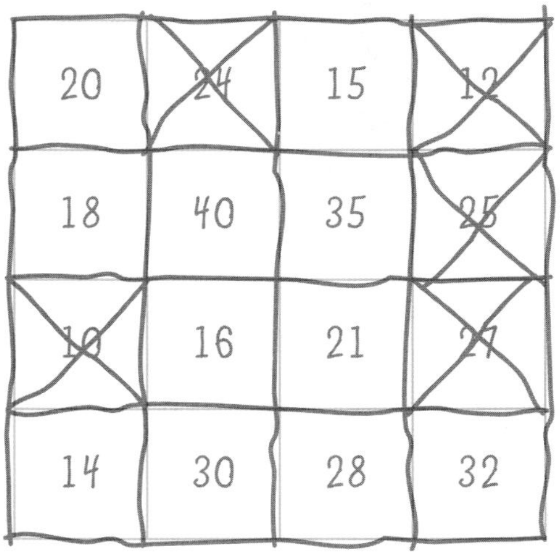

3. Suppose you were playing with the larger product card. Where would you place the 0? Explain.

Chapter 6
Lesson
9

Problem Solving

Compare Strategies: Look for a Pattern and Draw a Picture

You Will Learn
how to solve the same problem using different strategies

Learn

Plan a class picnic for 29 people! Decide how many blankets to bring. Each blanket seats 4 people. How many blankets do you need?

Maura's Way

I made a table and looked for a pattern.

I could bring 7 blankets for 28 people. But 29 people are coming, so I'll need 8 blankets.

Freddy's Way

I drew a picture.

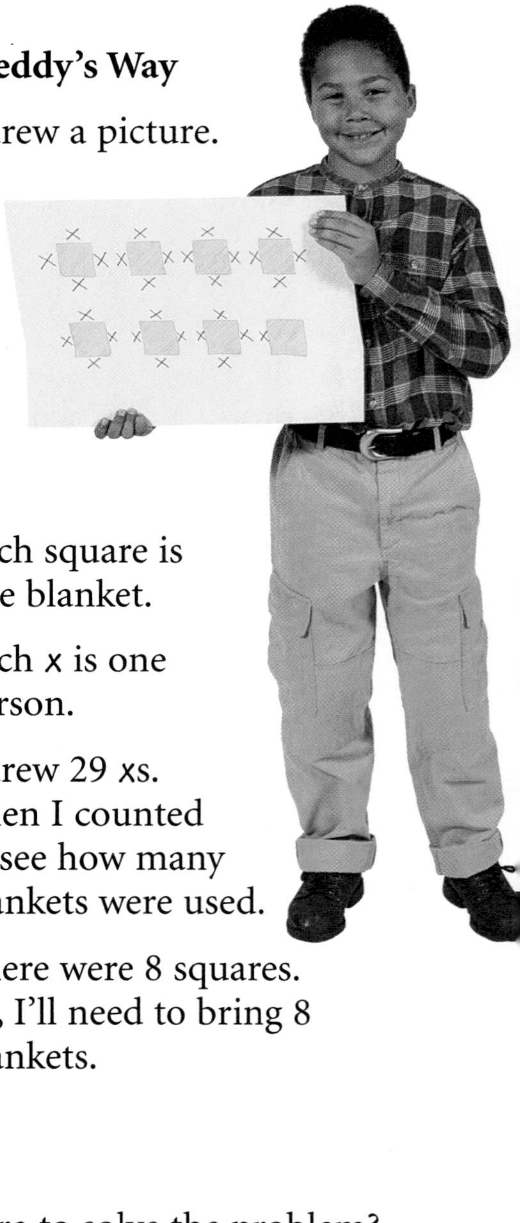

Each square is one blanket.

Each x is one person.

I drew 29 xs. Then I counted to see how many blankets were used.

There were 8 squares. So, I'll need to bring 8 blankets.

Talk About It

1. How did finding a pattern help Maura to solve the problem?

2. How did Freddy's picture help him find an answer?

Check

1. Suppose you are planning a picnic for 49 people. You must buy paper cups in packages of 12. How many packages of paper cups will you need?

Problem Solving
Understand
Plan
Solve
Look Back

Problem Solving Practice

Problem Solving Strategies

- Use Objects/Act It Out
- Draw a Picture
- Look for a Pattern
- Guess and Check
- Use Logical Reasoning
- Make an Organized List
- Make a Table
- Solve a Simpler Problem
- Work Backward

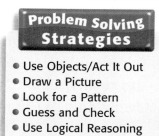

Choose a Tool

Use any strategy to solve each problem.

2. One package of pita bread makes 6 sandwiches. How many packages do you need to make 45 sandwiches?

3. For a scout barbeque, you must bring enough fruit drinks to serve 51 people. If fruit drinks come in cartons of 4, how many cartons should you buy?

4. **Critical Thinking** You must make pies for a family reunion. Each pie has 6 slices. If 62 people will be at the reunion, how many pies should you make so that each person gets one slice? How many slices will be left over?

5. You want to choose a sandwich with one filling from this menu. How many kinds of sandwiches can you choose?

6. **Social Studies** In 1993, a typical American ate about 400 pounds of vegetables and 25 pounds of cheese in a year. How many more pounds of vegetables than cheese did a typical American eat?

7. Suppose it rains on your picnic! Now you must set up inside tables that seat 8 people. If 49 people are coming, how many tables do you need?

Technology

Doubling with a Calculator

Materials
calculator

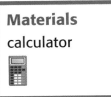

The manager of the Double Dollar Video Rental Store is trying to decide how much to charge for videos that are returned late. She wants to double the rental cost every day a video is late.

When you double a number, you make it twice its value. If you double \$1, you get \$2. If you double \$2, you get \$4. Notice that you are multiplying by 2. Use doubling to find the rental cost for a video that is returned 10 days late.

Work Together

You can use a calculator to double numbers.

1. Copy the table to record each cost.
2. Find the rental cost for a video that is returned 1 day late. Start by doubling \$1. Press 1 [×] 2 [=]. Record the cost.
3. Make sure the product of 1×2 still appears on your calculator. To find the rental cost for a video that is returned 2 days late, press [×] 2 [=]. Record the cost.
4. Continue doubling each rental cost. Record each cost.

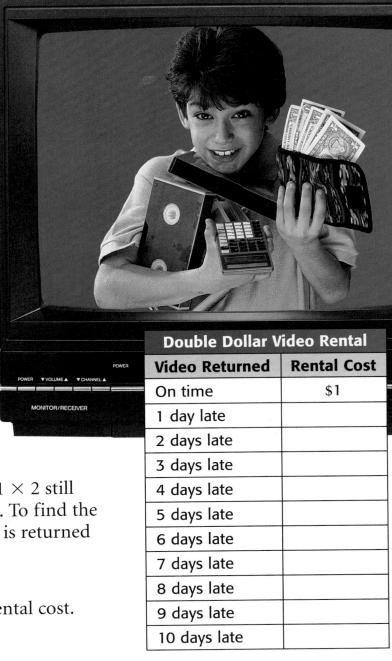

Double Dollar Video Rental

Video Returned	Rental Cost
On time	\$1
1 day late	
2 days late	
3 days late	
4 days late	
5 days late	
6 days late	
7 days late	
8 days late	
9 days late	
10 days late	

Exercises

Use your completed table of rental costs to answer **1–4.**

1. What is the rental cost for a video that is returned 5 days late?
2. What is the rental cost for a video that is returned 10 days late?
3. If the rental cost for a video is $128, how many days late was the video?
4. Do you think it's a good idea for the Double Dollar Video Store to double the cost every day a video is late? Why or why not?

Extensions

5. You can use the [Cons] key to double numbers. The [Cons] key remembers the operation you want so that you don't have to press the keys each time.
   - **a.** Since you want to multiply by 2 over and over, press [×] 2 [Cons]. Now you're ready to begin doubling numbers.
   - **b.** To double 3, enter 3 [Cons]. Record the result in a table.

Number to Double	Result
3	6
6	

   - **c.** Make sure the result still appears on your calculator. To double the result, enter [Cons].
   - **d.** Continue to double each result until you reach a number greater than 100. How many times did you need to double the result to get a result greater than 100?

The number on the right of the calculator display tells you the result.

The number on the left of the calculator display tells you how many times you've doubled.

SECTION B

Review and Practice

(Lesson 6) Write true or false. You may use a hundred chart to help.

1. 39 is a multiple of 3.

2. 57 is a multiple of 6.

3. 42 is a multiple of 6.

4. 45 is a multiple of 3.

5. 80 is a multiple of 6.

6. 52 is a multiple of 3.

(Lesson 7) **Patterns** Continue each pattern.

7. 88, 77, 66, ■, ■, ■

8. 36, 48, 60, ■, ■, ■

9. 100, 90, 80, ■, ■, ■

10. How can you tell without multiplying that 10×8 does not equal 85?

(Lesson 8) Find each product.

11. $5 \times 2 \times 1$

12. $(8 \times 0) \times 6$

13. $(6 \times 1) \times 4$

14. $3 \times 2 \times 3$

15. $2 \times 3 \times 2$

16. $9 \times (1 \times 9)$

17. $0 \times 7 \times 4$

18. $2 \times 4 \times 2$

19. **Reasoning** Vena and Rashan have each collected coins from 2 different countries. They each have 3 coins from each country. How many coins do they have all together?

(Lesson 9) Solve. Use any strategy.

20. You are planning a party for 44 people. You must set up tables that seat 6 people each. How many tables should you set up?

21. There are 26 students in a science class. Three students can share 1 microscope. How many microscopes does the class need?

22. **Journal** *11 times 7 is a fun fact; the product is 7s back to back!* Write your own poem or sentence that will help you remember a multiplication fact.

Skills Checklist

In this section, you have:

- ☑ **Explored Patterns on a Hundred Chart**
- ☑ **Explored Patterns on a Fact Table**
- ☑ **Multiplied with 3 Factors**
- ☑ **Solved Problems by Looking for a Pattern and Drawing a Picture**

YOUR CHOICE

Choose at least one. Use what you have learned in this chapter.

1 Bag It!

Use plastic bags and color cubes to show multiplication facts. Write a fact you want to show. Put equal groups of cubes into bags to show your fact.

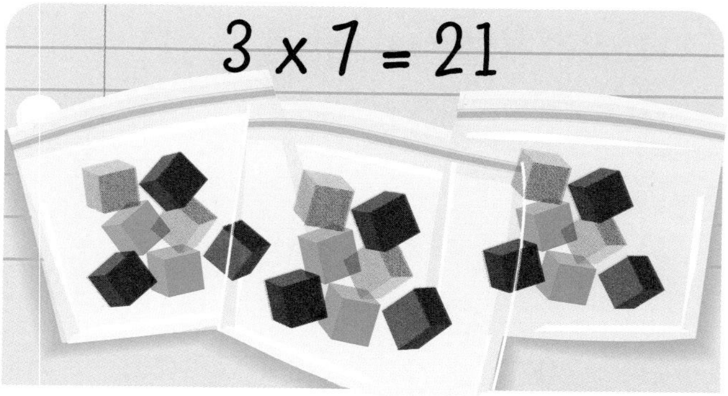

2 Goal 200

Play with at least one partner. Use two number cubes labeled 4–9. Take turns rolling the cubes. Find the product of the numbers you roll. Record the products. Add products to find your score. Try to be the first to score at least 200 points.

3 Computer Arrays

Draw arrays with a drawing program. Once you draw one □, you can copy and paste it. Label each array you draw.

4 Now You're Cooking

At Home Plan a meal for your family. Each person must be served 1 cup orange juice, 2 eggs or 2 grapefruit cups, 3 slices of bread, and 8 tablespoons granola. Make a table to show how much food you need.

CHAPTER 6
Review/Test

(Lessons 1–4) Find each product.

1. 3×6 **2.** 3×8 **3.** 4×4 **4.** 4×5 **5.** 6×9

6. 6×7 **7.** 7×7 **8.** 7×8 **9.** 8×2 **10.** 8×9

11. 9×4 **12.** 6×8 **13.** 4×3 **14.** 7×1 **15.** 4×7

16. $\begin{array}{r} 7 \\ \times 2 \\ \hline \end{array}$ **17.** $\begin{array}{r} 7 \\ \times 3 \\ \hline \end{array}$ **18.** $\begin{array}{r} 8 \\ \times 8 \\ \hline \end{array}$ **19.** $\begin{array}{r} 8 \\ \times 4 \\ \hline \end{array}$ **20.** $\begin{array}{r} 4 \\ \times 6 \\ \hline \end{array}$

21. $\begin{array}{r} 0 \\ \times 8 \\ \hline \end{array}$ **22.** $\begin{array}{r} 5 \\ \times 6 \\ \hline \end{array}$ **23.** $\begin{array}{r} 9 \\ \times 2 \\ \hline \end{array}$ **24.** $\begin{array}{r} 6 \\ \times 6 \\ \hline \end{array}$ **25.** $\begin{array}{r} 5 \\ \times 8 \\ \hline \end{array}$

26. $\begin{array}{r} 0 \\ \times 3 \\ \hline \end{array}$ **27.** $\begin{array}{r} 2 \\ \times 6 \\ \hline \end{array}$ **28.** $\begin{array}{r} 3 \\ \times 5 \\ \hline \end{array}$ **29.** $\begin{array}{r} 5 \\ \times 7 \\ \hline \end{array}$ **30.** $\begin{array}{r} 9 \\ \times 3 \\ \hline \end{array}$

31. Reasoning Explain how you could solve 7×9 if you know the product of 5×9.

(Lesson 6) Write true or false.

32. 21 is a multiple of 6. **33.** 24 is a multiple of 3 and a multiple of 6.

34. The ones digit in a multiple of 3 is always a 1, 3, or 6.

35. All multiples of 6 are also multiples of 3.

(Lesson 7) Patterns Continue each pattern.

36. 10, 20, 30, ■, ■, ■ **37.** 11, 22, 33, ■, ■, ■ **38.** 120, 110, 100, ■, ■, ■

39. 12, 24, 36, ■, ■, ■ **40.** 144, 132, 120, ■, ■, ■ **41.** 99, 88, 77, ■, ■, ■

(Lesson 8) Find each product.

42. $4 \times 1 \times 6$ **43.** $9 \times 9 \times 1$ **44.** $2 \times (3 \times 3)$ **45.** $5 \times 1 \times 2$

46. $3 \times 2 \times 4$ **47.** $(2 \times 2) \times 3$ **48.** $3 \times 0 \times 4$ **49.** $1 \times (8 \times 8)$

(Lesson 9) Solve. Use any strategy.

50. Suppose you must give 2 napkins to each guest at a family barbeque. There will be 13 people at the barbeque. How many napkins do you need?

CHAPTER 6

Performance Assessment

When you shake a piñon (PIN-yōn) pine tree, the ripe nuts from the pine cone fall to the ground. The Pueblo Indians of the southwest United States have a long tradition of including piñon nuts in meals. These nuts can be roasted and eaten by themselves or baked in cookies, pies, and cakes.

Piñon Cakes

Makes 8 cakes.

3 cups flour
1 cup piñon nuts
1 teaspoon salt
4 teaspoons baking powder
5 tablespoons sugar
4 tablespoons butter
3 cups water

1. **Decision Making** Suppose you need to make a cake for each person in your class. How many cakes will you make? How will you change the recipe so that it makes enough cakes?

2. **Recording Data** Copy and complete the table to show how much of each ingredient you'll need.

Ingredients for 8 Piñon Cakes	Ingredients for ____ Piñon Cakes
■ cups flour	■ cups flour
■ cup piñon nuts	■ cups piñon nuts
■ teaspoon salt	■ teaspoons salt
■ teaspoons baking powder	■ teaspoons baking powder
■ tablespoons sugar	■ tablespoons sugar
■ tablespoons butter	■ tablespoons butter
■ cups water	■ cups water

3. **Explain Your Thinking** How did you decide how much of each ingredient you would need?

4. **Critical Thinking** Will any cakes be left over? How do you know?

Math Magazine

The Amazing Maya

More than 2,000 years ago, people known as the Maya lived in Central America and southern Mexico. The Maya had a number system that allowed them to create an accurate calendar. They used symbols different from the ones we use.

Here are some of the symbols for Mayan numbers.

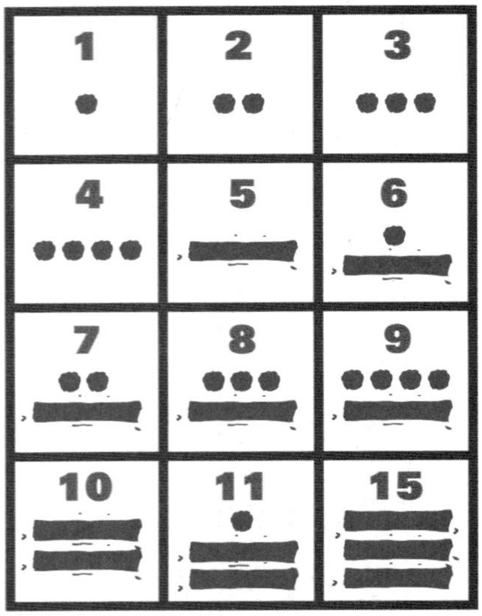

Can you figure out the key to Mayan numbers? Use the pattern in the table to try.

Try These!

Write the Mayan symbol for each number.

1. 12 **2.** 14 **3.** 18 **4.** 19

5. Reasoning How does skip counting by 5s help you understand Mayan numbers?

CHAPTERS 1–6

Cumulative Review

I can use patterns to decide which answer is correct. I know that products with 5 as a factor have a ones digit of 0 or 5. So, (B) is the only answer that makes sense.

Test Prep Strategy: Make Smart Choices

Look for patterns.

Which multiplication sentence is correct?

(A) $4 \times 5 = 9$ (B) $8 \times 5 = 40$

(C) $5 \times 5 = 36$ (D) $9 \times 5 = 14$

Test Prep Strategies

- Read Carefully
- Follow Directions
- Make Smart Choices
- Eliminate Choices
- Work Backward from an Answer

Write the letter of the correct answer. You may use any strategy to help.

1. What is 525 rounded to the nearest hundred?

   (A) 500 (B) 552 (C) 505 (D) 555

2. Estimate the sum of 629 and 328.

   (A) 800 (B) 900 (C) 2,000 (D) 600

3. What is the difference of 201 and 130?

   (A) 71 (B) 61 (C) 81 (D) 131

4. Lina buys cookies for her class. One box of cookies costs $3. How much will 6 boxes cost?

   (A) 6 (B) $18 (C) $30 (D) 12

5. Philip starts his homework at 6:00 P.M. He studies for 1 hour and 30 minutes. What time does he finish?

   (A) 6:30 P.M. (B) 7:00 A.M. (C) 7:30 A.M. (D) 7:30 P.M.

6. Which has the greatest sum?

   (A) $120 + 201$ (B) $501 + 120$ (C) $120 + 801$ (D) $701 + 120$

7. Which multiplication sentence is correct?

   (A) $6 \times 0 = 6$ (B) $6 \times 0 = 1$ (C) $6 \times 1 = 7$ (D) $6 \times 0 = 0$

8. Jean bought a bag of peanuts for $4 and a box of cereal for $5. Choose the operation you would use to find how much she spent all together.

   (A) add (B) subtract (C) multiply (D) not here

DATA FILE

Chapter 7
Division Concepts and Facts

COOL COLLECTIONS

SECTION A

Understanding Division 275

Rachel collects letters from around the world.
Page 275

Have you ever heard of a *rupee* or a *pula*? These are different kinds of money used in other countries. The rupee is used in India, and the pula is used in Botswana. Which country makes 8 different coins?

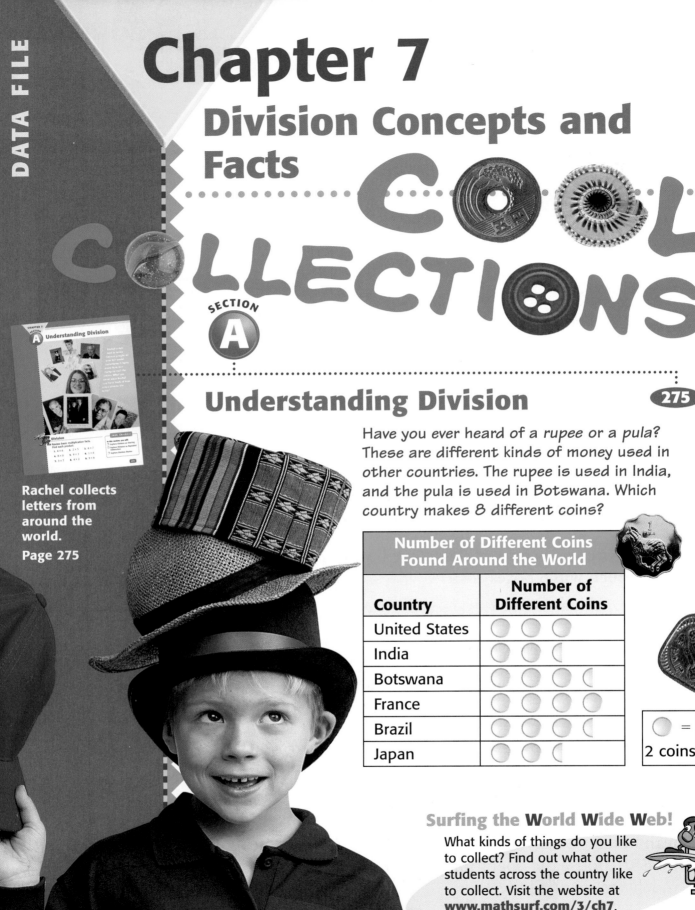

Number of Different Coins Found Around the World

Country	Number of Different Coins
United States	● ● ●
India	● ● ◐
Botswana	● ● ● ◐
France	● ● ● ●
Brazil	● ● ● ◐
Japan	● ● ◐

● = 2 coins

Surfing the World Wide Web!

What kinds of things do you like to collect? Find out what other students across the country like to collect. Visit the website at **www.mathsurf.com/3/ch7**. Use the data you find to report the top three things to collect.

SECTION B

Using Multiplication Facts to Find Division Facts

283

Do you know what a philatelist is? It's a person who collects stamps. Some stamps come in groups, or blocks, with different designs on each stamp. Which stamps have the greatest number of stamps in a block?

U.S. Stamps			
Stamp	Year Issued	Number in a Block	Value
Santa Maria	1893	6	3¢
Postal Service	1971	12	8¢
Indian Art	1980	4	15¢
Space	1981	8	18¢
Dinosaurs	1989	4	25¢
Kids Care	1995	4	32¢

Frank is a computer wiz.

Page 283

SECTION C

Finding More Division Facts

299

People have loved playing games for many years. Mill was most popular in Europe during the Middle Ages. People in India played Pachisi thousands of years ago. Which game uses the least number of pieces?

Game	Number of Players	Total Number of Pieces
Chess	2	32
Checkers	2	24
Pachisi	4	16
Mill	2	18

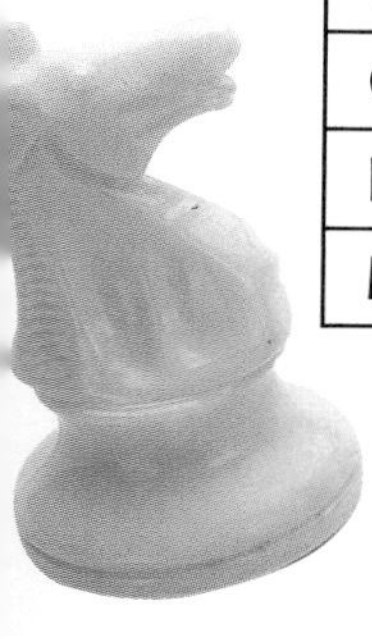

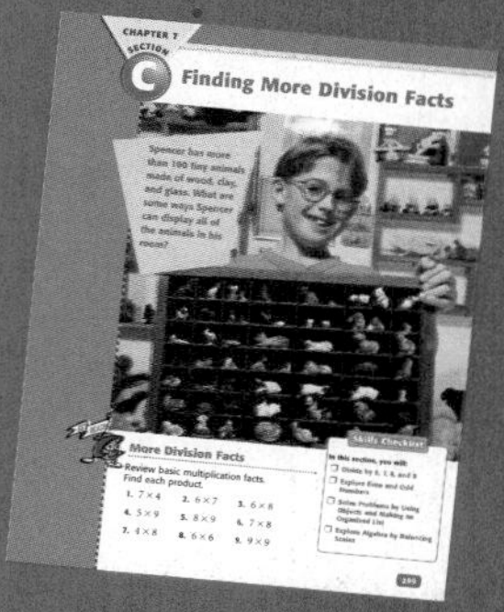

Spencer collects cool animals.

Page 299

TEAM PROJECT
Send & Deliver

Materials
grid paper, markers, scissors, paste

Set up a postal system in your classroom!

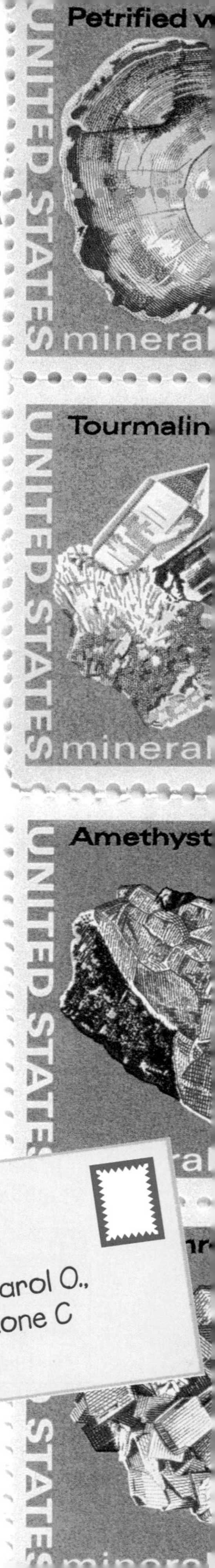

Make a Plan

- Draw a sketch of your classroom. On the sketch, divide your classroom into 4 zones. Label each zone A–D.

Carry It Out

1. Use grid paper to make a sheet of 4¢ stamps. Your sheet should have 24 stamps on it.

From Zone A	To Zone B 16¢	To Zone C 24¢	To Zone D 32¢
From Zone B	To Zone A 16¢	To Zone C 16¢	To Zone D 24¢
From Zone C	To Zone A 24¢	To Zone B 24¢	To Zone D 16¢
From Zone D	To Zone A 32¢	To Zone B 24¢	To Zone C 16¢

2. Send a letter to classmates in each of the other zones. Use the table to find the cost to mail letters to other zones.
3. Address the letters and paste the stamps. Don't forget to write your return address!

Talk About It

- How did you know how many stamps to put on each letter?

Present the Project

- Display the letters in your classroom.

CHAPTER 7

SECTION A

Understanding Division

Rachel sends mail to many famous people all over the world. Sometimes it takes more than one stamp to mail the letters. What are some ways Rachel can keep track of how many stamps she needs?

Division

Review basic multiplication facts.
Find each product.

1. 4×6	**2.** 2×5	**3.** 6×7
4. 8×0	**5.** 9×3	**6.** 1×6
7. 3×7	**8.** 4×2	**9.** 9×6

Skills Checklist

In this section, you will:

- ❒ **Explore Division as Sharing**
- ❒ **Explore Division as Repeated Subtraction**
- ❒ **Explore Division Stories**

Exploring Division as Sharing

Problem Solving Connection
- Use Objects/ Act It Out
- Draw a Picture

Materials
counters

Explore

What's this? It's snowing inside the house! Actually, this is a snow dome. Shake up a snow dome, and snow falls on the scene inside!

Work Together

Use counters or draw pictures to solve.

Remember
Equal groups have the same number of objects in each group.

1. Claude has 9 new snow domes in his collection. He wants equal groups of domes on each shelf.
   a. How many shelves are there?
   b. How many domes will he put on each shelf?

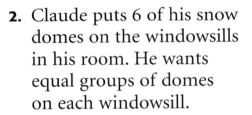

2. Claude puts 6 of his snow domes on the windowsills in his room. He wants equal groups of domes on each windowsill.
   a. How many windowsills are in Claude's room?
   b. How many domes will he put on each windowsill?

3. Write your own problem about 12 snow domes.

Talk About It

Tell how you found how many domes to put on each shelf or on each windowsill.

Connect

When you **share equally,** you can **divide.**

Laurie wants to share 8 pencils equally with Miko.
How many pencils will each person get?

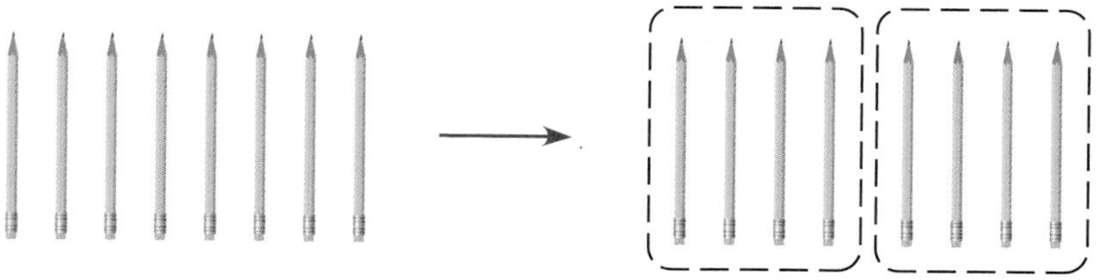

number of pencils		number of people		number for each	
8	$\div$	2	$=$	4	**division sentence**

Laurie and Miko will each get 4 pencils.

Practice

Copy and complete each division sentence.

1. $4 \div 2 = \square$

2. $12 \div 2 = \square$

Solve. You may use counters or draw pictures to help.

3. Reasoning Three friends shared some baseball cards. If they each got 3 cards, how many did they start with?

4. Tarik and 4 friends share 10 crackers equally. How many crackers does each person get?

5. Science The buckeye butterfly has 4 wings with the same number of spots on each wing. It has 8 spots total. How many spots are on each wing?

6. Mr. Walls passes out 15 markers to 5 students. If each student gets the same number of markers, how many markers does each student get?

7. Journal Suppose you want to arrange leaves in a scrapbook. You want the same number of leaves on each page. Draw a picture to show how you would arrange 12 leaves on 3 pages.

Chapter 7
Lesson
2

Exploring Division as Repeated Subtraction

Problem Solving Connection
- Use Objects/ Act It Out
- Draw a Picture

Materials
counters

Explore

Rachel writes letters to people all over the world. When they write back, she keeps the letters in a scrapbook. Her favorite question to ask is, "What is the most important lesson to learn from life?"

Rachel lives in Roanoke, Virginia. She gets mail from as far away as Russia.

Work Together

Use counters or draw pictures to solve.

1. Suppose Rachel writes 2 letters a day. She wants to know how many days it will take her to write 10 letters.

a. Show how many letters Rachel plans to write. Take away groups of 2. How many groups of 2 did you take away?

b. How many days will it take her to write 10 letters?

Problem Solving Hint
You can use objects to act out each problem.

2. Rachel needs 3 stamps to send each letter. She wants to know how many letters she can send with 15 stamps.

a. Show how many stamps Rachel has. Take away groups of 3. How many groups of 3 did you take away?

b. How many letters can she send?

Talk About It

Explain how you solved the problems about Rachel's letters.

Connect

When you **take away equal groups,** you can **divide.**

Pablo is putting out supplies for the art club. He has 12 crayons. If he wants to put 6 crayons in a cup on each table, how many cups can Pablo fill?

crayons		number in each cup		number of cups	
12	÷	6	=	2	**division sentence**

Pablo can fill 2 cups with crayons.

Practice

Solve. You may use counters or draw pictures.

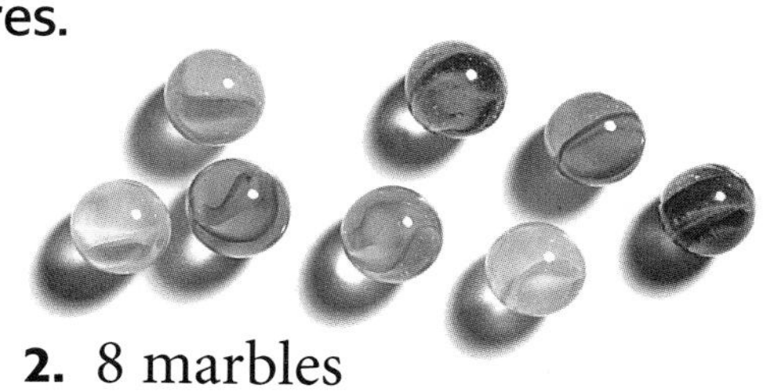

1. 6 stamps
3 on each envelope
How many envelopes?

2. 8 marbles
2 in each cup
How many cups?

3. Reasoning Suppose Pablo puts 4 markers in each cup. Could he have a total of 10 markers? Draw a picture and explain.

Use the table to solve **4** and **5.** You may use counters or draw pictures to help.

Item	Cost
Cap	$4
Whistle	$2
Ball	$5

4. Money Linn has $16 to spend on caps. How many can she buy?

5. Critical Thinking Carl has $17. He wants to buy 1 whistle and some balls. How many balls can he buy?

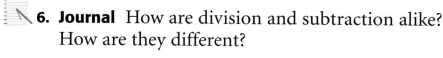

6. Journal How are division and subtraction alike? How are they different?

Chapter 7
Lesson
3

Exploring Division Stories

Problem Solving Connection
- Use Objects/ Act It Out
- Draw a Picture

Materials
counters

Explore

Marina wrote a division story to show 14 ÷ 2 = 7.

Marina gives her dog
2 dog treats eachday.
She has 14 dog treats.
How many days will the
dog treats last?
SPOT

Remember
When you divide, you share equally or take away equal groups.

Work Together

Try writing your own division stories. Use counters to solve.

1. Write your own story for 14 ÷ 2.

2. Write a division story for each.

a. 20 ÷ 4 **b.** 18 ÷ 9 **c.** 32 ÷ 4

Talk About It

3. Tell how your story for 14 ÷ 2 is like Marina's story. Tell how it is different.

4. Explain how you know your stories are division stories.

Connect

When you share equally or take away equal groups, you can divide.

Share Equally

Four friends share 12 sheets of paper. How many sheets of paper does each friend get?

$12 \div 4 = 3$

Each friend gets 3 sheets of paper.

Take Away Equal Groups

Jeff cut a submarine sandwich into 8 pieces. If each person gets 2 pieces, how many people can Jeff feed?

$8 \div 2 = 4$

Jeff can feed 4 people.

Practice

Write a division story for each. You may use counters to solve.

1. $25 \div 5$ **2.** $24 \div 6$ **3.** $27 \div 3$ **4.** $12 \div 4$

Algebra Readiness Complete each number sentence. You may use counters to solve.

5. $12 \div \square = 4$ **6.** $\square \div 2 = 3$ **7.** $24 \div \square = 3$ **8.** $\square \div 3 = 5$

Solve. You may use counters or draw pictures to help.

9. Shauna has 12 party favors. She wants to give 2 to each guest. How many guests can Shauna invite?

10. Ivan picked 16 peaches. He wants to share them equally with his sister. How many peaches will each person get?

11. **Using Data** Suppose you have one of each kind of coin made in France. You want to put four coins on each page of your scrapbook. How many pages will you need? Use the Data File on page 272 to help.

12. **Fine Arts** Japanese puppet theater called *bunraku* uses puppets like the one shown here. It takes 3 people to handle each puppet. How many puppets could 9 people handle?

13. **Journal** Draw a picture to show $24 \div 4$. Explain how your picture shows division.

Bunraku puppet theater

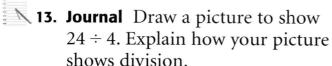

PRACTICE AND APPLY

SECTION A
Review and Practice

(Lessons 1 and 2) Copy and complete each division sentence.

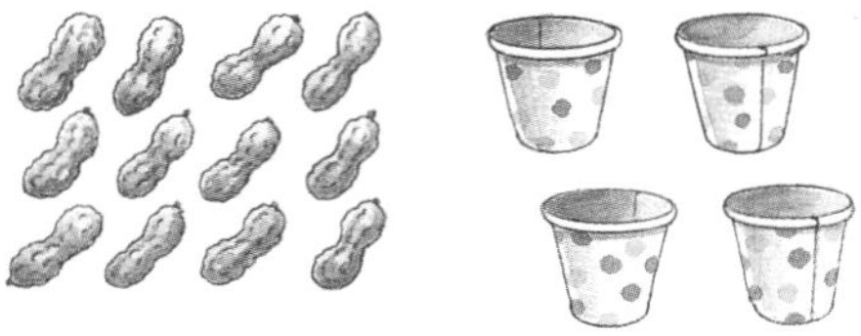

1. $12 \div 4 = \blacksquare$

2. $8 \div 2 = \blacksquare$

Solve. You may use counters or draw pictures.

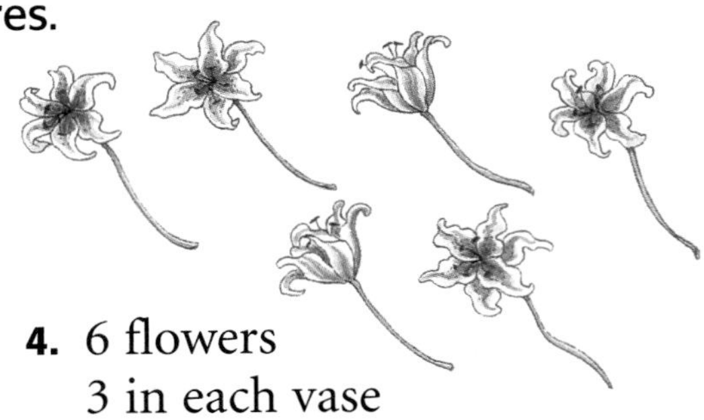

3. 10 pennies
5 in each group
How many groups?

4. 6 flowers
3 in each vase
How many vases?

5. **Reasoning** Keri and Nathan shared some crackers. Keri got 9 crackers and Nathan got 9 crackers. How many crackers did they share? Explain.

(Lesson 3) Write a division story for each. You may use counters to solve.

6. $24 \div 3$ **7.** $18 \div 6$ **8.** $14 \div 7$

Use the menu for **9** and **10.**

Lunch Menu	
Item	**Cost**
Hamburger	$2
Spaghetti	$3
Taco	$1

9. Mrs. Sheppard has $15 to spend on lunch for her family. How many plates of spaghetti can she buy?

10. **Write Your Own Problem** Use the menu to write your own division story. Draw a picture of your story to help you solve it.

11. **Journal** Suppose 21 students want to play a game with teams. They want 3 students on each team. Draw a picture to show how many teams they can make.

Skills Checklist

In this section, you have:

- ☑ **Explored Division as Sharing**
- ☑ **Explored Division as Repeated Subtraction**
- ☑ **Explored Division Stories**

CHAPTER 7

SECTION B

Using Multiplication Facts to Find Division Facts

Frank is a wiz with computers! He earns money to buy his own computer by fixing and testing computers in the lab at school. Can you think of how 6 students might separate into equal groups to share 2 computers?

Division Basic Facts

Review multiplication facts.
Find each product.

1. 2×3 **2.** 3×4 **3.** 4×6

4. 5×7 **5.** 1×6 **6.** 7×0

7. 4×7 **8.** 3×9 **9.** 5×3

Skills Checklist

In this section, you will:

- ❒ Connect Multiplication and Division
- ❒ Divide by 2, 3, 4, and 5
- ❒ Explore Dividing with 0 and 1
- ❒ Solve Problems by Choosing an Operation

Chapter 7
Lesson
4

Connecting Multiplication and Division

You Will Learn
how to use multiplication to divide

Vocabulary

fact family
a group of related facts

dividend
the number to be divided in a division number sentence

divisor
the number by which a dividend is divided

quotient
the answer to a division problem

Learn

Kellie just has to look at her collection to remember the fun places she's been. She collects a thimble from every place she visits.

Kellie lives in Norman, Oklahoma.

You can think about multiplication and fact families to divide.

Example

Kellie has 4 groups of 5 thimbles. How many thimbles does she have?

Multiply. Find 4×5.

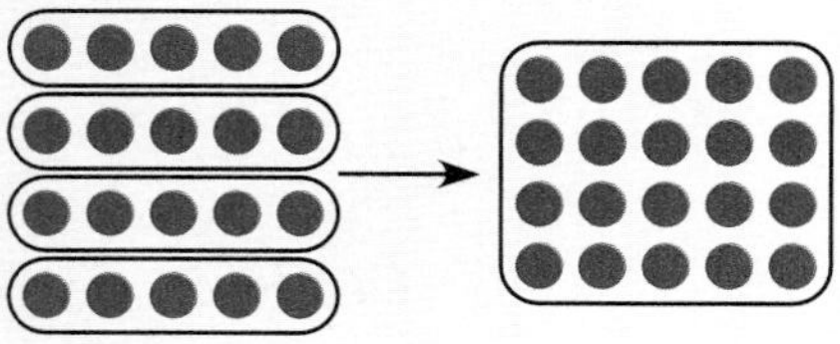

$4 \times 5 = 20$
So, she has 20 thimbles.

Kellie puts 20 thimbles in equal groups of 5. How many groups are there?

Divide. Find $20 \div 5$.

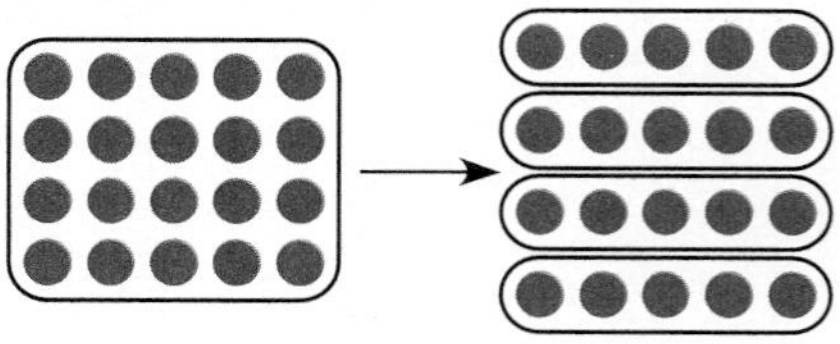

Think: 5 times what number equals 20? $5 \times \mathbf{4} = 20$

$20 \div 5 = \mathbf{4}$
So, there are 4 groups.

Math Tip
You use equal groups with multiplication and division.

Fact family:

factor	×	factor	=	product	**dividend**	÷	**divisor**	=	**quotient**
5	×	4	=	20	20	÷	5	=	4
4	×	5	=	20	20	÷	4	=	5

Talk About It

What multiplication fact can you use to find $28 \div 4$?

Check

Copy and complete. You may use counters to help.

1. $8 \times \blacksquare = 16$ $16 \div 8 = \blacksquare$

2. $5 \times \blacksquare = 15$ $15 \div 5 = \blacksquare$

3. $3 \times \blacksquare = 12$ $12 \div 3 = \blacksquare$

4. $2 \times \blacksquare = 6$ $6 \div 2 = \blacksquare$

5. Reasoning How could you use $3 \times 9 = 27$ to find $27 \div 3$?

Practice

Skills and Reasoning

Copy and complete. You may use counters to help.

6. $6 \times \blacksquare = 24$ $24 \div 6 = \blacksquare$

7. $4 \times \blacksquare = 12$ $12 \div 4 = \blacksquare$

8. $2 \times \blacksquare = 14$ $14 \div 2 = \blacksquare$

9. $3 \times \blacksquare = 9$ $9 \div 3 = \blacksquare$

10. $5 \times \blacksquare = 25$ $25 \div 5 = \blacksquare$

11. $3 \times \blacksquare = 18$ $18 \div 3 = \blacksquare$

12. $4 \times \blacksquare = 36$ $36 \div 4 = \blacksquare$

13. $7 \times \blacksquare = 21$ $21 \div 7 = \blacksquare$

14. What multiplication fact could you use to solve $10 \div 5$?

15. What are the number sentences in the fact family with $21 \div 7 = 3$?

Problem Solving and Applications

Solve. You may use counters to help.

16. Write Your Own Problem Write a division problem about a collection of thimbles or something else. Then solve.

17. What If Kellie puts 25 thimbles on 5 shelves. If she puts an equal number on each shelf, how many are on each shelf?

Mixed Review and Test Prep

Find each product.

18. 2×4 **19.** 2×7 **20.** 2×8 **21.** 2×3 **22.** 2×6

Patterns Continue each pattern.

23. 4, 8, 12, ■, ■, ■ **24.** 3, 6, 9, ■, ■, ■ **25.** 45, 40, 35, ■, ■, ■

26. Henry has 2 oranges. He cuts each orange into 4 pieces. How many pieces of orange does he have?

Ⓐ 8 Ⓑ 6 Ⓒ 2 Ⓓ 12

Chapter 7
Lesson
5

Dividing by 2

You Will Learn
how to divide by 2

Learn

Ka'Lena found her sea glass in Puerto Rico. Sea glass is glass that has been made smooth and dull by the ocean, a river, or a lake.

"Here's a green one!" Ka'Lena and her classmates in New York City spent lots of time with their heads bent to the sand over the summer. Why? They collected sea glass to study during the school year. What's the hardest color to find? Red!

Suppose students display 12 pieces of sea glass on 2 shelves. If they display an equal number of pieces on each shelf, how many pieces are on each shelf?

Remember
You can use fact families to help you divide.

Since you want to share equally, you divide.

Find $12 \div 2$.

Think: 2 times what number equals 12?

$2 \times \mathbf{6} = 12$

$12 \div 2 = \mathbf{6}$

So, there are 6 pieces on each shelf.

You can write a division number sentence in two ways.

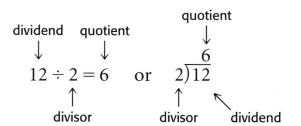

$$\underset{\text{dividend}}{12} \div \underset{\text{divisor}}{2} = \underset{\text{quotient}}{6} \quad \text{or} \quad \underset{\text{divisor}}{2}\overline{)\underset{\text{dividend}}{12}} \text{ with quotient } 6 \text{ above}$$

dividend → 12, divisor → 2, quotient → 6

Talk About It

What multiplication fact can help you find $8 \div 2$?

Check

Find each quotient.

1. $2\overline{)10}$ **2.** $2\overline{)16}$ **3.** $2\overline{)8}$ **4.** $2\overline{)4}$ **5.** $2\overline{)12}$

6. $4 \div 2$ **7.** $10 \div 2$ **8.** $12 \div 2$ **9.** $6 \div 2$ **10.** $16 \div 2$

11. Reasoning Raymond says, "I can solve $6 \div 2$ by using the fact $2 \times 6 = 12$." Do you agree or disagree? Explain.

PRACTICE AND APPLY

Practice

Skills and Reasoning

Find each quotient.

12. $2\overline{)18}$ **13.** $2\overline{)14}$ **14.** $2\overline{)16}$ **15.** $2\overline{)6}$ **16.** $2\overline{)8}$

17. $2 \div 2$ **18.** $8 \div 2$ **19.** $12 \div 2$ **20.** $18 \div 2$ **21.** $10 \div 2$

22. Divide 8 by 2. **23.** Divide 18 by 2. **24.** Divide 14 by 2.

25. How can you use multiplication to help you find $16 \div 2$?

26. Jerri says, "I can solve $8 \div 2$ by using the fact $2 \times 4 = 8$." Do you agree or disagree? Explain.

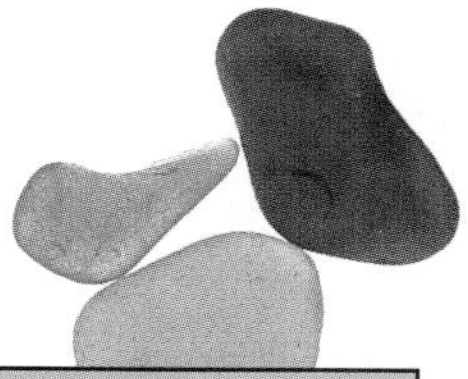

Problem Solving and Applications

Using Data Use the table to answer **27** and **28.**

27. How many green, blue, and brown pieces of sea glass did Ka'Lena's class collect?

28. If Ka'Lena's class put all the blue sea glass in equal groups of 2, how many groups of sea glass would they have?

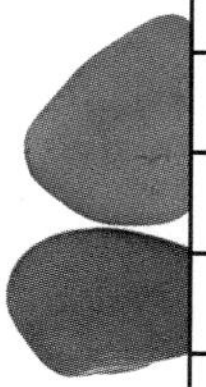

Sea Glass Collected

Color	Pieces
Clear	45
Blue	18
Turquoise	1
Purple	1
Green	170
Lavender	3
Red	0
Brown	97

Mixed Review and Test Prep

Find each product.

29. 5×4 **30.** 5×6 **31.** 5×8 **32.** 5×2 **33.** 5×5

Choose the correct number sentence.

34. Richard had 6 baseball cards and gave 2 away. How many baseball cards did he have left?

Ⓐ $6 + 2 = 8$ Ⓑ $6 \times 2 = 12$ Ⓒ $6 - 2 = 4$ Ⓓ $6 \div 2 = 3$

Chapter 7
Lesson
6

Dividing by 5

You Will Learn
how to divide by 5

Learn

What do you do when your computer crashes? Call Frank! He and some classmates earn money to buy their own computers by fixing and testing computers in the school lab.

Frank is from Oakland, California.

Problem Solving Hint
You can work backward to solve a problem.

Suppose there are 15 students in the lab. If there are 5 students working on each computer, how many computers are there?

Since students are in equal groups, you can divide.

Find $15 \div 5$.

Think: 5 times what number equals 15?

$5 \times \mathbf{3} = 15$

$15 \div 5 = \mathbf{3}$ $\qquad 5\overline{)15}$ with quotient $\mathbf{3}$

So, there are 3 computers.

Talk About It

What multiplication sentence can help you find $45 \div 5$?

Check

Find each quotient.

1. $5\overline{)25}$ **2.** $5\overline{)45}$ **3.** $5\overline{)20}$ **4.** $2\overline{)18}$ **5.** $5\overline{)15}$

6. $10 \div 5$ **7.** $12 \div 2$ **8.** $40 \div 5$ **9.** $35 \div 5$ **10.** $30 \div 5$

11. Reasoning Carlos says, "5×4 is 20, so $20 \div 5$ is 4." Do you agree or disagree? Explain.

Practice

Skills and Reasoning

Find each quotient.

12. $5\overline{)10}$ **13.** $5\overline{)15}$ **14.** $5\overline{)40}$ **15.** $5\overline{)20}$ **16.** $2\overline{)6}$

17. $5\overline{)35}$ **18.** $5\overline{)30}$ **19.** $5\overline{)25}$ **20.** $2\overline{)16}$ **21.** $5\overline{)45}$

22. $30 \div 5$ **23.** $15 \div 5$ **24.** $8 \div 2$ **25.** $25 \div 5$ **26.** $10 \div 5$

27. $10 \div 2$ **28.** $20 \div 5$ **29.** $40 \div 5$ **30.** $35 \div 5$ **31.** $45 \div 5$

32. Divide 40 by 5. **33.** Divide 25 by 5.

34. What multiplication fact can help you find $5\overline{)30}$?

35. How many groups of 5 are in 15?

Problem Solving and Applications

36. **What If** There are 5 computers in the lab and 20 students. If students work on computers in equal groups, how many students work on each computer?

37. **Money** Frank earns $5 an hour for fixing computers after school. If he earned $35, how many hours did he work?

38. **Time** Suppose Frank worked 3 days one week and 5 days the next week. If he worked for 2 hours each day, how many hours did he work?

39. **Science** Computer memory is measured in *bits* and *bytes*. There are 8 bits in one byte. How many bits are in 5 bytes?

Mixed Review and Test Prep

Find each product.

40. 3×5 **41.** 3×7 **42.** 3×4 **43.** 3×2 **44.** 3×6

45. 4×4 **46.** 4×8 **47.** 4×6 **48.** 4×7 **49.** 4×9

Subtract.

50. $679 - 457$ **51.** $323 - 152$ **52.** $191 - 118$ **53.** $522 - 389$

54. What is the value of the red digit in 167,293?

Ⓐ 20 Ⓑ 200 Ⓒ 2,000 Ⓓ 2

Chapter 7
Lesson
7

Dividing by 3 and 4

You Will Learn
how to divide by 3 and 4

Learn

Jorge holds his breath as he steps one foot closer to the praying mantis in the long grass. Click! He got the picture! He has another wildlife photo for his collection.

Did You Know?
America didn't always have the praying mantis, an insect which eats other insects in the garden. They were brought from Europe to America around 1900.

Example 1

Jorge wants to put an equal number of photos on 3 pages of a scrapbook. If he has 18 photos, how many photos should he put on each page?

Find $18 \div 3$.

Think: 3 times what number equals 18?

$3 \times \mathbf{6} = 18$

$18 \div 3 = \mathbf{6}$ $\quad \begin{array}{r}\mathbf{6}\\3\overline{)18}\end{array}$

So, he should put 6 photos on each page.

Example 2

Suppose Jorge wants to make a scrapbook with 4 photos on each page. He has 36 photos. How many pages will he need?

Find $36 \div 4$.

Think: 4 times what number equals 36?

$4 \times \mathbf{9} = 36$

$36 \div 4 = \mathbf{9}$ $\quad \begin{array}{r}\mathbf{9}\\4\overline{)36}\end{array}$

So, he needs 9 pages.

Talk About It

1. What multiplication fact can help you find $24 \div 3$?
2. What multiplication fact can help you find $16 \div 4$?

Check

Find each quotient.

1. $3\overline{)12}$ **2.** $4\overline{)8}$ **3.** $3\overline{)27}$ **4.** $2\overline{)12}$ **5.** $3\overline{)15}$

6. $12 \div 4$ **7.** $18 \div 3$ **8.** $32 \div 4$ **9.** $25 \div 5$ **10.** $28 \div 4$

11. Reasoning How many 3s are in 9?

Practice

Skills and Reasoning

Find each quotient.

12. $3\overline{)24}$ **13.** $5\overline{)40}$ **14.** $3\overline{)21}$ **15.** $4\overline{)36}$ **16.** $3\overline{)6}$

17. $4\overline{)32}$ **18.** $4\overline{)24}$ **19.** $4\overline{)28}$ **20.** $2\overline{)6}$ **21.** $4\overline{)12}$

22. $20 \div 4$ **23.** $9 \div 3$ **24.** $24 \div 4$ **25.** $21 \div 3$ **26.** $8 \div 2$

27. $6 \div 3$ **28.** $20 \div 5$ **29.** $27 \div 3$ **30.** $36 \div 4$ **31.** $16 \div 4$

32. Divide 12 by 3. **33.** Divide 16 by 4. **34.** How many 4s are in 20?

35. How could you take away equal groups to find $3\overline{)15}$?

Problem Solving and Applications

Using Data Use the Data File on page 273 to help answer **36** and **37.**

36. Suppose you have 3 blocks of Kids Care stamps. How many stamps do you have?

37. If there are 4 stamps in a row of the 1981 Space stamp block, how many rows are there?

38. Science A chicken can run 9 miles per hour. A dragonfly, the world's fastest insect, can fly 4 times as fast. How fast can a dragonfly fly?

Mixed Review and Test Prep

Find each product.

39. 1×3 **40.** 6×0 **41.** 1×9 **42.** 1×8 **43.** 5×0

44. Find $569 - 243$.

Ⓐ 812 Ⓑ 322 Ⓒ 326 Ⓓ 806

Exploring Dividing with 0 and 1

Problem Solving Connection

Look for a Pattern

Materials

calculator

Remember

You can think of a related multiplication sentence to divide.

Explore

You can find patterns when you divide with 0 and 1. You can also find patterns when you divide a number by itself.

Work Together

Use a calculator. Copy and complete each division sentence. Look for patterns.

1. Explore dividing by 1.

- **a.** $5 \div 1 = \square$
- **b.** $8 \div 1 = \square$
- **c.** $28 \div 1 = \square$
- **d.** $347 \div 1 = \square$

2. Explore dividing a number by itself.

- **a.** $3 \div 3 = \square$
- **b.** $5 \div 5 = \square$
- **c.** $29 \div 29 = \square$
- **d.** $454 \div 454 = \square$

3. Explore dividing with 0.

- **a.** $0 \div 6 = \square$
- **b.** $0 \div 8 = \square$
- **c.** $0 \div 52 = \square$
- **d.** $0 \div 106 = \square$

Talk About It

4. What pattern did you see when a number was divided by 1?

5. What pattern did you see when a number was divided by itself?

6. What pattern did you see when 0 was divided by a number?

Connect

Here are some division rules.

Rule	Example
• Any number divided by 1 equals that number.	$4 \div 1 = 4$
• Any number (except 0) divided by itself equals 1.	$4 \div 4 = 1$
• Zero divided by any number (except 0) equals 0.	$0 \div 4 = 0$
• You cannot divide by 0.	

Practice

Copy and complete each division sentence. Then match each division sentence to the rule that explains the answer.

1. $3 \div 1 = \square$
2. $0 \div 7 = \square$
3. $5 \div 5 = \square$
4. $6 \div 6 = \square$
5. $0 \div 4 = \square$
6. $7 \div 1 = \square$
7. $9 \div 1 = \square$
8. $0 \div 5 = \square$
9. $8 \div 8 = \square$
10. $9 \div 1 = \square$

a. Any number divided by 1 equals that number.

b. Any number (except 0) divided by itself equals 1.

c. Zero divided by any number (except 0) equals 0.

Find each quotient.

11. $4\overline{)4}$ **12.** $3\overline{)0}$ **13.** $2\overline{)18}$ **14.** $1\overline{)2}$ **15.** $3\overline{)3}$

16. $5 \div 1$ **17.** $24 \div 4$ **18.** $7 \div 7$ **19.** $6 \div 6$ **20.** $0 \div 9$

Copy. Write $<$, $>$, or $=$.

21. $2 \div 2$ ● $5 \div 5$ **22.** $15 \div 3$ ● $18 \div 3$ **23.** $6 \div 1$ ● $7 \div 1$

24. $9 \div 3$ ● $12 \div 4$ **25.** $32 \div 4$ ● $0 \div 2$ **26.** $14 \div 2$ ● $8 \div 1$

27. Algebra Readiness Copy and complete the table. Then write the rule.

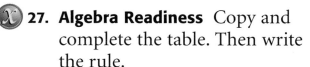

In	3	2	5	7	9	6
Out	9	6	15			

28. Critical Thinking Suppose you bake 2 sheets of cookies. There are 6 cookies on each sheet. You want to share the cookies equally with 12 friends. How many cookies will you give to each friend?

29. Journal Use pictures or words to explain why a number divided by 1 equals that number.

The Secret Divisor Game

Players 2

Object

The object of the game is to find the divisor with the fewest number of guesses.

How to Play

1. Player 1 thinks of a number from 1 to 5. This is the secret divisor. He or she writes it on a piece of paper so that Player 2 cannot see it.

   Divide by 3.

2. Make a table like the one below. Start with column number 1. Player 2 writes a number between 1 and 45 in the **In** row.

Guess	1	2	3
In			
Out			

3. Player 1 decides if that number divided by the secret number makes a basic division fact. If it does not, Player 1 writes an X in the **Out** row. If it does, Player 1 writes the quotient in the **Out** row.

4 Repeat until Player 2 has enough clues to guess the divisor. Player 2 gets 1 point for each guess.

5 Switch roles and repeat. Play until each player has had 5 turns thinking of a secret divisor. The player with the fewest points wins!

Talk About It

What strategy did you use to make guesses?

More Ways to Play

- Play another game. This time, Player 1 must think of a secret number from 0 to 9 to multiply. Player 2 must write numbers from 0 to 9 in the **In** row to find the secret factor.

- Play again. Player 1 thinks of two secret numbers from 0 to 5. One number is the secret addend and the other number is the secret factor. For example, Player 1 might choose:

  Add 3, multiply by 2.

  Player 2 thinks of numbers from 0 to 4. Player 2 must guess the secret addend and factor.

Reasoning

1. Suppose this is the table in the Secret Divisor Game.

Guess	1	2	3
In	17	15	14
Out	X	X	7

Do you have enough information to guess the divisor? Explain.

2. Which number would you rather pick as your first guess in the Secret Divisor Game: 17 or 18? Explain.

3. If you're playing the Secret Addend and Factor Game, do you have enough information to guess the addend and factor? Explain.

Guess	1	2	3
In	3	1	
Out	12	6	

Chapter 7
Lesson
9

Problem Solving

Analyze Word Problems: Choose an Operation

You Will Learn
how to choose the operation needed to solve a problem

Learn

Bonnie volunteers her time to help stray animals find a safe and happy place to live.

Suppose Bonnie agreed to spend 24 hours in 4 weeks helping at the animal shelter. She must work the same number of hours each week. How many hours will she work each week?

Bonnie from Clarinda, Iowa, was a finalist in the national Be Kind to Animals Kid Contest.

Work Together

▶ Understand

What do you know?

What do you need to find out?

▶ Plan

What operation should you choose?

Since you must separate the number of hours into 4 equal groups, you divide.

▶ Solve

Divide.

24	÷	4	=	6
hours		weeks		hours each week

So, she will work 6 hours each week.

▶ Look Back

Does your answer make sense?

Talk About It

Suppose Bonnie agreed to work 5 hours one week, 3 hours the next week, and 2 hours the next week. What operation would you use to decide how many hours she worked in 3 weeks?

Check

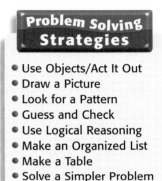

Problem Solving
Understand
Plan
Solve
Look Back

Which number sentence would you choose to solve the problem? Explain.

1. Suppose Bonnie worked 5 hours a week for 4 weeks. How many hours did she work?

   Ⓐ $4 + 5 = 9$ Ⓑ $5 - 4 = 1$ Ⓒ $4 \times 5 = 20$ Ⓓ $20 \div 5 = 4$

Write which operation you would use. Then solve the problem.

2. Suppose Bonnie buys a 4-pound bag of Bow-Wow dog food and a 5-pound bag of Doggie Delight dog food. How many pounds of dog food does she have?

Problem Solving Practice

Problem Solving Strategies

- Use Objects/Act It Out
- Draw a Picture
- Look for a Pattern
- Guess and Check
- Use Logical Reasoning
- Make an Organized List
- Make a Table
- Solve a Simpler Problem
- Work Backward

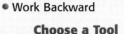

Choose a Tool

Which number sentence would you choose to solve the problem? Explain.

3. **Money** Suppose Bonnie sold \$8 in tickets to a fund-raiser. Each ticket cost \$2. How many tickets did she sell?

   Ⓐ $8 + 2 = 10$ Ⓑ $8 \div 2 = 4$

4. Suppose Bonnie's cat had 8 cat toys and lost 2 of them under the refrigerator. How many cat toys does he have now?

   Ⓐ $8 - 2 = 6$ Ⓑ $8 \times 2 = 16$

Write which operation you would use for 5 and 6. Then solve.

5. Suppose Bonnie bought a 5-pound bag of cat food for \$4.95. She also bought a 3-pound bag of bird seed for \$1.50. How much money did she spend?

6. Suppose you are joining a walk-a-thon to raise money to help animals. Your aunt says she will give you \$3 for every mile you walk. If you walk 5 miles, how much money will you raise?

7. **Journal** Write a problem that you would use addition, subtraction, multiplication, or division to solve. Write which operation you would use and explain why.

8. **Critical Thinking** A 5-pound bag of dog treats costs \$10. A 3-pound bag of puppy treats costs \$9. How much more does one pound of puppy treats cost than one pound of dog treats?

SECTION B

Review and Practice

Vocabulary Match each with its definition.

1. fact family	**a.** the number to be divided in a division number sentence
2. divisor	**b.** a group of related facts using the same set of digits
3. dividend	**c.** the number by which a dividend is divided
4. quotient	**d.** the answer in a division problem

(Lessons 5–8) Find each quotient.

5. $2\overline{)16}$	**6.** $3\overline{)27}$	**7.** $5\overline{)15}$	**8.** $4\overline{)20}$	**9.** $1\overline{)10}$
10. $2\overline{)10}$	**11.** $4\overline{)24}$	**12.** $4\overline{)32}$	**13.** $2\overline{)8}$	**14.** $3\overline{)18}$
15. $5\overline{)5}$	**16.** $4\overline{)16}$	**17.** $5\overline{)35}$	**18.** $3\overline{)9}$	**19.** $2\overline{)6}$
20. $12 \div 2$	**21.** $14 \div 2$	**22.** $20 \div 5$	**23.** $24 \div 3$	**24.** $40 \div 5$
25. $21 \div 3$	**26.** $0 \div 3$	**27.** $10 \div 5$	**28.** $45 \div 5$	**29.** $36 \div 4$
30. $6 \div 1$	**31.** $12 \div 3$	**32.** $8 \div 4$	**33.** $25 \div 5$	**34.** $18 \div 2$

35. June has 18 stamps. Each letter needs 2 stamps. How many letters can she mail?

36. **Social Studies** A U.S. president is elected every 4 years. President Reagan was in office for 8 years (1981–1989). How many times was he elected?

(Lesson 9) Write which operation you would use. Then solve.

37. **Time** If it takes Charles 5 minutes to make his bed each day, how much time does he spend making his bed in one week? (Hint: one week = 7 days)

38. Alma wants to give her 5 friends an equal number of muffins. If she makes 15 muffins, how many muffins will each friend get?

39. **Journal** Choose a division fact. Explain how you could use multiplication to solve.

Skills Checklist

In this section, you have:

- ☑ **Connected Multiplication and Division**
- ☑ **Divided by 2, 3, 4, and 5**
- ☑ **Explored Dividing with 0 and 1**
- ☑ **Solved Problems by Choosing an Operation**

CHAPTER 7

SECTION

C Finding More Division Facts

Spencer has more than 100 tiny animals made of wood, clay, and glass. What are some ways Spencer can display all of the animals in his room?

More Division Facts

Review basic multiplication facts. Find each product.

1. 7×4	**2.** 6×7	**3.** 6×8
4. 5×9	**5.** 8×9	**6.** 7×8
7. 4×8	**8.** 6×6	**9.** 9×9

Skills Checklist

In this section, you will:

- ❒ Divide by 6, 7, 8, and 9
- ❒ Explore Even and Odd Numbers
- ❒ Solve Problems by Using Objects and Making an Organized List
- ❒ Explore Algebra by Balancing Scales

Chapter 7
Lesson
10

Dividing by 6 and 7

You Will Learn
how to divide by 6 and 7

Math Tip
Think about multiplication facts to help you divide.

Learn

Spencer's room is full of animals, but it isn't crowded. That's because Spencer collects tiny animal figures. He tries to find containers with sections to display his animals.

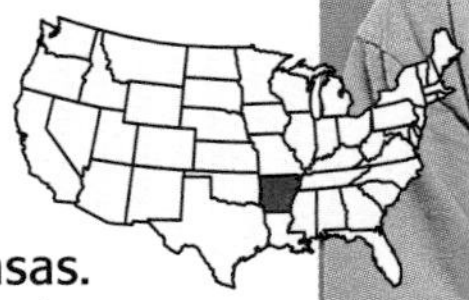

Spencer lives in Little Rock, Arkansas. He has more than 100 animals and gives each one a name.

Example 1

Suppose Spencer wants to display 24 animals in egg cartons. Each egg carton row holds 6 animals. How many rows will Spencer need?

Find 24 ÷ 6.

Think: 6 times what number equals 24?

$6 \times \mathbf{4} = 24$

$24 \div 6 = \mathbf{4}$ $\qquad 6\overline{)24}$ with quotient **4**

So, Spencer needs 4 rows.

Example 2

Spencer has a tray that holds 49 animals. It has 7 rows with an equal number of sections. How many sections are in each row?

Find 49 ÷ 7.

Think: 7 times what number equals 49?

$7 \times \mathbf{7} = 49$

$49 \div 7 = \mathbf{7}$ $\qquad 7\overline{)49}$ with quotient **7**

So, there are 7 sections in each row.

Talk About It

What multiplication fact can help you find 54 ÷ 6?

Check

Find each quotient.

1. $6\overline{)18}$ **2.** $7\overline{)28}$ **3.** $6\overline{)6}$ **4.** $6\overline{)30}$ **5.** $7\overline{)42}$

6. 14 ÷ 7 **7.** 42 ÷ 6 **8.** 63 ÷ 7 **9.** 12 ÷ 6 **10.** 21 ÷ 7

11. Reasoning Is the quotient of 35 ÷ 7 greater than or less than the quotient of 36 ÷ 6? Explain.

Practice

Skills and Reasoning

Find each quotient.

12. $7\overline{)35}$ **13.** $7\overline{)56}$ **14.** $6\overline{)42}$ **15.** $6\overline{)12}$ **16.** $7\overline{)7}$

17. $6\overline{)48}$ **18.** $7\overline{)63}$ **19.** $7\overline{)14}$ **20.** $6\overline{)18}$ **21.** $1\overline{)6}$

22. $42 \div 7$ **23.** $28 \div 7$ **24.** $24 \div 3$ **25.** $30 \div 6$ **26.** $12 \div 4$

27. $6 \div 6$ **28.** $25 \div 5$ **29.** $24 \div 6$ **30.** $0 \div 7$ **31.** $49 \div 7$

32. Divide 21 by 7. **33.** Divide 0 by 6. **34.** Divide 36 by 6.

35. Is the quotient of $54 \div 6$ greater than or less than the quotient of $56 \div 7$? Explain.

36. What multiplication fact can help you find $42 \div 7$?

Problem Solving and Applications

37. What If Spencer displays 30 animals in a box with 6 rows. He wants to put the same number of animals in each row. How many animals should he put in each row?

38. Time Jeremy agreed to feed his friend's fish for the next 35 days. For how many weeks will Jeremy feed the fish? (Hint: There are 7 days in a week.)

39. Money Sandy wants to buy rag dolls for her collection. Each doll costs $7. How much will she spend on 3 dolls?

40. Write Your Own Problem Write a division problem using 6 or 7 as a divisor. Trade problems with a classmate and solve.

41. Algebra Readiness Copy and complete the table. Write the rule.

In	14	21	35	42	63
Out	2	3	5		

Mixed Review and Test Prep

Find each product.

42. 8×9 **43.** 9×5 **44.** 8×4 **45.** 9×3 **46.** 2×8

47. 6×9 **48.** 7×8 **49.** 6×8 **50.** 9×9 **51.** 0×8

52. Find $2 \times 3 \times 3$.

Ⓐ 6 Ⓑ 9 Ⓒ 18 Ⓓ 8

Chapter 7 Lesson 11

Dividing by 8 and 9

You Will Learn
how to divide by 8 and 9

Remember
You can use a related multiplication fact to find a quotient.

Learn

Trading cards aren't just for sports. You can collect trading cards for superheroes, animals, movies, and even old cars and airplanes.

Example 1

Suppose you have 48 superhero cards. You want to give the same number of cards to 8 friends. How many cards should each friend get?

Find $48 \div 8$.

Think: 8 times what number equals 48?

$8 \times \mathbf{6} = 48$

$48 \div 8 = \mathbf{6}$ $\qquad \begin{array}{r}\mathbf{6}\\ 8\overline{)48}\end{array}$

So, each friend will get 6 cards.

Example 2

Suppose you have 72 airplane cards. Your album holds 9 cards on each page. How many pages do you need for your airplane cards?

Find $72 \div 9$.

Think: 9 times what number equals 72?

$9 \times \mathbf{8} = 72$

$72 \div 9 = \mathbf{8}$ $\qquad \begin{array}{r}\mathbf{8}\\ 9\overline{)72}\end{array}$

So, you need 8 pages.

Talk About It

1. What multiplication fact can help you find $45 \div 9$?
2. What multiplication fact can help you find $32 \div 8$?

Check

Find each quotient.

1. $8\overline{)56}$
2. $9\overline{)27}$
3. $8\overline{)16}$
4. $8\overline{)24}$
5. $9\overline{)36}$
6. $9 \div 9$
7. $72 \div 8$
8. $63 \div 9$
9. $40 \div 8$
10. $54 \div 9$
11. **Reasoning** Is the quotient of $64 \div 8$ greater than or less than the quotient of $81 \div 9$? Explain.

Practice

Skills and Reasoning

Find each quotient.

12. $8\overline{)8}$ **13.** $9\overline{)18}$ **14.** $5\overline{)35}$ **15.** $9\overline{)81}$ **16.** $9\overline{)27}$

17. $8\overline{)48}$ **18.** $8\overline{)24}$ **19.** $9\overline{)72}$ **20.** $8\overline{)64}$ **21.** $8\overline{)32}$

22. $45 \div 9$ **23.** $21 \div 7$ **24.** $56 \div 8$ **25.** $42 \div 6$ **26.** $36 \div 9$

27. $9 \div 9$ **28.** $0 \div 8$ **29.** $72 \div 8$ **30.** $63 \div 9$ **31.** $40 \div 8$

32. Divide 54 by 9. **33.** Divide 16 by 8. **34.** Divide 48 by 6.

35. How does knowing $8 \times 4 = 32$ help you solve $32 \div 8$?

36. What multiplication fact can help you find $0 \div 9$?

Problem Solving and Applications

37. **What If** You have 18 baseball cards to give to 9 friends. You want to give the same number of cards to each person. How many cards should each person get?

38. A checkerboard has a total of 64 squares. If each row has 8 squares, how many rows does the board have?

Using Data Use the Data File on page 273 for **39** and **40.**

39. Suppose you are playing Pachisi. How many pieces should each player have?

40. Suppose six people want to play games at the same time. What games could they play?

Mixed Review and Test Prep

Add or subtract.

41. \$2.34 + \$3.64 **42.** \$4.05 + \$5.95 **43.** \$6.52 − \$4.22

44. \$6.83 − \$0.90 **45.** \$2.67 − \$1.45 **46.** \$8.04 + \$1.92

47. Suppose 5 friends want to share 3 packs of movie cards equally. Each pack has 10 cards. How many cards should each friend get?

Ⓐ 10 cards Ⓑ 4 packs Ⓒ 6 cards Ⓓ 5 friends

STOP and Practice

Find each quotient.

1. $4\overline{)8}$	**2.** $3\overline{)27}$	**3.** $5\overline{)35}$	**4.** $6\overline{)36}$	**5.** $2\overline{)18}$
6. $5\overline{)45}$	**7.** $3\overline{)24}$	**8.** $4\overline{)32}$	**9.** $7\overline{)28}$	**10.** $9\overline{)9}$
11. $9\overline{)63}$	**12.** $8\overline{)48}$	**13.** $1\overline{)9}$	**14.** $8\overline{)56}$	**15.** $7\overline{)49}$
16. $7\overline{)35}$	**17.** $2\overline{)4}$	**18.** $3\overline{)6}$	**19.** $9\overline{)45}$	**20.** $3\overline{)15}$
21. $5\overline{)30}$	**22.** $4\overline{)28}$	**23.** $5\overline{)5}$	**24.** $8\overline{)24}$	**25.** $8\overline{)64}$
26. $1\overline{)7}$	**27.** $5\overline{)15}$	**28.** $7\overline{)7}$	**29.** $6\overline{)24}$	**30.** $1\overline{)5}$
31. $0 \div 8$	**32.** $54 \div 9$	**33.** $18 \div 9$	**34.** $6 \div 2$	**35.** $42 \div 7$
36. $0 \div 7$	**37.** $6 \div 6$	**38.** $16 \div 4$	**39.** $0 \div 4$	**40.** $54 \div 6$
41. $32 \div 8$	**42.** $14 \div 2$	**43.** $42 \div 6$	**44.** $12 \div 3$	**45.** $25 \div 5$
46. $20 \div 5$	**47.** $21 \div 7$	**48.** $24 \div 4$	**49.** $8 \div 2$	**50.** $18 \div 3$
51. $0 \div 9$	**52.** $9 \div 3$	**53.** $10 \div 2$	**54.** $6 \div 1$	**55.** $40 \div 8$
56. $81 \div 9$	**57.** $30 \div 6$	**58.** $36 \div 4$	**59.** $4 \div 1$	**60.** $56 \div 7$
61. $20 \div 4$	**62.** $40 \div 5$	**63.** $27 \div 9$	**64.** $18 \div 6$	**65.** $48 \div 6$

Error Search

Find each quotient that is not correct. Write it correctly and explain the error.

66. $0 \div 5 = 5$	**67.** $12 \div 2 = 10$	**68.** $8 \div 1 = 8$
69. $18 \div 2 = 20$	**70.** $56 \div 8 = 7$	**71.** $4 \div 4 = 0$

Remember the Facts!

Use these activities anytime to help you remember your division facts.

1. **Fact Challenge** Play this game with a partner. The first player calls out 2 factors. The second player completes the multiplication fact and gives a related division fact. Take turns calling out factors. Score 1 point for each correct response. How many points can you score?

2. **Fact Caterpillar** Work with a group. The first person writes a division fact, such as $12 \div 4 = 3$. The next person writes another fact, using a number from the first fact, such as $24 \div 3 = 8$. Take turns adding to your caterpillar. Try not to use the same fact twice.

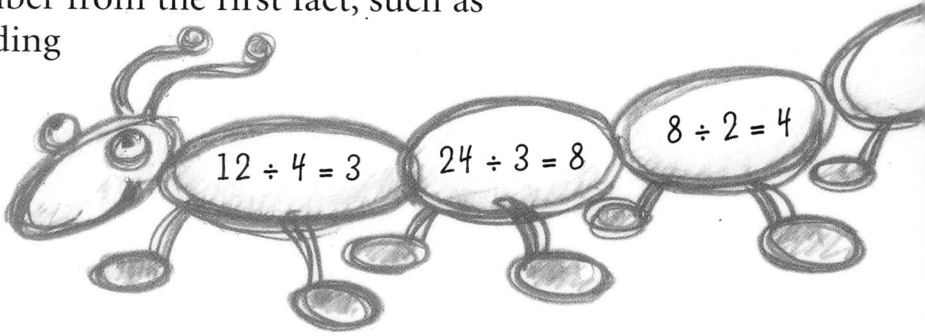

3. **Fish For Facts** Work with a partner to make 32 division fact cards. Make four cards with a quotient of 2, four cards with a quotient of 3, and so on.

- Shuffle the cards. Give each player 7 cards.
- Look for pairs of cards with the same quotient. When you find a matching pair of cards, set them aside.
- Player 1 calls out a fact on one card. If player 2 has a card with the same quotient, he or she gives the card to player 1. If player 2 doesn't have a matching card, player 1 picks a new card from the pile.
- Take turns calling out facts until one player has matched all cards. The player with the most matching pairs at the end of the game wins.

Chapter 7
Lesson
12

Exploring Even and Odd Numbers

Problem Solving Connection
- Use Objects/ Act It Out
- Look for a Pattern

Materials
color cubes

Vocabulary

even number
a whole number that has 0, 2, 4, 6, or 8 in the ones place

odd number
a whole number that has 1, 3, 5, 7, or 9 in the ones place

Problem Solving Hint
Look for a pattern in the digits in the ones place.

Explore

You can divide to decide if a number is even or odd.

An **even number** can be divided into two equal groups.

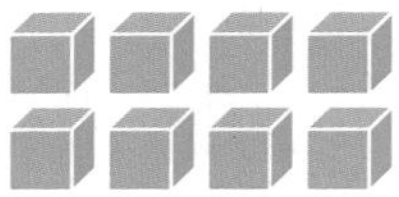

An **odd number** has one left over when you try to divide it into two equal groups.

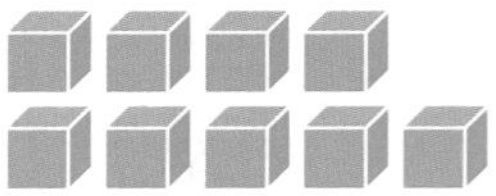

Work Together

1. Use color cubes to build the numbers 2 to 12. Try to divide each of the numbers into two equal groups.
   a. Which numbers can be divided into two equal groups?
   b. Which numbers have one left over?

2. Which of the numbers 2 to 12 are even numbers? Which of the numbers are odd numbers?

Talk About It

3. Can a number be both even and odd? Explain.

4. Suppose you build an odd number such as 7 with color cubes. How can you add or subtract cubes to show an even number?

Connect

An even number can be divided by 2 with no leftovers. An odd number has one left over when it is divided by 2.

You can find patterns in even and odd numbers.

Even numbers have a 0, 2, 4, 6, or 8 in the ones place.

Odd numbers have a 1, 3, 5, 7, or 9 in the ones place.

1	2	3	4	5	6	7	8	9	10
11	12	13	14	15	16	17	18	19	20
21	22	23	24	25	26	27	28	29	30
31	32	33	34	35	36	37	38	39	40
41	42	43	44	45	46	47	48	49	50
51	52	53	54	55	56	57	58	59	60
61	62	63	64	65	66	67	68	69	70
71	72	73	74	75	76	77	78	79	80
81	82	83	84	85	86	87	88	89	90
91	92	93	94	95	96	97	98	99	100

Practice

Write odd or even. You may use color cubes to help.

1. 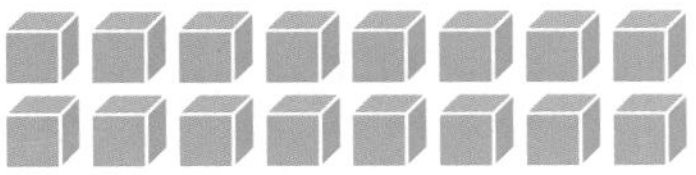

2. 

3. 22 **4.** 18 **5.** 15 **6.** 20 **7.** 21 **8.** 19

9. Start with 11 and write the next 5 odd numbers. Explain how you know which numbers are odd.

10. **Reasoning** Choose at least 2 questions to answer. Draw pictures to explain your answers.

a. If you add two odd numbers, will the sum be even or odd? Try $3 + 5$, $7 + 9$, $5 + 11$.

b. If you add an even number and an odd number, will the sum be even or odd? Try $5 + 4$, $12 + 7$, $9 + 8$.

c. If you multiply two odd numbers, will the product be even or odd? Try 5×7, 3×9, 7×9.

d. If you multiply an odd number by an even number, will the product be even or odd? Try 5×6, 3×8, 7×4.

11. Gary has 2 shelves to show his model cars. He put 8 cars on each shelf. Does he have an even or an odd number of cars? Explain.

12. **Collecting Data** Find at least 5 numbers in a newspaper or magazine. Copy the numbers and write if each is even or odd.

13. **Journal** Describe the patterns you see in even numbers. Describe the patterns you see in odd numbers.

Problem Solving

Compare Strategies: Use Objects and Make an Organized List

You Will Learn
how to choose strategies to help you solve problems

Problem Solving Hint
You can use different strategies to solve the same problem. Choose strategies that work best for you.

Learn

Rick and Katrina are planning the school yearbook. They want 24 pictures on each page. The pictures should be arranged in equal rows. What are all the ways to arrange the pictures?

Rick thinks:

I'll use objects to act out the problem.

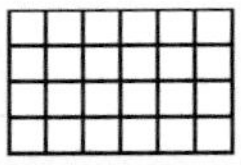

4 rows of 6 or 6 rows of 4

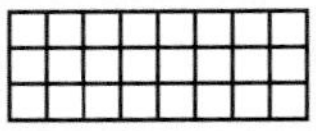

3 rows of 8 or 8 rows of 3

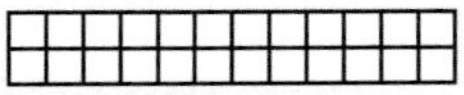

2 rows of 12 or 12 rows of 2

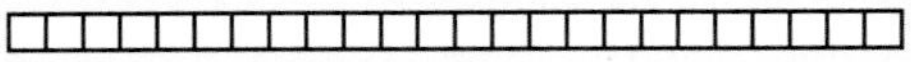

1 row of 24 or 24 rows of 1

Katrina thinks:

I'll make an organized list to find all the ways.

Rows	Pictures in Each Row	Total
1	24	24
2	12	24
3	8	24
4	6	24
6	4	24
8	3	24
12	2	24
24	1	24

Talk About It

Which strategy would you choose to solve the problem? Explain.

Check

Problem Solving
Understand
Plan
Solve
Look Back

Solve. Use objects or make an organized list to help.

1. David is planning the school magazine. He has 16 photos to include. He wants to put the same number of photos on each page. Find all the ways he can plan the magazine.
   a. How many pages could the magazine have?
   b. How many pictures could be on each page?
   c. List all the ways David can plan the magazine.

Problem Solving Practice

Problem Solving Strategies

- Use Objects/Act It Out
- Draw a Picture
- Look for a Pattern
- Guess and Check
- Use Logical Reasoning
- Make an Organized List
- Make a Table
- Solve a Simpler Problem
- Work Backward

Choose a Tool

Use any strategy to solve.

2. **What If** Rick and Katrina decide they want 32 pictures on each page. The pictures should be in equal rows. What are all the ways to arrange the pictures?

3. Kate wants to take a picture of 20 students in the band. She wants the students to stand in equal rows. What are all the ways she can arrange them?

4. Dante needs to choose an outfit to wear. Each outfit has 2 pieces of clothing. Find all the outfits he has to choose from.

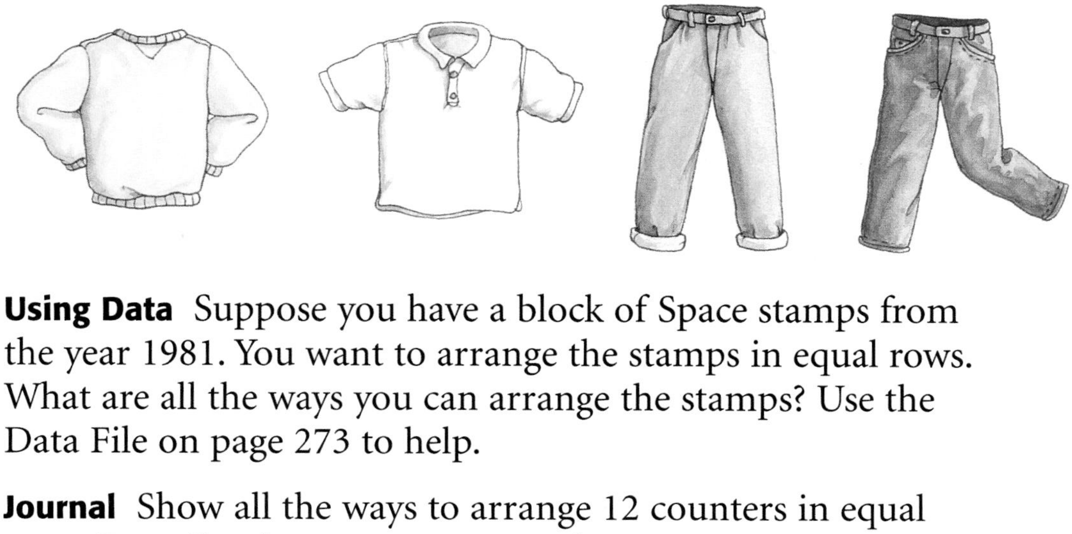

5. **Using Data** Suppose you have a block of Space stamps from the year 1981. You want to arrange the stamps in equal rows. What are all the ways you can arrange the stamps? Use the Data File on page 273 to help.

6. **Journal** Show all the ways to arrange 12 counters in equal rows. Describe the strategy you used.

Chapter 7
Lesson
14

Exploring Algebra: Balancing Scales

Problem Solving Connection

- Use Objects/ Act It Out
- Make a Table

Materials

color cubes

Problem Solving Hint

Use objects to help you show each way.

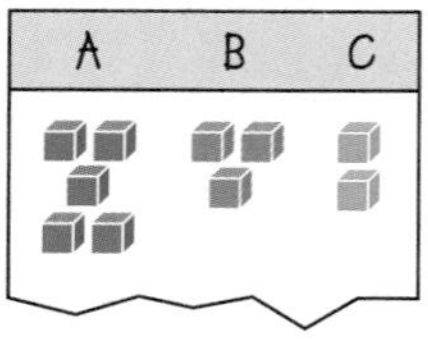

Since 3 + 2 = 5, both sides of the scale have the same amount.

Explore

A scale is balanced when the same amount is on both sides. Find all the ways to balance this scale. Boxes with the same letter have the same number of cubes.

Box A has 5 cubes inside. How many cubes can be in boxes B and C?

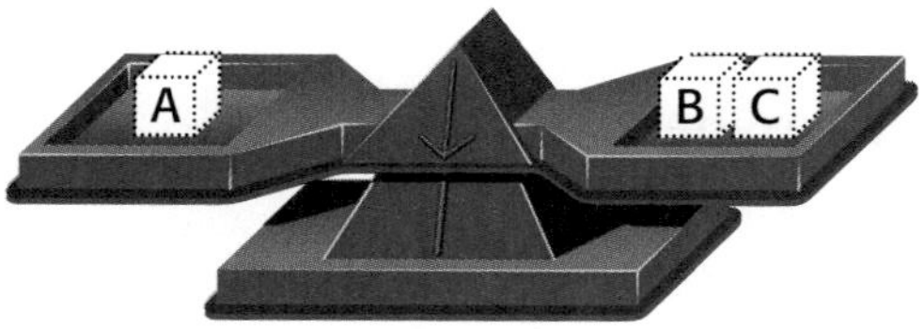

A	B	C
5	5	0
5	4	1
5	3	2
5	2	3
5	1	4
5	0	5

Work Together

Find all the ways to balance each scale. Make a table to record each way. You may use color cubes to help.

1. Box A has 7 cubes inside. How many cubes can be in boxes B and C?

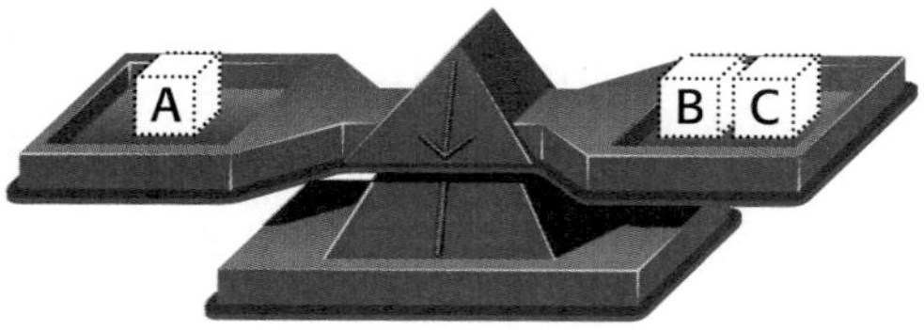

2. Each box A has 2 cubes inside. How many cubes can be in boxes B and C?

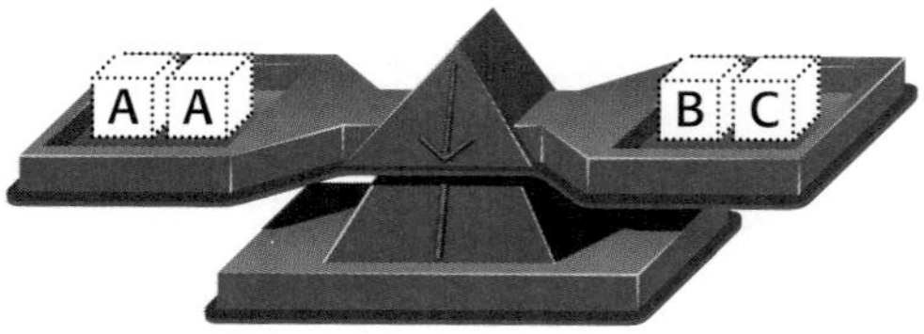

Talk About It

How did you find how many cubes could be in each box so that the scales balanced?

Connect

Making an organized list can help you make sure you have found all of the different ways to fill the boxes.

Each box A has 3 cubes inside. How many cubes can be in boxes B and C?

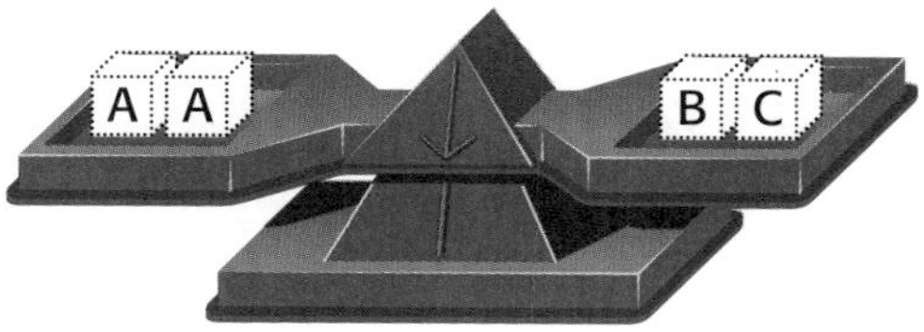

A	A	B	C
3	3	6	0
3	3	5	1
3	3	4	2
3	3	3	3
3	3	2	4
3	3	1	5
3	3	0	6

$6 + 0 = 6$
$5 + 1 = 6$
$4 + 2 = 6$
$3 + 3 = 6$
$2 + 4 = 6$
$1 + 5 = 6$
$0 + 6 = 6$

Practice

Solve. You may use color cubes to help.

1. Each box A has 6 cubes inside. How many cubes can be in boxes B and C? Make a table to record each way.

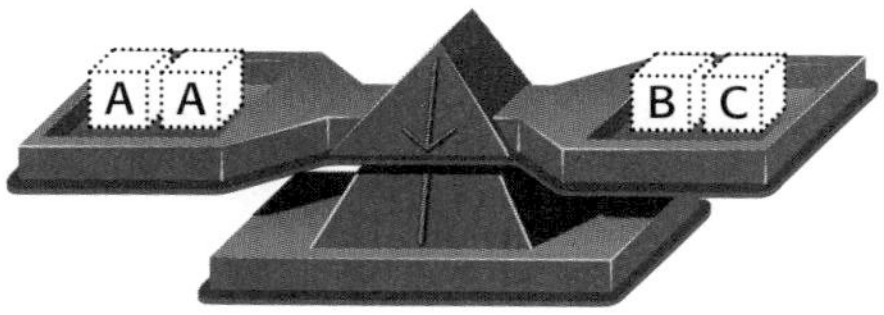

2. **Reasoning** Box B has 4 cubes inside. Box C has 6 cubes inside. How many cubes are in each box A?

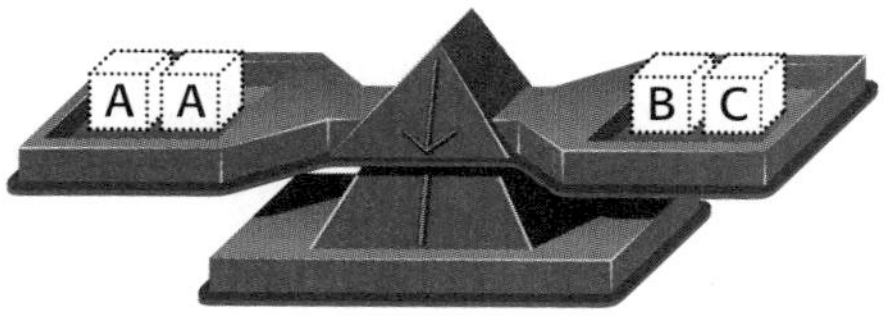

3. **Reasoning** Box A has 14 cubes inside. How many cubes are in each box B?

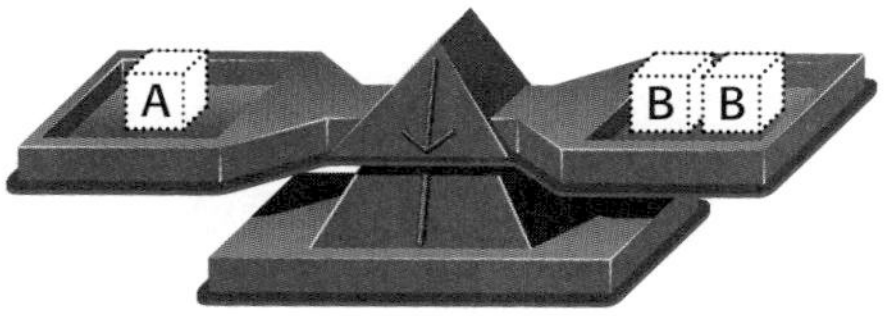

4. **Journal** Make a table or draw a picture to show all of the different ways to complete the number sentence, $9 = B + C$.

SECTION C

Review and Practice

Vocabulary

1. List 3 even numbers. **2.** List 3 odd numbers.

(Lessons 10 and 11) Find each quotient.

3. $8\overline{)16}$	**4.** $9\overline{)27}$	**5.** $7\overline{)49}$	**6.** $7\overline{)21}$	**7.** $6\overline{)30}$
8. $8\overline{)64}$	**9.** $6\overline{)36}$	**10.** $9\overline{)63}$	**11.** $7\overline{)14}$	**12.** $8\overline{)48}$
13. $42 \div 7$	**14.** $56 \div 8$	**15.** $24 \div 6$	**16.** $48 \div 6$	**17.** $72 \div 9$
18. $12 \div 6$	**19.** $18 \div 9$	**20.** $28 \div 7$	**21.** $45 \div 9$	**22.** $32 \div 8$

23. Divide 63 by 7. **24.** Divide 24 by 8. **25.** Divide 35 by 7.

(Lesson 12) Write odd or even. You may use color cubes to help.

26. 18 **27.** 25 **28.** 11 **29.** 6 **30.** 32

(Lesson 13) Use any strategy to solve.

31. Mary must decide what to wear. Find all the outfits she has to choose from. Each outfit has 2 pieces of clothing.

(Lesson 14) Solve. You may use color cubes to help.

32. Box A has 18 cubes inside. How many cubes are in each box B?

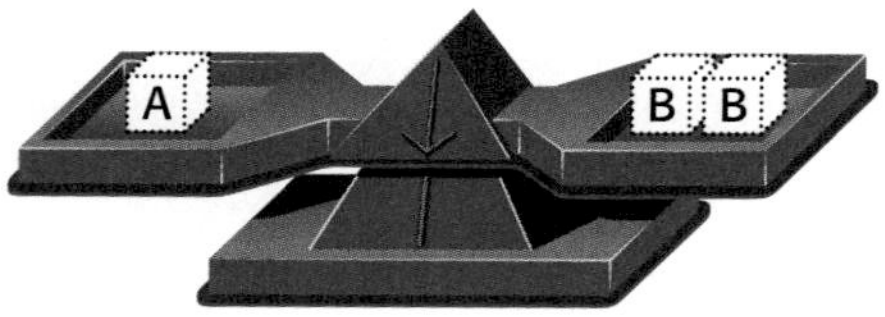

33. Journal Explain how you can use multiplication facts to divide. You may use $36 \div 9$ as an example or choose your own fact.

Skills Checklist

In this section, you have:

- ☑ **Divided by 6, 7, 8, and 9**
- ☑ **Explored Even and Odd**
- ☑ **Solved Problems by Using Objects and Making an Organized List**
- ☑ **Explored Algebra by Balancing Scales**

YOUR CHOICE

Choose at least one. Use what you have learned in this chapter.

1 Sticky Questions

Nancy has 24 stickers. Using that information, write a question for each answer.

a. 8 **b.** 3 **c.** 4

d. 6 **e.** 24 **f.** 12

2 Computer Collecting

Some museums, like the American Museum of Natural History, have fun collections. Use the World Wide Web at **www.mathsurf.com/3/ch7** to find out about museum collections. Make up two division stories using the data you find.

3 Guess the Fact

With a partner, take at least 32 counters. Make a division fact using some or all of the counters. Let your partner guess the fact. Take turns making facts with the counters and guessing.

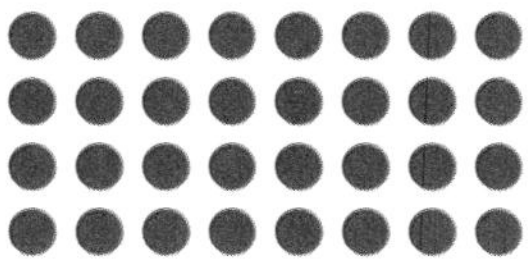

$32 \div 4 = 8$

4 Dividing Collections

At Home What do you like to collect? Divide your collection into equal groups. Make a poster to show what you did. Share the poster with your classmates.

5 Stamp It Out

Suppose you have 12 stamps in a collection. Draw all the ways you could arrange the stamps in equal rows on a page. Write a division sentence for each.

CHAPTER 7

Review/Test

Vocabulary Complete each sentence.

Word List
dividend
quotient
odd numbers
even numbers

1. Numbers with a 0, 2, 4, 6, or 8 in the ones place are ____.
2. Numbers with a 1, 3, 5, 7, or 9 in the ones place are ____.
3. The number to be divided is called the ____.
4. The ____ of $24 \div 3$ is 8.

(Lesson 4) Copy and complete.

5. $8 \times ■ = 16$ / $16 \div 8 = ■$
6. $3 \times ■ = 15$ / $15 \div 3 = ■$
7. $5 \times ■ = 20$ / $20 \div 5 = ■$
8. $4 \times ■ = 24$ / $24 \div 4 = ■$
9. $7 \times ■ = 21$ / $21 \div 7 = ■$
10. $6 \times ■ = 42$ / $42 \div 6 = ■$

(Lessons 5–8, 10–11) Find each quotient.

11. $5\overline{)30}$ 12. $6\overline{)18}$ 13. $4\overline{)36}$ 14. $2\overline{)16}$ 15. $9\overline{)18}$

16. $3\overline{)12}$ 17. $8\overline{)64}$ 18. $7\overline{)7}$ 19. $5\overline{)45}$ 20. $7\overline{)28}$

21. $20 \div 4$ 22. $6 \div 1$ 23. $14 \div 2$ 24. $49 \div 7$ 25. $81 \div 9$

26. $21 \div 3$ 27. $48 \div 8$ 28. $0 \div 9$ 29. $4 \div 1$ 30. $30 \div 6$

(Lesson 9) Choose the number sentence you would use to solve each problem. Explain.

31. Andy collected 12 rocks. He gave 3 rocks to a friend. How many rocks does Andy have left?

Ⓐ $12 \div 3 = 4$ Ⓑ $12 - 3 = 9$

32. Jason and Tami found 6 pieces of sea glass. They want to share them equally. How many pieces does each friend get?

Ⓐ $6 \div 2 = 3$ Ⓑ $6 \times 2 = 12$

(Lesson 13) Solve. Use any strategy.

33. Kira has 16 stamps to display in her album. She wants to put the same number of stamps on each page. What are all the ways Kira can display her stamps?

CHAPTER 7
Performance Assessment

An artist needs your help! The artist has been asked to draw a flip book of a bouncing ball. The publisher said the book should be 8, 16, 24, or 32 pages. The artist must tell the publisher how many times the ball will bounce in each book. Help the artist figure it out!

1. **Decision Making** Look at the drawings. How many pages does it take to show one bounce?

2. **Recording Data** Help the artist complete the table.

Number of Bounces for Each Book				
Book Length	8 pages	16 pages	24 pages	32 pages
Number of Bounces				

3. **Explain Your Thinking** How did you decide how many times the ball would bounce in each book?

4. **Critical Thinking** Now plan your own flip book. How many bounces will you show? How many drawings will you need to make? How did you figure it out?

Math Magazine

Poetry Power! **Poets think long and hard about their work. Some use math to help them build the rhythm of their poems. Robert Louis Stevenson (1850–1894) used numbers to create this poem. Count the syllables in each line to see how!**

When I was sick and lay abed,
I had two pillows at my head,
And all my toys beside me lay,
To keep me happy all the day.

And sometimes for an hour or so,
I watched my leaden soldiers go,
With different uniforms and drills,
Among the bedclothes, through the hills.

From "The Land of Counterpane,"
by Robert Louis Stevenson

Each line of this poem has 8 syllables!

Try These!

1. There are 32 syllables in a *stanza* of this poem. How many lines are in a stanza?
2. Write your own poem with equal groups of syllables in each line. How many syllables will you have in 2 lines, 3 lines, and 5 lines?

CHAPTERS 1–7

Cumulative Review

Test Prep Strategy: Eliminate Choices

Estimate.
What is the sum of 19, 9, 13, and 13?

Ⓐ 38 Ⓑ 54 Ⓒ 70 Ⓓ 89

Sometimes it is faster to choose the correct answer by estimating. 20 + 10 + 10 + 10 = 50. The correct answer should be close to 50. 54, Ⓑ, is a reasonable answer.

Write the letter of the correct answer. Estimate or use any strategy to help.

Test Prep Strategies

- Read Carefully
- Follow Directions
- Make Smart Choices
- Eliminate Choices
- Work Backward from an Answer

1. Tak saved \$11.45. Then he earned \$3.51. How much money does he have now?

Ⓐ \$12.16 Ⓑ \$16.06 Ⓒ \$7.94 Ⓓ \$14.96

2. What is 3,401 − 2,238?

Ⓐ 1,163 Ⓑ 5,639 Ⓒ 4,273 Ⓓ 163

Use the graph to answer **3** and **4.**

Players in the Soccer League

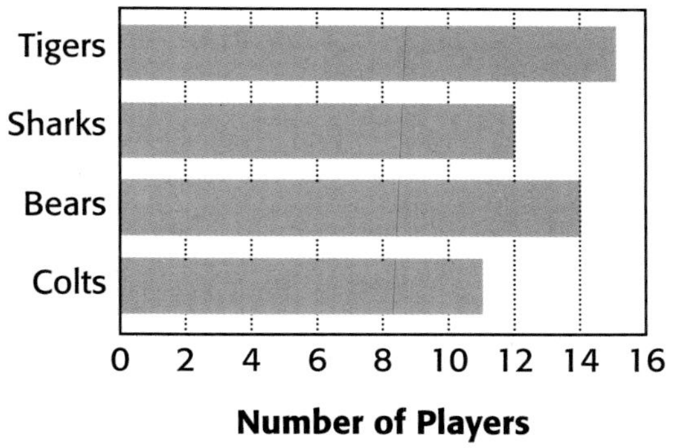

3. How many more players play for the Tigers than for the Colts?

Ⓐ 2 Ⓑ 4
Ⓒ 3 Ⓓ 1

4. How many players play for the 4 teams in the Soccer League?

Ⓐ 24 Ⓑ 32
Ⓒ 52 Ⓓ 74

5. At the Apple Festival, 9 people each bought 6 apples. How many apples did they buy?

Ⓐ 45 Ⓑ 54 Ⓒ 63 Ⓓ 96 Ⓔ not here

6. Art has 24 sheets of paper in his binder. He uses 4 pages each day. How many days until he runs out of paper?

Ⓐ 24 Ⓑ 20 Ⓒ 12 Ⓓ 6 Ⓔ not here

7. Find 42 ÷ 6.

Ⓐ 48 Ⓑ 36 Ⓒ 8 Ⓓ not here

DATA FILE

Chapter 8 Using Geometry

BUILDINGS AND STRUCTURES

SECTION A

Japanese Noh masks
Page 321

Shapes and Solids

Higher! Higher! This time line shows when each structure became the tallest in the world. In 1931, which structure was the tallest in the world?

321

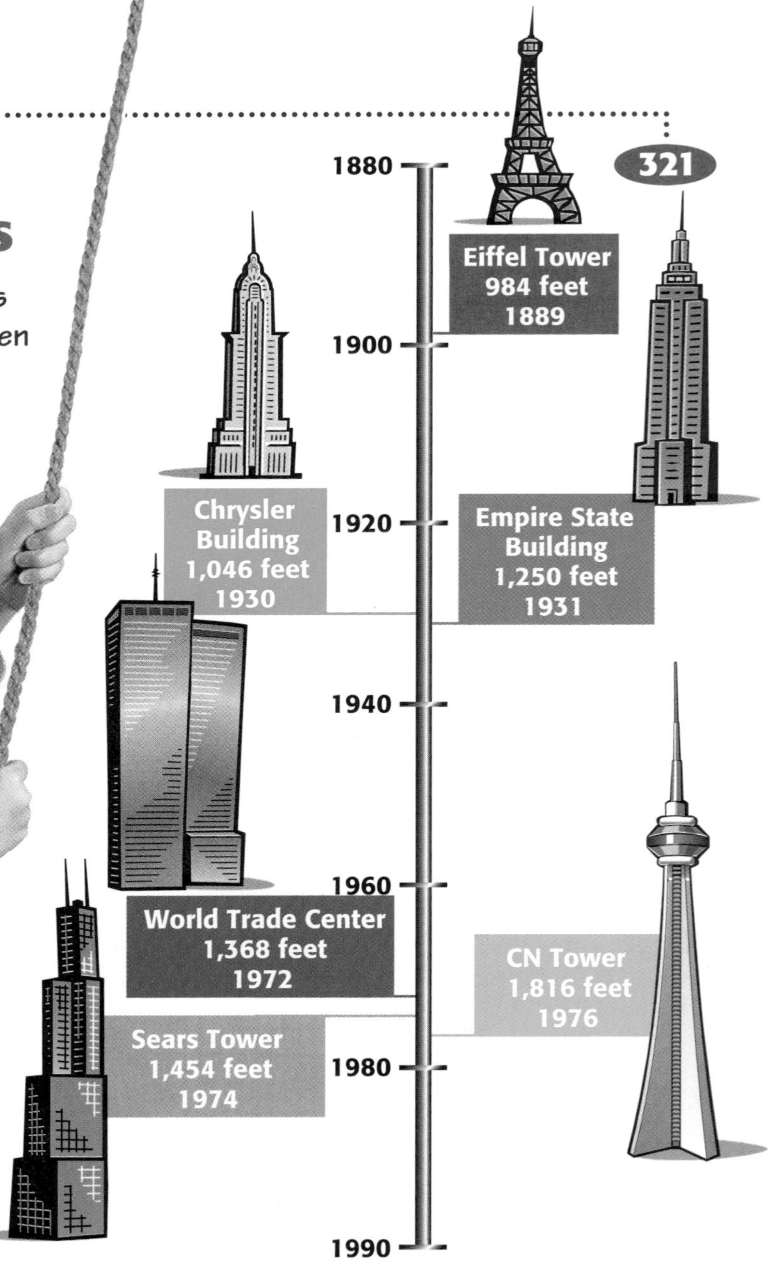

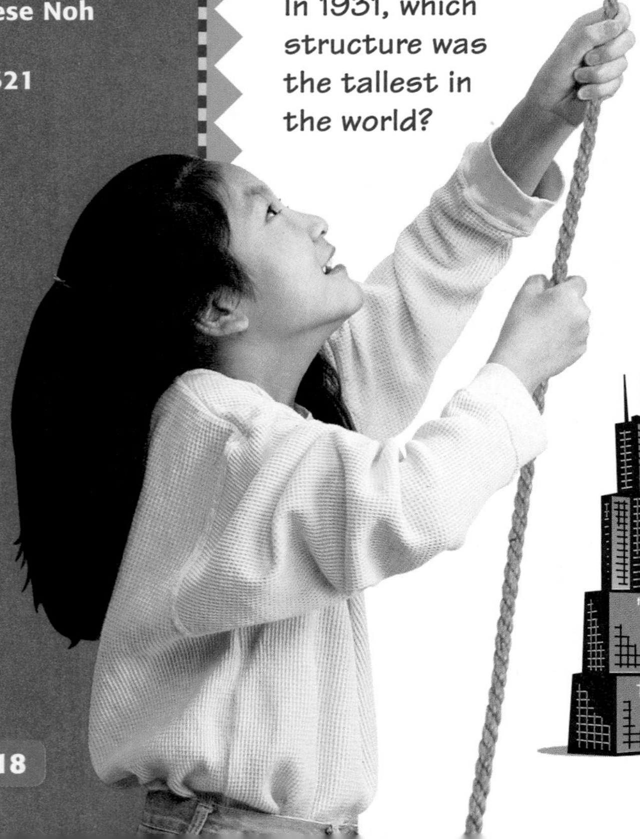

SECTION B

Perimeter, Area, and Volume

339

In 1791, George Washington decided to make the area we know as Washington, D.C., the capital of the United States. Benjamin Banneker was chosen to help measure the layout of the city. It took 9 years to build the city.

Name one street that crosses 12th Street.

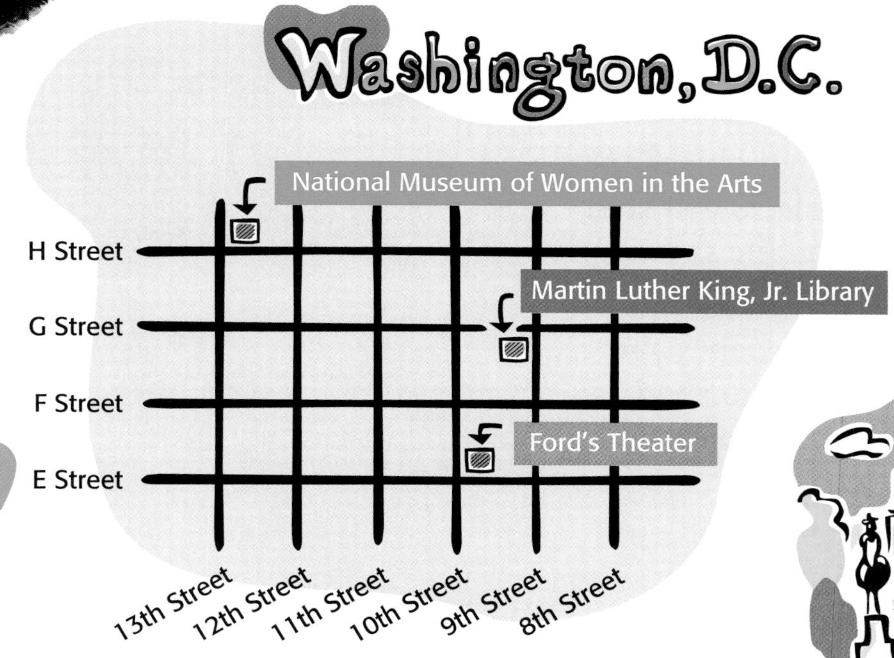

Playground designers
Page 339

Surfing the World Wide Web!

Want to visit a cool building, statue, or bridge? Go to **www.mathsurf.com/3/ch8** on the World Wide Web to see some interesting places.

TEAM PROJECT
Still Life COLLAGE

Materials
large sheet of white paper, markers, construction paper, scissors, paste

A still life is a picture of everyday objects. A Spanish painter named Pablo Picasso (1881–1973) created this still life using only simple and made-up shapes.

Create your own still life using shapes.

Pitcher, Bowl, Fruit 1931

Make a Plan

- What object or objects will your still life show?
- How will you use shapes and color to show your objects?

Carry It Out

1. Cut different colors of paper into the shapes you see in your objects.
2. Paste the shapes on white paper to show your still life.

Talk About It

- How does your still life look different from the objects you picked? How does it look the same?

Present the Project

- Share your still life with the class.
- See if your classmates can identify the shapes in your still life. See if they can tell what object or objects you wanted to show.

CHAPTER 8

SECTION A

Shapes and Solids

Japanese Noh masks date back hundreds of years. What do you notice about both sides of this mask?

Skills Checklist

In this section, you will:

- ❒ Explore Solids
- ❒ Explore Solids and Shapes
- ❒ Learn About Lines and Line Segments
- ❒ Explore Angles
- ❒ Explore Slides, Flips, and Turns
- ❒ Explore Symmetry
- ❒ Solve Problems by Solving a Simpler Problem

Shapes and Solids

Review patterns. Complete each pattern.

1. ● ▲ ● ▲ ____ ____ ____
2. ■● ■▲ ■● ■▲ ____ ____
3. ▲ ▲▲ ▲▲▲ ____ ____ ____

Chapter 8
Lesson
1

Exploring Solids

Problem Solving Connection
Use Objects/
Act It Out

Materials
Power Solids

Vocabulary

Solid Figures
cube
sphere
rectangular prism
cone
pyramid
cylinder

edge
where two faces of a solid figure meet

face
a flat surface of a solid figure

Math Tip
Sometimes *parts* of an object will match a solid figure.

Explore

Here are some solid figures.

Cube

Sphere

Rectangular Prism

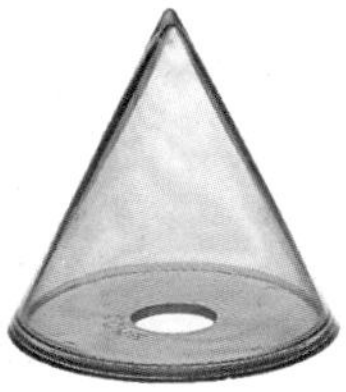

Cone

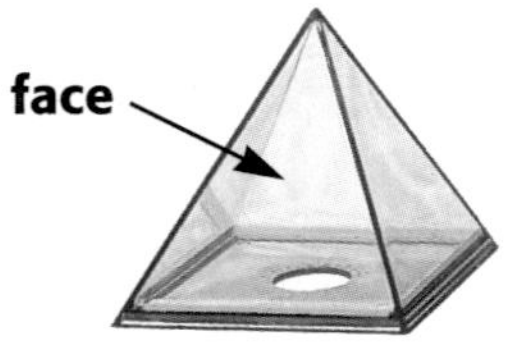

Pyramid

Cylinder

Work Together

1. Find at least one object in your classroom that matches each solid figure. Write why the objects match.
   a. cube
   b. sphere
   c. rectangular prism
   d. cone
   e. pyramid
   f. cylinder

Talk About It

2. How do you know your objects match?
3. What other objects can you think of that match some solid figures? Use the photo to help.

Connect

Here are some objects that match solid figures. You can describe solid figures in different ways.

These objects have flat faces.

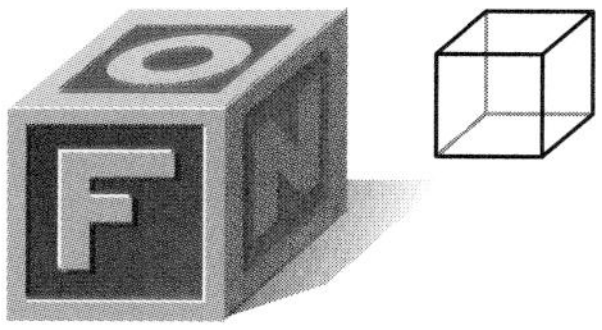
Cube

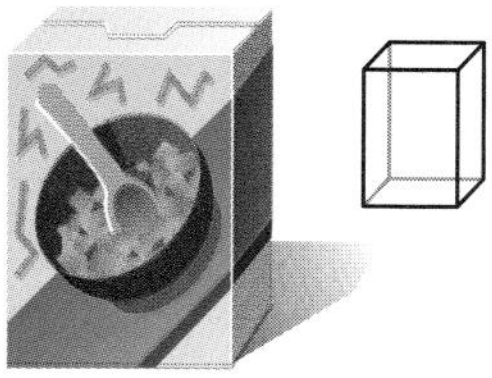
Rectangular Prism

Pyramid

These objects can roll.

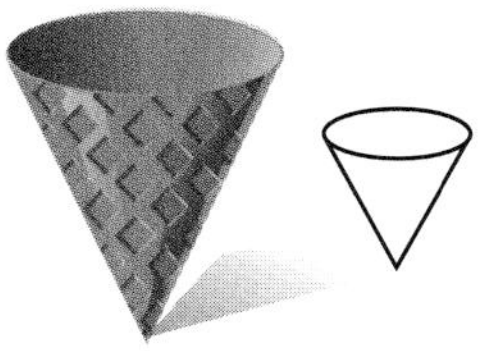
Cone

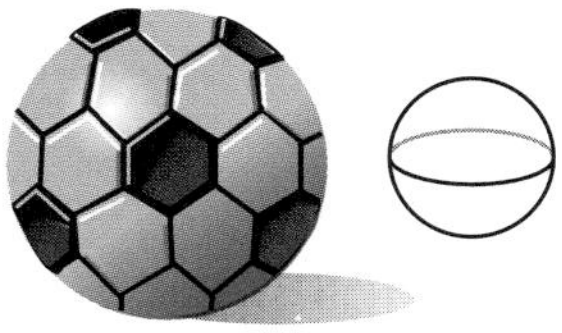
Sphere

Cylinder

Practice

Name the solid figure that each object looks like.

1.

2.

3.

4.

5.

6.

7. **Reasoning** How is a rectangular prism like a cube? How is it different?

8. **Logic** What solid figure has six faces and twelve edges?

9. **Using Data** Use a picture of two of the structures listed in the Data File on page 318. Name a solid that matches each.

10. **Journal** Choose two solid figures. Write the ways they are alike and different.

Exploring Solids and Shapes

Problem Solving Connection
- Use Objects/ Act It Out
- Draw a Picture

Materials
Power Solids

Vocabulary
Shapes
square
triangle
circle
rectangle

corner
the point where two sides meet

side
line segment forming part of a figure

Did You Know?
A square is also a rectangle.

Explore

Here are some shapes.

Square **Triangle** **Circle** **Rectangle**

Work Together

Use Power Solids or other objects.

1. Trace the faces of each solid figure. Then write the names of the shapes you've drawn.
   a. cube
   b. rectangular prism
   c. cylinder
   d. pyramid
   e. cone

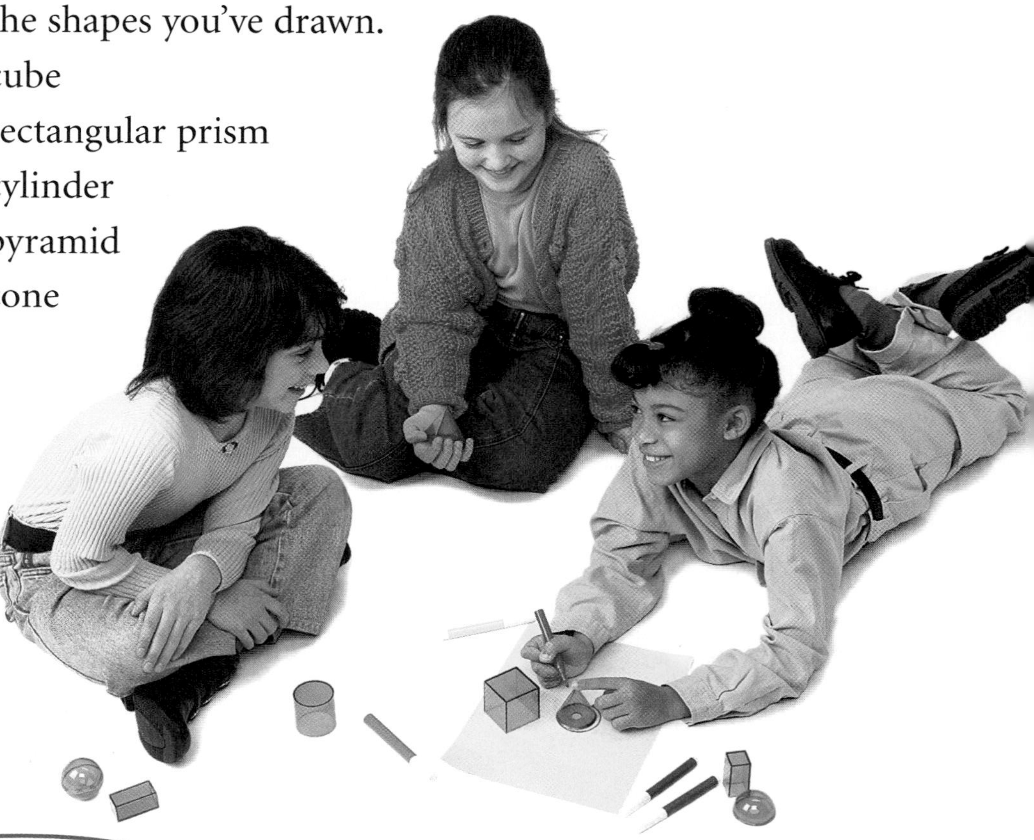

Talk About It

2. Which shapes have no corners? Which shapes have corners?
3. Look at the shapes you've drawn. Can you tell which solid figures would roll? Explain.

Connect

Each face of these solid figures is a familiar shape.

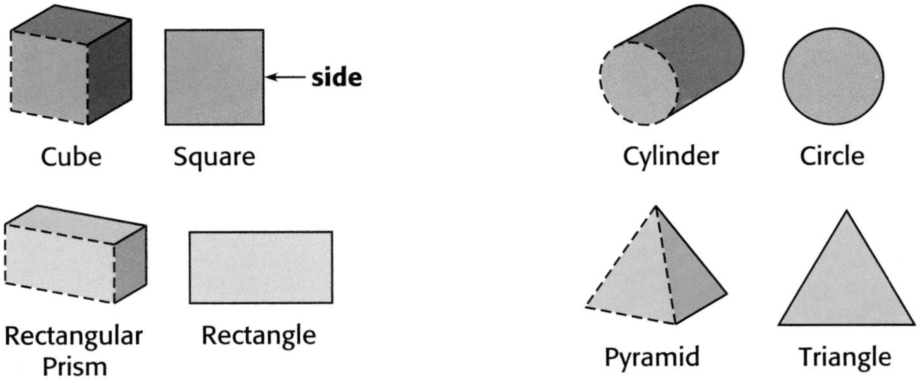

The sides of a square are the same length.

Practice

Name the shape that each object looks like.

1. 

2. 

3. 

4. 

Copy and complete.

	Shape	Number of Sides	Number of Corners
5.	Square		
6.	Triangle		
7.	Circle		
8.	Rectangle		

9. Critical Thinking Which solid figure could have these shapes as faces?

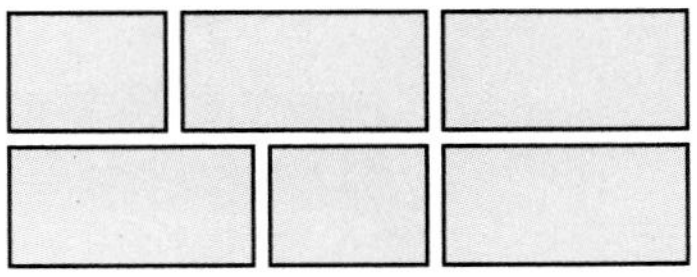

Ⓐ cube Ⓑ cylinder

Ⓒ pyramid Ⓓ rectangular prism

10. Patterns Continue the pattern.

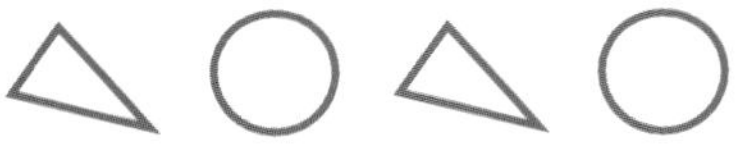 ____ ____ ____ ____

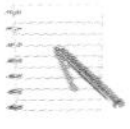 **11. Journal** How is a rectangle like a square? How is it different?

PRACTICE AND APPLY

Chapter 8
Lesson
3

Lines and Line Segments

You Will Learn
how to identify lines, line segments, rays, parallel lines, and intersecting lines

Vocabulary

line
a straight path that is endless in both directions

point
an exact position

line segment
part of a line

ray
part of a line that is endless in one direction

intersecting lines
lines that cross at one point

parallel lines
lines that do not cross

Learn

Have you ever drawn a picture of your house? Architects use intersecting lines and line segments to design buildings.

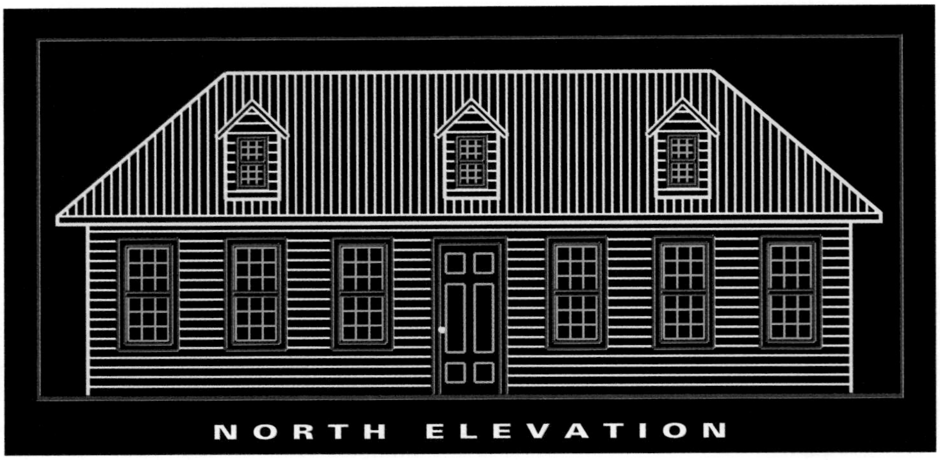

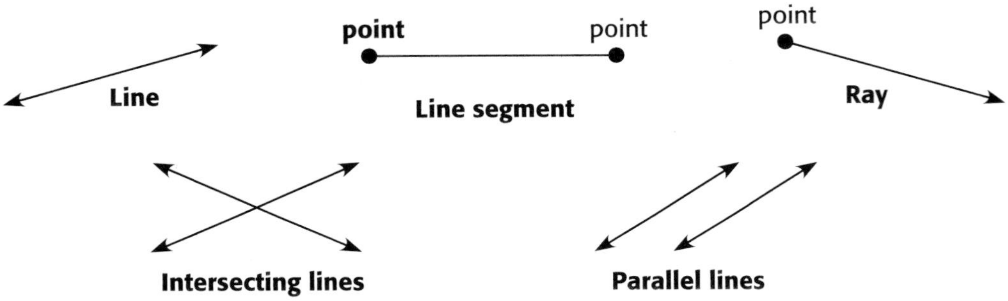

Talk About It

Where have you seen intersecting lines? Where have you seen parallel lines?

Check

Write the name for each.

1.  **2.**  **3.** 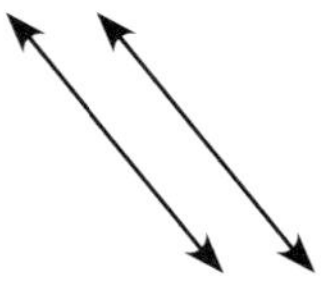 **4.** 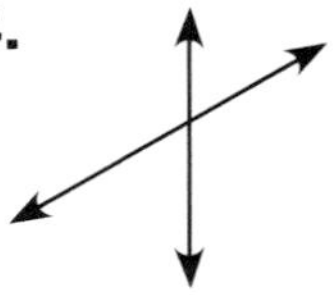

5. Reasoning How is a ray like a line? How is it different?

Practice

Skills and Reasoning

Write the name for each.

6. 

7. 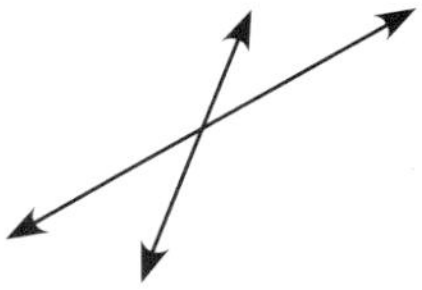

8. 

9. 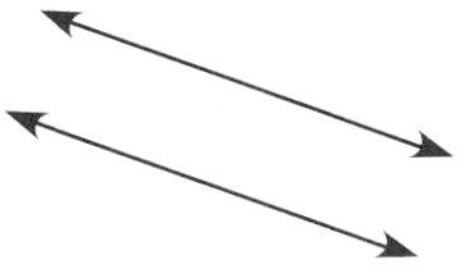

10. 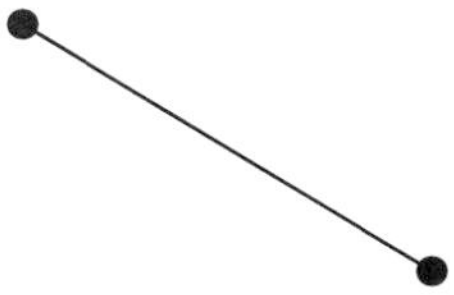

11. 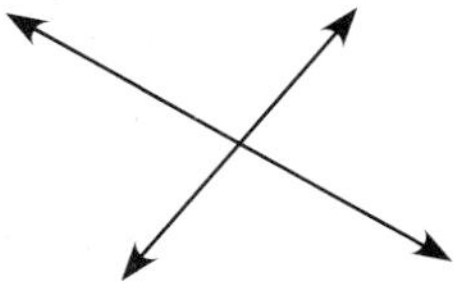

12. Can two rays intersect? Explain.

13. Can two lines be both parallel and intersecting? Explain.

Problem Solving and Applications

Write parallel or intersecting for each.

14. 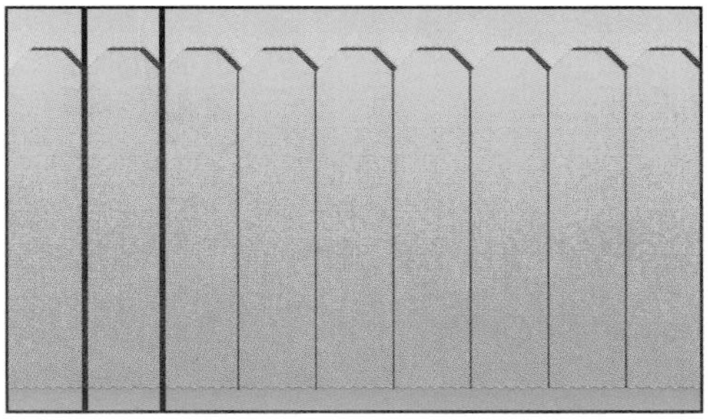

15.  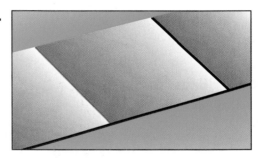

16. **Using Data** How many years ago was the Empire State Building built? Use the Data File on page 318 to solve.

Mixed Review and Test Prep

Multiply or divide.

17. 5×4 18. $81 \div 9$ 19. 2×6 20. $56 \div 8$

21. $35 \div 7$ 22. 7×9 23. 3×4 24. $36 \div 6$

25. Eric has 45 baseball cards to give to friends. If he wants to give the same number of cards to 5 friends, how many cards will each friend get?

Ⓐ 4 Ⓑ 5 Ⓒ 8 Ⓓ 9

Exploring Angles

Problem Solving Connection
Use Objects/
Act It Out

Materials
Power Polygons

Vocabulary

polygon
a closed figure with three or more sides made up of line segments

angle
formed by two rays or two line segments with a common end point

right angle
an angle that forms a square corner

Math Tip
Different polygons may have the same size angle.

Explore

This is a **polygon**. Each corner of a polygon forms an **angle**. In any polygon, the number of sides equals the number of angles.

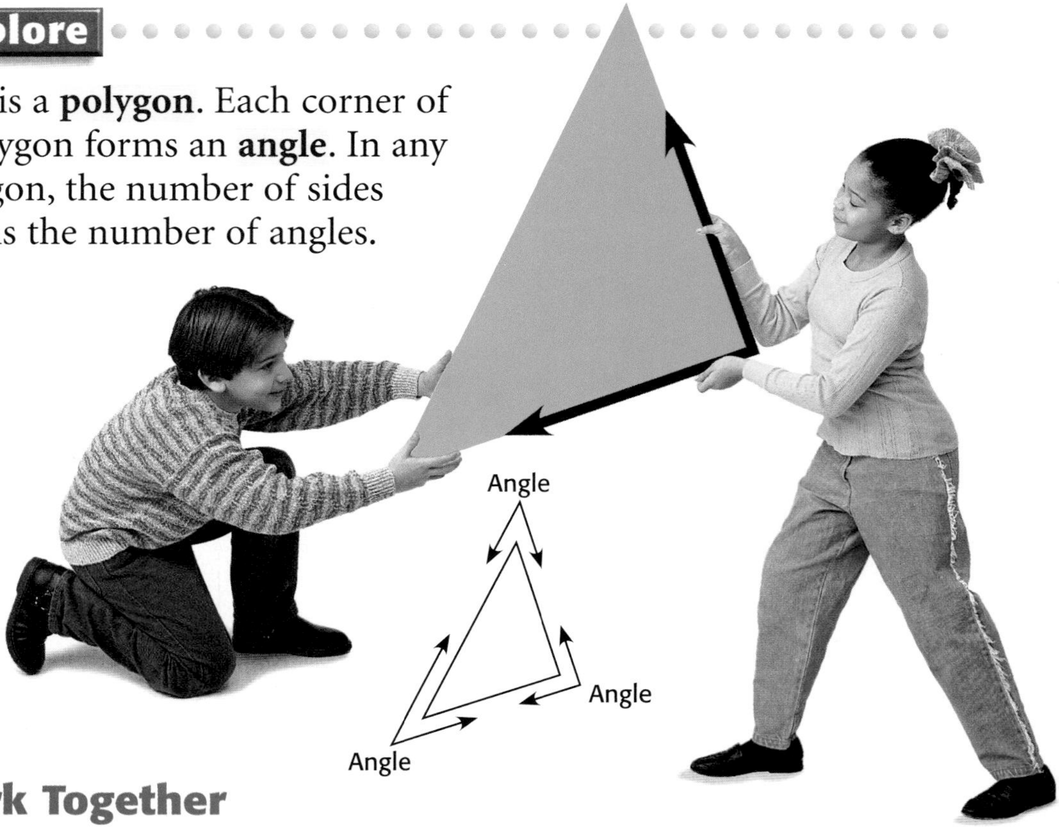

Work Together

Use these Power Polygon pieces.

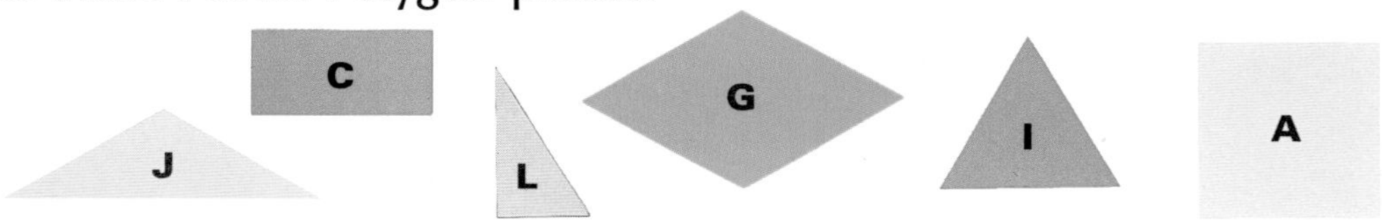

1. Record which pieces have angles that match each.

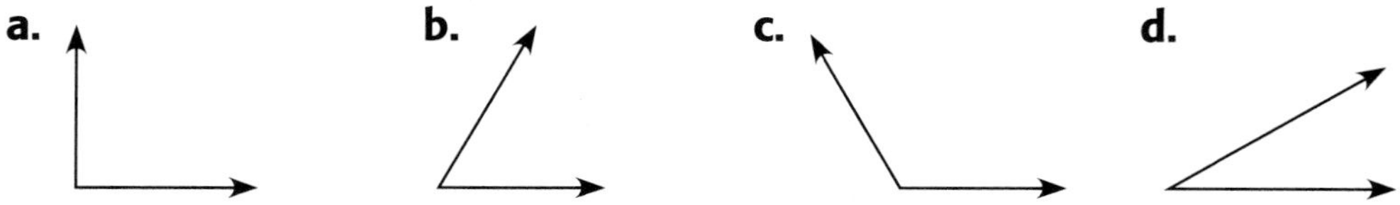

2. Find a shape with no angles that are the same.
3. Find a shape with two angles that are the same.
4. Find a shape with all angles the same.

Talk About It

How did you decide which pieces had angles that matched **a–d**?

Connect

Angles can be different sizes.

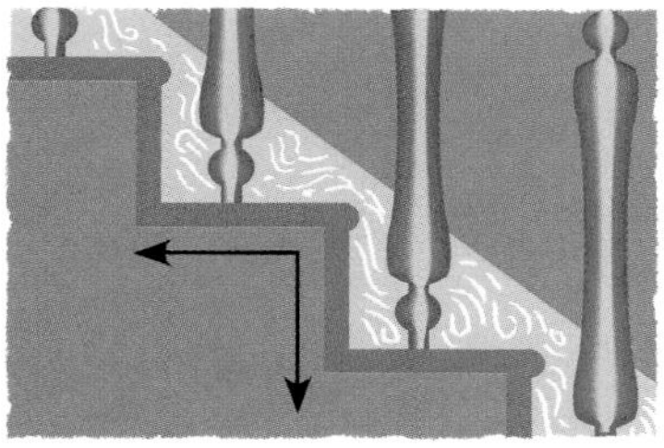

This is a **right angle**.

This angle is less than a right angle.

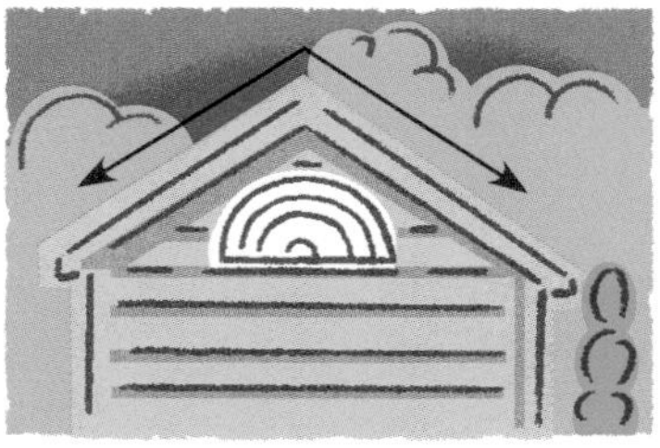

This angle is greater than a right angle.

Practice

Write whether each angle is a right angle, less than a right angle, or greater than a right angle.

1.

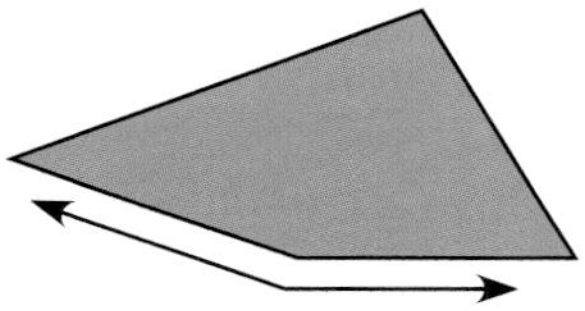

2.

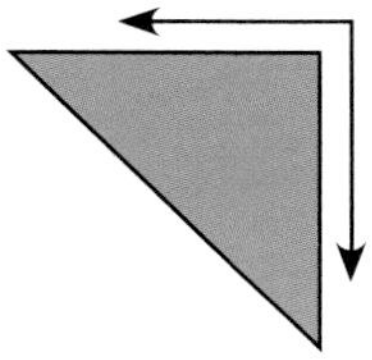

3.

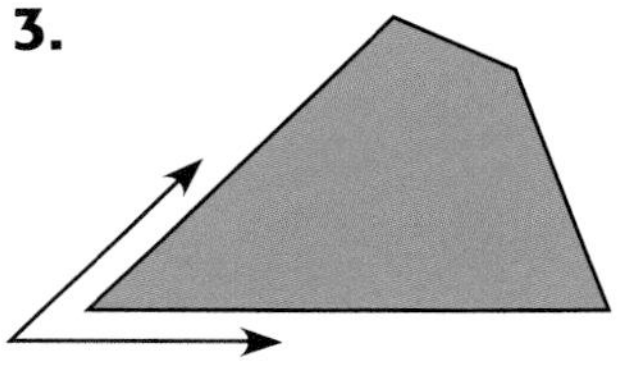

Write the number of right angles in each polygon. You may use the corner of a sheet of paper to help.

4.

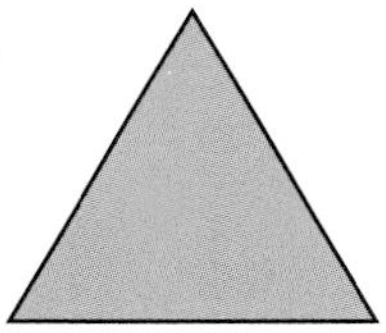

5.

6.

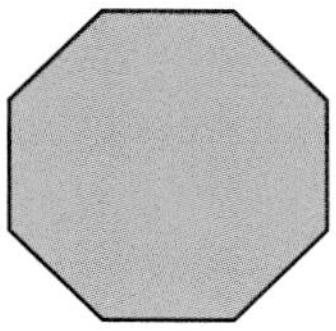

7.

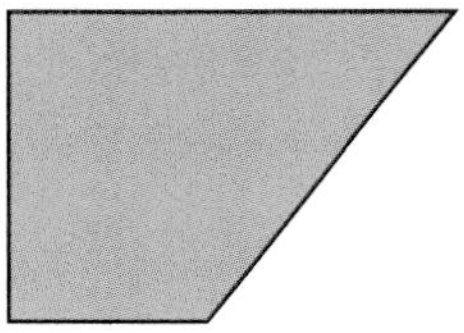

8. Reasoning Mattie says, "A pentagon has 5 sides so I know that it also has 5 angles." Do you agree? Explain.

9. Time Which clock has hands that form a right angle?

Ⓐ

Ⓑ

Ⓒ

10. Journal Look for examples of right angles and angles that are greater than and less than right angles. Choose at least one of each. Draw the angles and identify each.

Exploring Slides, Flips, and Turns

Problem Solving Connection
Draw a Picture

Materials
- Power Polygons
- grid paper

Vocabulary

slide
to move a figure in one direction

flip
to turn a figure over

turn
to rotate a figure

congruent
having the same size and shape

Explore

Here are three ways you can move a figure.

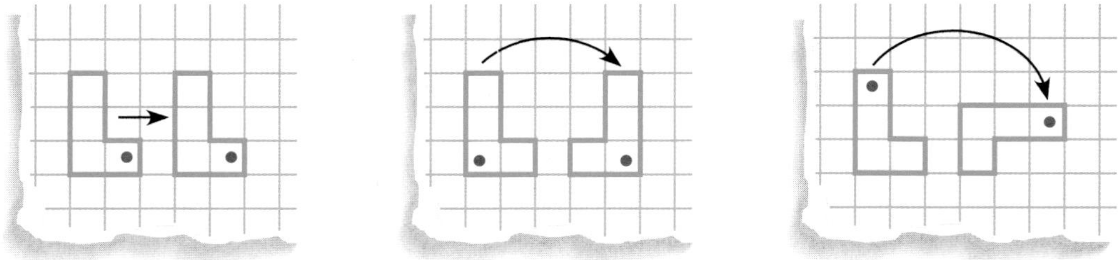

Slide **Flip** **Turn**

Work Together

1. Choose one of these Power Polygons. Make a design with slides, flips, and turns.

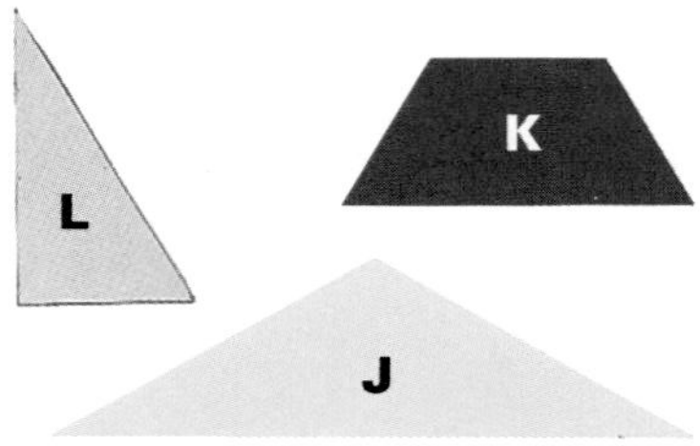

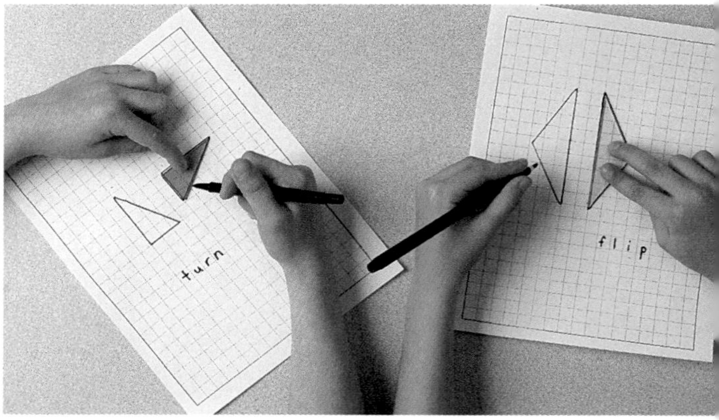

   a. Trace the piece on grid paper.
   b. Slide, flip, or turn the piece. Trace it again. Label the move.
   c. Make at least 5 more slides, flips, or turns. Label each move as you go.

2. Trace a different polygon on grid paper. Make 5 moves, but don't label them. Exchange your paper and your polygon with a classmate. Can you guess the other's moves?

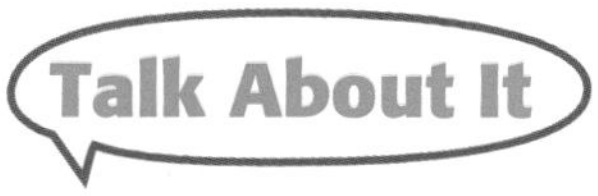

When you exchanged designs with a classmate, how could you tell how the piece was moved?

Connect

Any figure can be moved by using slides, flips, and turns.

This figure has been flipped and turned.

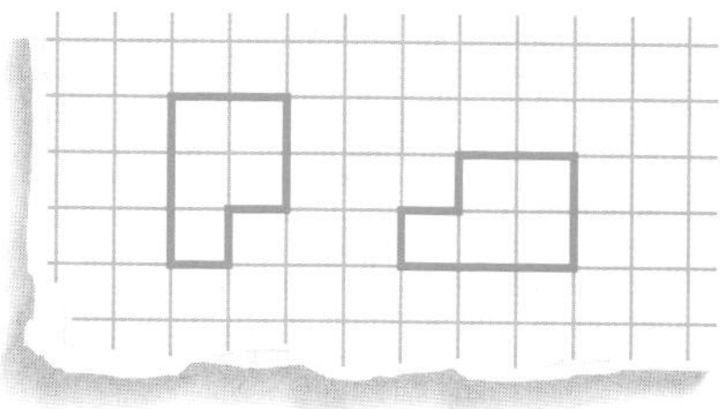

One way to tell if a figure has been moved is to see if the two figures are **congruent**.

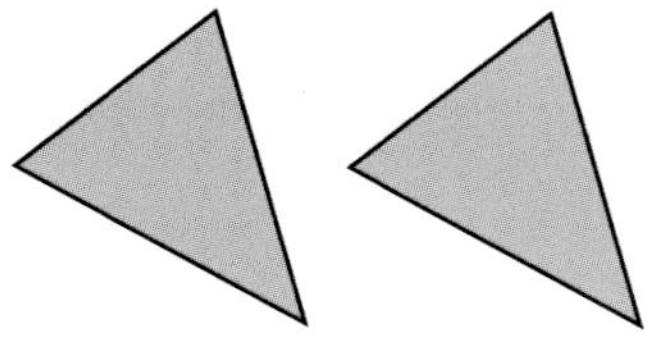

These two figures are congruent. They are the same size and same shape.

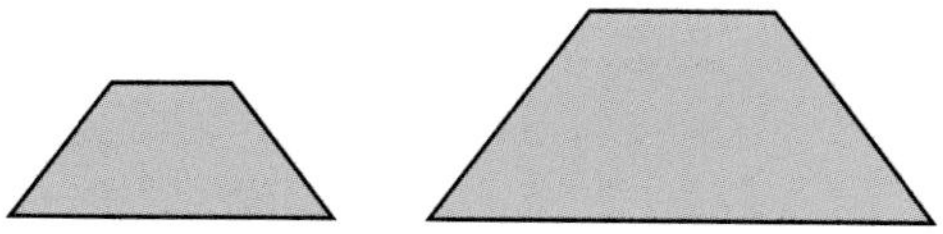

These figures are not congruent. If you cut one out, it would not fit on the other figure exactly.

Practice

Write slide, flip, or turn for each.

1. 

2. 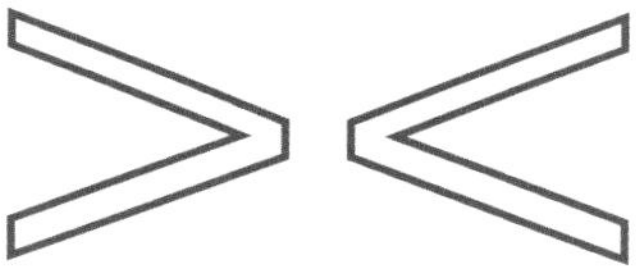

3. 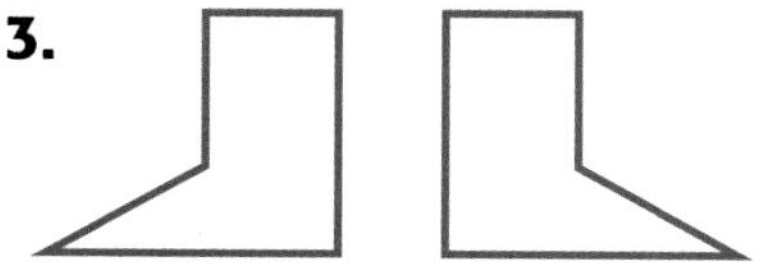

4. 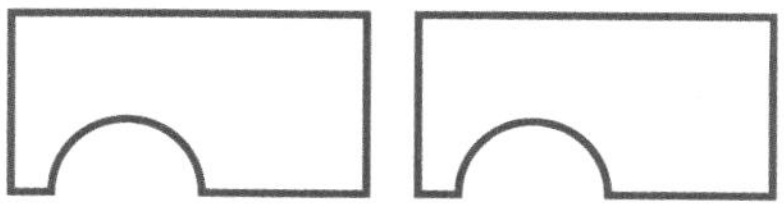

Write congruent or not congruent for each.

5. 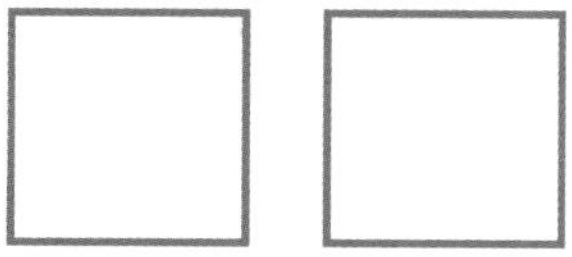

6. 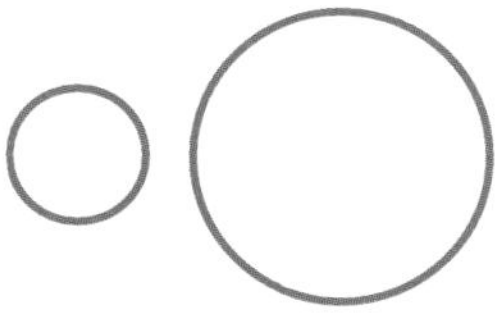

7. 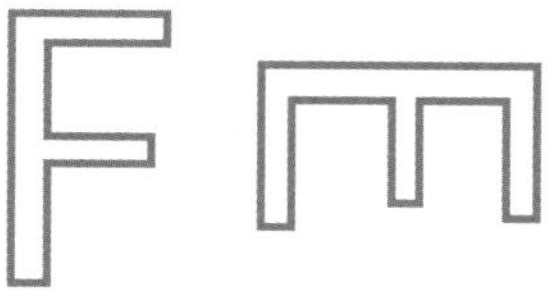

8. Reasoning Suppose you use this Power Polygon piece to create a design. Could a flip look like a slide? Explain.

9. Journal How can you tell whether two figures are congruent?

Chapter 8
Lesson
6

Exploring Symmetry

Problem Solving Connection

Use Objects/
Act It Out

Materials

- scissors
- paper

Vocabulary

line of symmetry
a line on which a figure can be folded so that both parts match exactly

Explore

Japanese Noh plays date back to the 1300s. In these plays, actors wear masks and use movement to tell stories.

A figure has a **line of symmetry** if you can fold the figure so both parts match exactly. This Noh mask appears to have a line of symmetry.

You can make a mask with a line of symmetry.

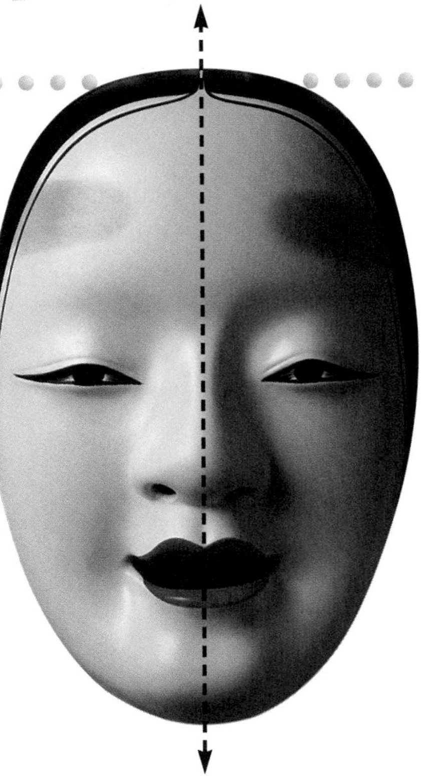

Work Together

1. Fold a sheet of paper in half.
2. Draw half of a face on the paper, using the fold as the line of symmetry.
3. With the paper folded, cut holes for the eyes, nose, and mouth. Cut out the shape of the face.
4. Unfold the paper. Color your mask the same on each side of the fold.

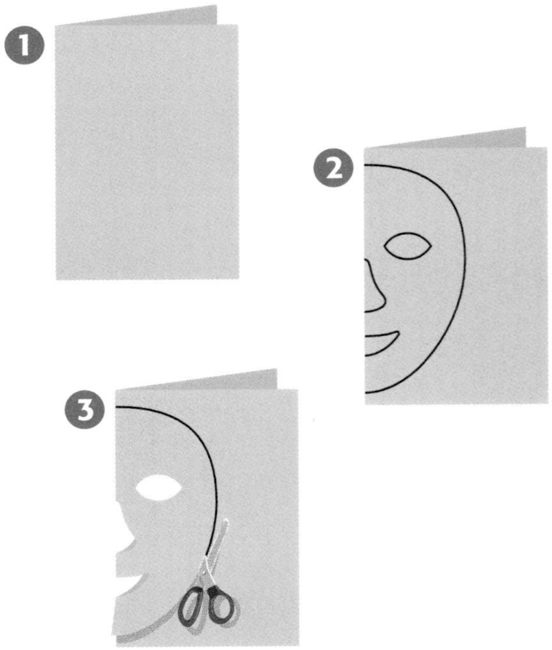

Math Tip
The left side of your mask should look exactly like the right side.

Talk About It

Where is the line of symmetry on your mask?

Connect

These objects appear to have a line of symmetry.

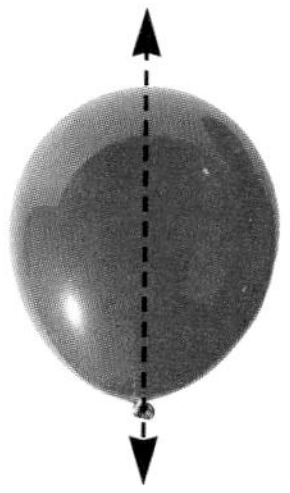

Some objects appear to have more than one line of symmetry.

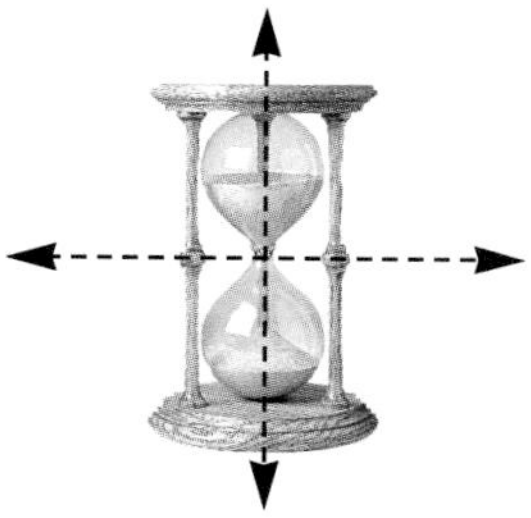

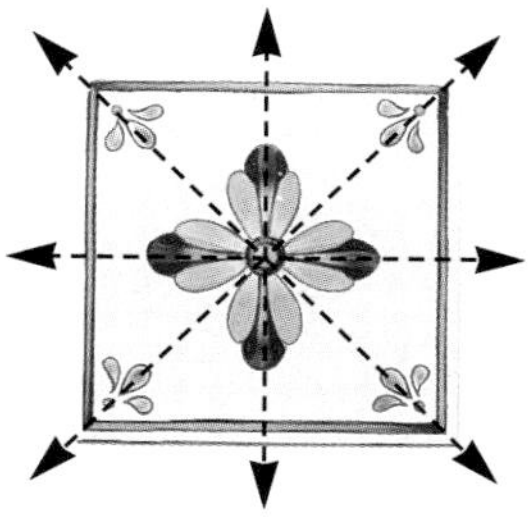

Practice

Does each object appear to have a line of symmetry? Write yes or no.

1. 

2. 

3. 

4. 

Does each line appear to be a line of symmetry? Write yes or no.

5. 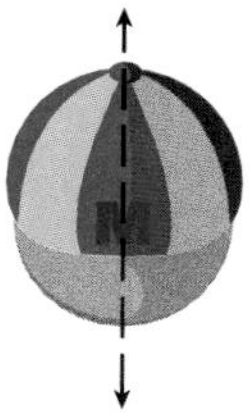

6. 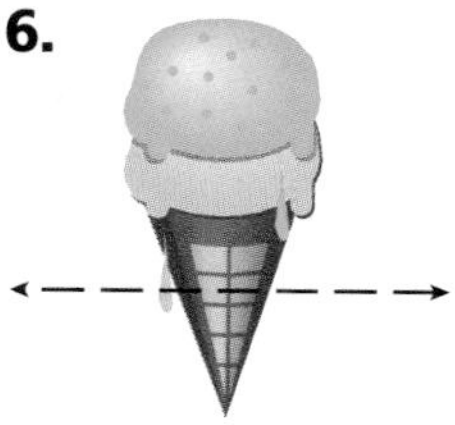

7. 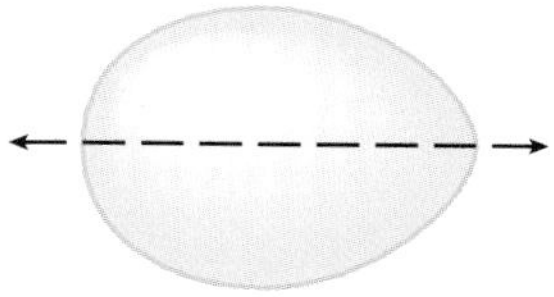

8. 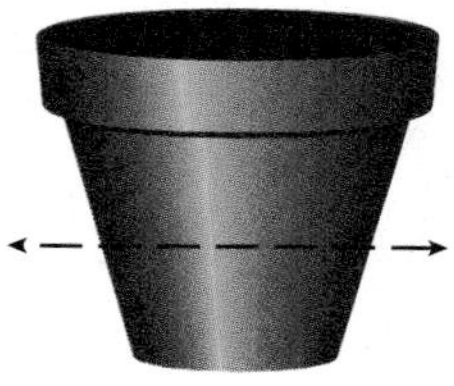

9. **Critical Thinking** Does a circle have more than one line of symmetry? Explain.

10. **Geography** Which of these states seem to have a line of symmetry?

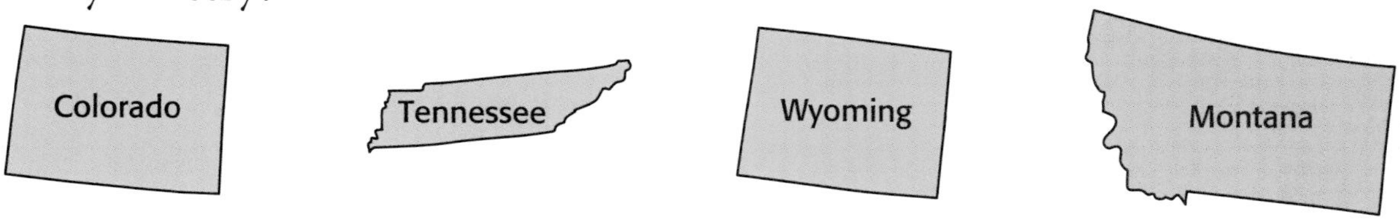

11. **Journal** Draw a polygon that has exactly one line of symmetry. Explain your drawing.

Technology

Congruence and Symmetry

You can use a computer drawing program to explore congruent figures and lines of symmetry.

> **Materials**
> a computer drawing program

Work Together

1 Open a new draw document. Make a figure.

- Choose the polygon tool.
- Move the mouse to the place you want to begin your figure. Click once to set the starting point of your figure.
- Move the mouse and click to make the first side of your figure.
- Repeat to make more sides.
- To close your figure, move the mouse back to the starting point and click.

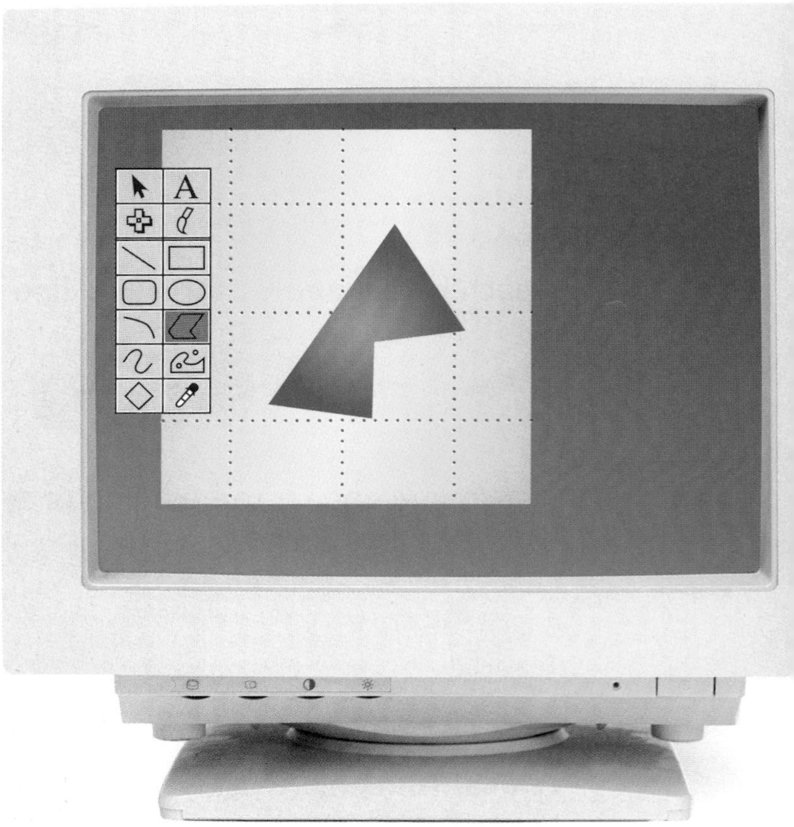

2 You can make a congruent figure by making a copy of the figure you drew above.

- Select your figure.

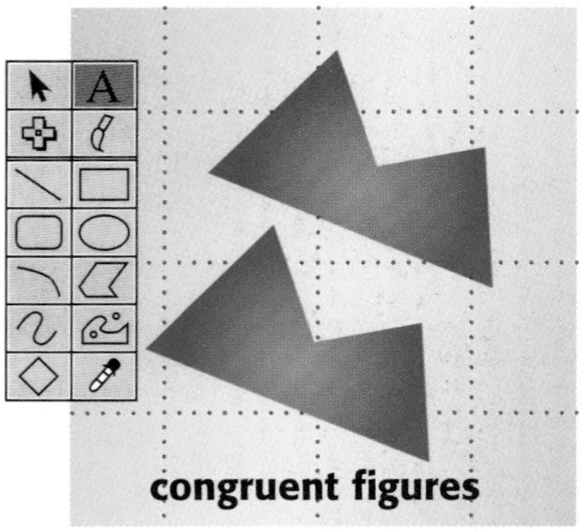

- Choose **Copy** from the Edit menu.
- Click on the place you want the copy to go. Choose **Paste** from the Edit menu.
- Label your figures by using the text tool.

3 You can copy and flip your figure to create a design that has a line of symmetry.

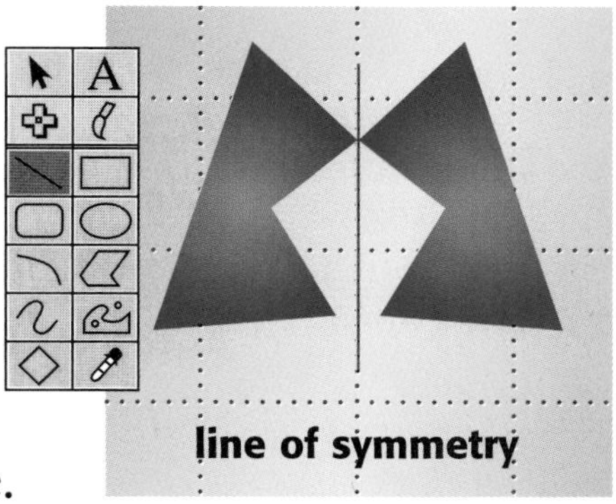

- Make two copies of your figure using the Copy and Paste functions.
- Select one copy. Choose **Transform: Flip Horizontally** from the Arrange menu.
- Slide the flipped figure next to the other figure.
- Use the line tool to show the line of symmetry.
- Use the text tool to label your design.

Exercises

1. Explain how you know your figures are congruent.
2. How did you know where to show the line of symmetry in your design?
3. **Reasoning** Fernando drew these figures. Are his figures labeled correctly? Explain.

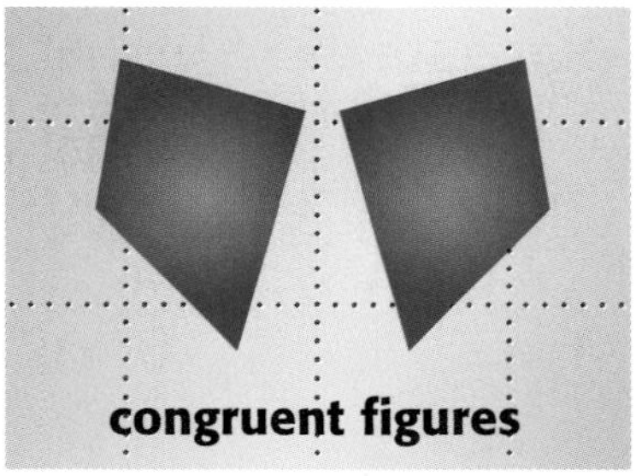

Extensions

4. Create a design that has more than one line of symmetry. Try the **Transform: Flip Vertically** function from the Arrange menu. Show all lines of symmetry in your design.
5. Draw a figure that does not change when it is flipped. You may want to try the rectangle or oval tools.
6. Try turning your figure. Choose **Free Rotate** from the Arrange menu. Click on a corner of your figure and drag the mouse. When you let go of the mouse button, your figure will be turned.

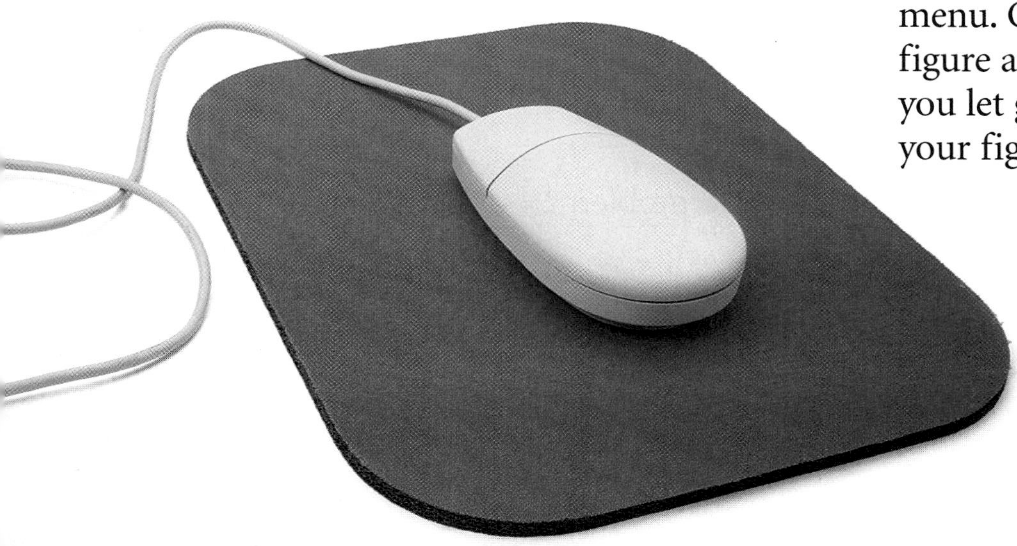

Chapter 8
Lesson
7

Problem Solving

Analyze Strategies: Solve a Simpler Problem

You Will Learn
how to look at a simpler part of a figure to solve a problem

Learn

Some figures show shapes within shapes. How many triangles are in this figure?

These pyramids were designed for the Louvre Museum in Paris, France, by I. M. Pei, a Chinese-American architect.

Work Together

▶ Understand

What do you know?

What do you need to find out?

▶ Plan

Break into simpler parts.

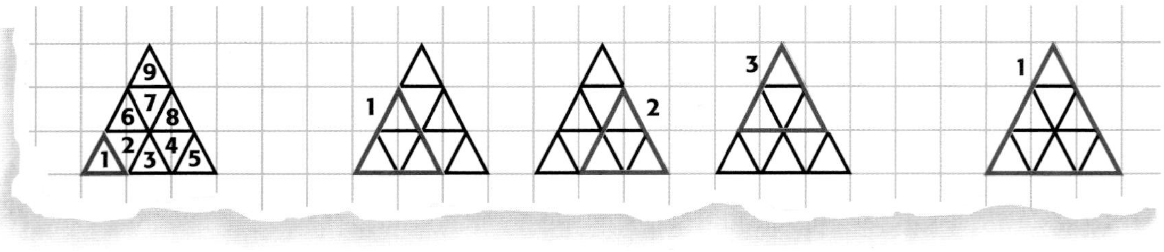

Triangles with a side of 1 unit

Triangles with a side of 2 units

Triangles with a side of 3 units

▶ Solve

Add to solve the harder problem.

$9 + 3 + 1 = 13$
There are 13 triangles in the figure.

▶ Look Back

How else could you solve the problem?

Talk About It

How does looking at only part of the figure help you solve this problem?

Check

Problem Solving: Understand, Plan, Solve, Look Back

1. How many squares can you find in this window? Draw the top left section of the window on grid paper.
   - **a.** How many squares are in this section of the window? (Hint: The section itself is 1 square.)
   - **b.** How many squares are in four sections of the window?
   - **c.** Now look at the whole window. How many more squares are there?
   - **d.** How many squares are there in all?

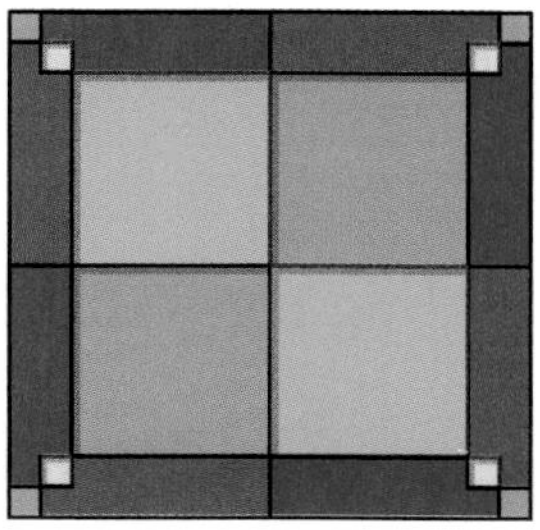

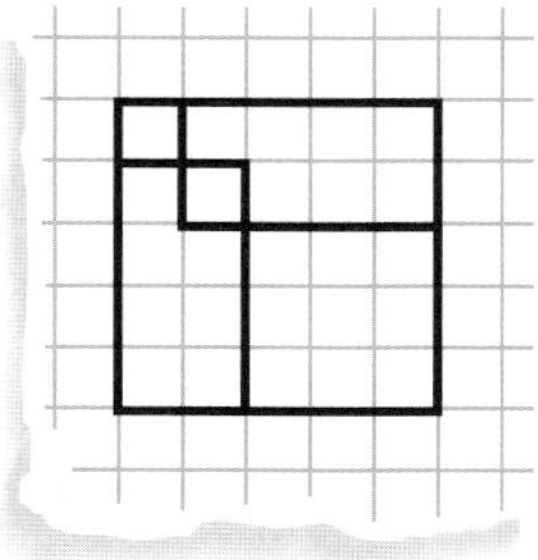

Problem Solving Practice

Use any strategy to solve each problem.

2. **Fine Arts** How many rectangles can you find in this painting?

This painting by Piet Mondrian (1872–1944) is called *Composition.*

Problem Solving Strategies

- Use Objects/Act It Out
- Draw a Picture
- Look for a Pattern
- Guess and Check
- Use Logical Reasoning
- Make an Organized List
- Make a Table
- Solve a Simpler Problem
- Work Backward

Choose a Tool

3. Elise packs boxes that hold 1 or 5 flowers each. If she has 25 flowers, how many ways can she pack the boxes?

4. Angela strings four beads. The blue bead is to the right of the red bead. The white bead is the only bead between the pink bead and the blue bead. Which bead is on the left?

5. Andre has 32 baseball cards. He gives 4 away, and places the rest in a card album. If he puts 7 cards on each page of the album, how many pages are in his album?

SECTION A
Review and Practice

Vocabulary Write true or false for each.

1. A sphere has no edges.
2. Parallel lines always meet.
3. Intersecting lines meet at a point.
4. A ray is a part of a line having two end points.

(Lesson 1) Name the solid figure that each object looks like.

5. 

6. 

7. 

(Lesson 2) Write the number of sides that each shape has.

8. 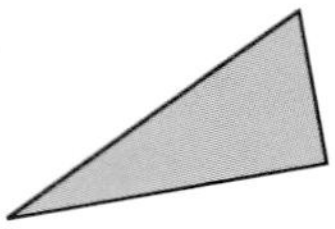

9. 

10. 

11. Reasoning If two same-sized squares are placed side by side, what shape will you see?

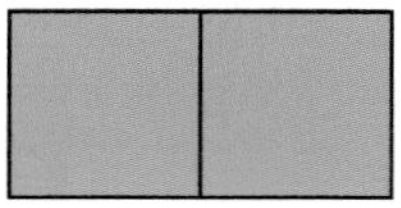

(Lesson 5) Write slide, flip, or turn for each.

12. 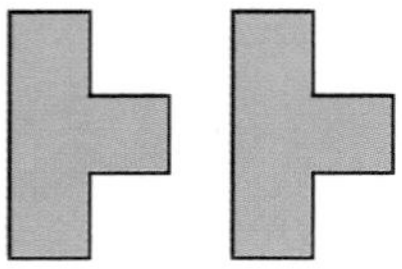

13. 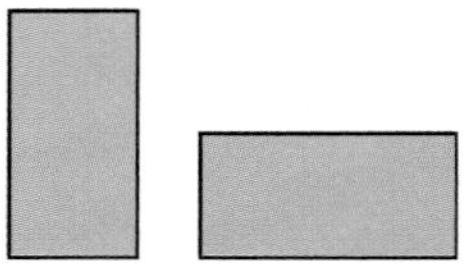

14. 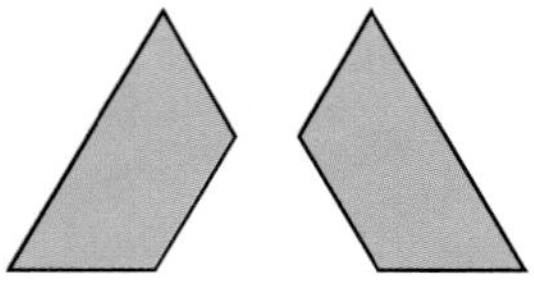

(Lesson 6) Is each line a line of symmetry? Write yes or no.

15. 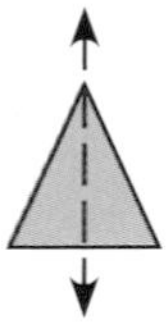

16. 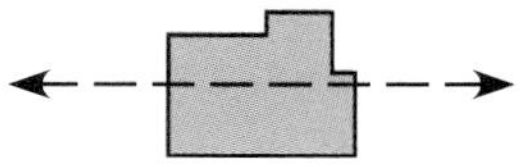

17. (Lesson 7) How many rectangles are in this figure?

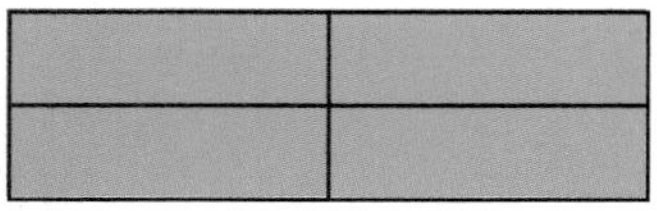

18. Journal Create a design. Include some shapes, intersecting lines, and congruent figures. Explain how you used what you learned in this section to create your design.

Skills Checklist

In this section, you have:

- ☑ Explored Solids
- ☑ Explored Solids and Shapes
- ☑ Learned About Lines and Line Segments
- ☑ Explored Angles
- ☑ Explored Slides, Flips, and Turns
- ☑ Explored Symmetry
- ☑ Solved Problems by Solving a Simpler Problem

CHAPTER 8

SECTION

B Perimeter, Area, and Volume

Some students in Folsom, California, helped design their own playground! How could you decide how many pieces of equipment would fit in a play area?

GET READY!

Measurement and Coordinate Grids

Review adding more than two addends. Find each sum.

1. $8 + 12 + 8 + 12$

2. $3 + 1 + 3 + 2 + 4$

3. $12 + 4 + 12 + 4$

Skills Checklist

In this section, you will:

- ❒ Explore Perimeter
- ❒ Explore Area
- ❒ Solve Problems by Making Decisions
- ❒ Explore Volume
- ❒ Learn About Coordinate Grids

Chapter 8
Lesson
8

Exploring Perimeter

Problem Solving Connection
Draw a Picture

Materials
grid paper

Vocabulary

unit
quantity used as a standard of measurement

perimeter
the distance around a figure

Explore

You can use grid paper to find the distance around a figure. Count the **units** along the outside of the rectangle. The distance around is 16 units.

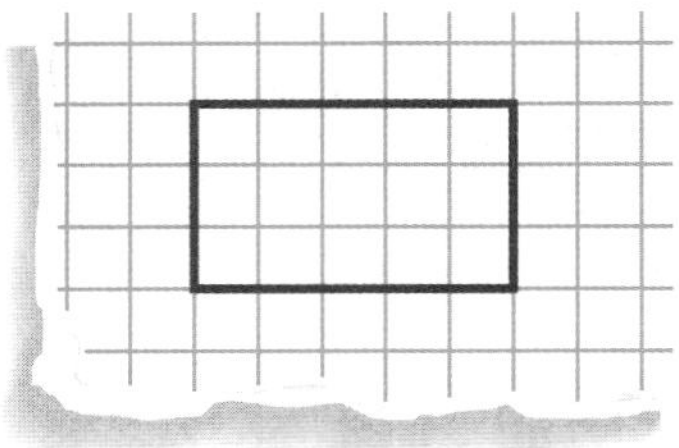

Work Together

1. Find the distance around each figure.

a.

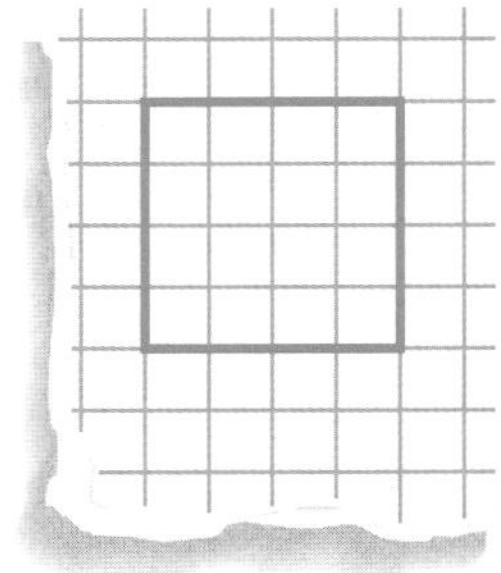

b.

c.

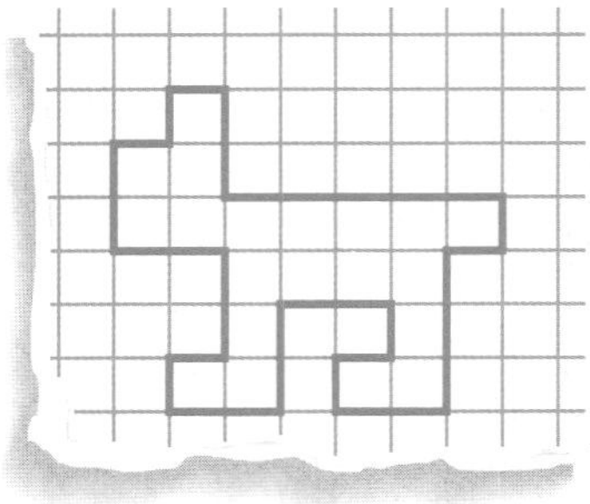

d.

Problem Solving Hint
You can use guess and check to decide what kind of figure to draw.

2. Use grid paper. Draw a figure with a distance around of

   a. 6 units **b.** 8 units **c.** 16 units **d.** 20 units

Talk About It

3. How did you find the distance around each figure?

4. Look at the square in **1a.** How could you add to find the total distance around? How could you multiply?

Connect

The distance around an object or figure is its **perimeter**.

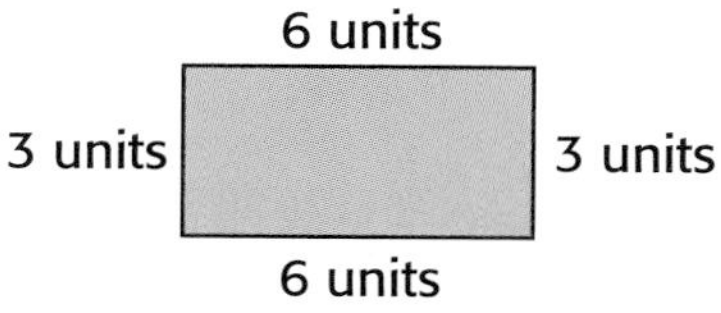

$3 + 6 + 3 + 6 = 18$

The perimeter is 18 units.

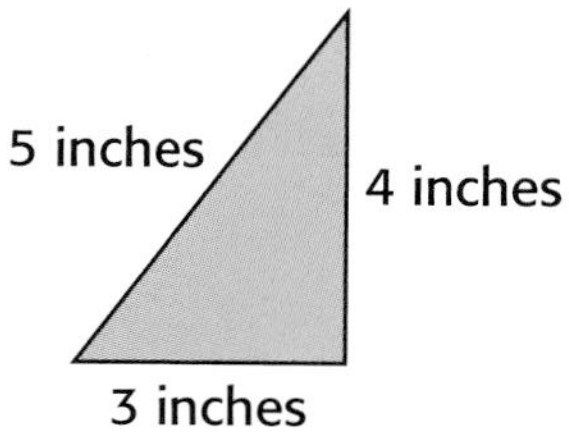

$3 + 4 + 5 = 12$

The perimeter is 12 inches.

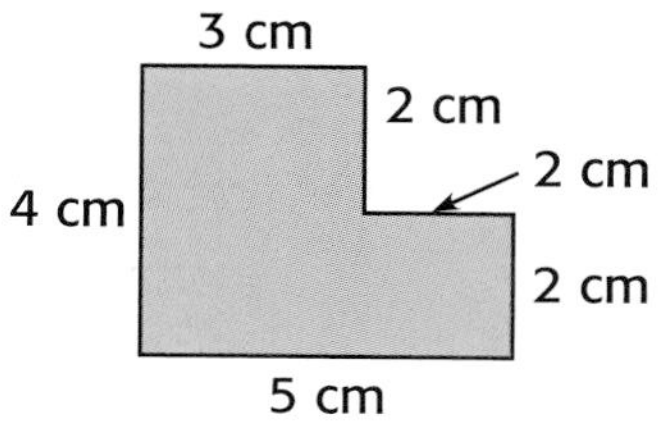

$3 + 2 + 2 + 2 + 5 + 4 = 18$

The perimeter is 18 cm.

Practice

Find the perimeter of each.

1.

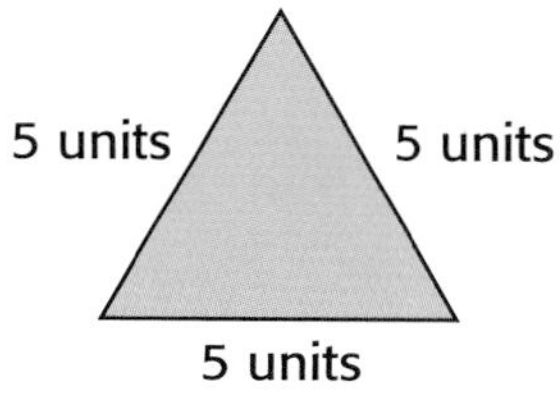

2.

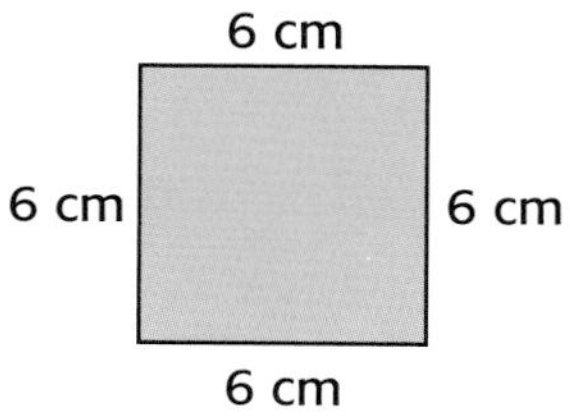

3.

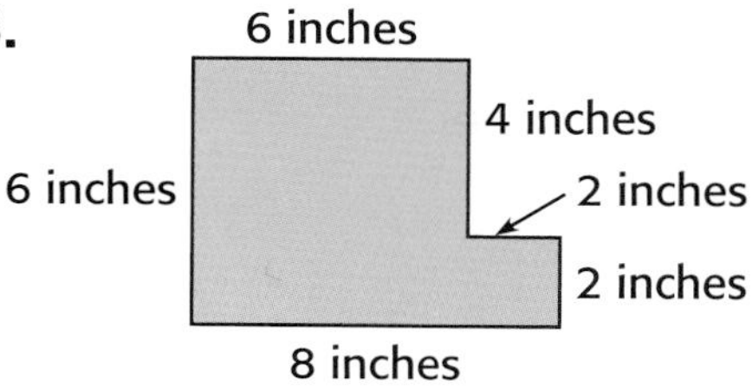

Use grid paper. Draw a figure with each perimeter.

4. 10 units **5.** 12 units **6.** 22 units **7.** 4 units

8. Social Studies The Great Pyramid of Cheops was built by Egyptians in about 2500 B.C. It has a square base that is 756 feet on each side. What is the perimeter of the base of the pyramid?

9. Algebra Readiness The perimeter of a square measures 20 units. How long is each side?

10. Journal Use grid paper to draw a square and a rectangle. Then write the perimeter of each shape.

The Great Pyramid of Cheops is located in Giza, outside of Cairo, Egypt.

Chapter 8
Lesson
9

Exploring Area

Problem Solving Connection
Draw a Picture

Materials
grid paper

Vocabulary
square unit
the unit used to measure area

area
the number of square units needed to cover the surface of a figure

Explore

You can use grid paper to measure the surface of a figure in **square units.**

Count the number of squares inside the figure.

There are 30 square units in the rectangle.

Work Together

1. Write the number of square units in each figure.

a.
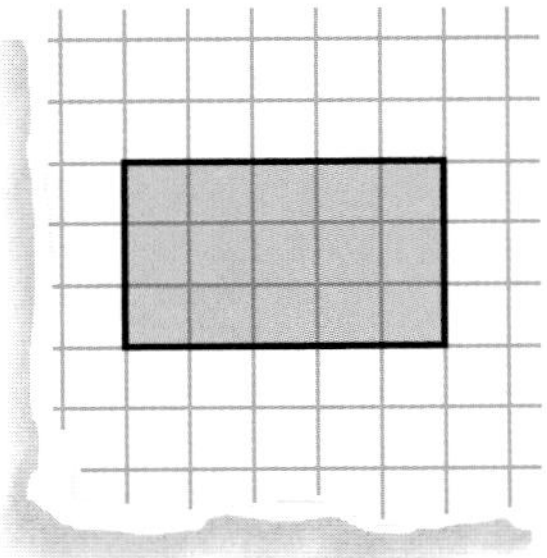

b.
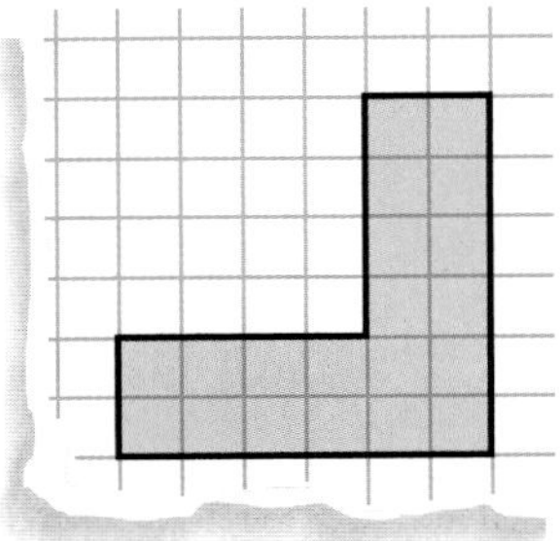

c.
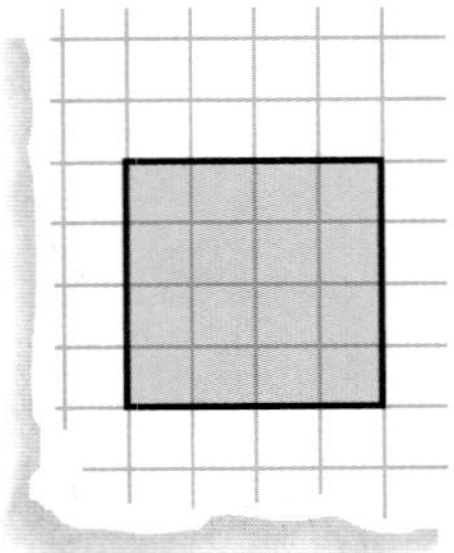

2. Use grid paper. Draw two different figures that measure 12 square units.

3. Estimate the number of square units in each figure.

a.
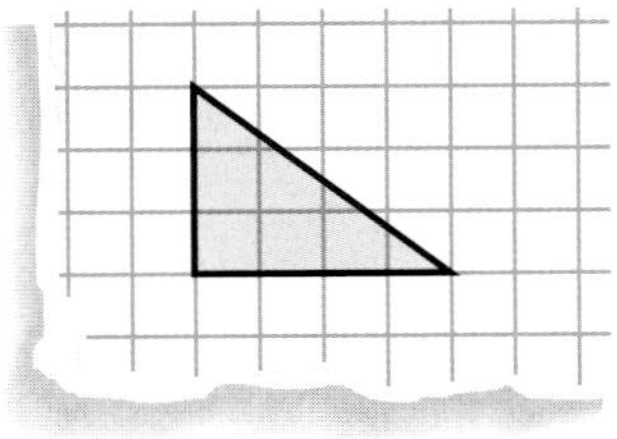

b.
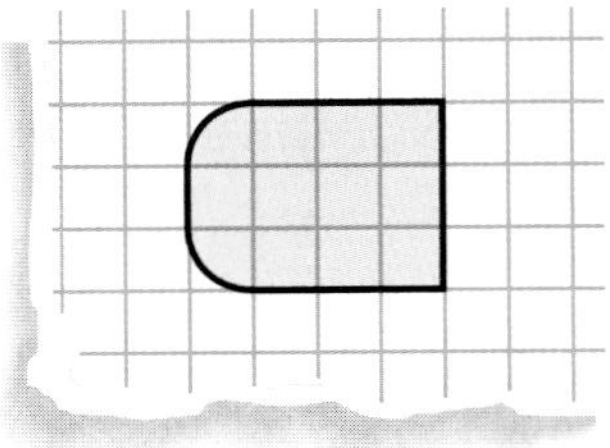

Math Tip
You can think of two partly covered squares as one whole square to help you estimate.

Talk About It

How could you multiply to find the number of square units inside the rectangle above?

Connect

The number of square units needed to cover the surface of a figure is the **area**.

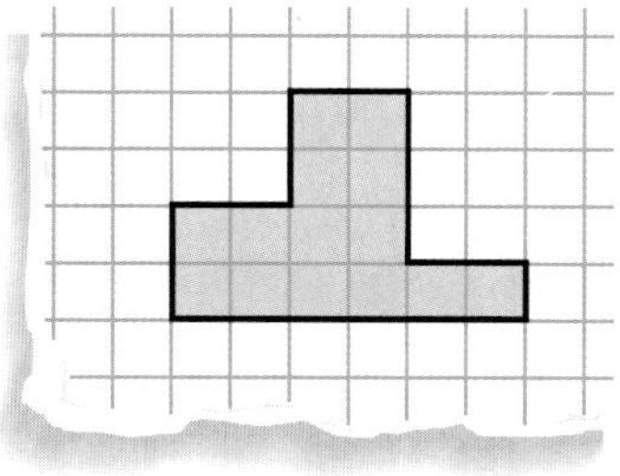

The area is 14 square units.

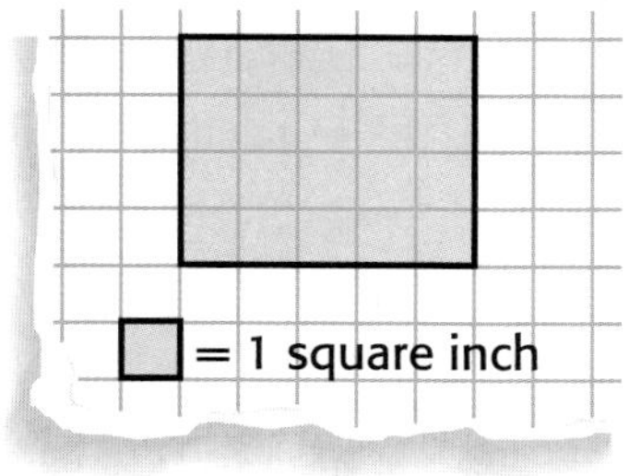

The area is 20 square inches.

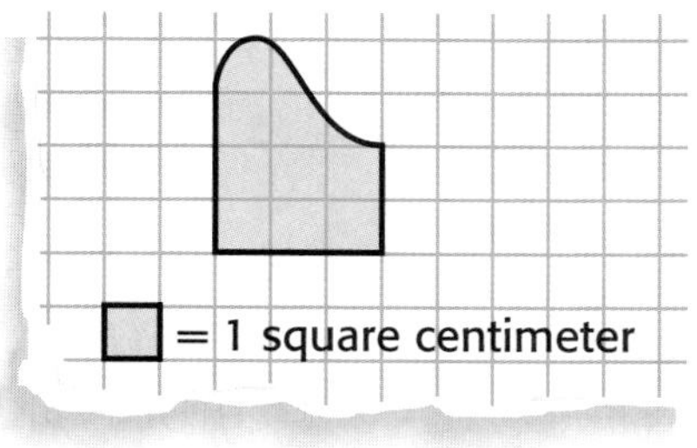

The area is a little more than 9 square centimeters.

Practice

Find each area. Write your answer in square units.

1.

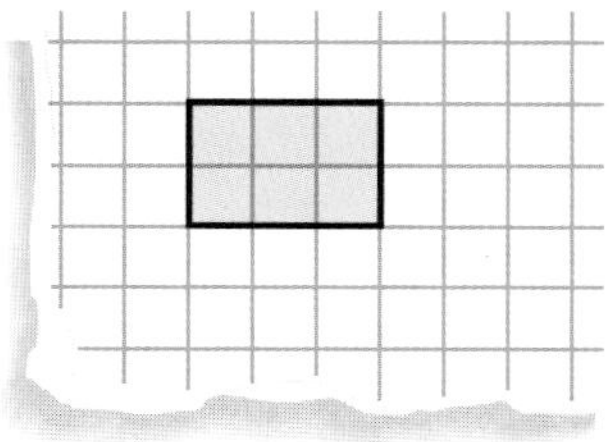

2.

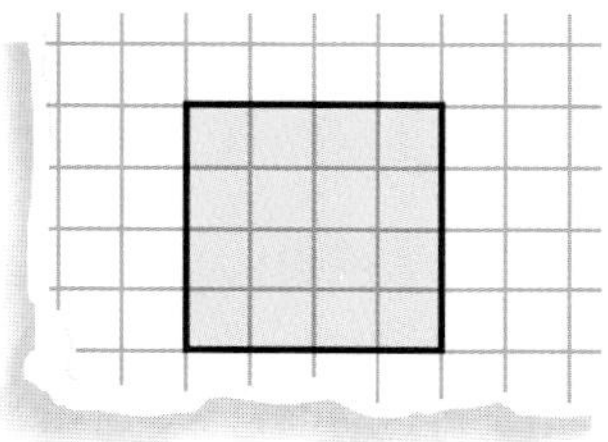

3.

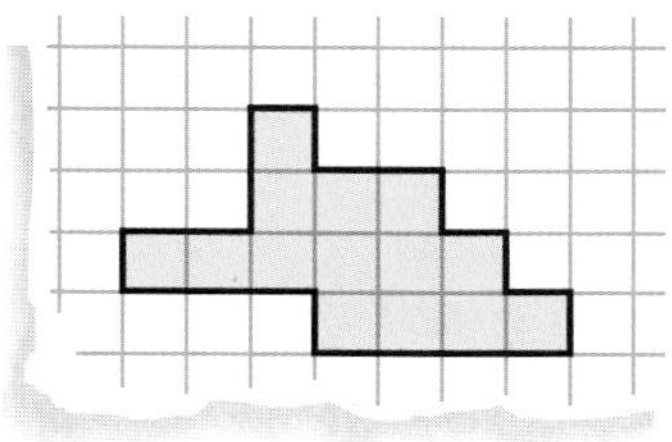

4. Use grid paper. Look at the rectangle shown in **1**.

a. Draw a figure with an area greater than the rectangle. Draw another figure with an area less than the rectangle.

b. What happens to the perimeter and area of the rectangle if you double the length of its sides?

5. Geography Use the map to estimate the area of Washington, D.C., in square miles.

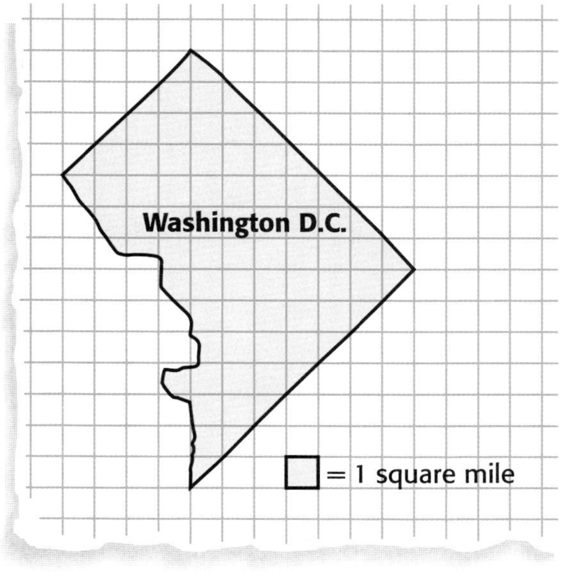

6. Journal Draw a figure on grid paper. Explain the difference between the area of the figure and the perimeter of the figure.

Problem Solving

Decision Making: Estimating Area

You Will Learn
how to estimate area to make a diagram

Explore

Students in Folsom, California, helped plan and build their own playground! They met with a playground architect and then helped build it. You can plan *your* own playground! What will it include?

Students in Folsom, California, with a playground diagram

Problem Solving Hint
You can estimate area to help decide what kind of equipment will fit.

Here are some things to think about:

- Your playground should be a rectangle. Two sides should each be 20 feet and two sides should each be 30 feet.
- You can choose the pieces of equipment! The area needed for each piece of equipment is shown below.

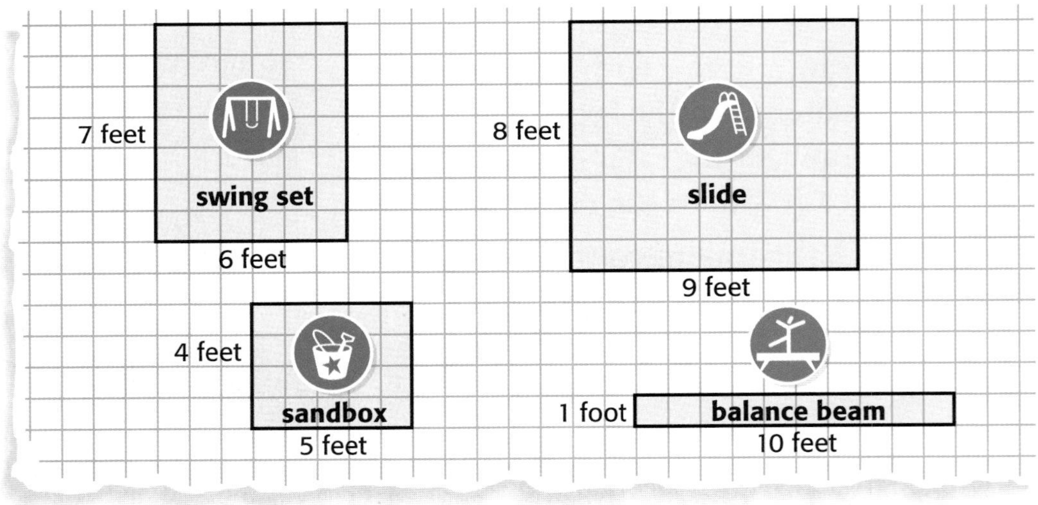

- If you want, you can think of another piece of equipment.
- Be safe! If you use the balance beam, make sure all sides of the beam are 6 feet away from the other equipment and the edge of the playground.

Work Together

▶ Understand

1. What do you know?
2. What do you need to decide?

▶ Plan and Solve

3. What kinds of equipment do you like?
4. Does some equipment take more area than others? Explain.
5. How can you decide if you have room for all the equipment you want?
6. Do you want to include equipment that's not on the list? If so, about how much area will it need? Where might it fit?

▶ Make a Decision

7. Use grid paper to outline a rectangle for your playground. One square on your grid paper should show 1 square foot.
8. Draw the area of each piece of equipment you want in the playground. Write the area inside each drawing.
9. Color your plan.

▶ Present Your Decision

10. Present your plan to the class. Explain how you decided what to include and where to place each item.
11. As a class, submit one plan to **www.mathsurf.com/3/ch8**. Compare your plan with those of other students. Did more students choose slides, swings, or some other piece of equipment?

Chapter 8
Lesson
11

Exploring Volume

Problem Solving Connection
Use Objects

Materials
color cubes

Vocabulary
volume
the number of cubic units in a solid figure
cubic unit
the unit used to measure volume

Explore

You can use cubes to measure the amount of space in a solid figure.

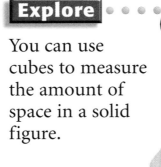

Work Together

1. Use color cubes to build each solid figure. Write how many cubes are in each.

Math Tip
Sometimes you have to decide how many cubes are hidden.

a.

b.

c.

d.

e.

f.

2. Use 4, 5, and 8 cubes to build three solid figures.

Talk About It

How can you count the number of units in a solid figure if not all of the cubes can be seen?

Connect

The number of cubes needed to fill a solid figure is the **volume**. The volume of a solid figure is measured in **cubic units**.

The volume is 10 cubic units.

The volume is 6 cubic units.

Practice

Find the volume of each. You may use cubes to help.

1.

2.

3.

4.

5.

6.

7. **Reasoning** Suppose you build a solid with 17 cubes. Then you use the same cubes to build a different solid. Are the volumes of the two solids different? Explain.

8. **Patterns** What is the volume of the solid figure that comes next in the pattern?

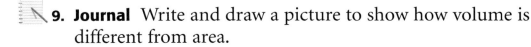

9. **Journal** Write and draw a picture to show how volume is different from area.

Coordinate Grids

You Will Learn
how to find and name a point on a coordinate grid

Vocabulary

coordinate grid
a graph used to locate points

ordered pair
a pair of numbers used to locate a point on a grid

Learn

Visit exhibits at the National Air and Space Museum in Washington, D.C.

A **coordinate grid** is a special graph with lines that intersect. Each point where lines intersect can be named by an **ordered pair** of numbers.

First Floor of the National Air and Space Museum

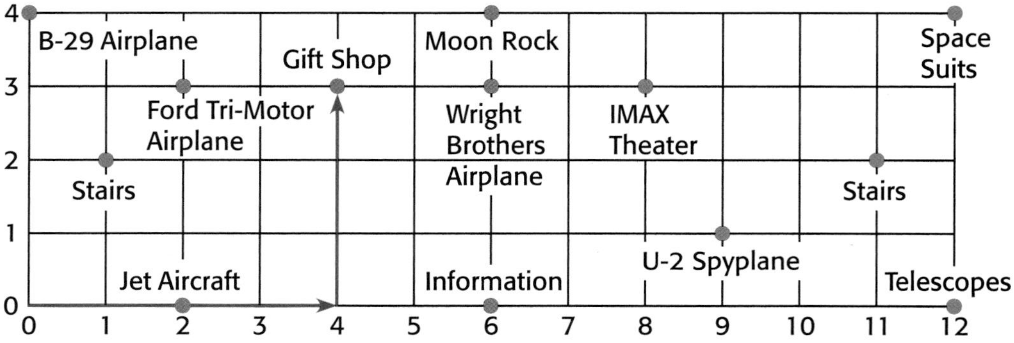

Example 1

What is located at the point (4, 3)?

Start at 0.

The first number shows how many spaces you move to the right.

The second number shows how many spaces you move up.

The gift shop is located at the point (4, 3).

Example 2

At what point are the space suits?

The space suits are located at the point (12, 4).

Talk About It

Find the point (1, 4) on the coordinate grid. Then find the point (4, 1). Are they the same point? Explain.

Check

Use the grid on page 348. Write the ordered pair for each.

1. B-29 airplane **2.** IMAX theater **3.** Information

4. **Reasoning** Arie said, "The first number in an ordered pair is the number of spaces you move to the right." Do you agree or disagree? Explain.

Practice

Skills and Reasoning

Use the grid on page 348. Write an ordered pair for each.

5. Telescopes **6.** Jet aircraft **7.** Moon rock **8.** Stairs

Write what is located at each ordered pair.

9. (9, 1) **10.** (6, 3) **11.** (11, 2) **12.** (2, 3)

13. Malcolm said, "To find the ordered pair (7, 0), I'll go to the right 7 spaces and up 0 spaces." Do you agree or disagree? Explain.

14. What ordered pair is two spaces to the right of (4, 3)?

Problem Solving and Applications

Using Data Use the Data File on page 319 to help answer **15** and **16**.

15. What streets intersect at the Martin Luther King, Jr. Library?

16. What is located at the corner of 10th St. and E St.?

Mixed Review and Test Prep

Mental Math Find the sum, difference, or product.

17. $30 + 60$ **18.** $140 - 70$ **19.** 8×4 **20.** $700 + 900$

21. Find the perimeter.

Ⓐ 16 feet Ⓑ 48 square feet

Ⓒ 12 feet Ⓓ 28 feet

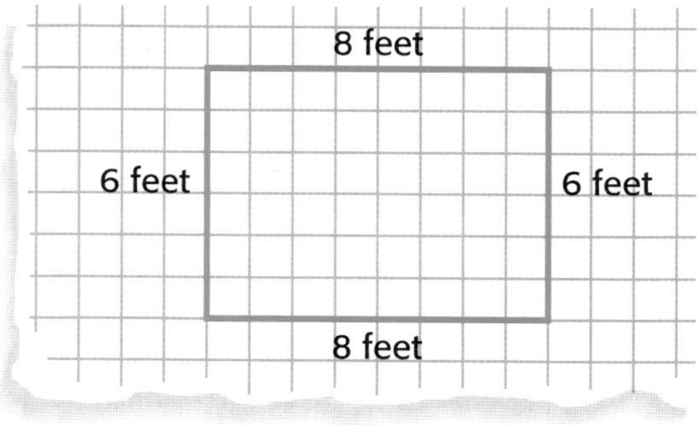

SECTION B
Review and Practice

Vocabulary Choose the correct word to complete each sentence.

Word List
perimeter
volume
area

1. The distance around a figure is its _____.
2. _____ is the number of square units needed to cover the surface of a shape.
3. The number of cubic units in a solid figure is the _____.

(Lessons 8 and 9) Find the area and perimeter of each shape.

4. 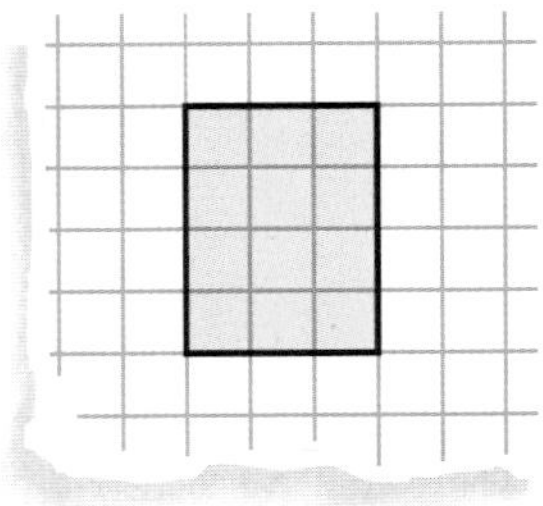

5. 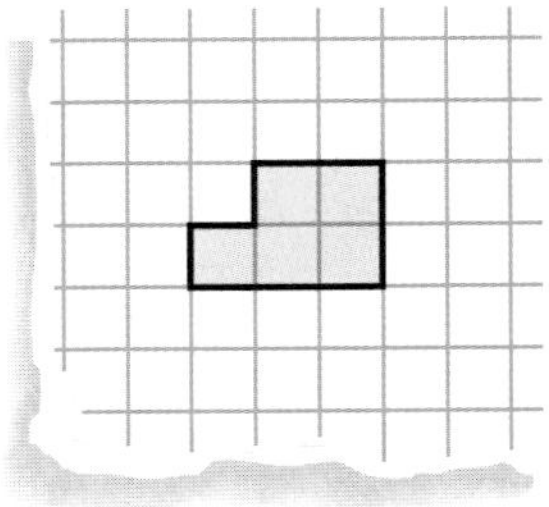

6. 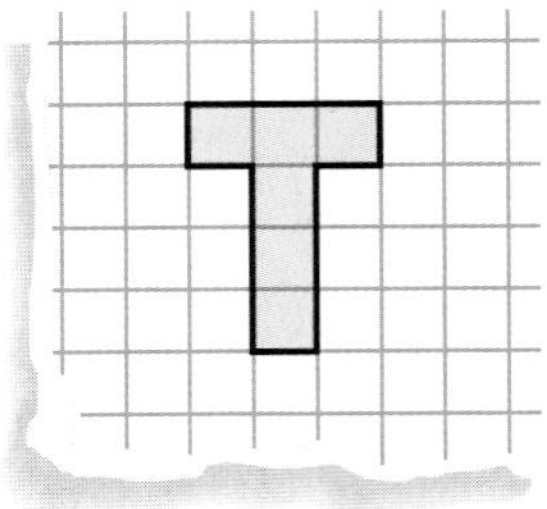

7. **Reasoning** If one side of a square measures 9 units, what is the perimeter?

(Lesson 11) Find the volume of each.

8. 

9. 

10. 

(Lesson 12) Write the ordered pair that locates each letter.

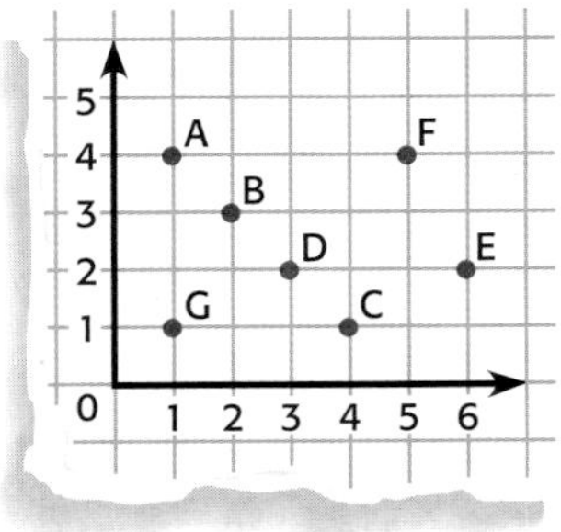

11. D
12. B
13. E
14. F
15. Which letter is located at (1, 1)?
16. **Journal** Use grid paper. Draw a rectangle and write its area and perimeter.

Skills Checklist

In this section, you have:

- ☑ **Explored Perimeter**
- ☑ **Explored Area**
- ☑ **Solved Problems by Making Decisions**
- ☑ **Explored Volume**
- ☑ **Learned About Coordinate Grids**

YOUR CHOICE

Choose at least one. Use what you have learned in this chapter.

1 Figure It Out

Build a solid figure using color cubes. Challenge a partner to draw your figure from the side or above. Take turns until each of you has made three drawings.

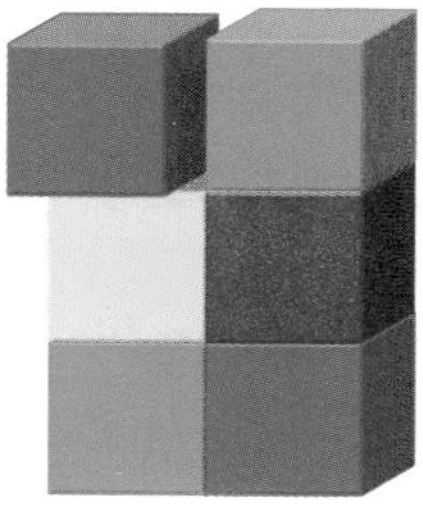

2 Counter Power

Estimate the area of your math book using counters. Then use your data to estimate the area of your desk, the chalkboard, and the ceiling. Explain how you made each estimate.

3 Searching for Solids

At Home Search for examples of solid figures where you live. Make a table or pictograph to show how many of each solid you found. Compare your results with classmates' results.

4 Sorts of Shapes

Work with a partner. Think of a rule to sort Power Polygons. You might sort by color, by number of corners, by number of sides, and so on. Challenge your partner to guess your rule. Take turns until both of you have guessed three times.

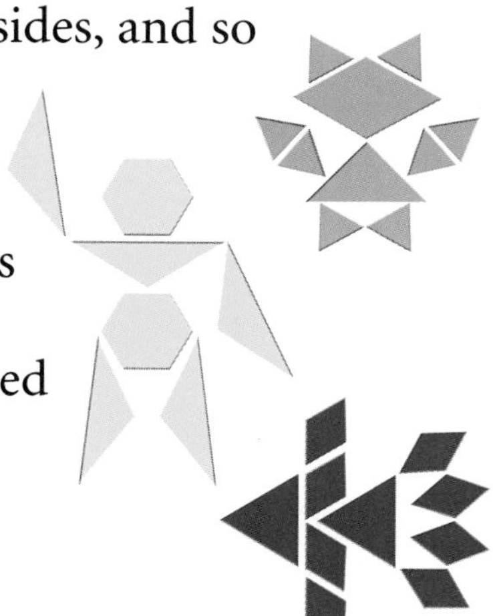

5 Pattern Paper

Make a pattern using Power Polygons. Then use a drawing program on a computer to copy your pattern. Print and color your pattern paper to decorate a wall or a notebook.

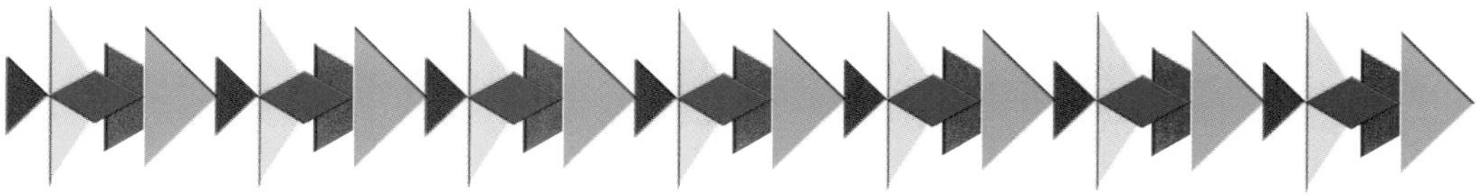

CHAPTER 8
Review/Test

Vocabulary Match each with its example.

a. ray
b. sphere
c. parallel lines
d. right angle

1. 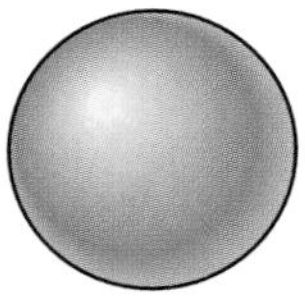

2. 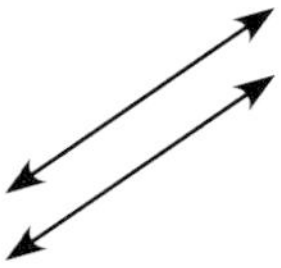

3. 

4. 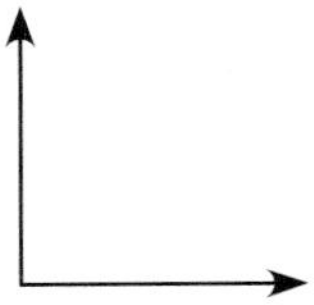

(Lessons 1 and 2) Name the solid figure or shape that each object looks like.

5. 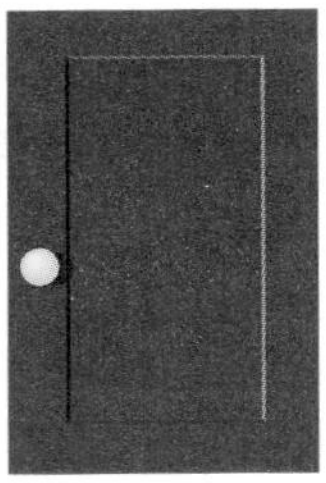

6. 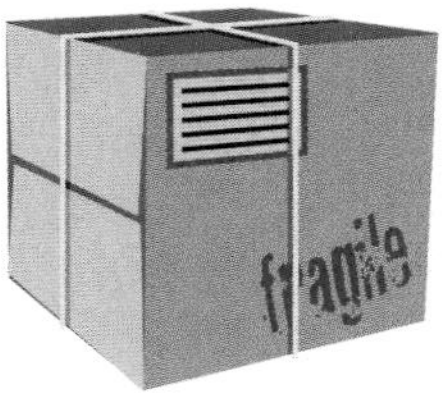

7. 

8. 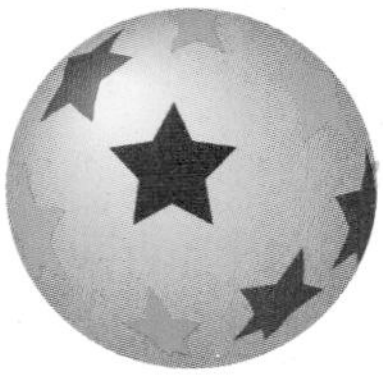

(Lesson 5) Write congruent or not congruent for each.

9. 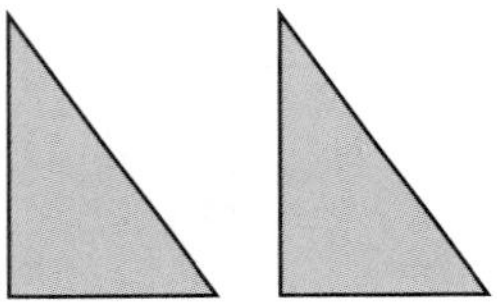

10. 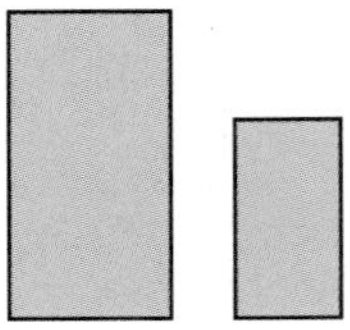

11. 

(Lesson 6) Is each a line of symmetry? Write yes or no.

12. 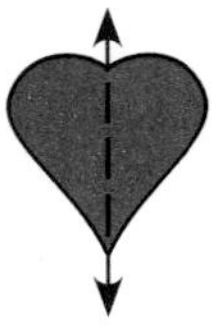

13. 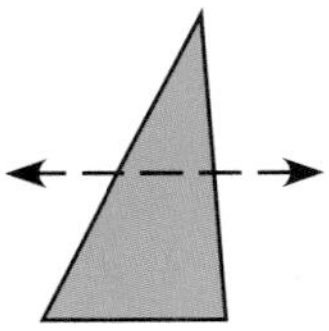

14. 

15. **(Lesson 7)** How many squares can you find in this design?

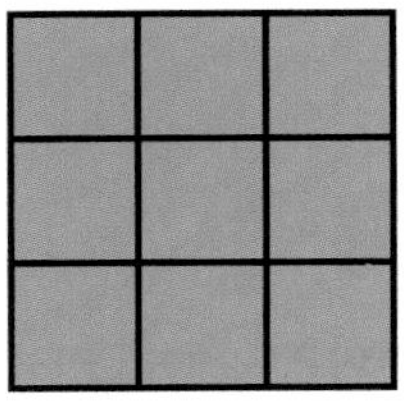

16. **(Lessons 8 and 9)** Find the perimeter and area of the figure.

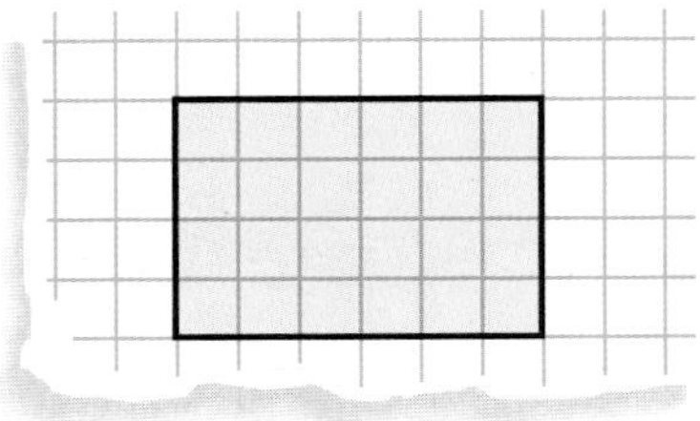

CHAPTER 8
Performance Assessment

Every year, the Ndebele (en-de-BEL-ee) women of Zimbabwe paint their houses and outer walls with brightly colored geometric shapes. Make a plan for your own wall painting. Use shapes you know and symmetry in your design. Then find the perimeter and area of your wall.

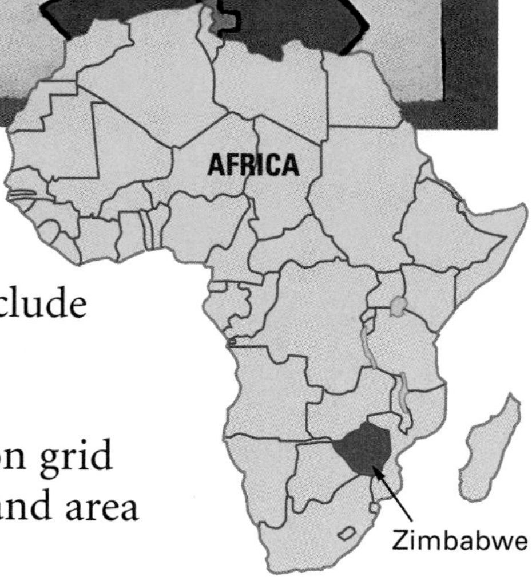

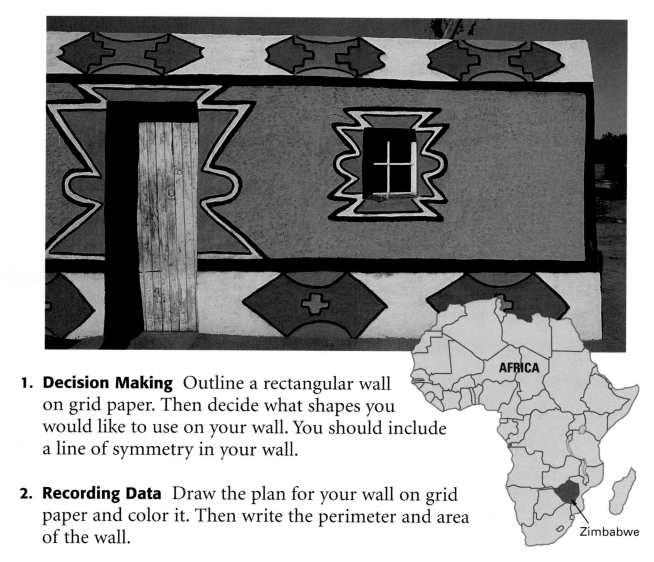

1. **Decision Making** Outline a rectangular wall on grid paper. Then decide what shapes you would like to use on your wall. You should include a line of symmetry in your wall.

2. **Recording Data** Draw the plan for your wall on grid paper and color it. Then write the perimeter and area of the wall.

3. **Explain Your Thinking** What kinds of shapes are in your design? Where is the line of symmetry?

4. **Critical Thinking** How did you find the perimeter and area of your wall? What units did you use?

Math Magazine

Chinese Kites Kites are much more than toys in China! Kites were invented in China 3,000 years ago. They were used for celebrations, good luck, and even protection. Today, people fly kites in contests or just for fun!

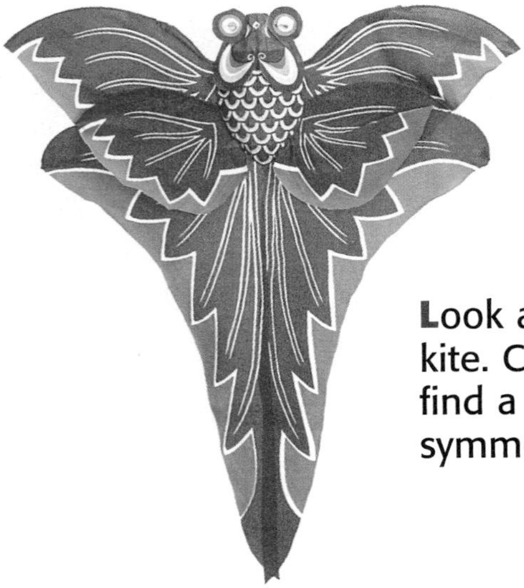

Look at this kite. Can you find a line of symmetry?

Try These!

Try designing a kite. You might want to use a traditional good luck symbol like a dragon or turtle. Make sure your kite has symmetry!

CHAPTERS 1–8
Cumulative Review

This question asks for the month with the *least* number of rainy days. September has the least number of rainy days, so Ⓑ is correct.

Test Prep Strategy: Follow Directions

Answer the question asked.
Which month had the least number of rainy days?

Ⓐ July Ⓑ September Ⓒ June Ⓓ August

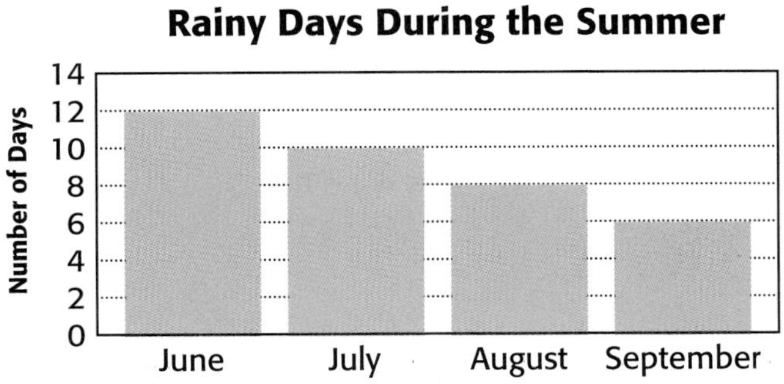

Test Prep Strategies

- Read Carefully
- Follow Directions
- Make Smart Choices
- Eliminate Choices
- Work Backward from an Answer

Write the letter of the correct answer. Use any strategy to help.

1. June has 30 days. How many days were NOT rainy in June?
   Ⓐ 12 Ⓑ 42 Ⓒ 18 Ⓓ 16
2. How many rainy days were there during July and September?
   Ⓐ 12 Ⓑ 16 Ⓒ 6 Ⓓ 18
3. Taisha's class has 32 students. How many pizzas would they need to buy so that everyone would get one slice?
   Ⓐ 9 Ⓑ 2
   Ⓒ 5 Ⓓ 4

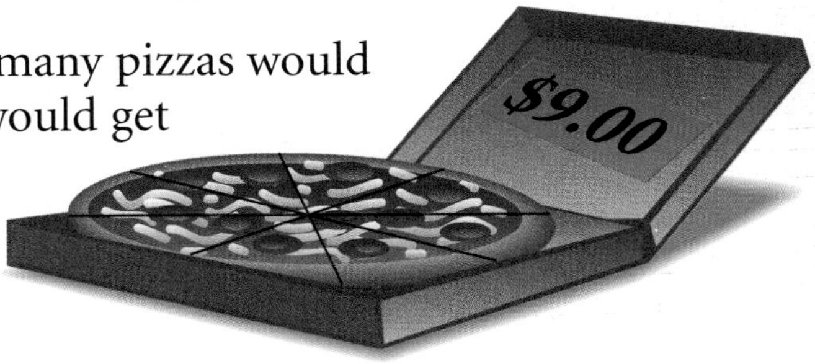

4. How much would it cost without tax to buy 7 pizzas?
   Ⓐ $63 Ⓑ $56 Ⓒ $64 Ⓓ not here
5. What solid figure is shown here?
   Ⓐ cylinder Ⓑ pyramid Ⓒ cone Ⓓ cube

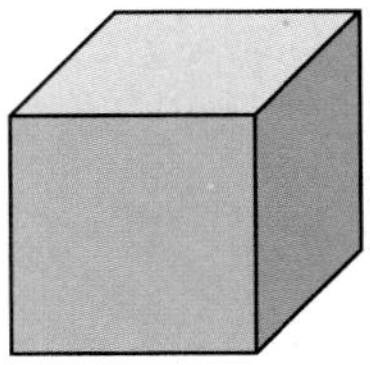

6. Which number is NOT a multiple of 5?
   Ⓐ 5 Ⓑ 20 Ⓒ 12 Ⓓ 15

REVIEW AND PRACTICE

DATA FILE

Chapter 9
Multiplying and Dividing

City Life

SECTION A

359

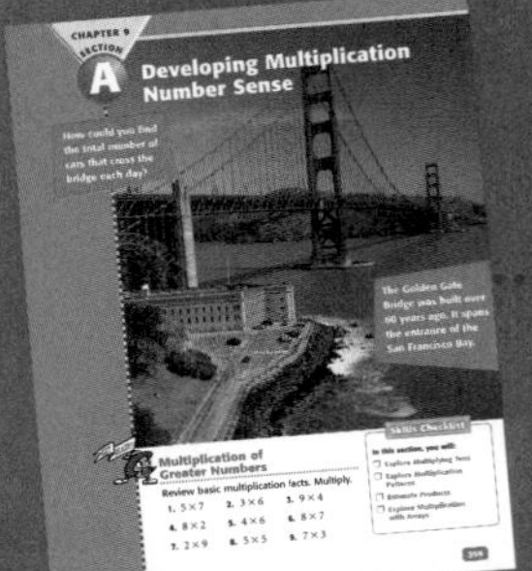

The Golden Gate Bridge in San Francisco, California
Page 359

Developing Multiplication Number Sense

People go to cities for work, school, shopping, and vacation.
There are many different ways to get there. Which type of transportation carries the most people at once?

Getting to the City	
Transportation	**Number of Passengers**
Car	4
Bus	44
Light rail	76
Commuter train car	150
Jet airplane	122

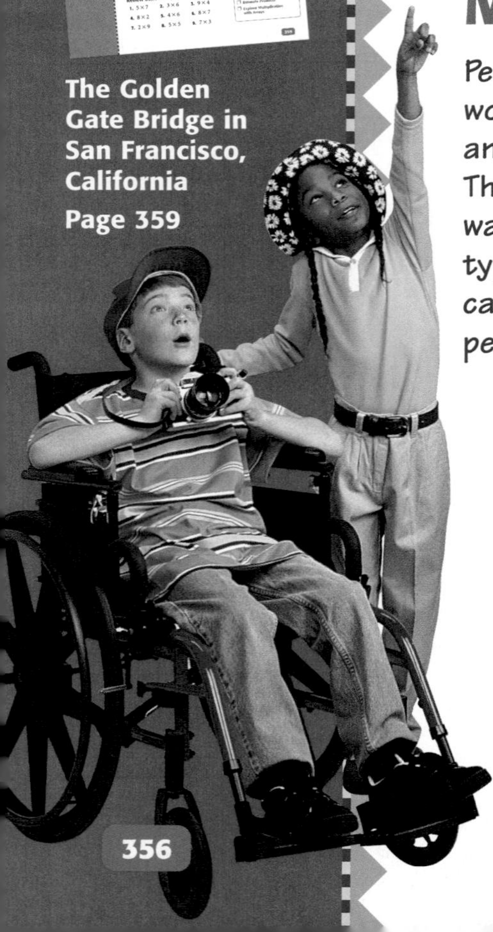

Surfing the World Wide Web!

What other ways can you find to get around a city? Use the World Wide Web to research different types of transportation around the world. Try to find information about the Bullet Train in Japan or the cable cars in California. Start at **www.mathsurf.com/3/ch9**.

SECTION B

Multiplying by 1-Digit Factors

369

Every year performers play at subway and commuter rail stations in New York City. They are part of a program called Music Under New York. Which type of music had the most performers?

Music Under New York Performers

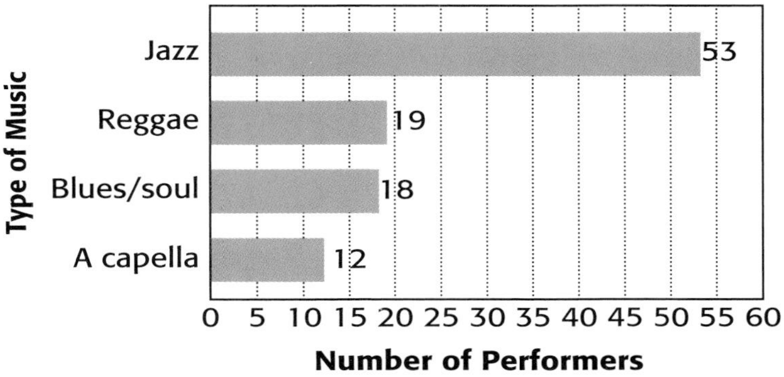

Future City competition

Page 369

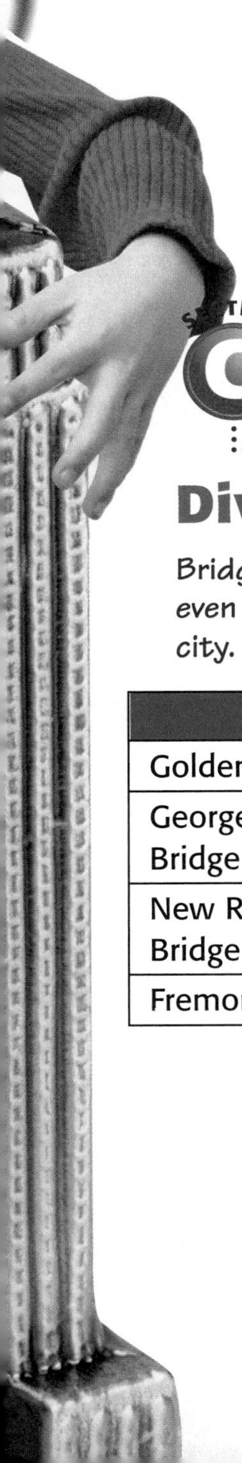

SECTION C

Dividing with 1-Digit Divisors

389

Bridges can help you get from city to city or even from one part to another part of the same city. Which of these bridges is the widest?

Bridge	State	Width	Length
Golden Gate Bridge	California	90 feet	8,981 feet
George Washington Bridge	New York	119 feet	4,760 feet
New River Gorge Bridge	West Virginia	70 feet	3,031 feet
Fremont Bridge	Oregon	68 feet	8,063 feet

Katie started a fund-raiser in Tulsa, Oklahoma.

Page 389

TEAM PROJECT
CITY PLANNING

Materials
construction paper, markers

People plan cities so that everyone has room to live, work, and play. This is the plan for the ancient Greek city of Miletus.

Design a city for the students in your class.

Make a Plan

- How many people live in your city?
- How will you show your city plan?

Carry It Out

1. Make a list of the different parts of your city. How much space will each part take?
2. Every city needs water. If each person in your city uses 4 gallons of water each hour, how many gallons of water does your city need each day?
3. Make a plan of your city on a large sheet of paper. Is there enough space for everyone in your city? Label the different parts of your city on your plan.

Talk About It

- How did you make sure your city would have enough water for each person?
- Explain how you planned your city.

Present the Project

- Display the plan for your city.
- Of all the cities your classmates created, which city would you want to live in? Why?

CHAPTER 9

SECTION

A Developing Multiplication Number Sense

How could you find the total number of cars that cross the bridge each day?

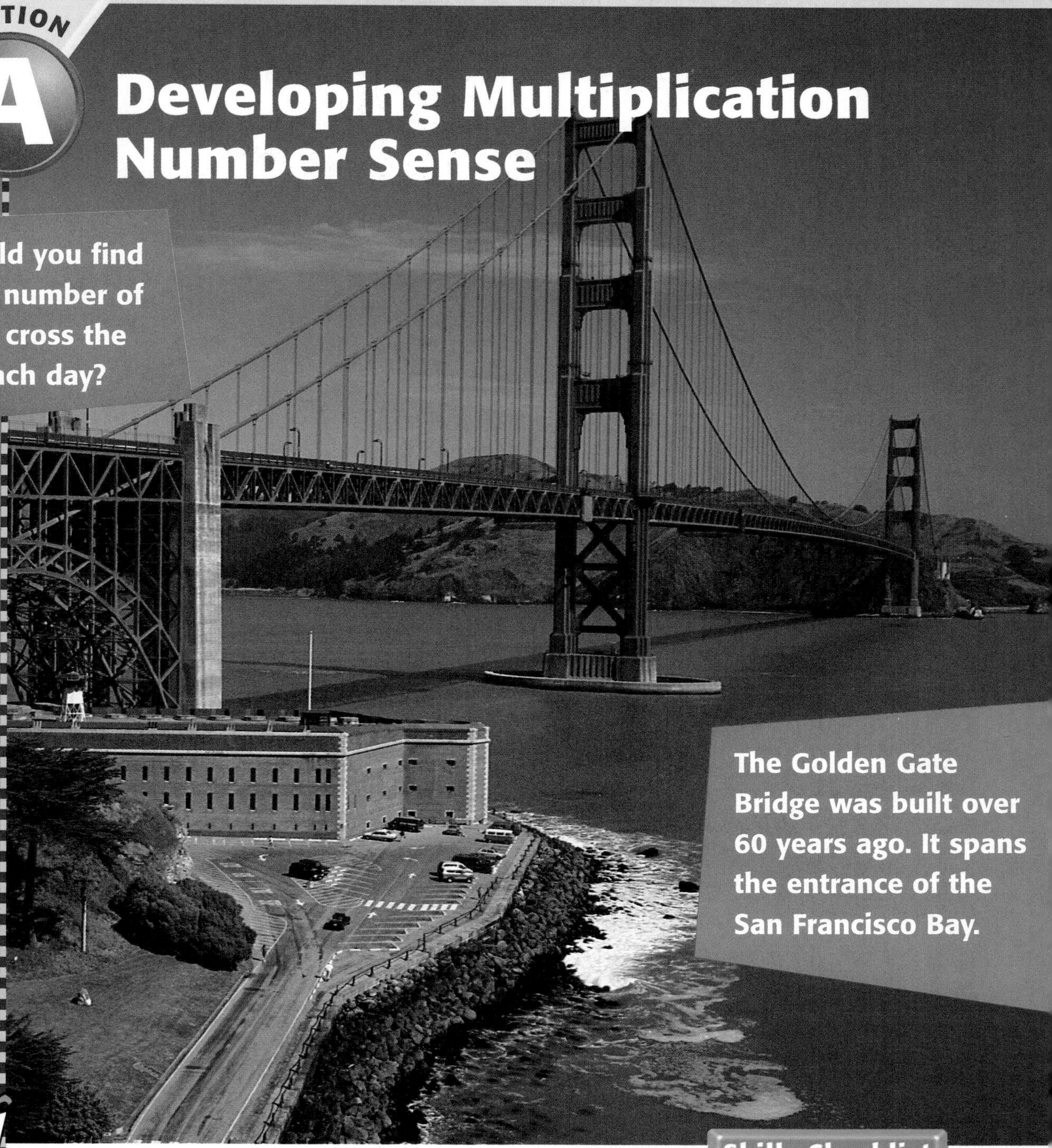

The Golden Gate Bridge was built over 60 years ago. It spans the entrance of the San Francisco Bay.

Multiplication of Greater Numbers

Review basic multiplication facts. Multiply.

1. 5×7	**2.** 3×6	**3.** 9×4
4. 8×2	**5.** 4×6	**6.** 8×7
7. 2×9	**8.** 5×5	**9.** 7×3

Skills Checklist

In this section, you will:

- ❒ Explore Multiplying Tens
- ❒ Explore Multiplication Patterns
- ❒ Estimate Products
- ❒ Explore Multiplication with Arrays

Chapter 9
Lesson
1

Exploring Multiplying Tens

Problem Solving Connection
Use Objects/
Act It Out

Materials
place-value blocks

Explore

What can be done with the millions of plastic bottles that are recycled each year? Some people have found a way to make fuzzy cloth out of them. Did you ever think plastic bottles could keep you warm?

These bottle flakes will be melted and then spun into yarn.

Math Tip
You can skip count by tens to find the total.

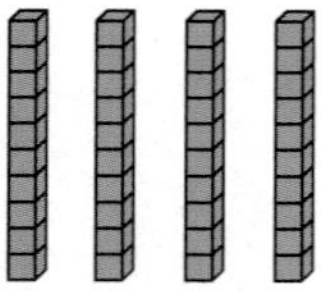

10, 20, 30, 40

Work Together

Use place-value blocks to find each product.

1. One pound of cloth can be made from 10 recycled plastic bottles. How many plastic bottles are needed to make 4 pounds of cloth?

2. If it takes 20 plastic bottles to make a sweatshirt, how many plastic bottles are needed for 3 sweatshirts?
3. Write your own problem about recycled plastic bottles. Then solve.

Talk About It

How did you find the total number of bottles needed for 4 pounds of cloth?

Connect

You can think about basic facts to help you multiply tens.

3 groups of 4
3×4 ones = 12 ones
$3 \times 4 = 12$

3 groups of 40
3×4 tens = 12 tens
$3 \times 40 = 120$

Practice

Copy and complete. You may use place-value blocks to help.

1. 7×1 ten = ■ tens
   $7 \times 10 =$ ■
2. 3×3 tens = ■ tens
   $3 \times 30 =$ ■
3. 5×4 tens = ■ tens
   $5 \times 40 =$ ■
4. 6×5 tens = ■ tens
   $6 \times 50 =$ ■
5. 4×2 tens = ■ tens
   $4 \times 20 =$ ■
6. 2×6 tens = ■ tens
   $2 \times 60 =$ ■
7. **Reasoning** How can you use 8×5 to help you find 8×50?
8. How many sheets are in 3 notepads?
9. How many hats are in 4 bags?
10. How many stickers are in 5 packs?

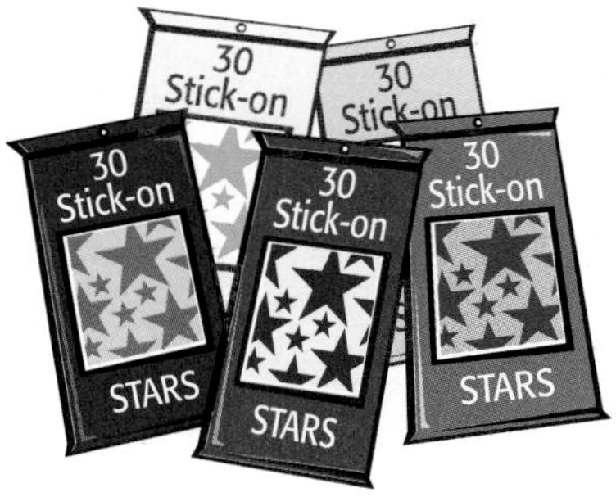

11. **Critical Thinking** Mr. Kwan's class makes puppets for a finger play. There are 6 groups of 4 students in the class. Students will make a puppet for each finger.
    a. How many students are in Mr. Kwan's class?
    b. How many puppets will each group make?
12. **Journal** Draw a picture that shows $7 \times 20 = 140$. Explain your drawing.

Chapter 9
Lesson
2

Exploring Multiplication Patterns

Problem Solving Connection
Look for a Pattern

Materials
calculator

Explore

Place-value patterns can help you multiply by tens and hundreds.

Math Tip
Think about basic facts to help you multiply greater numbers.

Work Together

1. Use a calculator to find each product. Look for patterns.

a.	b.	c.
$3 \times 5 =$ ▢	$4 \times 4 =$ ▢	$8 \times 3 =$ ▢
$3 \times 50 =$ ▢	$4 \times 40 =$ ▢	$8 \times 30 =$ ▢
$3 \times 500 =$ ▢	$4 \times 400 =$ ▢	$8 \times 300 =$ ▢

2. Use patterns to find each product. Check with a calculator.

a.	b.	c.
$2 \times 9 =$ ▢	$5 \times 6 =$ ▢	$3 \times 7 =$ ▢
$2 \times 90 =$ ▢	$5 \times 60 =$ ▢	$3 \times 70 =$ ▢
$2 \times 900 =$ ▢	$5 \times 600 =$ ▢	$3 \times 700 =$ ▢

d.	e.	f.
$6 \times 4 =$ ▢	$3 \times 3 =$ ▢	$4 \times 5 =$ ▢
$6 \times 40 =$ ▢	$3 \times 30 =$ ▢	$4 \times 50 =$ ▢
$6 \times 400 =$ ▢	$3 \times 300 =$ ▢	$4 \times 500 =$ ▢

Talk About It

3. Describe the patterns you found.

4. What basic fact can you use to find 5×70? Explain.

Connect

Basic facts and place-value patterns can help you multiply.

If you know $2 \times 4 = 8$, then you can use mental math to find 2×40 and 2×400.

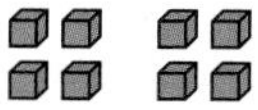

2×4 ones $= 8$ ones
$2 \times 4 = 8$

2×4 tens $= 8$ tens
$2 \times 40 = 80$

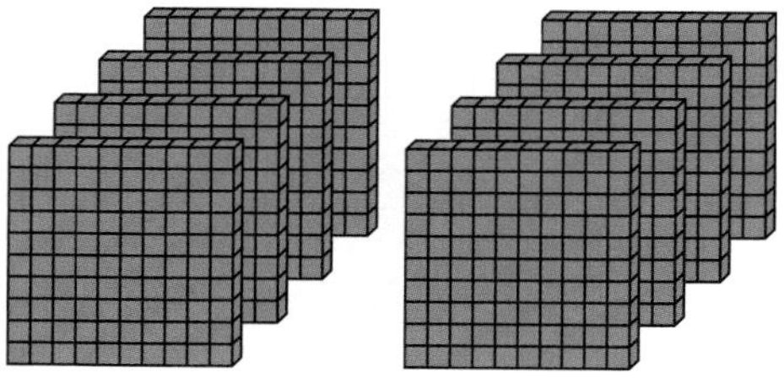

2×4 hundreds $= 8$ hundreds
$2 \times 400 = 800$

Practice

Copy and complete.

1. $4 \times 3 =$ ■
$4 \times$ ■ $= 120$
■ $\times 300 = 1{,}200$

2. $5 \times 2 =$ ■
■ $\times 20 = 100$
$5 \times$ ■ $= 1{,}000$

3. $5 \times$ ■ $= 25$
$5 \times 50 =$ ■
■ $\times 500 = 2{,}500$

Mental Math Find each product using mental math.

4. 2×60 **5.** 3×500 **6.** 7×200 **7.** 5×80

8. 9×300 **9.** 6×70 **10.** 4×700 **11.** 8×400

12. Reasoning Can you use the basic fact 3×8 to find 3×80? Explain.

13. Geometry Readiness Continue the pattern.

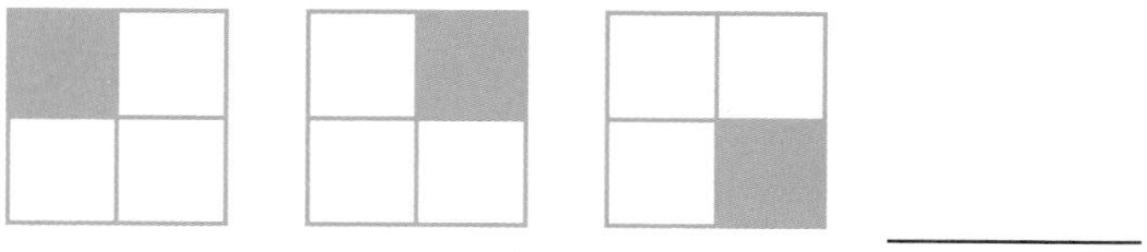

14. Using Data How many groups of 30 people will fit on a commuter train car? Use the Data File on page 356 to solve.

Elevated train in Chicago, Illinois

15. Geography The distance by airplane from Paris, France, to Rome, Italy, is about 700 miles. How many miles would you travel if you flew from Paris to Rome and back?

16. Journal How can you use $4 \times 6 = 24$ to help you find 4×600?

Chapter 9
Lesson
3

Estimating Products

You Will Learn
how to estimate products

Learn

The Golden Gate Bridge is a suspension bridge in San Francisco, California. It hangs from 2 huge cables. Each of these cables is made up of 61 strands of wire.

More than 21,000 cars cross the Golden Gate Bridge on a typical morning.

Example 1

You can estimate to find about how many strands of wire hold up the Golden Gate Bridge.

2×61

Round 61 to the nearest ten.

↓

$2 \times 60 = 120$

About 120 strands of wire hold up the Golden Gate Bridge.

Example 2

Suppose 104 cars cross the bridge in one minute. About how many cars will cross the bridge in 5 minutes?

5×104

Round 104 to the nearest hundred.

↓

$5 \times 100 = 500$

About 500 cars will cross in 5 minutes.

Remember
When you round numbers, you find a number that is close.

Talk About It

Explain how you would estimate the product of 8 and 206.

Check

Estimate each product.

1. 2×71 **2.** 3×68 **3.** 7×613 **4.** 9×54

5. Reasoning Estimate to decide if 5×59 is greater than or less than 6×59. Explain.

Practice

Skills and Reasoning

Estimate each product.

6. 3×62 **7.** 7×945 **8.** 8×462 **9.** 7×57 **10.** 4×75

11. 3×513 **12.** 6×253 **13.** 4×37 **14.** 9×68 **15.** 3×42

16. 8×387 **17.** 2×893 **18.** 2×13 **19.** 5×523 **20.** 6×82

21. Estimate the product of 7 and 42.

22. Estimate the product of 6 and 449.

23. Estimate to decide if 7×769 is greater than or less than 9×496. Explain.

24. The product of 4 and another number is about 320. Give two numbers that make this sentence true. Explain.

Problem Solving and Applications

25. **Using Data** Suppose 300 band members were going on a plane trip. Would everyone fit on 2 jet airplanes? Explain. Use the Data File on page 356 to solve.

26. **Careers** A city planner must decide how much parking space is needed in front of the library. A school bus is 47 feet long. About how many feet of space are needed for 3 buses?

27. **Algebra Readiness** Copy and complete the table. Then write the rule.

In	1	2	3	5	7	8
Out	10	20	30			

28. **Social Studies** The tunnel connecting England and France is 31 miles. About how far do you travel if you ride from England to France and back?

Mixed Review and Test Prep

Add or multiply.

29. 2×5 **30.** 6×3 **31.** $4 + 1$ **32.** 7×2 **33.** $3 + 3$

34. $5 + 4$ **35.** $6 + 3$ **36.** 8×4 **37.** $21 + 79$ **38.** 9×7

39. A chef needs 3 eggs for each cake that she makes. How many cakes can she make with 15 eggs?

Ⓐ 15 Ⓑ 5 Ⓒ 12 Ⓓ 2

Chapter 9
Lesson
4

Exploring Multiplication with Arrays

Problem Solving Connection
- Use Objects/ Act It Out
- Draw a Picture

Materials
place-value blocks

Math Tip
Think of numbers as groups of tens and ones.

14 = 1 ten, 4 ones

31 = 3 tens, 1 one

Explore

You can use place-value blocks to help you multiply.

Work Together

1. Find 5×14. Use place-value blocks to show an array.
   - **a.** Show 1 ten and 4 ones in a row. This shows 1×14.

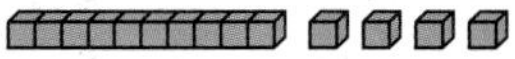

   - **b.** Put 4 more rows of 14 on your array. This shows 5×14.

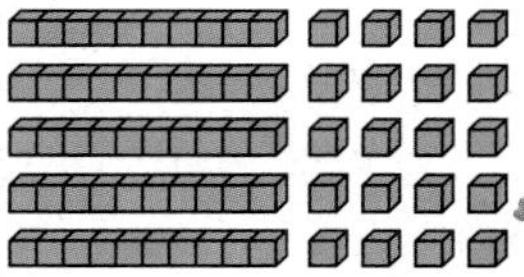

   - **c.** How many tens are in your array? How many ones?
   - **d.** Add the tens and ones. What is the product?
2. Use place-value blocks to find each product.

   a. 3×31 **b.** 4×24 **c.** 2×23

Talk About It

3. Describe the array you used to find 3×31.
4. Tell how you would use place-value blocks to find 7×16.
5. What multiplication sentence could you write to show 4 rows of 1 ten and 3 ones blocks? Explain.

Connect

Break apart numbers into tens and ones to help you multiply. You can use grid paper to help.

Find 3×16.

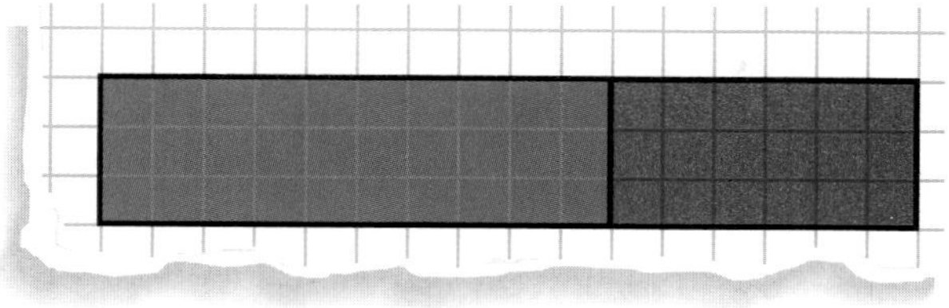

3 rows of 10
$3 \times 10 = 30$

3 rows of 6
$3 \times 6 = 18$

$30 + 18 = 48$

So, $3 \times 16 = 48$

Practice

Find each product. You may use place-value blocks or grid paper to help.

1. 2×15

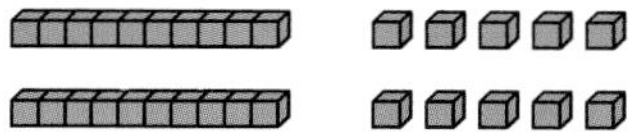

2 rows of 10
$2 \times 10 = 20$

2 rows of 5
$2 \times 5 = 10$

2. 3×23

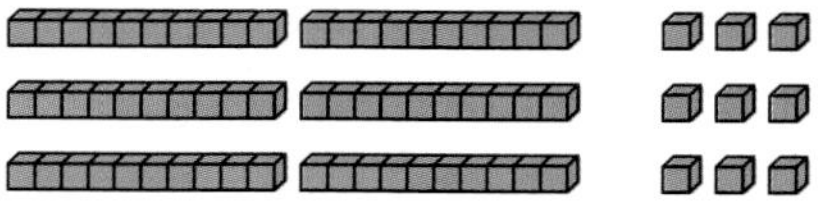

3 rows of 20
$3 \times 20 = 60$

3 rows of 3
$3 \times 3 = 9$

3. 4×13

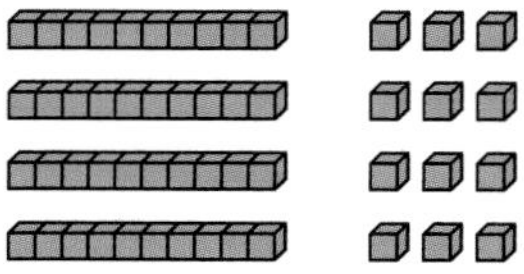

4×10 4×3

4. 3×25

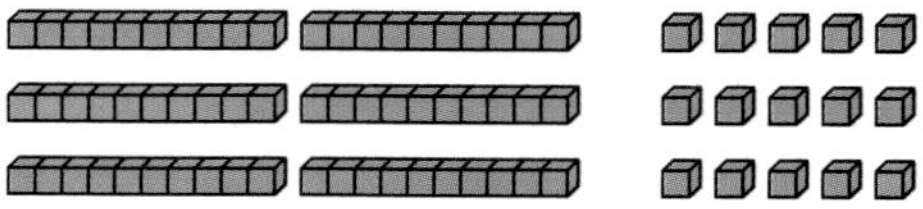

3×20 3×5

5. 5×12 **6.** 4×21 **7.** 3×22 **8.** 4×14 **9.** 6×13

10. 2×32 **11.** 5×17 **12.** 2×18 **13.** 1×15 **14.** 3×27

15. **Algebra Readiness** Find the missing number in $22 \times \blacksquare = 88$. You may use grid paper or place-value blocks to solve.

16. **Journal** Explain how to find the product of 3 and 26 by breaking apart the numbers.

SECTION A

Review and Practice

(Lesson 1) Copy and complete. You may use place-value blocks to help.

1. 8×1 ten $= \square$ tens
   $8 \times 10 = \square$
2. 4×3 tens $= \square$ tens
   $4 \times 30 = \square$
3. 9×2 tens $= \square$ tens
   $9 \times 20 = \square$
4. **Reasoning** How can you use 2×7 to help you find 2×70?

(Lesson 2) Copy and complete.

5. $7 \times 3 = \square$
   $7 \times \square = 210$
   $\square \times 300 = 2{,}100$
6. $8 \times 6 = \square$
   $\square \times 60 = 480$
   $8 \times \square = 4{,}800$
7. $5 \times \square = 20$
   $5 \times 40 = \square$
   $\square \times 400 = 2{,}000$

Mental Math Find each product using mental math.

8. 3×60
9. 2×500
10. 7×80
11. 5×700
12. 8×200
13. 4×90
14. 6×600
15. 5×30

(Lesson 3) **Estimation** Estimate each product.

16. 3×37
17. 5×22
18. 2×516
19. 8×693
20. 4×844
21. 9×76
22. 7×489
23. 6×93
24. Leroy reads books in a series of mysteries. Each book has 117 pages. About how many pages will Leroy read if he finishes 9 of these books?

(Lesson 4) Find each product. You may use place-value blocks or grid paper to help.

25. 3×24
26. 5×22
27. 2×17
28. 4×16
29. 6×15
30. 3×28
31. 5×12
32. 2×27
33. 1×18
34. **Journal** Draw an array on grid paper or use place-value blocks to show how to multiply 6×14.

Skills Checklist

In this section, you have:

- ☑ **Explored Multiplying Tens**
- ☑ **Explored Multiplication Patterns**
- ☑ **Estimated Products**
- ☑ **Explored Multiplication with Arrays**

CHAPTER 9

SECTION

B Multiplying by 1-Digit Factors

If you need 3 milk cartons to build a skyscraper, how many cartons do you need for 15 skyscrapers?

Jason and Carlos won a prize at the Future City Competition.

Skills Checklist

In this section, you will:

- ❒ Multiply Using Partial Products
- ❒ Multiply 2-Digit Numbers
- ❒ Multiply 3-Digit Numbers
- ❒ Multiply Money
- ❒ Multiply Using Mental Math
- ❒ Solve Problems by Making a Table

Multiplying by 1-Digit Factors

Review multiplying with patterns. Find each product.

1. 5×30	**2.** 6×200	**3.** 3×70
4. 8×400	**5.** 2×80	**6.** 9×500
7. 5×200	**8.** 4×60	**9.** 7×80

Chapter 9
Lesson
5

Multiplying: Partial Products

You Will Learn
how to multiply numbers using partial products

Learn

At the Public Gardens in Boston, Massachusetts, you can take a ride around the pond on a Swan Boat. Be sure to bring a bag of peanuts, because hungry ducks will follow you the whole way!

These visitors are trying to catch sight of the ducks.

Example 1

If it takes 13 minutes to go around the pond in a Swan Boat, how many minutes does it take to go around the pond twice?

Find 2×13.

$$\begin{array}{rl} 13 & \\ \times\ 2 & \\ \hline 6 & 2 \times 3 \text{ ones} \\ 20 & 2 \times 1 \text{ ten} \\ \hline 26 & \end{array}$$

So, it takes 26 minutes.

Example 2

If each Swan Boat holds 42 students, how many students could fit on 5 boats?

Find 5×42.

$$\begin{array}{rl} 42 & \\ \times\ 5 & \\ \hline 10 & 5 \times 2 \\ 200 & 5 \times 40 \\ \hline 210 & \end{array}$$

So, 210 students can fit on 5 boats.

Remember
You can use place-value blocks to help multiply.

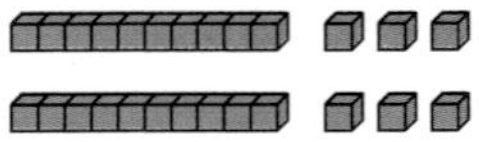

2×10 2×3

Talk About It

How is multiplying greater numbers like solving two simpler problems?

Check

Find each product.

1. $\begin{array}{r} 17 \\ \times\ 3 \\ \hline 21 \\ \square\square \\ \hline \square\square \end{array}$
2. $\begin{array}{r} 42 \\ \times\ 2 \\ \hline \square \\ 80 \\ \hline \square\square \end{array}$
3. $\begin{array}{r} 32 \\ \times\ 5 \\ \hline \square\square \\ \square\square\square \\ \hline \square\square\square \end{array}$
4. $\begin{array}{r} 29 \\ \times\ 7 \\ \hline \square\square \\ \square\square\square \\ \hline \square\square\square \end{array}$
5. $\begin{array}{r} 83 \\ \times\ 6 \\ \hline \square\square \\ \square\square\square \\ \hline \square\square\square \end{array}$

6. **Reasoning** Raymond says, "To find 4 × 13 I can add 12 and 40." Do you agree or disagree? Explain.

Practice

Skills and Reasoning

Find each product.

7. $\begin{array}{r} 39 \\ \times\ 5 \\ \hline \end{array}$
8. $\begin{array}{r} 56 \\ \times\ 3 \\ \hline \end{array}$
9. $\begin{array}{r} 23 \\ \times\ 2 \\ \hline \end{array}$
10. $\begin{array}{r} 77 \\ \times\ 8 \\ \hline \end{array}$
11. $\begin{array}{r} 63 \\ \times\ 5 \\ \hline \end{array}$

12. 14 × 4
13. 18 × 5
14. 3 × 22
15. 6 × 13
16. 8 × 71
17. 4 × 15
18. 2 × 59
19. 3 × 72
20. 54 × 4
21. 37 × 4

22. Explain why 7 × 14 is the same as 28 + 70.

23. How can you tell that 5 × 76 will be at least 3 digits?

Problem Solving and Applications

24. **What If** 250 adults want to ride the Swan Boats. If each boat holds 30 adults, will 8 boats be enough? Explain.

25. **Critical Thinking** There are 6 benches on a Swan Boat. If there are 2 people on each bench and 1 person in the back pedaling, how many people are on the boat?

Mixed Review and Test Prep

Add or subtract.

26. 19 + 12
27. 42 − 7
28. 239 + 48
29. 105 − 72
30. 67 + 89

31. Helen has 12 beads. If she puts 4 beads on each bracelet, how many bracelets will she make?

Ⓐ 12 Ⓑ 4 Ⓒ 16 Ⓓ 3

Chapter 9
Lesson
6

Multiplying 2-Digit Numbers

You Will Learn
how to multiply with regrouping

Learn

The Future City Competition lets students design a dream city of tomorrow. Jason and Carlos of Baton Rouge, Louisiana, took a prize for their city.

Jason and Carlos at the Future City Competition

Suppose you use 18 toothpicks for each foot of subway track. How many toothpicks do you need to make 4 feet of track?

Find 4×18.

Math Tip
Both methods work for multiplying!

We got the same answer, but our work looks different. What did you do?

First I multiplied 4×8 and got 32. I regrouped 32 into 3 tens, 2 ones.

Then I multiplied 4×1 ten and added the 3 extra tens. That made 7 tens.

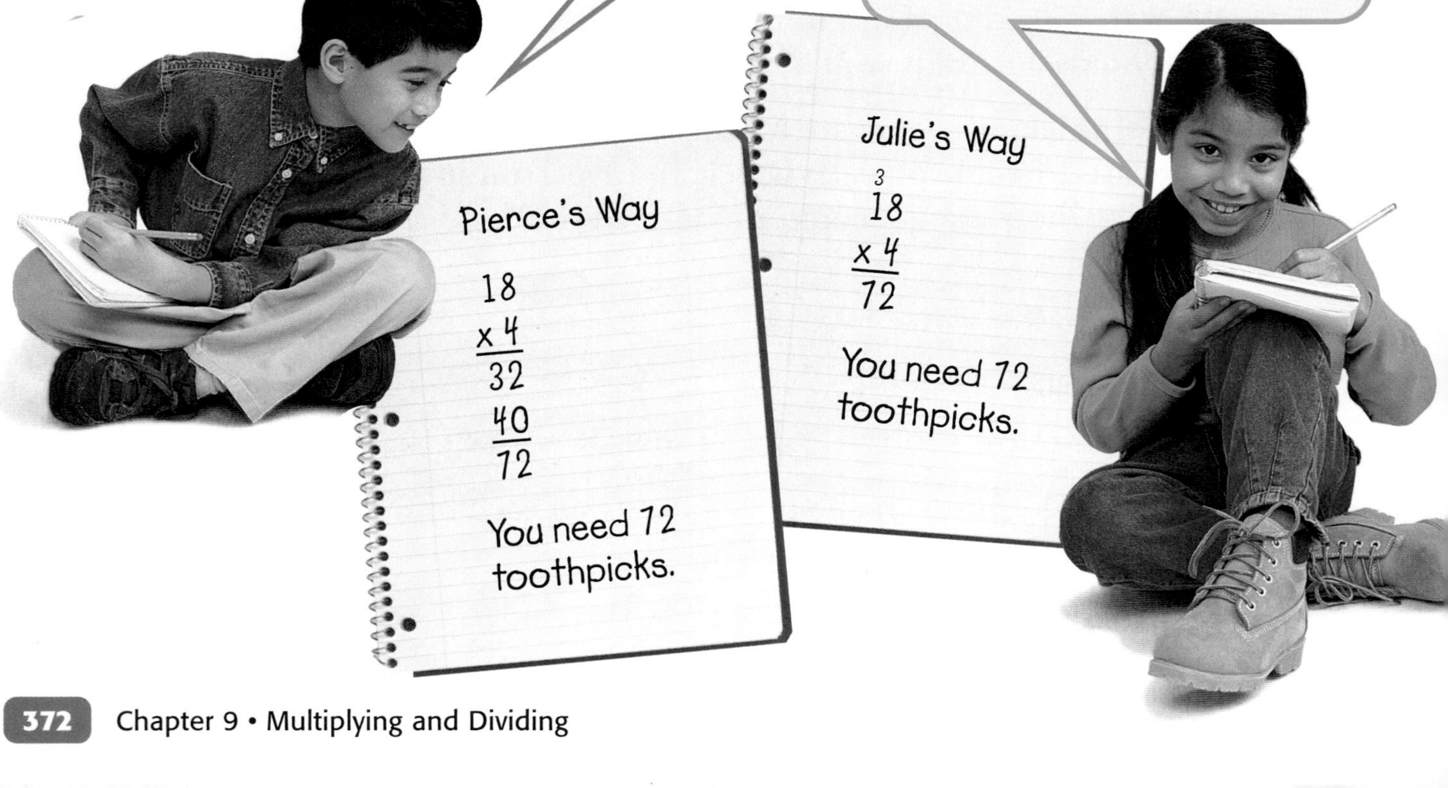

Example

Use Julie's method to find 2×67.

Step 1

Multiply the ones.
Regroup if needed.

$$\begin{array}{r} {}^{1} \\ 67 \\ \times\ 2 \\ \hline 4 \end{array}$$

2×7 ones $= 14$ ones
Regroup 14 ones as 1 ten, 4 ones.

Step 2

Multiply the tens.
Add the extra tens.

$$\begin{array}{r} {}^{1} \\ 67 \\ \times\ 2 \\ \hline 134 \end{array}$$

2×6 tens $= 12$ tens
12 tens $+ 1$ ten $= 13$ tens

$2 \times 67 = 134$

Estimate to check.

2×67 is close to 2×70. $2 \times 70 = 140$

Since 134 is close to 140, the answer is reasonable.

Talk About It

1. Where was the 1 ten recorded after 14 ones was regrouped as 1 ten, 4 ones?
2. How are Julie's and Pierce's ways alike? How are they different?

Check

Copy and complete.

1. $\begin{array}{r} \square \\ 13 \\ \times\ 6 \\ \hline \square 8 \end{array}$
2. $\begin{array}{r} \square \\ 23 \\ \times\ 4 \\ \hline \square\square \end{array}$
3. $\begin{array}{r} \square \\ 56 \\ \times\ 7 \\ \hline \square\square\square \end{array}$
4. $\begin{array}{r} \square \\ 35 \\ \times\ 7 \\ \hline \square\square\square \end{array}$
5. $\begin{array}{r} \square \\ 86 \\ \times\ 8 \\ \hline \square\square\square \end{array}$

Find each product. Estimate to check.

6. $\begin{array}{r} 24 \\ \times\ 2 \\ \hline \end{array}$
7. $\begin{array}{r} 38 \\ \times\ 8 \\ \hline \end{array}$
8. $\begin{array}{r} 71 \\ \times\ 3 \\ \hline \end{array}$
9. $\begin{array}{r} 84 \\ \times\ 2 \\ \hline \end{array}$
10. $\begin{array}{r} 67 \\ \times\ 5 \\ \hline \end{array}$

11. 3×32
12. 19×5
13. 68×7
14. 5×13
15. 57×2
16. 91×4
17. 62×9
18. 14×5
19. 3×25
20. 7×42
21. Multiply 46 by 2.
22. Find the product of 76 and 4.
23. **Reasoning** How can you tell what the ones digit of the product of 54×6 will be without solving the whole problem?

Practice

Skills and Reasoning

Find each product. Estimate to check.

24. $\begin{array}{r} 47 \\ \times\ 2 \\ \hline \end{array}$ **25.** $\begin{array}{r} 23 \\ \times\ 6 \\ \hline \end{array}$ **26.** $\begin{array}{r} 58 \\ \times\ 3 \\ \hline \end{array}$ **27.** $\begin{array}{r} 31 \\ \times\ 9 \\ \hline \end{array}$ **28.** $\begin{array}{r} 85 \\ \times\ 4 \\ \hline \end{array}$

29. $\begin{array}{r} 11 \\ \times\ 6 \\ \hline \end{array}$ **30.** $\begin{array}{r} 41 \\ \times\ 7 \\ \hline \end{array}$ **31.** $\begin{array}{r} 28 \\ \times\ 4 \\ \hline \end{array}$ **32.** $\begin{array}{r} 95 \\ \times\ 9 \\ \hline \end{array}$ **33.** $\begin{array}{r} 78 \\ \times\ 2 \\ \hline \end{array}$

34. 61×8 **35.** 45×2 **36.** 5×18 **37.** 4×39 **38.** 26×7

39. 73×5 **40.** 2×51 **41.** 96×8 **42.** 3×22 **43.** 82×4

44. Find the product of 82 and 5. **45.** Multiply 63 by 3.

46. Jan says, "When I regroup to find 65×4, I record a small 0 above the 6 in the tens place." Do you agree or disagree? Explain.

47. How can you tell without solving the whole problem whether 53×7 is less than or greater than 350?

Problem Solving and Applications

Using Data Use the pictograph to answer **48–50.**

48. How many milk cartons did Classroom 3A use for model cities?

49. How many more milk cartons than toothpicks did Classroom 3A use?

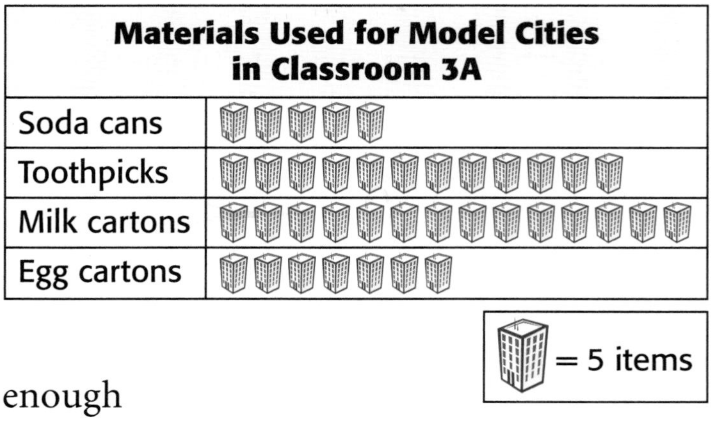

50. **Critical Thinking** If it takes 18 toothpicks to build a foot of subway track, are there enough toothpicks for 3 feet of track? Explain.

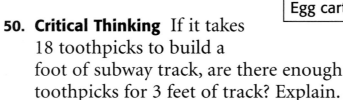

51. **Algebra Readiness** Copy and complete the table. Then write the rule.

In	2	4	6	8	12	16
Out	6	12	18			

Problem Solving and HEALTH

Your body is busier than you are! Even while you're sitting on the couch, your body is working.

Use the table for **52–56.**

52. How many breaths do the lungs take in 5 minutes?

53. How many times do you blink during a TV commercial break that is 2 minutes long?

54. **Critical Thinking** An adult takes about 18 breaths in a minute. How many more breaths do you take in 3 minutes than an adult?

55. A baby's heart beats about 120 times in a minute. How many more times does a baby's heart beat than yours in a minute?

Things Your Body Does in 1 Minute While Resting

Part of the Body	What It Does
Heart	Beats about 90 times
Lungs	Take in about 26 breaths
Eyes	Blink about 15 times

56. **Write Your Own Problem** Use the data from the table to write your own multiplication problem.

57. **Journal** Explain how you could use regrouping to solve 37×4.

Mixed Review and Test Prep

Find each product or quotient.

58. $10 \div 5$	**59.** $45 \div 9$	**60.** $9 \div 3$	**61.** $56 \div 7$	**62.** $72 \div 9$
63. $12 \div 2$	**64.** $15 \div 3$	**65.** $24 \div 6$	**66.** $18 \div 2$	**67.** $35 \div 7$
68. 3×6	**69.** 9×4	**70.** 7×6	**71.** 5×8	**72.** 4×4
73. 9×3	**74.** 2×8	**75.** 6×2	**76.** 8×6	**77.** 3×4

78. **Time** It takes Elena and her mother 22 minutes to drive to the store. If they leave at 9:00 A.M., what time will they arrive?

Ⓐ 10:22 A.M. Ⓑ 9:22 P.M. Ⓒ 9:22 A.M. Ⓓ not here

STOP and Practice

Find each product.

1. $\begin{array}{r} 42 \\ \times\ 2 \\ \hline \end{array}$	**2.** $\begin{array}{r} 31 \\ \times\ 3 \\ \hline \end{array}$	**3.** $\begin{array}{r} 12 \\ \times\ 3 \\ \hline \end{array}$	**4.** $\begin{array}{r} 23 \\ \times\ 4 \\ \hline \end{array}$	**5.** $\begin{array}{r} 51 \\ \times\ 6 \\ \hline \end{array}$
6. $\begin{array}{r} 14 \\ \times\ 6 \\ \hline \end{array}$	**7.** $\begin{array}{r} 27 \\ \times\ 4 \\ \hline \end{array}$	**8.** $\begin{array}{r} 83 \\ \times\ 6 \\ \hline \end{array}$	**9.** $\begin{array}{r} 71 \\ \times\ 5 \\ \hline \end{array}$	**10.** $\begin{array}{r} 53 \\ \times\ 6 \\ \hline \end{array}$
11. $\begin{array}{r} 54 \\ \times\ 7 \\ \hline \end{array}$	**12.** $\begin{array}{r} 72 \\ \times\ 9 \\ \hline \end{array}$	**13.** $\begin{array}{r} 15 \\ \times\ 3 \\ \hline \end{array}$	**14.** $\begin{array}{r} 67 \\ \times\ 5 \\ \hline \end{array}$	**15.** $\begin{array}{r} 94 \\ \times\ 7 \\ \hline \end{array}$
16. $\begin{array}{r} 86 \\ \times\ 6 \\ \hline \end{array}$	**17.** $\begin{array}{r} 78 \\ \times\ 8 \\ \hline \end{array}$	**18.** $\begin{array}{r} 65 \\ \times\ 9 \\ \hline \end{array}$	**19.** $\begin{array}{r} 39 \\ \times\ 6 \\ \hline \end{array}$	**20.** $\begin{array}{r} 47 \\ \times\ 4 \\ \hline \end{array}$
21. $\begin{array}{r} 59 \\ \times\ 2 \\ \hline \end{array}$	**22.** $\begin{array}{r} 97 \\ \times\ 3 \\ \hline \end{array}$	**23.** $\begin{array}{r} 35 \\ \times\ 6 \\ \hline \end{array}$	**24.** $\begin{array}{r} 74 \\ \times\ 8 \\ \hline \end{array}$	**25.** $\begin{array}{r} 92 \\ \times\ 3 \\ \hline \end{array}$
26. $\begin{array}{r} 75 \\ \times\ 5 \\ \hline \end{array}$	**27.** $\begin{array}{r} 89 \\ \times\ 3 \\ \hline \end{array}$	**28.** $\begin{array}{r} 48 \\ \times\ 6 \\ \hline \end{array}$	**29.** $\begin{array}{r} 68 \\ \times\ 4 \\ \hline \end{array}$	**30.** $\begin{array}{r} 22 \\ \times\ 9 \\ \hline \end{array}$
31. 6×16	**32.** 8×13	**33.** 77×4	**34.** 46×9	**35.** 7×64
36. 4×52	**37.** 37×2	**38.** 5×85	**39.** 96×8	**40.** 7×29
41. 5×33	**42.** 24×9	**43.** 88×6	**44.** 3×76	**45.** 5×44
46. 7×19	**47.** 34×8	**48.** 5×26	**49.** 58×9	**50.** 4×62

Error Search

Find each problem that is not correct. Write it correctly and explain the error.

51. $\begin{array}{r} 36 \\ \times\ 6 \\ \hline 1{,}836 \end{array}$	**52.** $\begin{array}{r} 48 \\ \times\ 3 \\ \hline 124 \end{array}$	**53.** $\begin{array}{r} 63 \\ \times\ 4 \\ \hline 252 \end{array}$	**54.** $\begin{array}{r} 82 \\ \times\ 5 \\ \hline 41 \end{array}$	**55.** $\begin{array}{r} 27 \\ \times\ 7 \\ \hline 149 \end{array}$

Animal Company

Multiply. Match each letter to its answer in the blank below to solve the riddle. Some letters are not used.

56. 7×55 [W]	**57.** 3×91 [U]	**58.** 79×6 [M]	**59.** 7×11 [I]
60. 22×8 [L]	**61.** 9×38 [Z]	**62.** 87×6 [C]	**63.** 8×43 [H]
64. 49×2 [O]	**65.** 7×63 [T]	**66.** 18×7 [S]	**67.** 49×5 [A]
68. 5×89 [S]	**69.** 8×62 [B]	**70.** 3×32 [J]	**71.** 17×6 [S]

___   ___ ___ ___
245   474 98 496

Number Sense Estimation and Reasoning

Write whether each statement is true or false. Explain your answer.

72. The product of 3 and 27 is greater than 60.

73. The product of 42 and 8 is less than 320.

74. The product of 7 and 19 is closer to 70 than to 140.

75. The product of 9 and 31 is less than 360.

76. The product of 2 and 40 is less than the product of 4 and 20.

Chapter 9 Lesson 7

Multiplying 3-Digit Numbers

You Will Learn
how to multiply 3-digit numbers

Learn

The young actors and actresses at the Story Book Theater in Deland, Florida, are getting ready for the bright lights of the big city!

The Story Book Theater can seat 237 people.

These students did a play based on *The Chronicles of Narnia* by C. S. Lewis.

Math Tip
You can also multiply this way:

```
 237
×  3
  21
  90
 600
 711
```

Example

If the Story Book Theater sells every seat for 3 performances, how many tickets are sold? Find 3 × 237.

Step 1
Multiply the ones. Regroup as needed.

$$\begin{array}{r} {}^{2} \\ 237 \\ \times\ \ 3 \\ \hline 1 \end{array}$$

Step 2
Multiply the tens. Add any extra tens. Regroup as needed.

$$\begin{array}{r} {}^{1\,2} \\ 237 \\ \times\ \ 3 \\ \hline 11 \end{array}$$

Step 3
Multiply the hundreds. Add any extra hundreds.

$$\begin{array}{r} {}^{1\,2} \\ 237 \\ \times\ \ 3 \\ \hline 711 \end{array}$$

So, 711 tickets are sold.

Other Examples

A. $\begin{array}{r} {}^{1} \\ 103 \\ \times\ \ 4 \\ \hline 412 \end{array}$ **B.** $\begin{array}{r} {}^{1} \\ 290 \\ \times\ \ 2 \\ \hline 580 \end{array}$ **C.** $\begin{array}{r} {}^{4\,5} \\ 568 \\ \times\ \ 7 \\ \hline 3{,}976 \end{array}$

Talk About It

In step 2 of the first example, what does the small 1 above the 2 in the hundreds place mean?

Check

Find each product.

1. $\begin{array}{r} 212 \\ \times\ 4 \\ \hline \end{array}$ 2. $\begin{array}{r} 309 \\ \times\ 2 \\ \hline \end{array}$ 3. $\begin{array}{r} 300 \\ \times\ 3 \\ \hline \end{array}$ 4. $\begin{array}{r} 151 \\ \times\ 5 \\ \hline \end{array}$ 5. $\begin{array}{r} 430 \\ \times\ 7 \\ \hline \end{array}$

6. 2×237 7. 4×313 8. 342×3 9. 8×123 10. 614×9

11. **Reasoning** How could you use mental math to find 3×200? Explain.

Practice

Skills and Reasoning

Find each product.

12. $\begin{array}{r} 354 \\ \times\ 2 \\ \hline \end{array}$ 13. $\begin{array}{r} 208 \\ \times\ 2 \\ \hline \end{array}$ 14. $\begin{array}{r} 132 \\ \times\ 3 \\ \hline \end{array}$ 15. $\begin{array}{r} 371 \\ \times\ 4 \\ \hline \end{array}$ 16. $\begin{array}{r} 400 \\ \times\ 6 \\ \hline \end{array}$

17. 2×428 18. 3×379 19. 5×342 20. 611×3 21. 405×5

22. 3×751 23. 4×122 24. 367×2 25. 8×534 26. 2×601

27. Multiply 6 and 238.

28. Find the product of 7 and 711.

29. How could you use mental math to find 2×411?

Problem Solving and Applications

Using Data Use the Data File on page 357 to answer **30** and **31.**

30. How many more jazz performers than reggae performers play for Music Under New York?

31. Are there more than 3 times as many jazz performers as a capella performers? Explain.

32. **Critical Thinking** In the first 3 weeks of play rehearsals, students practiced 3 days each week for 2 hours a day. How many hours did they practice in the first 3 weeks?

Mixed Review and Test Prep

Add or subtract.

33. $\$2.60 - \$0.45$ 34. $\$1.80 + \$5.00$ 35. $43 + 78$ 36. $865 - 78$

37. **Algebra Readiness** Find the missing factor. $\blacksquare \times 20 = 60$

Ⓐ 30 Ⓑ 60 Ⓒ 6 Ⓓ 3

Chapter 9
Lesson
8

Multiplying Money

You Will Learn
how to multiply money

Learn

Students who live in big cities sometimes take the city bus to school. It costs \$3.75 each week for Ted to take the bus to school.

Example

How much does it cost to take the bus for 2 weeks?

Math Tip
Here's why it works:

$$\begin{array}{r} \$3.75 \\ +\ \$3.75 \\ \hline \$7.50 \end{array}$$

Step 1
Multiply the same way you would with whole numbers.

$$\begin{array}{r} \overset{1}{\$3}.\overset{1}{7}5 \\ \times\ \ 2 \\ \hline 7\ 50 \end{array}$$

Step 2
Write the answer in dollars and cents.

$$\begin{array}{r} \$3.75 \\ \times\ \ 2 \\ \hline \$7.50 \end{array}$$

Estimate to check. $2 \times \$3.75$ is close to $2 \times \$4.00$.
$2 \times \$4.00 = \$8.00$
Since \$7.50 is close to \$8.00, the answer is reasonable.
So, it costs \$7.50.

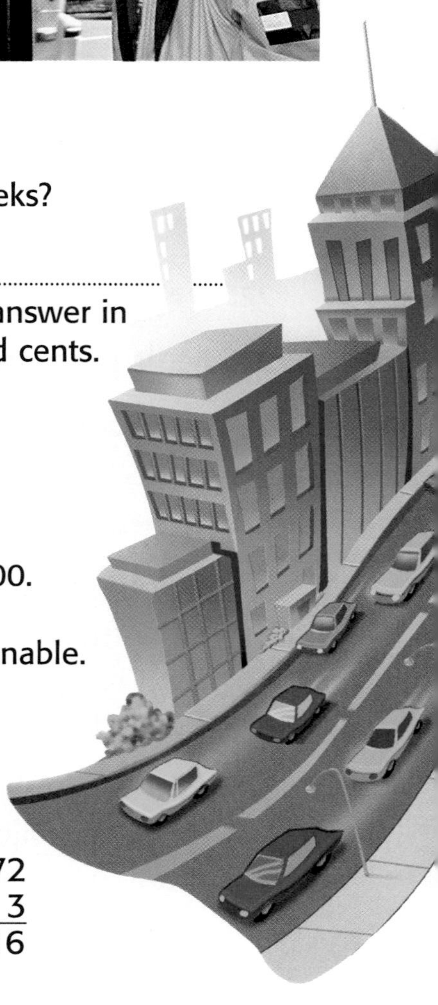

Other Examples

A. $\begin{array}{r} \$\overset{2}{0}.\overset{2}{8}7 \\ \times\ \ 3 \\ \hline \$2.61 \end{array}$ **B.** $\begin{array}{r} \$\overset{1}{2}.30 \\ \times\ \ 4 \\ \hline \$9.20 \end{array}$ **C.** $\begin{array}{r} \$4.\overset{2}{7}2 \\ \times\ \ 3 \\ \hline \$14.16 \end{array}$

Talk About It

Suppose you wrote \$750 instead of \$7.50 in the first example. Would your answer be reasonable? Explain.

Check

Find each product. Estimate to check.

1. $3 \times \$0.21$ **2.** $2 \times \$1.42$ **3.** $4 \times \$1.81$ **4.** $3 \times \$2.06$ **5.** $4 \times \$0.47$

6. **Reasoning** How is the product of \$6.30 and 3 like the product of 3 and 630? How is it different?

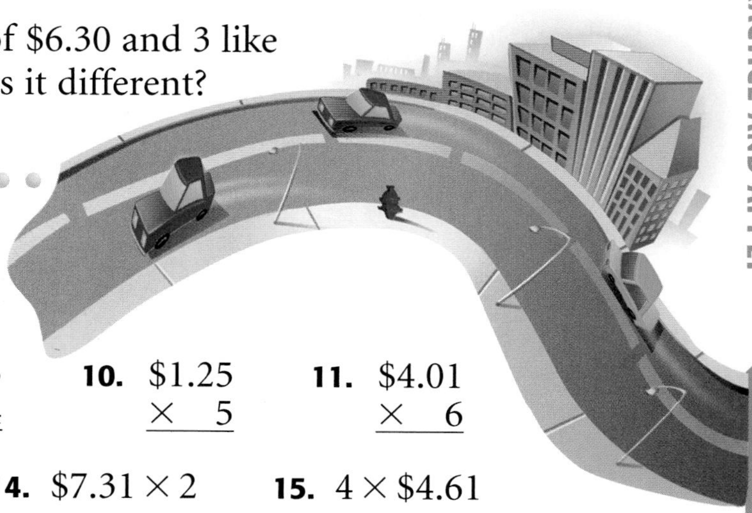

Practice

Skills and Reasoning

Find each product. Estimate to check.

7. $\$0.65 \times 2$ **8.** $\$2.30 \times 3$ **9.** $\$0.73 \times 4$ **10.** $\$1.25 \times 5$ **11.** $\$4.01 \times 6$

12. $4 \times \$3.11$ **13.** $5 \times \$0.64$ **14.** $\$7.31 \times 2$ **15.** $4 \times \$4.61$

16. $\$3.82 \times 2$ **17.** $5 \times \$3.16$ **18.** $3 \times \$1.11$ **19.** $\$2.03 \times 5$

20. What is the product of 4 and \$5.81?

21. Multiply 3 and \$6.14.

22. Is \$4.50 the same amount as \$0.45? Explain.

23. Max multiplied \$1.59 and 3. He recorded \$477. Is he correct? Explain.

Problem Solving and Applications

24. **What If** Ted rides in a car 2 days and rides the bus 3 days. The bus costs \$0.75 a day. How much will Ted spend on bus fare that week?

25. **Social Studies** In Toronto, the urban train costs \$2.00 for adults and \$0.50 for children. How much would it cost for 3 adults and 2 children to ride?

26. **Journal** How is multiplying money like multiplying whole numbers? How is it different?

Mixed Review and Test Prep

Add or subtract.

27. $25 + 63$ **28.** $415 + 98$ **29.** $522 - 351$ **30.** $19 + 88$ **31.** $58 - 12$

32. Which group includes all odd numbers?

Ⓐ 0, 3, 12, 9 Ⓑ 8, 15, 52, 90 Ⓒ 7, 13, 31, 5 Ⓓ 1,001, 1,002

Chapter 9
Lesson
9

Mental Math

You Will Learn
how to multiply mentally

Learn

It's Mental Math-letics Day! Manuel and Carrie are solving multiplication problems mentally.

Manuel solves 48×3.

Carrie solves 6×32.

Remember
You can use basic facts to help multiply 50×3.

$5 \times 3 = 15$

$50 \times 3 = 150$

48 is 2 less than 50.
50 × 3 = 150
I need to subtract 2 groups of 3, or 6.
150 − 6 = 144
So, 48 × 3 = 144.
Mental Math-letics Day
First I multiply the ones, then the tens.
6 × 2 = 12, and 6 × 30 = 180
Ones and tens together give me the product.
12 + 180 = 192
So, 6 × 32 = 192.

Talk About It

1. Why did Manuel subtract 2 groups of 3?
2. How could you solve 9×21 mentally?

Check

Find each product using mental math.

1. 51×4 **2.** 3×39 **3.** 22×5 **4.** 41×6 **5.** 52×8

6. Reasoning What addition sentence could help you solve 31×5?

Practice

Skills and Reasoning

Mental Math Find each product using mental math.

7. 41×5 **8.** 29×3 **9.** 19×7 **10.** 61×8 **11.** 59×5

12. 68×3 **13.** 32×5 **14.** 51×6 **15.** 43×2 **16.** 39×4

17. Multiply 72 and 4.

18. What is the product of 29 and 2?

19. Describe two ways to find the product of 28 and 4 mentally.

20. If you know $30 \times 2 = 60$, how could you solve 32×2 mentally?

Problem Solving and Applications

21. Science A typical female koala weighs 12 pounds. A typical male koala weighs twice as much. How much does a typical male koala weigh?

22. Social Studies The elevator in the Sears Tower in Chicago holds 66 people. How many people can this elevator carry in 5 trips?

23. Algebra Readiness Copy and complete the table. Then write the rule.

In	2	3	4	7	8	9
Out	24	36	48			

Mixed Review and Test Prep

Find each quotient.

24. $45 \div 9$ **25.** $24 \div 6$ **26.** $12 \div 3$ **27.** $36 \div 6$ **28.** $40 \div 5$

29. $63 \div 7$ **30.** $21 \div 3$ **31.** $56 \div 8$ **32.** $15 \div 3$ **33.** $18 \div 2$

34. $72 \div 9$ **35.** $14 \div 7$ **36.** $16 \div 4$ **37.** $64 \div 8$ **38.** $42 \div 6$

39. Measurement What is the perimeter of the square?

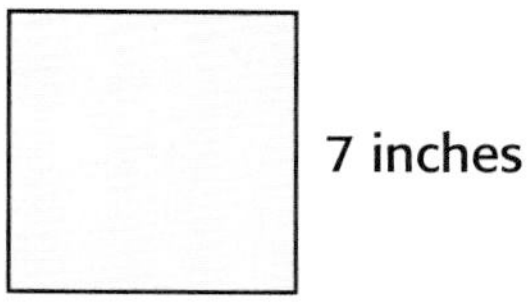

Ⓐ 56 inches Ⓑ 28 inches

Ⓒ 28 square inches Ⓓ 14 inches

Target Products!

Players
2 or more

Materials
set of digit cards 0–9

0	1	2	3	4
5	6	7	8	9

Object
The object of the game is to find products that make the highest score.

How to Play

1. Draw a circle board like the one shown.

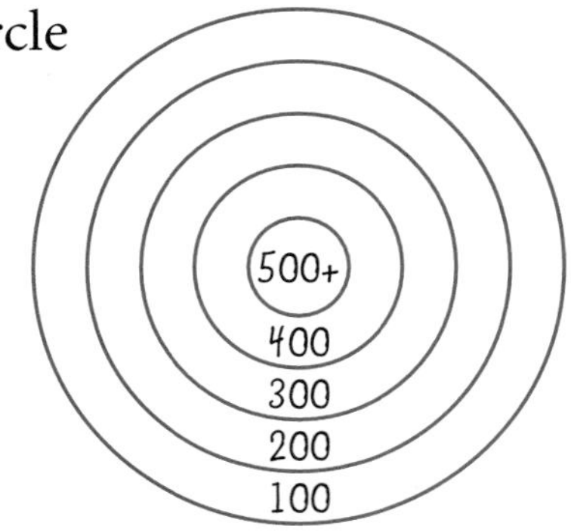

2. Player 1 turns over 3 digit cards and writes a 2-digit by 1-digit multiplication problem. Then Player 1 finds the product.

3 If the product is less than 100, the player scores zero points. If the product is in the 100s, the player scores 100 points. If the product is in the 200s, the player scores 200 points, and so on. If the product is in the 500s or greater, the player gets 500 points.

4 Player 1 writes his or her initial in the appropriate area of the circle grid, then fills in the score card.

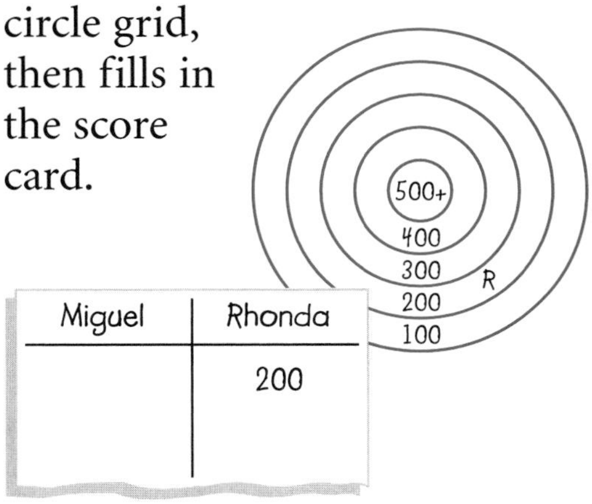

5 Players take turns until each player has found 3 products. Then they add their scores. The player with the greatest score wins!

Talk About It

1. What strategies did you use to get the greatest score?

2. Which card did you least like to turn over? Why?

3. How could you use estimation to place your initials?

More Ways to Play

- Play again. This time try to get the least score.

- Play again. This time, the winner is the player whose score is closest to 1,000.

Reasoning

1. Suppose you choose these digit cards in the first game. How would you arrange your cards for the greatest product?

9 2 7

2. Suppose you choose these cards in the game to get the least total score. How would you arrange them for the least product?

1 8 0

3. Suppose you are playing the Closest to 1,000 game. If your score were 800, how would you arrange these cards?

3 7 1

Problem Solving

Analyze Strategies: Make a Table

You Will Learn
how to make a table to help you solve problems

Learn

Construction crews are working hard to complete the new building. At the end of the first month, the building was 3 floors tall. At the end of the second month, it was 6 floors tall. At the end of the third month, it was 9 floors tall. If the pattern continues, how many months will it take to complete 18 floors?

Work Together

▶ Understand

What do you know?

What do you need to find out?

▶ Plan

Make a table. Fill in what you know.

Month	1	2	3			
Floors	3	6	9			

▶ Solve

Look for a pattern in the table.

3 new floors are built each month.

Use the pattern to complete the table.

Month	1	2	3	4	5	6
Floors	3	6	9	12	15	18

What is your answer?

It will take 6 months to complete 18 floors.

▶ Look Back

How can you check your answer?

Talk About It

How does using a table help you solve this problem?

Check

Problem Solving
Understand
Plan
Solve
Look Back

Make a table to solve.

1. At the end of the first week, workers finished painting the first 2 floors of the building. After the second week, 4 floors of the building were painted. After the third week, 6 floors were painted.

a. Make a table to show what you know. How many new floors do the workers finish each week?

Week	1	2	3						
Floors	2	4	6						

b. What pattern can help you complete the table?

c. How many weeks will it take workers to finish painting the 18 floors?

Problem Solving Practice

Problem Solving Strategies

- Use Objects/Act It Out
- Draw a Picture
- Look for a Pattern
- Guess and Check
- Use Logical Reasoning
- Make an Organized List
- Make a Table
- Solve a Simpler Problem
- Work Backward

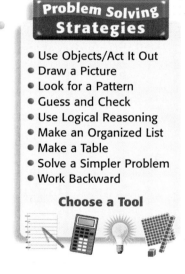

Choose a Tool

Make a table or use any strategy to solve.

2. A gardener can choose tulips, lilies, or daffodils for the center of the flower box. He can choose petunias or impatiens for the outside. How many different ways can he arrange the flower box?

3. Todd likes to use the stairs. If it takes him 2 minutes to walk down 5 floors, how long would it take him to walk down 15 floors?

4. **Money** Paula rents an apartment for $795 each month. How much will she pay to rent the apartment for 6 months?

5. There are 63 apartments in a building. After 1 month, 7 apartments were rented. After 2 months, 14 were rented. After 3 months, 21 were rented. If the pattern continues, how long will it take for all of the apartments to be rented?

Skills Practice Bank, page 526, Set 6

SECTION B

Review and Practice

(Lessons 5–8) Find each product.

1. 62×3
2. 73×4
3. 81×5
4. 13×3
5. 68×4
6. 22×6
7. 82×2
8. 29×8
9. 36×9
10. 92×7
11. 102×5
12. 431×3
13. 390×5
14. 442×2
15. 213×9

16. Suppose a theater has 36 rows of 9 seats each. How many people can sit in the theater?

17. Science A gibbon monkey can travel about 25 feet in a single swing. How far can it travel in 7 swings?

18. The school year has 185 days at Jeremy's school. There are 6 hours in each school day. How many hours of school are there in one school year?

19. $2.30 × 2 **20.** $9.61 × 3 **21.** 4 × $0.67

22. $3.55 × 5 **23.** 6 × $1.76 **24.** 7 × $0.51

25. Critical Thinking Suppose you bought 2 sandwiches and 2 drinks. How much would it cost without tax?

Food Prices	
Sandwich	$2.35
Drink	$0.99
Salad	$1.25
Ice cream cone	$0.75

(Lesson 9) Mental Math Find each product.

26. 29 × 6 **27.** 31 × 7 **28.** 52 × 5

29. 38 × 3 **30.** 18 × 3 **31.** 81 × 4

(Lesson 10) Use any strategy to solve.

32. Money Allison rakes leaves for her neighbors. The first week she earns $2.00. The next week she has $4.00. The next week she has $6.00. If the pattern continues, how many more weeks until she has $12.00?

33. Journal How would you regroup to find 43 × 8?

Skills Checklist

In this section, you have:

- ☑ Multiplied Using Partial Products
- ☑ Multiplied 2-Digit Numbers
- ☑ Multiplied 3-Digit Numbers
- ☑ Multiplied Money
- ☑ Multiplied Using Mental Math
- ☑ Solved Problems by Making a Table

CHAPTER 9

SECTION C

Dividing with 1-Digit Divisors

Katie earns money to help her community by selling lemonade.

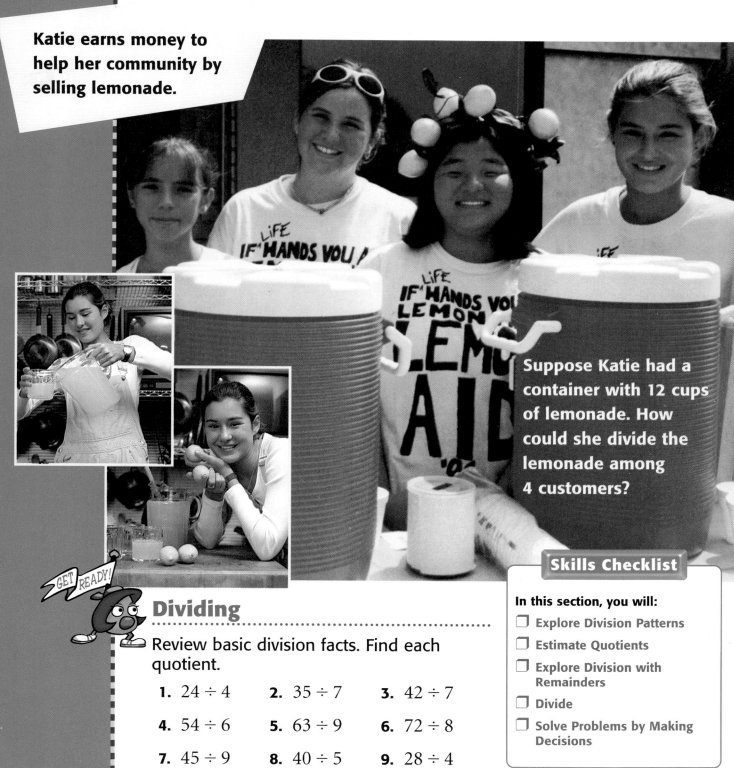

Suppose Katie had a container with 12 cups of lemonade. How could she divide the lemonade among 4 customers?

Dividing

Review basic division facts. Find each quotient.

1. $24 \div 4$	**2.** $35 \div 7$	**3.** $42 \div 7$
4. $54 \div 6$	**5.** $63 \div 9$	**6.** $72 \div 8$
7. $45 \div 9$	**8.** $40 \div 5$	**9.** $28 \div 4$

Skills Checklist

In this section, you will:

- ❒ Explore Division Patterns
- ❒ Estimate Quotients
- ❒ Explore Division with Remainders
- ❒ Divide
- ❒ Solve Problems by Making Decisions

Chapter 9
Lesson
11

Exploring Division Patterns

Problem Solving Connection
Look for a Pattern

Materials
calculator

Explore

Place-value patterns can help you divide greater numbers.

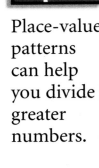

Math Tip
Think of basic division facts to help.

Work Together

1. Use a calculator to find each quotient. Look for patterns.

a. 8 ÷ 4 = ■
80 ÷ 4 = ■
800 ÷ 4 = ■

b. 9 ÷ 3 = ■
90 ÷ 3 = ■
900 ÷ 3 = ■

c. 6 ÷ 2 = ■
60 ÷ 2 = ■
600 ÷ 2 = ■

2. Use patterns to find each quotient. Check with a calculator.

a. 7 ÷ 7 = ■
70 ÷ 7 = ■
700 ÷ 7 = ■

b. 8 ÷ 2 = ■
80 ÷ 2 = ■
800 ÷ 2 = ■

c. 6 ÷ 3 = ■
60 ÷ 3 = ■
600 ÷ 3 = ■

d. 14 ÷ 2 = ■
140 ÷ 2 = ■
1,400 ÷ 2 = ■

e. 5 ÷ 1 = ■
50 ÷ 1 = ■
500 ÷ 1 = ■

f. 18 ÷ 9 = ■
180 ÷ 9 = ■
1,800 ÷ 9 = ■

Talk About It

3. Describe patterns you found.

4. What basic fact can you use to find 120 ÷ 4? Explain.

Connect

Basic facts and place-value patterns can help you divide mentally.

You can use $6 \div 3$ to find $60 \div 3$ and $600 \div 3$.

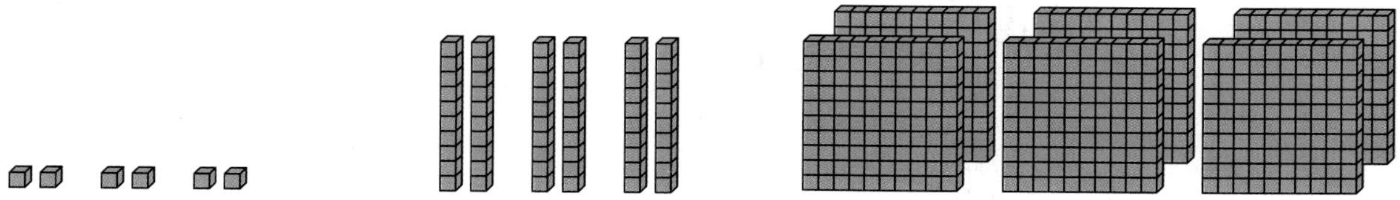

6 ones $\div$ 3 = 2 ones
$6 \div 3 = 2$

6 tens $\div$ 3 = 2 tens
$60 \div 3 = 20$

6 hundreds $\div$ 3 = 2 hundreds
$600 \div 3 = 200$

Practice

Copy and complete.

1. $3 \div 3 = ■$
$30 \div ■ = 10$
$■ \div 3 = 100$

2. $10 \div 5 = ■$
$■ \div 5 = 20$
$1{,}000 \div ■ = 200$

3. $12 \div 2 = ■$
$120 \div ■ = 60$
$1{,}200 \div 2 = ■$

Mental Math Find each quotient using mental math.

4. $400 \div 2$ **5.** $120 \div 6$ **6.** $600 \div 3$ **7.** $50 \div 5$

8. $180 \div 3$ **9.** $70 \div 7$ **10.** $200 \div 2$ **11.** $80 \div 4$

12. $350 \div 5$ **13.** $540 \div 9$ **14.** $900 \div 3$ **15.** $200 \div 4$

16. Reasoning How can you use $15 \div 3 = 5$ to help you find $150 \div 3$?

17. Measurement Hector sells bags of popcorn. He wants to put 160 ounces of popcorn into 4-ounce bags. How many bags will he need?

18. Time Mrs. Taba's class is 60 minutes long. She wants to divide her class time into 3 equal periods. How long will each period be?

19. There are 300 students going on a field trip. Each of the 6 teachers will have an equal number of students in a group. How many students will be in each group?

20. Journal Explain how you can use $6 \div 2$ to find $600 \div 2$.

Chapter 9
Lesson
12

Estimating Quotients

You Will Learn
how to estimate quotients

Math Tip
Think of basic facts that are close to help you estimate.

Learn

When Katie was 11 years old, she started a fund-raiser to help people in need. She and about 150 other students spent a weekend selling lemonade around their neighborhoods.

Every year, Katie's "Lemon-Aid" helps to raise money for people in Tulsa, Oklahoma.

Example 1

If Katie has 13 cups of lemonade to sell to 6 people, about how many cups should each person get?

Estimate the quotient of $13 \div 6$.

Think: 13 is close to 12.

$12 \div 6 = 2$

So, each person should get about 2 cups of lemonade.

Example 2

If Katie pours 80 cups of lemonade equally into 9 pitchers, about how many cups will be in each pitcher?

Estimate the quotient of $80 \div 9$.

Think: 80 is close to 81.

$81 \div 9 = 9$

So, there will be about 9 cups of lemonade in each pitcher.

Talk About It

In Example 1, will each person get more or less than 2 cups of lemonade? How do you know?

Check

Estimate each quotient.

1. $37 \div 9$ **2.** $41 \div 8$ **3.** $17 \div 3$ **4.** $18 \div 5$

5. **Reasoning** Is the quotient of $33 \div 4$ greater or less than 8? Explain.

Practice

Skills and Reasoning

Estimate each quotient.

6. $63 \div 8$ **7.** $41 \div 6$ **8.** $26 \div 3$ **9.** $16 \div 5$ **10.** $23 \div 6$

11. $24 \div 5$ **12.** $36 \div 5$ **13.** $50 \div 7$ **14.** $34 \div 6$ **15.** $55 \div 6$

16. $17 \div 4$ **17.** $9 \div 4$ **18.** $11 \div 2$ **19.** $21 \div 4$ **20.** $29 \div 5$

21. $28 \div 9$ **22.** $20 \div 7$ **23.** $50 \div 8$ **24.** $64 \div 7$ **25.** $25 \div 4$

26. $18 \div 8$ **27.** $29 \div 7$ **28.** $25 \div 3$ **29.** $36 \div 7$ **30.** $14 \div 5$

31. Estimate the quotient of $22 \div 3$.

32. Estimate the quotient of $39 \div 5$.

33. What basic division fact can you use to help you estimate the quotient of $29 \div 6$? Explain.

34. Is the quotient of $41 \div 7$ greater than or less than 6? Explain.

Problem Solving and Applications

35. Geometry Readiness How many triangles that do not touch could you make from 24 toothpicks?

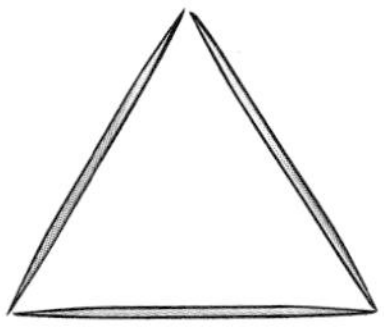

36. Money Suppose some students buy 7 cups of lemonade. If each cup costs $1.25, how much do they owe?

37. Measurement If you cut 36 inches of string into five equal pieces, about how long will each piece be?

38. Science A lemon tree can bear fruit for 50 years. If you pick lemons twice a year, how many times would you pick lemons over a tree's lifetime?

Mixed Review and Test Prep

Add or multiply.

39. 2×143 **40.** 3×27 **41.** $964 + 89$ **42.** 5×18

43. 658×3 **44.** $382 + 200$ **45.** $604 + 783$ **46.** $73 + 219$

47. $5.42 + $3.00 **48.** $34 + 29$ **49.** $123 + 111$ **50.** $508 + 67$

51. Estimation Estimate the product of 7×381.

Ⓐ 38,100 Ⓑ 2,100 Ⓒ 2,800 Ⓓ 380

Exploring Division with Remainders

People Mover in Detroit, Michigan

Problem Solving Connection
Use Objects/
Act It Out

Materials
counters

Vocabulary
remainder
the number left over after dividing

Explore

Greg has 25 tokens for the Detroit People Mover. He uses three tokens each week. Greg needs to plan how many weeks he can use the People Mover before he has to buy more tokens.

Work Together

1. Use 25 counters to show the tokens.
   a. Make groups of 3.
   b. How many weeks can Greg ride the People Mover?
   c. How many tokens will he have left over?
2. Suppose Katrina buys 18 tokens for her and her 3 sisters. If each of them gets an equal number of tokens, how many tokens will be left over? Use counters to solve.
   a. How many tokens will each receive?
   b. How many tokens will be left over?

Remember
You can estimate the quotient to help decide how many counters go in each group.

Talk About It

How did you find how many tokens were left over?

Connect

Sometimes when you divide there are leftovers. These leftovers are called **remainders**.

Find $5\overline{)33}$

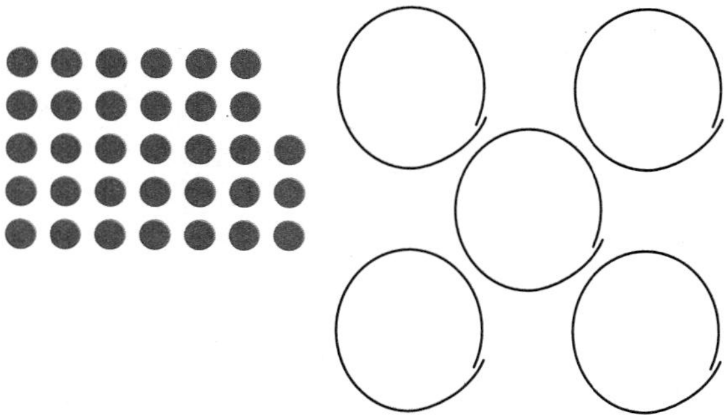

$\begin{array}{r} 6 \text{ R } 3 \\ 5\overline{)33} \end{array}$

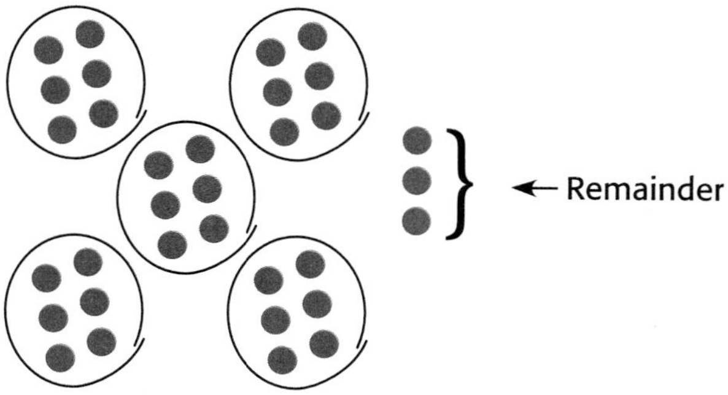

Practice

Find each quotient and remainder. You may use counters to help.

1. $5\overline{)34}$ ▢ R ▢ **2.** $8\overline{)41}$ ▢ R ▢ **3.** $3\overline{)16}$ ▢ R ▢ **4.** $6\overline{)28}$ ▢ R ▢

5. $9\overline{)17}$ **6.** $4\overline{)26}$ **7.** $9\overline{)74}$ **8.** $3\overline{)11}$ **9.** $4\overline{)9}$

10. $2\overline{)7}$ **11.** $8\overline{)51}$ **12.** $5\overline{)44}$ **13.** $6\overline{)39}$ **14.** $2\overline{)17}$

15. $4\overline{)22}$ **16.** $7\overline{)45}$ **17.** $6\overline{)19}$ **18.** $3\overline{)8}$ **19.** $7\overline{)67}$

20. Reasoning Arnold says, "If I want to learn 15 spelling words in 6 days, I can learn 2 words each day." Do you agree or disagree? Explain.

21. Mike cooked 32 cups of soup and poured it into containers that held 6 cups each. How many cups of soup were left over?

Ⓐ 2 cups Ⓑ 4 cups Ⓒ 5 cups Ⓓ 6 cups

22. History In 1913 Henry Ford added an assembly line to his car factory in Detroit. It took about 6 hours to make 1 car. About how many cars could a worker make in a 40-hour week?

23. Social Studies The cost of a Model T car dropped from $550 in 1913 to $290 in 1924. How much less did the 1924 car cost?

24. Journal Draw a picture or write a story about 3 friends sharing 14 tokens equally. Show or write whether there are tokens left over.

Chapter 9 Lesson 14

Dividing

You Will Learn
how to find quotients and remainders

Learn

When you are in a marching band, you have to stay in line! Suppose the band must form rows with 6 students in each row. If there are 55 students, how many rows can they form?

Example

Find 55 ÷ 6.

Step 1

Estimate the quotient.

$6\overline{)55}$

Think: 55 is close to 54.

$54 \div 6 = 9$

Step 2

Multiply.

$$\begin{array}{r} 9 \\ 6\overline{)55} \\ 54 \end{array} \leftarrow 9 \times 6$$

Step 3

Subtract.

$$\begin{array}{r} 9 \\ 6\overline{)55} \\ -\,54 \\ \hline 1 \end{array} \leftarrow \text{remainder}$$

Step 4

Compare. Write the remainder beside the quotient.

$$\begin{array}{r} 9\text{ R }1 \\ 6\overline{)55} \\ -\,54 \\ \hline 1 \end{array} \quad 1 < 6$$

The band can form 9 rows of 6 students, with 1 extra student as the leader.

Talk About It

Why should you estimate the quotient first? Explain.

Check

Remember
The R means remainder.

Find each quotient and remainder.

1. $3\overline{)13}$ **2.** $5\overline{)24}$ **3.** $7\overline{)28}$ **4.** $8\overline{)47}$ **5.** $6\overline{)38}$

6. Reasoning Suppose you want to share 17 cups of popcorn equally among 3 people. Will each person get more or less than 5 cups? Explain.

Practice

Skills and Reasoning

Find each quotient and remainder.

7. $4\overline{)27}$ **8.** $9\overline{)82}$ **9.** $6\overline{)38}$ **10.** $3\overline{)19}$ **11.** $6\overline{)63}$

12. $8\overline{)75}$ **13.** $3\overline{)18}$ **14.** $9\overline{)39}$ **15.** $9\overline{)59}$ **16.** $3\overline{)22}$

17. $33 \div 5$ **18.** $27 \div 9$ **19.** $49 \div 6$ **20.** $52 \div 7$ **21.** $64 \div 9$

22. $12 \div 5$ **23.** $36 \div 5$ **24.** $53 \div 6$ **25.** $46 \div 8$ **26.** $20 \div 3$

27. Divide 25 by 4. **28.** Divide 32 by 6. **29.** Divide 19 by 5.

30. Divide 8 by 3. **31.** Divide 54 by 7. **32.** Divide 63 by 8.

33. Molly says, "When you divide a number by 5, the remainder will always be less than 5." Do you agree or disagree? Explain.

34. Suppose you need to buy 14 cans of soda for a meeting. How many 6-packs will you need to buy?

Problem Solving and Applications

Using Data Use the Data File on page 357 for **35** and **36.**

35. **Critical Thinking** The Golden Gate Bridge has sidewalks that are 15 feet wide. There are 6 lanes on the bridge. How wide is each lane?

36. How much wider is the George Washington Bridge than the Fremont Bridge?

37. **Write Your Own Problem** Write a division word problem in which the remainder is:

a. 3 **b.** 5 **c.** 4 **d.** 0 **e.** 1

Mixed Review and Test Prep

Subtract or multiply.

38. $12 - 4$ **39.** 9×9 **40.** 7×8 **41.** $13 - 5$ **42.** $18 - 9$

43. **Measurement** What is the area of the rectangle?

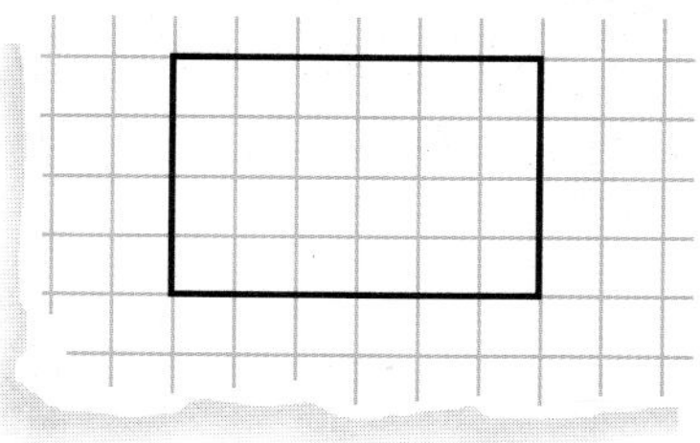

Ⓐ 20 square units Ⓑ 24 units

Ⓒ 24 square units Ⓓ 20 units

Chapter 9 Lesson 15

Problem Solving
Decision Making: Plan a Marathon

You Will Learn
how to make decisions to help you solve problems

Explore

The New York City Marathon has more than 29,000 runners, including wheelchair racers! The participants drink more than 500,000 cups of juice, and it takes 1,000 tables to hold all the cups! Runners in the marathon start in separate groups, so they don't get too crowded.

Suppose you have to plan a mini-marathon. You must decide how many juice stations you will have, how many cups of juice you need, and how many people will be in each group of runners.

Here are some things to think about:

- The length of your course must be between 13 and 19 miles.
- You must have a juice station every 2 miles.
- Each juice station should have 1 cup of juice for each runner.
- There are 48 runners. They must be separated into equal starting groups.

Work Together

Understand

1. What do you know?
2. What do you need to decide?

Plan and Solve

3. Draw a course on grid paper. Let the length of a square show one mile.

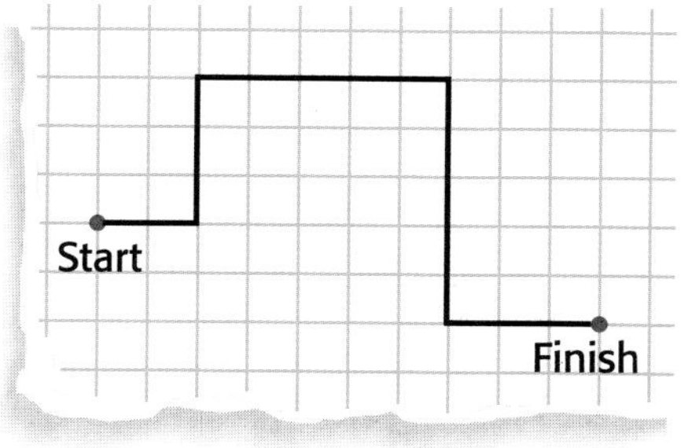

4. Show the juice stations on your map.

Make a Decision

5. How many juice stations will you have?
6. How many cups of juice will you need?
7. How many runners will be in each group?

Present Your Decision

8. Share your decisions with the class. Explain how you decided where the juice stations should go and how many cups of juice you will need. Tell how you decided how many runners should be in each group.

PROBLEM SOLVING PRACTICE

Technology

Dividing with a Calculator

There are different ways to divide with a calculator.

Materials
calculator

Work Together

1. You can divide by subtracting equal groups. The [Cons] key helps you keep track of the number of groups you've subtracted.

   Divide 78 by 6.

   - Since you want to subtract 6 over and over, press [−] 6 [Cons]. Now you're ready to begin dividing.
   - Enter 78 [Cons] to subtract 1 group of 6.
   - To subtract another group of 6 press [Cons] again. The calculator displays the total number of groups subtracted and the amount left.
   - Continue to subtract groups of 6 by pressing the [Cons] key. Stop when you reach 0. How many groups of 6 did you subtract from 78? What is 78 ÷ 6?

2. Some calculators will divide numbers and display the quotient and the remainder.

   Divide 25 by 4.

   - To have the calculator divide 25, enter 25 [INT÷].
   - Since you are dividing by 4, enter 4.
   - Press [=]. What is the quotient and remainder?

Exercises

1. Use the [Cons] key to find 42 ÷ 3.
   a. How many groups of 3 did you subtract from 42? What is 42 ÷ 3?
   b. How does using the [Cons] key to divide show repeated subtraction?
2. **Reasoning** Kara helps out in the computer lab. She needs to put 95 floppy disks into disk holders. Each holder takes 5 disks. How many holders will she need? Use the [Cons] key to solve.
3. Use the [INT÷] key to find 79 ÷ 8. What is the quotient? What is the remainder?

Extensions

4. Make a table like this one. Use the [INT÷] key to complete.

	Divide	Quotient	Remainder
a.	55 ÷ 4		
b.	54 ÷ 4		
c.	53 ÷ 4		
d.	52 ÷ 4		
e.	51 ÷ 4		
f.	50 ÷ 4		
g.	49 ÷ 4		
h.	48 ÷ 4		

9. **Reasoning** Use the [INT÷] key to find the quotient of 97 ÷ 8. Then predict what 96 ÷ 8 will be. Write your prediction, then test it.

5. What patterns do you notice in the table?
6. **Reasoning** What was the greatest remainder in your table? Why do you think no remainders were greater?
7. Make a new table. This time divide 9 numbers by 3. You may start with any number. Don't forget to make each number you divide 1 less.
8. What patterns do you notice in the remainders when you divide by 3?

SECTION C
Review and Practice

Vocabulary Write true or false.

1. The remainder is the product of two factors.

(Lesson 11) Mental Math Find each quotient.

2. $800 \div 2$ 3. $150 \div 3$ 4. $40 \div 2$ 5. $700 \div 7$ 6. $140 \div 7$

7. A videotape is 90 minutes. Lena watches it in three equal time periods. How long is each time period?

8. **Science** A panda will eat about 90 pounds of bamboo stems in 3 days. If it eats the same amount of food each day, how many pounds of bamboo stems does it eat each day?

(Lesson 12) Estimation Estimate each quotient.

9. $65 \div 7$ 10. $35 \div 9$ 11. $27 \div 4$ 12. $43 \div 6$ 13. $32 \div 6$

14. **Reasoning** If you divided 13 cups of juice equally among 4 people, about how many cups would each person have?

(Lessons 13 and 14) Find each quotient and remainder.

15. $3\overline{)7}$ 16. $7\overline{)22}$ 17. $6\overline{)51}$ 18. $8\overline{)26}$ 19. $4\overline{)18}$

20. $3\overline{)21}$ 21. $9\overline{)79}$ 22. $5\overline{)42}$ 23. $5\overline{)16}$ 24. $4\overline{)38}$

25. $4\overline{)13}$ 26. $6\overline{)37}$ 27. $2\overline{)5}$ 28. $8\overline{)50}$ 29. $9\overline{)39}$

30. $45 \div 7$ 31. $29 \div 9$ 32. $11 \div 2$ 33. $80 \div 9$ 34. $77 \div 8$

35. A box can hold 8 books. How many boxes are needed for 67 books? Will all the boxes be full? Explain.

36. Otis wants to share 35 baseball cards among four cousins. He wants to give the same number to each cousin. He will keep what is left. How many cards will each cousin get? How many cards will Otis have left?

37. **Journal** Explain how to use a basic fact to estimate a quotient.

Skills Checklist

In this section, you have:

- ☑ Explored Division Patterns
- ☑ Estimated Quotients
- ☑ Explored Division with Remainders
- ☑ Divided
- ☑ Solved Problems by Making Decisions

YOUR CHOICE

Choose at least one. Use what you have learned in this chapter.

1 Cliff Dwellers

Some falcons build their nests on the tops of skyscrapers. Tall buildings remind them of their natural homes on cliffs. Write a story about how high a falcon flies to reach its nest on top of a building. How many floors does the building have? How many feet tall is each floor?

2 Poster Product

Make a poster that shows how to multiply a 3-digit number by a 1-digit number.

ShinyLight Bulbs
Shine for 31 Weeks!!

EverBright Bulbs
Last 8 Months!!

3 Build a Building

At Home Use grid paper to plan a model skyscraper. How many floors will your skyscraper have? How tall is each floor? Fly to the World Wide Web to find information about skyscrapers. Start at **www.mathsurf.com/3/ch9.**

4 Night Lights

Suppose you are helping to decide which light bulbs to buy for the street lamps in your neighborhood. Which kind of light bulb would you choose? Explain.

CHAPTER 9

Review/Test

(Lesson 3) Estimate each product.

1. 4×21 **2.** 6×132 **3.** 3×83 **4.** 5×212 **5.** 6×72

6. 4×256 **7.** 2×51 **8.** 7×361 **9.** 8×614 **10.** 5×33

(Lessons 5–8) Find each product.

11. $\begin{array}{r} 14 \\ \times\ 6 \\ \hline \end{array}$ **12.** $\begin{array}{r} 71 \\ \times\ 9 \\ \hline \end{array}$ **13.** $\begin{array}{r} 59 \\ \times\ 3 \\ \hline \end{array}$ **14.** $\begin{array}{r} 18 \\ \times\ 4 \\ \hline \end{array}$

15. 32×2 **16.** 3×86 **17.** 74×8 **18.** 2×99

19. 65×7 **20.** 24×3 **21.** 9×31 **22.** 47×7

23. $\begin{array}{r} 244 \\ \times\ \ 6 \\ \hline \end{array}$ **24.** $\begin{array}{r} 536 \\ \times\ \ 5 \\ \hline \end{array}$ **25.** $\begin{array}{r} 259 \\ \times\ \ 3 \\ \hline \end{array}$ **26.** $\begin{array}{r} 310 \\ \times\ \ 6 \\ \hline \end{array}$

27. 120×3 **28.** 349×4 **29.** $\$3.98 \times 4$ **30.** $\$2.21 \times 2$

31. $\$0.78 \times 5$ **32.** $\$3.33 \times 7$ **33.** $\$4.05 \times 4$ **34.** $\$0.26 \times 3$

35. **Science** A six-inch kangaroo rat traveling at top speed can cover 72 inches in one jump. How many inches could it cover in 2 jumps at top speed?

(Lesson 9) Find each product using mental math.

36. 31×7 **37.** 19×8 **38.** 51×3 **39.** 38×5

(Lesson 11) Use any strategy to solve.

40. Ollie is learning spelling words. The first night, he learned 6 words. By the second night, he had learned 12 words. By the third night, he had learned 18 words. If the pattern continues, in how many more nights will he have learned 72 words?

(Lesson 12) Estimate each quotient.

41. $70 \div 9$ **42.** $59 \div 8$ **43.** $12 \div 5$ **44.** $26 \div 7$ **45.** $50 \div 7$

(Lessons 13 and 14) Find each quotient and remainder.

46. $23 \div 9$ **47.** $41 \div 8$ **48.** $64 \div 7$ **49.** $35 \div 8$ **50.** $22 \div 7$

CHAPTER 9
Performance Assessment

Medieval cities were protected by walls. Florence, Italy, knocked down and rebuilt its city walls three times as the city grew. Plan a city. How many stones will you need to make a wall around it?

Dalmation Coast, Yugoslavia

1. **Decision Making** A stone wall can be from 2 to 9 stones high. How high will your city's walls be?

2. **Recording Data** Now plan your city wall. Suppose each stone is the same size as a square on your grid paper. How many stones will you need?

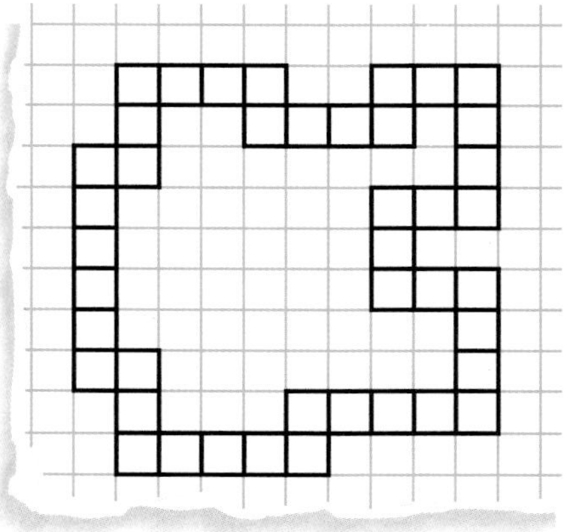

3. **Explain Your Thinking** How did you figure out how many stones you would need?

4. **Critical Thinking** Suppose your city grows. Show how you would make your city bigger. Then find the number of stones you would need to build a new wall around your city.

Carcassonne, France

Math Magazine

Ancient Egyptian Multiplication

Since the ancient Egyptians used pictures and symbols as numbers, they didn't multiply numbers the way you do. They used doubling to find products.

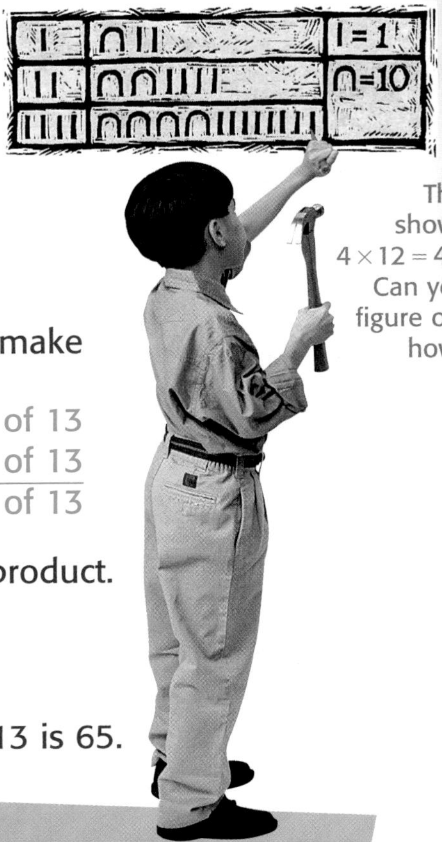

This shows $4 \times 12 = 48$. Can you figure out how?

You don't have to use Egyptian numbers to multiply the way they did.

Find 5×13.

1. Make a doubling table. The numbers in each row are twice as much as the row before.

Groups of 13	Total
1	13
2	26
4	52

2. Look for a way to make 5 groups of 13.

   Think: 4 groups of 13
   + 1 group of 13
   5 groups of 13

3. Add to find the product.

$$\begin{array}{r} 52 \\ +\,13 \\ \hline 65 \end{array}$$

So, 5 groups of 13 is 65.

Try These!

Multiply the ancient Egyptian way.

1.

Groups of 17	Total
1	17
2	
4	

$6 \times 17 = ■$

Think: $4 + 2 = 6$

2.

Groups of 23	Total
1	23
2	
4	

$7 \times 23 = ■$

Think: $4 + 2 + 1 = 7$

CHAPTERS 1–9
Cumulative Review

Test Prep Strategy: Make Smart Choices

Use mental math.
What is the product of 202 and 7?

Ⓐ 14,014 Ⓑ 209 Ⓒ 1,414 Ⓓ 2,734

You can use mental math to help you make smart choices.

$7 \times 200 = 1{,}400$
$7 \times 2 = 14$
$1{,}400 + 14 = 1{,}414$

So, the correct answer is Ⓒ.

Write the letter of the correct answer. Use mental math or any strategy to help.

1. Estimate the sum of 438 and 792.

   Ⓐ 400 Ⓑ 1,200 Ⓒ 11,000 Ⓓ 12,000

2. What is the sum of 674 + 193?

   Ⓐ 500 Ⓑ 900 Ⓒ 481 Ⓓ 867

3. What is the total value of 2 quarters, 3 dimes and 2 pennies?

   Ⓐ \$0.07 Ⓑ \$2.32 Ⓒ \$0.82 Ⓓ \$0.87

4. What is the area of this rectangle?

   Ⓐ 7 units
   Ⓑ 14 units
   Ⓒ 12 square units
   Ⓓ 14 square units

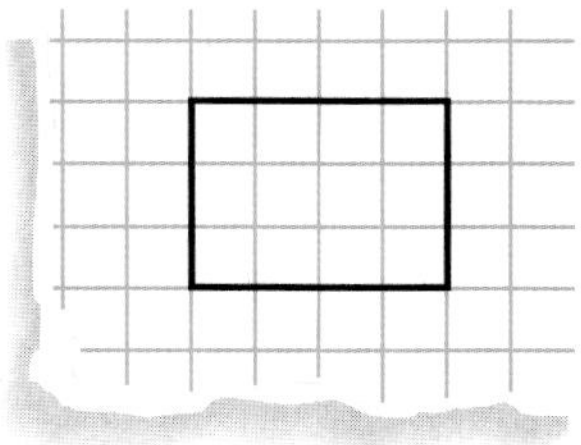

5. Find 400 − 120.

   Ⓐ 280 Ⓑ 520 Ⓒ 380 Ⓓ 420

6. Estimate the product of 7 and 523.

   Ⓐ 350 Ⓑ 3,500 Ⓒ 420 Ⓓ 530

7. What is the product of 89 and 4?

   Ⓐ 356 Ⓑ 93 Ⓒ 22 R 1 Ⓓ 85

8. Divide 58 by 6.

   Ⓐ 8 R 10 Ⓑ 7 R 2 Ⓒ 8 R 2 Ⓓ 9 R 4

Test Prep Strategies

- Read Carefully
- Follow Directions
- Make Smart Choices
- Eliminate Choices
- Work Backward from an Answer

DATA FILE

Chapter 10

Fractions and Customary Linear Measurement

SPORTS AND GAMES

SECTION A

Understanding Fractions

411

Athletes in the Olympic games proudly display their country's flag. Which flag looks like it has the most red?

Bahrain

Colombia

Congo

Tanzania

Poland

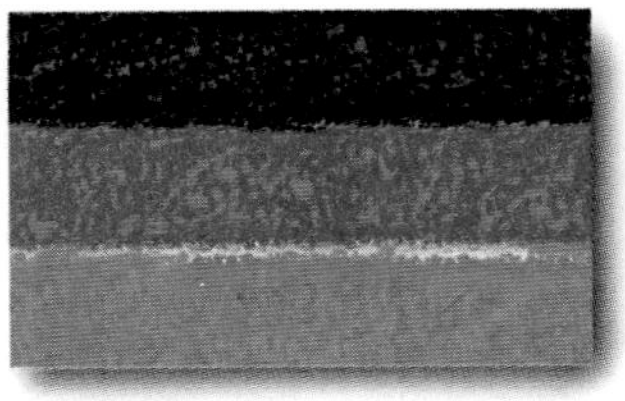

Germany

Estonia

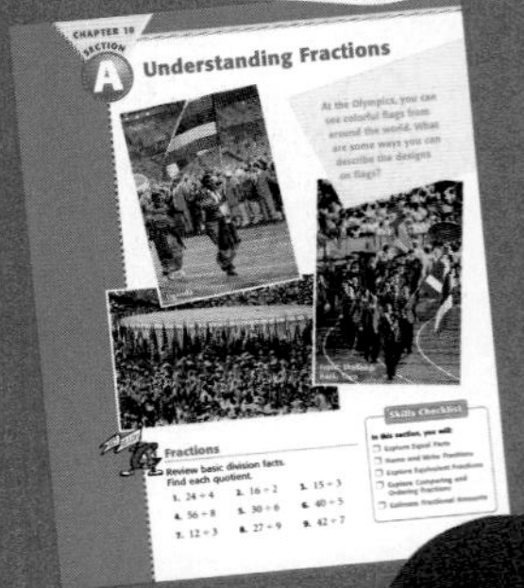

Olympic flags
Page 411

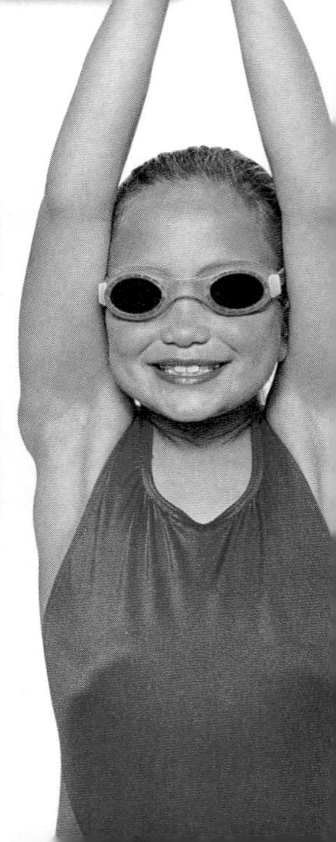

SECTION B

Extending Fraction Concepts

423

You might be surprised at all the places you can find fractions! How many equal parts do you see on a field hockey field?

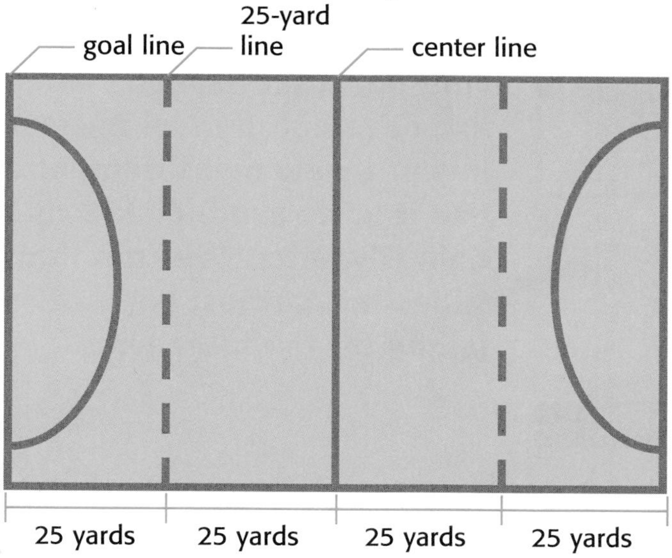

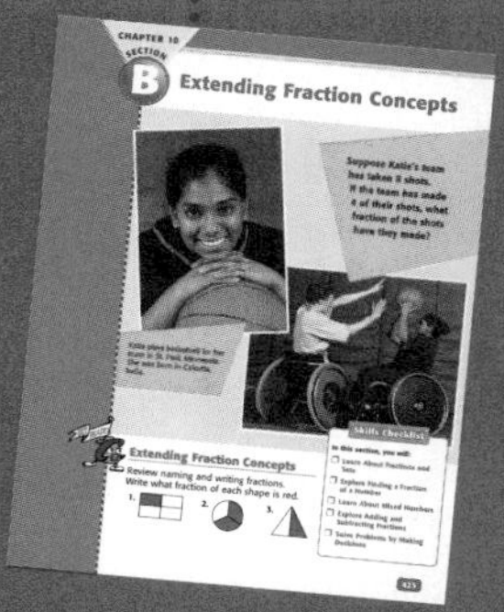

Katie plays basketball in St. Paul, Minnesota

Page 423

SECTION C

Customary Linear Measurement

435

These athletes can jump! What is the world record distance for the long jump?

World Records		
Event	**Athlete**	**Record**
High jump	Javier Sotomayor (Cuba)	8 feet, $\frac{1}{2}$ inch
Pole vault	Sergey Bubka (Ukraine)	20 feet, $1\frac{3}{4}$ inches
Long jump	Mike Powell (United States)	29 feet, $4\frac{1}{2}$ inches

How long is a football?

Page 435

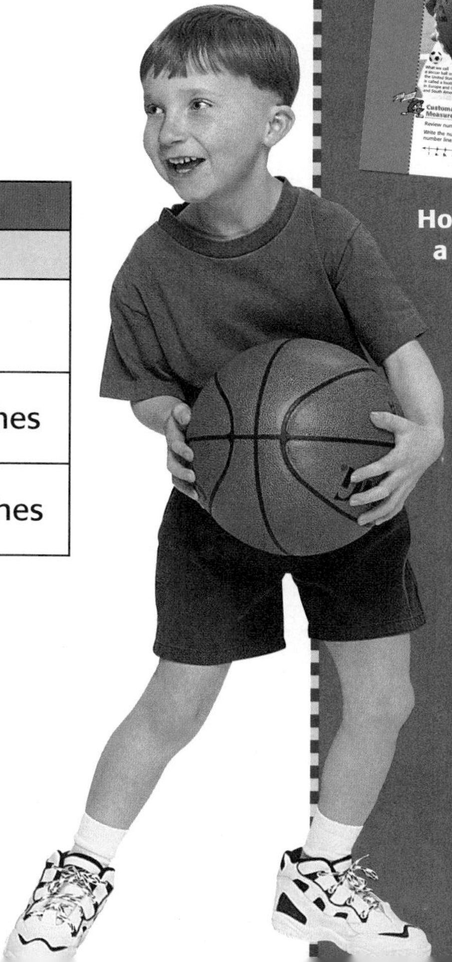

Surfing the World Wide Web!

What is your favorite sport or game to play? Does the field or board you play on have equal parts? Search the World Wide Web for information about sports and games. Visit the website at **www.mathsurf.com/3/ch10** to share your favorites.

TEAM PROJECT

COIN OLYMPICS

Materials
coin or counter

Find out what happens when people use different units of measurement! Invent a new measurement unit. Use it to measure distances in Coin Olympics. The coin that slides the farthest without falling off the table wins.

Make a Plan

- What will your new measurement unit be?
- Decide where the starting line should be.

Carry It Out

1. Make and name your new unit. You may want a number of smaller units to equal one larger unit. For example, 8 glibbos make a glin.
2. Make a ruler using your units.
3. Play Coin Olympics with your group. Measure and record the distance of each coin slide using your ruler.

Talk About It

- Were you able to measure each coin slide exactly? Explain.

Present the Project

- Display the results of your Coin Olympics.
- Compare your group's results with those of the rest of the class. Who had the longest or shortest slide? How can you tell?

CHAPTER 10

SECTION A

Understanding Fractions

Uganda

Front: Thailand;
Back: Togo

At the Olympics, you can see colorful flags from around the world. What are some ways you can describe the designs on flags?

Fractions

Review basic division facts.
Find each quotient.

1. $24 \div 4$ **2.** $16 \div 2$ **3.** $15 \div 3$

4. $56 \div 8$ **5.** $30 \div 6$ **6.** $40 \div 5$

7. $12 \div 3$ **8.** $27 \div 9$ **9.** $42 \div 7$

Skills Checklist

In this section, you will:

- ❒ Explore Equal Parts
- ❒ Name and Write Fractions
- ❒ Explore Equivalent Fractions
- ❒ Explore Comparing and Ordering Fractions
- ❒ Estimate Fractional Amounts

Chapter 10
Lesson
1

Exploring Equal Parts

Problem Solving Connection
- Use Objects/ Act It Out
- Draw a Picture

Materials
- geoboard
- rubber bands

Vocabulary
Ways to Name Equal Parts
halves
thirds
fourths
fifths
sixths
eighths
tenths
twelfths

Explore

There are different ways to divide a geoboard into equal parts. Here is one way to divide a geoboard into 2 equal parts.

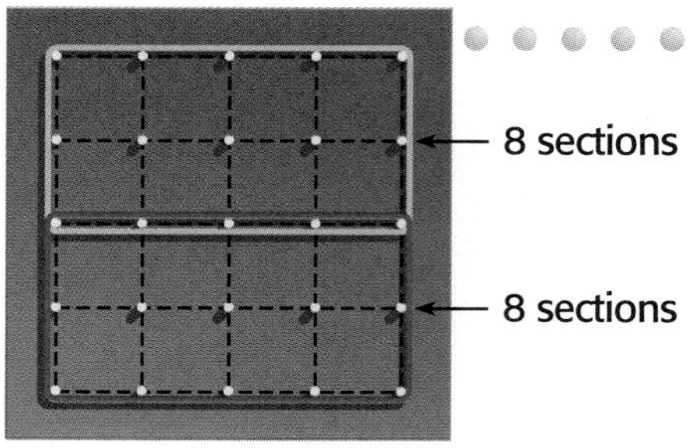

Work Together

Use a geoboard and rubber bands.

1. Find at least 3 other ways to divide a geoboard into 2 equal parts.
2. Find at least 3 ways to divide a geoboard into 4 equal parts.
3. Find at least 3 ways to divide a geoboard into 8 equal parts.

Talk About It

4. How did you decide the parts were equal?
5. How many sections were in each part when you divided the geoboard into 2 equal parts? 4 equal parts? 8 equal parts?

Math Tip
Equal parts must be the same size, but they don't have to be the same shape.

Connect

Here are some ways to divide a whole into equal parts.

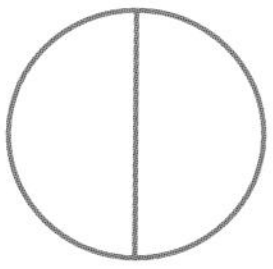
halves

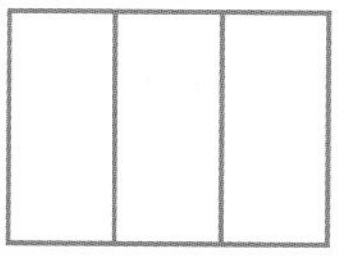
thirds

fourths

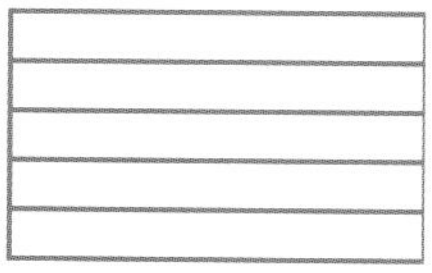
fifths

sixths

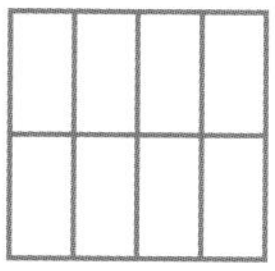
eighths

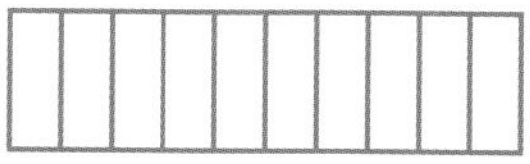
tenths

twelfths

Practice

Write whether each has equal parts or unequal parts.

1. 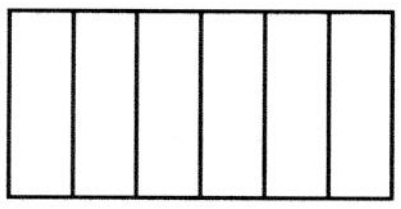

2. 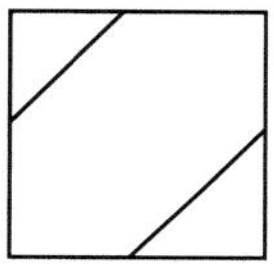

3. 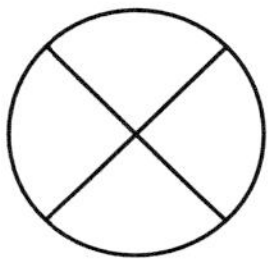

4. 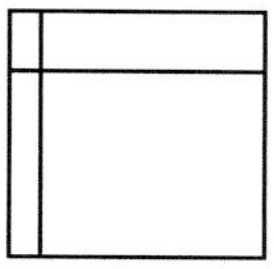

Name the equal parts of each whole.

5. 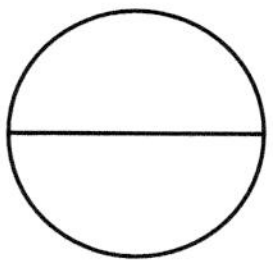

6. 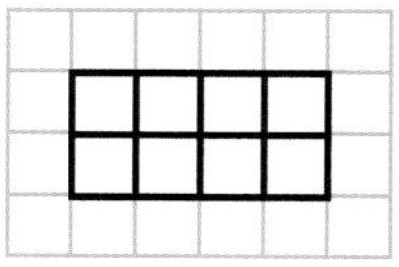

7. 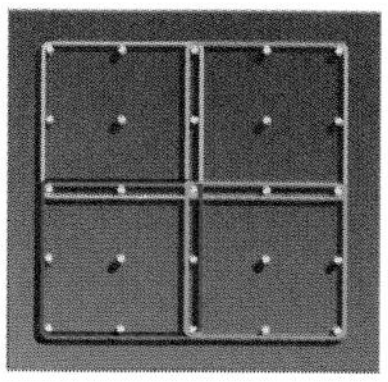

8. 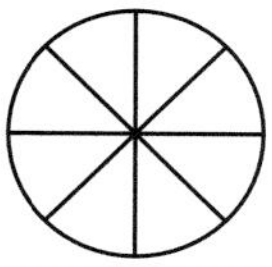

Draw a picture to show each. You may use grid paper to help.

9. fifths **10.** thirds **11.** sixths **12.** fourths

13. **History** Table tennis was invented in England about 100 years ago. Name the equal parts of the table top.

14. **Reasoning** Suppose two pizzas are the same size. One pizza is divided into eighths and the other pizza is divided into tenths. Which pizza has larger pieces?

15. **Journal** Show 3 different ways to divide a square into fourths. You may use grid paper to help.

China won gold and silver medals at the 1996 Olympics.

Chapter 10
Lesson
2

Naming and Writing Fractions

You Will Learn
how to name and write fractions

Vocabulary

fraction
comparison of equal parts to a whole

numerator
top number of a fraction that tells the number of equal parts considered

denominator
bottom number of a fraction that tells the number of equal parts in all

Learn

The Olympic Games start with a march of all the athletes. An athlete from each country carries the country's flag.

You can use **fractions** to name equal parts of a whole.

Monaco

1 part red　　1 ← **numerator**
2 equal parts in all　　2 ← **denominator**

$\frac{1}{2}$, or one half, of Monaco's flag is red.

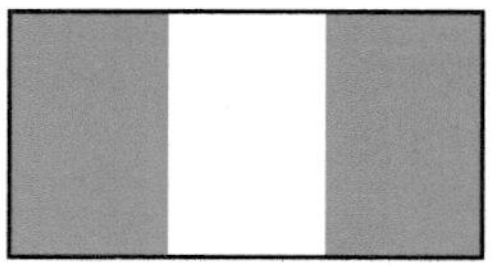

Nigeria

2 parts green　　2 ← numerator
3 equal parts in all　　3 ← denominator

$\frac{2}{3}$, or two thirds, of Nigeria's flag is green.

Talk About It

Problem Solving Hint
You may draw a picture to help you think about $\frac{4}{4}$ of a sandwich.

Karl ate $\frac{4}{4}$ of his sandwich. Jenny said, "You ate the whole sandwich!" Was Jenny right? Explain.

Check

Write the fraction of each figure that is blue.

1. 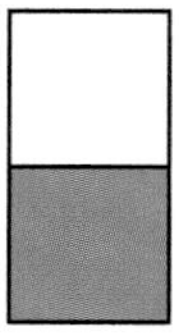

2. 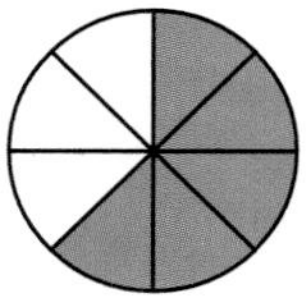

3. 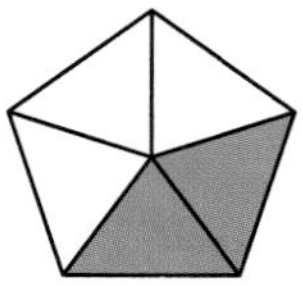

4. Reasoning The German flag is $\frac{1}{3}$ red. How many equal parts are there in the flag? How many of the parts are red?

Practice

Skills and Reasoning

Write the fraction of each figure that is red.

5. 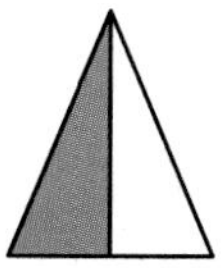

6. 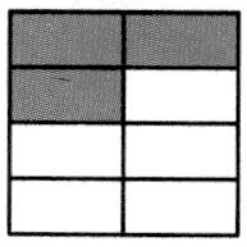

7. 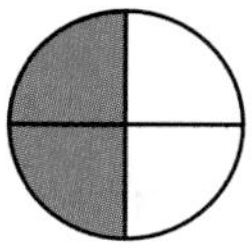

8. 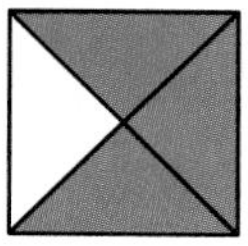

9. 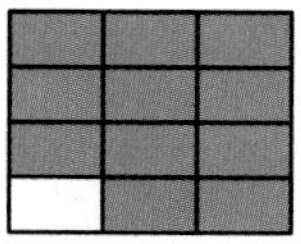

10. 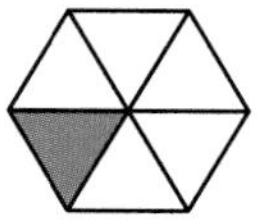

11. 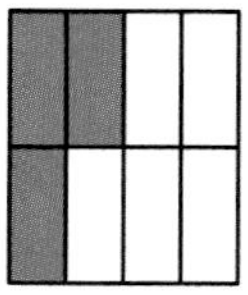

12. 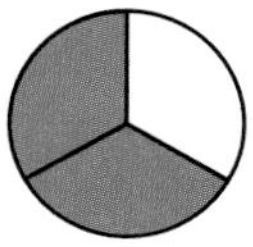

Draw a picture to show each fraction.

13. $\frac{4}{5}$ blue **14.** $\frac{1}{8}$ green **15.** $\frac{6}{10}$ red **16.** $\frac{3}{4}$ blue

17. You have two oranges of the same size. One orange is cut into 6 slices. The other orange is cut into 8 slices. Which orange has larger slices?

18. Jody says, "One half of Taiwan's flag is red." Do you agree or disagree? Explain.

Taiwan

Problem Solving and Applications

Write the fraction for the part that is left.

19. 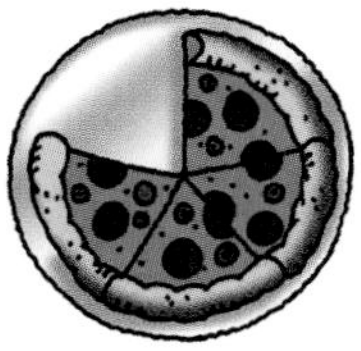

20. 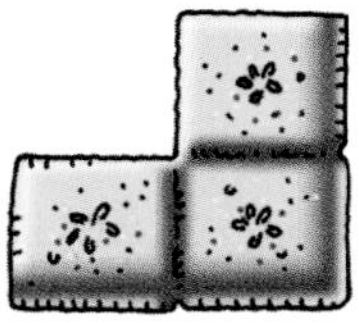

21. 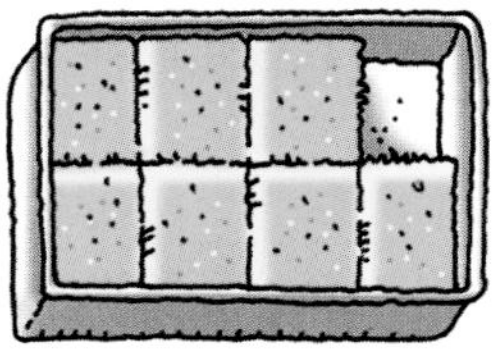

22. 

Using Data Use the Data File on page 408 to solve.

23. What fraction of Poland's flag is white?

24. What fraction of Estonia's flag is blue?

Mixed Review and Test Prep

Multiply.

25. 6×72 **26.** 34×8 **27.** 6×28 **28.** 27×5 **29.** 7×49

30. Divide 37 by 4.

Ⓐ 10 Ⓑ 9 R 1 Ⓒ 33 Ⓓ 8 R 5

Chapter 10
Lesson
3

Exploring Equivalent Fractions

Problem Solving Connection
- Use Objects/ Act It Out
- Look for a Pattern

Materials
fraction strips

Vocabulary
equivalent fractions fractions that name the same amount

Explore

Different fractions can name the same amount.

Work Together

Use fraction strips.

1. Find a $\frac{1}{2}$ fraction strip. Line up the other fraction strips so they match the $\frac{1}{2}$ strip exactly. How many of each strip do you need?

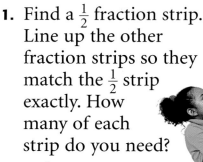

a. $\frac{1}{4}$ strips

b. $\frac{1}{6}$ strips

c. $\frac{1}{8}$ strips

d. $\frac{1}{10}$ strips

e. $\frac{1}{12}$ strips

Math Tip
Make sure that the strips match exactly.

2. Find a $\frac{1}{3}$ fraction strip. Line up fraction strips so they match exactly. How many of each strip do you need?

a. $\frac{1}{6}$ strips **b.** $\frac{1}{12}$ strips

3. Put together three $\frac{1}{4}$ strips to show $\frac{3}{4}$. How many $\frac{1}{8}$ strips do you need to match $\frac{3}{4}$?

4. Can you use $\frac{1}{3}$ strips to match $\frac{1}{2}$ exactly? Explain.

Talk About It

How do you know two fractions name the same amount?

Connect

Fractions that name the same amount are called **equivalent fractions**. Here are some equivalent fractions.

$\frac{1}{5} = \frac{2}{10}$

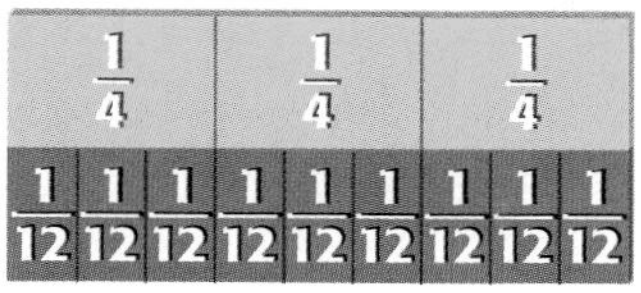

$\frac{3}{4} = \frac{9}{12}$

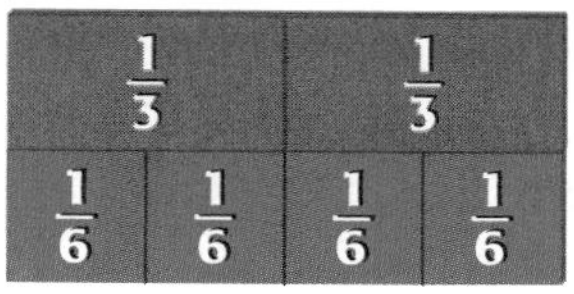

$\frac{2}{3} = \frac{4}{6}$

Practice

Copy and complete. You may use fraction strips to help.

1. 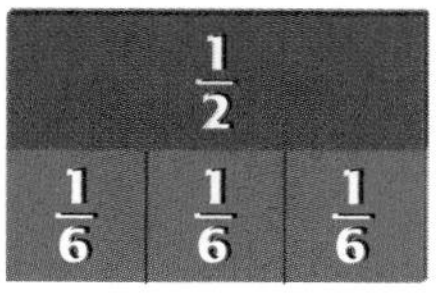

$\frac{1}{2} = \frac{\square}{6}$

2. 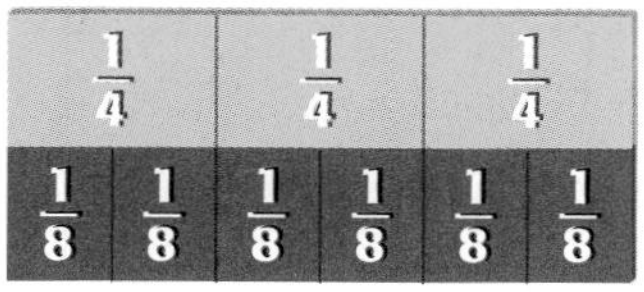

$\frac{3}{4} = \frac{\square}{8}$

3. 

$\frac{1}{4} = \frac{\square}{8}$

4. 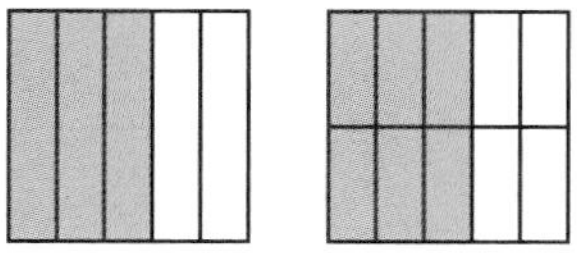

$\frac{3}{5} = \frac{\square}{10}$

5. 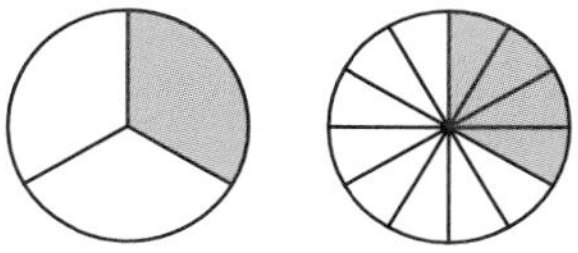

$\frac{1}{3} = \frac{\square}{12}$

6. 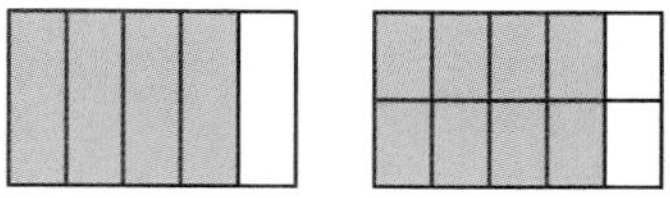

$\frac{4}{5} = \frac{\square}{10}$

Write if the fractions are equivalent or not equivalent. You may use fraction strips to help.

7. 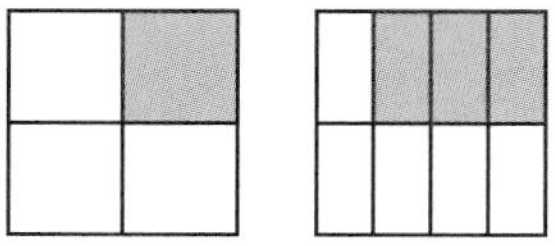

8. 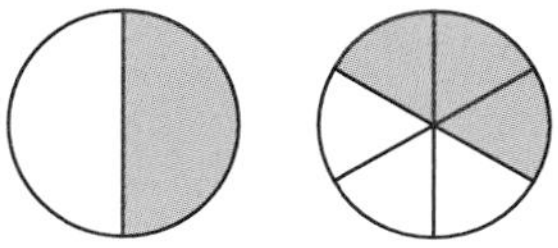

9. 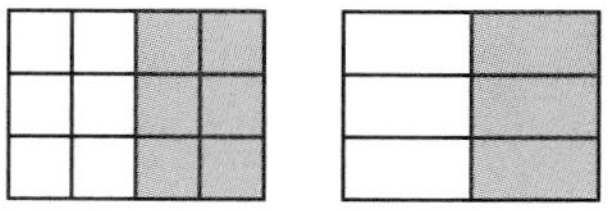

10. Patterns Look for a pattern. Complete the next three fractions.

a. $\frac{1}{4}, \frac{2}{8}, \frac{3}{12}, \frac{4}{\square}, \frac{5}{\square}, \frac{6}{\square}$ **b.** $\frac{2}{3}, \frac{4}{6}, \frac{6}{9}, \frac{\square}{12}, \frac{\square}{15}, \frac{\square}{18}$

11. Critical Thinking The total time of a football game is divided into 4 equal parts called quarters. If there are 2 quarters in half of the game, how many halves are there in a full game?

12. Journal Draw a picture to show that $\frac{1}{2}$ and $\frac{5}{10}$ are equivalent fractions. You may use grid paper to help.

Exploring Comparing and Ordering Fractions

Problem Solving Connection
- Use Objects/ Act It Out
- Look for a Pattern

Materials
fraction strips

Vocabulary
unit fraction
a fraction with a numerator of 1

Math Tip
Be sure to line up the strips when you compare them.

Explore

You can use objects to compare and order fractions.

Work Together

Use fraction strips.

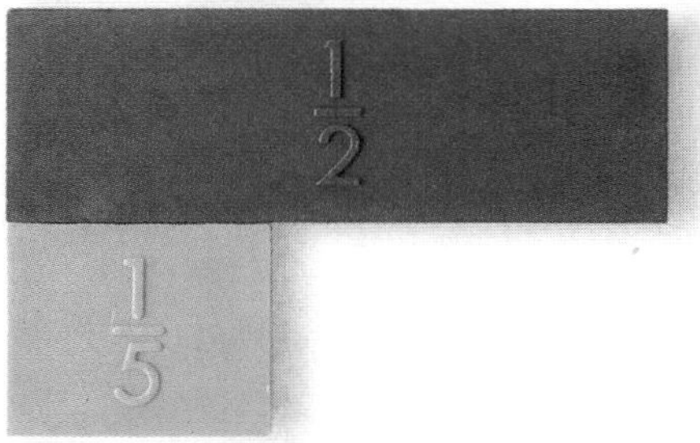

1. Compare **unit fractions** with each fraction in the table. List the unit fractions that are greater and that are less.

		Unit Fractions That Are Greater	Unit Fractions That Are Less
a.	$\frac{1}{2}$		
b.	$\frac{1}{4}$		
c.	$\frac{1}{3}$		
d.	$\frac{1}{6}$		
e.	$\frac{2}{6}$		
f.	$\frac{2}{3}$		

2. Arrange the unit fractions shown in the fraction strips in order from greatest to least. List the unit fractions in order.

Talk About It

Look at your arrangement of unit fractions. What do you notice about the denominators and the size of fraction strips?

Connect

You can compare fractions using <, >, or =.

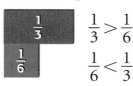

$\frac{1}{3} > \frac{1}{6}$

$\frac{1}{6} < \frac{1}{3}$

$\frac{1}{3}$ is greater than $\frac{1}{6}$.

$\frac{1}{6}$ is less than $\frac{1}{3}$.

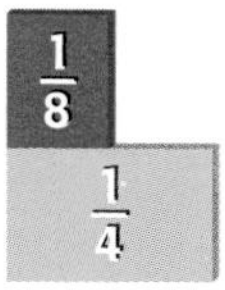

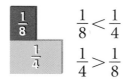

$\frac{1}{8} < \frac{1}{4}$

$\frac{1}{4} > \frac{1}{8}$

$\frac{1}{8}$ is less than $\frac{1}{4}$.

$\frac{1}{4}$ is greater than $\frac{1}{8}$.

$\frac{1}{5} = \frac{2}{10}$

$\frac{1}{5}$ is the same as $\frac{2}{10}$.

Use fraction strips to help you order fractions.

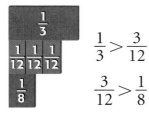

$\frac{1}{3} > \frac{3}{12}$

$\frac{3}{12} > \frac{1}{8}$

In order from greatest to least:

$\frac{1}{3}, \frac{3}{12}, \frac{1}{8}$

$\frac{1}{10} < \frac{2}{6}$

$\frac{2}{6} < \frac{1}{2}$

In order from least to greatest:

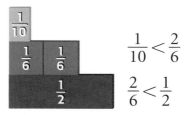

$\frac{1}{10}, \frac{2}{6}, \frac{1}{2}$

Practice

Compare. Write <, >, or =. You may use fraction strips to help.

1. 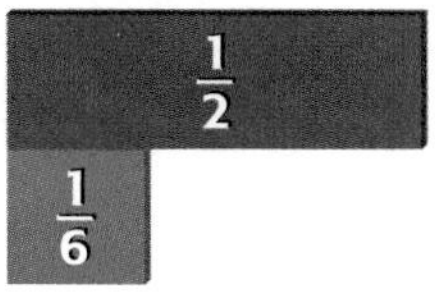

$\frac{1}{2}$ ● $\frac{1}{6}$

2. 

$\frac{1}{8}$ ● $\frac{1}{3}$

3. 

$\frac{1}{4}$ ● $\frac{2}{8}$

4. 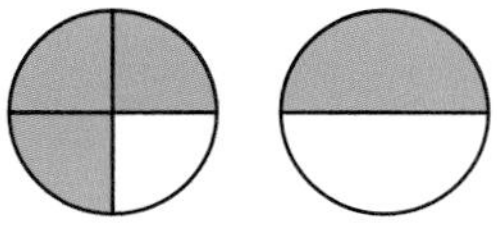

$\frac{3}{4}$ ● $\frac{1}{2}$

5. 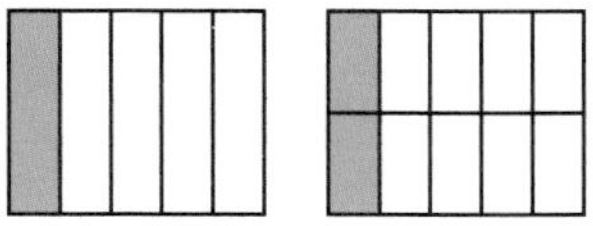

$\frac{1}{5}$ ● $\frac{2}{10}$

6. 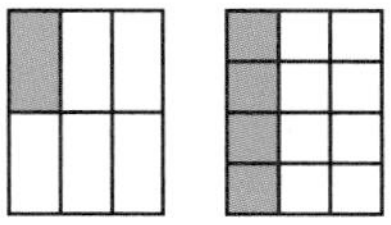

$\frac{1}{6}$ ● $\frac{4}{12}$

7. Music In music, there are $\frac{1}{4}$ notes and $\frac{1}{8}$ notes. A $\frac{1}{4}$ note is played for the same amount of time as two $\frac{1}{8}$ notes. Which is played longer, a $\frac{1}{4}$ note or three $\frac{1}{8}$ notes?

8. Journal Draw a picture to show three different fractions. You may use fraction strips to help. Explain how to order them from least to greatest.

Estimating Fractional Amounts

You Will Learn
how to estimate fractional amounts

Learn

You can estimate fractional amounts by thinking of fractions you know.

You know		So you can estimate	
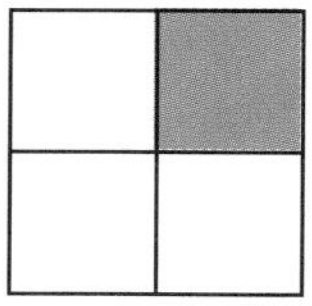	$\frac{1}{4}$	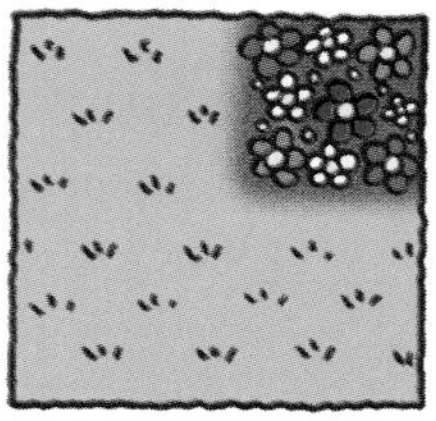	less than $\frac{1}{4}$
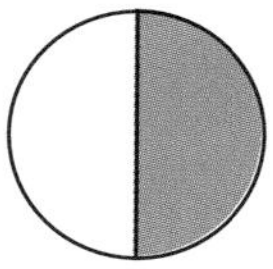	$\frac{1}{2}$	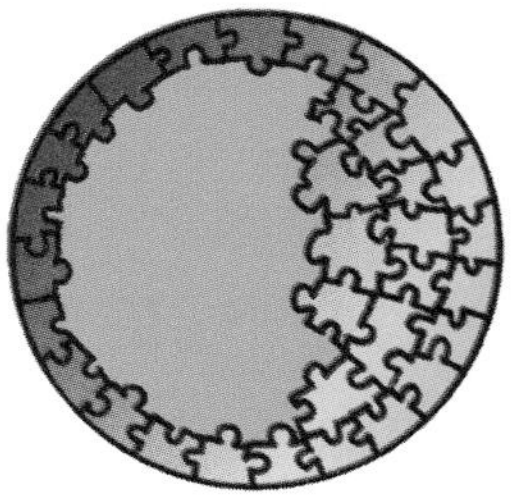	about $\frac{1}{2}$
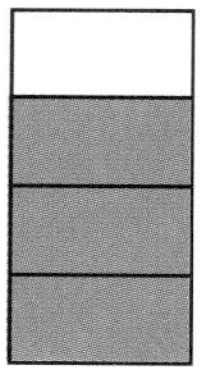	$\frac{3}{4}$	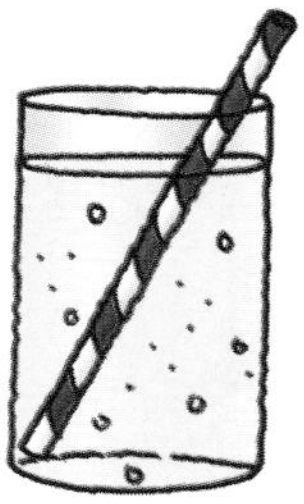	more than $\frac{3}{4}$

Math Tip
Think of a fraction that is close.

Talk About It

What fraction would you use to estimate the shaded amount? Explain.

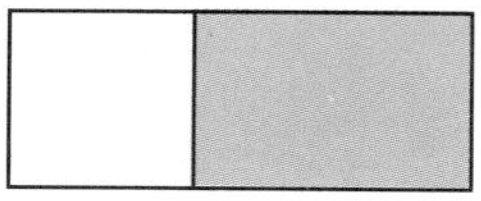

Check

Estimate the amount that is shaded.

1. 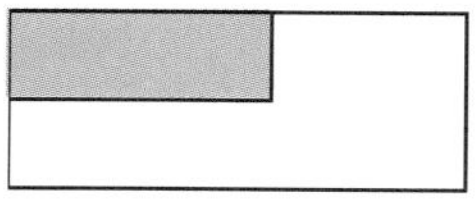
2. 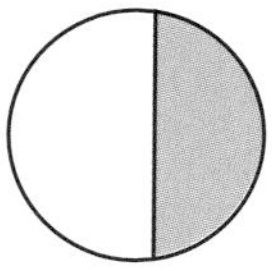
3. 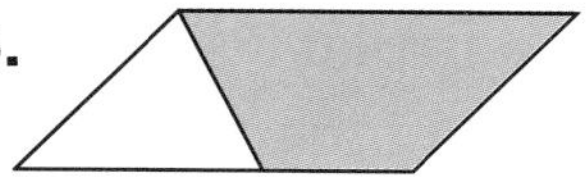

4. **Reasoning** Is the shaded amount closer to 1 or to $\frac{1}{2}$? Explain.

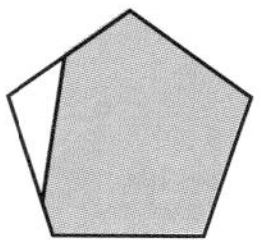

Practice

Skills and Reasoning

Estimate the amount that is shaded.

5. 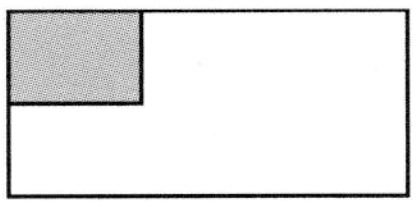

6. 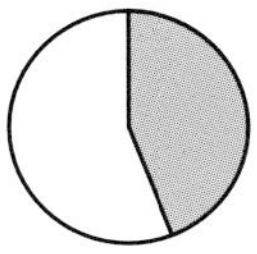

7. 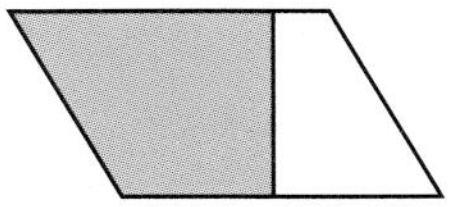

8. 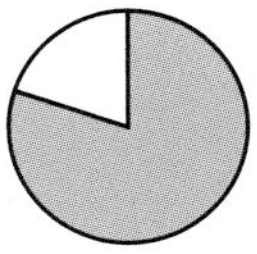

9. 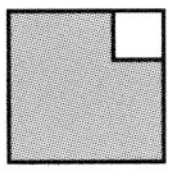

10. 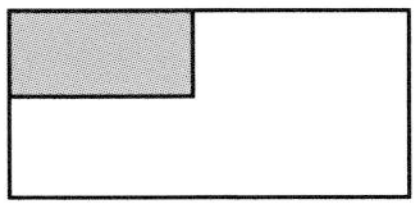

11. 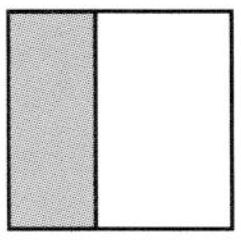

12. 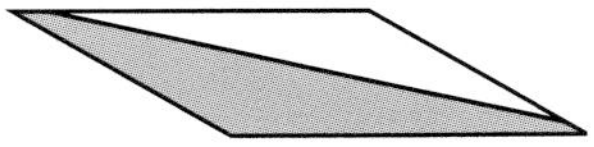

13. Cris says the amount shaded is about the same on each circle. Do you agree or disagree? Explain.

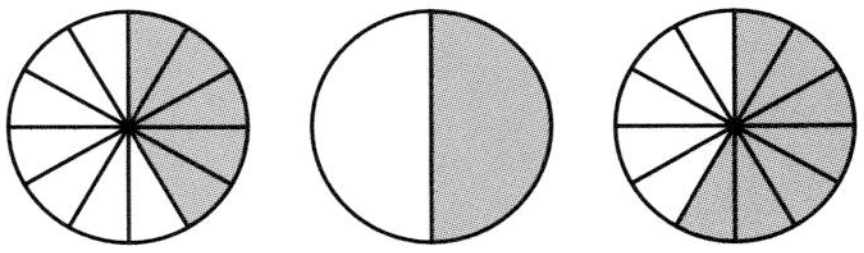

14. Suppose LaShonda needs about $\frac{1}{2}$ of a pizza for her friends. Is there enough pizza left? Explain.

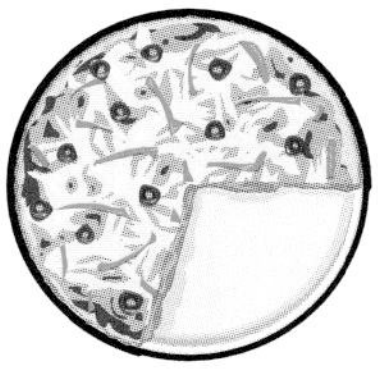

Problem Solving and Applications

Estimate the amount that is left.

15. 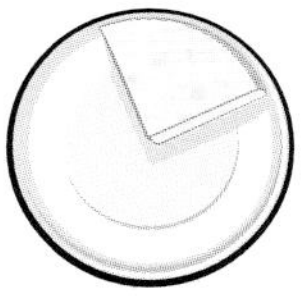

16. 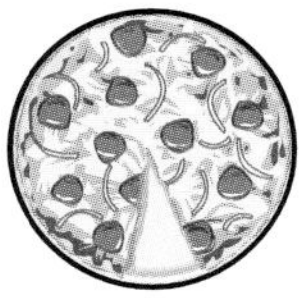

17. 

18. 

Using Data Use the Data File on page 408 for **19–21.**

19. About what fraction of Colombia's flag is red?

20. About what fraction of Tanzania's flag is blue?

21. About what fraction of the flag of Bahrain is red?

22. Time About what fraction of an hour has passed?

Mixed Review and Test Prep

Write the quotient and remainder for each.

23. $46 \div 6$ **24.** $37 \div 7$ **25.** $33 \div 4$ **26.** $64 \div 9$ **27.** $55 \div 8$

28. Algebra Readiness Choose the missing number. $6 \times \blacksquare = 42$

Ⓐ 4 Ⓑ 36 Ⓒ 7 Ⓓ 8

SECTION A

Review and Practice

Vocabulary Match each with its meaning.

1. numerator	**a.** bottom number of a fraction
2. denominator	**b.** fraction with a numerator of 1
3. unit fraction	**c.** top number of a fraction
4. fraction	**d.** a comparison of equal parts to a whole

(Lesson 1) Name the equal parts of each whole.

5. 

6. 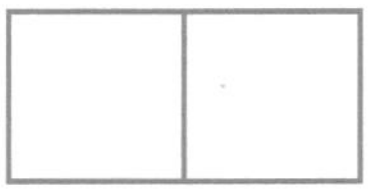

7. 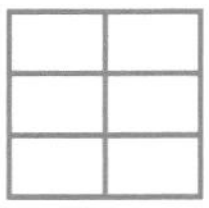

8. 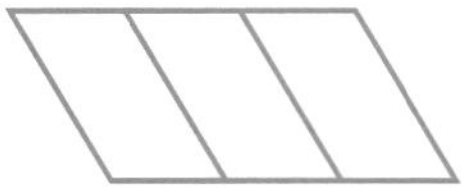

(Lesson 2) Write the fraction of each figure that is green.

9. 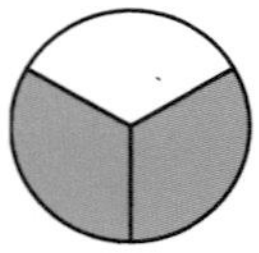

10. 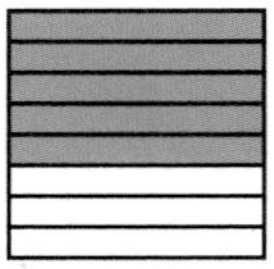

11. 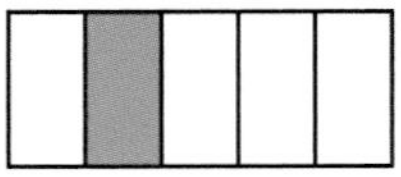

12. 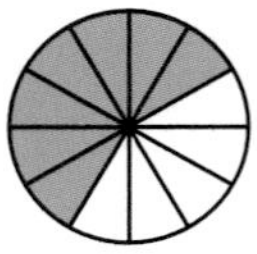

13. What fraction of the Mauritius flag is yellow?

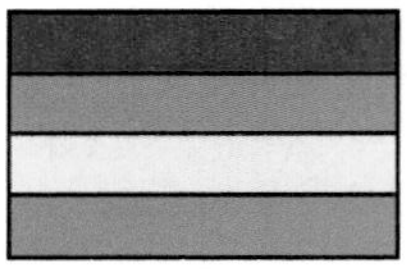

Mauritius

(Lesson 4) Compare. Write <, >, or =.
You may use fraction strips to help.

14. 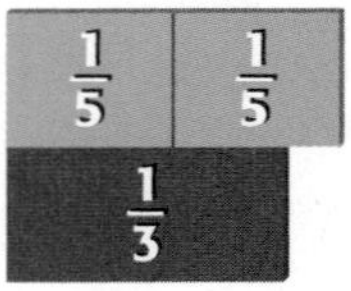

$\frac{2}{5} \bullet \frac{1}{3}$

15. 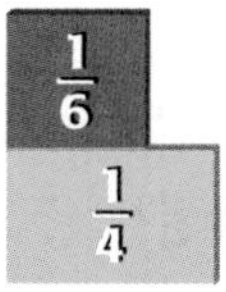

$\frac{1}{6} \bullet \frac{1}{4}$

16. 

$\frac{1}{4} \bullet \frac{2}{8}$

(Lesson 5) Estimate each shaded amount.

17. 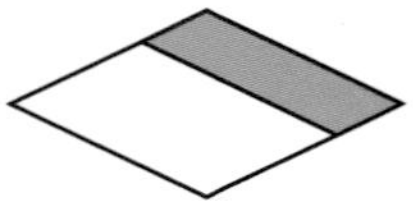

18. 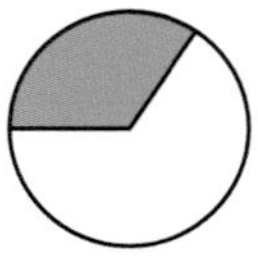

19. 

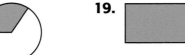

20. Journal Look at the flag of Congo on page 408. Can you use fractions to describe the part of the flag that is green? Why or why not?

Skills Checklist

In this section, you have:

- ☑ **Explored Equal Parts**
- ☑ **Named and Written Fractions**
- ☑ **Explored Equivalent Fractions**
- ☑ **Explored Comparing and Ordering Fractions**
- ☑ **Estimated Fractional Amounts**

CHAPTER 10
SECTION B

Extending Fraction Concepts

Suppose Katie's team has taken 8 shots. If the team has made 4 of their shots, what fraction of the shots have they made?

Katie plays basketball for her team in St. Paul, Minnesota. She was born in Calcutta, India.

Extending Fraction Concepts

Review naming and writing fractions.
Write what fraction of each shape is red.

1. 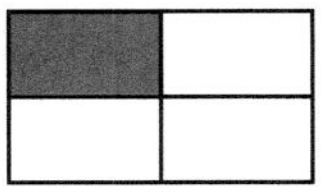

2. 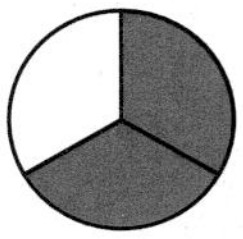

3. 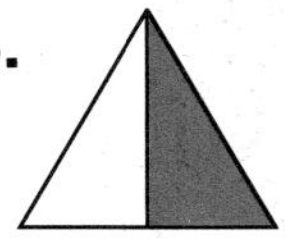

Skills Checklist

In this section, you will:

- ❐ Learn About Fractions and Sets
- ❐ Explore Finding a Fraction of a Number
- ❐ Learn About Mixed Numbers
- ❐ Explore Adding and Subtracting Fractions
- ❐ Solve Problems by Making Decisions

Fractions and Sets

You Will Learn
how to find a fraction of a set

Learn

A fraction may name part of a set or a group.

Did You Know?
Checkers probably came from a Spanish game called *alquerque.*

$\frac{7}{10}$ of the checkers are red.

$\frac{7}{10}$ ← 7: number of red checkers; 10: total number of checkers

$\frac{2}{5}$ of the game pieces are green.

Talk About It

Suppose you had 1 more blue game piece. What fraction of the pieces would be green? Explain.

Check

Write a fraction to tell what part of the set is circled.

1.

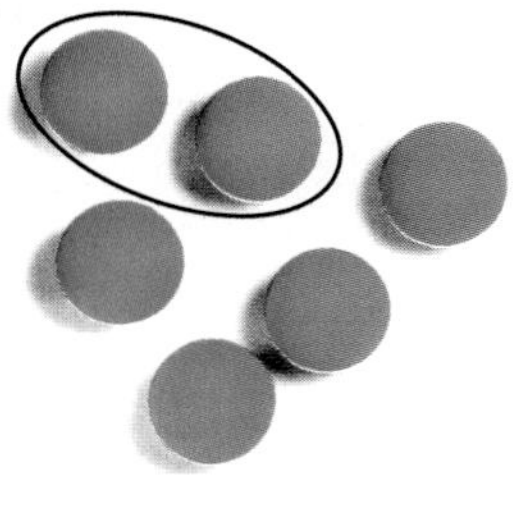

2.

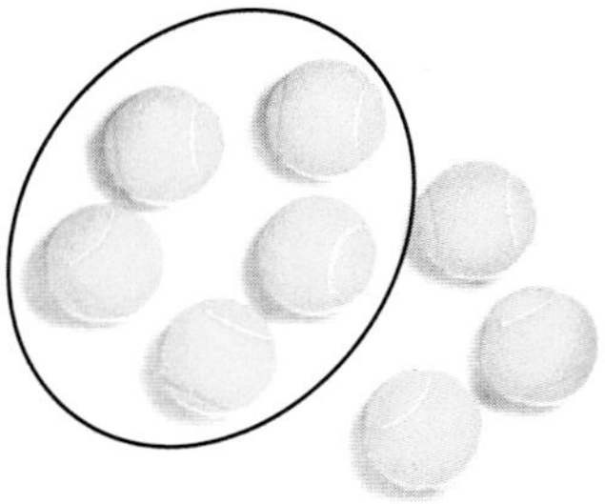

3.

4. Reasoning Suppose a bowl has green and red apples. Three of the apples are green. What additional information do you need to write a fraction to show how many green apples are in the bowl? Explain.

Practice

Skills and Reasoning

Write a fraction to show what part of each set is circled.

5.

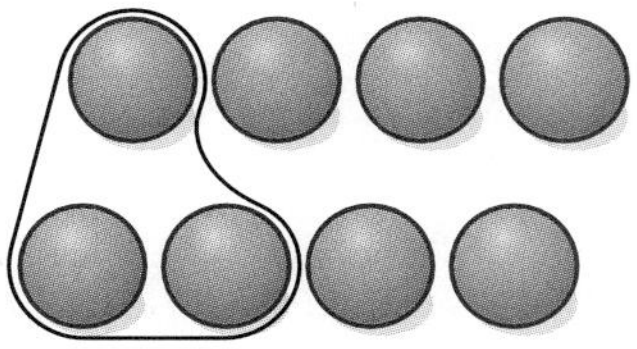

6.

7.

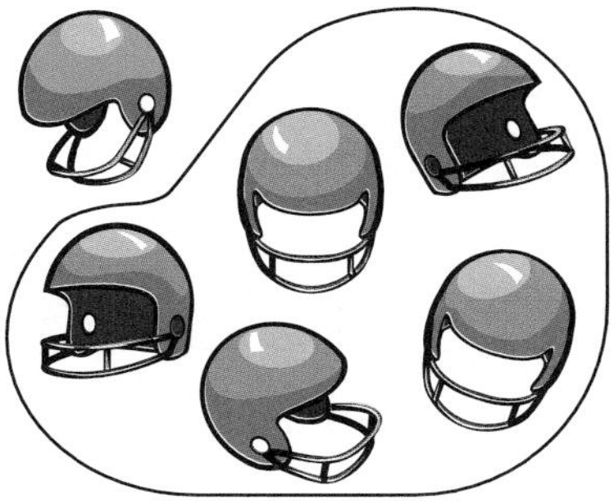

Write a fraction to complete each sentence.

8.

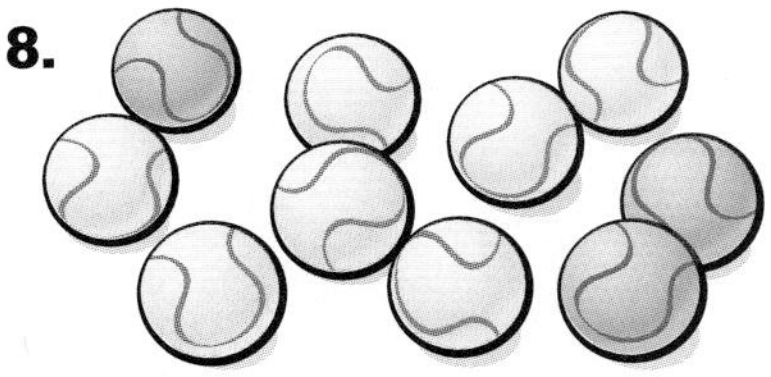

▒ of the tennis balls are yellow.

9.

▒ of the peanuts are in the bowl.

10.

▒ of the bowling pins are standing up.

11. $\frac{1}{10}$ of Rita's 10 marbles are blue. The rest are red. How many are red?

12. Jorge has 3 white shirts and 1 blue shirt. If he buys another blue shirt, what fraction is blue?

Problem Solving and Applications

13. **Time** What fraction of a week is one day?

14. **Critical Thinking** Marcus has 12 marbles. He gives 3 marbles to a friend and 4 marbles to his sister. What fraction is left?

15. **Write Your Own Problem** Draw a picture to show a fraction of a set of baseballs. Write a sentence that names the fraction.

16. Carole ate $\frac{1}{8}$ of her sandwich. Bob ate $\frac{1}{6}$ of his sandwich. Who ate more?

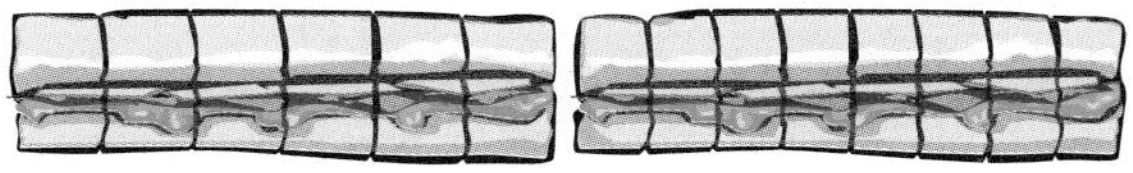

Mixed Review and Test Prep

Find each product or quotient.

17. 32×4 **18.** 45×7 **19.** 670×6 **20.** 912×3 **21.** 405×2

22. $9\overline{)45}$ **23.** $3\overline{)27}$ **24.** $4\overline{)32}$ **25.** $2\overline{)16}$ **26.** $7\overline{)42}$

27. Find 35 + 987.

Ⓐ 1,012 Ⓑ 953 Ⓒ 922 Ⓓ not here

Exploring Finding a Fraction of a Number

Problem Solving Connection
Use Objects/
Act It Out

Materials
counters

Explore

Suppose in the first half of the championship game, Katie's basketball team scored 15 points. If Katie scored $\frac{1}{3}$ of the points, how many points did she score?

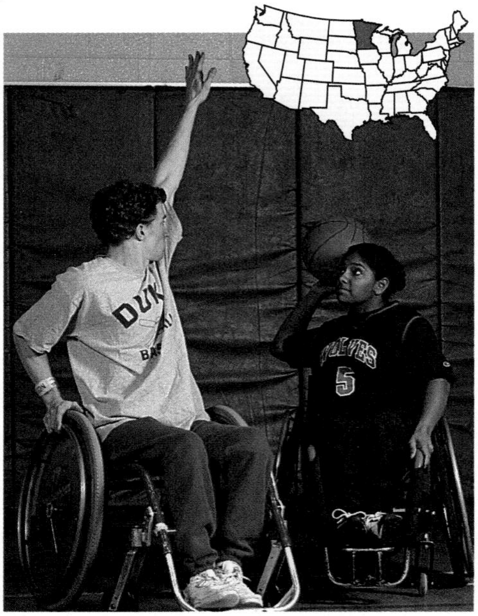

Katie plays basketball with her team in St. Paul, Minnesota.

Work Together

1. Use counters to find $\frac{1}{3}$ of 15.
   a. Show 15 counters.
   b. Arrange the counters in 3 equal groups to show thirds.
   c. How many are in each group?
   d. How many points did Katie score?

Math Tip
Be sure to arrange the counters in equal groups!

2. Use counters to help solve.
   a. Darren had 12 pennies and gave away $\frac{1}{4}$ of them. How many pennies did he give away?
   b. Amrita had 10 pencils. She sharpened $\frac{1}{5}$ of them. How many pencils did she sharpen?

Talk About It

How did dividing the counters into 3 equal groups help you find $\frac{1}{3}$ of 15?

Connect

You can think about division to find a fraction of a number.

Find $\frac{1}{3}$ of 21.

Divide 21 into 3 equal groups.

$21 \div 3 = 7$

$\frac{1}{3}$ of $21 = 7$

Find $\frac{1}{4}$ of 24.

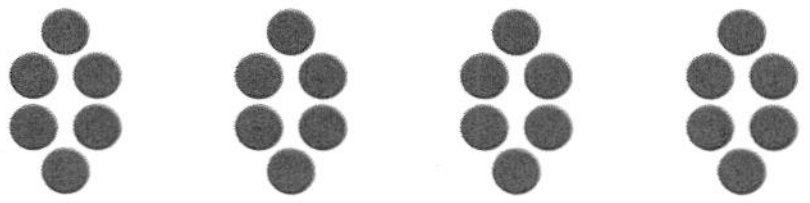

Divide 24 into 4 equal groups.

$24 \div 4 = 6$

$\frac{1}{4}$ of 24 is 6

Practice

Solve. You may use counters or draw a picture to help.

1.

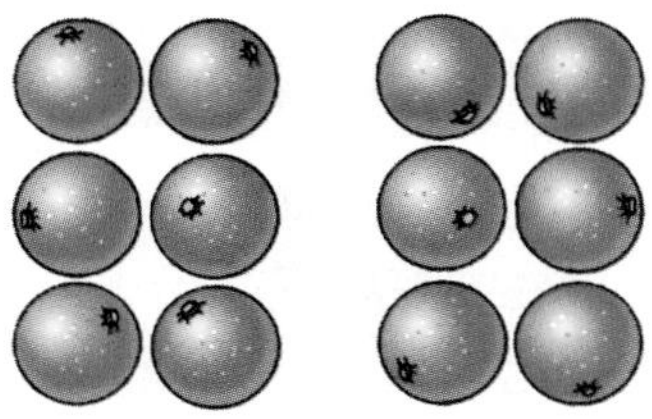

$\frac{1}{2}$ of $12 = \square$

2.

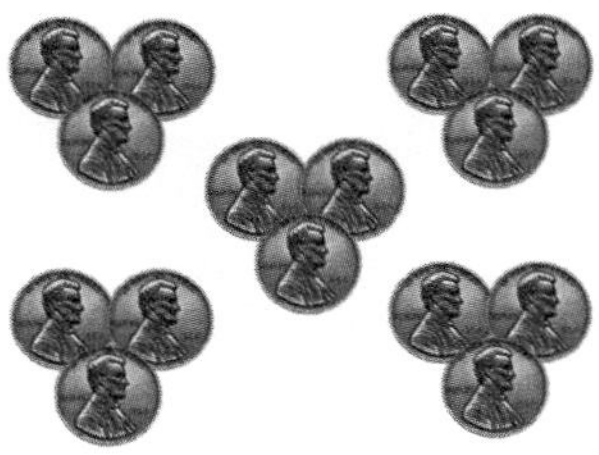

$\frac{1}{5}$ of $15 = \square$

3.

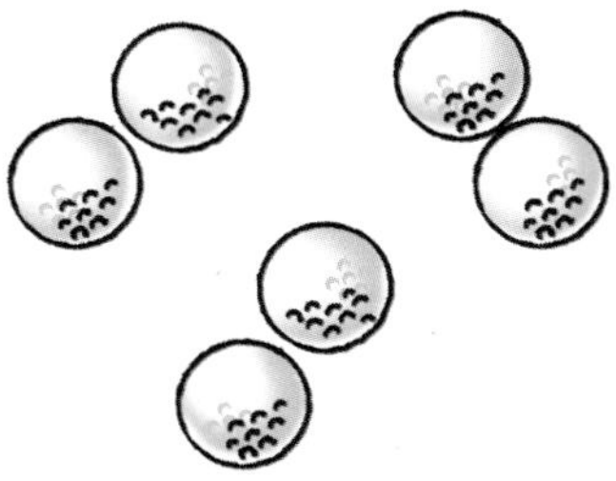

$\frac{1}{3}$ of $6 = \square$

4. Find $\frac{1}{6}$ of 18.

5. Find $\frac{1}{4}$ of 36.

6. Find $\frac{1}{5}$ of 25.

7. Find $\frac{1}{3}$ of 27.

8. Find $\frac{1}{4}$ of 16.

9. Find $\frac{1}{8}$ of 24.

10. **Science** Summer lasts for $\frac{1}{4}$ of the year. How many months does summer last? (Hint: A year has 12 months.)

11. **Time** Suppose you slept for $\frac{1}{3}$ of a 24-hour day. How many hours did you sleep?

12. **Money** Aaron and his sister will each get $\frac{1}{2}$ of the money they make selling lemonade. If they make \$12, how much money will they each get?

13. What fraction of the objects are:

a. caps?

b. balls?

c. mitts?

14. **Journal** Draw a picture to show $\frac{1}{5}$ of 20 basketballs.

Chapter 10
Lesson
8

Mixed Numbers

You Will Learn
how to write fractions greater than one

Vocabulary
mixed number
a number that has a whole number and a fractional part

Math Tip
$\frac{4}{4}$ pizza is the same as 1 pizza.

Learn

You can use whole numbers and fractions to name amounts greater than 1. You write a **mixed number** using a whole number and a fraction.

Example 1

How many pizzas are shown?

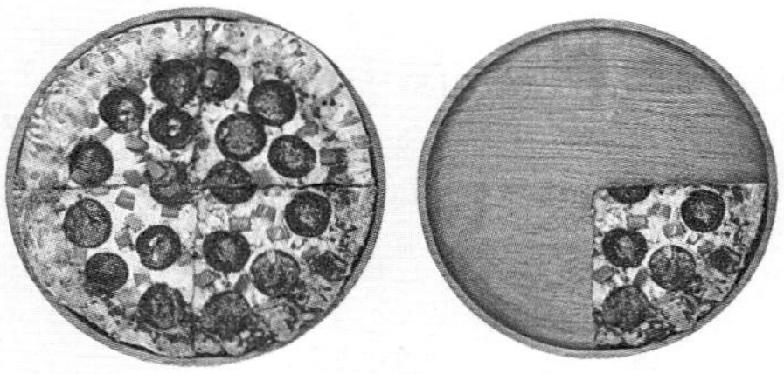

There is 1 whole pizza and $\frac{1}{4}$ of a pizza.

$1\frac{1}{4}$

one and one fourth

There are $1\frac{1}{4}$ pizzas.

Example 2

How many sandwiches are shown?

There are 2 whole sandwiches and $\frac{2}{3}$ of a sandwich.

$2\frac{2}{3}$

two and two thirds

There are $2\frac{2}{3}$ sandwiches.

Talk About It

What does $3\frac{3}{4}$ mean?

Check

Write a mixed number for each.

1. 

2. 

3. **Reasoning** Is $2\frac{2}{3}$ more or less than $2\frac{1}{2}$? Explain. You may use Example 2 to help.

Practice

Skills and Reasoning

Write a mixed number for each.

4. 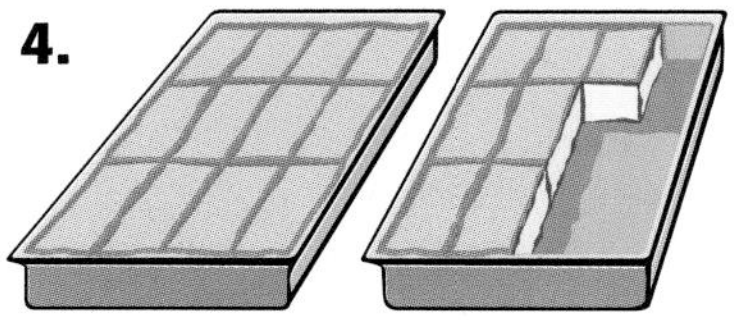

5. 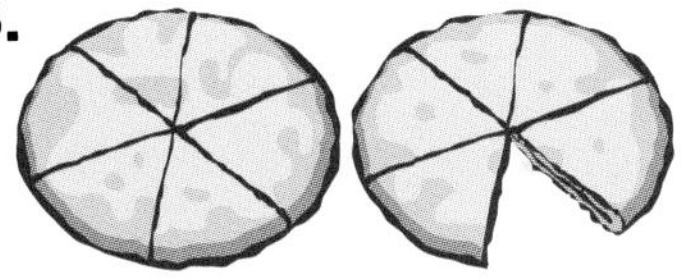

6. 

7. 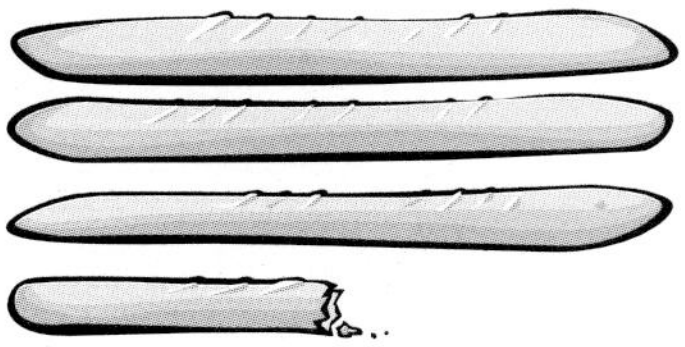

8. 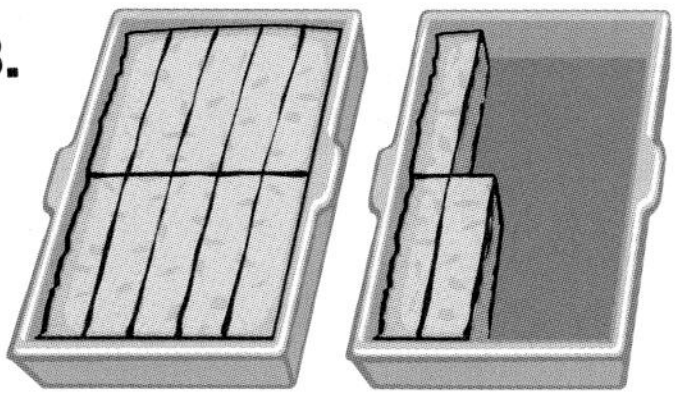

9. 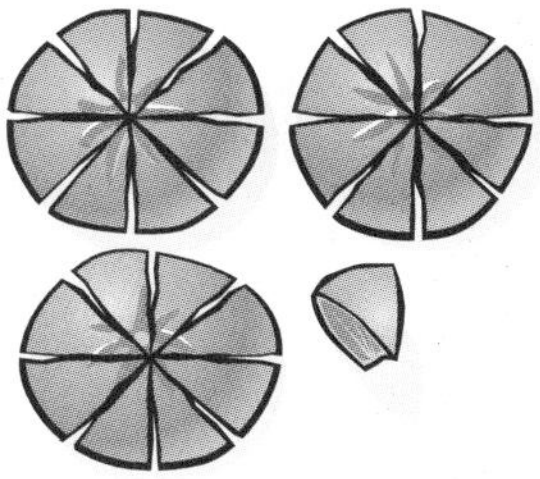

10. Is there more or less than $1\frac{3}{4}$ cakes? Explain.

11. David says, "$1\frac{4}{8}$ is the same as $1\frac{1}{2}$." Do you agree or disagree? Explain.

Problem Solving and Applications

12. Draw a picture to show each mixed number.

a. $2\frac{1}{2}$ **b.** $1\frac{3}{4}$ **c.** $3\frac{1}{3}$ **d.** $2\frac{2}{3}$

13. **Science** A newly hatched ostrich is $\frac{1}{8}$ as tall as an adult ostrich. An adult ostrich is 8 feet tall. How tall is a newly hatched ostrich?

14. **Critical Thinking** Suppose each pizza has 8 slices. You have $1\frac{3}{8}$ pizzas left. How many slices is that?

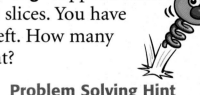

Problem Solving Hint
You can draw a picture to help!

Mixed Review and Test Prep

Add or subtract.

15. $54 + 27$ **16.** $78 - 19$ **17.** $67 + 904$ **18.** $409 - 216$

Algebra Readiness Find each missing number.

19. $3 \times \blacksquare = 24$ **20.** $9 \times \blacksquare = 81$ **21.** $\blacksquare \times 6 = 18$ **22.** $\blacksquare \times 7 = 63$

23. Find the product of 7 and 15.

Ⓐ 735 Ⓑ 105 Ⓒ 75 Ⓓ 95

Exploring Adding and Subtracting Fractions

Problem Solving Connection

- Use Objects/ Act It Out
- Look for a Pattern

Materials

fraction strips

Explore

You can use fraction strips to add and subtract fractions.

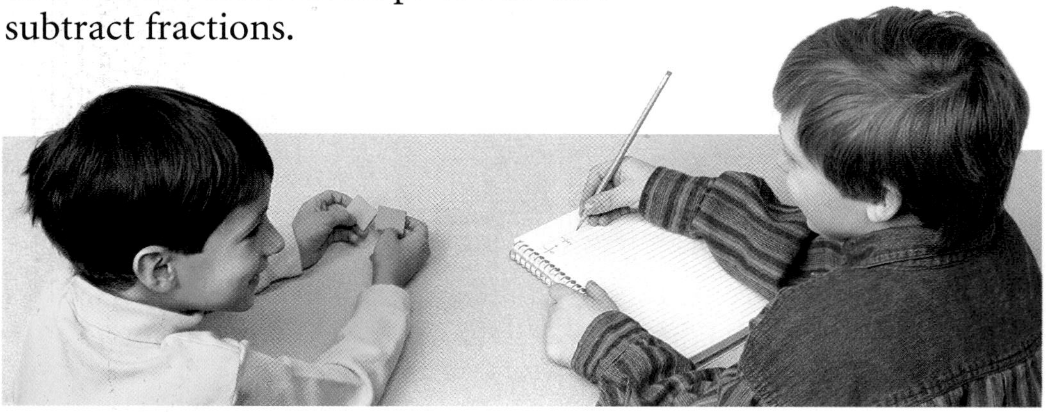

Work Together

1. Add fractions using fraction strips.

a. Put together 1 fifth and 1 fifth. How many fifths do you have?

b. Put together 1 sixth and 1 sixth. How many sixths do you have?

c. Put together 1 fourth and 2 fourths. How many fourths do you have?

Remember

To show 2 fourths, put together a $\frac{1}{4}$ piece and a $\frac{1}{4}$ piece.

2. Subtract fractions using fraction strips.

a. Show 4 fifths. Take away 2 fifths. How many fifths are left?

b. Show 2 thirds. Take away 1 third. How many thirds are left?

c. Show 6 twelfths. Then show 3 twelfths. Compare. What is the difference?

Talk About It

What is $\frac{5}{10}$ take away $\frac{2}{10}$? Tell how you would find out.

Connect

Here is a rule for adding and subtracting fractions with the same denominators.

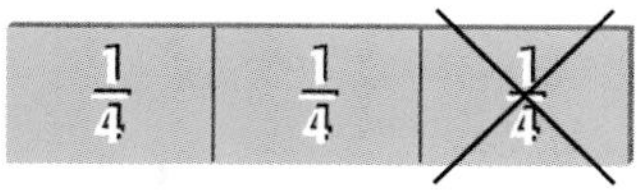

To add fractions with the same denominators:

$\frac{3}{6} + \frac{1}{6} = \frac{4}{6}$ ← add the numerators
← use the same denominator

To subtract fractions with the same denominators:

$\frac{3}{4} - \frac{1}{4} = \frac{2}{4}$ ← subtract the numerators
← use the same denominator

Practice

Find each sum or difference. You may use fraction strips or draw a picture to help.

1. 

$\frac{1}{3} + \frac{1}{3}$

2. 

$\frac{4}{5} - \frac{1}{5}$

3. 

$\frac{4}{8} - \frac{1}{8}$

4. $\frac{7}{12} - \frac{6}{12}$ **5.** $\frac{2}{8} + \frac{5}{8}$ **6.** $\frac{1}{5} + \frac{3}{5}$ **7.** $\frac{3}{10} + \frac{6}{10}$

8. $\frac{7}{8} - \frac{3}{8}$ **9.** $\frac{3}{12} + \frac{4}{12}$ **10.** $\frac{3}{6} - \frac{2}{6}$ **11.** $\frac{4}{8} + \frac{3}{8}$

12. $\frac{7}{8} - \frac{2}{8}$ **13.** $\frac{5}{10} + \frac{3}{10}$ **14.** $\frac{4}{5} - \frac{3}{5}$ **15.** $\frac{6}{9} + \frac{2}{9}$

16. **Using Data** Playing field hockey, Leticia ran from the goal line to the center line. Then she ran back for $\frac{1}{4}$ of the field. Did she end up at the goal line, the center line, or the 25-yard line? Use the Data File on page 409 to help.

17. Suppose you knocked over 7 of 10 bowling pins. What fraction of the bowling pins would still be standing?

18. **Journal** Draw a picture to show what fraction of the cheese will be left after 4 more slices are eaten. Write a subtraction sentence to go with your picture.

Problem Solving

Decision Making: Plan a Team Party

You Will Learn
to use a table to make decisions

Explore

Suppose the soccer team is having a party, and your group is in charge of the food. The team has 12 players. You must decide which kinds of food to serve and how much of each type of food to buy. You can serve all or some of these foods.

Work Together

▶ Understand

1. What do you know?
2. What do you need to decide?

▶ Plan and Solve

3. How many people will you serve?
4. What kinds of food will you choose?
5. How many servings of each food do you need for each player? For example, how many slices of pizza will each player get? How many juice boxes will each player get?

▶ Make a Decision

6. Use a table like this one to help plan the party. Draw a picture to show the amount of food needed.

Food	Servings for 1 Player	Total Servings for 12 Players	Amount of Food Needed	Amount of Food to Order
Submarine sandwich	1 piece	12 pieces	$2\frac{2}{5}$ sandwich 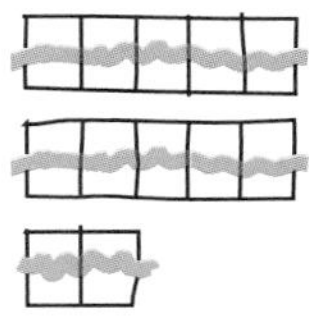	3 submarine sandwiches
Pizza	2 slices	24 slices	3 pizzas 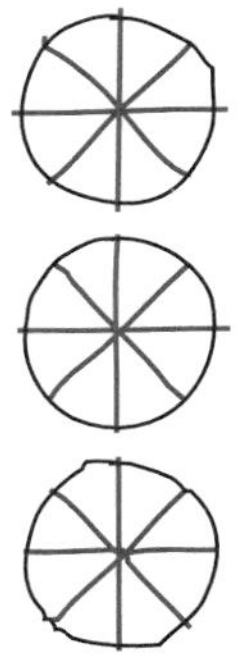	3 pizzas

▶ Present Your Decision

7. Tell the class about your table. Are there some ways you could change your table so that you would not have as much food left over?

SECTION B

Review and Practice

(Lesson 6) Write a fraction that tells what part of the set is circled.

1.

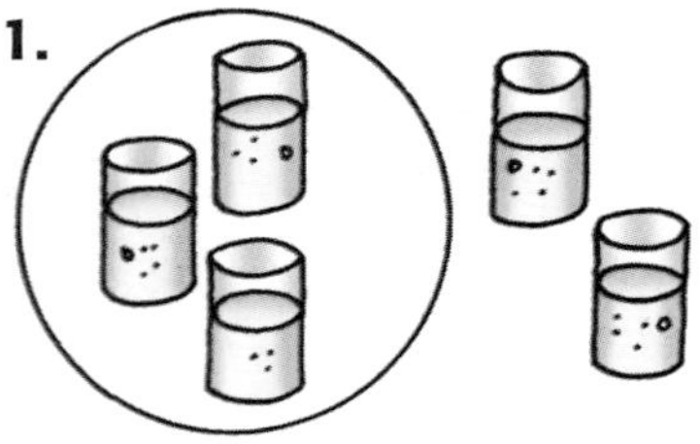

2.

3.

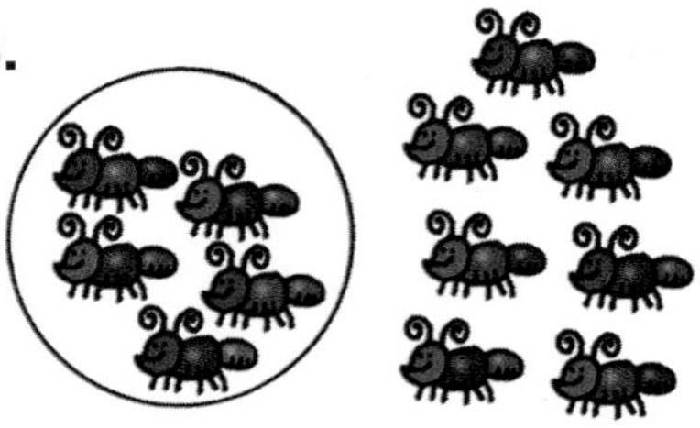

(Lesson 7) Solve. You may use counters or draw a picture to help.

4. Find $\frac{1}{3}$ of 9. **5.** Find $\frac{1}{5}$ of 30. **6.** Find $\frac{1}{2}$ of 18.

7. Find $\frac{1}{6}$ of 24. **8.** Find $\frac{1}{4}$ of 20. **9.** Find $\frac{1}{4}$ of 12.

10. Reasoning Darryl had $12. He spent $\frac{1}{3}$ of the money on baseball cards. How much did Darryl spend on cards?

(Lesson 8) Write a mixed number for each.

11.

12.

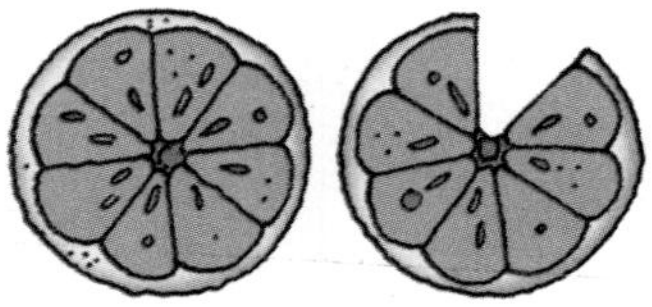

13

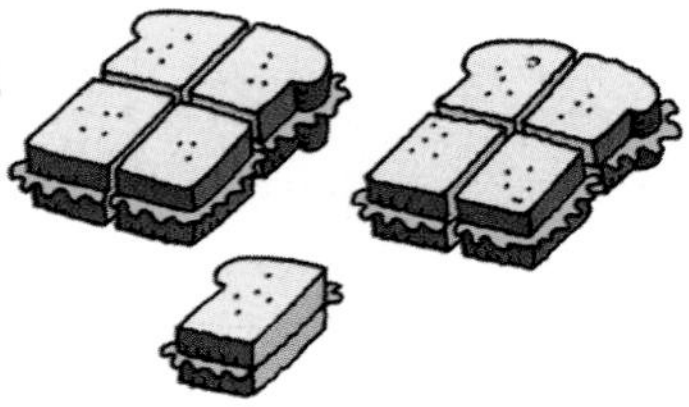

(Lesson 9) Find each sum or difference. You may use fraction strips or draw a picture to help.

14. $\frac{2}{3} - \frac{1}{3}$ **15.** $\frac{7}{10} - \frac{2}{10}$ **16.** $\frac{2}{5} + \frac{2}{5}$

17. $\frac{5}{12} + \frac{2}{12}$ **18.** $\frac{5}{6} - \frac{4}{6}$ **19.** $\frac{9}{9} - \frac{7}{9}$

20. Critical Thinking Suppose you need $\frac{3}{4}$ cup of milk to make pancakes. You only have $\frac{1}{4}$ cup of milk. How much more milk do you need?

21. Journal Draw a picture to show how many strawberries are left after $\frac{1}{3}$ have been eaten.

Skills Checklist

In this section, you have:

- ☑ **Learned About Fractions and Sets**
- ☑ **Explored Finding a Fraction of a Number**
- ☑ **Learned About Mixed Numbers**
- ☑ **Explored Adding and Subtracting Fractions**
- ☑ **Solved Problems by Making Decisions**

CHAPTER 10

SECTION C

Customary Linear Measurement

About how long is a football— a foot, an inch, or a mile?

What we call a soccer ball in the United States is called a football in Europe and Central and South America.

Customary Linear Measurement

Review number lines.

Write the number for each letter on the number line.

1 **a.** **b.** 4 **c.** 6 **d.** **e.** 9 **f.** 11 **g.**

Skills Checklist

In this section, you will:

- ❐ **Explore Length**
- ❐ **Measure to the Nearest $\frac{1}{2}$ Inch and $\frac{1}{4}$ Inch**
- ❐ **Explore Length in Feet and Yards**
- ❐ **Learn About Feet, Yards, and Miles**
- ❐ **Solve Problems by Using Logical Reasoning**

Chapter 10
Lesson
11

Exploring Length

Problem Solving Connection
- Use Objects/ Act It Out
- Look for a Pattern

Materials
- paper clip
- pencil

Vocabulary

inch
a standard unit used to measure length

Explore

You can measure the lengths of objects using nonstandard units. Try measuring objects with a pencil and a paper clip.

Work Together

Choose five items in your classroom. Estimate each length, then measure each with a pencil and paper clip. Copy and complete the table to record your measurements.

	Item	Length Using a Paper Clip	Length Using a Pencil
1.			
2.			
3.			
4.			
5.			

Math Tip
Make sure you start at one end of the item you are measuring.

Talk About It

6. Look at each measurement. Was the number of pencils in each measurement more or less than the number of paper clips?

7. Suppose you used your arm instead of a paper clip or pencil to measure. Would the number of arms be more or less than the number of pencils? Explain.

8. When a length was a little more or less than a pencil, what did you do?

Connect

An **inch** is a standard unit of measure.
You can measure length using inches.

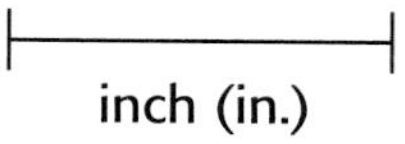

Line up the object with the left end of the ruler.

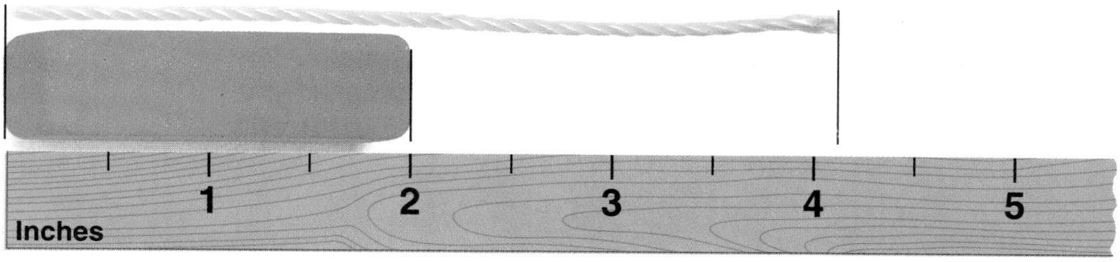

The eraser is 2 inches long to the nearest inch.

The string is 4 inches long to the nearest inch.

Practice

Estimate each length. Then measure to the nearest inch.

1. 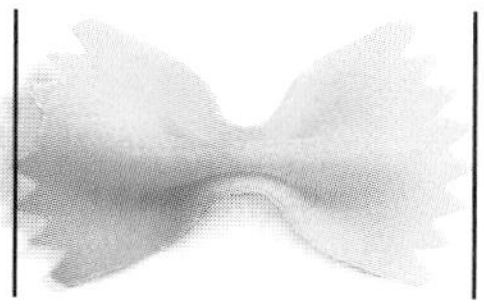

2. 

3. 

4. 

5. **Reasoning** Suppose you need at least 4 inches of ribbon for a craft project. Is this enough ribbon?

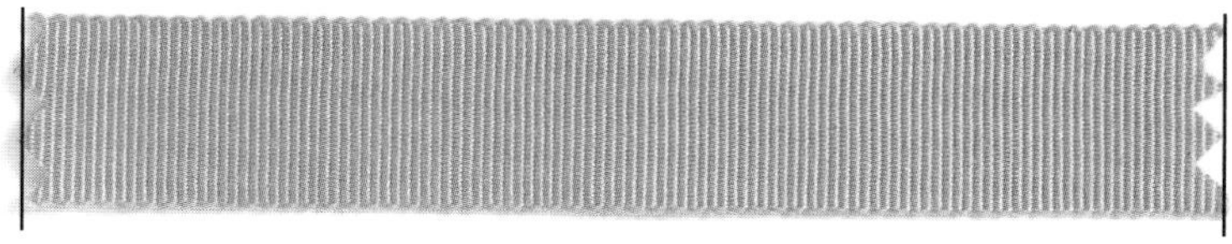

6. Measure a sheet of paper, your shoe, and your desk. Write each measurement in order from greatest to least.

7. Use a ruler. Draw a line to show each length.

a. 3 inches **b.** 4 inches **c.** 1 inch **d.** 2 inches

8. **Collecting Data** Find something in class or at home that is about an inch. Measure to check your estimate.

9. **Journal** Choose something to measure. Explain how to measure the item to the nearest inch using a ruler.

Chapter 10
Lesson
12

Measuring to the Nearest $\frac{1}{2}$ Inch and $\frac{1}{4}$ Inch

You Will Learn
how to measure to the nearest $\frac{1}{2}$ and $\frac{1}{4}$ inch

Learn

Sometimes objects are a little more or less than an inch. You can find a measurement that is closer to the actual length by measuring to the nearest $\frac{1}{2}$ or $\frac{1}{4}$ inch.

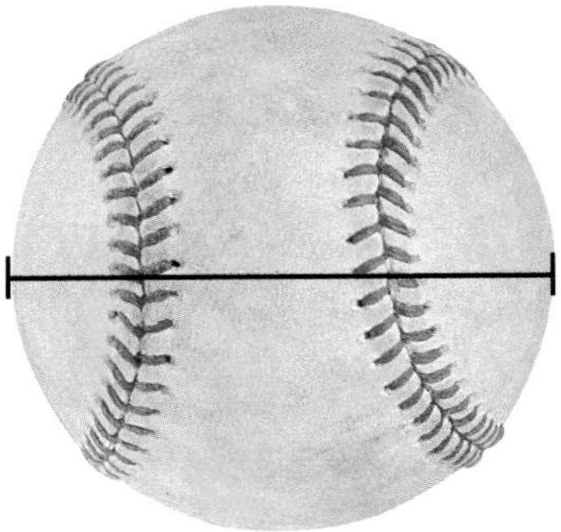

Example

How long is the peanut to the nearest $\frac{1}{2}$ inch?

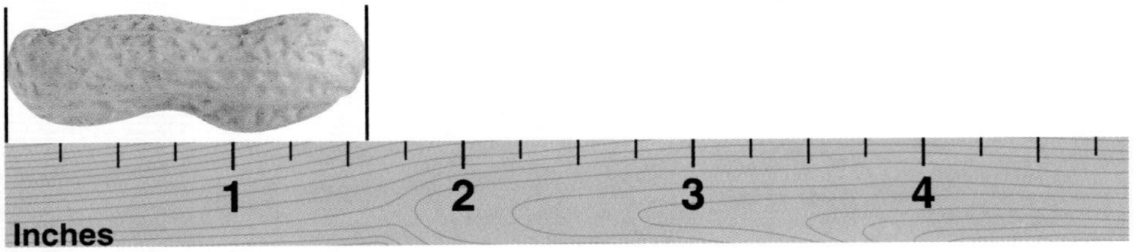

The peanut is $1\frac{1}{2}$ inches long.

How long is the ticket stub to the nearest $\frac{1}{4}$ inch?

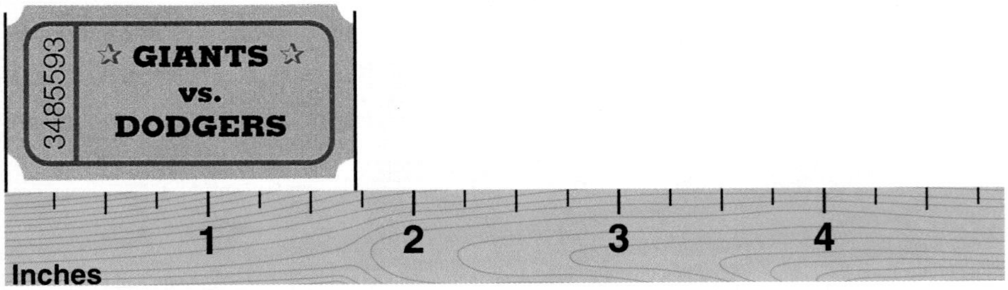

The ticket stub is $1\frac{3}{4}$ inches long.

Math Tip
When you see $1\frac{1}{2}$ inches, read "one and one half inches."

Talk About It

1. How many $\frac{1}{2}$ inches are in one inch? How many $\frac{1}{4}$ inches are in one inch? Explain.

2. Find the measurement of the baseball to the nearest $\frac{1}{4}$ inch. Would you say the baseball is about 2 inches wide or 3 inches wide? Explain.

Check

Measure the length of each object to the nearest $\frac{1}{2}$ inch.

1. 

2. 

Measure the length of each object to the nearest $\frac{1}{4}$ inch.

3. 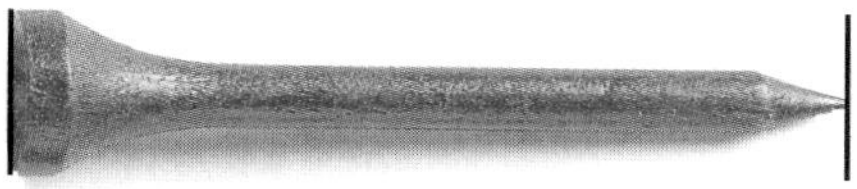

4. 

5. **Reasoning** To buy the smallest beads, should Alice buy $\frac{1}{2}$-inch, $\frac{1}{4}$-inch, or $\frac{3}{4}$-inch beads?

Practice

Skills and Reasoning

Measure the length of each object to the nearest $\frac{1}{2}$ inch.

6. 

7. 

Measure the length of each object to the nearest $\frac{1}{4}$ inch.

8. 

9. 

10. You need to measure an ant for a science project. Does it make more sense to measure to the nearest $\frac{1}{2}$ inch or $\frac{1}{4}$ inch?

Problem Solving and Applications

11. **Reasoning** Measure the perimeter of the square to the nearest inch.

12. **Collecting Data** Find objects in the room that you estimate are about 6 inches long. Measure the objects to check your estimates.

Mixed Review and Test Prep

Write the fraction of each figure that is shaded.

13. 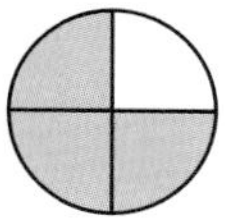

14. 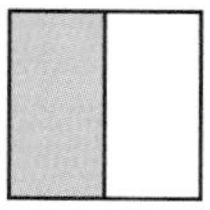

15. 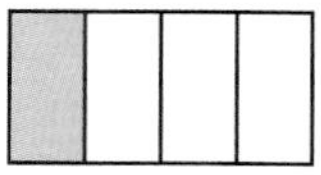

16. Find 9×54.

Ⓐ 486 Ⓑ 456 Ⓒ 6 Ⓓ not here

Chapter 10
Lesson
13

Exploring Length in Feet and Inches

Problem Solving Connection
Use Objects

Materials
inch ruler

Vocabulary
foot
unit of measure equal to 12 inches

Explore

You can measure length in **feet** as well as inches.

12 inches = 1 foot (ft)

Work Together

1. Use feet and inches to measure length.
   a. Estimate the length of your desk in feet and inches. Then record the length in a table.
   b. Use a ruler to measure the length of your desk in feet and inches. Record your measurement. Was your estimate close to the actual measurement?

Math Tip
Look at your ruler before you estimate, so you have an idea of the distance of a foot.

Item	Estimated Length	Measured Length

2. Choose other objects in the room that look longer than 1 foot. Fill in the table to record your estimates and measurements.

Talk About It

Describe how you used the ruler to measure feet.

Connect

You can multiply to write measurements in feet as measurements in inches.

How many inches are in 3 feet?

1 foot = 12 inches

So, 3 feet = 3×12 inches

$3 \times 12 = 36$

3 feet = 36 inches

There are 36 inches in 3 feet.

How many inches are in 2 feet, 4 inches?

1 foot = 12 inches

So, 2 feet = 2×12 inches

$2 \times 12 = 24$

2 feet = 24 inches

24 inches + 4 inches = 28 inches

2 feet 4 inches = 28 inches

There are 28 inches in 2 feet, 4 inches.

Practice

Write each measurement in inches.

1. 6 feet **2.** 2 feet **3.** 5 feet

4. 3 feet, 1 inch **5.** 4 feet, 2 inches **6.** 7 feet, 6 inches

7. Shridhar Chillal of India has the longest fingernails in the world. His thumbnail is 4 feet, 5 inches long! How long is that in inches?

8. **Estimation** Write three items in the room that are shorter than 1 foot. Write three items that are longer than 3 feet.

9. **Reasoning** Does it make more sense to measure the length of your hand in feet or inches? Explain.

Using Data Use the Data File on page 409 to help solve **10** and **11.**

10. A refrigerator is 67 inches tall. Did Javier Sotomayor jump higher than a refrigerator when he set the high jump record? Explain.

11. Was the length of Mike Powell's record jump in 1991 longer than the length of six 5-foot bikes standing end to end? Explain.

12. **Journal** Measure the length of an object that is longer than 1 foot. Write the measurement in feet and inches. Then write the measurement in inches.

Javier Sotomayor of Cuba at the 1996 Olympic Games in Atlanta, Georgia

Feet, Yards, and Miles

You Will Learn
how to estimate and compare measurement in inches, feet, yards, and miles

Vocabulary

yard
unit of measure equal to 36 inches or 3 feet

mile
unit of measure equal to 5,280 feet or 1,760 yards

Learn

Robert won first place at his school's Field Day for running the 50-yard dash.

How long is a yard?

Robert from Martinsburg, West Virginia, likes science, math, in-line skating, and football.

A football is about 1 foot long.

A baseball bat is about 1 **yard** long.

Most people can walk 1 **mile** in about 25 minutes.

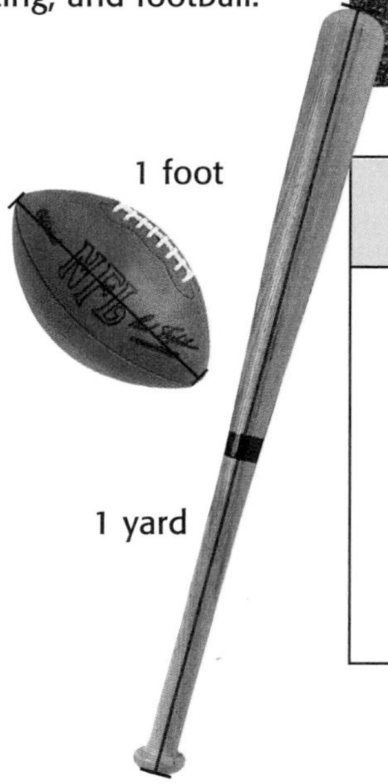

Customary Units of Length
12 inches = 1 foot (ft)
3 feet = 1 yard (yd)
36 inches = 1 yard
5,280 feet = 1 mile (mi)
1,760 yards = 1 mile

Did You Know?
Noureddine Morceli of Algeria holds the world record for running a mile in 3 minutes, 44 seconds.

Talk About It

1. What is another real-world object that is about a foot? What is another object that is about a yard?
2. Would it make more sense to measure the length of the classroom in yards or miles? Explain.

Check

Compare. Write <, >, or =.

1. 12 in. ● 1 ft 2. 4 feet ● 1 yard 3. 1,000 ft ● 1 mi
4. **Reasoning** Why do you think people's heights are usually given in feet and inches instead of yards?

Practice

Skills and Reasoning

Compare. Write <, >, or =.

5. 3 yards ● 1 foot **6.** 5,280 ft ● 1 mi **7.** 2 yd ● 7 ft

8. 3 feet ● 1 yard **9.** 1 mile ● 5 yards **10.** 4 yd ● 144 in.

Choose an estimate for each.

11. height of a wall	**a.** 1 mile
12. length of your math book	**b.** 1 foot
13. distance driven in the car	**c.** 3 yards
14. height of a table	**d.** 1 yard

15. Would it make sense to measure your math book in yards? Explain.

16. Allan says, "If I lay 3 footballs end to end, they would measure about a yard." Do you agree or disagree? Explain.

Problem Solving and Applications

17. Measurement Find the perimeter in yards.

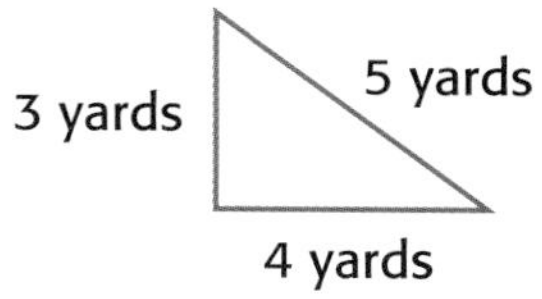

18. Science A red kangaroo can jump 40 feet. Is this more or less than 14 yards?

19. Science A tiger can grow to be 3 yards long. How long is that in inches?

20. Health At his school's Health Fair, Robert showed how to exercise to improve the heart. He did 5 sets of 22 jumping jacks. How many jumping jacks is that?

Mixed Review and Test Prep

Multiply or divide.

21. 9×6 **22.** 5×4 **23.** $8\overline{)56}$ **24.** $6\overline{)48}$ **25.** $7\overline{)49}$

26. Patterns Write the next number in the pattern: 45, 36, 27, ■.

Ⓐ 15 Ⓑ 16 Ⓒ 14 Ⓓ 18

Chapter 10 Lesson 15

Problem Solving

Analyze Strategies: Use Logical Reasoning

You Will Learn

how to use logical reasoning to solve problems

Learn

Salim, Mia, Lorenzo, and Odetta marked their heights but forgot to write their names next to each mark. Odetta knows she is 50 inches tall. Mia is the tallest. Lorenzo is taller than Salim. How tall is each person?

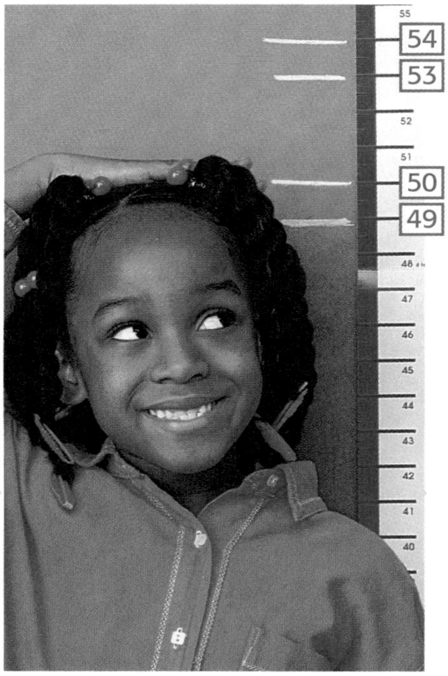

Work Together

▶ Understand

What do you know?

What do you need to find out?

▶ Plan

How will you find out? You can use logical reasoning to help you find the information that is missing.

▶ Solve

Make a table to record what you know. Use the clues to help complete the table.

	49 in.	50 in.	53 in.	54 in.
Mia	No	No	No	Yes
Salim	Yes	No	No	No
Odetta	No	Yes	No	No
Lorenzo	No	No	Yes	No

So, Salim is 49 inches tall, Odetta is 50 inches tall, Lorenzo is 53 inches tall, and Mia is 54 inches tall.

▶ Look Back

How can you check your answer?

Talk About It

How could you use reasoning to decide how tall each person is?

Check

Problem Solving
Understand
Plan
Solve
Look Back

Use logical reasoning to solve.

1. Help Rosa figure out which swim team finished in first, second, third, and fourth places. The Penguins finished in second place. The Dolphins were the last to finish. The Sharks beat the Waves.

	First	Second	Third	Fourth
Penguins				
Dolphins				
Waves				
Sharks				

2. Dolores, Mira, Chris, and Isaac are brothers and sisters. Mira is the youngest. Chris is 11 years old. Isaac is younger than Dolores. If each person is either 9, 10, 11, or 12 years old, how old is each person?

Problem Solving Practice

Use any strategy to solve.

3. Geometry Readiness I have 4 corners. I only have 1 right angle. Which figure am I?

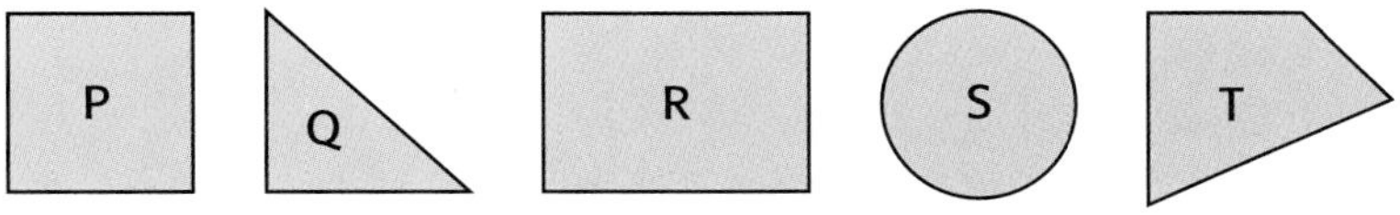

4. Satoshi, Erica, Joshua, and Lani are planning a party. Each person will take either pizza, lemonade, cookies, or plates. Erica wants to take cookies. Lani wants to take lemonade. Joshua doesn't want to take pizza. Help decide what each person should take.

5. Copy and complete the grid. Use the digits 1, 2, 3, and 4 to fill in the grid so that each diagonal has a sum of 10. Use each digit only once.

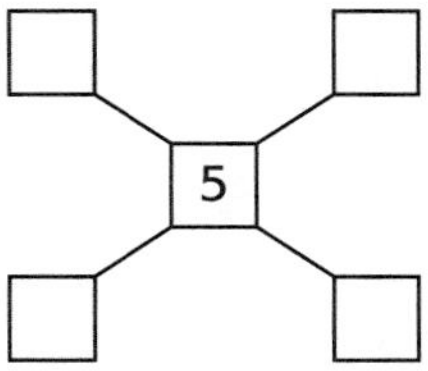

6. Money Roger has 4 coins. The total value of the coins is 40¢. He doesn't have any dimes. What coins does Roger have?

Problem Solving Strategies

- Use Objects/Act It Out
- Draw a Picture
- Look for a Pattern
- Guess and Check
- Use Logical Reasoning
- Make an Organized List
- Make a Table
- Solve a Simpler Problem
- Work Backward

Choose a Tool

SECTION C
Review and Practice

Vocabulary Match each with its example.

1. 1 inch	**a.** the distance you can walk in about 25 minutes
2. 1 foot	**b.** about the width of a bottle cap
3. 1 yard	**c.** about the height of a doorknob
4. 1 mile	**d.** about the length of a football

(Lesson 11) Estimate each length. Then measure to the nearest inch.

5. 

6. 

(Lesson 12) Measure each object to the nearest $\frac{1}{2}$ inch.

7. 

8. 

(Lesson 12) Measure each object to the nearest $\frac{1}{4}$ inch.

9. 

10. 

(Lesson 13) Write each measurement in inches.

11. 4 feet **12.** 1 foot, 2 inches **13.** 4 feet, 6 inches

(Lesson 14) Compare. Write <, >, or =.

14. 3 feet ● 24 inches **15.** 1 yd ● 36 in. **16.** 3 yd ● 9 ft

(Lesson 15) Use any strategy to solve.

17. **Logic** Stacy, Marc, Jordan, and Letisha each buy a red, blue, green, or yellow T-shirt. Letisha buys a blue T-shirt. Jordan does not buy a red or yellow T-shirt. Stacy does not buy a red or a green T-shirt. If they each buy a different color T-shirt, which color T-shirt did each person buy?

18. **Journal** Name something that you would measure in inches, feet, and yards.

Skills Checklist

In this section, you have:

- ☑ Explored Length
- ☑ Measured to the Nearest $\frac{1}{2}$ Inch and $\frac{1}{4}$ Inch
- ☑ Explored Length in Feet and Yards
- ☑ Learned About Feet, Yards, and Miles
- ☑ Solved Problems by Using Logical Reasoning

YOUR CHOICE

Choose at least one. Use what you have learned in this chapter.

1 Fraction Family

At Home Interview a friend or family member about how he or she uses fractions in everyday life. Make a poster and present your example to the class.

2 Shell Out

Philip came back from vacation with 12 seashells for his friends. Using this information, write a question for each answer.

a. $\frac{1}{2}$

b. $\frac{4}{12}$

c. 9

3 Design an Olympic Flag

Design a striped flag. Draw a rectangle on grid paper. Then draw 8 equal sized stripes. Color the flag $\frac{2}{8}$ blue, $\frac{1}{2}$ red, and $\frac{2}{8}$ yellow.

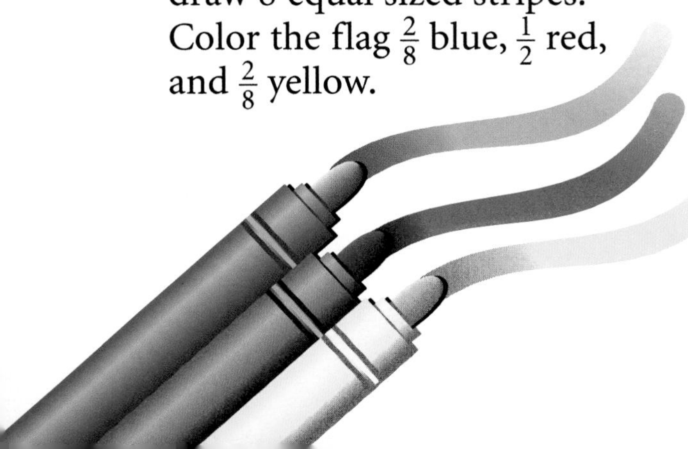

4 Walk the Block

Write a story about going from Germaine's house to the grocery store. Write whether you walked more or less than a mile.

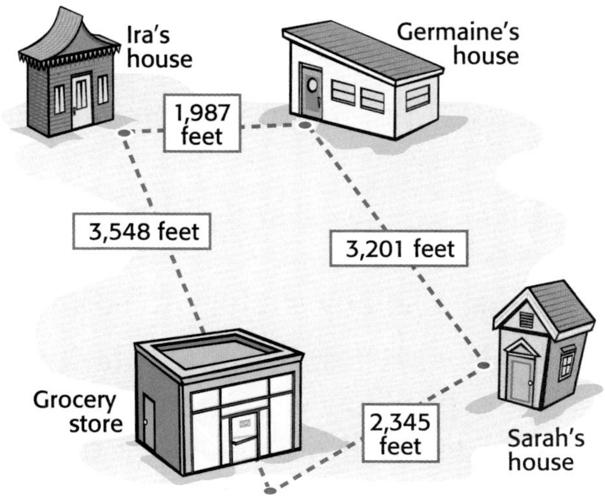

CHAPTER 10
Review/Test

(Lesson 2) Write the fraction of the figure that is orange.

1.

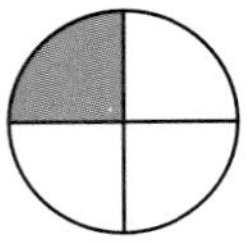

(Lesson 3) Write if the fractions are equivalent or not equivalent.

2.

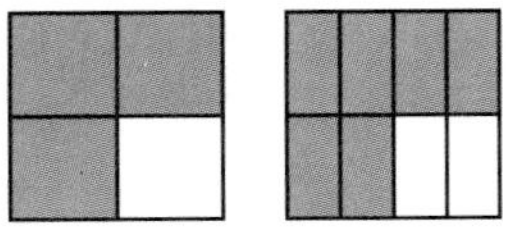

(Lesson 4) Compare. Write <, >, or =.

3.

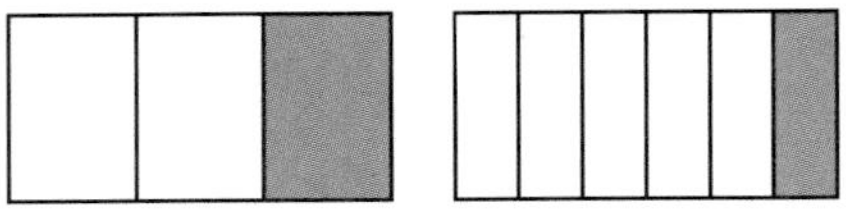

$\frac{1}{3} \bigcirc \frac{1}{6}$

(Lesson 5) Estimate the shaded amount.

4.

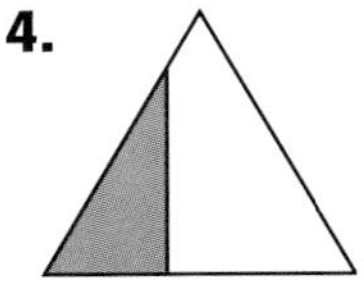

(Lesson 6) Write a fraction to show what part of the set is circled.

5.

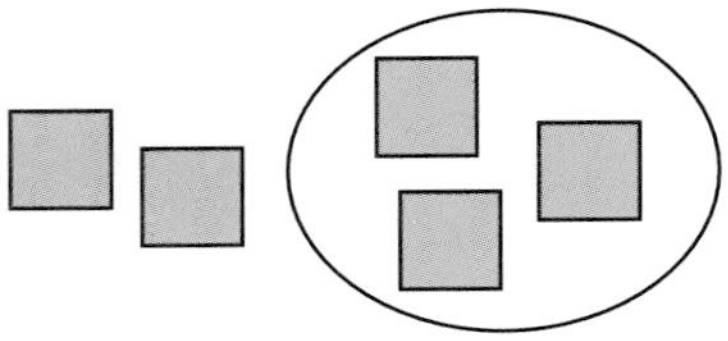

(Lesson 7) Solve. You may draw a picture to help.

6. Find $\frac{1}{4}$ of 12.

(Lesson 8) Write a mixed number for the picture.

7.

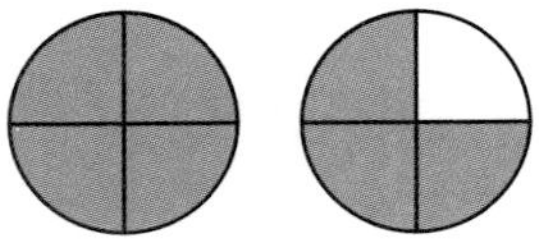

(Lesson 9) Find each sum.

8. $\frac{2}{5} + \frac{1}{5}$ **9.** $\frac{1}{3} + \frac{1}{3}$

(Lesson 11) Measure to the nearest inch.

10.

(Lesson 12) Measure to the nearest $\frac{1}{2}$ inch.

11.

(Lesson 13) Write the measurement in inches.

12. 4 feet **13.** 1 foot, 5 inches

(Lesson 14) Compare. Write <, >, or =.

14. 2 yards $\bigcirc$ 2 feet

(Lesson 15) Use any strategy to solve.

15. Logic Charles, Belinda, Rita, and Darryl will each work at the school car wash on different days. Charles will work on Tuesday. Belinda will work the day after Rita. If each person works on either Monday, Tuesday, Wednesday, or Thursday, on which day does each person work?

CHAPTER 10

Performance Assessment

You can use fractions to describe designs. This design is divided into 10 equal parts. $\frac{1}{10}$ is green, $\frac{6}{10}$ are yellow, and $\frac{3}{10}$ are red.

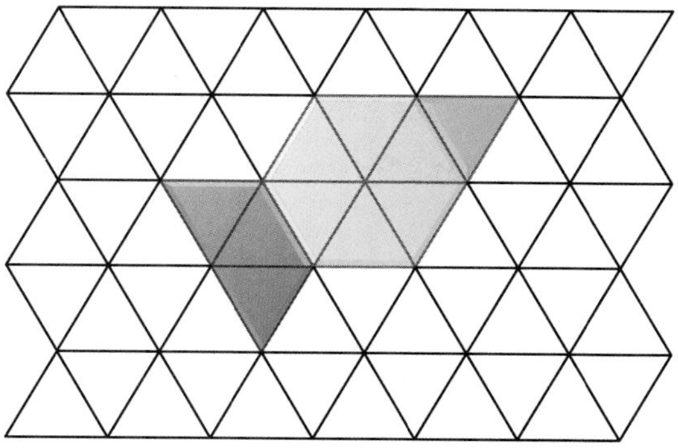

1. **Decision Making** Use triangle paper and any of these Power Polygon pieces to create your own designs. Make designs that show eighths, tenths, and twelfths.

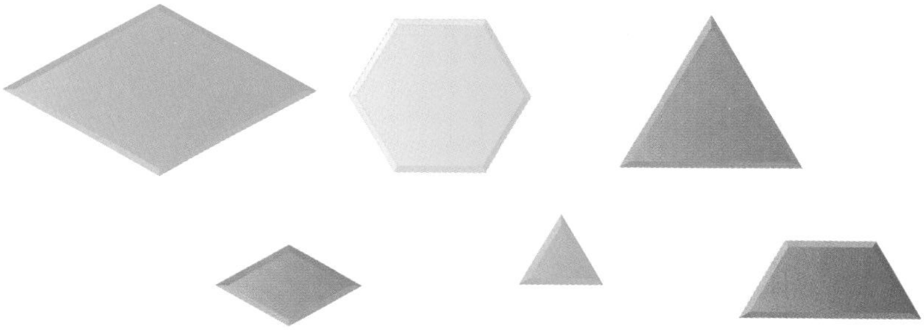

2. **Recording Data** Trace and color your designs. Then use fractions to describe each design.

3. **Explain Your Thinking** How did you know what fraction of your design was red, green, blue, or yellow?

4. **Critical Thinking** Make a design with Power Polygon pieces that is $\frac{4}{8}$ blue, $\frac{3}{8}$ red, and $\frac{1}{8}$ green.

Math Magazine

Measuring with Hands and Feet **Just as you can use paper clips or pencils to measure objects, people long ago used everyday objects to measure length. Do you recognize any of these measurement units?**

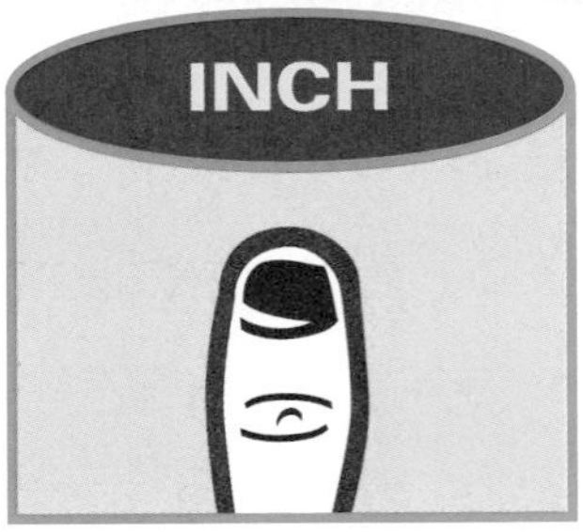

The width of the thumb

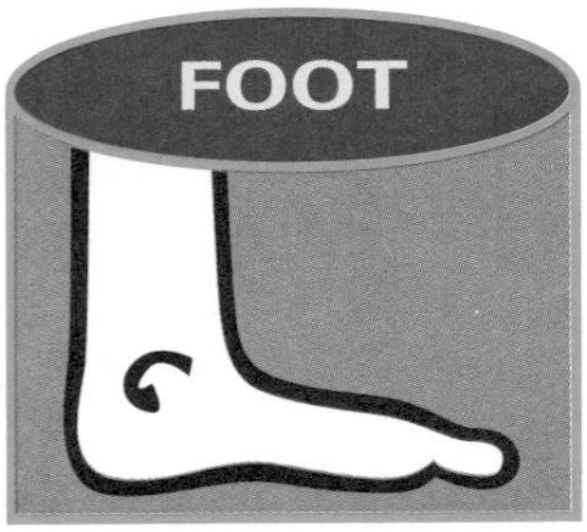

The length of a foot

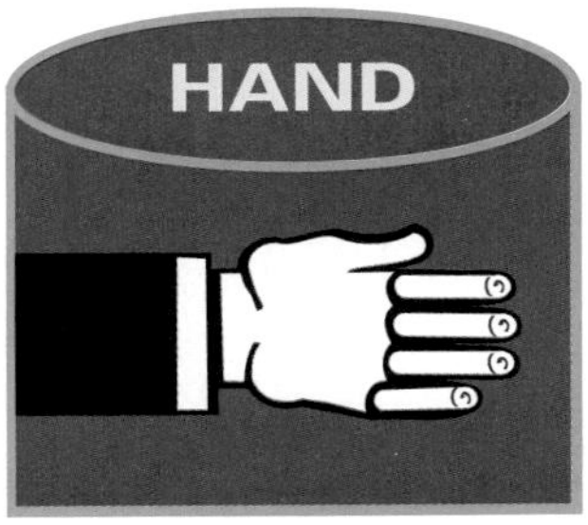

The width of a hand

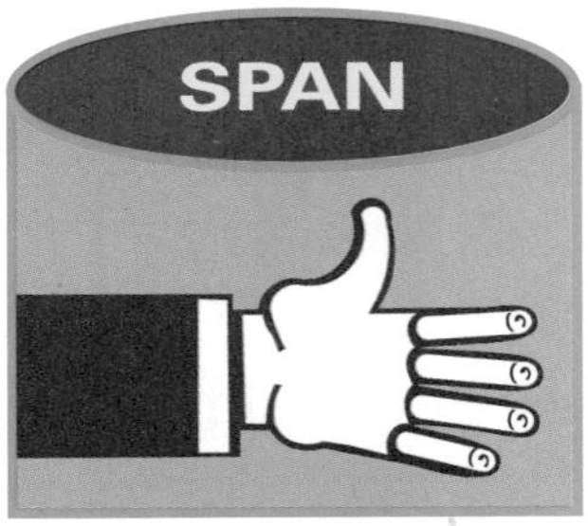

The distance between the thumb and pinkie

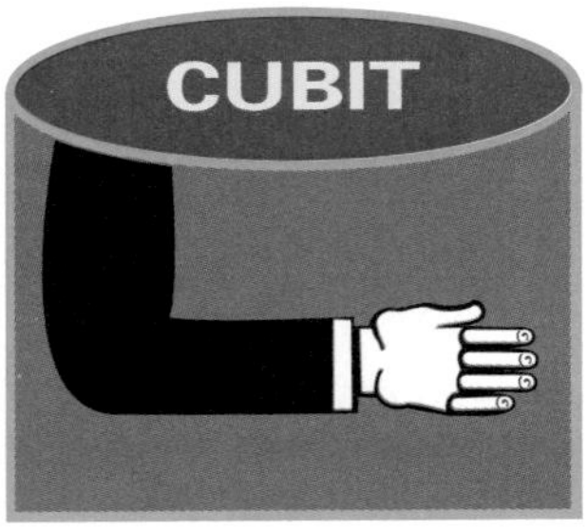

The distance between the elbow and the tip of the middle finger

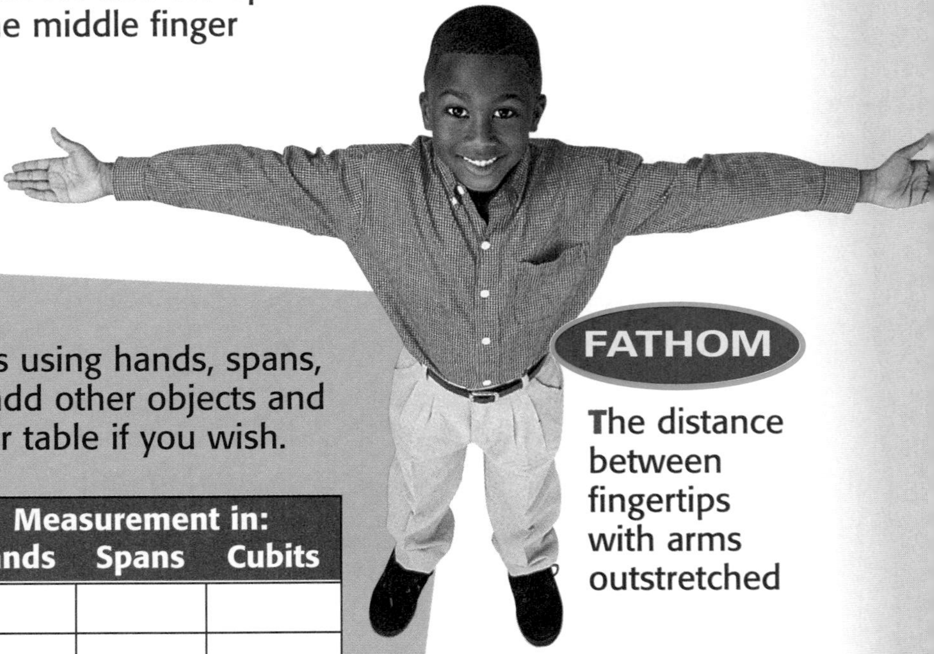

The distance between fingertips with arms outstretched

Try These!

Measure these objects using hands, spans, and cubits. You may add other objects and measurements to your table if you wish.

	Object Measured	Measurement in:		
		Hands	Spans	Cubits
1.	Desk			
2.	Chair			
3.	Book			

CHAPTERS 1–10

Cumulative Review

Test Prep Strategy: Make Smart Choices

Use Logical Reasoning.

Kaylie, Roger, and Jon shared a pizza with 8 slices. Kaylie ate $\frac{3}{8}$ of the pizza. Roger ate the same amount as Kaylie. Jon ate the rest of the pizza. What fraction of the pizza did Jon eat?

Ⓐ $\frac{8}{8}$ Ⓑ $\frac{1}{2}$ Ⓒ $\frac{3}{5}$ Ⓓ $\frac{2}{8}$

Add to find the total part of the pizza Kaylie and Roger ate.

$\frac{3}{8} + \frac{3}{8} = \frac{6}{8}$

To find the fraction of the pizza Jon ate, subtract.

$\frac{8}{8} - \frac{6}{8} = \frac{2}{8}$

So, the correct answer is Ⓓ.

Write the letter of the correct answer. Use logical reasoning or any strategy to help.

1. Sean found 6 shells at the beach. He gave $\frac{1}{2}$ of the shells to his sister. How many shells did Sean give?

Ⓐ 12 Ⓑ 6 Ⓒ 3 Ⓓ 2

2. Twelve inches is the same as ____.

Ⓐ 1 yard Ⓑ 2 feet Ⓒ 1 mile Ⓓ 1 foot

3. I am an even number between 15 and 25. The sum of my digits is 9. What number am I?

Ⓐ 16 Ⓑ 9 Ⓒ 36 Ⓓ 18

4. Jared bought a book for $6.49. How much change should he get from $10.00?

Ⓐ $3.49 Ⓑ $3.51 Ⓒ $4.51 Ⓓ not here

5. Delaware became a state in 1787. Hawaii became a state 172 years later. What year did Hawaii become a state?

Ⓐ 1859 Ⓑ 1872 Ⓒ 1959 Ⓓ 1939

6. What is the perimeter of the figure?

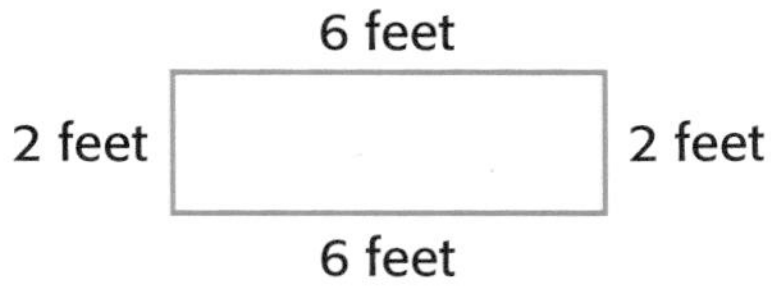

Ⓐ 36 inches Ⓑ 16 feet

Ⓒ 12 square feet Ⓓ 8 feet

7. Elliot started playing kickball at 3:00 P.M. The game ended at 5:15 P.M. How long did the game last?

Ⓐ 2 hours 15 minutes Ⓑ 1 hour 45 minutes

Ⓒ 2 hours 45 minutes Ⓓ 3 hours 45 minutes

Test Prep Strategies

- Read Carefully
- Follow Directions
- Make Smart Choices
- Eliminate Choices
- Work Backward from an Answer

DATA FILE

Chapter 11

Decimals and Metric Linear Measurement

On the Fast Track

SECTION A

Understanding Decimals

455

Whoosh! In speed skating, winners might be only a few hundredths of a second faster than their opponents. Which athlete was fastest in the 500-Meter Women's Speed Skating event?

World Middle School Olympics
Page 455

Results from the 1994 Winter Olympics

500-Meter Women's Speed Skating	
Athlete	**Time (seconds)**
Susan Auch	39.61
Bonnie Blair	39.25
Franziska Schenk	39.70

500-Meter Men's Speed Skating	
Athlete	**Time (seconds)**
Manabu Horii	36.53
Sergej Klevtsjenja	36.39
Aleksandr Golubev	36.33

SECTION B

Metric Linear Measurement

Some animals leap, some run, and others just waddle along! This table shows the length of strides of some animals. Which animal has the shortest stride?

Stride Lengths of Animals	
Animal	**Length of Stride**
Badger	30 cm
Beaver	15 cm
Porcupine	16 cm
Black bear	50 cm
Skunk	20 cm
Grizzly bear	46 cm
Raccoon	16 cm
Coyote	40 cm
Cougar	50 cm

Surfing the World Wide Web!

Roller coasters, airplanes, spaceships, and downhill skiers all have something in common: they're fast! Visit the website at **www.mathsurf.com/3/ch11** to find information on some record breaking speeds. You're bound to find some fast-inating facts!

469

Speedy elevators
Page 469

TEAM PROJECT

Treasure Hunt

Materials
centimeter grid paper, scissors

Have you ever tried to give someone directions for getting from one place to another? Send your classmates on a treasure hunt to see if they can find an object in the classroom.

Make a Plan

- What object will you choose?
- Where will your classmates start the treasure hunt? What path will they take to find the object?

Carry It Out

1. Make a meter strip to help you measure distances.

   a. Cut out 10 strips of centimeter grid paper that are each 10 centimeters long. Label the end of each strip 10, 20, 30, 40, and so on until you reach 100.

   b. Tape the strips together in order from 10 to 100.

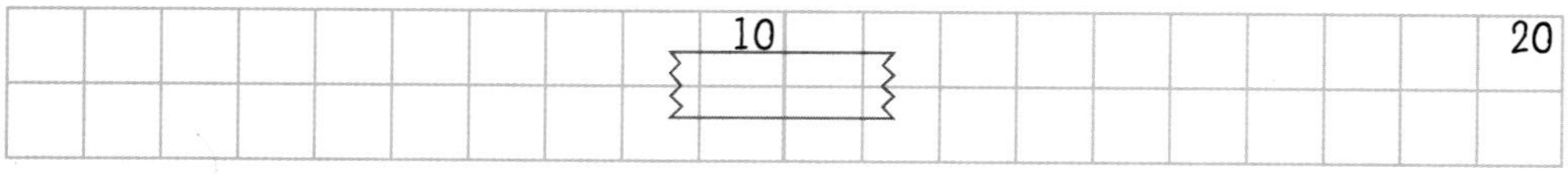

10
20

2. Write directions to get to the object. Measure distances and include them in your directions.
3. Trade directions with your classmates and go on a treasure hunt! Don't forget to bring your meter strip with you.

Talk About It

- Did your classmates find the object?
- How could you improve your directions?

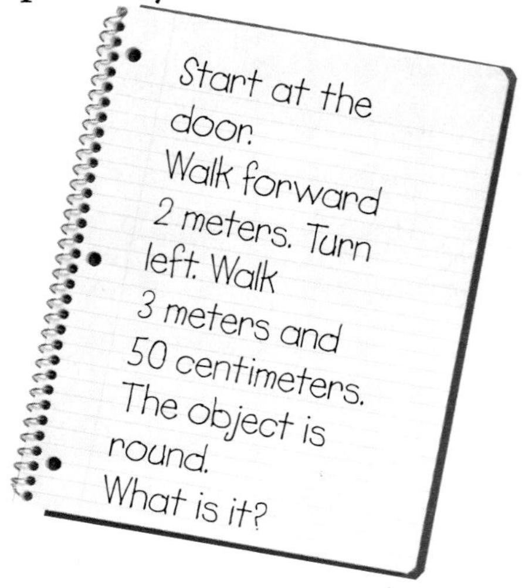

Start at the door.
Walk forward 2 meters. Turn left. Walk 3 meters and 50 centimeters.
The object is round.
What is it?

Present the Project

- Put your treasure hunt directions on a bulletin board for other classmates to try.

CHAPTER 11

SECTION

A Understanding Decimals

Students from all over the world compete at the World Middle School Olympics and post their results on the World Wide Web. How can you tell which student wins a race?

Decimals

Review place value. Copy and complete.

1. 1 ten = ▢ ones
2. 1 hundred = ▢ ones
3. 1 hundred = ▢ tens

Skills Checklist

In this section, you will:

- ❒ Explore Tenths
- ❒ Learn About Hundredths
- ❒ Explore Adding and Subtracting Decimals
- ❒ Connect Decimals and Money
- ❒ Solve Problems by Making Decisions

Exploring Tenths

Problem Solving Connection
- Use Objects/ Act It Out
- Draw a Picture

Materials
tenths grids

Vocabulary

tenth
one of 10 equal parts of a whole

decimal
a number that uses place value and a decimal point to show tenths, hundredths, and so on

decimal point
a symbol used to separate ones from tenths in decimals

Remember
$\frac{10}{10} = 1$
10 tenths = 1 whole

Explore

You can show **tenths** using grids.

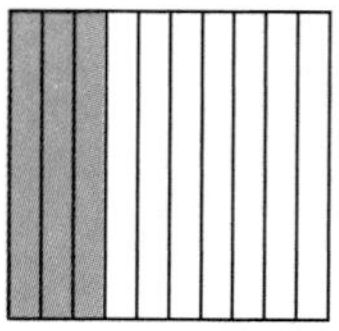

$\frac{3}{10}$

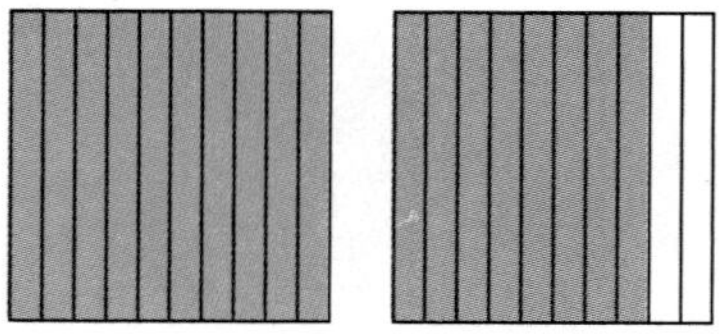

$1\frac{8}{10}$

Work Together

1. Use tenths grids to show each fraction or mixed number.
   a. $\frac{7}{10}$ **b.** $\frac{1}{10}$ **c.** $1\frac{5}{10}$ **d.** $2\frac{3}{10}$
2. Think of 3 other fractions or mixed numbers using tenths. Show each with tenths grids.
3. Arrange all of the grids you made in order from least to greatest. List the fractions and mixed numbers in order.

Talk About It

4. How did you show 1 whole with a tenths grid?
5. Explain how you arranged the grids in order from least to greatest.

Connect

Any number in tenths can be written as a fraction or as a **decimal**.

Tenths Grid	Fraction or Mixed Number	Decimal	Word Name
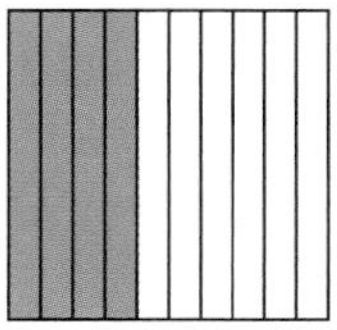	$\frac{4}{10}$	0.4 (**decimal point**)	four tenths
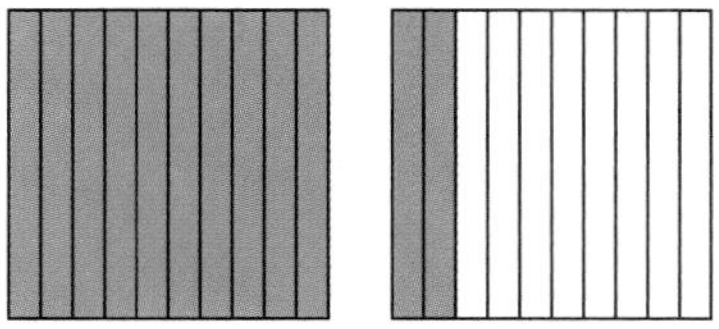	$1\frac{2}{10}$	1.2	one and two tenths

Practice

Write the fraction and the decimal to name each shaded part.

1. 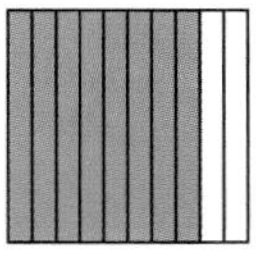

2. 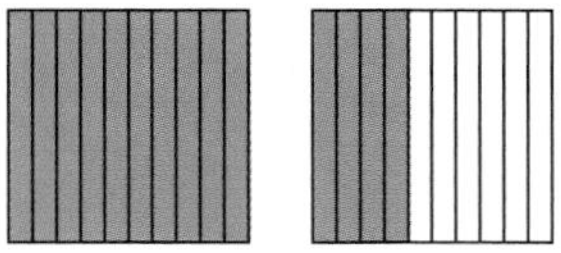

3. 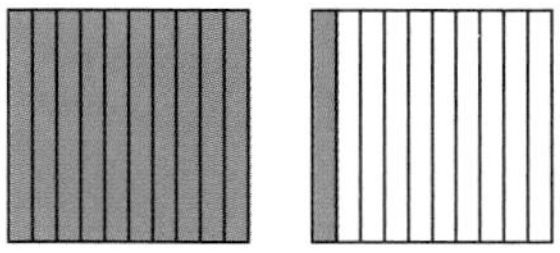

4. 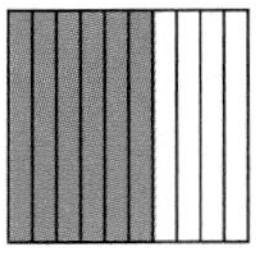

Write each as a decimal.

5. seven tenths **6.** one and five tenths **7.** two and eight tenths

8. $\frac{5}{10}$ **9.** $1\frac{3}{10}$ **10.** $2\frac{4}{10}$ **11.** $1\frac{6}{10}$ **12.** $\frac{9}{10}$

13. Write each part of the circle as a fraction and as a decimal.

		Fraction	Decimal
a.	**Red**		
b.	**Blue**		
c.	**Green**		

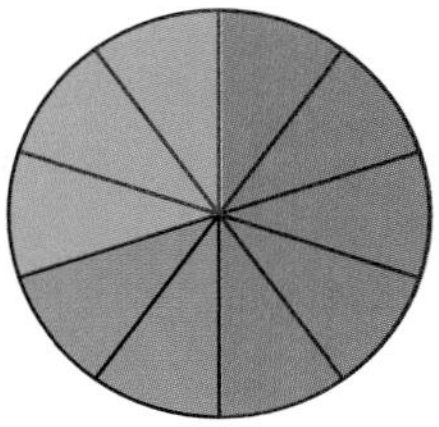

14. Science A rabbit's ears can be as long as 6.9 centimeters. Does it make sense to say a rabbit's ears can be a little less than 7 centimeters long? Explain.

15. Journal Think of a number in tenths. Draw a picture to show that number. Then write the number as a fraction and as a decimal.

Chapter 11
Lesson
2

Hundredths

You Will Learn
to name and write hundredths as decimals

Vocabulary
hundredth
one of 100 equal parts of a whole

Math Tip

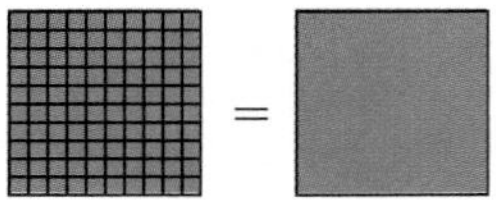

$\frac{100}{100} = 1$

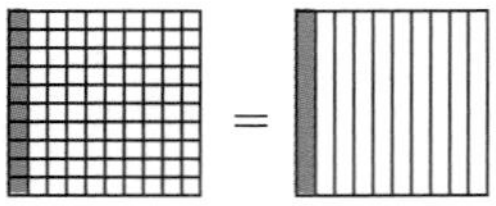

$\frac{10}{100} = \frac{1}{10}$

Learn

The World Middle School Olympics is for school-age athletes. In 1996, Kris beat her schoolmate, Tracy, in a race. Kris ran $\frac{69}{100}$ of a second faster than Tracy.

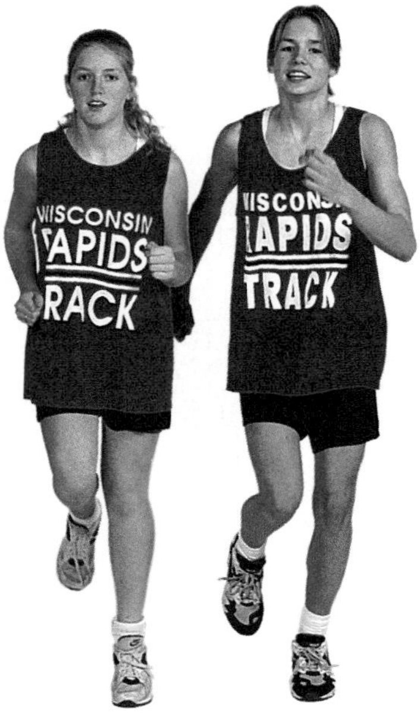

Tracy and Kris from Wisconsin Rapids, Wisconsin, competed in the 1996 World Middle School Olympics.

You can use decimals to show **hundredths**.

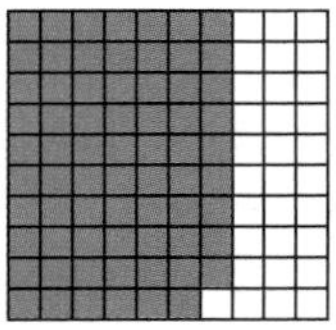

$\frac{69}{100} = 0.69$

sixty-nine hundredths

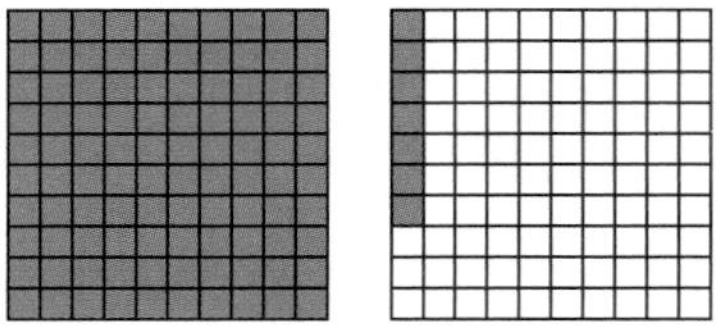

$1\frac{7}{100} = 1.07$

one and seven hundredths

ones		tenths	hundredths
0	.	6	9
1	.	0	7

You can name the same amount in different ways.

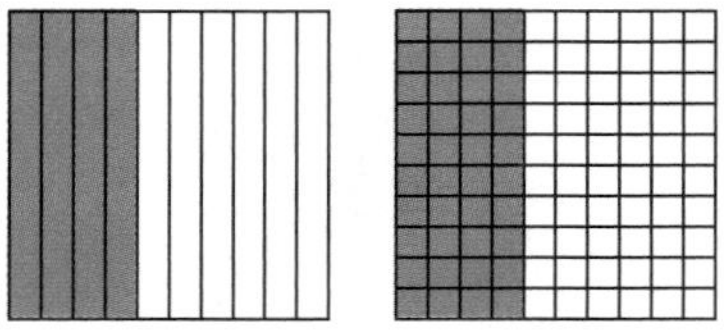

$\frac{4}{10} = \frac{40}{100}$

four tenths = forty hundredths

$0.4 = 0.40$

Talk About It

Why does 0.4 name the same amount as 0.40?

Check

Write the fraction and the decimal to name each shaded part.

1. 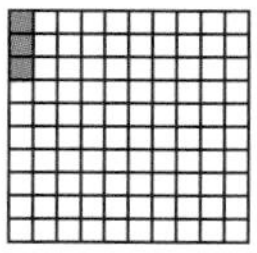

2. 

3. 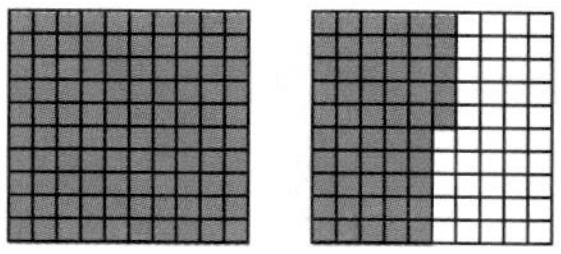

4. 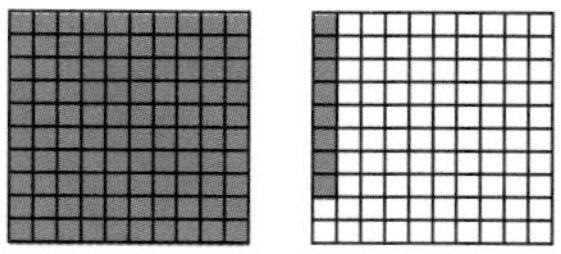

5. **Reasoning** Is 0.3 greater than or less than 0.35? Explain. You may use hundredths grids to help.

Practice

Skills and Reasoning

Write the fraction and the decimal to name each shaded part.

6. 

7. 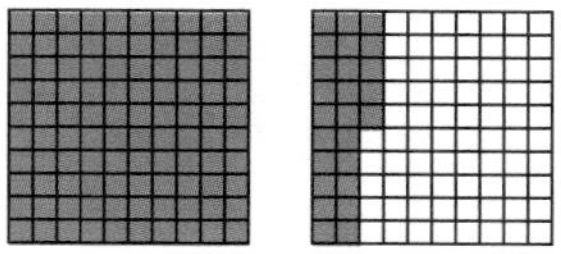

8. 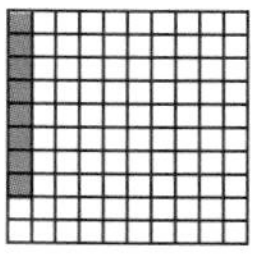

9. 

Write each as a decimal.

10. seven hundredths **11.** nineteen hundredths **12.** one and two hundredths

13. $\frac{34}{100}$ **14.** $\frac{5}{100}$ **15.** $2\frac{4}{100}$ **16.** $1\frac{89}{100}$ **17.** $3\frac{14}{100}$

18. Is 0.60 greater than, less than, or equal to 0.06? Explain.

19. What is the value of each red digit?

a. 0.27 **b.** 1.36 **c.** 2.54 **d.** 1.02 **e.** 0.59

Problem Solving and Applications

Using Data Use the Data File on page 452 for **20** and **21.**

20. Write the word name for Aleksandr Golubev's time in the men's 500-meter speed skating race.

21. Who won the women's 500-meter speed skating race? Explain how you know.

Mixed Review and Test Prep

Find each sum or difference.

22. $14 + 36$ **23.** $23 - 12$ **24.** $38 + 26$ **25.** $56 - 32$ **26.** $40 - 22$

27. There are 12 inches in a foot. How many inches are in 3 feet?

Ⓐ 15 Ⓑ 36 Ⓒ 9 Ⓓ 24

Chapter 11
Lesson
3

Exploring Adding and Subtracting Decimals

Problem Solving Connection
- Use Objects/ Act It Out
- Draw a Picture

Materials
- tenths grids
- color pencils

Problem Solving Hint
Using grids or drawing pictures can help you put together or take away tenths.

Explore

You can use grids to add and subtract decimals.

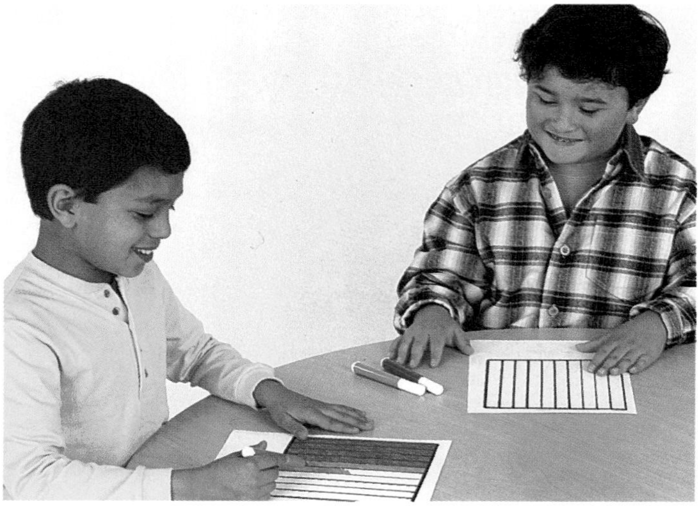

Work Together

1. Find the sum of 0.4 and 0.7.

a. Shade 0.4 on a tenths grid.

b. On the same grid, shade 0.7 in another color. Use another grid if you need to.

c. Write the sum as a decimal.

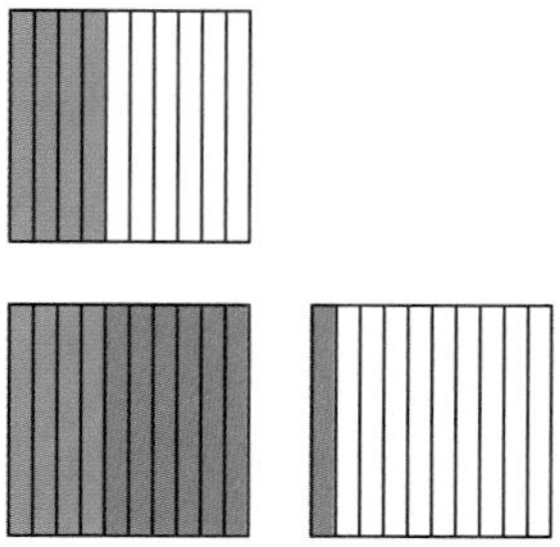

2. Subtract 0.4 from 1.6.

a. Shade 1.6 on tenths grids.

b. Cross out 0.4 of the shaded part.

c. Write the difference as a decimal.

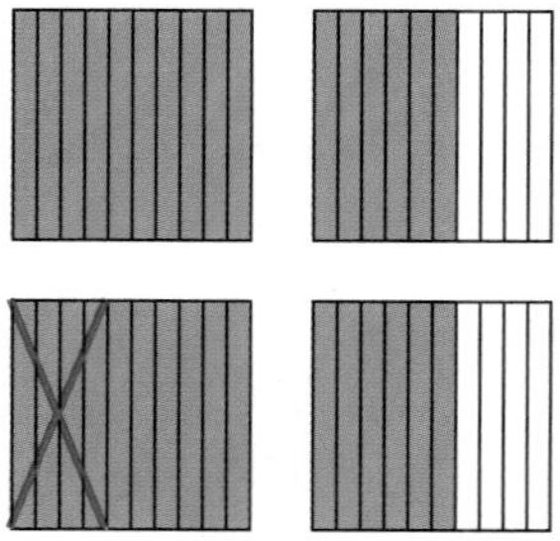

3. Use tenths grids to find each sum or difference.

a. 0.5 + 0.3 **b.** 1.1 + 0.9 **c.** 1.4 + 0.5

d. 0.4 − 0.2 **e.** 1.3 − 0.2 **f.** 1.7 − 0.5

Talk About It

When adding decimals, do you always need to use an extra grid? Explain.

Connect

You can add and subtract decimals using place value.

Add 1.6 and 0.5.	Line up the decimal points.	Add tenths. Regroup if needed.	Add ones.
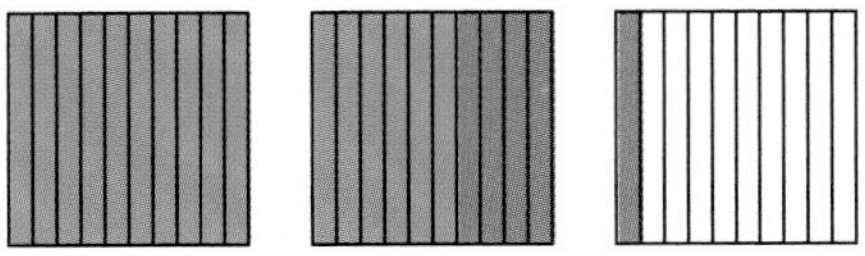	$\begin{array}{r} 1.6 \\ +\ 0.5 \\ \hline \end{array}$	$\begin{array}{r} \scriptstyle 1 \\ 1.6 \\ +\ 0.5 \\ \hline 1 \end{array}$	$\begin{array}{r} \scriptstyle 1 \\ 1.6 \\ +\ 0.5 \\ \hline 2.1 \end{array}$

Subtract 1.8 from 2.5.	Line up the decimal points.	Subtract tenths. Regroup if needed.	Subtract ones.
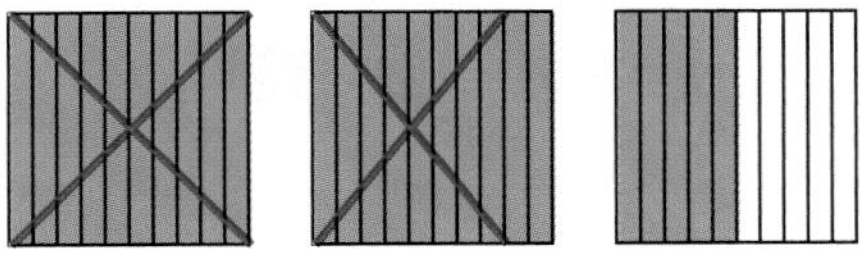	$\begin{array}{r} 2.5 \\ -\ 1.8 \\ \hline \end{array}$	$\begin{array}{r} \scriptstyle 1\ 15 \\ \not{2}.\not{5} \\ -\ 1.8 \\ \hline 7 \end{array}$	$\begin{array}{r} \scriptstyle 1\ 15 \\ \not{2}.\not{5} \\ -\ 1.8 \\ \hline 0.7 \end{array}$

Practice

Find each sum or difference. You may use tenths grids to help.

1. $\begin{array}{r} 4.2 \\ +\ 2.4 \\ \hline \end{array}$ **2.** $\begin{array}{r} 1.7 \\ +\ 5.6 \\ \hline \end{array}$ **3.** $\begin{array}{r} 7.3 \\ -\ 4.1 \\ \hline \end{array}$ **4.** $\begin{array}{r} 8.4 \\ -\ 3.7 \\ \hline \end{array}$ **5.** $\begin{array}{r} 0.6 \\ +\ 0.3 \\ \hline \end{array}$

6. $\begin{array}{r} 2.5 \\ +\ 1.8 \\ \hline \end{array}$ **7.** $\begin{array}{r} 6.2 \\ -\ 5.1 \\ \hline \end{array}$ **8.** $\begin{array}{r} 5.2 \\ -\ 1.7 \\ \hline \end{array}$ **9.** $\begin{array}{r} 8.3 \\ +\ 1.6 \\ \hline \end{array}$ **10.** $\begin{array}{r} 9.2 \\ -\ 5.5 \\ \hline \end{array}$

11. History In 1783, the first hot-air balloon flew 5.5 miles across Paris, France. Write this decimal number as a fraction.

12. Health Ray's body temperature is normally 98.6 degrees. Today, his temperature is 1.6 degrees higher than normal. What is his temperature today?

13. Reasoning Is the difference between 1.8 and 0.5 greater than or less than 1? You may use tenths grids to explain.

14. Patterns Write the next three numbers in the pattern:

1.0, 1.2, 1.4, ▒, ▒, ▒

15. Journal How is adding and subtracting decimals like adding and subtracting whole numbers? How is it different?

Connecting Decimals and Money

You Will Learn
how to connect money amounts and decimals

Learn

Money amounts are written like decimals. You can think of cents as fractional parts of whole dollars.

100 pennies = $1.00

$1¢ = \frac{1}{100}$ of $1.00

1¢ = $0.01

10 dimes = $1.00

$10¢ = \frac{10}{100}$ of $1.00

10¢ = $0.10

You can also use place value to help you understand money amounts as decimals.

Math Tip
You can think of 35 cents as 35 hundredths of a dollar.

35 hundredths = 0.35

35 hundredths of $1.00 = $0.35

Decimal Place Value	ones		tenths	hundredths
Money	dollars		dimes	pennies
	2	.	3	5

$2.35 or two dollars and thirty-five cents

Talk About It

How is 1 hundredth the same as 1 cent?

Check

Write each as a money amount.

1. $\frac{24}{100}$ of $1.00 2. $\frac{8}{100}$ of $1.00 3. $\frac{63}{100}$ of $1.00

4. **Reasoning** How are 0.54 and $0.54 the same and different?

Practice

Skills and Reasoning

Write each as a money amount.

5. $\frac{82}{100}$ of \$1.00 **6.** $\frac{41}{100}$ of \$1.00 **7.** $\frac{19}{100}$ of \$1.00 **8.** $\frac{59}{100}$ of \$1.00

9. forty-nine cents

10. thirty-two cents

11. six dollars and fifty-five cents

12. two dollars and sixty-seven cents

13. eighty-six hundredths of \$1.00

14. two and forty-five hundredths of \$1.00

15. Copy and complete the table.

		Fraction of \$1.00	Decimal Part of \$1.00
a.	\$0.68		
b.	\$0.06		
c.	\$0.13		

Problem Solving and Applications

16. Joey bought a model racing car that cost \$3.76. If he pays with \$5.00, how much change should he get back?

17. **Money** What coin is worth $\frac{25}{100}$ of a dollar?

18. Mr. Cole is writing a check to pay for some toys. Help him complete the check by writing the money amount.

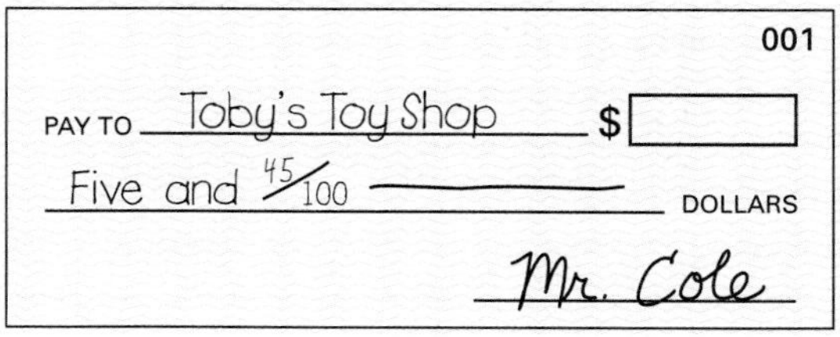

Mixed Review and Test Prep

Algebra Readiness Copy and complete each number sentence.

19. $6 \times \square = 60$ **20.** $6 \times \square = 24$ **21.** $27 \div \square = 9$ **22.** $8 \times \square = 800$

23. Find the difference of $472 - 395$.

Ⓐ 123 Ⓑ 867 Ⓒ 77 Ⓓ not here

Technology

Fractions and Decimals on a Calculator

Use a calculator to count by fractions or by decimals.

Materials
calculator

Work Together

1 Use your calculator to count by tenths using fractions.

- Start with $\frac{1}{10}$. Enter [+] 1 [/] 10 [=]. Record the result in a table.
- Press [=]. The display will show the sum of $\frac{1}{10} + \frac{1}{10}$. Record.
- Continue to press [=] and record each sum. Stop when you have counted 9 tenths.

Number of Tenths	Sum of Fractions	Sum of Decimals
1	$\frac{1}{10}$	
2	$\frac{2}{10}$	
3		

- If you count on one more tenth, what fraction do you think you will get? Press [=] to check.
- The [Ab/c] key shows a fraction as a whole number or a mixed number. What whole number is 10 tenths the same as? Press [Ab/c] to find out.

2 Use your calculator to count by tenths using decimals.

- Start with 0.1. Enter [+] 0.1 [=]. Record the result in the table.
- Press [=]. The display will show the sum of 0.1 + 0.1. Record the sum.
- Continue to press [=] and record each sum. Stop when you have counted 9 tenths.

Number of Tenths	Sum of Fractions	Sum of Decimals
1	$\frac{1}{10}$	0.1
2	$\frac{2}{10}$	0.2
3		

- If you count on one more tenth, what number will you get? Press [=] to check.

Exercises

1. Use your calculator to count by hundredths using decimals. Stop when you have counted 9 hundredths. If you count one more hundredth, what decimal will you get?

2. Use your calculator to count by eighths using fractions. Stop when you have counted 7 eighths.
   a. What fraction will come next if you count on one more eighth?
   b. How many eighths are the same as 1? Explain how you know.

Extensions

You can use your calculator to change fractions to decimals and decimals to fractions.

3. To show a decimal as a fraction, enter the decimal. Then press [F↔D]. Try these decimals. Record the fractions in a table.

	Decimal	Fraction
a.	0.5	
b.	1.4	
c.	2.05	

4. To show a fraction as a decimal, enter the fraction. Then press [F↔D]. Try these fractions. Record the decimals in a table.

	Fraction	Decimal
a.	$\frac{1}{4}$	
b.	$1\frac{5}{10}$	
c.	$1\frac{85}{100}$	

5. **Reasoning** How would you write 2.25 as a mixed number? Explain.

Chapter 11
Lesson
5

Problem Solving

Decision Making: Plan a Day

You Will Learn
to use a table to make decisions

Explore

Plan a trip to Zoom City Fun Park! You must decide how long you will stay at the park and what you will do there. You should also keep track of how much your trip will cost.

ZOOM CITY FUN PARK

Open 11:00 A.M. to 5:00 P.M.

Tickets
1 for $1.50
6 for $8.00
15 for $18.75

Ride	Tickets Needed	Wait
Rocket Coaster	3	15 minutes
Ferris Wheel	1	5 minutes
Dizzy Machine	2	10 minutes
Bumper Cars	1	5 minutes
Water Slide	2	10 minutes

Each ride lasts about 4 minutes.

FOOD SHOP

Hamburger	$3.45
Turkey and cheese sandwich	$2.65
French fries	$0.85
Apple juice	$0.45
Lemonade	$0.55
Ice cream bar	$1.15

Work Together

Understand

1. What do you know?
2. What do you need to decide?

Plan and Solve

3. What time will you get to the park? When will you leave?
4. Which rides do you want to take? How many tickets will you need?
5. In what order will you take the rides?
6. Will you take a break for lunch? If so, what will you order?

Make a Decision

7. Make a schedule like this one. Be sure to include everything you will do.

Time	Ride	Tickets
11:00 A.M.	Rocket Roller Coaster	3
11:30 A.M.	Lunch	0
12:00 P.M.	Wild Water Slide	2

8. How many tickets will you need? What is the best way to buy the tickets?
9. What is the total cost of your trip to the park? Do you need to change any of your plans?

Present Your Decision

10. Share your schedule with the class.
11. Who planned the longest visit? Who planned the shortest visit?
12. Did the person who planned the longest visit also spend the most money?
13. **What If** The park offers a special day pass. You may take all the rides you want for $25.00. Would you buy the day pass? Explain.

Skills Practice Bank, page 528, Set 6

SECTION A
Review and Practice

Vocabulary Choose the best word to complete each sentence.

Word List
decimal
decimal point
hundredth

1. A fraction in tenths or hundredths can be written as a ____.
2. A ____ is one of 100 equal parts of a whole.
3. The ____ separates the ones from the tenths.

(Lessons 1 and 2) Write the fraction and the decimal to name each shaded part.

4. 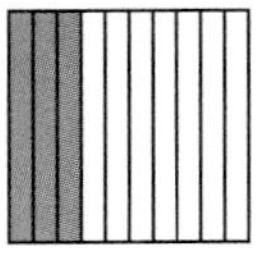

5. 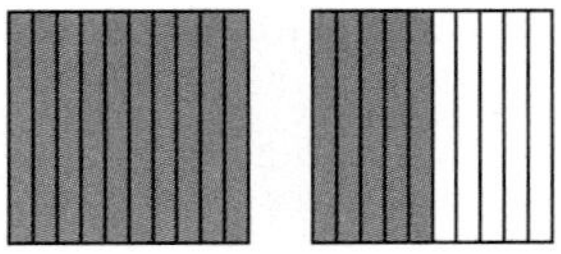

6. 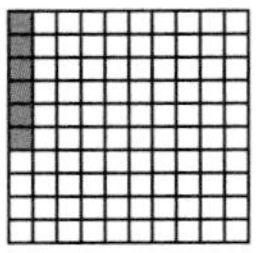

7. 

Write each as a decimal.

8. nine tenths **9.** sixty-five hundredths **10.** one and seven tenths

11. $\frac{12}{100}$ **12.** $1\frac{6}{10}$ **13.** $2\frac{1}{100}$ **14.** $\frac{1}{10}$ **15.** $\frac{34}{100}$

(Lesson 3) Find each sum or difference. You may use tenths grids to help.

16. $\begin{array}{r} 2.9 \\ +\ 4.2 \\ \hline \end{array}$ **17.** $\begin{array}{r} 9.4 \\ -\ 8.3 \\ \hline \end{array}$ **18.** $\begin{array}{r} 1.7 \\ +\ 4.5 \\ \hline \end{array}$ **19.** $\begin{array}{r} 7.4 \\ -\ 3.9 \\ \hline \end{array}$ **20.** $\begin{array}{r} 3.6 \\ +\ 4.5 \\ \hline \end{array}$

21. Jeri ran the 40-yard dash in 6.4 seconds. Bo ran it in 9.3 seconds. How many seconds faster was Jeri than Bo?

(Lesson 4) Write each as a money amount.

22. $\frac{32}{100}$ of \$1.00 **23.** $\frac{44}{100}$ of \$1.00

24. $3\frac{59}{100}$ of \$1.00 **25.** $\frac{5}{100}$ of \$1.00

26. Journal Think of a number in tenths or hundredths. Draw a picture or use grids to show that number. Then write the number as a fraction and as a decimal.

Skills Checklist

In this section, you have:

- ✔ Explored Tenths
- ✔ Learned About Hundredths
- ✔ Explored Adding and Subtracting Decimals
- ✔ Connected Decimals and Money
- ✔ Solved Problems by Making Decisions

CHAPTER 11

SECTION

B Metric Linear Measurement

Some elevators can travel about 600 meters in a minute! Do you think 600 meters is greater or less than 600 feet?

Metric Linear Measurement

Review measurement. Match each with its estimate.

1. height of a doorknob — **a.** 10 feet
2. height of a wall — **b.** 1 yard
3. length of a pencil — **c.** 8 inches

Skills Checklist

In this section, you will:

- ❒ Explore Centimeters and Decimeters
- ❒ Learn About Meters and Kilometers
- ❒ Solve Problems by Using Objects and Drawing a Picture

Chapter 11
Lesson
6

Exploring Centimeters and Decimeters

Problem Solving Connection
Use Objects/
Act It Out

Materials
centimeter ruler

Vocabulary
centimeter
a standard unit used to measure length in the metric system
decimeter
a metric unit of measure equal to 10 centimeters

Remember
Begin measuring at one end of the item.

Explore

The metric system of measurement was invented in France in the 1790s. Today, it is used in almost all countries.

A **centimeter** (cm) is a unit of measure in the metric system. You can measure length using centimeters.

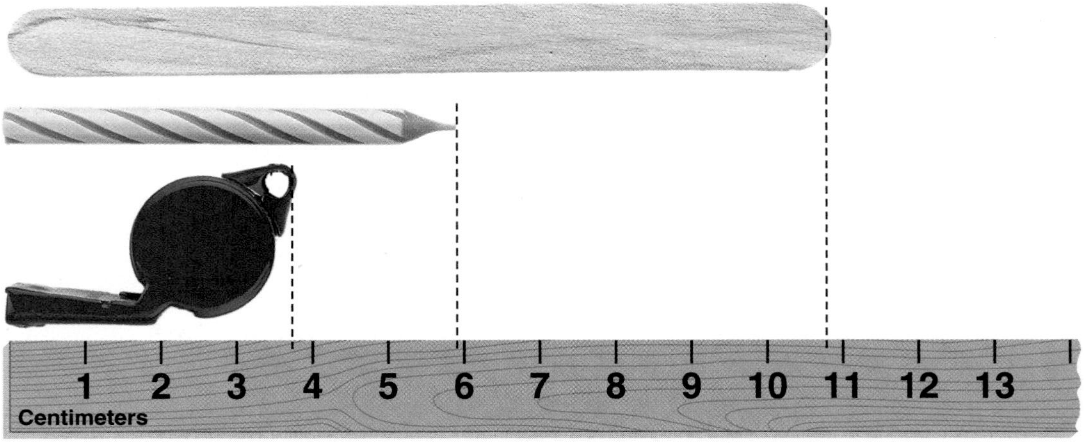

The whistle is 4 cm to the nearest cm.

The candle is 6 cm to the nearest cm.

The ice cream stick is 11 cm to the nearest cm.

Work Together

1. Use a centimeter ruler. Measure each object to the nearest centimeter. Record each measurement.

a. pencil **b.** thumb **c.** math book

2. Use estimation to find an object close to each length. Then measure each object and record the actual length to the nearest centimeter.

a. 10 cm **b.** 20 cm **c.** 30 cm

Talk About It

When an object was a little more or less than a centimeter, how did you record its length?

Connect

Here are some ways to think about a centimeter.

1 centimeter is about:

the width of a toothbrush

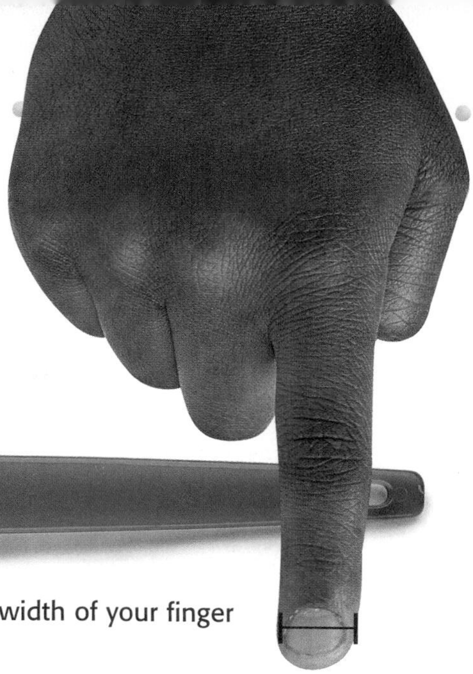

the width of your finger

A **decimeter** (dm) is 10 centimeters.

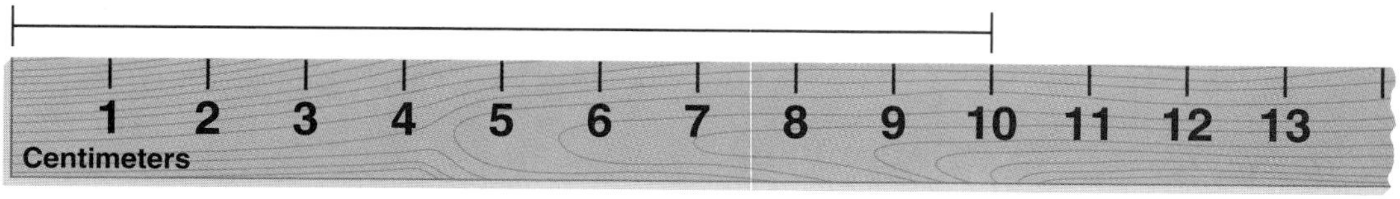

10 cm = 1 dm

Practice

Estimate the length of each object. Then measure to the nearest centimeter.

1. 

2. 

Match each with its estimate.

3. length of your desk	**a.** 6 dm
4. length of a cassette tape	**b.** 1 cm
5. length of a ladybug	**c.** 1 dm

6. Geometry Use a ruler to measure the perimeter of the square to the nearest centimeter.

7. Collecting Data Name two objects that are about 1 dm long.

8. Journal Find an object in the room and estimate its length to the nearest centimeter. Record your estimate. Then measure the object to the nearest centimeter and record the actual measurement.

Chapter 11
Lesson
7

Meters and Kilometers

You Will Learn
how to estimate and compare measurements in meters and kilometers

Vocabulary

meter
a metric unit of measure equal to 100 centimeters

kilometer
a metric unit of measure equal to 1,000 meters

Learn

Meters (m) and **kilometers** (km) are metric units of measure. They are used to measure length.

A meter is about the width of a doorway.

A kilometer is about the distance you walk in 15 minutes.

100 centimeters = 1 meter

1,000 meters = 1 kilometer

Math Tip
One meter is a little more than one yard.

One kilometer is a little more than half a mile.

Talk About It

1. What is another real-world object that is about a meter?
2. Give examples of some distances you would measure in kilometers.

Check

Match each with its estimate.

1. height of a wall — **a.** 2 km
2. distance you travel in a car — **b.** 1 m
3. length of a baseball bat — **c.** 3 m
4. **Reasoning** If something is 7 meters long, how many centimeters long is it? Explain.

Practice

Skills and Reasoning

Match each with its estimate.

5. height of a tall tree — **a.** 6 m

6. length of your math book — **b.** 3 km

7. distance of a bus ride — **c.** 30 cm

Write whether you would measure each in cm, m, or km.

8. length of your foot

9. length of a playground

10. distance of a 60-minute walk

11. height of a cat

12. Is an 80-cm-long tennis racket longer or shorter than a meter? Explain.

13. Suppose you walked 50 meters to a neighbor's house and then 50 meters back again. Did you walk 1 kilometer? Explain.

Problem Solving and Applications

Using Data Use the Data File on page 453 to answer **14** and **15.**

14. How much longer is the stride of a badger than the stride of a beaver?

15. What animal has a stride that is twice the length of a skunk's stride?

16. Geometry Write the perimeter of the playground in meters.

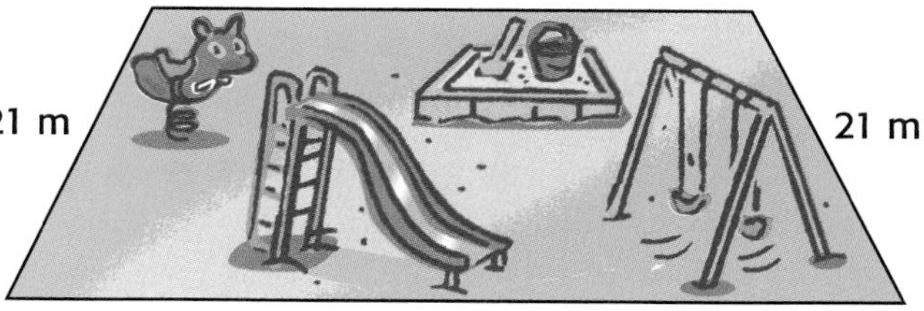

Mixed Review and Test Prep

Multiply or divide.

17. 8×38 **18.** $54 \div 6$ **19.** 6×109 **20.** $16 \div 4$ **21.** 23×4

22. Algebra Readiness If  is 3, what is  ?

 +  = 12

Ⓐ 3 Ⓑ 12 Ⓒ 9 Ⓓ 15

Problem Solving

Compare Strategies:
Use Objects and Draw a Picture

You Will Learn
how to use objects and draw a picture to solve problems

Learn

Suppose you are riding the elevator in a hotel. You get in the elevator on the ninth floor. The elevator goes down 7 floors. Then it goes up 6 floors. It goes up 3 more floors, then down 5 floors, and you get off. On what floor did you get off?

Miguel thinks:

I'll use counters. Each counter shows one floor. Start on the ninth floor.

When I go down, I'll take away counters. When I go up, I'll add counters.

down 7 floors

up 6 floors

up 3 floors

down 5 floors

I got off on the sixth floor.

John thinks:

I'll draw a picture to help.

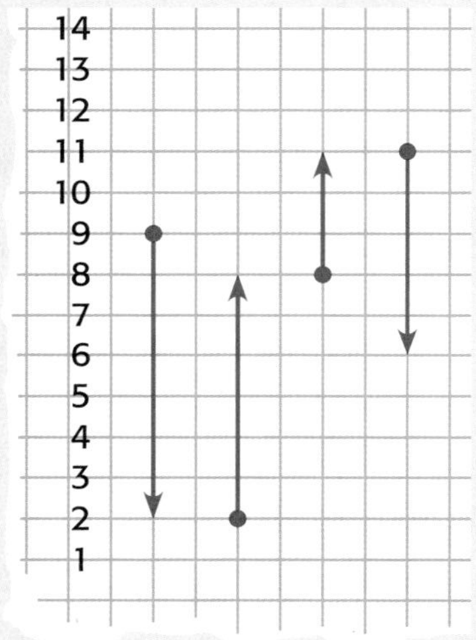

Down 7 floors.

Up 6 floors. Up 3 floors.
Down 5 floors.

I got off on the sixth floor.

Problem Solving Hint
Using objects or drawing a picture can help you see the problem more clearly.

Talk About It

When do you think it makes sense to draw a picture or use objects to solve a problem?

Check

Use objects, draw a picture, or use any strategy to solve.

Problem Solving
Understand
Plan
Solve
Look Back

1. Suppose you get on an elevator on the fifth floor. You go up 14 floors, then up 2 more floors. Then you go down 8 floors and up 1 floor. Then you get off. On what floor do you get off?

Problem Solving Practice

Use any strategy to solve.

Problem Solving Strategies

- Use Objects/Act It Out
- Draw a Picture
- Look for a Pattern
- Guess and Check
- Use Logical Reasoning
- Make an Organized List
- Make a Table
- Solve a Simpler Problem
- Work Backward

Choose a Tool

2. An elevator moves from the second floor to the sixth floor. Then it moves up 3 floors and down 8 floors. On what floor is it now?

3. **Geometry** Suppose you want to build a square pen for your pet turtle out of eight 1-meter-long boards. How many boards must you use on one side of the pen? What is the perimeter of the pen?

4. In the Quick-Check checkout line you must have no more than 11 items. A shopper has 4 cans of juice, 3 cartons of milk, 4 loaves of bread, and a magazine in his shopping cart. How many items must be put back?

5. Suppose an elevator can hold 23 people. There are 6 people on the elevator on the first floor. On the second floor, 1 person gets off and 13 people get on. On the fifth floor 5 people get off and 9 people get on. Can more people fit? Explain.

6. Victor, Jenny, Cassandra, and Enrico have a bicycle race. Jenny comes in second. Victor comes in 1 place ahead of Enrico. What place did each person come in?

7. You have 13 baseball cards. You trade 5 of your cards for 12 of your friend's cards. Then you lose some cards so you have 11. How many cards did you lose?

SECTION B
Review and Practice

Vocabulary Match each with its meaning.

1. centimeter
2. decimeter
3. meter
4. kilometer

a. a metric unit of measure equal to 100 centimeters

b. a metric unit of measure equal to 10 centimeters

c. a metric unit of measure equal to 1,000 meters

d. a standard metric unit of measure that is about the width of a toothbrush

(Lesson 6 and 7) Match each with its estimate.

5. height of a street light
6. length of a housefly
7. length of a color marker

a. 1 cm

b. 3 m

c. 1 dm

Write whether you would measure each in cm, m, or km.

8. height of a tricycle
9. height of a building
10. airplane trip
11. distance across the room
12. caterpillar
13. distance of a 3-hour hike
14. **Reasoning** Find an object in the room that is more than 1 meter in length. Estimate its length to the nearest meter.

(Lesson 8) Solve. Use any strategy.

15. Suppose you get on an elevator on the tenth floor. The elevator goes up 7 floors, then up 4 more floors. It goes down 13 floors, and then down 2 more floors. What floor are you on now?
16. **Journal** Explain how you would find how wide your desk is to the nearest centimeter.

Skills Checklist

In this section, you have:

- ☑ Explored Centimeters and Decimeters
- ☑ Learned About Meters and Kilometers
- ☑ Solved Problems by Using Objects and Drawing a Picture

YOUR CHOICE

Choose at least one. Use what you have learned in this chapter.

1 Decimal Dilemma

At Home Ask a family member to show you a few coins. Write what coins you see. Then write the value as a money amount and a fraction. Try three more times, using different combinations of coins each time.

2 Fable Fun

In the fable *The Tortoise and the Hare,* the tortoise beats the hare in a race. Write your own story about an ant and a snail in a 100-cm race. Draw a track like this one and show which crosses the finish line first.

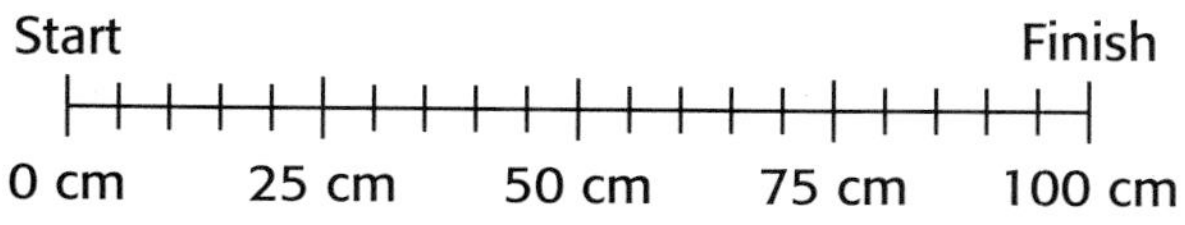

a. Which is ahead at 25 cm?

b. Which is ahead at 50 cm?

c. Which crosses the finish line at 100 cm first? By how many centimeters did it win?

3 Garden Plan

Suppose you are planning a space for a garden. You have 12 boards that are each 1 meter long. You must make a rectangle or square by placing the boards so that their ends touch. Use grid paper to show how many ways you can form a rectangle or square with the boards. Write the perimeter and area for each.

4 Right on Time

Sometimes the winning times in races are shown in tenths or hundredths of a second. Go to **www.mathsurf.com/3/ch11** for 3 winning times written as decimals. Then write each time as a fraction.

CHAPTER 11
Review/Test

Vocabulary Write true or false.

1. A doorway is about one centimeter wide.
2. 1 kilometer equals 1,000 meters.
3. 1 meter equals 1,000 centimeters.
4. In a decimal, the decimal point separates the ones from the tenths.

(Lessons 1 and 2) Write each as a decimal.

5. three tenths
6. nine tenths
7. one and two tenths
8. $\frac{1}{10}$
9. $3\frac{7}{10}$
10. $\frac{4}{10}$
11. $1\frac{2}{10}$
12. $\frac{9}{10}$
13. three hundredths
14. four and thirteen hundredths
15. $\frac{8}{100}$
16. $\frac{25}{100}$
17. $8\frac{72}{100}$
18. $2\frac{5}{100}$
19. $1\frac{99}{100}$

(Lesson 3) Find each sum or difference.

20. $0.2 + 1.3$
21. $2.4 + 1.1$
22. $3.2 - 0.1$
23. $4.5 - 2.6$
24. $5.3 + 3.9$

25. **Reasoning** Brandy ran a race in 9.5 seconds. Jo ran the race in 8.2 seconds. By how many seconds did Jo win the race?

(Lesson 4) Write each as a money amount.

26. $\frac{78}{100}$ of \$1.00
27. $\frac{2}{100}$ of \$1.00
28. $3\frac{45}{100}$ of \$1.00
29. $\frac{50}{100}$ of \$1.00

(Lessons 6 and 7) Write whether you would measure each in cm, m, or km.

30. your hand
31. parking lot
32. distance of a long car ride

(Lesson 8) Use any strategy to solve.

33. There are 24 people on a bus. At the first stop, 3 people get on and 7 get off. At the next stop, 12 people get off and 4 get on. At the next stop, 9 get off and no people get on. How many people are on the bus now?

CHAPTER 11
Performance Assessment

Have you ever wanted to design your own flag? This flag is 0.40 white, 0.24 blue, 0.30 green and 0.06 red.

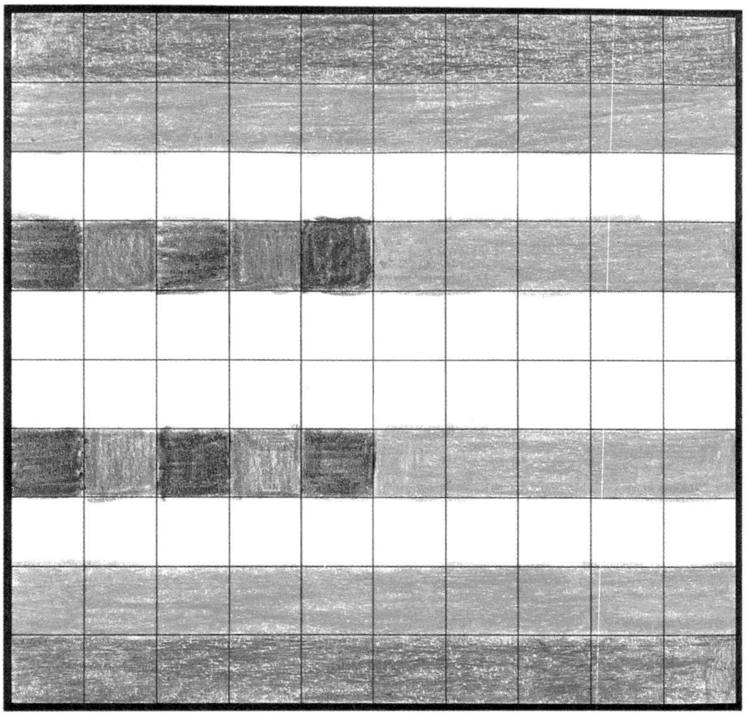

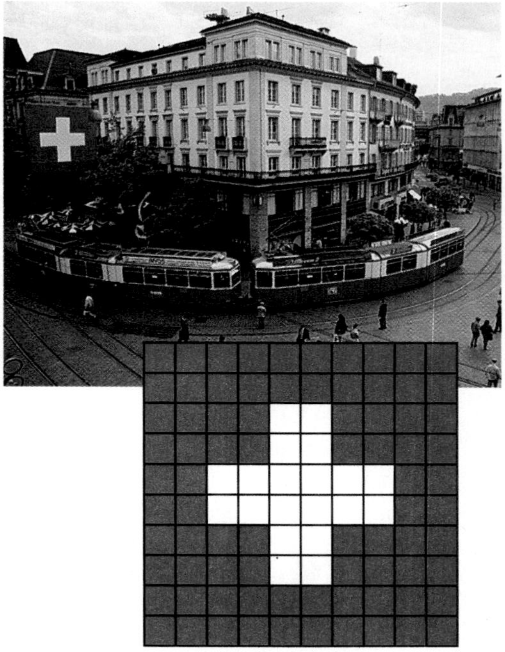

The flag of Switzerland is 0.20 white and 0.80 red.

1. **Decision Making** Design your own flag on hundredths grid paper. The flag must be at least 0.40 white and must use at least 2 colors.

2. **Recording Data** Write a description of your flag using decimals. You may use a table like this one to help.

Color	Decimal Part of Flag
White	0.40

3. **Explain Your Thinking** How did you know which decimals to use to describe your flag? How did you make sure your flag was at least 0.40 white?

4. **Critical Thinking** Design a flag on hundredths grid paper that is 0.60 blue, 0.12 green, and 0.28 red.

Math Magazine

Multi-axis trainer at Huntsville, Alabama, Space Camp

Liftoff! **Guion S. Bluford, Jr. was the first African American astronaut in space. He took many math and science courses in college, then joined the Air Force. Since he has become an astronaut, he has spent more than 513 hours in space.**

The final seconds before liftoff are exciting! Here is the order of events Guion Bluford expects when waiting to take off:

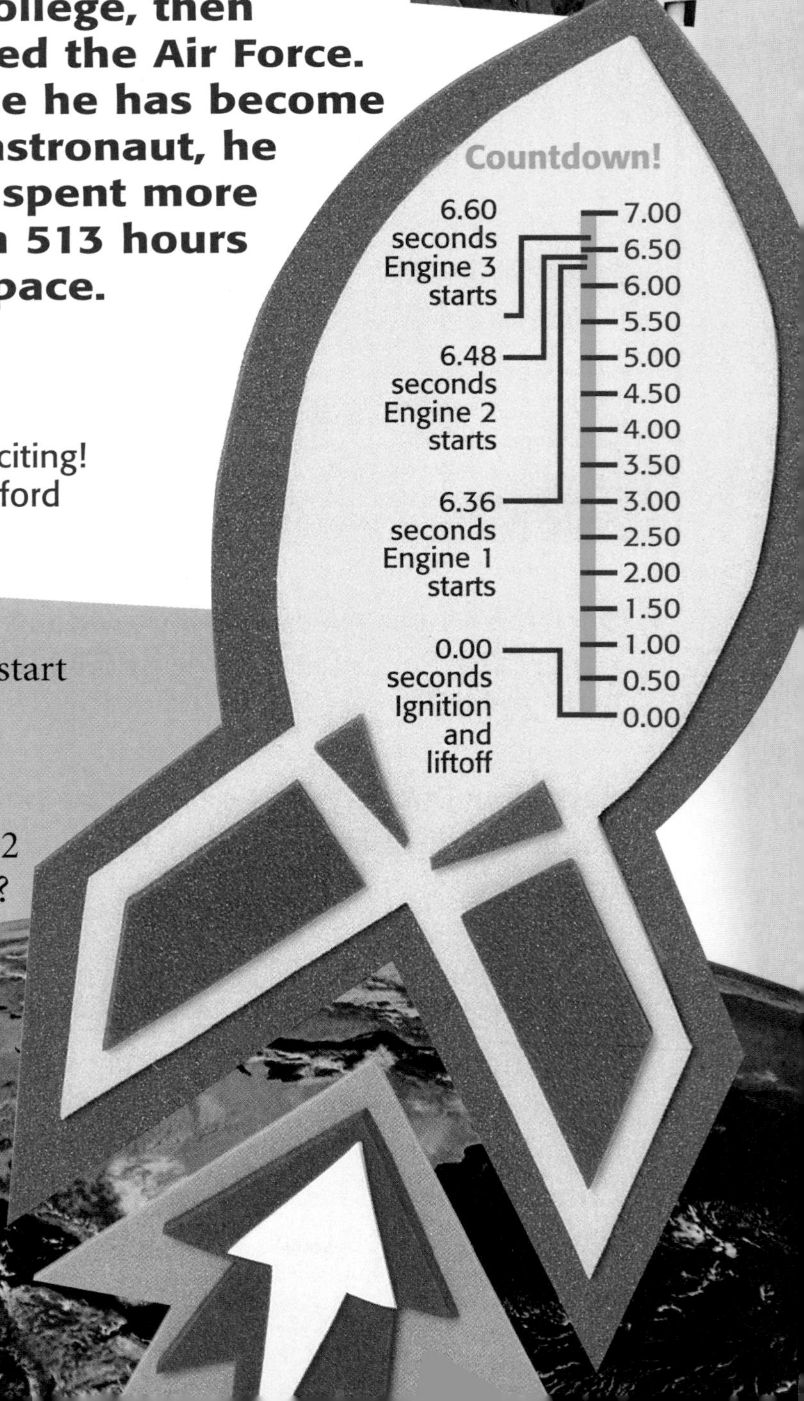

Try These!

1. Which happens first, the start of Engine 2 or liftoff?

2. How many seconds pass between the time Engine 2 starts and Engine 1 starts?

CHAPTERS 1–11

Cumulative Review

At first I thought the length of a paper clip was about 4 inches. When I reread the problem, my answer didn't make sense. Since the problem asks for the length in centimeters, the answer is (C).

Test Prep Strategy: Read Carefully

Reread the problem with your answer. Does it make sense? Choose the best estimate for the length of a paper clip in centimeters.

(A) 4 meters (B) 4 paper clips
(C) 4 centimeters (D) 4 inches

Test Prep Strategies

- Read Carefully
- Follow Directions
- Make Smart Choices
- Eliminate Choices
- Work Backward from an Answer

Write the letter of the correct answer. Read carefully and use any strategy to help.

1. Erica has $5.25. If she buys a magazine for $2.29, how much money does she have left?

   (A) $7.54 (B) $2.96 (C) 754 (D) $2.33

2. What is the product of 17×7?

   (A) 89 (B) 149 (C) 24 (D) 119

3. What is the place value of the red digit in 5.34?

   (A) tenths (B) ones (C) hundredths (D) tens

4. Which mixed number is the same as 3.21?

   (A) $3\frac{21}{10}$ (B) 321 (C) 32.1 (D) $3\frac{21}{100}$

5. Find the product of 34×8.

   (A) 26 (B) 272 (C) 4 R 4 (D) 42

6. At the station, 122 people were on the first train, 115 were on the second train, and 189 were on the last train. About how many people in all were on the three trains?

   (A) about 200 people (B) 3 trains
   (C) about 400 people (D) not here

7. Find the quotient of $32 \div 4$.

   (A) 128 (B) 8 (C) 28 (D) 7

DATA FILE

Chapter 12

Measurement and Probability

Around the HOUSE

SECTION A

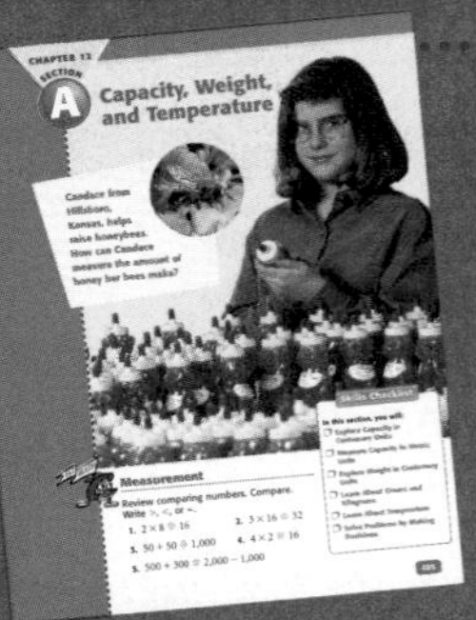

Candace is a beekeeper in Hillsboro, Kansas.

Page 485

Capacity, Weight, and Temperature

485

Labels on food can tell you how much of the food you are buying. Which do you think is heavier, a pound of butter or an ounce of cheese?

SECTION

B

Probability

499

You can use objects found around the house to explore probability. If you flip a coin, what are the different ways it can land?

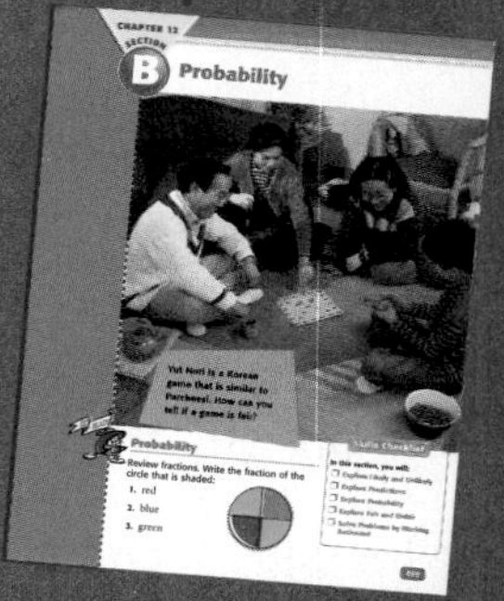

Yut Nori game
Page 499

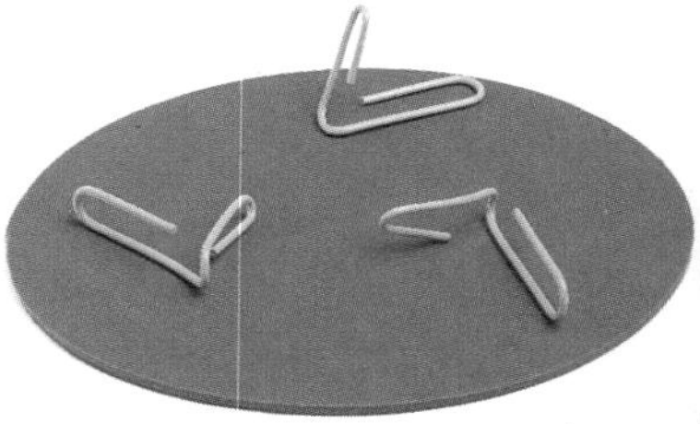

Surfing the World Wide Web!

To find what the temperature is all around the country, go to **www.mathsurf.com/3/ch12** for weather data.

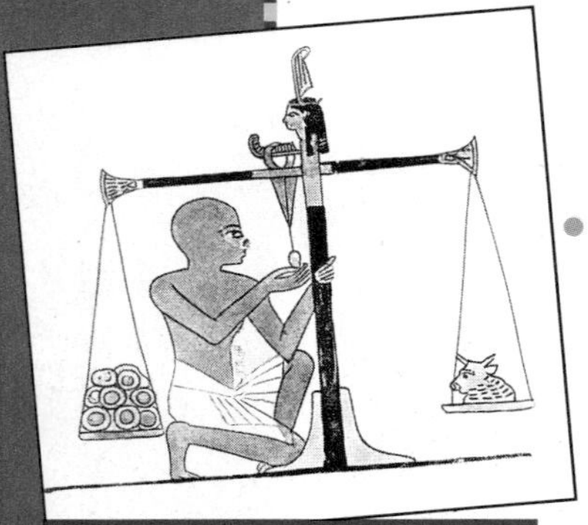

TEAM PROJECT
Penny Weight

Materials
cardboard, ruler, string, small paper cups, pennies, scissors

Find an object's weight in pennies! Make a balance scale like these ancient Egyptian scales.

Make a Plan

- How do you think a scale works?
- What object will you weigh?

Carry It Out

1. Punch holes in the middle and at both ends of a piece of cardboard.
2. Cut 7 equal lengths of string. Tie 3 strings at each end of the scale to paper cups. Tie the last string to the middle.
3. Put an object in one of the cups. How many pennies does it take to balance the scale?
4. Use other objects and record their weights in pennies.

Talk About It

- How did you know if the scale was balanced?

Present the Project

- Share your scale and list of weights with the class.
- Did other groups find the same weights for similar objects?

CHAPTER 12

SECTION

A Capacity, Weight, and Temperature

Candace from Hillsboro, Kansas, helps raise honeybees. How can Candace measure the amount of honey her bees make?

Measurement

Review comparing numbers. Compare. Write >, <, or =.

1. 2×8 ● 16

2. 3×16 ● 32

3. $50 + 50$ ● 1,000

4. 4×2 ● 16

5. $500 + 300$ ● $2{,}000 - 1{,}000$

Skills Checklist

In this section, you will:

- ❒ Explore Capacity in Customary Units
- ❒ Measure Capacity in Metric Units
- ❒ Explore Weight in Customary Units
- ❒ Learn About Grams and Kilograms
- ❒ Learn About Temperature
- ❒ Solve Problems by Making Decisions

Chapter 12
Lesson
1

Exploring Capacity: Customary Units

Problem Solving Connection
Use Objects/
Act It Out

Materials
- cup, pint, quart, gallon, and other containers
- water

Vocabulary
capacity
the amount a container can hold

Customary Units of Capacity
cup quart
pint gallon

Math Tip
To measure 1 cup, fill the measuring cup to the line that shows 1 cup.

Explore

Capacity is the amount a container will hold. A **cup** (c), **pint** (pt), **quart** (qt), and **gallon** (gal) are units used to measure capacity.

Work Together

1. Use estimation to learn about 1 cup.
   a. Choose a container that you think holds about 1 cup.
   b. Check your estimate. Fill a measuring cup with 1 cup of water and pour it into the container you chose.
   c. Does the container hold more or less than 1 cup?
2. Choose a container that you think matches each capacity. Then measure to check your estimate.
   a. pint b. quart c. gallon

Talk About It

Do you think containers with different shapes can have the same capacity? Explain.

Connect

Cups, pints, quarts, and gallons are related units of capacity.

2 cups = 1 pint

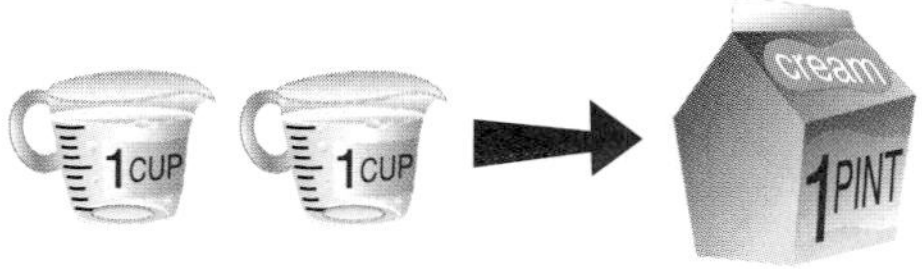

4 cups = 2 pints = 1 quart

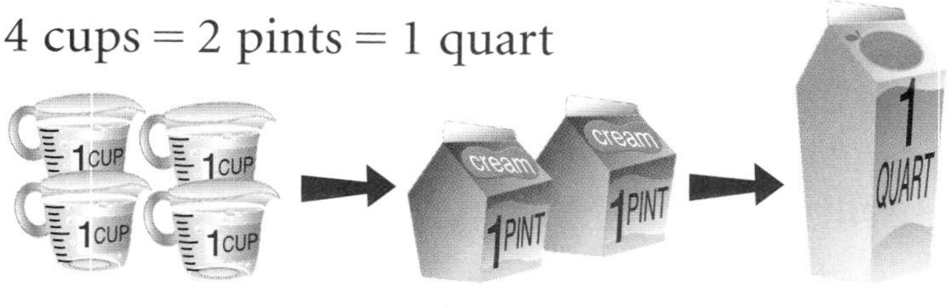

16 cups = 8 pints = 4 quarts = 1 gallon

Practice

Choose the best estimate for each.

1.

Ⓐ 1 cup
Ⓑ 1 quart
Ⓒ 1 pint

2.

Ⓐ 1 cup
Ⓑ 1 quart
Ⓒ 1 gallon

3.

Ⓐ 1 cup
Ⓑ 1 pint
Ⓒ 1 gallon

4.

Ⓐ 1 pint
Ⓑ 1 quart
Ⓒ 1 gallon

Compare. Write <, >, or =.

5. 1 gallon ● 2 quarts 6. 1 cup ● 1 pint 7. 4 quarts ● 1 gallon

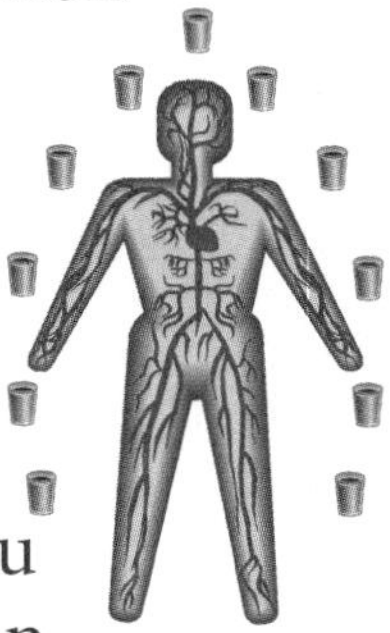

8. **Health** Children should drink about 3 pints of water each day. About how many cups of water is that?

9. **Science** An adult's body has about 11 pints of blood. Is that more or less than a gallon?

10. **Journal** Write a story or draw a picture about how you might use cup, pint, quart, and gallon containers to measure.

11. **Reasoning** Suppose you want to give everyone in your class 1 cup of juice. Will 1 gallon of juice be enough? Will 2 gallons be enough? Explain.

Chapter 12
Lesson
2

Measuring Capacity: Metric Units

You Will Learn
how to estimate and compare measurement in liters and milliliters

Vocabulary
milliliter
a metric unit of capacity

liter
a metric unit of capacity equal to 1,000 mL

Remember
The capacity of a container is how much it can hold.

Learn

A **milliliter** (mL) and a **liter** (L) are units of capacity in the metric system.

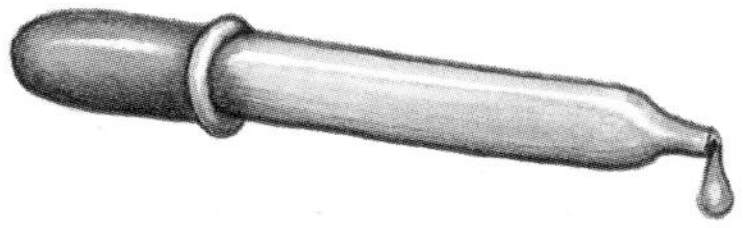

about 1 milliliter

1 liter

There are 1,000 milliliters in 1 liter.

Example 1

About how much soup does this soup spoon hold: 15 mL or 15 L?

Think: A liter bottle holds much more than a soup spoon. So, 15 mL is a better estimate.

Example 2

About how much water will the pail hold: 7 mL or 7 L?

Think: The pail is bigger than the liter bottle. The pail will hold several liters.

So, 7 L is a better estimate.

Talk About It

Would you measure the amount of water in a full bathtub in liters or milliliters? Explain.

Check

Choose the better estimate for each.

1.

Ⓐ 2 mL Ⓑ 2 L

2.

Ⓐ 50 mL Ⓑ 50 L

3.

Ⓐ 250 mL Ⓑ 250 L

4. Reasoning What kind of container might hold a few milliliters of water? What kind of container might hold a few liters?

Practice

Skills and Reasoning

Choose the better estimate for each.

5.

Ⓐ 1 mL Ⓑ 1 L

6.

Ⓐ 5 mL Ⓑ 5 L

7.

Ⓐ 150 mL Ⓑ 150 L

8. Suppose you estimated that you made about 1 liter of punch. How could you check your estimate?

Problem Solving and Applications

9. Critical Thinking Jack drank 1,300 mL of water. How much more or less than 1 L did he drink?

10. Science You breathe about 6 liters of air every minute. How many liters of air do you breathe in 5 minutes?

Mixed Review and Test Prep

Multiply or divide.

11. 7×8 **12.** 3×6 **13.** 6×9 **14.** 4×7 **15.** 9×9

16. $6\overline{)36}$ **17.** $7\overline{)42}$ **18.** $9\overline{)63}$ **19.** $3\overline{)24}$ **20.** $5\overline{)40}$

21. Find the product of 7×48.

Ⓐ 343 Ⓑ 2,856 Ⓒ 84 Ⓓ 336

Chapter 12
Lesson
3

Exploring Weight: Customary Units

Problem Solving Connection
- Use Objects/ Act It Out
- Make a Table

Materials
- classroom objects to weigh
- scale

Vocabulary

pound
a standard unit of weight equal to 16 ounces

ounce
a standard unit used to measure weight

Did You Know?
A person's brain weighs about 3 pounds.

Explore

A **pound** (lb) is a unit used to measure weight.

Thinking about how much a stapler weighs can help you estimate the weight of other items.

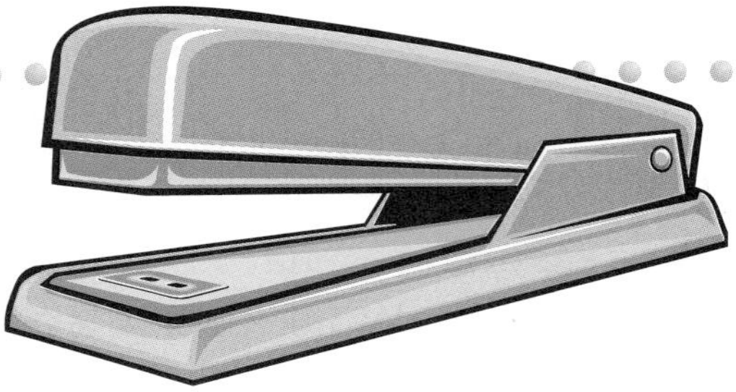

about 1 pound

Work Together

1. Choose 5 items in the classroom that you think weigh about 1 pound.
2. Place a pound weight on one side of the scale. Place an item on the other side of the scale. Record whether the weight of the item is more than, less than, or equal to 1 pound.
3. Repeat for each item.

Item	More Than 1 Pound	1 Pound	Less Than 1 Pound

Talk About It

Name an item besides a stapler that is about 1 pound.

Connect

An **ounce** (oz) is a unit of weight that is less than a pound.

about 1 ounce

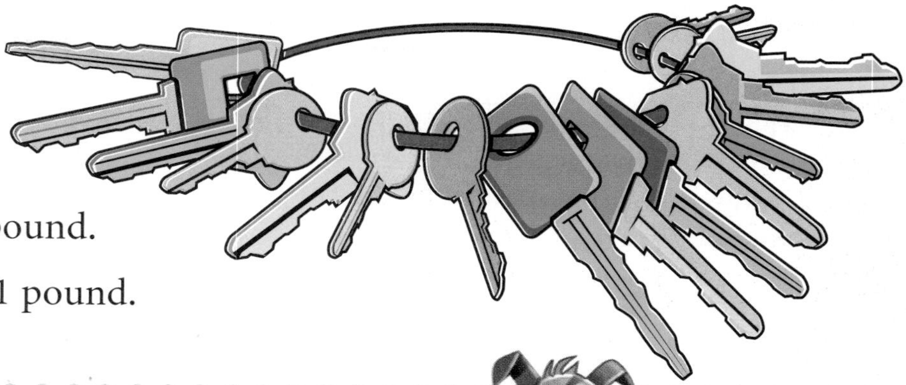

16 keys weigh about 1 pound.

There are 16 ounces in 1 pound.

Practice

Choose the better estimate for each.

1.

Ⓐ 1 oz
Ⓑ 1 lb

2.

Ⓐ 6 oz
Ⓑ 6 lb

3.

Ⓐ 2 oz
Ⓑ 2 lb

4.

Ⓐ 10 oz
Ⓑ 10 lb

Write whether each is less than or more than a pound.

5.

6.

7.

8.

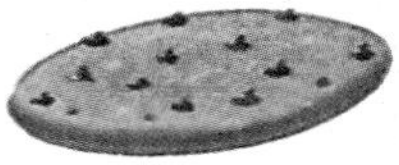

9. Reasoning Suppose a kitten weighs 2 pounds. How many ounces does it weigh?

10. Patterns Copy and complete the table.

Pounds	1	2	3	4	5	6
Ounces	16	32	48			

11. Using Data Use the fact from *Did You Know?* on page 490 to help you answer the question. A dolphin's brain weighs about 30 ounces. Does a person's brain weigh more or less than a dolphin's brain?

12. Journal Draw a picture of an item that weighs about an ounce. Draw a picture of an item that weighs about a pound. Label each drawing with its estimate.

Chapter 12
Lesson
4

Grams and Kilograms

You Will Learn
how to estimate and compare measurements in grams and kilograms

Vocabulary

gram
a metric unit used to measure mass

kilogram
a metric unit of measure equal to 1,000 grams

Learn

Candace has a *bzzzzy* life! She and her dad raise bees and store their honey. A jar holds 227 grams of honey.

How much is a gram?

Candace and her dad raise bees in Hillsboro, Kansas.

Grams (g) and **kilograms** (kg) are metric units of measure. You can think about the heaviness of a paper clip and a bunch of bananas to help understand grams and kilograms.

Did You Know?
The prefix *kilo* means "1,000."

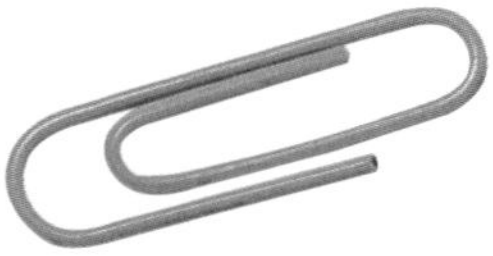

about 1 gram

about 1 kilogram

1,000 grams = 1 kilogram

Talk About It

Think about the heaviness of a balloon compared with the heaviness of a stapler. Do you think larger objects are always heavier than smaller objects? Explain.

Check

Choose the better estimate for each.

1.

Ⓐ 30 g Ⓑ 30 kg

2.

Ⓐ 1 g Ⓑ 1 kg

3.

Ⓐ 10 g Ⓑ 10 kg

4. Reasoning Would you measure a large watermelon in grams or kilograms? Explain.

Practice

Skills and Reasoning

Choose the better estimate for each.

5.

Ⓐ 100 g Ⓑ 100 kg

6.

Ⓐ 6 g Ⓑ 6 kg

7.

Ⓐ 1 g Ⓑ 1 kg

8. Jeremy says, "The number of grams in 3 kilograms is $3 \times 1{,}000$." Do you agree or disagree? Explain.

9. Which is heavier, a 1-kilogram cake or a 900-gram cake? Explain.

Problem Solving and Applications

Using Data Use the Data File on page 482 to answer **10** and **11.**

10. How many sticks of butter are in 1 pound?

11. How many 1-cup containers of water would it take to fill the milk container?

Mixed Review and Test Prep

Add or subtract.

12. $879 - 54$ **13.** $34 + 499$ **14.** $265 - 127$ **15.** $78 + 75$

16. Find the product of 34×5.

Ⓐ 170 Ⓑ 150 Ⓒ 155 Ⓓ 172

Chapter 12
Lesson
5

Temperature

You Will Learn
how to estimate and compare temperature in degrees Fahrenheit and Celsius

Vocabulary

Units of Temperature
degrees Celsius
degrees Fahrenheit

Learn

A thermometer measures temperature. **Degrees** (°) of **Celsius** (C) and **Fahrenheit** (F) are units of temperature.

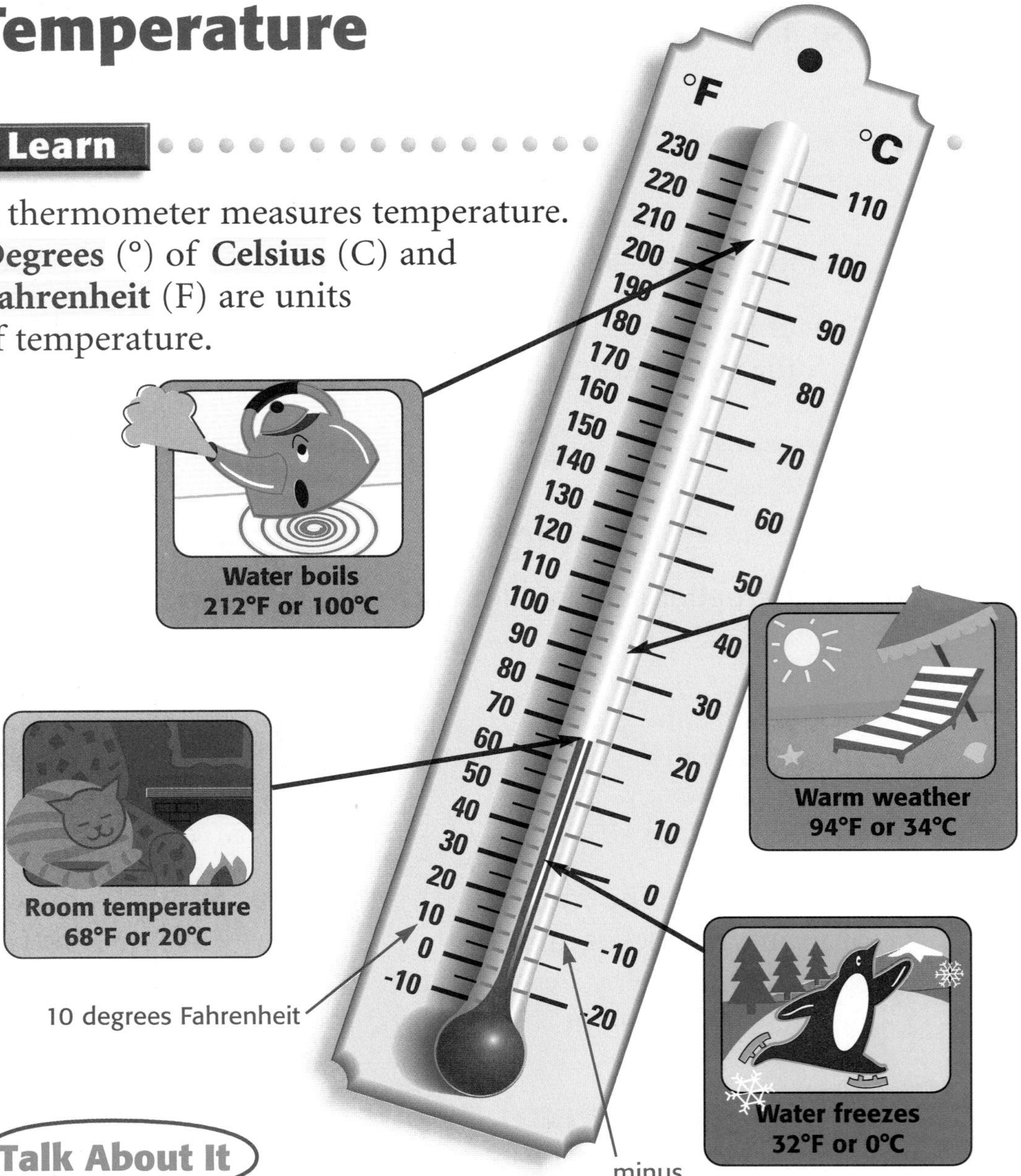

Did You Know?
The surface of the sun is 9,626°F.

Talk About It

Is 25°C warmer or cooler than 14°C?

Check

Write each temperature using °C.

1. 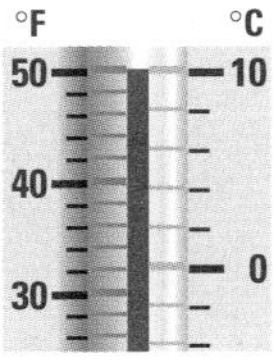

2. 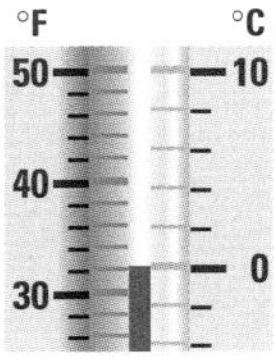

3. 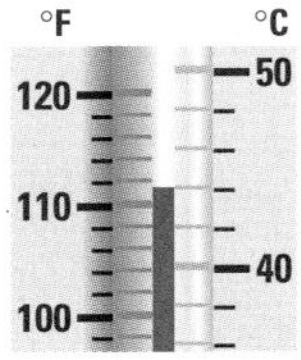

4. 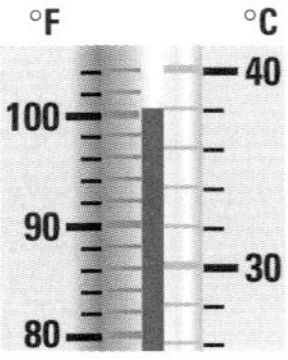

5. **Reasoning** If it is 12°F outside, is it warm or cold?

Practice

Skills and Reasoning

Write each temperature using °F.

6. 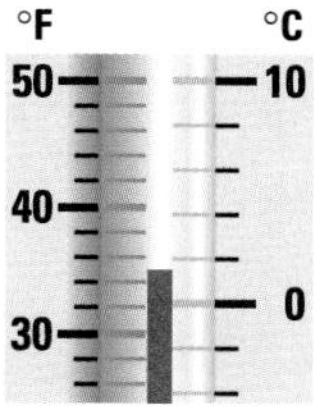

7. 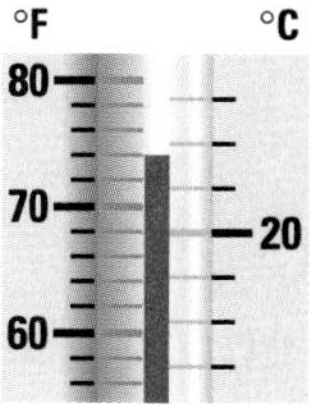

8. 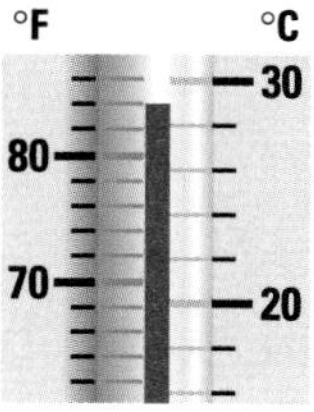

9. 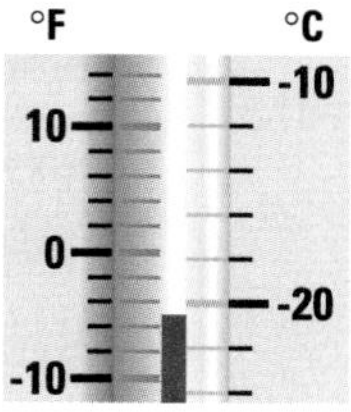

Choose the better estimate for each.

10. 

Ⓐ 2°C Ⓑ 20°C

11. 

Ⓐ 32°F Ⓑ 72°F

12. 

Ⓐ −10°C Ⓑ 90°C

13. Suppose it is 89°F outside. Should you wear a sweater? Explain.

14. If it is 15°C in the morning and 25°C in the afternoon, by how many degrees did the temperature increase?

Problem Solving and Applications

15. Collecting Data Use a thermometer to measure the temperature inside and outside the classroom. Which is hotter? Explain.

16. Geography The highest temperature in the shade ever recorded was 136°F in Libya, Africa. How many degrees hotter is this than room temperature?

Mixed Review and Test Prep

Add or subtract.

17. $9.54 + $2.32

18. $15.11 + $3.29

19. $22.45 + $36.58

20. $5.87 − $2.36

21. $87.93 − $76.35

22. $15.94 − $10.98

23. Geometry Find the perimeter.

Ⓐ 37 inches Ⓑ 74 inches

Ⓒ 74 feet Ⓓ 330 inches

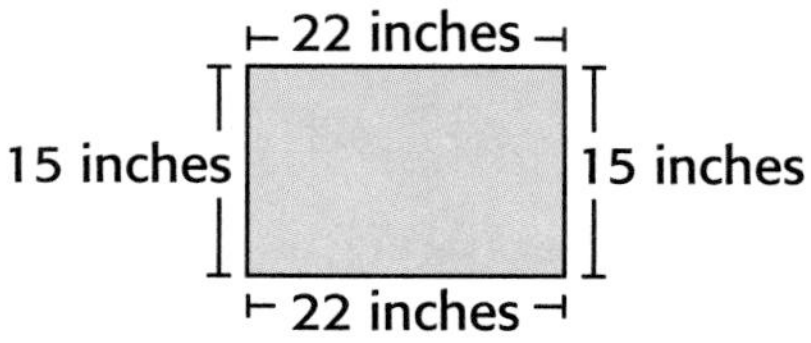

Skills Practice Bank, page 529, Set 4

Problem Solving

Decision Making: Packing for Backpacking

You Will Learn
how to solve problems by making decisions

Explore

Suppose you and a friend are going backpacking with a school group for three days. You and your friend must decide what to take.

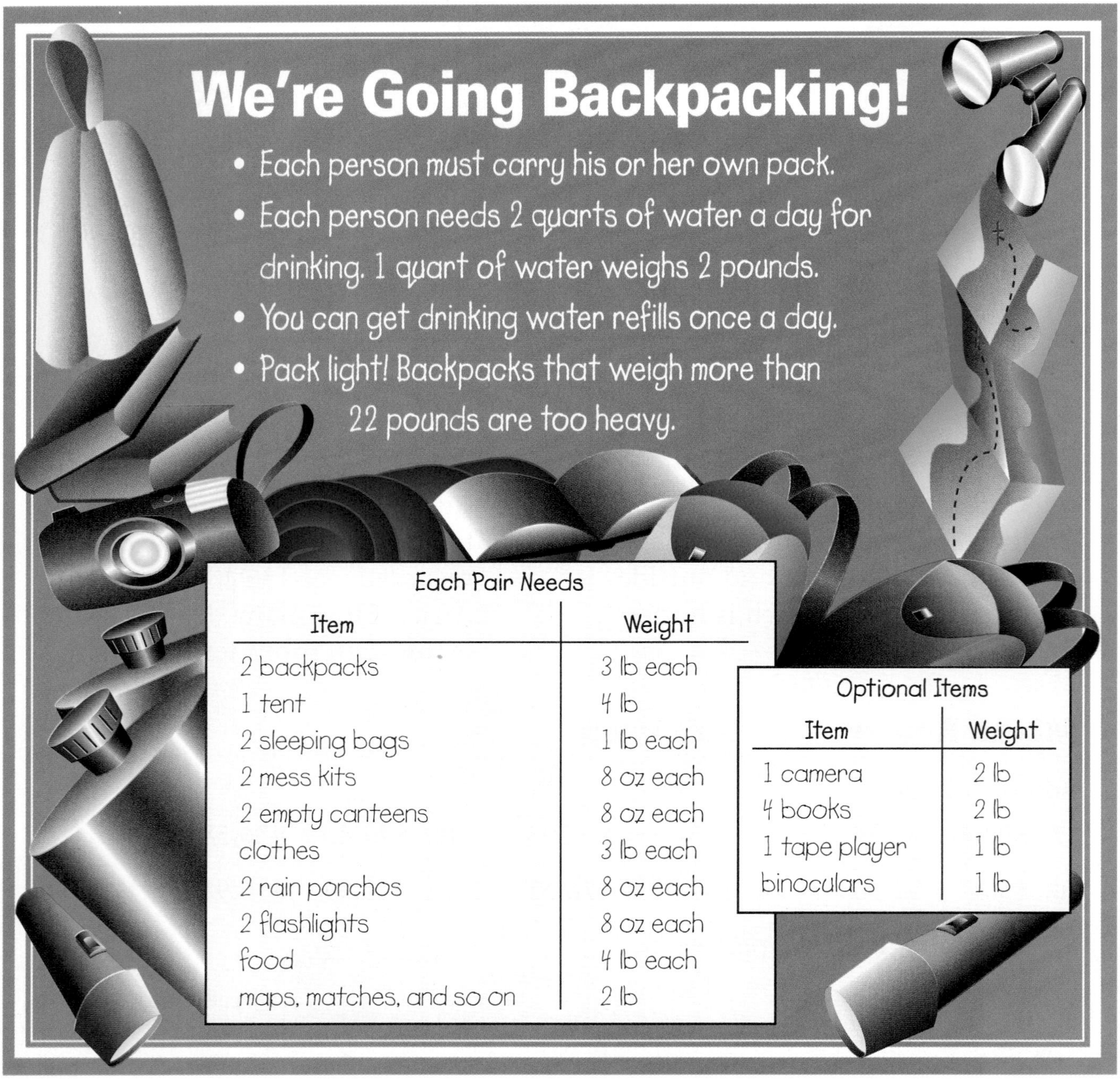

We're Going Backpacking!

- Each person must carry his or her own pack.
- Each person needs 2 quarts of water a day for drinking. 1 quart of water weighs 2 pounds.
- You can get drinking water refills once a day.
- Pack light! Backpacks that weigh more than 22 pounds are too heavy.

Each Pair Needs

Item	Weight
2 backpacks	3 lb each
1 tent	4 lb
2 sleeping bags	1 lb each
2 mess kits	8 oz each
2 empty canteens	8 oz each
clothes	3 lb each
2 rain ponchos	8 oz each
2 flashlights	8 oz each
food	4 lb each
maps, matches, and so on	2 lb

Optional Items

Item	Weight
1 camera	2 lb
4 books	2 lb
1 tape player	1 lb
binoculars	1 lb

Work Together

Understand

1. What do you know?
2. What do you need to find out?

Plan and Solve

3. How much water will you need to carry? How many pounds will it weigh?
4. Look at all of the things you and your friend will need. Don't forget your water. How many pounds will everything weigh?
5. How can you split up the items so that both backpacks weigh about the same amount?
6. How many pounds will each of you *need* to carry?
7. How much more weight can you carry?
8. What things would you like to take with you?

Make a Decision

9. Make a list of the items each person will carry and the total weight for each.

Present Your Decision

10. Share the decisions you have made with your classmates. Did other students make different decisions? Did anyone think about things you didn't think about?

PROBLEM SOLVING PRACTICE

SECTION A
Review and Practice

(Lessons 1 and 2) Choose the best estimate for each.

1.

Ⓐ 1 cup
Ⓑ 1 quart
Ⓒ 1 gallon

2.

Ⓐ 1 cup
Ⓑ 1 quart
Ⓒ 1 gallon

3.

Ⓐ 30 mL
Ⓑ 30 L

4.

Ⓐ 1 L
Ⓑ 1 mL

(Lessons 3 and 4) Choose the better estimate for each.

5.

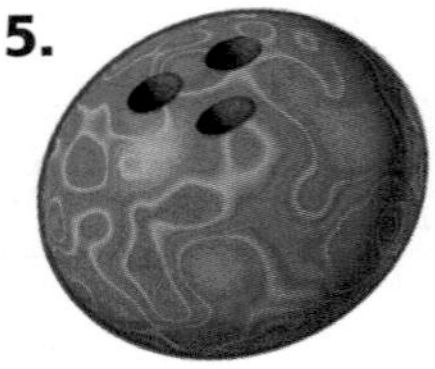

Ⓐ 12 oz
Ⓑ 12 lb

6.

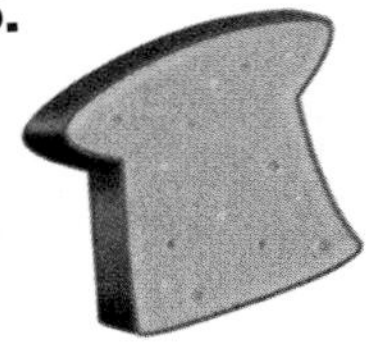

Ⓐ 1 oz
Ⓑ 1 lb

7.

Ⓐ 500 g
Ⓑ 500 kg

8.

Ⓐ 500 g
Ⓑ 500 kg

9. Reasoning Jeff had 2 stacks of newspapers. Each stack weighed 600 g. If he carried both stacks together, would he be carrying more or less than 1 kg? Explain.

(Lesson 5) Write each temperature using °F.

10.

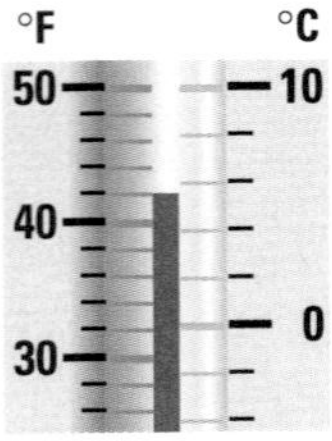

11.

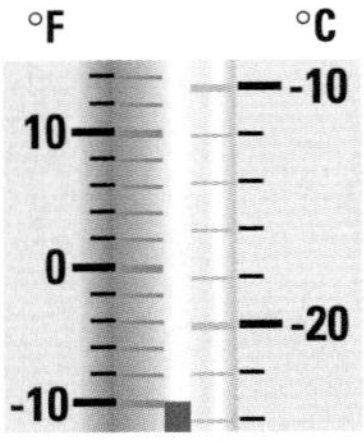

12. Journal Choose 3 units of measure you learned in this chapter. Draw a picture to help you remember the size of each.

Skills Checklist

In this section, you have:

- ☑ Explored Capacity in Customary Units
- ☑ Measured Capacity in Metric Units
- ☑ Explored Weight in Customary Units
- ☑ Learned About Grams and Kilograms
- ☑ Learned About Temperature
- ☑ Solved Problems by Making Decisions

B Probability

Yut Nori is a Korean game that is similar to Parcheesi. How can you tell if a game is fair?

GET READY!

Probability

Review fractions. Write the fraction of the circle that is shaded:

1. red

2. blue

3. green

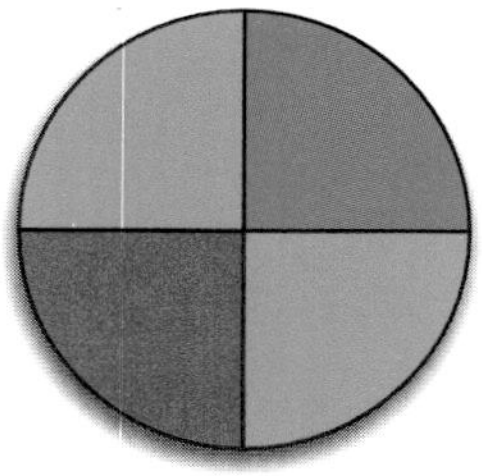

Skills Checklist

In this section, you will:

- ❒ Explore Likely and Unlikely
- ❒ Explore Predictions
- ❒ Explore Probability
- ❒ Explore Fair and Unfair
- ❒ Solve Problems by Working Backward

Chapter 12
Lesson
7

Exploring Likely and Unlikely

Problem Solving Connection
- Make a Table
- Use Logical Reasoning

Vocabulary

impossible
cannot happen

certain
sure to happen

possible
able to happen

likely
probably will happen

unlikely
probably will not happen

Explore

Some events are **impossible**.

Could you find a tree that walks?

Some events are **certain**.

Will the day after Monday be Tuesday?

Events that can happen are **possible**.

Work Together

1. Make a table like this one.

Impossible	Possible	Certain

2. Write each statement under the word in your table that best describes it.

a. You will see the sun today.

b. One hour after 3:00 P.M. it will be 4:00 P.M.

c. You can jump as high as a 10-story building.

d. If you drop your pencil, it will fall.

e. A dog can grow wings and fly.

f. You will hear a plane fly overhead today.

3. Think of at least 3 other statements to add to your table.

Math Tip
Think carefully! Some events may happen often but are not certain.

Talk About It

How did you decide where to place each statement?

Connect

There are many events that are possible. If an event has a good chance of happening, then it is **likely**. If an event probably won't happen, it is **unlikely**.

Impossible	Unlikely	Likely	Certain
The sun will rise in the west tomorrow.	School will be canceled next Thursday.	It is raining somewhere in the world.	There are fish swimming in an ocean today.

Practice

Write whether each is impossible, possible, or certain.

1. You can be in two different places at the same time.
2. Some students in your school will walk home.
3. Water will become ice if it is frozen.

Write whether each is likely or unlikely.

4. You will find a ten-dollar bill today.
5. You will step outside tomorrow.
6. You will win a trip to Australia.
7. You will be asleep at 2:00 A.M.
8. You will change your name tomorrow.
9. **Reasoning** Reid says, "It is likely to rain in our town every day." Do you agree or disagree? Explain.
10. **Collecting Data** Suppose you dropped a paper cup on the floor. Is it likely or unlikely to land standing up? Try dropping a cup 10 times to see.
11. **Journal** Make a list of events that are impossible, unlikely, likely, and certain.

Chapter 12
Lesson
8

Exploring Predictions

Explore

When you make a **prediction**, you make a guess about how likely or unlikely something is. Try to use what you know to help you make a good guess. Then test your prediction by doing an **experiment**.

Problem Solving Connection
- Guess and Check
- Use Objects/ Act It Out

Materials
- bag
- red and blue color cubes

Vocabulary

prediction
a guess about what will happen

experiment
a test or trial

possible outcomes
all results that could occur

Remember
Tally marks can help you keep track of the number of times each color is picked.

| = 1

𝍸 = 5

Work Together

1. Put 7 red cubes and 3 blue cubes in a bag.
   a. Predict which color you are more likely to pull out of the bag. Tell why you think so.
   b. Now test your prediction. Pull out 1 cube. Record its color on a tally table.

Color	Tally	Number
Red		
Blue		

   c. Put the cube back into the bag. Pull again and record the color on the tally table. Repeat this at least 20 times. Make sure to put the cube back into the bag each time.
   d. Did red cubes or blue cubes come out more often?
2. Put 1 red cube and 7 blue cubes in a bag. Predict which color you are more likely to pull out of the bag. Then test your prediction with another tally table. Did the color you predicted come out more often?

Talk About It

How did you make your predictions?

Connect

Before you make a prediction, it is helpful to list the **possible outcomes**. Then you can use words like *more, fewer, all,* or *no* to help you describe your prediction.

	Possible Outcomes	Predictions
	red blue	There will be *more* blue cubes picked than red cubes. There will be *fewer* red cubes picked than blue cubes.
	red	*All* of the cubes picked from this bag will be red. There will be *no* blue cubes picked from this bag.

Practice

Suppose you put these cubes in a bag. Predict which color you are more likely to pull out.

1. 

2. 

3. 

4. 

5. **Reasoning** Would it be easier to guess a number between 1 and 10 or a number between 1 and 1,000? Explain.

6. **Using Data** Use the Data File on page 483. Choose an object that you could flip in the air. List all possible outcomes of how the item could land.

7. **Journal** Suppose you put 4 red cubes and 8 blue cubes in a bag. Do you think you are more likely to pick a blue cube or a red cube? Explain.

Exploring Probability

Problem Solving Connection
- Guess and Check
- Use Objects/ Act It Out

Materials
- blank spinners
- colored markers

Vocabulary

probability
the chance that an event will happen

Explore

Spin a spinner.
Where will it stop?

Work Together

1. Make spinners like these. Don't forget to label each.

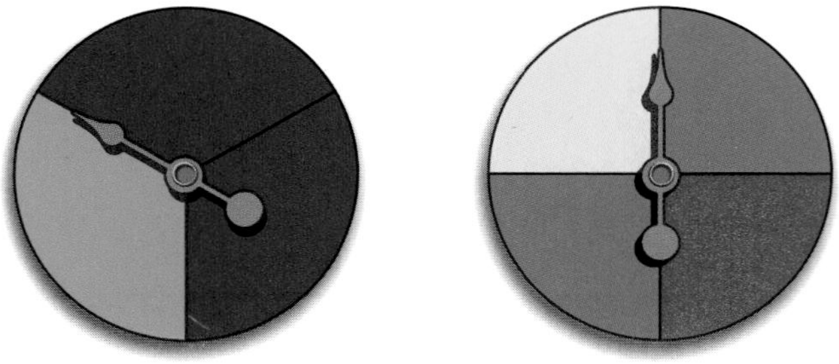

Spinner A   Spinner B

2. List the possible outcomes for each spinner. What colors can Spinner A stop on? What colors can Spinner B stop on?
3. Predict which color Spinner A is more likely to stop on. Spin the spinner at least 20 times. Record each result in a tally table. Did the color you predicted come up more often?
4. Predict which color Spinner B is more likely to stop on. Spin the spinner at least 20 times. Record each result in a tally table. Did the color you predicted come up more often?
5. Make a spinner with white, green, and red. Make it so that it is more likely to stop on green.

Math Tip
If you aren't sure if the spinner has stopped on one color or another, spin again.

Talk About It

6. How did you make your predictions for Spinners A and B?
7. How did you make a spinner that was more likely to stop on green?

Connect

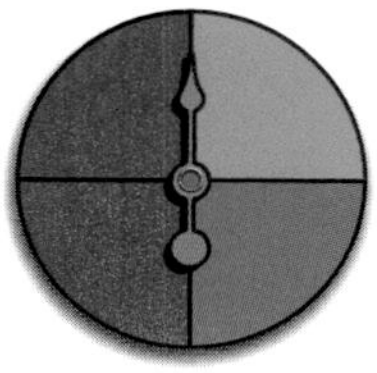

You can use what you know about fractions to write **probability** and make predictions. This spinner is divided into 4 equal sections. Predict which color the spinner is more likely to stop on.

2 out of 4 equal sections are red.

So, the probability of spinning red is $\frac{2}{4}$.

1 out of 4 equal sections is green.

So the probability of spinning green is $\frac{1}{4}$.

1 out of 4 equal sections is blue.

So the probability of spinning blue is $\frac{1}{4}$.

$\frac{2}{4} > \frac{1}{4}$

So, the spinner is more likely to stop on red than green or blue.

Practice

Copy and complete.

1.

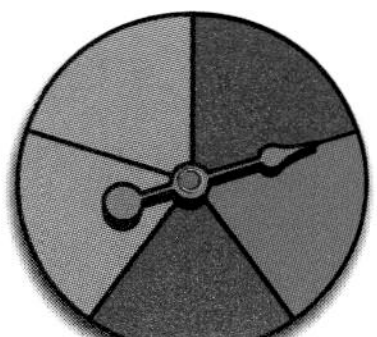

Red	___ out of 5 or	$\frac{\_\_\_}{5}$
Blue	___ out of 5 or	$\frac{\_\_\_}{5}$
Orange	___ out of 5 or	$\frac{\_\_\_}{5}$

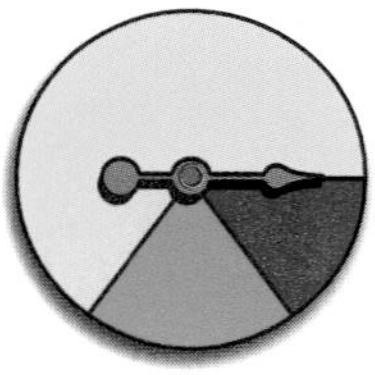

2. Reasoning What color do you predict this spinner is more likely to stop on?

3. In the Korean game Yut Nori, four sticks are tossed. Each stick has a round side and a flat side. Here are the names of each possible outcome and the probabilities of each.

Yut	Keol	Kae	Do	Mo

$\frac{1}{16}$	$\frac{4}{16}$	$\frac{6}{16}$	$\frac{4}{16}$	$\frac{1}{16}$

a. Which outcome are you most likely to toss?

b. Which outcomes are you least likely to toss?

4. Journal Draw a spinner with 4 equal sections. Color the spinner so that the probability of spinning green is $\frac{1}{4}$, the probability of spinning blue is $\frac{2}{4}$, and the probability for spinning white is $\frac{1}{4}$.

Exploring Fair and Unfair

Problem Solving Connection
- Use Objects/ Act It Out
- Guess and Check

Materials
- blank spinners
- colored markers

Vocabulary

fair
a game is fair if each player has an equal chance of winning

equally likely
just as likely to happen as not to happen

Did You Know?
Games with spinners are usually games of chance. Chess is a game of skill.

Explore

A game is **fair** if each player has an equal chance of winning.

Arielle and Amelia play chess at their school in New York City.

Work Together

Play a spinner game. You score a point each time the spinner stops on red. Your classmate scores a point each time it stops on blue. Spin the spinner 20 times. Make a tally table to record your scores.

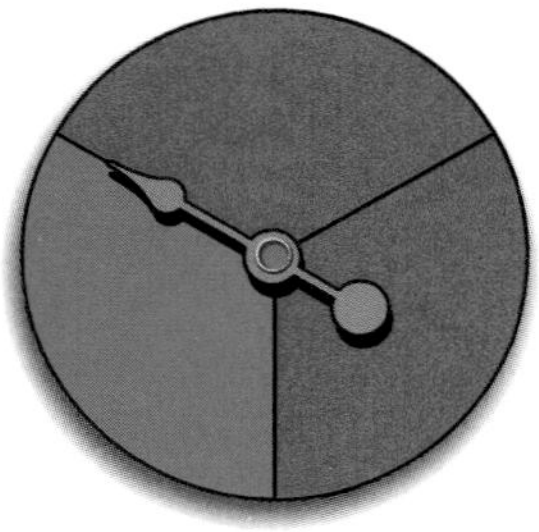

Spinner A

1. Make Spinner A. Predict who you think will win the game. Then play the game.
   a. Who scored more points?
   b. Did you predict the winner?

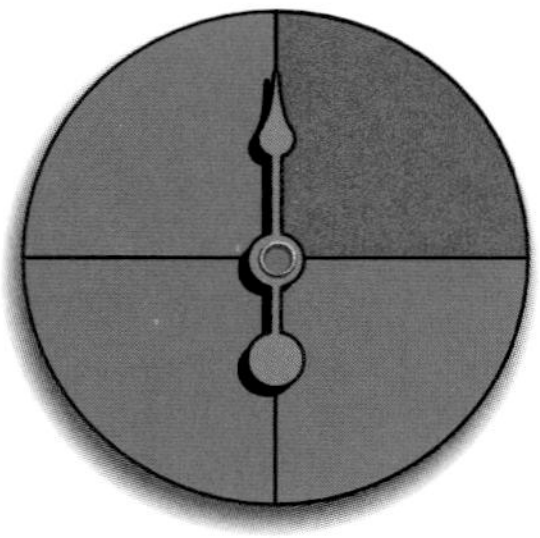

Spinner B

2. Make Spinner B. Predict who you think will win this game. Then play the game.
   a. Who scored more points?
   b. Did you predict the winner?

3. Make a spinner that is fair to both players. Then test your spinner by playing the game.

Talk About It

4. Were Spinners A and B fair or unfair? Tell how you know.
5. How did you make a fair spinner?

Connect

The two possible outcomes for this spinner are yellow and green. The spinner is fair if it is **equally likely** to stop on yellow or green.

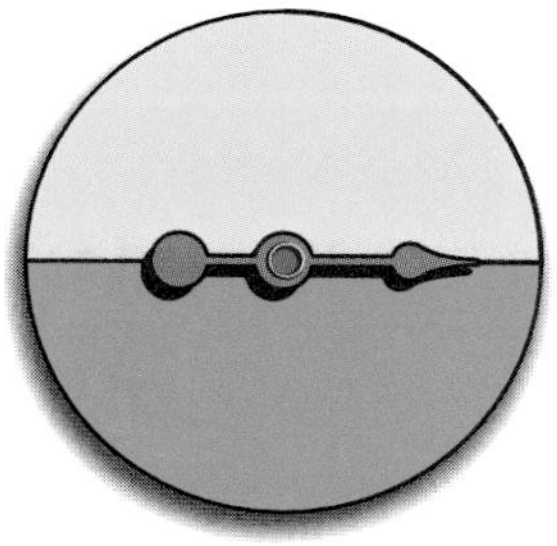

1 out of 2 equal sections is yellow. So, the probability of spinning yellow is $\frac{1}{2}$.

1 out of 2 equal sections is green. So, the probability of spinning green is $\frac{1}{2}$.

Since $\frac{1}{2} = \frac{1}{2}$, both possible outcomes are equally likely to happen.

The spinner is fair.

Practice

Write whether each spinner is fair or unfair.

1. 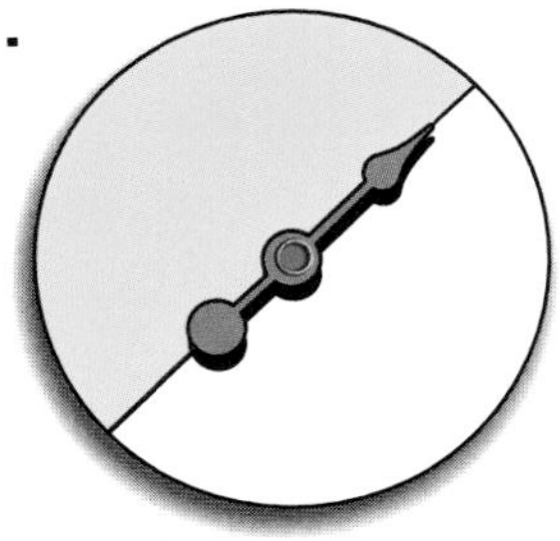

2. 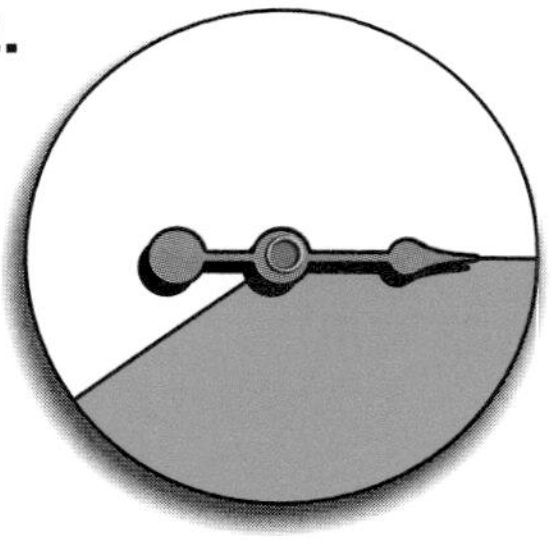

3. 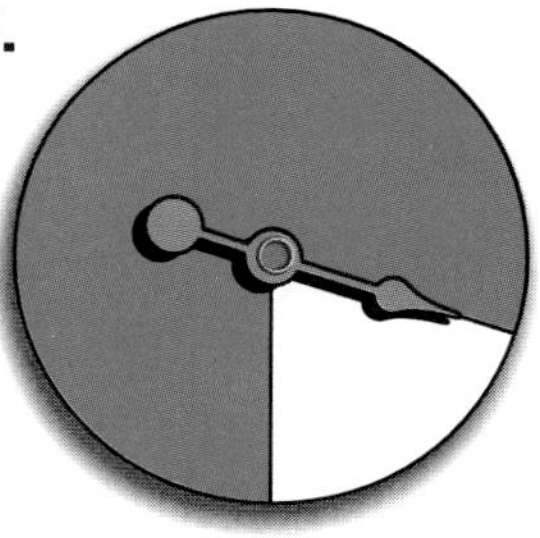

4. 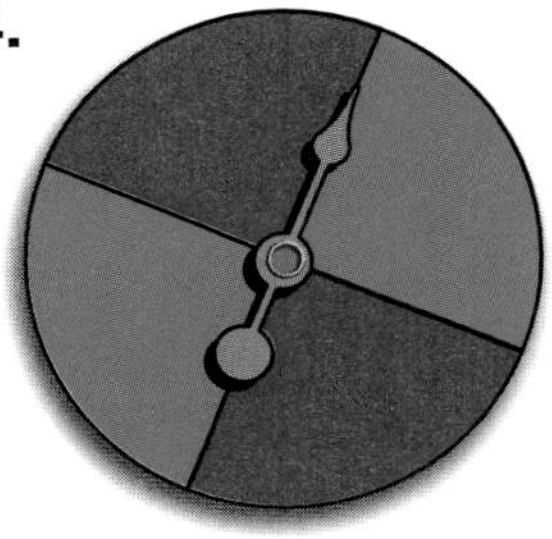

5. Reasoning Are the chances of picking a red cube likely, unlikely, or equally likely? Explain.

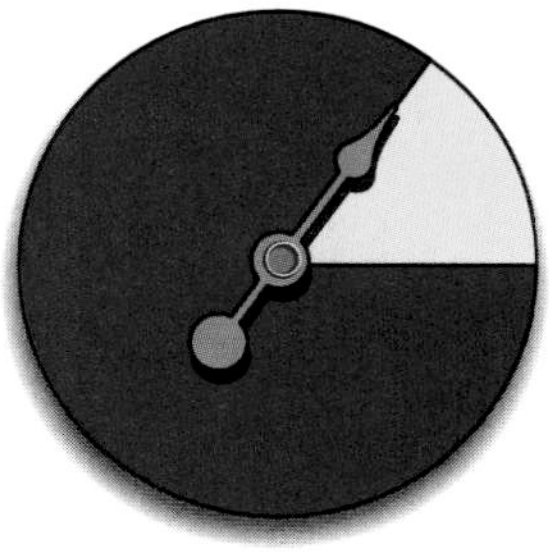

6. Critical Thinking Ricardo plays a board game with this spinner. A purple spin moves him forward one space. A yellow spin moves him back one space. After many spins is he more likely to be ahead or behind where he started? Explain.

7. Journal Draw a fair spinner using 4 colors.

Technology

Testing Predictions

Sometimes the results of an experiment don't match your prediction. Often, if you run more trials you are more likely to get the result you expect. Computers can run many trials in just a few seconds.

Materials
DataWonder! or other random number generator software

Work Together

Suppose you put 1 red cube, 5 blue cubes, and 2 yellow cubes in a bag. Predict which color you are more likely to pull out of the bag. Then use your software to help you test your prediction.

1. Create a Full Data Table.
   - Copy these titles.

Testing Predictions

		Test 1	Test 2	Test 3	Test 4	Test 5
1	Red					
2	Blue					
3	Yellow					

2. Record your prediction.
   - From the Report menu choose **Show Report.**
   - Which color do you think will come out more often?
3. Return to your data table to test your prediction.
   - Click on the data table window.
   - From the Calculate menu, choose **Random Data.**
   - Select Simple Probability. Then click OK.
   - Use A for red, B for blue, and C for yellow. Use the pull-down menus next to A, B, and C to select how many of each you want in the bag. Then click OK.
   - Enter 50 trials. This tells the computer to pull a cube from the bag 50 times.
   - Click Run Trial. The number of times each cube was picked should appear in the window.

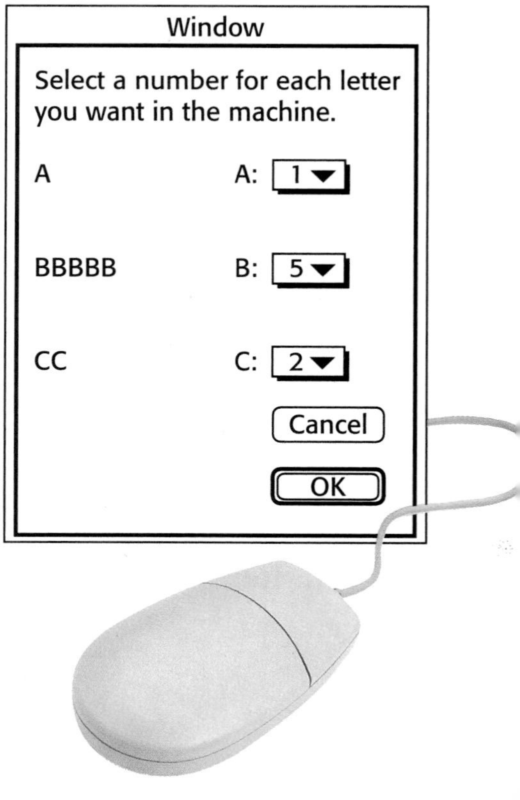

4 Insert the results in your data table.

- Click Insert Result.
- Click on the cell under Test 1.

Testing Predictions

		Test 1	Test 2	Test 3	Test 4	Test 5
1	Red	4				
2	Blue	30				
3	Yellow	16				

5 Run 4 more tests.

- Repeat steps 3 and 4. Make sure to insert the results of each test in the correct column of your data table.

6 Insert the table into the Report Window.

Exercises

Answer **1** and **2** in the Report window below your table. When you are finished, choose **Print Report** from the File menu.

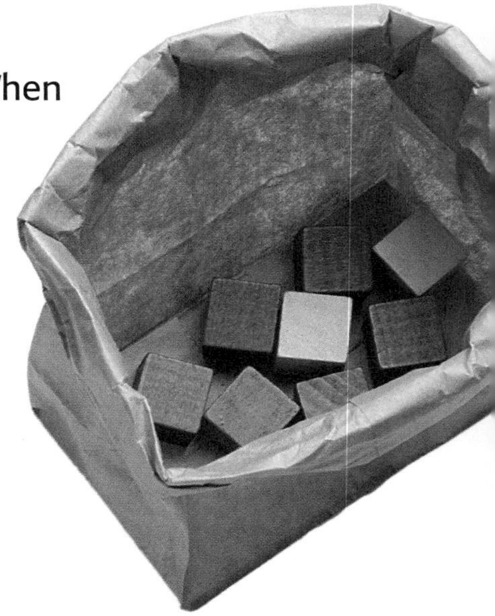

1. Did the color you predicted come out more often in each test?

2. Compare your results with a classmate's. Were the results of each test the same? Did the same color come out more often?

Extensions

Choose **New** from the File menu. Answer **3–5** in the Report window. **Print Report** when you are finished.

3. Suppose you put 3 red cubes, 4 blue cubes, and 2 yellow cubes in a bag. Predict which color you are more likely to pull out of the bag.

5. Did the color you predicted come out more often in each test?

4. Use the Random Data function to help you test your prediction. Run at least 3 tests. Insert your data table into the Report Window.

6. **Reasoning** Think of a combination of red, blue, and yellow cubes to put in a bag so that yellow is more likely to be pulled out. Run a test to see if your combination works.

Problem Solving

Analyze Strategies: Work Backward

You Will Learn
how to solve problems by working backward

Learn

Gwen cuts a piece of ribbon into 2 equal pieces. Then she cuts 15 inches off one of the pieces. This piece of ribbon is now 24 inches long. How long was the original piece of ribbon?

Work Together

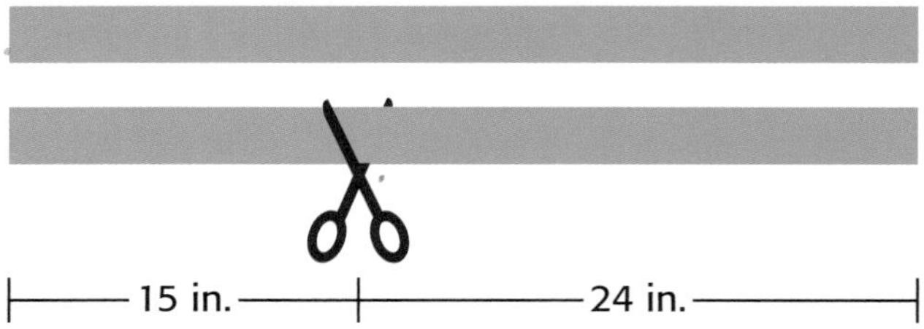

▶ Understand

What do you know?

What do you need to find out?

▶ Plan

List the steps Gwen took.

Step 1: Gwen cut the ribbon into 2 equal pieces.

Step 2: She cut 15 inches off one of the pieces.

Work backward by undoing each step. Start with the last step.

a. Add 15 inches to the 24-inch piece.
b. Double the length to find the length of the original piece.

▶ Solve

Follow your plan to find the length of the original piece of ribbon.

a. 24 inches + 15 inches = 39 inches
b. 39 inches + 39 inches = 78 inches
So, the original piece of ribbon was 78 inches long.

▶ Look Back

How can you check your answer?

Talk About It

1. How did working backward help to solve this problem?
2. What other strategy could you use to solve this problem? Explain.

Check

Problem Solving
Understand
Plan
Solve
Look Back

1. Gwen and Bernard use a box of floor tiles. Gwen uses $\frac{1}{2}$ of them in the entry. Bernard uses 60 tiles in the kitchen. They used 50 tiles for the bathroom. There are 10 tiles left. They want to know how many tiles they started with.

a. List the steps Gwen and Bernard took.

b. List the steps you will take to work backward.

c. How many tiles did they start with?

Problem Solving Practice

Problem Solving Strategies

- Use Objects/Act It Out
- Draw a Picture
- Look for a Pattern
- Guess and Check
- Use Logical Reasoning
- Make an Organized List
- Make a Table
- Solve a Simpler Problem
- Work Backward

Choose a Tool

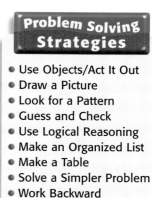

2. Gwen cuts 36 in. off of a board to make a shelf. Then she cuts the rest of the board into 4 equal sections. Each section is 9 in. long. How long was the original board?

3. Sandy likes number riddles. She picked a number to start with. Then she added 16, subtracted 4, and added 5. If Sandy ended up with 45, what number did she start with?

4. Candice needs to get to school at 8:30 A.M. It will take her 30 minutes to get to school. It will take her 45 minutes to get ready in the morning. What time should Candice wake up?

5. Gwen wants to cover her patio with square tiles. If each tile is 1 square foot, how many tiles will Gwen need? Use the patio plan to help.

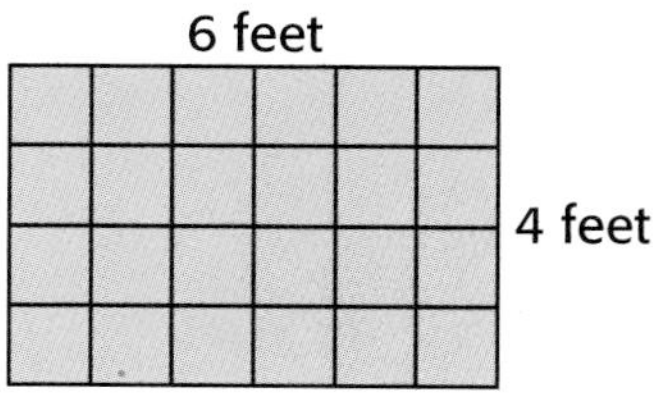

Patio Plan

6. Keri and Jon are playing a game. If the spinner stops on red, the player moves ahead 4 spaces. If the spinner stops on blue, the player moves back 1 space. What spins does Keri need to land on the cherry square exactly, without reaching Home?

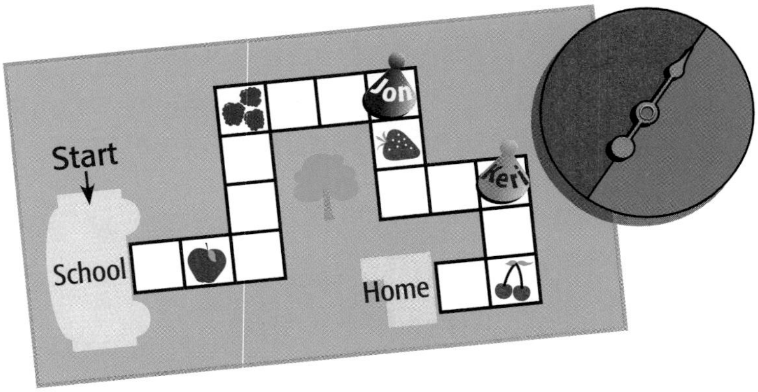

SECTION B

Review and Practice

Vocabulary Match each with its meaning.

1. unlikely
2. possible outcomes
3. probability

a. all results that could occur
b. probably will not happen
c. the chance that an event will happen

(Lesson 8) Suppose you put these cubes in a bag. Predict which color you are more likely to pull out.

4. 

5. 

6. 

(Lesson 9) Copy and complete.

7. 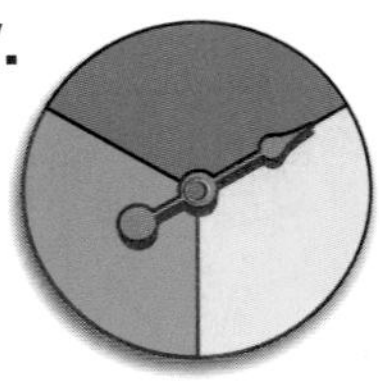

Blue ___ out of 3 or $\frac{\_\_}{3}$

Green ___ out of 3 or $\frac{\_\_}{3}$

Yellow ___ out of 3 or $\frac{\_\_}{3}$

8. 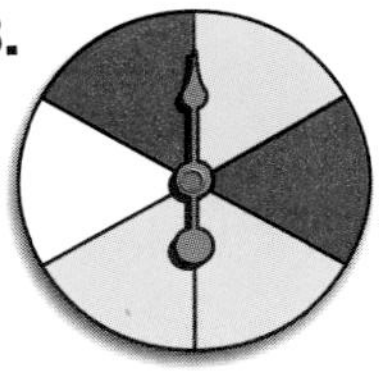

Red ___ out of 6 or $\frac{\_\_}{6}$

White ___ out of 6 or $\frac{\_\_}{6}$

Yellow ___ out of 6 or $\frac{\_\_}{6}$

(Lesson 10) Write whether each spinner is fair or unfair.

9. 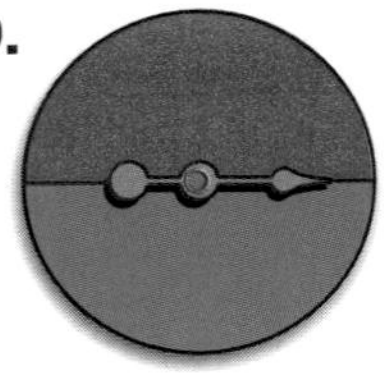

10. 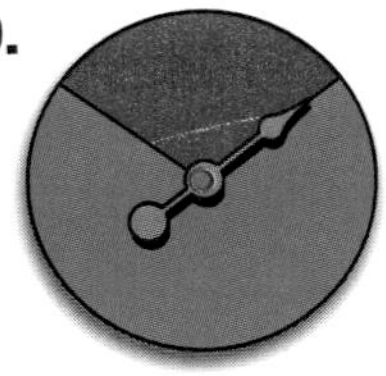

11. 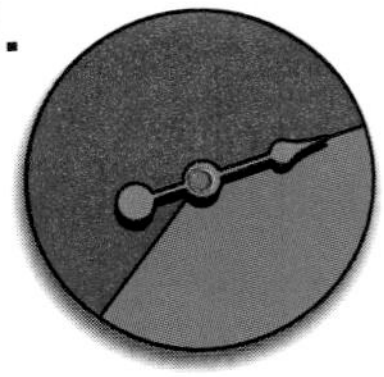

(Lesson 11) Use any strategy to solve.

12. Josie is selling lemonade. She sold 2 cups to her friends and 5 cups to her neighbors. She added 4 cups to the pitcher. Now she has 5 cups. How many cups did Josie start with?

13. Journal Draw a spinner for each.

a. Likely to stop on red.

b. Unlikely to stop on red.

Skills Checklist

In this section, you have:

- ☑ Explored Likely and Unlikely
- ☑ Explored Predictions
- ☑ Explored Probability
- ☑ Explored Fair and Unfair
- ☑ Solved Problems by Working Backward

YOUR CHOICE

Choose at least one. Use what you have learned in this chapter.

1 Picture This

At Home Use a thermometer to measure the temperature outside. Draw a picture to show what the weather is like and what you like to do on days like this. Write the date and temperature.

2 Fill'er Up

Suppose you have 2 empty milk containers. One container can hold 1 quart of milk and the other can hold 1 gallon of milk. How can you use the 2 containers to measure 3 quarts of milk?

3 A Weighty Tale

Write a story that includes an ounce, a pound, a gram, and a kilogram. Use these units so the reader can understand their sizes.

4 Roll 'Em

Roll 2 number cubes labeled 1–6 and find the sum of the numbers. Repeat this at least 20 times. Record the sums in a tally table. Which sum did you roll the most? Which did you roll the least?

5 Are You Game?

Create a game. Will you go on a wildlife expedition or will you take a trip to an amusement park? Draw your game board. Use a number cube or make a spinner to decide how many spaces each player will move. Make sure your game is fair.

CHAPTER 12
Review/Test

(Lessons 1–5) Choose the best estimate for each.

1. 

Ⓐ 1 cup
Ⓑ 1 quart

2. 

Ⓐ 8 lb
Ⓑ 8 oz

3. 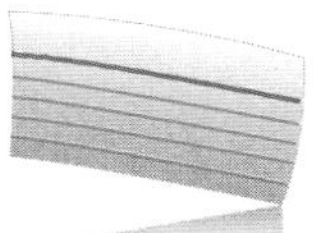

Ⓐ 1 kg
Ⓑ 1 g

4. 

Ⓐ 30°C
Ⓑ 0°C

(Lessons 7 and 8) Suppose you put these cubes in a bag. Predict which color you are more likely to pull out.

5. 

6. 

7. 

8. 

(Lesson 9) Copy and complete.

9. 

Yellow ▢ out of 4 or $\frac{▢}{4}$
Green ▢ out of 4 or $\frac{▢}{4}$
Blue ▢ out of 4 or $\frac{▢}{4}$

(Lesson 10) Write whether each spinner is fair or unfair.

10. 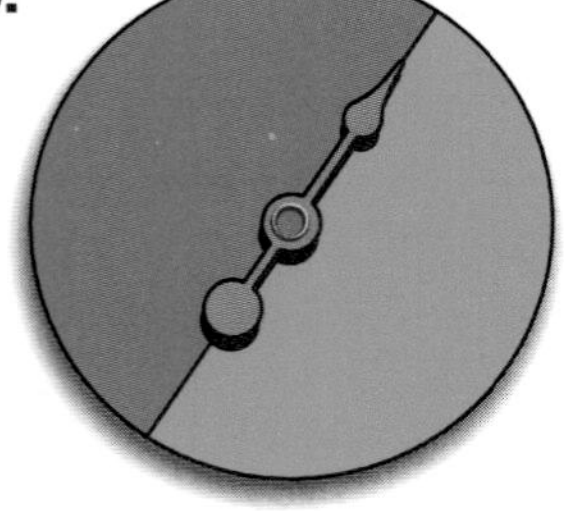

11. 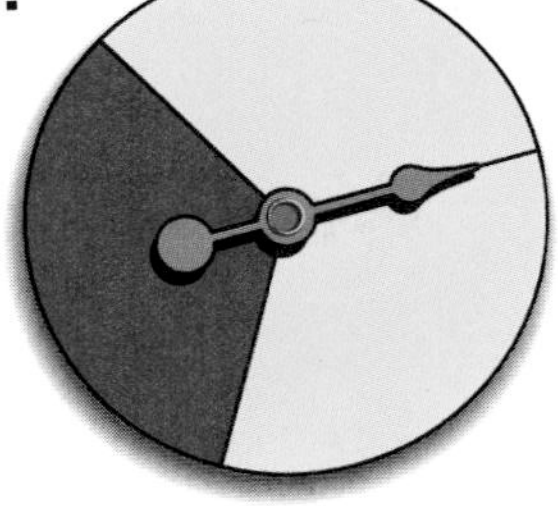

12. 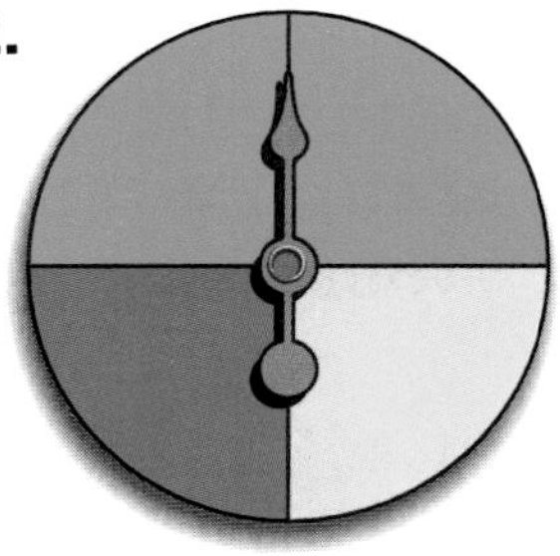

(Lesson 11) Use any strategy to solve.

13. Marvin has some lemons. He uses $\frac{1}{2}$ of them to make lemonade. He uses 6 of them to make lemon cake. Four lemons are left. How many lemons did Marvin start with?

CHAPTER 12
Performance Assessment
A. Measurement

Dwayne works in a grocery store. He is filling the dairy case with these items. Help Dwayne put the prices on the containers.

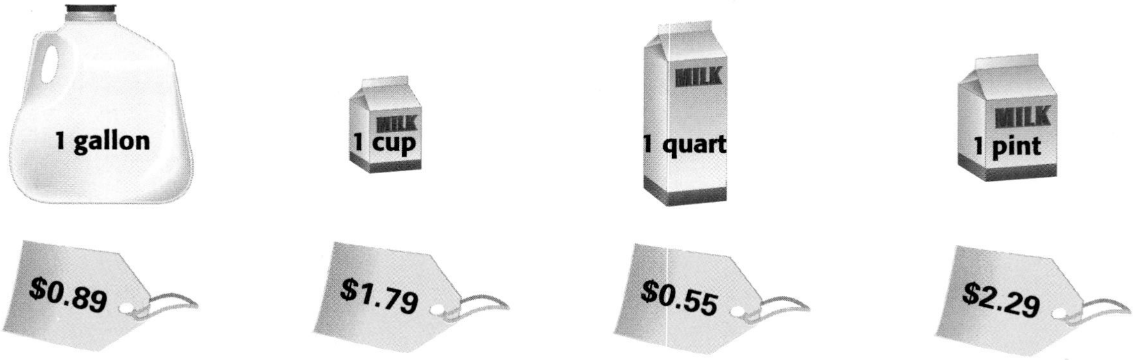

1. **Decision Making** Decide how much each item should cost.

2. **Explain Your Thinking** How did you decide which label went on each item? Explain.

3. **Critical Thinking** Suppose the temperature in the dairy case is about 30°C. Should Dwayne be worried? Explain.

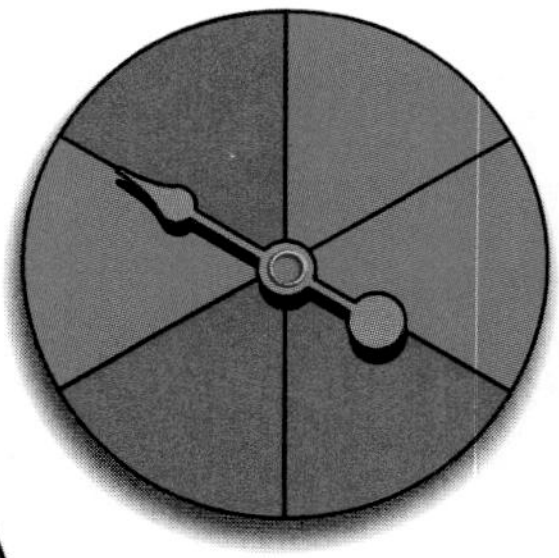

Spinner C

B. Probability

Suppose you and a friend play a game using a spinner. If the spinner stops on blue, you get a point. If it stops on red, your friend gets a point.

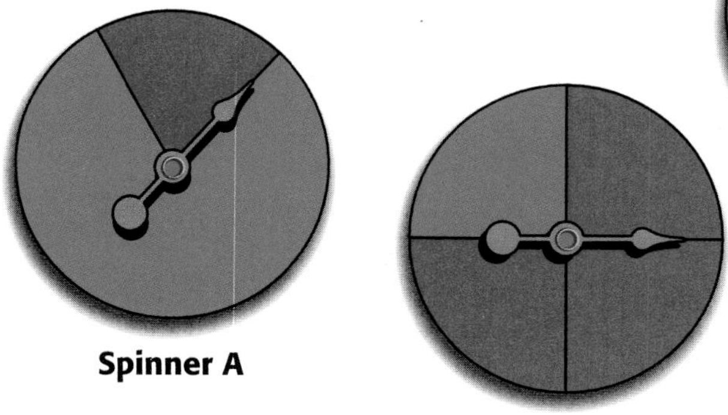

Spinner A

Spinner B

4. **Decision Making** Which spinner will you choose for the game?

5. **Explain Your Thinking** How did you decide which spinner to choose? Is the spinner you chose a fair spinner? Would your friend agree?

6. **Critical Thinking** Draw a different spinner for this game that is fair.

Math Magazine

Yut Nori In Korea, families celebrate the lunar new year by playing a game called Yut Nori. Players toss 4 special sticks in the air to move around a game board. Each player tries to be the first one Home.

round side   flat side

Here's how to play Yut Nori.

- Choose a corner to be Home. Toss the sticks to see how many spaces you can move your marker. If you don't have sticks, you can use 4 counters instead. Use the red side for *round* and the yellow side for *flat.*
- If you land on corners B or C you can take a shortcut Home.
- If you land on another player's marker, send the player back to his or her Home to start over.
- Take turns tossing the sticks. Try to be the first player to return Home.

Toss	Moves
Mo	**5**
Yut	**4**
Keol	**3**
Kae	**2**
Do	**1**

Sample Board

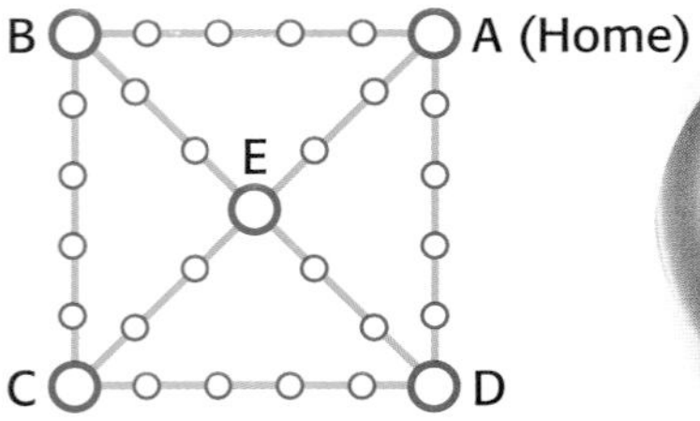

Try These!

Write the number of spaces you can move with each toss.

1. **2.**  **3.**

CHAPTERS 1–12

Cumulative Review

Test Prep Strategy: Follow Directions

Watch for words like *not*.

Which spinner is not fair?

(A)

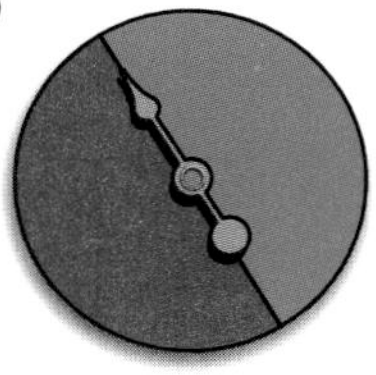

(B)

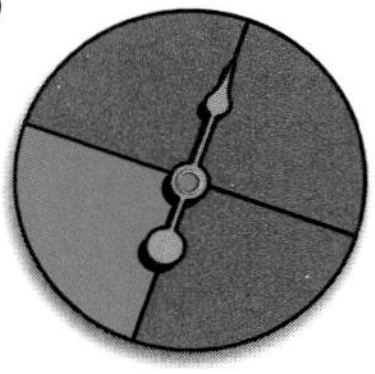

(C)

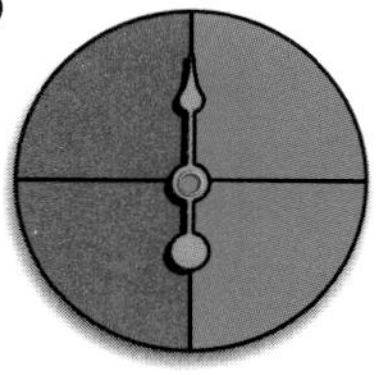

When a question uses words like *not*, you must think carefully about your answer. (A) and (C) are fair spinners, and (B) is unfair. Since the question asks for the spinner that is not fair, the answer is (B).

Write the letter of the correct answer. Use any strategy to help.

Test Prep Strategies

- Read Carefully
- Follow Directions
- Make Smart Choices
- Eliminate Choices
- Work Backward from an Answer

1. Daniela buys a book for \$4.85 and a tape for \$13.92. How much does she spend for both items?

(A) \$9.07 (B) 1,877 (C) \$17.77 (D) \$18.77

2. Which is not the same as 4 cups?

(A) 2 pints (B) 1 quart (C) 1 pint

3. What is the product of 19×8?

(A) 27 (B) 152 (C) 72 (D) 2 R 3

4. Billie arranges 54 photos in her photo album. She puts 6 photos on each page. How many pages does she need?

(A) 8 pages (B) 48 pages (C) 324 pages (D) 9 pages

5. Ed builds a fence around his square garden. Each side of his garden is 45 feet long. How much fencing does he need?

(A) 180 feet (B) 90 feet (C) 45 feet (D) 450 feet

6. Which does not name the part that is shaded?

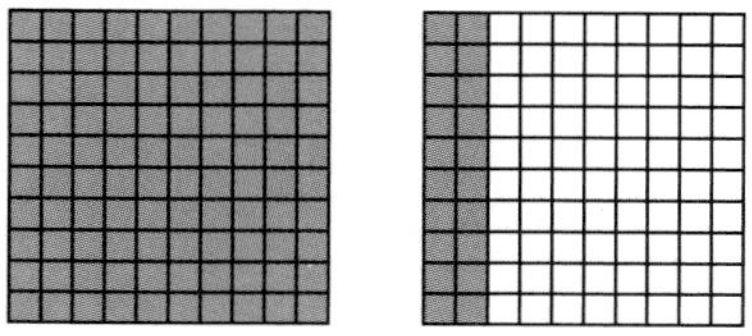

(A) 0.12 (B) 1.2

(C) 1.20 (D) $1\frac{20}{100}$

7. Hector jogs 5 km every morning. How many kilometers does Hector jog in 1 week?

(A) 12 km (B) 40 km (C) 35 km (D) 30 km

REVIEW AND PRACTICE

Set 1 For use after pages 11 and 28.

Use the pictograph to answer each question.

1. What is the most common dog's name?
2. How many dogs are named Rugby?
3. Which name do 15 dogs have?
4. Suppose there are 20 dogs named Fifi. Copy the graph and include symbols and a label for dogs named Fifi.

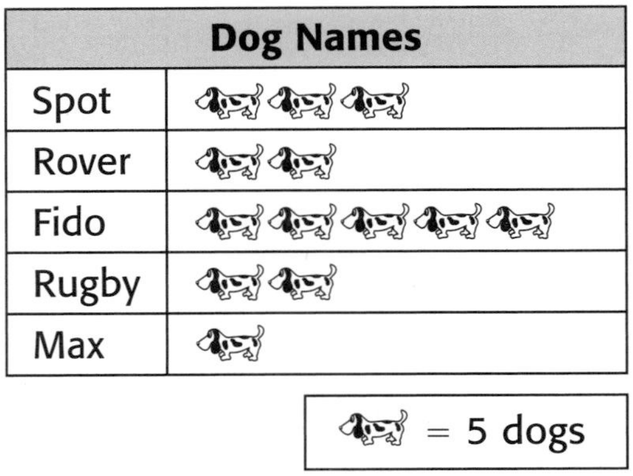

Set 2 For use after pages 13 and 31.

Use the bar graph to answer each question.

1. How many pounds of broccoli were sold?
2. Which vegetable did Millie sell 20 pounds of?
3. Suppose there were 10 pounds of cabbage sold. Copy the graph and include a label and bar to show how much cabbage was sold.

Vegetables Sold at Millie's Shop

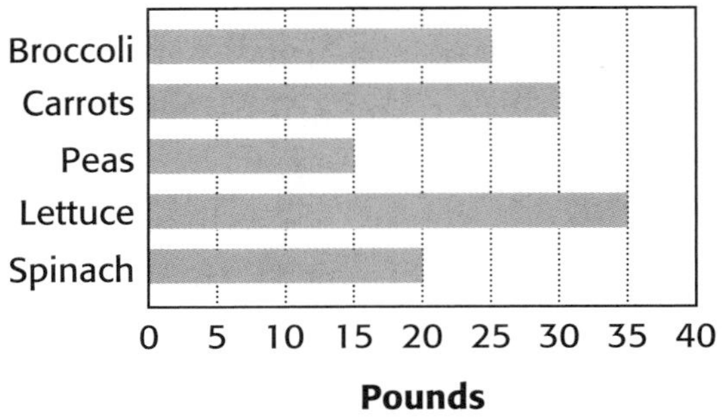

Set 3 For use after page 15.

Use the line graph to answer each question.

1. How tall was Sandy's plant in February?
2. If the pattern continues, how tall do you think the plant will be in May?

Height of Sandy's Plant

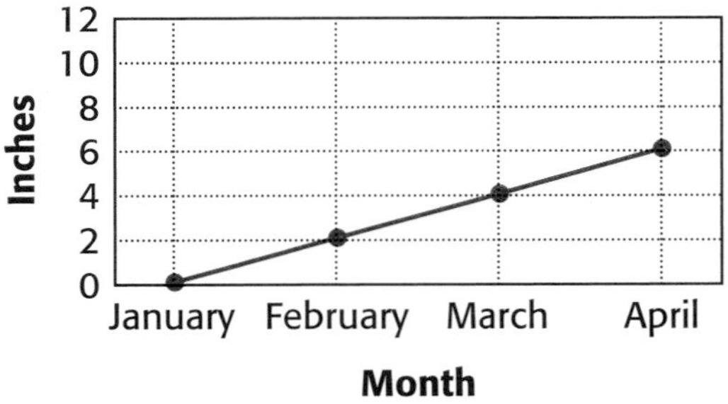

Set 4 For use after pages 19 and 41.

1. **(Page 19)** Steph had 12 crackers and ate 5 of them. How many does she have now? What operation did you use to solve?
2. **(Page 41)** John ran for 50 minutes on Monday. He ran for 40 minutes on Tuesday and 30 minutes on Wednesday. If the pattern continues, how many minutes will he run on Saturday?

Set 1 For use after page 59.

Write each number in standard form.

1. five hundred ninety 2. 100,000 + 3,000 + 50 3. sixty-seven

Set 2 For use after page 67.

Compare. Use <, >, or =.

1. 132 ○ 123 2. 2,999 ○ 3,259 3. 8,201 ○ 8,201 4. 99 ○ 104

Order from least to greatest.

5. 546, 465, 456 6. 1,097, 1,907, 1,079 7. 235, 892, 103

Set 3 For use after page 71.

Round to the nearest ten.

1. 21 2. 51 3. 185 4. 403 5. 67

Round to the nearest hundred.

6. 249 7. 68 8. 170 9. 311 10. 550

Set 4 For use after page 75.

Write each time two ways.

1. 

2. 

Set 5 For use after page 79.

Write each time two ways. Write A.M. or P.M.

3. 

sleeping

4. 

doing homework

Set 6 For use after pages 61 and 85.

Use any strategy to solve each problem.

1. **(Page 61)** Wanda wants to buy 30 ounces of raisins. There are 10-ounce boxes and 1-ounce boxes. How many ways can she buy the raisins?

2. **(Page 85)** The Alvarez family went to a concert at 8:00 P.M. The concert lasted 1 hour and 20 minutes. What time did the concert end?

Set 1 For use after page 109.

Add. Estimate to check.

1. 38 + 7 2. \$15 + \$23 3. 80 + 19 4. 55 + 29 5. 77 + 44 6. 37 + 25

Set 2 For use after page 115.

Add. Estimate to check.

1. 321 + 456
2. 131 + 280
3. 574 + 396
4. 246 + 62
5. 18 + 160
6. 943 + 289
7. Find the sum of 440 and 860
8. Find the sum of 876 and 105

Set 3 For use after page 119.

Choose a tool 

Add.

1. 4,271 + 1,135
2. 1,234 + 3,918
3. 9,010 + 886
4. 1,150 + 74
5. 2,000 + 1,300
6. Find the sum of 43, 258, and 712.
7. Find the sum of 27, 831, and 117.

Set 4 For use after page 129.

Write the total value in dollars and cents.

1. 

2. 

3. What are 3 coins that total \$0.45?

Set 5 For use after page 135.

Add. Estimate to check.

1. \$3.25 + 1.80
2. \$8.46 + 0.95
3. \$7.39 + 4.23
4. \$2.71 + 1.59
5. \$0.60 + 5.75

Set 6 For use after pages 121 and 139.

1. **(Page 121)** Janet and her younger brother Jared are 5 years apart in age. The sum of their ages is 13. How old is each?
2. **(Page 139)** Ana has \$5 to spend on stickers. Dog stickers are \$2.25 a pack, star stickers are \$1.50 a pack, and rainbow stickers are \$1.15 a pack. Can she buy one pack of each? Explain. Do you need an exact answer or an estimate? Why?

Skills Practice Bank Chapter 4

Set 1 For use after page 165.

Subtract. Check each answer.

1. 27 − 12 2. 56 − 8 3. \$80 − \$19 4. 75 − 25 5. 96 − 47

Set 2 For use after page 169.

Subtract. Check each answer.

1. 456 − 123 2. 541 − 280 3. 392 − 116 4. 246 − 82 5. 767 − 677 6. 931 − 925

Set 3 For use after page 173.

Subtract. Check each answer.

1. 271 − 185 2. 342 − 78 3. 940 − 896 4. 715 − 317 5. 681 − 394 6. 847 − 539

7. 230 − 56 8. 165 − 109 9. 110 − 72 10. 345 − 165 11. 871 − 482 12. 443 − 356

Set 4 For use after page 175.

Subtract. Check each answer.

1. 305 − 234 2. 408 − 169 3. 702 − 493 4. 500 − 26 5. 910 − 682 6. 600 − 201

Set 5 For use after page 189.

Subtract. Check each answer.

1. \$3.53 − 1.48 2. \$7.62 − 4.77 3. \$9.05 − 5.38 4. \$15.00 − 8.64 5. \$24.00 − 9.09

Set 6 For use after pages 185 and 193.

Use any strategy to solve.

1. **(Page 185)** A matinee at the movies costs \$2.00. Regular price is \$7.00. How much will 3 friends save by going to a matinee instead of paying regular price?

2. **(Page 193)** Cheryl played 18 minutes of a basketball game, sat on the bench, then played the last 13 minutes. If the basketball game was 40 minutes, how many minutes did Cheryl sit on the bench?

Set 1 For use after page 207.

Copy and complete.

1. 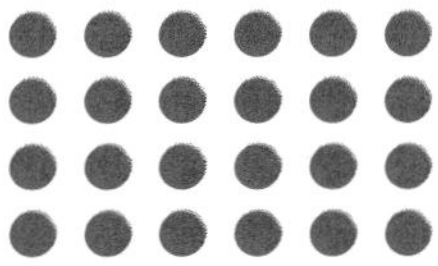

   a. ■ + ■ + ■ + ■ = ■

   b. ■ × ■ = ■

2. 

   a. ■ + ■ + ■ + ■ = ■

   b. ■ × ■ = ■

3. 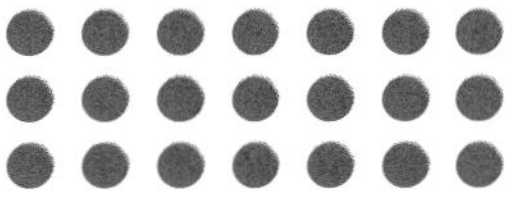

   a. ■ + ■ + ■ = ■

   b. ■ × ■ = ■

Set 2 For use after page 213.

Find each product.

1. 2×7 **2.** 2×2 **3.** 6×2 **4.** 9×2 **5.** 2×8 **6.** 2×3

Set 3 For use after page 215.

Find each product.

1. 5×8 **2.** 9×5 **3.** 1×5 **4.** 5×6 **5.** 5×5 **6.** 2×4

7. 5×2 **8.** 5×4 **9.** 5×7 **10.** 5×3 **11.** 8×5 **12.** 1×2

Set 4 For use after page 219.

Find each product.

1. 3×0 **2.** 0×7 **3.** 1×4 **4.** 8×1 **5.** 6×0 **6.** 1×9

Set 5 For use after page 221.

Find each product.

1. 9×4 **2.** 3×9 **3.** 9×8 **4.** 9×7 **5.** 9×9 **6.** 9×2

7. 5×9 **8.** 4×2 **9.** 9×1 **10.** 5×3 **11.** 6×9 **12.** 8×2

Set 6 For use after pages 225 and 229.

Use any strategy to solve.

1. **(Page 225)** It costs $2 an hour to park on 12th Ave. A car is parked there for 5 hours. How much will it cost?

2. **(Page 229)** A parking lot has cars arranged in 5 rows. There are 9 cars in the first row, 8 cars in the second row, 9 cars in the third row, and so on. How many cars are there in the lot?

Set 1 For use after page 241.

Find each product.

1. 7×3 2. 3×4 3. 5×8 4. 1×3 5. 6×3 6. 3×3

7. 2×9 8. 8×3 9. 3×0 10. 2×3 11. 9×3 12. 3×5

Set 2 For use after page 243.

Find each product.

1. 5×4 2. 4×1 3. 4×8 4. 9×4 5. 9×6 6. 4×3

7. 4×4 8. 3×8 9. 4×7 10. 8×4 11. 4×2 12. 4×6

Set 3 For use after page 245.

Find each product.

1. 6×4 2. 7×6 3. 6×8 4. 3×6 5. 6×9 6. 6×2

7. 5×6 8. 0×6 9. 8×6 10. 6×6 11. 9×9 12. 5×7

Set 4 For use after page 247.

Find each product.

1. $\begin{array}{r} 8 \\ \times 7 \\ \hline \end{array}$ 2. $\begin{array}{r} 7 \\ \times 7 \\ \hline \end{array}$ 3. $\begin{array}{r} 8 \\ \times 8 \\ \hline \end{array}$ 4. $\begin{array}{r} 7 \\ \times 5 \\ \hline \end{array}$ 5. $\begin{array}{r} 8 \\ \times 9 \\ \hline \end{array}$ 6. $\begin{array}{r} 4 \\ \times 8 \\ \hline \end{array}$

7. 4×7 8. 7×9 9. 3×8 10. 8×5 11. 8×6 12. 7×2

Set 5 For use after page 259.

Find each product.

1. $(2 \times 2) \times 4$ 2. $2 \times (2 \times 3)$ 3. $6 \times 1 \times 7$ 4. $9 \times (5 \times 0)$

5. $4 \times (2 \times 3)$ 6. $8 \times 6 \times 1$ 7. $3 \times 3 \times 3$ 8. $(6 \times 0) \times 5$

Set 6 For use after page 265.

Use any strategy to solve.

1. Max needs 68 paper plates for a picnic. If plates are sold in packs of 6, how many packs are needed?

2. Suppose 68 people each need a cup. Cups come in packs of 5. How many packs should Max buy?

SKILLS PRACTICE BANK

Skills Practice Bank Chapter 7

Set 1 For use after page 287.

Find each quotient.

1. $8 \div 2$ **2.** $10 \div 2$ **3.** $6 \div 2$ **4.** $18 \div 2$ **5.** $14 \div 2$

6. $2\overline{)4}$ **7.** $2\overline{)12}$ **8.** $2\overline{)16}$ **9.** $2\overline{)6}$ **10.** $2\overline{)10}$

Set 2 For use after page 289.

Find each quotient.

1. $25 \div 5$ **2.** $40 \div 5$ **3.** $15 \div 5$ **4.** $35 \div 5$ **5.** $20 \div 5$

6. $5\overline{)45}$ **7.** $2\overline{)10}$ **8.** $5\overline{)30}$ **9.** $5\overline{)25}$ **10.** $5\overline{)10}$

Set 3 For use after page 291.

Find each quotient.

1. $15 \div 3$ **2.** $36 \div 4$ **3.** $6 \div 3$ **4.** $16 \div 4$ **5.** $18 \div 3$

6. $3\overline{)27}$ **7.** $4\overline{)24}$ **8.** $3\overline{)12}$ **9.** $4\overline{)32}$ **10.** $4\overline{)12}$

Set 4 For use after page 301.

Find each quotient.

1. $6 \div 6$ **2.** $49 \div 7$ **3.** $63 \div 7$ **4.** $48 \div 6$ **5.** $0 \div 7$

6. $6\overline{)54}$ **7.** $7\overline{)21}$ **8.** $6\overline{)36}$ **9.** $7\overline{)35}$ **10.** $6\overline{)18}$

Set 5 For use after page 303.

Find each quotient.

1. $81 \div 9$ **2.** $56 \div 8$ **3.** $27 \div 9$ **4.** $32 \div 8$ **5.** $54 \div 9$

6. $8\overline{)8}$ **7.** $8\overline{)72}$ **8.** $9\overline{)45}$ **9.** $9\overline{)36}$ **10.** $8\overline{)24}$

Set 6 For use after pages 297 and 309.

Use any strategy to solve.

1. **(Page 297)** Shelly sold nine \$6 tickets and five \$4 tickets to the school play. How much money did she collect? What operation or operations did you use to solve?

2. **(Page 309)** There are 24 seats for the play. How could the seats be arranged in equal rows?

Set 1 For use after page 325.

Name each shape or solid figure.

1. 

2. 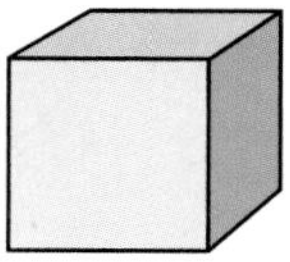

3. 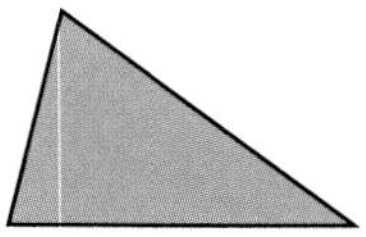

4. 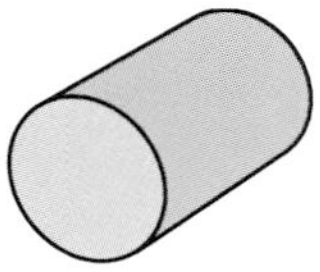

Set 2 For use after page 329.

Write the name for each.

1. 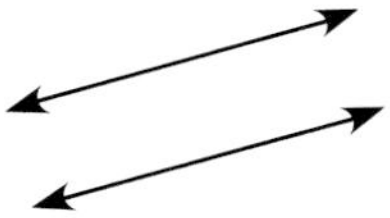

2. 

Write whether each is greater or less than a right angle.

3. 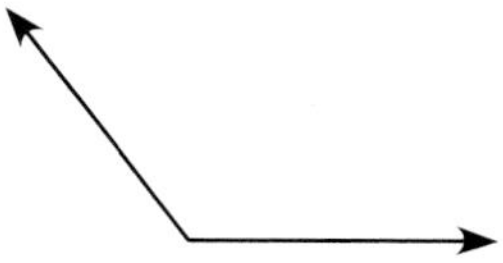

4. 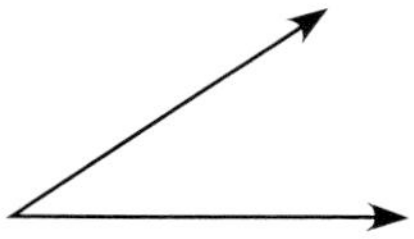

Set 3 For use after page 341.

Find the perimeter of each figure.

1. 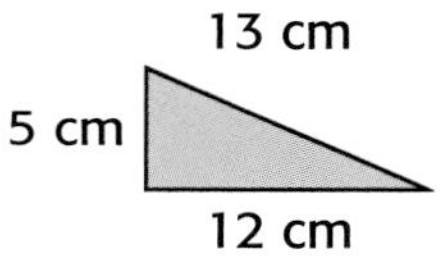

2. 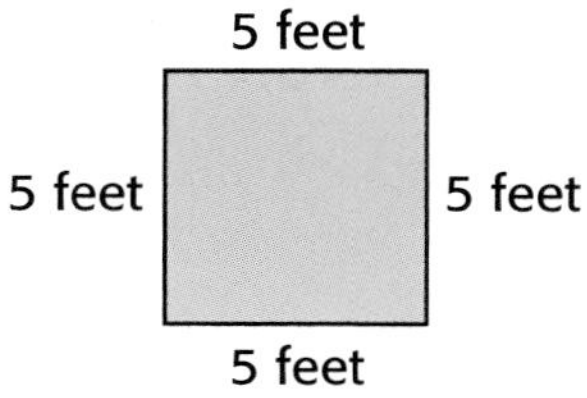

3. 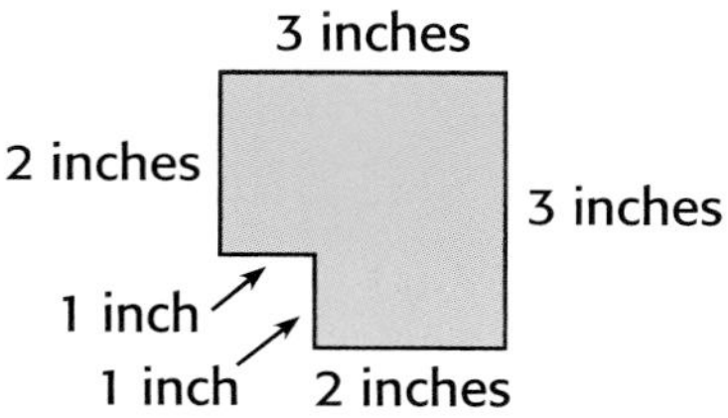

Set 4 For use after page 343.

Find each area. Write your answer in square units.

1. 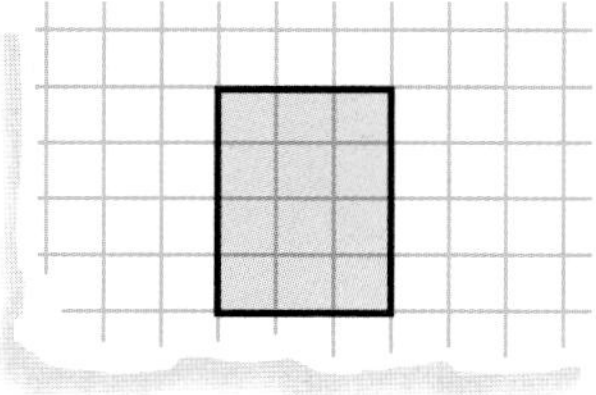

2. 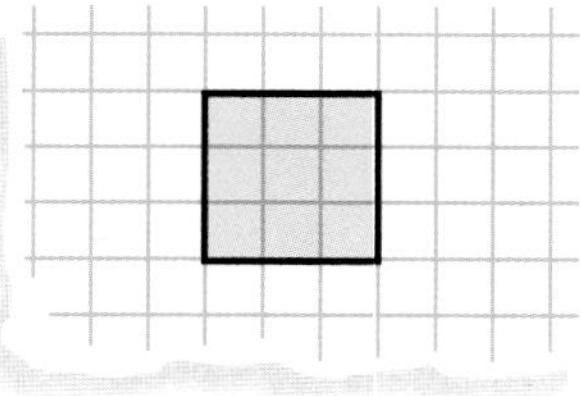

3. 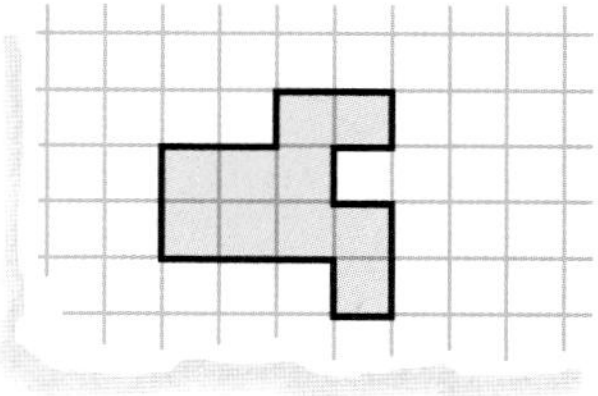

Set 5 For use after page 347.

Find each volume. Write your answer in cubic units.

1. 

2. 

3. 

Set 6 For use after page 337.

Use any strategy to solve.

1. How many triangles are in the figure?

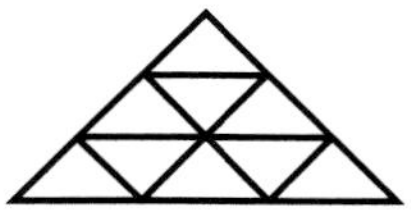

Set 1 For use after page 375.

Find each product. Estimate to check.

1. 20×8
2. 27×5
3. 43×7
4. 51×9
5. 38×6
6. 92×4
7. 48×7
8. 82×9
9. 25×6
10. 32×5
11. 83×3
12. 45×7
13. 21×4
14. 6×87
15. 72×8
16. 5×39
17. 13×6

Set 2 For use after page 379.

Find each product. Estimate to check.

1. 492×3
2. 312×2
3. 504×3
4. 670×5
5. 248×4
6. 432×9
7. 625×3
8. 885×5
9. 109×4
10. 9×320
11. 582×8

Set 3 For use after page 381.

Find each product. Estimate to check.

1. $0.78 × 3
2. $1.50 × 4
3. $3.42 × 5
4. $2.69 × 2
5. $9.28 × 7
6. $9.98 × 2
7. 5 × $0.87
8. $3.09 × 2
9. 9 × $1.01
10. $4.30 × 3

Set 4 For use after page 395.

Find each quotient and remainder. You may use counters to help.

1. $5\overline{)21}$
2. $4\overline{)11}$
3. $6\overline{)34}$
4. $7\overline{)24}$
5. $9\overline{)44}$

Set 5 For use after page 397.

Find each quotient and remainder.

1. $4\overline{)30}$
2. $5\overline{)33}$
3. $3\overline{)5}$
4. $9\overline{)70}$
5. $3\overline{)28}$

Set 6 For use after page 387.

Make a table to solve.

1. Bruce had 16 baseball cards in September. The next month he had 20 cards. The next month he had 24 cards, and the month after that he had 28 cards. If the pattern continues, in how many more months will he have 52 cards?

Set 1 For use after page 415.

Write the fraction of each figure that is shaded.

1. 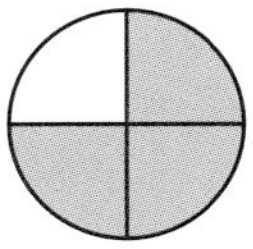

2. 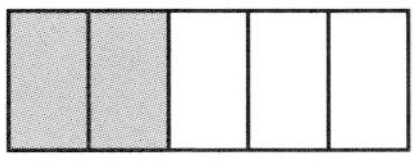

3. 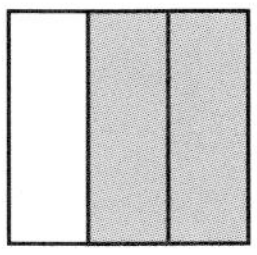

4. 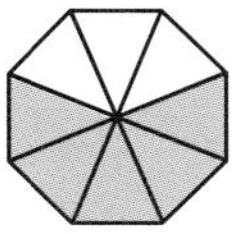

Set 2 For use after page 419.

Compare. Write <, >, or =. You may use fraction strips to help.

1. 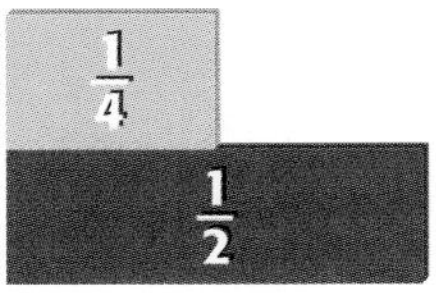

$\frac{1}{4} \bigcirc \frac{1}{2}$

2. 

$\frac{1}{3} \bigcirc \frac{2}{6}$

3. 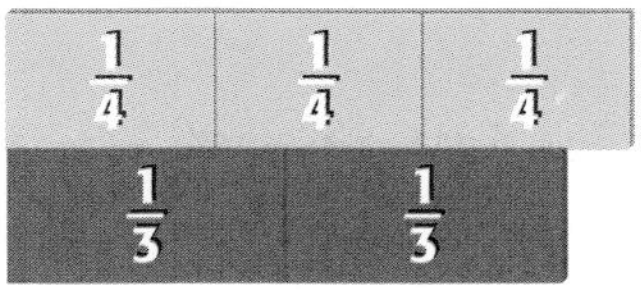

$\frac{2}{3} \bigcirc \frac{3}{4}$

4. 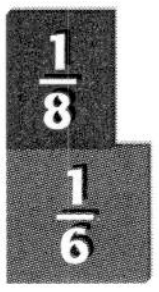

$\frac{1}{6} \bigcirc \frac{1}{8}$

Set 3 For use after page 425.

Write a fraction to show what part of each set is circled.

1. 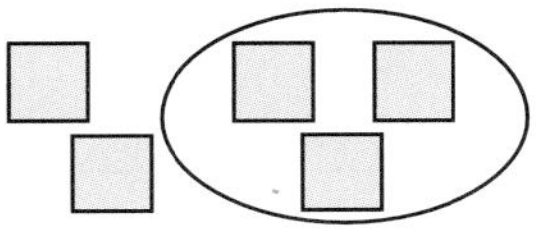

2. 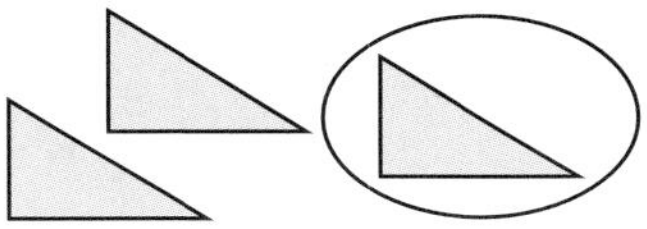

3. 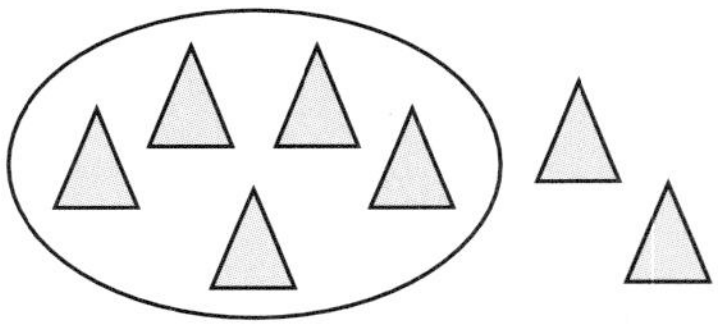

Set 4 For use after page 431.

Find each sum or difference. You may use fraction strips or draw a picture to help.

1. $\frac{2}{4} + \frac{1}{4}$ 2. $\frac{2}{3} - \frac{1}{3}$ 3. $\frac{1}{7} + \frac{4}{7}$ 4. $\frac{9}{10} - \frac{6}{10}$ 5. $\frac{1}{8} + \frac{3}{8}$

Set 5 For use after page 439.

Measure the length to the nearest $\frac{1}{2}$ inch.

1. 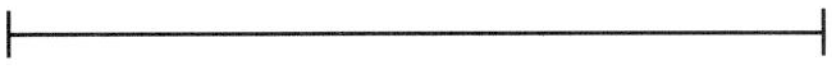

2. 

Set 6 For use after page 445.

Use any strategy to solve.

1. Frank, Bill, Tom, Jean, and Pat are 8, 9, or 10 years old. $\frac{3}{5}$ of them are 9 years old. Tom is 1 year older than Pat. Bill is 1 year younger than Pat. Pat is the same age as Jean and Frank. How old is each person?

Set 1 For use after page 459.

Write each as a decimal.

1. seven tenths 2. $1\frac{1}{10}$ 3. one hundredth 4. $\frac{27}{100}$ 5. $6\frac{92}{100}$

Set 2 For use after page 461.

Find each sum or difference. You may use tenths grids to help.

1. $\begin{array}{r} 2.4 \\ +\,5.5 \\ \hline \end{array}$ 2. $\begin{array}{r} 3.7 \\ -\,0.6 \\ \hline \end{array}$ 3. $\begin{array}{r} 4.8 \\ +\,3.7 \\ \hline \end{array}$ 4. $\begin{array}{r} 7.6 \\ -\,3.9 \\ \hline \end{array}$ 5. $\begin{array}{r} 5.3 \\ +\,3.8 \\ \hline \end{array}$ 6. $\begin{array}{r} 2.3 \\ -\,0.7 \\ \hline \end{array}$

Set 3 For use after page 463.

Write each as a money amount.

1. seventy-five cents 2. $\frac{64}{100}$ of \$1.00 3. $\frac{99}{100}$ of \$1.00

4. $\frac{16}{100}$ of \$1.00 5. six dollars and five cents

Set 4 For use after page 471.

Copy and complete with cm or dm.

1. length of a fork 2 ____ 2. length of a sewing needle 4 ____

3. length of a comb 13 ____ 4. length of a calculator 1 ____

Set 5 For use after page 473.

Write whether you would measure each in cm, m, or km.

1. height of ceiling 2. length of bar of soap

3. thickness of door 4. distance of long car ride

Set 6 For use after pages 467 and 475.

Use any strategy to solve.

1. **(Page 467)** You spent \$9.00 on rides at the amusement park. Some rides cost \$2.00, some cost \$1.75, and some cost \$1.50. If you went on exactly 5 rides, which rides did you go on?

2. **(Page 475)** You go on a go-cart, Ferris wheel, roller coaster, and water ride. The Ferris wheel is your second ride. You rode the roller coaster right before the go-cart. In what order did you take the rides?

Set 1 For use after page 487.

Compare. Use <, >, or =.

1. 2 cups ● 1 quart
2. 1 quart ● 2 pints
3. 1 gallon ● 3 quarts

Set 2 For use after page 489.

Choose the better estimate for each.

1. can of soda
   Ⓐ 355 L
   Ⓑ 355 mL
2. large pot of soup
   Ⓐ 2 L
   Ⓑ 2 mL
3. water used to brush teeth
   Ⓐ 200 L
   Ⓑ 200 mL

Set 3 For use after page 493.

Choose the better estimate for each.

1. television set
   Ⓐ 60 ounces
   Ⓑ 60 pounds
2. head of lettuce
   Ⓐ 1 ounce
   Ⓑ 1 pound
3. stack of books
   Ⓐ 5 g
   Ⓑ 5 kg
4. penny
   Ⓐ 5 g
   Ⓑ 5 kg

Set 4 For use after page 495.

Choose the better estimate for each.

1. sunny day
   Ⓐ 70°F
   Ⓑ 20°F
2. ice cube
   Ⓐ 30°C
   Ⓑ 0°C
3. snowy day
   Ⓐ 10°F
   Ⓑ 100°F
4. hot cocoa
   Ⓐ 95°C
   Ⓑ 15°C

Set 5 For use after page 503.

Predict which color you are more likely to pull out of a bag.

1. 
2. 
3. 
4. 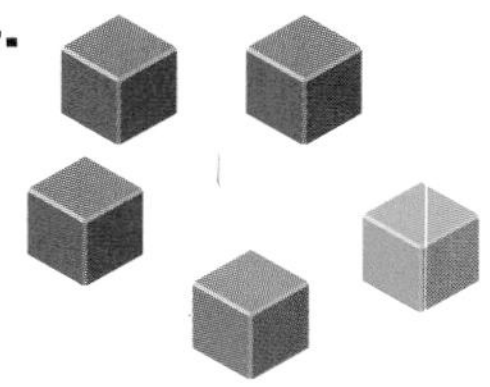

Set 6 For use after page 511.

Use any strategy to solve.

1. Jan picked a number, added 12, divided by 3, and ended up with 5. What numbers did she pick?

Table of Measures

Customary Units of Measure

Length

1 foot (ft)	= 12 inches (in.)
1 yard (yd)	= 36 inches (in.)
	= 3 feet (ft)
1 mile (mi)	= 5,280 feet (ft)
	= 1,760 yards (yd)

Area

1 square foot (ft^2)	= 144 square inches (in^2)

Volume

1 cubic foot (ft^3)	= 1,728 cubic inches (in^3)

Capacity

1 cup (c)	= 8 fluid ounces (fl oz)
1 pint (pt)	= 2 cups (c)
1 quart (qt)	= 2 pints (pt)
	= 4 cups (c)
1 gallon (gal)	= 4 quarts (qt)
	= 16 cups (c)

Weight

1 pound (lb)	= 16 ounces (oz)

Fahrenheit Temperature

32°F	= freezing point of water
98.6°F	= normal body temperature
212°F	= boiling point of water

Metric Units of Measure

Length

1 centimeter (cm)	= 10 millimeters (mm)
1 decimeter (dm)	= 10 centimeters (cm)
1 meter (m)	= 1,000 millimeters (mm)
	= 100 centimeters (cm)
	= 10 decimeters (dm)
1 kilometer (km)	= 1,000 meters (m)

Area

1 square meter (m^2)	= 10,000 square centimeters (cm^2)
	= 100 square decimeters (dm^2)

Volume

1 cubic decimeter (dm^3)	= 1,000 cubic centimeters (cm^3)

Capacity

1 liter (L)	= 1,000 milliliters (mL)

Mass

1 gram (g)	= 1,000 milligrams (mg)
1 kilogram (kg)	= 1,000 grams (g)

Celsius Temperature

0°C	= freezing point of water
37°C	= normal body temperature
100°C	= boiling point of water

Time

1 minute (min)	= 60 seconds (sec)
1 hour (hr)	= 60 minutes (min)
1 quarter hour	= 15 minutes (min)
1 half hour	= 30 minutes (min)
1 day (d)	= 24 hours (hr)
1 week (wk)	= 7 days (d)
1 month (mo)	= about 4 weeks (wk)
1 year (yr)	= 365 days (d)
	= 52 weeks (wk)
	= 12 months (mo)

Glossary

A.M. (p. 78) Times from midnight to noon.

addend (p. 102) A number added to find a sum.
Example: 2 + 7 = 9
↑ Addend ↑ Addend

addition (p. 96) An operation that gives the total number when you put together two or more numbers.

analog clock (p. 74) A clock that displays time using hands.

angle (p. 328) Two rays with a common endpoint.

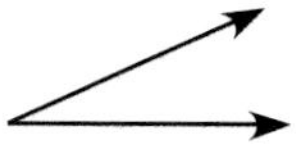

area (p. 343) The number of square units needed to cover a closed figure.

array (p. 206) Objects arranged in rows and columns.

bar graph (p. 12) A graph that uses bars to show data.

calendar (p. 82) A chart that shows months, days, and dates.

capacity (p. 486) The amount a container can hold.

cent (¢) (p. 126) Unit of money. 100 cents equals 1 dollar.

centimeter (cm) (p. 470) A unit for measuring length in the metric system. *See also* Table of Measures, page 530

1 centimeter

certain (p. 500) Definitely will happen.

chances (p. 501) The probability that a particular event will occur.

change (p. 130) The amount of money you receive back when you pay with more money than something costs.

circle (p. 324) A plane figure in which all the points are the same distance from a point called the center.

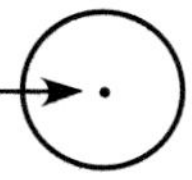

compare (p. 64) To decide which of two numbers is greater.

cone (p. 322) A solid figure that has a circle for its only base.

congruent figures (p. 331) Figures that have the same size and shape.

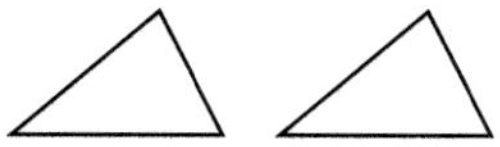
Congruent triangles

coordinate grid (p. 348) A graph used to locate points.

corner (p. 324) Where two sides meet.

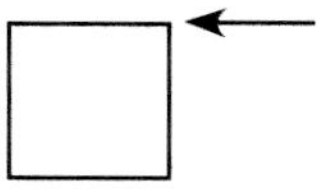

cube (p. 322) A solid figure that has squares for its six faces.

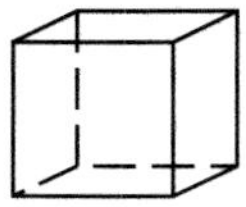

cubic centimeter (p. 347) A cube with edges 1 centimeter long. Unit for measuring volume.

cubic inch (p. 347) A cube with edges 1 inch long. Unit for measuring volume.

cubic unit (p. 347) A cube with edges 1 unit long. Unit for measuring volume.

cup (c) (p. 486) A unit for measuring capacity in the customary system. *See also* Table of Measures, page 530

customary units of length, weight, capacity, and temperature *See* Table of Measures, page 530

cylinder (p. 322) A solid figure that has congruent circles for its two faces.

data (p. 10) Information used to make calculations.

decimal (p. 457) A number that uses a decimal point to show tenths and hundredths. *Example:* 3.14

decimal point (p. 457) A symbol used to separate the ones place from the tenths place in decimals, or dollars from cents in money. *Example:* 4.57 (↑ Decimal point)

decimeter (dm) (p. 471) A unit for measuring length in the metric system. *See also* Table of Measures, page 530

degree Celsius (°C) (p. 494) A unit for measuring temperature in the metric system. *See also* Table of Measures, page 530

degree Fahrenheit (°F) (p. 494) A unit for measuring temperature in the customary system. *See also* Table of Measures, page 530

denominator (p. 414) The bottom number of a fraction that tells the number of equal parts in the whole. *Example:* $\frac{7}{8}$ ← Denominator

difference (p. 152) The number that is the result of subtracting one number from another. *Example:* $6 - 4 = 2$ ← Difference

digits (p. 52) The symbols used to show numbers: 0, 1, 2, 3, 4, 5, 6, 7, 8, and 9.

digital clock (p. 74) A clock that displays time using numbers.

display (p. 265) The window on a calculator that shows the numbers as they are entered and the results of the calculations.

dividend (p. 284 The number to be divided in a division number sentence. *Example:* $63 \div 9 = 7$ (↑ Dividend: 63)

division (p. 276) An operation that tells how many groups there are or how many are in each group.

divisor (p. 284) The number by which a dividend is divided. *Example:* $63 \div 9 = 7$ (↑ Divisor: 9)

dollar ($) (p. 128) A bill or coin worth 100 cents.

edge (p. 322) A line segment where two faces of a solid figure meet.

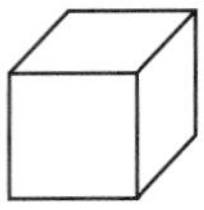

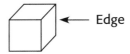

elapsed time (p. 80) The difference between two times.

end point (p. 326) A point at the end of a ray or line segment.

equally likely (p. 507) Just as likely to happen as not to happen.

equivalent fractions (p. 417) Fractions that name the same amount. *Example:* $\frac{1}{2}$ and $\frac{2}{4}$

estimate (p. 68) To find a number that is close to an exact answer.

even number (p. 306) A whole number that has 0, 2, 4, 6, or 8 in the ones place.

expanded form (p. 52) A way to write a number that shows the place value of each digit. *Example:* $9{,}000 + 300 + 20 + 5$

experiment (p. 502) A test or trial.

face (p. 322) A flat surface of a solid figure.

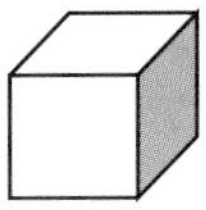

fact family (p. 284) A group of related facts.
Example: $4 + 3 = 7$
$3 + 4 = 7$
$7 - 3 = 4$
$7 - 4 = 3$

factors (p. 206) Numbers that are multiplied together to obtain a product. *Example:* $7 \times 3 = 21$ (↑ Factor: 7, ↑ Factor: 3)

fair (p. 506) All results are equally likely to happen.

fair game (p. 506) A game where each player has an equal chance of winning.

flip (p. 330) To turn a plane figure over.

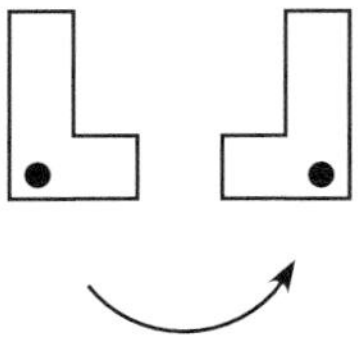

foot (ft) (p. 440) A unit for measuring length in the customary system. *See also* Table of Measures, page 530

fraction (p. 414) A way to compare equal parts to a whole. *Example:* $\frac{3}{10}$ is 3 equal parts out of 10 equal parts.

front-end estimation (p. 136) A way to estimate a sum by adding the first digit of each addend.

gallon (gal) (p. 486) A unit for measuring capacity in the customary system. *See also* Table of Measures, page 530

gram (g) (p. 492) A unit for measuring mass in the metric system. *See also* Table of Measures, page 530

graph (p. 10) A picture that shows data in an organized way.

greater than (>) (p. 64) The relationship of one number being farther to the right on a number line than another number.
Example: $7 > 3$
"Seven is greater than three."

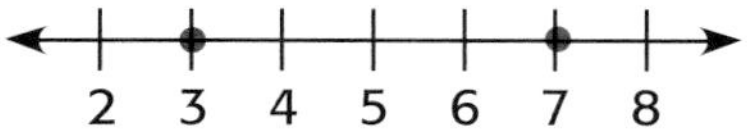

grouping (associative) property (p. 258) When the grouping of addends or factors is changed, the sum or product stays the same.
Examples: $(5 + 2) + 3 = 5 + (2 + 3)$
$(3 \times 2) \times 1 = 3 \times (2 \times 1)$

hundredth (p. 458) One out of 100 equal parts of a whole.

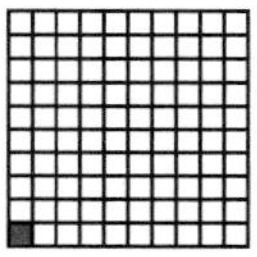

impossible (p. 500) Cannot happen.

inch (in.) (p. 437) A unit for measuring length in the customary system. *See also* Table of Measures, page 530

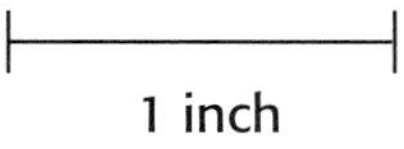

intersecting lines (p. 326) Lines that cross at a point.

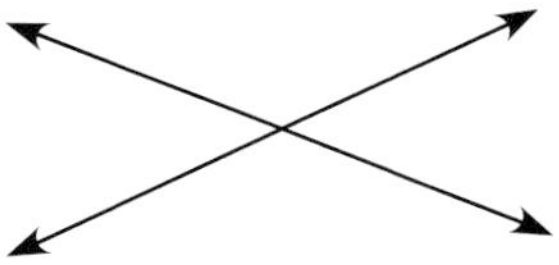

key (p. 10) Part of a pictograph that tells what each symbol stands for. *See also* symbol

kilogram (kg) (p. 492) A unit for measuring mass in the metric system. *See also* Table of Measures, page 530

kilometer (km) (p. 472) A unit for measuring length in the metric system. *See also* Table of Measures, page 530

less than (<) (p. 64) The relationship of one number being farther to the left on a number line than another number.
Example: $3 < 7$
"Three is less than seven."

likely (p. 501) Probably will happen.

line (p. 326) A straight path that is endless in both directions.

line graph (p. 14) A graph that connects points to show how data changes over time.

line of symmetry (p. 332) A line on which a figure can be folded so that both halves are congruent.

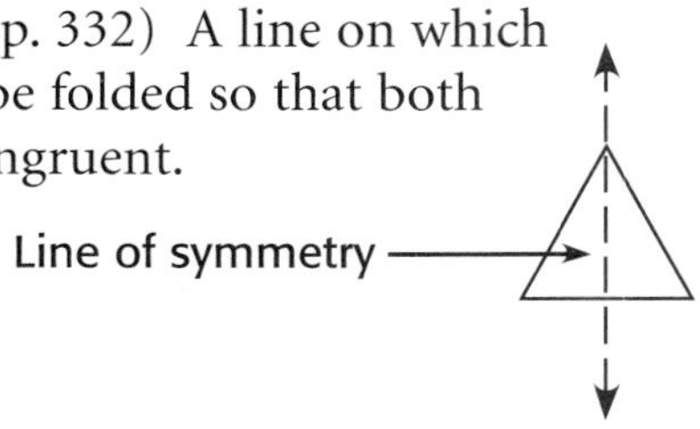

line segment (p. 326) Part of a line that has two end points.

liter (L) (p. 488) A unit for measuring capacity in the metric system. *See also* Table of Measures, page 530

mass (p. 492) The amount of matter that something contains.

mental math (p. 124) Performing calculations without using pencil and paper or a calculator.

meter (m) (p. 472) A unit for measuring length in the metric system. *See also* Table of Measures, page 530

metric units of length, weight, mass, capacity, and temperature *See* Table of Measures, page 530

mile (mi) (p. 442) A unit for measuring length in the customary system. *See also* Table of Measures, page 530

milliliter (mL) (p. 488) A unit for measuring capacity in the metric system. *See also* Table of Measures, page 530

mixed number (p. 428) A number that has a whole-number part and a fractional part. *Example:* $2\frac{3}{4}$

multiple (p. 216) The product of a given whole number and any other whole number.

multiplication (p. 206) An operation that gives the total number when you put together equal groups.

number line (p. 66) A line that shows numbers in order using a scale.

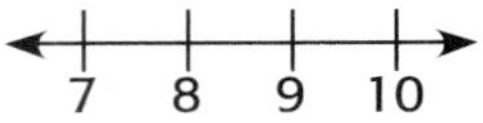

number sentence (p. 150) A way to show a relationship between numbers. *See also* equation
Examples: $2 + 5 = 7$
$6 \div 2 = 3$

numerator (p. 414) The top number of a fraction that tells the number of equal parts considered.
Example: $\frac{7}{8}$ ← Numerator

odd number (p. 306) A whole number that has 1, 3, 5, 7, or 9 in the ones place.

one property (p. 219) In multiplication, the product of a number and 1 is that number. In division, a number divided by 1 is that number. *Examples:* $5 \times 1 = 5$
$3 \div 1 = 3$

operation (p. 18) Addition, subtraction, multiplication, and division.

order (p. 66) To arrange numbers from least to greatest or from greatest to least.

ordered pair (p. 348) A pair of numbers used to locate a point on a coordinate grid.

order (commutative) property (p. 99) Changing the order of addends or factors does not change the sum or product.
Examples: $8 + 5 = 5 + 8$
$3 \times 6 = 6 \times 3$

ordinal number (p. 82) A number used to tell order. *Examples:* first, thirteenth, 1st, 4th

ounce (oz) (p. 491) A unit for measuring weight in the customary system. *See also* Table of Measures, page 530

outcome (p. 503) A possible result of an experiment.

P.M. (p. 78) Times from noon to midnight.

parallel lines (p. 326) Lines that do not intersect.

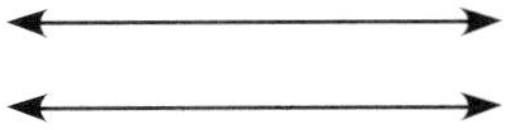

pattern (p. 38) A sequence of objects, events, or ideas that repeat.

perimeter (p. 341) The distance around a closed figure.

period (p. 58) A group of three digits in a number, separated by a comma.

pictograph (p. 10) A graph that uses symbols to show data.

pint (pt) (p. 486) A unit for measuring capacity in the customary system. *See also* Table of Measures, page 530

place value (p. 52) The value given to the place a digit has in a number. *Example:* In 6,928, the place value of the digit 9 is hundreds.

plane figure (p. 324) A figure that lies on a flat surface.

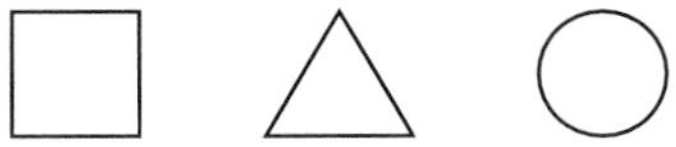

point (p. 326) An exact position often marked by a dot.

polygon (p. 328) A closed plane figure made up of line segments.

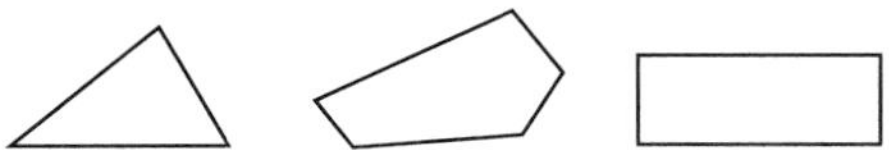

possible (p. 500) Able to happen.

pound (lb) (p. 490) A unit for measuring weight in the customary system. *See also* Table of Measures, page 530

prediction (p. 502) A guess about what will happen.

probability (p. 505) The chance that an event will happen.

problem solving guide (p. 16) A process for solving a problem: Understand, Plan, Solve, Look Back.

product (p. 206) The number that is the result of multiplying two or more factors. *Example:* $5 \times 6 = 30$
↑ Product

pyramid (p. 322) A solid figure whose base is a polygon and whose faces are triangles with a common point.

quart (qt) (p. 486) A unit for measuring capacity in the customary system. *See also* Table of Measures, page 530

quotient (p. 284) The number other than the remainder that is the result of dividing. *Example:* $63 \div 7 = 9$
↑ Quotient

ray (p. 326) Part of a line that begins at a point and is endless in one direction.

rectangle (p. 324) A polygon that has four sides and four right angles.

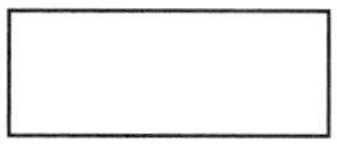

rectangular prism (p. 322) A solid figure whose six faces are all rectangles.

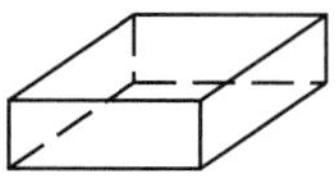

regroup (p. 106) To name a whole or decimal number in a different way. *Example:* 28 is the same as 1 ten and 18 ones.

remainder (p. 395) The number left over after dividing. *Example:* $31 \div 7 = 4$ R3
↑ Remainder

right angle (p. 329) An angle that forms a square corner.

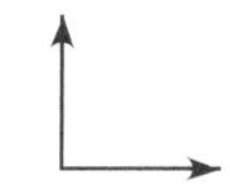

Roman numerals (p. 46) Numerals in a number system used by ancient Romans.
Examples: I = 1
IV = 4
V = 5
VI = 6

rounding (p. 68) Replacing a number with a number that tells about how much or how many. *Example:* 42 rounded to the nearest 10 is 40.

scale (p. 12) The numbers that show the units used on a graph.

schedule (p. 84) A list that shows the times events occur.

side (p. 325) A line segment forming part of a plane figure.

skip counting (p. 3) Counting by a number other than 1. *Example:* To skip count by 2s, think: 2, 4, 6, 8, ….

slide (p. 330) To move a plane figure in one direction.

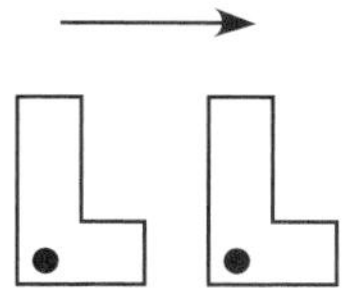

solid figure (p. 322) A figure that has three dimensions and volume.

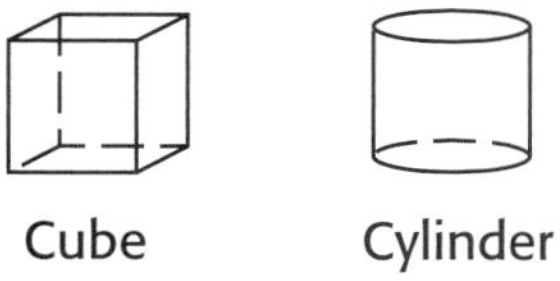

sphere (p. 322) A solid figure that has the shape of a round ball.

square (p. 324) A polygon that has four equal sides and four right angles.

square centimeter (p. 343) A square with 1 centimeter sides. Unit used for measuring area.

square inch (p. 343) A square with 1 inch sides. Unit used for measuring area.

square number (p. 246) The product of a number multiplied by itself. *Example:* $6 \times 6 = 36$
↑
Square number

square unit (p. 342) The unit used to measure area.

standard form (p. 52) A way to write a number that shows only its digits. *Example:* 9,325

strategy (p. 4) A plan or method used to solve a problem. *Example:* Draw a Picture

subtraction (p. 150) An operation that tells the difference between two numbers or how many are left when some are taken away.

sum (p. 96) The number that is the result of adding two or more addends.
Example: $7 + 9 = 16$
↑
Sum

survey (p. 26) Question or questions answered by a group of people.

symbol (p. 10) A picture in a pictograph that stands for a given number of objects.

symmetry (p. 332) A figure has symmetry if it can be folded along a line so that both parts match exactly. *See also* line of symmetry

tally mark (p. 27) A mark used to record data.

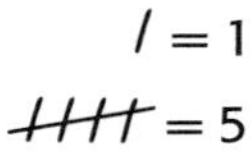

tenth (p. 456) One out of 10 equal parts of a whole.

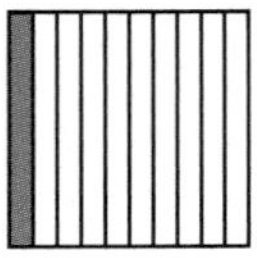

triangle (p. 324) A polygon that has three sides.

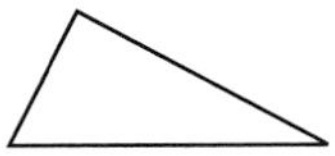

turn (p. 330) To rotate a plane figure.

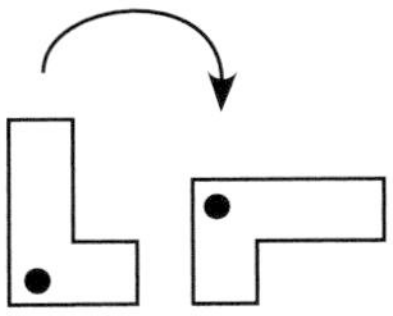

unit (p. 340) A quantity used as a standard of measure.

unit fraction (p. 418) A fraction with a numerator of 1. *Example:* $\frac{1}{2}$

units of time (pp. 74, 82) Minute, hour, day, week, month, year.

unlikely (p. 501) Probably will not happen.

volume (p. 347) The number of cubic units needed to fill a solid figure.

word name (p. 52) A way to show a number using words. *Example:* nine thousand, three hundred twenty-five

yard (yd) (p. 442) A unit for measuring length in the customary system. *See also* Table of Measures, page 530

zero property (p. 219) In addition, the sum of a number and 0 is that number. In multiplication, the product of a number and 0 is 0. *Examples:* $7 + 0 = 7$
$7 \times 0 = 0$

GLOSSARY

Credits

Photographs

Cover Steve Ewert*

Front Matter **i** Steve Ewert* **iiiTR** Jenny Thomas* **iiiC** Jenny Thomas* **iiiB** John Lei* **ivTL** R. J. Erwin/DRK Photo **ivTR** Stephen Cooper/Tony Stone Images **vB** Katrine Naleid* **viT(background behind "Fun")** Douglas T. Mesney/The Stock Market **viT(background behind "Places")** Paul Steel/ The Stock Market **viT(background behind "To")** ZEFA Germany/The Stock Market **viT(background behind "visit")** Keyphotos/ The Stock Market **viB** Katrine Naleid* **viiiTC** George B. Fry III* **viiiTR** George B. Fry III* **ixTR & TC** Ken Lax* **xCL** Katrine Naleid* **xCC** Katrine Naleid* **xiiTC** Katrine Naleid* **xiiBC** Katrine Naleid* **xiiB** Katrine Naleid* **xiiiTL** Bruce Fritz* **xivCL** Katrine Naleid* **1TL** John Shaw/Bruce Coleman Inc. **1TR** Explorer Krafft/Photo Researchers **1BL** Scala/Art Resource, NY

Chapter 1 **6** Jenny Thomas* **7** Jenny Thomas* **9B** Lori Cool* **10** Lori Cool* **13** Laguna Photo/Liaison International **14** John Lei* **16** Jeff Foott/DRK Photo **18** Corbis-Bettmann **25T** Greg Kiger* **26** John Lei* **30** Greg Kiger* **32T** L. Kolvoord/ The Image Works **32BL** Bob Daemmrich/ Stock, Boston **33** Jeffry Myers/Stock, Boston **34R** Jenny Thomas* **35** Jenny Thomas* **38** Jenny Thomas* **41T** National Museum of The American Indian **41B** Terry E. Eiler

Chapter 2 **48TL** Art Wolfe/Tony Stone Images **48TR** Art Wolfe/Tony Stone Images **48BL** R. J. Erwin/DRK Photo **48BR** James Carmichael Jr./The Image Bank **48BR** Stephen Cooper/Tony Stone Images **49T** Carol Hughes/ Bruce Coleman Inc. **49C** J. H. Robinson/Photo Researchers **49B** Zig Leszczynski/Animals, Animals **51** Ron Sanford/Tony Stone Images **52** Tom McHugh/Photo Researchers **56T** John Shaw/Bruce Coleman Inc. **56B** David Cavagnaro/DRK Photo **57** Joe McDonald/ Animals, Animals **58TL** Royal Ontario Museum, Toronto **58TR** James Carmichael Jr./ The Image Bank **58B** J. C. Carton/Bruce Coleman Inc. **61** Renee Lynn/Davis-Lynn Images **63T** Francois Gohier/Photo Researchers **63B** Renee Lynn* **64** Tom Walker/Tony Stone Images **65** Steven David Miller/Animals, Animals **66** D. Robert Franz/Ron Kimball Stock Agency **68** Margarette Mead/The Image Bank **73T** Jane Burton/Dorling Kindersley **73C** Jane Burton-Kim Taylor/Dorling Kindersley **73B** Jane Burton-Kim Taylor/Dorling Kindersley **76** Rachel Holland* **76(border)** Rachel Holland* **80T** Dorling Kindersley **80B** Jane Burton/Dorling Kindersley **84T** S. Dimmitt/ Photo Researchers **84C** M Browning/Photo Researchers **84B** Tim Davis/Davis-Lynn Images

Chapter 3 **92** Katrine Naleid* **93T** Rod Planck/Photo Researchers **94BR** Rob Levine* **95** Stephen R. Swinburn/Stock, Boston **100TR** Tim Davis* **100TL** Renee Lynn* **100B** Renee Lynn* **103** John Elk III/Stock, Boston **105** Joe Traver* **108** The Griffith Institute, Ashmolean Museum, Oxford **109L** Photography by Egyptian Expedition, The Metropolitan Museum of Art **109R** The Griffith Institute, Ashmolean Museum, Oxford **110** Rob Levine* **111** Rob Levine* **112** Cynthia Johnson/Liaison International **113** Jany Sauvanet/Photo Researchers **116R** Joe Traver* **117** Anthony Mercieca/Photo Researchers **118** Davis Barber* **120** Tim Davis* **124** Dan Lamont* **130** Tim Davis* **138T** Renee Lynn* **139L** Renee Lynn* **139C** Geoffrey Nilsen Photography* **139R** Renee Lynn* **144B** Renee Lynn/Davis-Lynn Images

Chapter 4 **146TR** Katrine Naleid* **146(background behind "Fun")** Douglas T. Mesney/The Stock Market **146(background behind "Places")** Paul Steel/The Stock Market **146(background behind "To")** ZEFA Germany/The Stock Market **146(background behind "Visit")** Keyphotos/The Stock Market **146B** Katrine Naleid* **149** Björn Bölstad/ Photo Researchers **161** Hank Morgan/Rainbow **164T** David Leeson* **164B** Geoffrey Nilsen Photography* **168** Gregory G. Dimijian/Photo Researchers **170** Dan Feicht/Cedar Point **171** Porter Gifford/Liaison International **173L** Focus on Sports **173R** Corbis-Bettmann **174** John Lei* **179** Explorer Krafft/Photo Researchers **180T** Collier-Condit/Stock, Boston **180B** Pat & Tom Leeson/Photo Researchers **184T** David Schultz/Tony Stone Images **184B** Gary Holscher/Tony Stone Images **185** Francois Gohier/Photo Researchers **190** Patricia Caulfield/Photo Researchers **193** Lee F. Snyder/Photo Researchers **196L** Joseph Sohm/Tony Stone Images **196R** Tobias Everke/Liaison International

Chapter 5 **202B** Renee Lynn/Tony Stone Images **203** Tony Novak-Clifford* **204T** Tony Novak-Clifford* **207** Jeff Foott **209** Stephen Dalton/Photo Researchers **211(background)** Jeff Gnass/The Stock Market **214** Kevin Horan **224** Alan G. Nelson/ Animals, Animals **225** John Cancalosi/Stock, Boston **229R** Walker Collection, Indiana Historical Society Library **234T** Joe Quever* **234CR** Joe Quever*

Chapter 6 **239** Rick Friedman* **240** Rick Friedman* **241** Renee Lynn* **245** E. R. Degginger/Bruce Coleman Inc. **246** James A. Sugar/Black Star **247** Renee Lynn* **253** George B. Fry III* **255C** J. Shaw/Bruce Coleman Inc. **255B** Scott Camazine/Photo Researchers **256** John Lei* **262** John Lei* **264(frame)** George B. Fry III* **269** Renee Lynn* **270T** David L. Brown/Tom Stack & Associates **270BR** Photo © Michael Holford/ Coll. British Museum

Chapter 7 **272TR & TC** Ken Lax* **272BCR** Ken Lax* **273B** Ken Lax* **275** Bill Campbell* **278** Bill Campbell* **279TL** Ken Lax* **279TR** Ken Lax* **281** Jack Vartoogian **283** Jenny Thomas* **284** Keith Ball* **285** Keith Ball* **286T** James Keyser* **288T** Jenny Thomas* **290R** Peter Steiner/The Stock Market **296** Roger Banes* **299** Lloyd Litsey* **300** Lloyd Litsey* **301** Lloyd Litsey* **302TL** PCD/Frozen Images/The Image Works. Cards photographed by GHP Studio* **302TC** NASA. Cards photographed by GHP Studio* **302TR** Tom McHugh/Photo Researchers. Cards photographed by GHP Studio* **302BCL** The Kobal Collection/Superstock, Inc. Card photographed by GHP Studio* **302BL** Trading card courtesy of TOPPS. Card photographed by GHP Studio* **303** Ken Lax* **316T** Corbis-Bettmann **316R** Jenny Thomas*

Chapter 8 **319T** The Research Libraries, New York Public Library **319B** Annie Griffiths Belt/DRK Photo **320T** ©1957 Rene Burri/ Magnum Photos, Inc. **320B** Giraudon/ Art Resource, NY **321** ©1997 photo by Masumi Yamaguchi/ORION PRESS, Tokyo **321(inset)** ©1997 photo by Numasaki/ORION PRESS, Tokyo **332** Garry Gay/The Image Bank **336** David Simson/Stock, Boston **337** Scala/Art Resource, NY **339** Terrence McCarthy* **341** Will & Deni McIntyre/Tony Stone Images **344** Terrence McCarthy* **345** Terrence McCarthy* **348T** Joseph Nettis/Stock, Boston **348B** NASA **353** Jeremy Woodhouse/DRK Photo **354** Katrine Naleid*

Chapter 9 **359** Andrea Pistolesi/The Image Bank **360T** Phil Degginger/Bruce Coleman Inc. **363** Randy Faris/Westlight **364** Larry Ulrich/ DRK Photo **366** John Lei* **369** Art Stein/ National Engineers Week Future City Competition **369(background)** Jose Fuste Raga/The Stock Market **370L** David J. Sams/Stock, Boston **370R** Marco Cristofor/The Stock Market **372T** Art Stein **375** John Lei* **378** Bill Bachmann* **382BL** John Lei* **382BR** John Lei* **383** Bill Ross/Westlight **386** Steve Uzzell/Woodfin Camp & Associates **389L** Bob McCormack* **389C** Bob McCormack* **389R** Courtesy Katie Eiler **392** Bob McCormack* **394T** Doris DeWitt/ Tony Stone Images **398TL** David Pollack/ The Stock Market **398TR** Owen Franken/Stock, Boston **398BL** Martha Cooper/Peter Arnold, Inc. **398BR** Katsuyoshi Tanaka/Woodfin Camp & Associates **399L** Ernesto Bazan/Liaison International **399R** Jim Anderson/Woodfin Camp & Associates **405T** Jonathan Blair/ Woodfin Camp & Associates **405B** Owen Franken/Stock, Boston **406L** Michael Holford

Chapter 10 **408TL** Katrine Naleid* **408TR** Katrine Naleid* **408BL** Katrine Naleid* **408BR** Katrine Naleid* **409** Katrine Naleid* **411T** Doug Pensinger/Allsport **411C** Jamie Couire/Allsport **411B** Michael Cooper/ Allsport **413** Doug Pensinger/Allsport **414** Jamie Couire/Allsport **423** Eric Miller* **426T** Eric Miller* **428L** Renee Lynn* **428C** Renee Lynn* **428TR** George B. Fry III* **428BR** George B. Fry III* **431** George B. Fry III* **435** George B. Fry III* **435(inset)** George B. Fry III* **439TL** Pat Lynch/Photo Researchers **439TR** Scott Camazine/Photo Researchers **441** Stephen Dunn/Allsport **442T** Harriet Wise*

Chapter 11 **452–453** Pierre Longnus/ Liaison International **453T** John Shaw/Bruce Coleman Inc. **453C** John Shaw/Bruce Coleman Inc. **453B** Jeff Lepore/Photo Researchers **455** Bruce Fritz* **458** Bruce Fritz* **461** Corbis-Bettmann **469** Jenny Thomas* **470** Ken Lax* **471C** Ken Lax* **471BL** Ken Lax* **471BR** Kjell B. Sandved/Bruce Coleman Inc. **472** Jenny Thomas* **475** Joseph Quever* **479** Gilles Bassignac/Liaison International **480TL** Richard T. Nowitz **480TR** NASA **480B** NASA

Chapter 12 **482L** Katrine Naleid* **484TL** Corbis-Bettmann **484TR** Photo © Michael Holford/Coll. British Museum **485L** Nigel Cattlin/Photo Researchers **485R** Charles Riedel* **492T** Charles Riedel* **493R** Jenny Thomas*

Cheryl Fenton* ixTL, xiiTR, 1BR, 28, 72, 92R, 94T, 94TC, 94CC, 94BCL, 94B, 126, 143B, 188, 189, 192, 195, 202T, 204, 205, 226, 227, 233, 238, 242, 249R, 257, 263, 272TL, 272BR, 286B, 287, 289, 333TL, 333BL, 333BR, 408TCR, 424, 437, 438, 439TCL, 439TCR, 439BCL, 439BCR, 439BL, 439BR, 442BL, 442BR, 446, 482R, 483TCL, 483TCR, 483BCL, 483BCR, 483BL, 488T, 492BL, 492BR, 493L, 493C, 513 **GHP Studio*** viiTL, 9T, 20–21, 25, 39, 45B, 70L, 70R, 78, 131, 136, 200TL, 201T, 201C, 228, 234CL, 234B, 236TL, 237T, 249L, 273TL, 274, 276, 279BR, 288T(frame), 288B, 291, 374, 395, 400B, 401, 462, 480C **Ken Karp*** ivBL, ivBC, ivBR, vT, viC, viiTR, viiC, viiB,viiiTL, viiiCL, viiiCR, viiiBC, viiiBR, ixC, ixB, xT, xCR, xB, xi, xiiTL, xiiiTR, xiiiB, xivT, xivCR, xivB, 2T, 4T, 4B, 5L, 5R, 20, 21, 32BR, 34L, 46, 74, 90, 96, 98, 106, 116L, 123, 128, 132, 138B, 144T, 148, 166, 182, 183, 191, 198, 200TR, 200-201B, 218, 229B, 236TC, 236-237T, 236-237B, 237BL, 237R, 244, 250, 251, 258, 260, 264, 265, 270BL, 272BL, 273TR, 290L, 292, 294, 306, 308, 318, 322, 324, 328, 330, 331, 333TR, 334, 334-335, 340, 342, 346, 356, 357, 360CL, 360CR, 372BL, 372BR, 380, 400T, 406R, 408TCL, 410, 412, 416, 418, 426B, 430, 432, 436, 440, 444, 450, 452T, 452B, 465, 471T, 483T, 483BR, 484B, 486, 488B, 490, 497, 499, 501, 502, 504, 506, 509, 516 **Parker/Boon Productions and Dorey Sparre Photography*** ivC, 48C, 54, 85, 152, 154, 158, 162, 186L,186R, 206, 211, 212, 216, 220, 254, 255T, 360B, 362, 382T, 384, 390, 394B, 396, 456, 460

*Photographed expressly for Scott Foresman - Addison Wesley.

Illustrations

Barbara Hoopes Ambler 443b **John Amoss** 40a–40c, 130b, 226b, 318c, 489a–489f **Scott Angle** 380c, 381a, 491b–491i, 498a–498h, 500a **Sam Assefa** 326a **Christine Benjamin** 6c, 10b, 11a, 17a, 20b, 21a, 24a, 29a–29d, 38b, 41b–41h, 42a, 43a, 44a, 46b, 92c, 93d–93k, 161b, 198e–98j, 200c, 200d, 201a–201d, 216b, 235a–235c, 269a, 505d, 510a, 513c **John Berg** 37b, 43b, 403c **Lisa Blackshear** 319b, 319d **Ken Bowser** iiid, 26b, 26f, 276b, 276c, 277b, 277c, 415j–415l, 420b, 420d, 420f, 427c, 427e, 427f, 428c, 428d, 434a–434g, 466a, 477d–477f **Elizabeth Brandt** 408f **Mark Busacca** 141b **Cameron Eagle** 3a, 3c, 19a, 23a, 115a, 223a, 305a **Rob Ebersol** 61a, 82a, 184c, 188a, 197a, 278d, 279b, 305c, 315a, 315b, 361c–361e, 370e, 374a, 393a, 421j–421n, 425a–425g, 429a–429h, 447b, 490a, 491a, 500b **Barb Friedman** 391d **Frank Frisari** 39e, 53c, 56b, 75i, 231a, 486b, 487a–487c, 496a, 514a–514d **Alan Guansing** 208a **Gary Hallgren** 160a, 177a, 178a, 263b, 377a **Eric Hill** 127e **Susan Jaekel** 150a –150c, 278c, 282a, 282b, 282d, 309a, 309b, 312a **Paul Jermann** 406b **Dave Jonason** 15b, 250a, 323a–323d, 338a, 375b **Christopher Kelly** 50d, 50g–50i **Jill Kongabel** 479a **Paul Koziarz** 28c, 332b, 348a, 349a, 363b, 367a, 397a, 399a, 405b, 463b, 467a, 473b–473e **Campbell Laird** 141c **Patrick Merewether** 231b **Karen Minot** 387a **Mas Miyamoto** 432a **Chris Mussselman** 27a **Hiber Nelson** 149a, 156a **Bill Pasini** 1d, 95b, 102a, 113a, 163c, 168b, 242b 353b **Marina Roth Patton** 280a, 280b, 479b **Ann Pickard** 229b, 229c, 231c, 249b, 267c, 488a, 488b, 495e–495g, 513d **Cary Rillo** 513b **Saul Rosenbaum** 17c, 60a, 87a–87c, 195a, 195d, 267a, 267b, 327g, 327h, 333e–333l, 337a, 351b, 351c, 352e–352h, 447a, 447c, 487d–487g, 493d–493f, 513a, 515a, 515b **Brooke Scudder** 39d **Rosalind Solomon** 89a **Gordon Silveria** 494g–494j **Linda Stinchfield** 1a, 433a, 433b **Jennifer Thermes** 358b **Bill Thompson** 50b–50f **Nancy Tobin** 134a–134c, 135a **Joe VanderBos** 40d, 325e–325h, 329a–329c, 463a, 473a **Thomas Ward** 37a, 193b, 355b, 403d, 487h **Jil Weil** 6b, 8a, 8b, 34b, 34d, 48g, 48h, 50a, 92b, 92d, 94a, 132f, 146c, 146e, 147a, 148a, 182b, 198a, 200b, 201e, 202a, 236b, 238a, 238c, 265b, 265c, 270d, 272b, 272e, 274a, 274c, 294d, 316c, 318b, 320a, 334c, 334d, 335b, 335c, 356a–357b, 358a, 384g, 408a, 409b, 410a, 450b–450f, 452b, 454a, 454b, 480d, 480e, 482b, 482d–482g, 484a, 508b, 508c, 509a, 516a, 516c–516e **Qin-Zhong Yu** 494a– 494e, 495a–495d, 495m, 498i, 498j, 511a **Precision Graphics, Paul Koziarz and QYA Design Studio** All technical artwork throughout; all generated electronically

Text and Art

Chapter 6 pp. 236, 269, from *Pueblo Indian Cookbook* (1977), ©Museum of New Mexico Press.

CREDITS

Index

A

Abacus, 90
Addend, 102, 103, 118
Addition, 92–145
- column, 118–119, 122
- decimals, 460–461, 468, 478
- extending, 123–140
- 4-digit numbers, 116–117, 122
- fractions, 430–431, 434, 448
- greater numbers, 105–122
- on a hundred chart, 98–99
- money, 105–122, 134–135, 140
- patterns in, 96–97
- with regrouping, 106–107, 108, 111, 122
- 3-digit numbers, 110–113, 122
- 2-digit numbers, 108–109, 122
- whole numbers, 92–145

Algebra
- balancing scales, 310–311, 312
- coordinate grid, 348–349, 350
- equality/inequality symbols (<, >), 64–65, 66–67, 69, 72, 115, 117, 127, 145, 173, 177, 187, 193, 293, 442, 446, 485, 487
- finding a rule, 20–21, 59, 137, 231, 245, 293, 294–295, 301, 365, 374, 383
- missing numbers, 100–101
- number sentences and, 59, 65, 75, 119, 155, 173, 219, 223, 247, 314, 367, 379, 421, 429, 463, 473
- patterns and, 96–97, 100–101, 104, 125, 135, 144, 152–153, 160, 165, 211, 213, 221, 230, 245, 257, 266, 268, 292–293, 362–363, 368, 386–387, 390–391, 417, 443

Algebra readiness, 59, 65, 67, 75, 81, 99, 119, 127, 137, 153, 155, 173, 193, 245, 247, 255, 259, 281, 293, 301, 341, 365, 367, 374, 379, 383, 421, 429, 463, 473
A.M., 78
Angle, 328–329
- right, 328, 329

Applications
- Real-life applications of mathematics are found throughout this book. A few instances are shown below. *See also* specific subject areas.
- animals, 16, 52, 56, 64, 80, 168, 193, 224, 225, 296, 492
- archaeology, 108
- architecture, 326, 336, 344, 364, 372
- birds, 66, 80, 116, 193
- carnivorous plants, 60
- collections, 30, 164, 284, 286, 300
- environment, 118, 168, 360
- food, 28, 237, 238, 240, 242, 246, 250, 269, 428
- fund-raisers, 124, 392
- games, 148, 273, 410, 454, 506, 516
- hobbies, 123, 203, 278
- inventions, 229
- parks, 156, 184, 370
- recreation, 76, 170, 173, 398, 414, 442, 458
- rocks, 138, 164
- space exploration, 165, 175, 480
- time capsule, 110
- volcanoes, 147, 179, 180, 187

Area, 342–343, 344–345, 350
Array, 206, 366–367
Art. *See* Fine arts

B

Bar graph, 12, 113
- making, 30–31, 42
- and problem solving, 16–18
- reading, 12–13, 24
- using, 13, 24, 43, 47, 49, 53, 113, 145, 146, 168, 199, 317, 355, 357, 389

Basic facts. *See also* Memorization activities
- addition, 95
- division, 389, 411
- fact family, 150
- mixed review, 11, 13, 15, 27, 29, 31
- multiplication, 211–234, 236–271, 275, 283, 299, 359
- place value, 455
- remember the facts, 23, 37, 249
- reviewing skills, 2-3
- stop and practice, 22–23, 36–37, 222–223, 248–249, 305
- subtraction, 149–151

C

Calculator. *See also* Tool, Choose a
- addition, 96, 116, 117, 141
- ancient abacus as, 90
- decimals, 464–465
- division, 292, 390, 400–401
- doubling with, 264–265
- factors, 218
- missing numbers, finding, 101
- for fractions, 464–465
- for multiplication, 362
- for subtraction, 152

Calendar, 82–83, 86, 270
Capacity
- customary units, 486–487, 498
- metric units, 488–489, 498

Careers, 81, 175, 365

Cents, 126, 127, 128–129, 140, 142, 462
Certain, 500, 501
Change (making), 130–131, 140, 142. *See also* Money
Circle, 324, 325
Clock. *See* Time
Coins, 126–127, 140
Column addition, 118–119, 122
Communication. *See also* Journal
In every lesson, students are encouraged to talk about what they have learned and to explain their thinking.
classroom conversation, 116, 124, 174, 180, 186, 220, 262, 308, 372, 382, 474
Write Your Own Problem, 11, 15, 17, 21, 41, 109, 113, 135, 151, 165, 169, 181, 189, 282, 285, 301, 375, 397, 425
Comparing
fractions, 418–419, 422
numbers, 64–65, 72, 88
ordering numbers and, 66
Computers. *See also* World Wide Web
congruent figures, 334–335
drawing arrays, 267
drawing patterns, 351
lines of symmetry, 334–335
making graphs, 34–35
testing predictions, 508–509
Cone, 322, 323
Congruent/congruence, 330, 331, 334–335
Consumer math, 17, 34–35, 40, 44, 71, 93, 97, 121, 124, 127, 130–131, 134–139, 140, 142–143, 153, 155, 157, 175, 184, 188–189, 191, 194, 200, 209, 213, 230, 232–233, 254, 263–264, 271, 279, 282, 297, 301, 317, 355, 380–381, 392–395, 397, 434, 451, 463, 466–467, 482, 515, 517
Cooperative learning, 8, 16, 18, 20, 26, 28, 30, 33, 34, 38–39, 50, 54, 60, 76, 84–85, 94, 96, 98, 100, 106, 120, 130, 138, 148, 152, 154, 158, 162, 166, 184, 190, 202, 204, 208, 216, 218, 224–225, 226–228, 238, 251, 254, 256, 274, 276, 278, 280, 292, 296, 306, 310, 320, 322, 324, 328, 330, 332, 334–335, 336, 340, 342, 345, 346, 358, 360, 362, 366, 386, 390, 394, 399, 400, 410, 412, 416, 418, 426, 430, 433, 436, 440, 444, 454, 456, 460, 464, 467, 470, 484, 486, 490, 497, 500, 502, 504, 506, 510
Coordinate grid, 348–349, 350
Corner, 324
Critical thinking, 11, 71, 75, 77, 89, 97, 139, 143, 189, 197, 229, 233, 263, 269, 279, 293, 297, 315, 325, 333, 353, 361, 371, 374, 375, 379, 388, 397, 405, 417, 425, 429, 434, 449, 479, 489, 507, 515
Cube, 322, 323, 325
Cubic unit, 346
Cubit, 450
Cultural connection, 28, 38, 41, 46, 48, 51, 58, 72, 90, 92, 95, 102–103, 108–109, 126, 147, 164, 168, 175, 198, 204, 229, 234, 236, 238, 240, 242, 269, 270, 272, 273, 281, 286, 290, 321, 332, 336, 341, 353, 354, 358, 405, 406, 408, 409, 411, 414, 415, 422, 435, 441, 479, 484, 495, 499, 505, 516
Cumulative Review, 47, 91, 145, 199, 235, 271, 317, 355, 407, 451, 481, 517. *See also* Mixed Review and Test Prep; Review/Test
Customary units
cup, 486–487
Fahrenheit, 494
foot, 440–443, 446, 450
gallon, 486–487
inch, 436–441, 446, 450
mile, 442–443
ounce, 490–491
pint, 486–487
pound, 490
quart, 486–487
yard, 442–443, 446
Cylinder, 322, 323, 325

D

Data, 11, 17, 19, 26–27, 31, 59, 65, 71, 81, 83, 89, 103, 117, 121, 127, 129, 135, 139, 140, 143, 157, 165, 172, 181, 189, 193, 194, 197, 209, 213, 221, 229, 233, 241, 259, 269, 281, 287, 291, 303, 307, 309, 315, 323, 327, 349, 353, 363, 365, 374, 379, 397, 405, 415, 421, 431, 437, 439, 441, 449, 459, 473, 471, 479, 491, 493, 495, 501, 503
Data File, 6–7, 48–49, 92–93, 146–147, 200–201, 236–237, 272–273, 318–319, 356–357, 408–409, 452–453, 482–483
Decimal point, 456, 468
Decimals, 455–468, 456, 468
adding and subtracting, 460–461, 468
calculator for counting by, 464–465
hundredths, 458–459, 468
money and, 462–463, 468
tenths, 456–457, 468
Degrees, Celsius and Fahrenheit, 494
Denominator, 414
Did You Know?, 16, 58, 76, 82, 126, 128, 164, 170, 180, 290, 324, 424, 442, 490, 492, 494, 506
Difference, 152, 156–157, 160. *See also* Subtraction
Digit, 52
Dime, 126
Dividend, 284
Division, 272–317, 396–397
with a calculator, 400–401
estimating in, 392–393, 402
even and odd numbers and, 306–307, 312

and multiplication, 283–298
patterns in, 390–391
remainders and, 394–395, 402
rules for, 293
as sharing, 276–277, 282
and subtraction, 278–279, 282
with 1-digit divisors, 389–402
writing stories using, 280–281, 282
Divisor, 284, 294
Dollars. *See* Money
Doubling, 152, 242–243, 406
with a calculator, 264–265

E

Edge, 322
Eighths, 412
Elapsed time, 80–81, 86
Equal groups, 205, 210
Equally likely, 506, 507
Equal parts, 412–413, 422
Equivalent fractions. *See* Fractions
Error Search, 22, 36, 114, 176, 222, 248, 304, 376
Estimation, 68, 102. *See also* Rounding
addition, 102–103, 104, 108, 109, 110, 111, 112, 116, 117, 187, 189
division, 392–393, 402
fractions, 420–421, 422
front-end, 136–137, 140, 142
measurement, 441
multiplication, 364–365, 368, 373, 380
number sense and, 115, 177, 377
rounding to tens, 68
subtraction, 156–157, 160, 163, 168, 170, 175, 181, 196
time, 77
vs. exact answer, 138–139, 140, 142
Even numbers, 306–307, 312
Expanded form of numbers, 52, 56, 58, 370–371, 388
Experiment, 502
Explore, 20, 28, 30, 32, 54, 76, 84, 96, 98, 106, 130, 152, 154, 158, 162, 166, 204, 208, 216, 218, 250, 254, 256, 276, 278, 280, 292, 306, 310, 322, 324, 328, 330, 332, 340, 342, 344, 346, 360, 362, 366, 390, 394, 412, 416, 418, 426, 430, 432, 436, 440, 456, 460, 466, 470, 486, 490, 496, 500, 504, 506

F

Face, 25, 322
Fact family, 284
Factor, 206, 210, 211–230, 232
Facts. *See* Basic facts
Fact table, 256–257, 266
Fair, 506–507, 512
Fathom, 450
Fibonacci numbers, 144
Fifths, 412
Fine arts, 281, 320, 336, 337, 357, 378
Flip, 330–331, 338
Four-digit numbers
adding, 116–117, 122
subtracting, 180–181, 194
Fractions, 411–434, 414
addition, 430–431, 434
calculator and, 464–465
comparing and ordering, 418–419, 422
decimals and, 457, 459, 468
equal parts, 412–413, 422
equivalent, 416–417
estimation, 420–421, 422
extending, 423–434
finding, 426–427, 434
mixed numbers and, 428–429, 434
naming and writing, 414–415, 422
sets and, 424–425, 434
subtraction, 430–431, 434
unit, 418
Front-end estimation. *See* Estimation

G

Games. *See* Practice Game
Geography, 69, 113, 122, 177, 178, 194, 333, 343, 363, 495. *See also* Maps
Geometry, 318–355, 471, 473
angles, 328–329
area, 342–343, 350
coordinate grids, 348–349
flips, 330–331, 338
lines and line segments, 326–327
perimeter, 340–341, 350
shapes, 324–325, 338
slides, 330–331, 338
solid figures, 322–323, 324–325, 338
symmetry, 332–333, 338
turns, 330–331, 338
volume, 346–347, 350
Geometry readiness, 40, 55, 97, 107, 205, 219, 255, 363, 393, 445
Graphs/graphing
bar graphs, 12–13, 30–31
line graphs, 14–15
making, 25–42
pictographs, 10–11, 28–29
reading, 9–24
Grouping property, 258
Guess and check strategy, 120–121, 122

H

Halves, 412
Health, 219, 229, 247, 375, 443, 461, 487
History, 71, 72, 163, 167, 173, 185, 197, 229, 341, 395, 413, 461
Home connection, 43, 87, 141, 195, 231, 267, 313, 351, 403, 447, 477, 513
Hundredths, 458–459, 468

I

Impossible, 500, 501
Internet. *See* World Wide Web

J

Journal, 9, 13, 17, 19, 21, 24, 27, 29, 31, 53, 55, 57, 59, 77, 79, 86, 97, 99, 101, 104, 107, 113, 117, 122, 131, 153, 155, 159, 160, 163, 166, 178, 181, 187, 193, 194, 205, 209, 210, 219, 229, 230, 252, 255, 257, 266, 277, 279, 281, 282, 293, 297, 298, 307, 309, 311, 323, 325, 329, 331, 333, 338, 341, 343, 347, 350, 361, 363, 367, 368, 375, 381, 388, 391, 395, 402, 413, 417, 419, 422, 427, 430, 434, 437, 441, 446, 457, 461, 468, 471, 476, 487, 491, 498, 501, 503, 505, 507, 512

K

Key for pictograph, 10

L

Language arts, 213
Length, 436–437, 442, 446. *See also* Linear measurement
Likely, 500–501, 506, 507
Linear measurement, 435–446, 469
- foot, 440–441, 442–443, 446
- inch, 440–441, 446
- metric, 469–476
- mile, 442–443
- to nearest fraction of inch, 438–439, 446
- yard, 442–443

Line graph, 14, 15, 24, 44
Lines, 326–327
- intersecting, 326, 338
- parallel, 326, 338

Line segment, 326–327
Line of symmetry, 332–333, 334–335, 338
List making, 60–61, 62, 88, 308–309
Literature, 49, 53, 70, 78, 79, 112, 189, 201, 221, 316, 378
Logic, 59, 67, 104, 187, 323, 444–445, 446, 448, 451, 500

M

Magic Squares, 198
Manipulatives. *See* Materials; Tool, Choose a
Maps, 56, 95, 113, 149, 156, 161, 163, 197. *See also* Geography
- Africa, 242, 353
- ancient Greece, 358
- Chaco Canyon, 102
- Death Valley, California, 178
- Great Lakes, 113
- Morocco, 242
- Rancho Nuevo, Mexico, 168
- real people locations, 10, 30, 76, 110, 116, 118, 124, 128, 164, 204, 214, 240, 278, 284, 286, 288, 296, 300, 344, 372, 378, 392, 426, 442, 458, 492, 506
- Washington, D.C., 319

Materials
- calculators, 96, 101, 152, 180, 218, 264, 292, 362, 390, 400, 464
- centimeter grid, 454
- color cubes, 100, 101, 104, 306, 310, 346, 351, 502
- computer drawing program, 334
- containers, 486
- counters, 20, 204, 208, 276, 278, 280, 394, 410, 426
- *DataWonder!,* 34, 508
- digit cards, 132, 384
- fraction strips, 416, 418, 430
- geoboard, 412
- grid paper, 28, 30, 260, 274, 330, 340, 342
- hundred chart, 98–99, 104, 154–155, 160, 216–217, 230, 254, 266
- money, 130, 410, 484
- number cubes, 54, 182, 260
- place-value blocks, 54, 106, 158, 162, 166, 360, 366
- Power Polygons, 328, 330, 351
- Power Solids, 322, 324
- ruler, 440, 470, 484
- scale, 490
- software random number generator, 508
- spinners, 504, 506
- tenths grids, 456–457, 460–461

Math Magazine, 46, 90, 144, 198, 234, 270, 316, 354, 406, 450, 480, 516
Math Tip, 12, 14, 26, 30, 54, 64, 68, 70, 78, 98, 116, 118, 124, 134, 136, 154, 206, 208, 212, 216, 220, 240, 242, 244, 256, 284, 300, 322, 328, 332, 342, 346, 360, 362, 366, 372, 378, 380, 390, 392, 412, 416, 418, 420, 426, 428, 436, 438, 440, 458, 462, 472, 486, 500, 504
Mayan numbers, 270
Measurement, 485–498. *See also* Capacity; Linear measurement; Weight
- differences, estimating, 157
- division, 391, 393
- metric, 469–476, 488–489, 492–493, 498
- missing numbers, finding, 101
- multiplication, 257, 383, 397
- place value, 53
- temperature, 494–495, 498

Memorization activities, 23, 37, 249, 305
Mental math. *See also* Tool, Choose a
- addition, 97, 99, 124–125, 140, 142, 187
- division, 391, 402
- multiplication, 363, 368, 382–383, 388
- subtraction, 153, 155, 186–187, 194, 196

Metric units
- Celsius, 494
- centimeter, 470–471, 476
- decimeter, 470–471, 476
- gram, 492–493
- kilogram, 492–493
- kilometer, 472–473, 476
- liter, 488
- meter, 472–473, 476
- milliliter, 488

INDEX

Missing numbers, 100–101, 104
Mixed numbers, 428–429, 434
Mixed Review and Test Prep, 11, 13, 15, 27, 29, 31, 41, 53, 57, 59, 65, 67, 69, 71, 75, 79, 81, 83, 103, 109, 113, 117, 119, 125, 127, 129, 135, 137, 151, 157, 165, 169, 173, 175, 181, 187, 189, 193, 207, 213, 215, 221, 229, 241, 243, 245, 247, 259, 285, 287, 289, 291, 301, 303, 327, 349, 365, 371, 375, 379, 381, 383, 393, 397, 415, 421, 425, 429, 439, 443, 459, 463, 473, 489, 493, 495. *See also* Cumulative Review; Review/Test
Money
- addition, 105–122, 125, 134–135, 140
- change, making, 130–131, 140, 142
- counting coins, 126–127, 140
- decimals and, 462–463, 468
- division, 279, 289, 301, 393
- dollars and cents, using, 128–129, 140, 142
- fractions, 427
- multiplication, 209, 215, 230, 252, 380–381, 388
- subtraction, 153, 155, 162–178, 163, 175, 188–189, 194

Multicultural connection. *See* Cultural connection
Multiple, 216, 232
Multiplication, 200–235, 236–271, 406
- arrays for, 366–367
- and division, 284–285
- Egyptian, 406
- equal groups in, 204–205, 210
- expanded form, 370–371, 388
- money, 380–381, 388
- and 1-digit factors, 369–388
- patterns in, 362–363, 368
- sentences, 206–207, 210
- stories, 208–209, 210
- tens, 360–361, 368
- and 3-digit numbers, 378–379, 388
- with 3 factors, 258–259, 266
- and 2-digit numbers, 372–375, 388

Music, 29, 99, 155, 215, 243, 419

N

Naming
- fractions, 414–415, 422
- numbers, 51–62, 87, 88. *See also* Numbers

Nickel, 126
Numbers
- comparing, 64–65, 72, 88
- expanded form of, 52, 56, 58
- fraction of, 426–427, 434
- mixed, 428–429, 434
- naming and writing, 51–62, 87, 88
- ordering, 66–67, 72, 88
- ordinal, 82–83, 88
- standard form of, 52, 53, 55, 56, 57, 58, 59, 62
- word name of, 52, 53, 56, 57, 58, 62

Number sense, 63–72
- addition, 95–104
- comparing numbers, 64–65, 72, 88
- estimation and reasoning, 115, 177, 377
- multiplication, 359–368
- operations and properties, 223
- ordering numbers, 66–67, 72, 88
- rounding to hundreds, 70–71, 72, 88
- rounding to tens, 68–69, 72, 88
- subtraction, 149–160

Numerator, 414

O

Objects, solving problems using, 190–193, 194, 308–309
Odd number, 306–307, 312
One-digit factor, 369–388
Operations, 18–19, 151, 223, 296–297, 298
Ordered pair, 348
Ordering
- fractions, 418–419
- numbers, 66–67, 72, 88

Ordinal number, 82–83, 88
Outcome, possible, 502, 503, 512

P

Pair, ordered, 348
Parallel lines, 326
Patterns
- addition, 96–97, 119
- communication and, 39, 216
- decimal, 461
- division, 285, 390–391
- on a fact table, 256–257, 266
- fraction, 417
- geometry, 325, 347
- on a hundred chart, 216–217, 230, 254–255, 266
- looking for, 20, 38–41, 42, 96, 98, 106, 231, 262–263
- in measurement, 491
- of missing numbers, 101
- multiplication, 220, 241, 255, 257, 266, 362–363, 368
- and place value through hundreds, 53
- subtraction, 152–153, 160, 165, 187
- in tables, 20

Penny, 126, 484. *See also* Cents
Performance Assessment, 45, 89, 143, 197, 233, 269, 315, 353, 405, 449, 479, 515
Perimeter, 340–341, 350
Period, 58
Pictograph, 10
- making, 28–29, 42
- reading, 10–11, 24
- using, 6, 11, 17, 24, 44, 91, 92, 201, 235, 272, 374

Place value, 51–62, 52, 88
- groups of ten as basis for, 55
- numbers, comparing, 64
- relationships in, 54–55, 62

P.M., 78
Point, 326
Polygon, 328

Possible, 500, 502, 503, 512
Practice Game, 132–133, 182–183, 260–261, 294–295, 384–385
Prediction, 502–503, 512
Prism, rectangular, 322, 323
Probability, 499–512
exploring, 504–505, 512
fair and unfair, 506–507, 512
likely and unlikely, 500–501
predictions, 502–503, 512
Problem solving. *See also* Problem solving, analyze word problems; Problem solving, compare strategies; Problem solving, decision making; Problem solving strategies
and geography, 113
and health, 375
and history, 173, 229
and science, 16, 193, 224–225
and social studies, 41
Problem solving, analyze word problems
determining important information, 224–225
exact or estimate, 138–139
introduction to problem solving, 16–17
multiple-step problems, 184–185, 194
operation selection, 18–19, 296–297
Problem Solving and Applications, 11, 13, 15, 53, 57, 59, 65, 67, 69, 71, 75, 79, 81, 83, 103, 109, 112, 117, 119, 125, 127, 129, 135, 137, 151, 157, 165, 169, 172, 175, 181, 187, 189, 207, 213, 215, 221, 241, 243, 245, 247, 259, 285, 287, 289, 291, 301, 303, 327, 349, 365, 371, 374, 379, 381, 383, 393, 396, 397, 415, 421, 425, 429, 439, 443, 459, 463, 473, 489, 493, 495
Problem solving, compare strategies, 262–263, 308–309, 474–475
Problem Solving Connection
draw a picture, 28, 30, 204, 208, 276, 278, 280, 324, 330, 340, 342, 366, 412, 456, 460
guess and check, 76, 100, 130, 502, 504, 506
look for a pattern, 20, 54, 96, 98, 106, 152, 154, 158, 162, 166, 216, 218, 254, 256, 292, 306, 362, 416, 418, 430, 436
make a table, 20, 26, 28, 30, 256, 310, 490, 500
use logical reasoning, 500
use objects/act it out, 54, 76, 98, 100, 106, 130, 152, 154, 158, 162, 166, 204, 208, 216, 276, 278, 280, 306, 310, 322, 324, 328, 332, 346, 360, 366, 394, 412, 416, 418, 426, 430, 436, 440, 456, 460, 470, 486, 490, 502, 504, 506
Problem solving, decision making, 32–33, 45, 84–85, 89, 143, 187, 197, 233, 250–251, 269, 315, 344–345, 353, 398–399, 405, 432–433, 449, 466–467, 479, 496–497, 515
Problem Solving Hint, 18, 20, 100, 101, 152, 190, 204, 218, 278, 288, 306, 308, 310, 340, 344, 414, 429, 460, 474
Problem solving strategies
draw a picture, 226–228
guess and check, 120–121
look for a pattern, 38–41
make an organized list, 60–61, 62
make a table, 386–387
solve a simpler problem, 336–337
use logical reasoning, 444–445
use objects, 190–193
work backward, 510–511
Product, 206, 210, 232, 364–365, 368
Properties, 206, 218–219, 223, 258–259, 292–293
Pyramid, 322, 323, 325, 336

Q

Quarter, 126
Quotient, 284, 392–393, 396, 402. *See also* Division

R

Ray, 326
Reasoning. *See also* Skills and Reasoning
addition, 97, 99, 101, 103, 104, 107, 108, 111, 116, 118, 122, 124, 134
algebra, 311
decimals, 459, 461, 462, 465, 478
division, 277, 279, 282, 285, 287, 288, 291, 295, 300, 302, 391, 392, 395, 396, 401, 402
estimation, 136
even and odd numbers, 307
fractions, 413, 414, 420, 424, 428, 434, 465
geometry, 323, 326, 329, 331, 335, 338, 347, 349, 350
making/reading graphs, 10, 14, 24, 27, 29, 35
measurement, 437, 439, 441, 442, 444–445, 472, 476, 478, 487, 489, 491, 493, 494, 498
mental math, 124, 383
metric system, 472, 476, 478, 489
mixed numbers, 428
money, 129, 131, 134
multiplication, 205, 207, 210, 212, 214, 219, 220, 230, 240, 242, 244, 247, 258, 266, 270, 361, 363, 364, 368, 371, 373, 379, 381, 383

number sense, 67, 69, 70, 115, 177, 377
patterns, 39, 217
place value, 52, 56, 58
probability, 501, 503, 505, 507, 509
problem solving, 444–445
rounding, 68, 70
subtraction, 151, 153, 155, 156, 164, 169, 171, 174, 180, 186, 188
time, 74, 77, 79, 81, 83
Rectangle, 324, 325
Rectangular prism, 322, 323, 325
Regrouping, 106
addition, 106–107, 108, 111, 122
multiplication, 372
subtraction, 158–159, 160, 170–173
Remainder, 394–395, 396, 402
Remember, 28, 52, 56, 66, 80, 96, 102, 106, 110, 130, 150, 156, 162, 166, 174, 188, 214, 215, 254, 276, 280, 286, 292, 302, 364, 370, 382, 394, 396, 430, 456, 470, 488, 502
Review/Test, 44, 88, 142, 196, 232, 268, 314, 352, 404, 448, 478, 514. *See also* Cumulative Review; Mixed Review and Test Prep
Right angle, 328, 329
Roman numeral, 46
Rounding, 68, 72, 88. *See also* Estimation
estimate differences, 156–157
estimate sums, 102
to hundreds, 70–71, 72, 88
to tens, 68–69, 72, 88
to thousands, 116
Rules, 20–21

S

Scale, 12, 490
balancing, 310–311, 312
Science, 13, 53, 56, 57, 58, 60–61, 63, 66, 71, 73, 80, 89, 137, 139, 149, 150, 156, 157, 165, 169, 179, 180, 185, 187, 193, 207, 209, 210, 221, 225, 229, 245, 255, 277, 289, 290, 291, 348, 383, 388, 393, 402, 404, 427, 429, 443, 453, 457, 480, 487, 489
Sets, fractions and, 424–425, 434
Shapes, 324–325, 338
Sharing, division and, 276–277, 282
Side, 324, 325
Sixths, 412
Skills Practice Bank, 518–529
Skills and Reasoning. *See also* Reasoning
addition, 109, 112, 117, 119, 135
decimals, 459, 463
division, 285, 287, 289, 291, 301, 303, 393, 397
estimation, 103, 137
fractions, 415, 421, 425, 429
geometry, 327
graphs, 11, 13, 15
measurement, 439, 443, 472, 489, 493, 495
mental math, 125, 383
metric system, 472, 489
mixed numbers, 429
money, 127, 129
multiplication, 207, 212, 215, 221, 241, 243, 245, 247, 259, 365, 371, 374, 379, 381, 383
number sense, 65, 67, 69, 71
place value, 53, 57, 59
rounding, 68, 71
subtraction, 151, 157, 165, 169, 172, 175, 181, 187, 189
time, 75, 79, 81, 83
Skip counting
finding patterns on a hundred chart, 216
multiplication and, 212, 214
Slide, 330–331, 338
Social studies, 41, 209, 252, 263, 298, 341, 365, 381, 395
Solids, 322–323, 324–325, 338
Span, 450
Sphere, 322, 323
Sports, 153, 408, 414, 415, 422, 435
Square, 324, 325, 337
Square number, 246
Square unit, 342, 343
Standard form of numbers, 52, 53, 55, 56, 57, 58, 59, 62
Stop and Practice, 22–23, 36–37, 114–115, 176–177, 222–223, 248–249, 304–305, 376–377
Subtraction, 146–199
across zero, 174–175
decimals, 460–461, 468, 478
differences, 156–157, 160
four-digit numbers, 180–181, 194
fractions, 430–431, 434
greater numbers, 162–178
on a hundred chart, 154–155, 160
money, 162–178, 188–189, 194
patterns in, 152–153, 160
regrouping in, 158–159, 160, 170–173
repeated, division as, 278–279, 282
3-digit numbers, 166–167, 168–169
2-digit numbers, 162–163, 164–165
whole numbers, 146–199
Sum, 96, 102–103, 104. *See also* Addition
Symbol, in pictograph, 10
Symmetry, line of, 332–333, 334–335, 338

T

Table, making, 386–387
Tally mark, 26, 27
Tally table, 27, 28, 29, 35, 42, 44
Team Project, 8, 50, 94, 148, 202, 238, 274, 320, 358, 410, 454, 484
Technology. *See* Calculator; Computer; World Wide Web

Temperature, 494–495, 498
Tens, multiplying, 360–361, 368
Tenths, 412, 456–457, 468
Test Prep Strategies. *See also* Mixed Review and Test Prep; Review/Test
eliminate choices, 199, 317
follow directions, 91, 355, 517
make smart choices, 271, 407, 451
read carefully, 145, 235, 481
use logical reasoning, 451
working backward from an answer, 47
Thermometer, 494, 495
Thirds, 412
Three-digit numbers
adding, 110–113, 122
multiplying, 378–379, 388
rounding to nearest ten, 68–69
subtracting, 166–167, 168–169, 174–175
Time, 73–86, 88
division, 289, 298, 301, 391
elapsed, 80–81, 86
fractions, 425, 427
geometry, 329
to half and quarter hour, 78–79, 86
to nearest five minutes, 74–75, 86
to nearest minute, 76–77, 86
subtraction, 153, 157, 173
Tool, Choose a
calculator, 17, 19, 40, 61, 121, 122, 139, 181, 185, 192, 225, 228, 263, 297, 309, 337, 387, 445, 475, 511
manipulatives, 17, 19, 40, 61, 121, 139, 185, 192, 225, 228, 263, 297, 309, 337, 387, 445, 475, 511
mental math, 17, 19, 40, 61, 121, 122, 139, 181, 185, 192, 225, 228, 263, 297, 309, 337, 387, 445, 475, 511
Triangle, 324, 325
Turn, 330–331, 338
Two-digit numbers
adding, 108–109, 122
multiplying, 372–375, 388
rounding to nearest ten, 68–69
subtracting, 162–163, 163–164

U

Unfair, 506–507, 512
Unit, 530. *See also* Area; Capacity; Length; Time; Weight; Volume
Unit fraction, 418
Unlikely, 500–501, 512

V

Volume, 346–347, 350

W

Weight
customary units, 490–491, 498
metric units, 492–493, 498
What If, 131, 205, 209, 215, 259, 285, 289, 301, 303, 309, 371, 381, 467
Word name for number, 52, 53, 56, 57, 58, 62
Work Together. *See* Cooperative Learning
World Wide Web, 7, 43, 49, 93, 147, 195, 201, 237, 272, 313, 319, 345, 356, 403, 409, 453, 477, 483
Write Your Own Problem, 11, 15, 17, 21, 41, 109, 113, 135, 151, 165, 169, 181, 189, 282, 285, 301, 375, 397, 425
Writing
fractions, 414–415, 422
numbers, 51–62, 87, 88. *See also* Numbers

Y

Your Choice, 43, 87, 141, 195, 231, 267, 313, 351, 403, 447, 477, 513

Z

Zero
division, 292–293, 298
as a factor, 218–219, 230
subtraction, 174–175

INDEX